ALSO BY KITTY KELLEY

HIS WAY: THE UNAUTHORIZED BIOGRAPHY OF
FRANK SINATRA
ELIZABETH TAYLOR: THE LAST STAR
JACKIE OH!
THE GLAMOUR SPAS

KITTY KELLEY

SIMON & SCHUSTER

NANCY REAGAN

The Unauthorized Biography

NEW YORK · LONDON · TORONTO · SYDNEY · TOKYO · SINGAPORE

Simon & Schuster
Simon & Schuster Building
Rockefeller Center
1230 Avenue of the Americas
New York, New York 10020

Designed by Eve Metz
Photo research by Vincent Virga
Manufactured in the United States of America

The lyrics from "Make with the Maximum" that appear on page 54 are reprinted through
the courtesy of Smith College.

Picture Credits

1, 2, 28, 47–49, 75: White House.

3–5: Kathleen Young.

6, 11, 22, 23, 26, 27, 29, 31, 43, 46, 50–53, 70, 72, 73: Wide World.

8, 9: Smith College.

10, 12–16, 18, 21, 24, 25, 37, 38, 44, 45, 54–57, 59, 62, 63, 69, 74: UPI/Bettmann.

17, 19: Lester Glassner Collection.

20: University of Southern California Library.

30, 32–34, 36, 39–42, 58, 60, 61, 64–66: *Women's Wear Daily*.

35: Fred Sweets/*Washington Post*.

67, 68: Ellen Pollon, formerly of Gucci.

71: Bernie Boston/*Los Angeles Times*.

Acknowledgments

I was once convinced that *His Way: The Unauthorized Biography of Frank Sinatra* (Bantam Books, 1986) was the hardest book I would ever write. Some people were so terrified by the subject that they refused to talk to me for fear of physical reprisals. But that fright paled alongside the terror sparked by Nancy Reagan. This, at first, made no sense. Unlike Frank Sinatra, the former First Lady was not connected to organized crime; nor was she known to fly into violent rages. So I could not understand why people were so afraid of her. Yet anxiety was palpable on the part of many who were more than reticent to talk about her.

"She will ruin me," said a former employee. "She will have me audited," said a former neighbor. "She will get my husband fired," said a former White House secretary.

It seemed preposterous that such power, real or imagined, could be exercised by the wife of the President of the United States, which Nancy Reagan was when I started researching this book. So I dismissed people's fears as unfounded and shrugged off their warnings of intimidation—until July 20, 1988.

On that day I received a strange phone call from Mr. Frank Underwood of the FBI in Washington, D.C. He asked whether I was writing a book on Mrs. Reagan and whether the files requested under the Freedom of Information Act on the late Edith Davis, her mother, were for this book. I was stunned by the call because the FOIA requests had been submitted by my research assistant under her name. I said that the information was being gathered for this biography, and then asked the reason for such a telephone inquiry, which was highly unusual. "We just want to know if the information is for *your* book," he said. He refused to elaborate. Was he acting on his own initiative or at the behest of his superiors, who may or may not have been reporting to the First Lady? I don't know because he refused to say. After five more letters and two administrative appeals, my assistant's request for information on Mrs. Davis and her undercover police activities was denied. After that, I began paying more attention to the pervasive influence of Nancy Reagan.

Some people's fear of the former First Lady was real and understandable; the fear of others was just plain silly, as in the case of the chief White House usher, Gary Walters. He was called with two simple questions:

(1) What type of lilies did the First Lady use in the White House family quarters?

(2) What kind of white orchid did Mrs. Reagan leave for Mrs. Bush before departing the White House in 1989?

"That information is privileged and private," said Walters. "I am not at liberty to release that information to you."

Thinking the questions harmless, I ventured that the White House belonged to everyone, even those writing biographies. Since our taxes bought the flowers used by the First Family, I didn't feel out of line asking about them. Besides, writers believe—as the architect Mies van der Rohe used to say—that God is in the details, as seemingly insignificant as they may be, but the White House usher was not persuaded.

"This is classified information," he said, "and you have absolutely no right to it."

I wrote to Mrs. Reagan seven times while researching this book, explaining that I was trying to do an in-depth biography that I hoped would stand the test of history. In each letter I requested an interview and even offered to submit questions in advance. I never received a response until last year when the director of planning for the Nancy Reagan Foundation answered my seventh letter by saying: "Mrs. Reagan is unable to comply with your request at this time and we do not foresee a time in the future when an interview could be arranged."

Having been bruised in print myself, I know how it feels to be depicted unfairly and inaccurately, and I would never want to inflict that kind of pain on someone else. To be fair, accurate, and thorough, my research assistants and I tried to interview as many people as possible who had known and worked with Nancy Reagan throughout her life. We contacted friends, acquaintances, relatives, schoolmates, co-stars, neighbors, employees, and political aides of Ronald Reagan in California and

Washington, D.C. Some of those who appreciated that history is best served by truthful recollection spoke openly and on the record; others spoke only on condition that their names not be used. In the end, the number of tape-recorded interviews reached 1,002, most of which are documented in the chapter notes at the end of the book.

I drew from presidential documents, FBI files, financial disclosures, IRS returns, letters, diaries, memoirs, oral histories, film archives, personal recollections, calendars, and correspondence. I tried to go beyond "the clothes and buttons of a person," which is how Mark Twain defined biography, to answer that everlasting question: "What's she really like?" Throughout the writing, I followed the creed of the preacher in John Steinbeck's *The Grapes of Wrath* who left the cloth: "There ain't no sin and there ain't no virtue. There's just stuff people do. It's all part of the same thing. And some of the things folks do is nice, and some ain't nice, but that's as far as any man got a right to say."

A few years ago Stuart Applebaum, vice president of publicity and public relations for Bantam Doubleday Dell, showed me the value of a publishing *mishpocah* (Yiddish for family), and throughout this project I've been blessed with the best. My gifted researcher, Melissa D. Smalling, coordinated the massive files for this book, and for four years she has worked indefatigably, bringing superior intelligence and immense good cheer to all her tasks. Without this extraordinary young woman, I would have no book. I also received expert assistance from Pamela Warrick on the West Coast and Aura Lippincott, Elena Gleckas, Sam Dixon, and Lisa Melmed in Washington. In New York City, Henri Astier researched old city directories and telephone books while Mervin Block did the research work of ten men. In London I was helped by Angela Murphy; Nicholas Gordon of *YOU* magazine; by my British literary agent, Deborah Rogers of Rogers, Coleridge & White, Ltd.; and my British publisher, Mark Barty-King, managing director of Bantam Press.

Within my literary agency, International Creative Management, I'm most grateful to Wayne Kabak, Sam Cohn, Esther Newberg, Suzanne Gluck, Heather Schroder, and Adele Fisher. At Simon & Schuster I've been buoyed by the support of C.E.O. Richard Snyder, the phenomenal editorial talent of Alice Mayhew, and the marketing genius of Charlie Hayward, Jack McKeown, and Judy Lee; plus Victoria Meyer in publicity; Marcella Berger in subsidiary rights; Eve Metz and Rick Willett in production; Frank Metz, head of the art department; Marcia Peterson, Sophie Sorkin, and Sarajane Herman in copy editing; Marie Florio in serial rights; Washington editor Marie Arana-Ward; George Hodgman, Adelle Stan, and Vincent Virga, who compiled the photographs for the book. Irwyn Applebaum, president and publisher of Pocket Books, deserves special thanks for providing one of the book's most important sources, and my deepest gratitude to Jeanne Bernkopf, who patiently smoothed the rough edges of an unwieldy manuscript. I also appreciate the time her husband, Michael Bernkopf, Ph.D., donated on his word processor. My thanks, also, to the most important lawyers in my life: my father, William V. Kelley of Witherspoon, Kelley, Davenport & Toole in Spokane, Washington, and Benjamin L. Zelenko and Robert L. Wald of Nussbaum and Wald in Washington, D.C.

Librarians, curators, and archivists contributed greatly to this project, and I'm indebted to the Academy of Motion Picture Arts and Sciences in Los Angeles; Alexandria Public Library's librarians in Virginia; Carol Applegate, Princeton High School, Princeton, New Jersey; Jeanne Baron, editorial librarian of *Washingtonian;* Bill Barrett of ACTION; Jack Begg, librarian of the *New York Post;* Diana R. Brown and Roger Mayer of Turner Entertainment for providing access to the MGM legal files; Nettie Brown, librarian of the *Modesto Bee,* Modesto, California; Marshall Bullock, reference librarian, Petersburg Public Library, Petersburg, Virginia; Larry Campbell, Registry of Charitable Trusts of California; the Chicago Historical Society; Church of Latter Day Saints Family History Center's staff, Kensington, Maryland; Ned Comstock and Gary Bryson, Cinema Library of the University of Southern California; Brian Daly, the Little Brown Church, Studio City, California; Daughters of the American Revolution Library, Washington, D.C.; Conley Edwards, head of public services, Virginia State Library, Richmond, Virginia; Martin I. Elzy, assistant director, Jimmy Carter Presidential Library; Judy Gerritts, librarian, the *San Francisco Examiner;* Regina Greenwell, archivist, Lyndon Baines Johnson Presidential Library; Greenwood Memorial Park, Phoenix, Arizona; Carol Hale, Ziegfeld Club of New York City; John Hanley, Congressional Cemetery, Washington, D.C.; John Haydon, *Washington Times;* Linda Henzell, University of Wisconsin Center for Film; Richard L. Holzhausen, audiovisual archivist, Gerald R. Ford Presidential Library; Sue Hornik of Common Cause, Washington, D.C.; Joan Howard, Nixon Presidential Materials Project, Alexandria, Virginia; Just Say No Foundation, Walnut Creek, California; the John F. Kennedy Presidential Library, Boston, Massachusetts; Fred Klose, archivist, National Archives Regional Branch, Los Angeles, California; the Library of Congress, Washington, D.C.; Mark Locher, public relations director, Screen Actors Guild, Los Angeles, California; Marion Marshall, Tax Analysts, Falls Church, Virginia; Martin Luther King, Jr., Public Library's Washingtonian Room staff, Washington, D.C.; Velma Martin, St. Mary's Church, Washington, D.C.; Mrs. McGinty, St. Patrick's Church, Washington, D.C.; Anne Moffett, *Time,* Washington, D.C.; Barry Morrison, Chicago Anti-Defamation

League; Nan Mould, Fourth Presbyterian Church, Chicago; the National Archives, Washington, D.C.; the National Geographic Society's library, Washington, D.C.; Marc Pachter and the Washington Biography Group; Maria Parisi, the National Portrait Gallery, Smithsonian Institution; Tony Phipps, film society manager, Screen Actors Guild, Los Angeles, California; Emily Piper, Berkshire Athenaeum, Pittsfield, Massachusetts; Phoenix Public Library; Princeton Seminary, Princeton, New Jersey; Mary Reyner, Sidwell Friends School of Washington, D.C.; Roscan Richmond, Screen Actors Guild, Los Angeles, California; Faigie Rosenthal and Bob Athons, *New York Daily News* library; Rick Ryan, Princeton University; the *Sacramento Bee* librarians and public relations office; Larry Salmon, Junior League of Chicago; Caroline Schaffner, curator, theater museum of the Museum of Repertoire Americana; Ann Schlosser, Warner Bros. Collection, University of Southern California; Tom Shorebird, archivist, the National Theatre, Washington, D.C.; Margery Sly, college archivist, Smith College, Northampton, Massachusetts; William J. Stewart, acting director, Gerald R. Ford Presidential Library; Mark Swartz, Shubert Archives, New York City; Dorothy Swerdlove, curator, theater division, New York Public Library; Merle Thomason, librarian, Fairchild Publications; William Lewis Tucker, president/founder of Uniphoto, Washington, D.C.; Adelaide Tyson, Chi Phi Fraternity, Atlanta, Georgia; University of Southern California University Library Special Collections Department; Connie Stokes and all the volunteers at the Columbia Historical Society, Washington, D.C.; Barclay Walsh, *The New York Times,* Washington, D.C.; Carol Perry Wilson, Office of External Affairs, National Spiritual Assembly of the Bahais of the United States; George Wilson, Pittsfield High School, Pittsfield, Massachusetts; Nona Yates, *Los Angeles Times* library.

Editors, writers, and reporters across the country took the time to answer questions and share their stories. For this and much more, I'm grateful to Roy Aarons, *Oakland Tribune;* R. W. Apple, *The New York Times;* Deborah Armida, *Oakland Tribune;* Roberta Ashley, *Cosmopolitan;* Lissa August, *Time;* Eileen Bailey, editor and publisher, *V Magazine,* Phoenix, Arizona; Fred Barnes, *New Republic;* Laurence Barrett, *Time;* Edward Baumann, *Chicago Tribune;* Jim Bellows, vice president/news, MediaNews Group; Leslie Bennetts, *Vanity Fair;* Beverly Beyette, *Los Angeles Times;* Marie Brenner, *Vanity Fair;* Ian Brodie, *Daily Telegraph* of London; Christopher Buckley; John Buckley; Lou Cannon; Otis Chandler, chairman of the board, *Los Angeles Times;* Garry Clifford, *People;* Joan Connelly, *Time;* Ken Cummins, *City Paper,* Washington, D.C.; Lisa Dallos, CNN; Tom DeFrank, *Newsweek;* Brian Doyle, *Time;* Margaret Engel, director, Alicia Patterson Foundation; Peter Fares, *New York Post;*

Murray Gart, *Time;* Vera Glaser, *Washingtonian;* Nicholas Gordon, *YOU Magazine;* Joel Greenberg, *Los Angeles Times;* David Grogan, *People Magazine;* Anthony Haden-Guest, *Vanity Fair;* Peter Hayes, editorial page editor, *Sacramento Union;* William Hifner, *The Washington Post;* Warren Hinckle, associate editor, *San Francisco Examiner;* Eleanor Harris Howard; Peter Kalikow, owner, *New York Post;* Charles Kelly, *Arizona Republic;* Ron Kessler; Jerry Knight, *The Washington Post;* Jesse Kornbluth, *Vanity Fair;* Irv Kupcinet, *Chicago Sun Times;* Jane Lane, *M;* Annie Leibovitz, *Vanity Fair;* Madeline L'Engle; Lee Lescaze, *The Wall Street Journal;* Bettyjane Levine, *Los Angeles Times;* Barbara Lieber, *People;* Lorrie Lynch, *USA Today;* Julia Malone, Cox Newspapers; John Mashek, *Boston Globe;* Robert Massie; Chris Matthews, *San Francisco Chronicle;* Bea Maxwell, *Los Angeles Times;* Jane Mayer, *The Wall Street Journal;* Colman McCarthy, *The Washington Post;* Sandra McElwaine; Gordon McKenzie, *London Daily Mail;* Bill McPherson; Marianne Means, Hearst Newspapers; Elizabeth Mehren, *Los Angeles Times;* Jack Nelson, bureau chief, *Los Angeles Times,* Washington, D.C.; Johanna Neuman, *USA Today,* William Norwich, *New York Daily News;* Jerry O'Leary, *The Washington Times;* Peter Osterlund, *Christian Science Monitor;* Bob Pack, *Washingtonian Magazine;* John Pekkanen, *Reader's Digest;* Charlie Peters, *Washington Monthly;* Jay Peterzel, *Time;* Bill Plante, CBS News; Donnie Radcliffe, *The Washington Post;* Peter Range, *U.S. News & World Report;* Bill Regardie, *Regardie's;* Cathy Rehl, "Good Morning America"; David Richards, *The New York Times,* and Orville Richards; Phyllis Richman, *The Washington Post;* Sue Riley, *Los Angeles Daily News;* Phyllis Rose; Mike Royko, *Chicago Tribune;* John Sansing, executive editor, *Washingtonian;* Robert Scheer, *Los Angeles Times;* Neang Seng, *Time;* Lloyd Shearer, *Parade;* Ira Silverman, NBC-TV; Barbara Simmonds, *The Berkshire Eagle;* Peggy Simpson, Hearst Newspapers; Martin Smith, *Sacramento Bee;* Robert J. Smith, *Chicago Tribune;* Lesley Stahl, CBS-TV; Susan Stamberg, National Public Radio; Jack Star; Warren Steibel, producer, William Buckley's "Firing Line"; Basil Talbott; Strobe Talbott, *Time;* Nan and Gay Talese; Michael Thomas; Robert Thompson, former D.C. bureau chief, Hearst Newspapers; Dennis Troute, ABC-TV; R. Emmett Tyrrell, Jr., *The American Spectator;* Owen Ullman, Knight-Ridder Newspapers; Nicholas von Hoffman; Denny Walsh, *San Jose Mercury-News;* Ellen Warren, Knight-Ridder Newspapers; Paul Wieck, *Albuquerque Journal;* Louis Wolf, co-editor, *Covert Action Information Bulletin;* Bob Woodward, *The Washington Post;* Judy York, *Avenue M.*

My sources made the most important contribution to this book, and I'm grateful to all for their help. Not every interview could be used, but I appreciate the time and consideration of everyone who cooperated, including several of Nancy Reagan's relatives, primarily her cousins and some of her children, who so generously shared their recollections.

My thanks to Patricia James Ackerley, Bess Abel, Mary (Dolly) Rochester Adams, Bill Adler, Elizabeth Prince Allen, Jay Allen, Rupert Allen, June Allyson, Joan Maxwell Alvarez, Jean Drake Alvord, Anne Amernick, Helen Anderson, Patrick Anderson, Alex Armstrong, Scott Armstrong, Terry Arthur, Charlotte Austin, Lew Ayres, Jackie Babbin, Judy Bachrach, Doris Barry, Ken Barun, Kate Beardsley, Jonathan Beatty, Marilyn Beck, Dr. Gerry Becker, Amy Ward Beir, Joanna Bendheim, Ron Berkheimer, Mike Berman, Pandro Berman, Jay Bernstein, Gladys W. Blackett, Mary Blackett, Joan Blake, Chris Blazakis, Sidney Blumenthal, Helen Boehm, Frances Borden, Patricia Bosworth, John Bradford, Ann Teal Bradley, David Bradley, Debby Bradley, Colleen Brady, Alice Braemer, Warner Brandt, Linda Breakstone, Cate Breslin, Richard Brooks, Bernice Brown, Edmund "Jerry" Brown, Kathleen Brown, Frank Browning, Ron Brownstein, Anne Buchholz and family, Jill Buckley, Dorothy Stimson Bullitt, Sally Bulloch, Anne Burford, Kitty Burke, Doris Burns, Helen Burroughs, Marion Burrows, Jo Ann Burton, Don Campbell, Judy Canter, Joe Canzeri, Tom Capra, Evelyn Adams Carpenter, Lucille Ryman Carroll, Joanne Carson, Tom Carter, Frank Casey, Matt Caufield, Carlo Celoni, Kevin Chaffee, Winnie Chambers, Mona Charon, Shirley Knight Chase, Tom Chauncey, Linda Chavez, Debbie Chenoweth, Tony Childs, Helen Chinoy, Nancy Clark, Tony Clifford, Richard Coe, Lee Cohen, Sheldon Cohen, Joseph Cohn, Judy Coleman, Nancy Collins, Patsy Bullitt Collins, David Columbia, Norma Connolly, Sarah Booth Conroy, John Cook, Maxine Cooke, Esther Coopersmith, Paul Corbin, Sylvia Costaños, Roger Courtney, Norman Cousins, Jeff Cowan, Jack Cox, Jayne Coyne, Diana Crane, Rosemary Cribben, Jane Beckwith Crowe, Jack Cummings, Judy Dallenmere, Brian Daly, Barbara Dana, Marian Darmsted, Iris Rainer Dart, Saul David, Bill Davidson, Gordon Davidson, Debra Davis, Jerry Davis, Nancy Davis, Patti Davis, Sheldon Davis, Susan Davis, Jane Dawson, Eddie de Celle, Oscar de Lavin, Janet Oliver DeCamp, Rosemary DeCamp, Janet de Cordova, Richard DeFelice, Jeff DeMontier, Sally Denton, Murray Deutchman, Alan DeValerio, Brad Dexter, Mary Bogdonovich Dexter, Mary Heald Dickert, Joan Kay Diebow, Maria DiMartini, Debby Dingall, Jill Dixon, Monsignor Robert Donohoe, Ann Doran, Rev. John Doran, David Dorsen, Anne Douglas, Linda Douglas, Mary Newhauser Dove, Alex Dudasik, Amanda Dunne, Philip Dunne, Fred and Nancy Dutton, Tom Eastham, Nancy Ebson, Beverly Ecker, Anne Edwards, John Ehrlichman, Judy Eisenhower, Teresa Elmore, Alan Emory, Richard Epstein, Henry Erlich, Michael Evans, John Farrington, Jr., Penny Farthing, Susie Farris,

Margot Feiden, Nikki Fink, Philip Finn, David Fischer, Justin Fishbein, Larry Fishman, Jim Fitzgerald, Bill Fitzpatrick, Frip Flanigan, Sally Fleg, Anne Fleming, Karl Fleming, Rhonda Fleming, Heather Foley, Joe Foote, Glenn Ford, Gary Foster, Barbara Fouch, Matt Franich, Pat Franich, Gay Palmer Frank, Donald Freed, Betty Friedan, Dr. Morris Friedell, J. Robert Friedman, Robert Fryer, Jim Fuller, Ken Galante, Yetta Galiber, Bill Galston, Anne Garbeff, Patricia Gayman, Paul and Martha Gibson, Joel Glickman, Virginia Dougherty Glover, Vic Gold, Howard Goldberg, Bonnie Goldstein, Richard Goldstone, Joanne Goldwater, Robert Goldwater, Stanley Gordon, Harry Gosset, Jim Grady, Susan Granger, Miriam Grant, Kathryn Grayson, Judy and Don Green, Billy Frank and J.M.J., Nina Green, Hildi Greenson, John Greenya, Henry Gris, Genie Grohman, Mary Ann Guitar, Richard Gully, Juliette Harvey Guthrie, Joyce Haber, Betsy Forsythe Hailey, Diane Hales, Steve Halpern, Thula Hampton, Lucy Hand, David Harney, Sr., Garry Harris, Jean Struben Harris, Ann Hart, Mrs. Nathan Hatch, Anne Wilder Hausner, Chuck Hawley, Sarah Dunn Hawley, Pat O'Brian Hayes, Julius Hegeler, Beth Heifetz, Edward Helin, Doris Heller, Sally Hempstead, Bill Henkel, Harriet Hentges, Audrey Herring, Lenore Hershey, Irene Hervey, Charles Higham, Judy Hilsinger, Alan Hilton, Jacquelyn Snow Hinds, Sanford Hollander, Judith Richards Hope and her father Dr. Joseph Richards, Sue Hornick, David Horowitz, John Howard, Mary Finch Hoyt, Ellen Hume, Nancy Davis Hunt, Marie Windsor Hupp, Harline Ward Hurst, Jayne Ikard, Rick Ingersoll, Jody Jacobs, Anne Hale Johnson, Beth Johnson, Julie Johnston, Barbara Hopkins Jones, Geoffrey Jones, John Judis, Phyllis Kaminsky, Jimmy Karen, Sally Katzen, Anne Keagy, David Keene, Sidney Meeker Keith, Gene Kelly, Steve Kelly, Cynthia Kempler, David Kennerly, LeRoy King, Kenny Kingston, Jean Kinney, Julia Knickerbocker, Jack Kotz, Mary Lynn Kotz, Elizabeth Gillespie Kramer, Kenyon Kramer, Larry Kramer, Judith Krantz, Denise Kreetzberg, John Kriaris, Carol Krute, Sylvia Rosenberg Lader, Robert Lamont, Richard Lamparski, Dr. Raymond LaScola, Betty Lasky, Cheryl Lavin, Laurence Leamer, Barney Leason, Virginia Lehman, Janet Leigh, Wendy Leigh, Helen Lerner, Joan Levine, Chuck Lewis, Drew Lewis, Jack Lewis, Jim Lewis, Jane Ley, Doris Lilly, Sally Perry Limberg, Eleanor Terry Lincoln, Miriam Nash Lindhe, Cynthia Lindsay, Jason Lindsey, Barbara Ling, Barbara and Robert Liotta, Frank Lorson, Ruta Lee Lowe, Kenneth Lynn, May Maas, Joyce Hagen Macy, Ben Maddow, Matty Maguire, Scott Malone, Dorothy Manners, Rita Marker, Fletcher Markle, Robert Marquardt, Buff Cobb-Martin, Jack Martin, Steve Martindale, Sam Marx, Suzanne Massie, George Masters, Florence Faas Mastin, Gilbert Mathieu, Timothy May, Jewell Jackson McCabe, Jim

McCahey, Abigail McCarthy, Robert McCloud, John McClure, Jerry Mc-Coy, Peter McCoy, Jan Davis McGuffie, Mrs. Albert McIntyre, Terry McKinnon, Eloise McNamara, Florence Meers, Jim Mendelo, Peter Menegas, Chet Migden, Barbara Pooley Miller, Casey Miller, Judy Miller, Marc Miller, Dr. George Millington, Lee Minelli, Meren Mitchell, John Monahan, Rev. Donn Moomaw, Anne Mooney, Gratsiella Moriano, Ann Morin, Barry Morrison, E. J. Mudd, Donald Murchison, Rose Murchison, Senator George Murphy, Helen Morgan Murray, Susan Myer, Tony Myerberg, Enoch Nappen, Joe Narr, Alana Nash, Simon Nathan, Gene Nelson, John Nelson, Judy Nelson, Roy Newbert, Barbara Newman, Clarence Newton, Lt. Fred Nixon, Phil Nobile, Lyn Nofziger, Kitty Nordstrom, Sally Nordstrom, Herb Nusbaum, David Obst, Andy Ockershausen, Joel Odum, Lilyan Neiman Ordower, Charles Orme, Robin Orr, Robbie Owen, Charles Palmer, Norman Panama, Patti Pancoe, Jacqueline Park, Dick Partee, Richard Pate, Ward Patton, Jan Paulk, Anna Perez, Newton Perry, Dr. Morton Smith-Peterson, Mary Pettus, David Pickford, Joan Pierce, Marion Pike, Tony Podesta, Ellen Pollon, Gretchen Poston, Jody Powell, St. Clair Pugh, Betty Shallberg Quely, Joan Quigley, Judy Quine, Tom Quinn, Frank Raccone, Charlotte Galbraith Ramage, Ann Keyser Rawley, Sonny Rawls, Paula Raymond, Bess Reagan, Michael Reagan, Barbara Rebori, Coates Redman, Helen Rees, Jim Reginato, Kathy Reid, Gottfried Reinhardt, Silvia Reinhardt, Oliver "Buck" Revell, Nancy Reynolds, Ray Rhinehart, John Riley, Art Robbins, Flora Roberts, John Roberts, Dolores Robinson, Jill Schary Robinson, Marian Robinson, Bill Roemer, Alex Rogers, Priscilla Blackett Rogers, Ed Rollins, George Romanos, Phyllis Rose, Jim Rosebush, J. B. Ross, Rep. John Rousselot, Milton A. "Mickey" Rudin, Dr. Daniel Ruge, Barbara Rush, George Rush, Jackie Rush, Bob Ryan, Cindy Maduro Ryan, Patricia Sagon, Enedina Salazar, Grace Salvatori, Henry Salvatori, Yvonne Sangiacomo, David Sargent, Jean Upham Sauter, Ursula Taylor Schacker, Jerry Schecter, Bob Schiller, Sabrina Schiller, Karl Schoumacher, Ted Schwartz, Marion Berry Scott, Barbara Seaman, John Sears, Sally Gavin See, Arlene Sellers, Danny Selznick, Susan Seward, Carl Anthony Sferrazza, Barbara Shailor, Karen Shaner, Elizabeth Shannon, Maggie Shannon, Marilyn Sharron, Alex Sheftell, Jerri Shenson, Julie Sherman, Joe Shimon, Donna Shor, Tom Shorebird, Lillian Burns Sidney, Sharon Sier, Irene Silbey, Diane Simon, Mary Sinclair, Shirley Singer, Jean Sisco, Paul Sluby, Jeannette Smalling, Walter Smalling, Jr., Jean Hagen Smith, Kenny Soames, Leonard Sorgi, Peter Sorum, Ann Sothern, Larry Speakes, Anne Spivak, Robert Stack, Susan Stalick, Michaela Stansfield, Patty Sue Stanton, Gloria Stewart, Jimmy Stewart, Larry Stinchcomb, Dean Stockwell, Pat Stolar,

Ann Straus, Daniel Stuckey, Madeline Kushman Stuckey, Marguerite Sullivan, Ce Ce Summers, Jean Swain, Nick Swano, Terry Sweeney, Gay Talese, Nan Talese, Jack Taylor, Patricia Taylor, Tessa Taylor, Jerry terHorst, Dennis Thomas, Merle Thomason, Anna Danzert Tilghman, Gertrude Tirrell, Lucy Toberman, Sue Tolchin, Reva Tooley, Emily Torcia, Nancy Traver, Stanley Tretick, Dr. Hugh Trout, Garry Trudeau, Jane Tucker, Racine Tucker, William Tucker, Greg Tweed, Ralph Tyler, Frank Ursomorso, Elizabeth Val Kanier, Kitsie Valatin, Juanita Valencia, Jessica Vartoughian, Alma Viator, Michael Viner, Robert Vogel, William von Rabb, Capt. Kenneth Wade, Irving Wallace, Sylvia Wallace, Blaine Waller, Gary Walters, Selene Walters, Shirley Watkins, Diane Wattenberg, Warren Weaver, Charis Webb, Les Weinrott, Rozanne Weisman, Steve Weisman, Ruth Jeffers Wellington, Carolyn Huddle Wells, John West, Dr. Ray Weston, Paul Weyrich, Bob White, O. Z. Whitehead, James Whitmore, Geraldine Whitt, Les Whitten, Faith Ryan Whittlesey, Bill Whorf, Charles Wick, Suzanne Wickham, Jon Wiener, Barbara Balensweig Wilk, Max Wilk, Al Williams, Charles Williamson, Marion Willing, Cleo Willoughby, John Wilson, Page Wilson, Michael Winters, Audrey Wolf, Helen Wolford, Jim Wrightson, Kathleen Young, Laura Young, Narda Zaccino, Bill Zwecker.

Kitty Kelley
Washington, D.C.
January 1991

FOR MERVIN BLOCK AND WAYNE KABAK AND MARVIN MCINTYRE—
THE THREE MEN MOST IMPORTANT TO THE LIFE OF THIS BOOK
AND, NOT INCIDENTALLY, TO ITS AUTHOR

Nancy Davis Reagan Family Tree

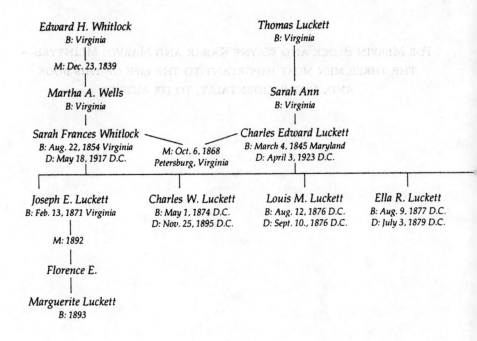

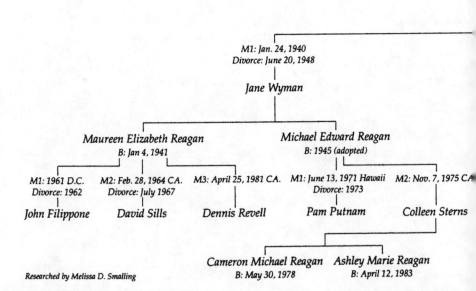

Researched by Melissa D. Smalling

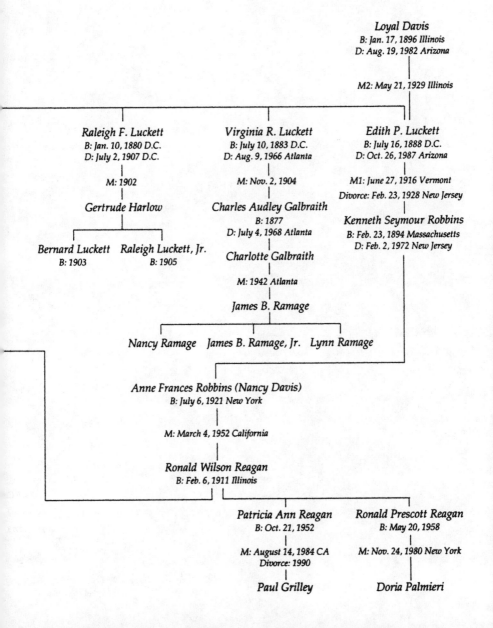

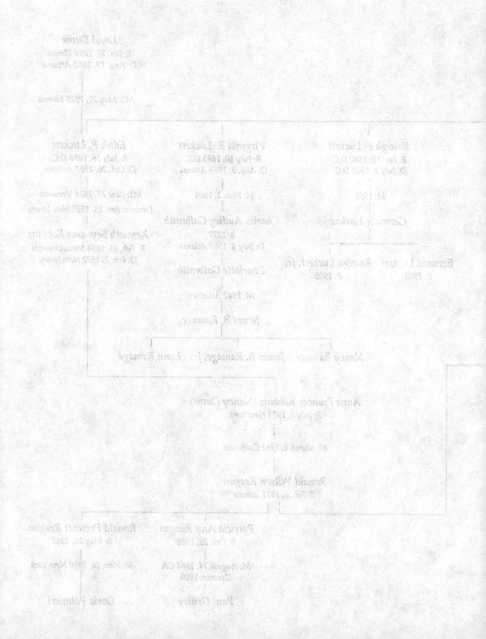

It is easier to pretend to be what you are not than to hide what you really are; but he that can accomplish both has little to learn in hypocrisy.

Charles Caleb Colton
Lacon
1825

1

STATE OF NEW YORK

CERTIFICATE AND RECORD OF BIRTH   32579

OF

Robbins Anne Frances

Sex	female	Color	White	Mother's Marriage Name	Mrs Edith L Robbins
Date of Birth	July 6·21			Mother's Name Before Marriage	Edith Luckett
Place of Birth Street, No. and Borough	Sloane Hospital			Mother's Residence	Flushing, L.I.
Father's Name	Kenneth Seymour Robbins			Mother's Birthplace	Petersburg Va.
Father's Residence	412 Amity St. Flushing L.I.			Mother's Age	29 Color White
Father's Birthplace	Pittsfield, Mass.			Mother's Occupation	Housewife
Father's Age	28	Color	White	Number of Children Born to this Mother including Present Birth	1
Father's Occupation	Automobile Business			Number of Children of this Mother Now Living	1

I, the undersigned, hereby certify that I attended professionally at the above birth and I am personally cognizant thereof, and that all the facts stated in said certificate and report of birth are true to the best of my knowledge, information and belief.

Signature ....

Date of Report   July 7,   1921   Reside at   347 W. 57 St.

This is to certify that the foregoing is a true copy of a record on file in the Department of Health. The Department of Health does not certify to the truth of the statements made thereon, as no inquiry as to the facts has been provided by law.

IRENE A SCANLON
CITY REGISTRAR

Do Not accept this transcript unless it bears the raised seal of the Department of Health. The reproduction or alteration of this transcript is prohibited by Section 3.21 of the New York City Health Code.

BUREAU OF VITAL RECORDS   DEPARTMENT OF HEALTH   THE CITY OF NEW YORK

TWO ENTRIES ON Nancy Reagan's birth certificate are accurate—her sex and her color. Almost every other item has been invented. In truth, the certificate itself gave birth to two generations of lies.

The original facts about the infant Anne Frances Robbins, now Nancy Reagan, were carefully rewritten:

She revised her date of birth, concealed her birthplace, and cast aside her father.

In her memoirs, she asserted she forgot the name of the hospital where she was born and added that "it burned down years ago." In fact, not only did Sloane Hospital in New York City not burn down, but according to its official history it did not have a fire.

As for her date of birth, Nancy said coyly at the age of sixty-nine, "I still haven't made up my mind." The certificate says she was born July 6, 1921. But when she grew up, she altered the date to 1923—thereby taking off two years.

When her mother gave her own age on her daughter's birth certificate, she took off four years; she was thirty-three at Nancy's birth. Her husband was twenty-seven, but she listed him as twenty-eight.

Edith Luckett's birthplace is recorded as Petersburg, Virginia. In fact, she was born in Washington, D.C. She is listed as a housewife, but she was an actress, a déclassé profession in those days.

Anne Frances Robbins fabricated not only a new background for herself, but also a new foreground. She was named for her father's great-great-great-grandmother, Anne Ayres, and her maternal grandmother, Sarah Frances. The baby girl was nicknamed Nancy by her mother. At the age of seventeen, Anne Frances went to court to change her entire name. She dropped her father's name and eventually dropped him.

Her father was "a Princeton graduate from a well-to-do family," she asserted in her memoirs. In fact, he did not attend Princeton—or any college. His family, from Pittsfield, Massachusetts, was not well-to-do. But even after disowning him, Nancy clung to those pretensions.

When the brown-haired, brown-eyed Anne Frances was born, her parents were living in a poor section of Flushing, Queens, an outer borough of New York City. They were renting one floor of a two-story frame house on Amity Street near the railroad tracks.

Nancy Reagan spent so many years redesigning the facts of her life that she came to accept her masquerade as real. By the time she became First Lady, the mask had become the face. History was about to be deceived.

"The truth is rarely pure," wrote Oscar Wilde in *The Importance of Being Earnest*, "and never simple." The retrieval of Nancy Reagan's birth certificate—the one tie to her past that she has been unable to shed—provides the country with an opportunity to take a second look at its former First Lady. A look at the face behind the mask.

2

"To UNDERSTAND NANCY, you've got to understand her mother and the life she invented for herself," said Lester Weinrott, a Chicago friend of Edith's. "Her mother made it up out of whole cloth. She invented herself. She created the stage, the scenery, and all the props. She constructed it out of spit. I shake my head in admiration because Edie, or Deedle as I called her, was a phenomenon. Unfortunately, her daughter did not lay claim to the best part of her gene pool, but at least she learned enough to make her husband President of the United States.

"What a mouth she [Edith] had," Weinrott went on. "Edie had the foulest mouth in the world and she told the dirtiest, filthiest jokes you ever heard in your life, but she played the role of a Southern belle to the hilt." Edith punctuated her musical drawl with every four-letter word known to stevedores, but always added a gracious "by your leave," "please," and "thank you."

Edith Prescott Luckett was born in Washington, D.C., on July 16, 1888, in an era so prim that books by male and female authors were still separated on library shelves. But this seventh and last child of Sarah Frances Whitlock and Charles Edward Luckett would never be a part of her straitlaced generation.

Edith was born when Benjamin Harrison was President of thirty-eight states and twenty-two territories. She arrived before the advent of the automobile and the telephone, when the typewriter was new on the market and the average American worker earned 22 cents an hour. In those days, where one came from determined who one was. Which is why she later concocted a Southern aristocracy for herself and social affluence for her family. Her mother had been born in Petersburg, Virginia, and prided herself on being a Southerner. By the time Edith grew up, she had adopted a honeyed accent and fabricated a magnolia lineage to the First Families of Virginia. She put herself forward as a daughter of the Confederacy, a product of ante-bellum gentry. This despite the fact that Edith's mother, Sarah Luckett, ran boardinghouses in the teeming Irish Catholic section of Washington, D.C., known as Swampoodle ("a swamp filled with puddles," wrote a newspaperman of the time), and her father, Charles Luckett, worked by the railroad tracks as a clerk for the Adams Express Company.

In later years, Edith would spin tales of her elegant family plantation background in Virginia, where she claimed to have attended a private boarding school. In fact, she was reared on the poverty-filled streets of the District of Columbia, where her poor, hard-working parents moved from one little red-brick row house to another, and she attended public school, but did not graduate from high school. In the first ten years of her life, her family moved five times within a four-block area, never able to better themselves in the process. The introduction of horsecars and electric trolleys brought noise to the downtown area of the nation's capital, and so the more prosperous residents followed the elegant carriages north to quieter locales. The Lucketts could not afford to move, so they remained downtown in dismal rental units over buggy stables, near the place where Abraham Lincoln died.

Throughout her life, Edith beguiled reporters with her phony genealogy. "I'm Southern, and that's the cute part about it," she told one writer a few years before she died. "My father and mother had to move up [north], but my mother went back to Petersburg to have all of her children born so that they wouldn't be born damn Yankees. Don't you love that?"

Actually, all of Sarah's children were born in Washington, D.C. except for her first. Traveling 130 miles from the District of Columbia to Petersburg, Virginia, for seven pregnancies was beyond the means of the Lucketts at the turn of the century, but not beyond Edith's imagination.

In 1907, Charles Luckett was promoted to manager of the F Street branch of the Adams Express Company, and with all the children working, including the two daughters, the family's fortunes finally improved enough so they could move into one of Washington's new apartment buildings. Unfortunately, what the gods of good fortune bestowed, they also snatched away.

At eleven o'clock on the morning of July 1, 1907, Edith's twenty-seven-year-old brother, Raleigh, walked into the Garrick Club on Pennsylvania Avenue and ordered a drink. When it was served, he pushed it away and left the table, heading for one of the reading rooms in the back. There he sat down on a sofa, pulled out a handgun, and shot himself in the chest. Hearing the blast, club members assumed it was merely the beginning of an early Fourth of July celebration, but minutes later they found Raleigh slumped over in a bloody heap, the smoking gun dangling from his left hand. "It's all over now," he gasped. "Telephone Joe."

His brother Joseph, the manager of the Columbia Theater, was immediately summoned, as were his father, mother, and two sisters. They rushed to the hospital, where they found Raleigh conscious but in critical condition. The bullet had penetrated his right breast and lay lodged in the membranes of his spinal cord, paralyzing him below the waist.

"Pop, it's all over, it's all over," he said when his father entered the room. Pouring out his despair over being separated from his wife and two sons, Raleigh said his life was no longer worth living. He refused to be consoled by reassurances that he would survive if the doctors could perform the surgery necessary to remove the bullet. Rather, he seemed determined to die.

"It's no use, Pop. It's no use," he said.

Hoping to rally the will of his son, the senior Luckett sent for Raleigh's young wife, Gertrude, who was staying with her parents at their summer home in Laurel, Maryland. She hastened to the hospital with her two little children and her father, Colonel M. R. Harlow. By then, Raleigh had lost so much blood that he was slipping in and out of consciousness. Heartsick and hysterical, Gertrude rushed to his side and apologized over and over for whatever she had done to offend him. She begged his forgiveness.

By 6:00 the next evening, the doctors admitted it was hopeless to attempt surgery and told the family that death was imminent. As she sat by her husband's side, Gertrude was inconsolable.

"Are you glad to see me, Raleigh? Are you glad to see me?" she asked.

"I'm awfully glad," he whispered at one point. He made a feeble effort to put his arms around her, but his lungs were so filled with blood that he fell back on the pillows, no strength left. His two-year-old son, Raleigh Jr., sat on the bed, near the father he had not seen for two months.

At fifty-three, Sarah Luckett had already buried two sons: Louis a month after he was born and Charles of tuberculosis when he was twenty-one years old. Her baby daughter Ella had died of cholera in infancy, and now she was watching her fourth child succumb—a suicide. Rocking back and forth in a chair, she buried her head in her hands and sobbed. Edith, nineteen, and her twenty-three-year-old sister, Virginia, also turned away, too agitated to watch their brother's deathbed reconciliation with his wife and children.

Raleigh died at 9:20 that night. On the Fourth of July, Charles and Sarah Luckett accompanied their son's coffin to Congressional Cemetery, where so many of their children lay buried.

Three years later, the city of Washington would read about the Lucketts again, but this time the stories would feature Edith, the youngest, who finally had persuaded her brother Joe to allow her to appear on stage at the Columbia Theater.

"I had no lines to say. I just laid [sic] there in the bed looking sad," she said years later. "When the curtain went down, I hopped out of bed and said, 'Don't cry. I'm alive!' I talked to the audience!"

The winsome young girl with angelic blond hair and larkspur blue eyes thrived on the applause she received that evening and decided then, despite her family's objections, to pursue her future in front of the footlights.

She began by understudying the leading ladies who performed at the Columbia Theater, where romances and comedies of doubtful merit made up the bulk of the stock company's offerings. Tickets at the Columbia sold for 25, 50, and 75 cents, while at the more established (respectable) National Theater orchestra seats cost $2.

One of her first notices read: "Little Edith Luckett has beauty, wit and talent. . . . Her prattle is as merry as the chirp of the cricket on the hearth, her eyes blue and her hair wavy. She has been brought to public notice by her remarkable cleverness, her grace and her sweet, pretty face."

The hallmark of Edith's life would be that "remarkable cleverness." At an early age, she grasped the value of meeting the right people and making the right connections. She quickly learned to advance herself. She began by using the theatrical contacts of her brother Joe, who got her placed with a revival of *The Crisis* in New York. Later, she became a member of a stock company in Minneapolis for a season. She returned to New York in 1910 to act in *Drifting,* a play soon to be forgotten.

Undeterred, Edith returned to Washington in 1911 to play in *The Fortune Hunter,* where she was mentioned by the *Washington Star* as an actress "whose steady progress promises a speedy fulfillment of the predictions of her numerous friends."

"The will to grow was everywhere written large, and to grow at no matter what or whose expense," wrote Henry James, characterizing the start of the twentieth century. He might just as well have been describing the ambition of Edith Prescott Luckett, who was determined to become an actress no matter what the cost. She accepted every job that came her way, toured in summer stock, and spent all her money on hobble skirts, cloche hats, silk stockings, and osprey plumes so that she could dress the part of a soubrette. "In stock, you know, one has to have a new gown every week," she told the *Boston Traveler and Evening Herald.* "It would never do to wear the same one twice. It takes a lot of time and thought and, what is more, a lot of money. But I don't begrudge either. The experience has been worth all it cost me."

At that time, stock companies covered the country like dewdrops, and every city that had an opera house turned it into a theater in the winter to pay the bills. Even a city as small as Pittsfield, Massachusetts—population 25,000 in the early 1900s—had a permanent stock company. It played the Colonial Theater (capacity: 1,400), where Edith Luckett, known to her stage friends as Lucky, was described as "an actress who is forging ahead rapidly."

With four years' experience, Edith took her career very seriously. When her boss, William Parke of Pittsfield's Parke Stock Company, insisted she play Mary in *If You're Only Human* in Boston, she refused. She said the role would damage her professional reputation.

William Parke threatened to fire her if she didn't accept. She held her ground, offering instead to obtain a substitute actress from New York and pay her salary and expenses. "I even offered to provide her gowns," said Edith.

When Parke told her to consider herself fired, she called her brother's friend Jack S. Connolly of the *Boston Herald* and asked for help. He, in turn, called producer George M. Cohan in New York City, who offered Edith a part in the new company of *Broadway Jones.* Edith accepted immediately and announced her departure from Pittsfield.

The road show of *Broadway Jones* was George M. Cohan's farewell to acting and Edith's chance to be associated with the most dynamic figure in American theater during the early 1900s. She seized the opportunity, hoping that Cohan would later cast her in one of his Broadway shows. He never did, but she mastered the publicity game by getting her name in the paper in every city the company toured. She never failed to regale male reporters with one of her "whizzers," as she called her gritty bathroom jokes, and always posed willingly for photographers. One day she walked into a restaurant with the dog that was in the play. She sat down and ordered two meals, one for herself and one for her mongrel co-star. The waiter, who could hardly believe his eyes, said that it was against the rules to allow dogs to eat out of restaurant plates.

"That's all right," chirped Edith. "I have my own plate." She opened her bag and brought out a little bib, a silver plate, and an Irish linen napkin. Later, she complained to the cashier. "This is not a regular dog," she said. "She is an actress and plays one of the principal parts in *Broadway Jones* and has taken several ribbons in Boston and New York at dog shows. She is very sensitive and I think your waiter has insulted her. In the future we will have to go elsewhere."

Edith received surprisingly good reviews in *Broadway Jones.* A Toledo, Ohio, theater critic applauded her "girlish and interesting work." The critic of the *Minneapolis Journal* even reviewed her gowns. "Like most Southern girls, Miss Luckett has a natural taste for clothes," he wrote, "and is always most attractively gowned. Among the younger actresses, she has risen to a conspicuous place within a half dozen years. Perhaps the next time she comes she will be heading her own company."

In 1913, when Edith was twenty-five years old but claiming to be twenty, she announced her engagement to Edward A. R. Brown, from "a wealthy, well-known New York family." She said she would leave the stage when they married and live happily ever after in Pittsfield. The engagement did not last, but Edith remained in Pittsfield, continuing her career. She thrived on being in a profession barely considered reputable at a time when signs still hung in hotels saying, "No Actors or Dogs Allowed."

Edith remained single long after most of her contemporaries were married and having children, and she flaunted her friendship with actress Alla Nazimova, one of the theater's most prominent lesbians. She was an ardent suffragist, saying that if American women were given the vote they could eliminate child labor in the United States.

Bawdy, raucous, and full of outrageous fun, Edith flouted conventions —smoking and swearing openly—but she made friends with everyone, including William Parke, who later asked her to rejoin his company. It was in Pittsfield that she met and fell in love with a handsome man six years her junior and decided, once again, to get married.

Kenneth Seymour Robbins came from an old New England family. He was the only son of John N. and Anne Ayres Robbins, who lived in a large house on Brenton Terrace. Ken was a salesman for the Berkshire Life Insurance Company. His father was vice president of W. E. Tillotson Manufacturing Company, and his mother was the great-great-niece of the first Episcopal nun in America, Sister Anne Ayres, who helped found St. Luke's Hospital in New York City. The family took pride in their ancestors, including Ken's maternal grandfather, Captain Frederick August Francis, a Civil War hero, who was married to Elizabeth Root, daughter of a general and granddaughter of one of the founders of Pittsfield.

Ken's parents were hardly overjoyed with their twenty-two-year-old son's courtship of an actress, especially one so much older than he. But Ken was enchanted with the local leading lady who showed the same drive and verve as his mother. "He'd be naturally attracted to someone strong-willed like his mother because while Ken was sweet and charming, he was a weak man and most definitely a mama's boy," said a cousin.

On June 27, 1916, Edith and Ken slipped off to Burlington, Vermont, to be married by a Congregational minister. The twenty-seven-year-old bride claimed to be twenty-four years old on her marriage certificate so she would appear to be only two years older than her twenty-two-year-old groom.

After their honeymoon, Edith and Ken returned to the Berkshires, where they started their married life in a farmhouse in Brainard, New York, owned by Ken's father.

Nine months later, President Woodrow Wilson called for a declaration of war against Germany. Ken enlisted in the army and served as a sergeant in the quartermaster corps until he was released on January 22, 1919. His honorable discharge papers said that he was a man of "excellent" character, "honest and faithful."

Ken's father had died in 1917 and left him some money, so he and Edith moved to New York City, where he worked as an agent for a life insurance company. Edith was given a small part by her friend Alla Nazimova in *'Ception Shoals.*

In 1920, after four years of marriage, Edith, who was thirty-two years old, became pregnant, and Ken wanted to return to Pittsfield to raise their child. Edith would not hear of it. Having tried and failed to get into the movies, she was now determined to pursue her dreams on Broadway. Ken acceded to the wishes of his remarkably clever wife and remained in New York with her for as long as he could stand it.

3

"NANCY HAS TRIED to destroy her father's good image by saying that he was a ne'er-do-well who sold used cars, deserted her at birth, and left her mother destitute," said Kathleen Young, a cousin of Kenneth Robbins, who met Nancy as a child. "It breaks my heart to read those things because they're simply not true."

"She has made some very nasty remarks about her father and how he mistreated her, but he was a kind, dear person," said Marian Swingle, who was married to Ken's brother-in-law by his later marriage.

In the opinion of his family, Kenneth Seymour Robbins was maligned by his one and only child, who resented the disintegration of her parents' marriage that left her a ward of relatives for the formative years of her youth. She later spoke of those years to Susan Crosland of the *Sunday Times* of London.

"The early childhood certainly left its mark," Nancy said in 1985. "But everything leaves its mark on you. Doesn't it? I'm not terribly good at psychoanalyzing myself."

Throughout her life, Nancy avoided any kind of self-analysis. Always declining to answer questions about her early childhood, she spoke only in glossy generalities. "Those were good old times in the good old days, a peaceful time in a peaceful place," she wrote in her autobiography. By then she had drawn a shade over the remembered reality, blocking out unpleasant, uncomfortable memories. She fully embraced the concept of *corriger la fortune*—the French expression meaning to correct one's fortune through denial of the past. Still, she never could camouflage the laceration of growing up without her mother and father. A thin layer of sadness seemed to envelop her like a shroud, causing her to cry easily and often at the most trivial things. "I puddle up reading the phone book," she admitted many years later. That scar left her with gnawing insecurities all of her life, rendering her unable to give and receive love naturally, which, in turn, seared her own children.

For the first year or so after giving birth, Edith tried to accommodate herself to the rituals of domesticity, but she could never quite shake the stardust of the stage. When she decided that Nancy should be properly christened, she shocked her puritan mother-in-law by choosing her lesbian friend Alla Nazimova to be the godmother. "Zim," as Edie called her, was a famous silent screen star renowned for the seances she held at her Hollywood palace, which became the Garden of Allah Hotel. Nazimova so dazzled Rudolph Valentino that he married, serially, two of the lesbians from her coterie.

"Edith told me that she and Alla Nazimova were very close friends, but whether there was ever a lesbian relationship between them, I don't know," said Les Weinrott. "There could have been in those early theater days, but once Deedle remarried and moved to Chicago, I think she probably flew pretty straight."

As a new mother, Edith reveled in showing off her baby. "Oh, you must come to dinner and meet my husband and see our new baby," Edith told Dorothy Stimson Bullitt, the founder of King Broadcasting Company in Seattle, who replied, "I'd like that very much. I'd also like to bring a present for your new baby. What does she need?"

"I want my baby to have a book," said Edith. "I'm asking all my friends to give the baby a book."

"A book? A baby book?"

"No, I don't want a book that the baby would like. I want a book that you like, because then, when my baby grows up, she'll have a proper diversified library. So please bring one of your favorite books."

Refusing to be confined by her new responsibilities, Edith continued accepting every invitation that came her way, appearing with or without her husband at cocktail parties, and sometimes carrying her baby in her arms. By 1923, her enchantment with motherhood had worn as thin as her marriage, so Kenneth Robbins returned to Pittsfield and lived with his mother while Edith rented a room on West 49th Street in Manhattan, determined to resume her career with a traveling stock company. She took two-year-old Nancy to Bethesda, Maryland, to be reared by her older sister, Virginia, and her husband, C. Audley Galbraith, a good, solid man who had been devoted to the Luckett family since marrying

Edith's sister in 1904. Edith felt that he and Virginia could provide a much more stable environment for her child than she could.

For the next five years, Nancy lived in a cramped little Dutch colonial house in the Battery Park section of Bethesda with her aunt, uncle, five-year-old cousin, Charlotte, and their wire-haired terrier, Ginger. The house had only two bedrooms, but a small sleeping space was made for Nancy on the upstairs porch. "We lived in a tiny, tiny house, which I can describe today down to the last detail," she said many years later.

She has repressed the rest of the details of her childhood or else rearranged them for public consumption. She wrote that when she was four or five years old, she had double pneumonia, was "seriously ill," and cried in misery for her mother. Her cousin Charlotte, who was three and a half years older than Nancy, does not recall this illness at all. Nor does she remember Nancy ever missing her mother. "But if she wrote it, I guess it must be true," she said dutifully. Nancy also wrote that on one of her visits her mother had brought her a Mary Pickford wig of blond curls, which she loved to wear. Perplexed by the story, Charlotte said, "No . . . no, I don't remember that either, but if Nancy wrote it, I guess . . . well, I guess it must've happened."

In her selective recollections of childhood, Nancy never relates the many attempts her father made to stay in touch with her, but Charlotte remembers the visits to Bethesda by Kenneth Robbins and his mother, whom Nancy lovingly called Nanee. A handsome, gray-haired woman who splashed herself with violet toilet water, Anne Ayres Robbins cherished her only grandchild and never wanted to lose contact with her. She always remembered Nancy's birthday, sent her presents for Christmas, cards for Thanksgiving, and candy for Halloween.

Every summer of her childhood, Nancy visited her father and grandmother at their house in Verona, New Jersey. Family photographs show that Ken and Nanee took Nancy to the beach shortly after Charles Lindbergh's nonstop solo transatlantic flight in 1927 because Nancy, holding her father's hand, is wearing a swimsuit emblazoned with Lindbergh's famous plane, *The Spirit of St. Louis.*

The one person both Nancy and Charlotte recollect vividly is Nancy's larger-than-life mother—the glamorous blond actress who occasionally swept into town swathed in a raccoon coat and loaded with presents, who danced through the night streets of Bethesda and told wild stories of her life on the road with stars like Spencer Tracy, Colleen Moore, Walter Huston, and ZaSu Pitts. "I loved Aunt Dee Dee," recalled Charlotte. "She was great. When she was in a play in New York, my mother took us up to see her. . . . We went up a number of times."

Nancy, too, remembers those trips with fondness. "The visits with

Mother were wonderful. I loved to dress up in her stage clothes, put on her makeup and pretend I was playing her parts. I saw her shows over and over again and never tired of them. Usually, I sat in the audience, but sometimes I watched from the wings. I don't remember the names of the plays, but I do remember the faces of the actors and actresses and the stagehands. The stagehands were especially nice to me."

In 1925, Nancy Robbins began accompanying her cousin Charlotte on the school bus to Sidwell Friends to attend kindergarten classes. The first year, the Galbraiths paid the $150 tuition, but then her mother took over the payments, believing it important for her daughter to attend one of Washington's finest private schools and to associate with upper-class children. Sidwell Friends' alumni include such prominent people as Charles Lindbergh and the children of President Theodore Roosevelt and Supreme Court Justice William O. Douglas. Edith wanted her daughter to have these associations early in life. Nancy attended the Quaker school for three years but did not impress her classmates.

"I don't recall the name at all," said Mary Neuhauser Dove.

"Never heard of her," said Carolyn Huddle Wells.

"I remember General Thomas Holcombe's daughter; he used to be commandant of the Marine Corps," said LeRoy O. King. "And Setsu Ko Matsudaira. She was a princess in the royal house of Japan. I remember the Mexican ambassador's son, but, I'm sorry, I don't remember any Nancy Robbins or Anne Frances Robbins. Who in the world was she?"

She was a plump little girl with sad brown eyes who played quietly with her dolls and gave pretend parties with her toy dishes. She said that her biggest treat came every Saturday night when her Uncle Audley gave her and her cousin a large piece of milk chocolate. "When you don't have a lot, small treats loom large," she recalled. Eating seemed to fill an emptiness for the little girl, who looked as round as a butterball next to her tall, wiry cousin. Years later, Charlotte still remembered Nancy sitting by herself, gobbling a box of chocolates her mother had brought to Bethesda. The box had been put high atop a cabinet after the girls had had their candy quota for the day. Then Charlotte and her mother and Edith had gone downtown; when they returned, they found Nancy sitting alone stuffing herself with candy. A memorable picture of a little girl who would grow up to be skeleton thin.

The dazzling career that Edith Luckett envisioned for herself never materialized beyond second-rate parts in poorly received plays. While she earned $60 a week, she watched with envy as her betters headed for Hollywood, where they were given railroad expenses and paid hundreds of dollars each day they worked, including rehearsals. By 1928, it was obvious that the motion picture, not the stage, was the way to national acclaim, but at the age of forty, Edith knew that the glorious road to stardom was no longer open to her.

"So she got smart," said her friend Lester Weinrott. "She was touring Chicago in George M. Cohan's *The Baby Cyclone* and someone introduced her to Loyal Davis, an unsuccessful but dedicated doctor—pisspot poor —who had been cuckolded by his first wife and was living in a drafty hotel after his humiliating divorce. Edith took it from there. She saw Loyal as her lifeline and grabbed on without letting go. She wanted to legitimize herself and give her daughter a break. Over the years, she transformed herself and this dour little man from the wrong side of the tracks in Galesburg, Illinois, into something that Chicago society had to pay attention to. It was the greatest performance she ever gave, and I salute her for it."

The remarkably clever actress knew that a poor doctor could become rich with the right patients, which she, with her socializing, could provide. So when she returned to Chicago a few months later with Walter Huston in *Elmer the Great*, she remained in the city in a rented apartment on East Pearson Street to court her doctor. His wife, Pearl, had recently divorced him in Reno, taken their son, Richard, and moved to Beverly Hills to remarry. The previous year, Ken Robbins had asked Edith for a divorce so he could marry Patsy Cross, and Edith, who had stayed on good terms with her husband through their eleven years of marriage, agreed. They filed a routine petition for an uncontested divorce on November 21, 1927, in Trenton, New Jersey, on the grounds of desertion; the final decree was granted on February 23, 1928, and a few months later Ken remarried in New Jersey. He lived there for the rest of his life, and he continued to see his daughter regularly until she was twenty years old. Edith made sure that Nancy spent part of every summer in New Jersey with him, his wife, and Nanee Robbins.

In 1928, when Audley Galbraith learned he was going to be transferred to Atlanta, he and Virginia took Nancy to be with her mother in Chicago, where Edith introduced them all to Loyal Davis. This was the man, she said, who could rescue Nancy from hand-me-down clothes and borrowed toys, and eventually transport her from the poor-relative environs of Bethesda to Chicago's shimmering Gold Coast. With him, she could look forward to her own bedroom, private schools, and debutante parties. Naturally, Nancy wanted her mother to get married as soon as possible.

Dr. Allen B. Kanavel, chief of surgery at Wesley Memorial Hospital, was not so enthusiastic. As Loyal Davis's mentor, he had advised him "never to hug a bad bargain with a deathlike grip," and Kanavel was not convinced that this forty-one-year-old divorced actress with a young daughter was the best bargain for his assistant. Kanavel wondered whether Loyal Davis, who had wanted to be an actor himself, might simply be infatuated with Edith's theatrical background and all the stars she knew. Dr. Kanavel insisted on finding out for himself by having Edith cook dinner for him at her apartment one night to see just how dedicated she was to becoming a doctor's wife. Instantly domestic, Edith charmed the elderly surgeon and assured him that she was ready to give up the theater to devote herself entirely to her husband and his career in medicine. "I shall never consider returning to the stage," she vowed. "Some actresses may make a success of marriage and a stage career, but I for one will not risk it." Dr. Kanavel was impressed.

Edith and Loyal were married on May 21, 1929, in a small chapel at the socially prestigious Fourth Presbyterian Church on Chicago's North Michigan Avenue. Their only attendants: Dr. Kanavel and seven-year-old Nancy. Dr. Davis, associate professor of experimental surgery at Northwestern University, was thirty-three; the bride was forty-one. The news was duly trumpeted in the society section of the *Chicago Tribune* the next day, along with the statement: "Both Dr. Davis and his bride gave their ages as 33 years."

Although Edith was older than her husband, she seemed much younger because of her happy-go-lucky insouciance. Uninhibited, she had no compunction about asking a doorman to button the back of her dress or stopping a passing stranger to get help zipping a tight skirt. She talked openly to everyone from cabdrivers to janitors, while Loyal Davis rarely spoke to people he considered his inferiors.

"He was an austere, forbidding man," said Lester Weinrott, "tight-assed and straitlaced."

When Edith embarked on her marriage, she embraced all the institutions that the establishment held dear. She endeared herself to Loyal's medical colleagues by making hospital rounds with him on a regular basis, befriending his students, visiting his patients, and working as a volunteer. She even started the gift shop at Passavant Hospital.

Then she joined the Fourth Presbyterian Church and dedicated herself to fund-raisers, benefits, and charity balls. If there was a socialite to be courted, a committee to be joined, a worthy cause to be championed, Edith was there. She pursued the grandes dames of Chicago society, wooed the meat packing princesses of Swift and Armour and Cudahy, and courted heiresses like Abra Rockefeller and Helen Wrigley. As a doctor's wife, she had entrée into the best circles and made good use of her access. Although it would take her thirty-three years to be sanctified enough for the Social Register, and then only when she was moving to

Arizona, she did manage to get herself and her husband invited to join the exclusive Casino Club.

"That was simply a little eating club," said Robert McCloud, a scion of a Chicago family and a 1937 graduate of Boys Latin School. McCloud, offended by Edith's profanity, never recognized her contributions to her husband's career. "She was never a member of the Women's Athletic Club and the doctor never belonged to the Chicago Club, which was the most exclusive club in the city. Dr. Davis was a very fine doctor, though. He studied under Dr. Harvey Cushing of Boston and he was respected by the people who counted, like my father, who was president of the First National Bank of Chicago and on the board of Passavant Hospital. Still, I think Mrs. Davis held him back socially. I . . . ah . . . never really understood how he ever . . . uh . . . married her anyway. She was so . . . well . . . no one could respect her foul mouth, and she was such a social climber. Very coarse. I just don't think she was up to the doctor's standards as a person. She did not have the breeding and social graces and character."

"She was vulgar," said one of Nancy's classmates at Girls Latin. "My father was a surgeon, and he did not think much of Dr. Davis for getting a divorce and remarrying. In those days, doctors were supposed to be married to medicine first and their wives second, and they were never to divorce. That's the way it was then."

Edith married her husband on the eve of the Great Depression, when Loyal Davis was barely making enough money to support himself, let alone a new family. To pay the rent on their apartment on East Delaware Place, buy her husband cashmere jackets so he could dress the part of a great surgeon, upgrade the wardrobe of her working-class mother-in-law, and enroll her own daughter in the exclusive Girls Latin School, Edith worked full time in broadcasting as a radio soap opera actress.

While her husband was paid $150 for performing prefrontal lobotomies, she brought in $500 to $1,000 a month working on "The Betty and Bob Show" on NBC Radio, a coast-to-coast soap opera. A master of mimicry, she played Bob's socialite mother, Mrs. Drake, who spoke with an affected British accent, and then she doubled as Mattie, the poor black maid. She was paid $15 for a standard broadcast to the East Coast, $10 for a repeat broadcast to the West Coast, plus $10 night work for stations not in the network. She made $175 a week, plus her salaries for "Ma Perkins," "Broadway Cinderella," and "Stepmother"—other soaps she did until 1944.

In addition, Edith worked indefatigably to ingratiate herself with the city's society editors. She cultivated them with luncheons and teas and cocktail parties, and called them regularly with tidbits of high-society gossip. Every Christmas she gave them a special mustard, which she made and put in jars labeled "From the kitchen of Mrs. Loyal Davis." Not surprisingly, her name appeared frequently on the social pages as "the wife of Dr. Loyal Davis, one of the city's leading neurosurgeons."

Despite her husband's rock-hard Republican politics, Edith managed to align herself with Chicago's powerful Democratic mayor, Edward J. Kelly. As an actress with a facility for elocution, she helped the mayor with public speaking, a favor that later would pay handsome financial rewards. She and Nancy accompanied the Kellys to the Democratic National Convention that was held in Chicago in 1932. Her picture appeared in the papers, the caption stating that she was teaching her eleven-year-old daughter the intricacies of convention politics.

"When Edie married Loyal, she was like Michelangelo looking at the Sistine Chapel for the first time. She was going to create herself a masterpiece," said Lester Weinrott. "Loyal had the credentials and she had the moxie. They both got a good deal when they married each other. He got himself a dynamo who would pay the bills and introduce him to the right people, and she got a security blanket for herself and her daughter. Without Edie, Loyal would never have made it in Chicago. Without him, she wouldn't have been accepted. They each got what they paid for. She was determined to make him the most prestigious physician in the city and get them into the Social Register, which she felt would pave the way for Nancy to be a lady of social graces.

"Edie worked for the first fifteen years of her marriage to get them an apartment on East Lake Shore Drive, which is the most exclusive block in Chicago. Surgeons didn't make that much money in those days, and so she needed to work. I once asked her why she was killing herself and I'll never forget her answer: 'Even if I have to eat acres of shit, I'll make Loyal the best damn society doctor in this town and Nancy will make her debut at the Casino Club.' Edith would do whatever she had to do to survive and prosper. She had pioneer guts, first-class American frontier grit. The kind where, if you saw a bear with two cubs, you killed the bear to eat and took the two cubs so they could grow up, and you could kill them later. That's the kind of guts she had."

Having finally put Swampoodle behind her, Edith could start blotting out Bethesda's deprivation by giving Nancy summers at Camp Kechuwa in northern Michigan, Easters in Bermuda, and trips to Europe. For Nancy's sixteenth birthday, Edith gave her a black Mercury convertible with red leather upholstery. She now believed that people could be admired solely for their looks, their clothes, and their material possessions, and she raised her daughter accordingly. "Pretty is as pretty does—that's what my mother taught me and that's what I taught Nancy," she said.

"I met Nancy when I was twelve years old, and I was in awe of everything she had," said Kathleen Young, a cousin who visited the Davises' home when she was a child. "I was returning to America after living in France for several years and being in a convent school. Nancy seemed so sophisticated to me because she had angora socks hanging in her bathroom and I had never met anyone who was rich enough to afford angora socks. I thought that was quite something. I always loved Edith because she was a lot of fun, but she changed when she married Loyal Davis. I think she probably married for security and . . . well . . . she was still great, but she'd changed. . . . She just wasn't as carefree as she'd once been."

Edith had become as bigoted as her husband. "And Loyal was the worst bigot in the world," said Lester Weinrott. "He was a racist who called all blacks niggers, and an anti-Semite who called all Jews kikes. He hated every Catholic he ever met. His mother, a railroad engineer's wife, was president of the Eastern Star [a Masonic order], and she spat on the floor every time a Catholic entered the room.

"Loyal was the same way. We had a federal judge in Chicago named Mike Igoe who married a nice Catholic girl from Galesburg, and Loyal never referred to Mrs. Igoe as anything but 'that Catholic bitch.' Not to her face, of course, just behind her back."

The prejudices of Loyal Davis were not hidden from the medical community, or from the interns and residents who worked for him. Some were so appalled by his virulent racism that when they went into the Chicago ghetto to deliver babies, they persuaded the black mothers to name their children "Loyal" out of spite.

Edith was as outspoken as he on the subject of "nigrahs," as she put it. At a party she gave at her Lake Shore Drive apartment to announce plans for the first Chicago International Film Festival, the festival's public relations director arrived with Gwendolyn Brooks, the black poet who later won the Pulitzer Prize. After Mrs. Brooks walked into her home, Edith drew the publicist aside.

"Who is that nigrah woman?" she said.

"Why, that's Gwendolyn Brooks," said the director. "She's just been named poet laureate of the state of Illinois."

"I don't care," snapped Edith. "I won't even allow colored help in my house. Please get her out."

"I'm sorry, I can't do that, Mrs. Davis."

"You'll do it, or I'll have your job."

"Since I only get paid a dollar a year for this job, you're welcome to it," said the publicist, standing her ground. Many years later she said,

"We stayed at the party, and I never said anything to Gwendolyn Brooks, but I don't think she felt very comfortable being there."

The only other black person known to enter the Davises' home was the singer Eartha Kitt, and her visit, too, was unintentional. She came as the guest of Carol Channing, whom Edith had invited over for drinks, telling her to bring "a theater crowd" with her of whoever was touring Chicago. When Channing walked in with the exotic black singer, she was severely berated by Dr. and Mrs. Davis for bringing "that woman" into their home.

Edith once gave a radio interview in Phoenix during which she laughed about Nancy's favorite color being red. "It makes her furious when I say this . . . but like I tell you—like the niggers—any color, so long as it's red."

Movie stars like Spencer Tracy, who shared the Davises' right-wing politics, felt comfortable with them; others did not. Myrna Loy once became so angry that she walked out of a dinner party in their home. "When they began reviling Adlai Stevenson and his humanitarian policies," she said, "I stood up from their table, scornfully surveyed that gathering of plutocrats, and headed straight for the door."

"The anti-Semitism of Loyal Davis was well known to everyone," said Dr. Ray Weston, a Chicagoan practicing in Los Angeles. "But that was during the days when there were quotas on Jews in all the medical schools. Northwestern probably had only eight or nine percent Jewish enrollment."

One Jewish student who felt the sting of Loyal Davis's biases grew to respect the man. "In fairness to my old mentor, I wouldn't say that his anti-Semitism was vicious, but I will admit that he had a hang-up," he said. "He could not say the word *Jew*. In the thirty-five years that I knew him, I never heard him say the word. He just couldn't do it. He'd say, 'your people.' If you read his autobiography, *A Surgeon's Odyssey*, you'll see where that anti-Semitism came from. When Loyal did his internship at Cook County Hospital, there was a Jewish doctor in his class who sold autopsies to bereaved families for $35, which was highly unethical, and Loyal figured that if one Jew will do it, they'll all be a bunch of crooks. He once admitted that to me. . . . In his own way, though, he had great integrity.

"When I was his personal clerk at Passavant Hospital, he checked out my uniform and my table manners and said, 'Good. I'm not so aware of the fact that you're a little West Side kike.' After three months working with him, I said I'd like to stay on at Passavant. I had worked hard— twenty hours a day—and everybody like me, but Loyal said, 'I think you had better go with your own people,' which meant I should go to Michael Reese Hospital, which was a haven for Jewish boys in those days.

"Edith was at the hospital a lot in the early days, and sometimes when Loyal got mad and called me a kike in front of patients, she would see me in the corridor at Passavant and put her arm around me and buy me a Coke. So I loved her."

Despite her beliefs, Edith's personality drew people to her like a magnetic force. "I first met Edith when we were working for NBC in a show sponsored by Standard Oil of Indiana," said Joan Kay Diebow. "Edith and Don Ameche were in the cast, and she told the coarsest jokes in the world, but everyone loved her. I had made some little yarn dolls for each member of the cast and took them down to the studio one day. When Edith saw them, she said, 'I'd love to have some of those for my kid,' so I made a set for Nancy, who was collecting dolls at the time. I did it just because I adored Edith."

"You couldn't help but love her," said Lester Weinrott. "She was this adorable darling little woman with a phony theatrical Southern accent who always made you feel good just being around her. Yes, she swore like a drafted Turkish sailor and told smutty toilet jokes, but Loyal pretended not to hear because she was paying all the bills and introducing him to the right people. I was so crazy about her I ended up being her educated slave for forty years. She could get people to do anything for her, and I have to say that Nancy, who never had her mother's spontaneous charm and warmth, certainly learned how to manipulate from a genius. She was schooled by a social mechanic of the first order."

The lessons were not lost on the youngster as she set about trying to win the love of Loyal Davis. She did everything to please him so that he would adopt her. "I used to go on trips with him, driving in our car to see patients in Gary or Cicero. Or on weekends . . . go to his office and laboratory at Northwestern and I would watch him work," she said. She watched silently because no one was allowed to speak when he was operating.

"I remember Nancy telling me that when Dr. Davis took her to surgery on Saturdays, she was always so afraid she would get sick and vomit during those neurological operations and embarrass him," said Jody Jacobs, former society editor of the *Los Angeles Times.* "Usually she watched from a glassed-in balcony, but sometimes the doctor actually took her into the operating room to stand near him as he was operating. She said she went because she wanted to make him proud of her; she never let on that it made her feel squeamish and sick to her stomach."

To please Loyal Davis, Nancy emulated him, adopting his compulsion for neatness, his obsession with clothes, his mania for discipline. She even embraced his conservative politics. He promised her $1,000 if she didn't smoke or drink until her twenty-first birthday, and she collected. While some children would have chafed under his strict regimen, Nancy seemed to thrive on it. Many saw Dr. Davis as a brilliant but formidable martinet, a humorless man undeserving of love, but Nancy adored him and wanted to become his daughter. Still, he would not agree to adoption for many years.

She later asserted that he had made her his daughter as soon as the law allowed, but that wasn't true. She had wheedled and cajoled and begged to be adopted from the beginning, but Dr. Davis had resisted. He treated her well and said he loved her, but he refused to initiate legal proceedings. Among his reservations, he said, was that her father and paternal grandmother were still alive. Nancy, however, did not care. The humiliation of going through high school as the daughter that Dr. Loyal Davis would not adopt was almost worse than being Anne Frances Robbins. Finally, her mother, worried about her daughter's future debut, prevailed upon her husband because she did not want to send out engraved invitations that read: "Dr. and Mrs. Loyal Davis invite you to a tea dance in honor of Mrs. Davis's daughter, Anne Frances Robbins."

Still, the doctor held back. So Nancy took the initiative. In 1938, when she was seventeen years old and a junior in high school, she consulted Orville Taylor, an attorney who lived in the same building, about the steps needed to get herself adopted. He told her that she would have to get a signed agreement from her natural father, so she made a trip East, met Ken Robbins at the Waldorf-Astoria in New York, and insisted that he sign the requisite legal papers. This he did, with sadness. With the papers in hand, Nancy returned to Chicago and presented them to her lawyer.

Nancy's adoption papers, still sealed, show that a petition was filed in Cook County Circuit Court on April 19, 1938, stating "that the natural parents of said child are divorced, and that the mother of said child has since married Loyal Davis . . . and that the father of said child, Kenneth S. Robbins, consents in writing to the adoption of said child by the petitioners, and waives the issuance of process, that said minor child being more than 14 years of age likewise consents in writing to her adoption."

The court papers show that Nancy not only wanted to be adopted by Loyal Davis, she also wanted to get rid of all traces of Anne Frances Robbins. So in her adoption petition, she asked that her name be legally changed to Nancy Davis. The next day, the court agreed to her petition. She never again referred to herself as Anne Frances Robbins. Yet she despised the word *adopted* and became angry at anyone who used it for her relationship to Loyal Davis. "It makes her so damn mad when people call Loyal her adopted father," said her mother. "Oh, God, he hates that, too! He's always been a father to her, and he doesn't like anybody to say he's her adopted father. Burns the tail feathers off him, he gets so mad."

"The day after she was legally adopted, she came prancing into school telling all of us, 'You can call me Nancy Davis from now on,' " recalls a classmate from Girls Latin School. "God, she was unbearable then, just unbearable. She had made a big deal out of leaving school in the middle of the week to go to court for two days, and frankly we were all kind of curious because we'd never heard of such a thing as getting yourself adopted. At that time, everyone in our class was the birth child of natural parents, and there were no parents who were divorced and remarried like Nancy's mother."

Only the children of privilege attended the private schools Girls Latin and Boys Latin (which merged in 1952 to become the Latin School). Girls Latin, which Nancy attended from 1929 to 1939, stood at 59 East Scott Street in one of Chicago's finest neighborhoods, a few blocks from where the Davises lived. The classes were small; there were only fourteen girls in Nancy's graduating class, and the school required strict adherence to the dress code—uniforms, no makeup, no jewelry. There was a classical curriculum of academics and sports to prepare students for college.

"She played field hockey, but she just didn't excel on the athletic field because she was too chubby," said Jane Beckwith Crowe, a classmate. "She worked real hard on her grades—she was a plodder—and managed to get a B-minus average. . . . The thing she was really interested in, though, was the movies and talking about movie stars. Her idol was Tyrone Power. She took dramatics and wanted to be an actress like her mother."

Another classmate, Jean Wescott Marshall, recalled going to the movies with Nancy every Saturday afternoon and Sundays after church. "We bought every movie magazine," she said. "She liked Bing Crosby. I liked Ronald Reagan. She said, 'I don't know what you see in Ronald Reagan.' "

With her husband's encouragement, Edith kept up her theatrical connections, and regularly entertained the stars who toured Chicago. Spencer Tracy frequently used the Davises' home to dry out from his alcoholic binges, and Walter Huston was a regular visitor who spent a good deal of time with the Davises in Arizona and at his ranch in California.

"When Nancy came back from her first trip to Hollywood," said Jane Beckwith Crowe, "that's when everyone wanted to talk to her. Up to then no one paid much attention to her, but we wanted to find out about the stars she had met and she had met quite a few. I remember her telling us about Greta Garbo and how Garbo was so cheap she'd cut her cigarettes in half. That's really saving your pennies, isn't it? Nancy knew Walter Huston and Spencer Tracy and Colleen Moore and ZaSu Pitts and Alla Nazimova, who were all friends of her mother."

"I remember that trip very well," said a classmate whose father was a surgeon, "because we were all in the locker room and we asked Nancy, or La Belle as I sarcastically called her then, how the trip went, and she said, 'Well, Uncle Walter [Huston] told me that I didn't have much hope of becoming a movie star because my legs are so bad.' I nearly fell off the bench when she said that because it was the only time I ever heard her be honest about herself or halfway funny. Nancy was not one to let her guard down."

Even as a teenager, she seemed "self-contained"; her classmates thought she was "nice but very determined to get what she wanted." Few of them remember spending much time after school in her home, which struck them as unusual.

"I never went to Nancy's house, even though I went to school with her from the fifth grade through high school," said Elizabeth Gillespie Kramer.

"I spent the night at Nancy's once," said Jane Beckwith Crowe, "and her mother sneaked into our bedroom after midnight and said, 'Okay. He's asleep now. Let's go into the kitchen and drink the champagne,' so we did, but we never went to their house after school because it was either too immaculate or the doctor might have been there. He was very difficult—cold and scary to us kids. Whatever, it just wasn't the place to hang out and have fun. . . . Nancy didn't even have a pet of any kind. There wasn't a dog or a cat or a bird or even a goldfish at her house."

"I only went to Nancy's one time and that was for lunch on a Saturday," said a surgeon's daughter. "I remember being looked over by her parents and that irritated me no end. I felt like I was being checked out. . . . I was so flustered that I started stammering and said something about not hearing with my eyes and seeing with my ears instead of the other way around . . . it was awful. . . . I was never asked back."

Although Nancy had a stepbrother, Richard, from Loyal Davis's first marriage, they did not grow up together. She saw him only during vacations until he came to live with his father after his mother died in 1939. So for most of her life, Nancy was reared as an only child and displayed the self-possessed characteristics associated with only children, who are usually more mature, more advanced, and more ambitious than children brought up with siblings. In one area of social development, though, Nancy seemed to lag behind the rest of her contemporaries.

"She did not date very much in high school, and I can't remember any boys who were ever interested in her," said Jane Beckwith Crowe. "I had a hard time getting her dates. She wanted to go out with Bobby Crane of the R. T. Crane plumbing family, but he wasn't interested in her. . . . I tried to get him to take her to the country club dance, but he wouldn't do it. Then there was Buddy Baird of Baird and Warner Real Estate, but he wasn't interested either. Nancy only liked the boys who came from prominent families, which is okay, I guess, but she was just so obvious about it."

"She was not as popular with the boys as some of the other girls in her class because she was a little unsophisticated," said Robert McCloud. "She was nice, though."

"A little prim," said Augustus Maxwell, Jr., another Chicago family scion who was graduated from Boys Latin.

Within a few years, that primness would somersault into promiscuity, but during high school, Nancy concentrated on meeting only the most suitable boys at the Fortnightly Club dances she attended with her class-mates.

"Most of us traveled in groups with the guys from Boys Latin," said a surgeon's daughter. "We would go over to Gin Skinner's house after school to listen to records or make fudge or something like that. But not Nancy. She never hung around with us. . . . She was always at home plotting and scheming and trying to get anchored to some guy like a barnacle on a boat. . . . She even bought herself orchid corsages so the rest of us would think she had a rich boyfriend who was crazy about her, but we caught on to that scam after we saw her going in and out of the flower shop at the Drake Hotel."

In writing about those days at Girls Latin, Nancy later admitted to scheming when it came to men, saying she "always had a crush on some-one," including "a tall blond policeman named Tommy on duty [near our apartment]. I was secretly in love with him. He was nice to all of us. I would tell him I was having trouble [getting across the windy street near Lake Michigan], and he'd help me cross while I hung on to his belt."

The need to appear special to others was gratified at school, where she was active in the glee club, president of her sophomore class, and presi-dent of the drama club. After being defeated for the office of student body president, she was elected student judge of her senior class. That post gave her responsibility for enforcing the school's dress code, a role that her classmates said she relished.

Her high school yearbook cites Nancy's "social perfection [as] a source of constant amazement to others," and in a senior prophecy she was remembered for her good manners, her good clothes, and her total incomprehension of science.

The highlight of her days at Girls Latin occurred during her senior year, when she had the lead in the class play, *First Lady*. The comedy by Katharine Dayton and George S. Kaufman, one of the most popular plays of the day, depicts a war between two formidable women determined to put their man into the White House. One woman backs a politician described as "Good-looking. Western. And doesn't know a thing."

Nancy's character cannot abide the thought of this other woman becoming First Lady. Nor can she stand to see her husband lose the presidency to the good-looking dolt from the West, so she sets out to sabotage the other candidate. At one point, Nancy's character becomes so frustrated with all the scheming necessary to achieve her goal that she says, "They ought to elect the First Lady and then let her husband be President."

Nancy's character wins in the end by treachery. "It was a great part," she said years later. "I loved it."

4

IN 1939, one-third of America was, in the words of President Franklin Delano Roosevelt, "ill-housed, ill-clad, ill-nourished." The other two-thirds of the country lived well enough to survive the crippling Depression around them and the approaching shadow of war, which would soon embroil most of the globe. The Nazis crushed Poland in 1939, but Hitler quickly reassured the world that he was not interested in further conquest. He said he cared only about his easel and the life of the artist. "I have wanted to be a great painter in oils, and as soon as I have carried out my program for Germany, I shall take up my painting," he said.

Much relieved, Americans headed for the New York World's Fair, listened to "Amos 'n' Andy" on the radio, and bought their children Superman comic books. They listened to John L. Lewis crusade for unions in the coal mines; they read *Grapes of Wrath* by John Steinbeck, the decade's most compelling social document; they swarmed into movie theaters to see *Gone With the Wind*, *Wuthering Heights*, *Dark Victory*, and *Goodbye, Mr. Chips*—some of the pictures that Hollywood produced at the height of its glory.

In 1939, the gangster Al Capone was released from prison after serving six years for tax evasion, and the comedian Jack Benny was convicted for smuggling $1 million worth of jewelry into the country for his wife.

In Chicago, Edith Davis braced herself for the arrival from California of her husband's twelve-year-old son, Richard, who was moving in with the Davises because his mother had died. By decree of Dr. Davis, she promptly enrolled the youngster in Boys Latin School as the mandatory first step for young Richard to become a doctor like his father.

This was also the year that Edith would achieve her social apotheosis with Nancy's debut at the Casino Club. By dint of sheer hard work, she had established herself and her husband as a social presence in Chicago, and on December 28 she would pass this prize on to her daughter by formally introducing her to society.

That fall, Nancy enrolled in Smith College, the largest women's resident liberal arts college in the world and one of the Seven Sisters, the elite schools known as the female Ivy League.

Although determined to be an actress, Nancy did not select Smith because of its theater department—it had none. Rather, she applied because her parents felt it was a socially correct school and one that would put her in contact with the right people. As the largest of the Seven Sisters, it was the one most likely to accept Nancy, whose grades were not good enough for admission to Vassar, Wellesley, or Radcliffe.

"Remember, this was during the Depression and on the eve of the war, so the admission standards weren't all that tough," said Mary Ann Guitar, one of Nancy's Smith classmates. "As long as you could afford the $500 tuition and the $500 room and board and were, as the phrase went, 'college material,' you went to college. If you weren't college material, you chopped off your head and went to work in a dime store. . . . Nancy didn't do something dopey like go to Pine Manor or Sweet Briar or Connecticut College for Women—one of those silly finishing type of schools. She wanted to be part of the ruling class, so she went to Smith."

"Most of us who went to Smith were considered in the top ten percent of society," said Sally Gavin See, another classmate. "Nancy had money —I remember she got an allowance of $100 a month, and I only got $1 a week—but she was from the Midwest, and she had nothing in terms of family background. I'm speaking as a frightful snob, but in the New England scale of things, Nancy didn't have culture; she didn't have social standing. She didn't have background. . . . We all knew about her theatrical ambitions—she name-dropped Uncle Walter and ZaSu Pitts and Alla Nazimova all the time, but she really did know these people—and while the stage was glamorous, it still was not quite *comme il faut* [as it should be], if you know what I mean."

Nancy did not much care about a college diploma. She wanted to go to work in the theater and become a star as soon as possible. Dr. and Mrs. Davis, on the other hand, wanted her to have the prestigious Ivy League credential that a degree from Smith would confer. Being a dutiful daughter, she complied.

"My parents wanted me to graduate from college before I started on my chosen career," she said. "I was so anxious to get stage experience that I wanted to quit after my second year at Smith, but I did what my mother and father wished, and now I'm glad. I just couldn't see spending four years in school at that time."

Arriving on campus at Northampton, Massachusetts, in the fall of 1939, Nancy was assigned to Talbot House. She roomed with Jean Wescott, a wealthy Chicago friend from Girls Latin who also lived on East Lake Shore Drive.

Without sororities, the college operated on the "cottage system" as stipulated in the will of Sophia Smith, its founder. All students lived on campus in assigned houses of no more than seventy girls to a house. Most of the socializing took place within a student's house, with the exception of those who took part in extracurricular activities. Meals were served at the houses by uniformed maids, and dinners were usually formal.

Nancy Davis was one of 528 freshmen, most of whom were the upper-middle-class daughters of successful businessmen; 51 fathers were doctors, 42 fathers were lawyers, and 11 were bankers. The women in Nancy's class were largely Episcopalian, with mothers committed to homemaking. Edith Davis was one of the few mothers who worked, and the only one engaged in radio soap operas.

Those freshmen, who would become the class of 1943, embraced a wide range of ambitions, the most popular being social service, teaching, and journalism. Several young women wanted to write and three students wanted to enter the diplomatic service. A few chose sculpturing, mineralogy, architecture, fashion design, and geology. But only one was determined to be an actress.

"Some of us talked about going to New York and getting an apartment to try the stage, but in the end my mother wasn't about to let me do something like that," said Jane Upham Sauter, class of 1943.

"It was frowned on at the time," said Harline Ward Hurst, another classmate. "There was a Victorian prohibition against it. You know . . . [the] 'Don't put your daughter on the stage, Mrs. Worthington' type of thing."

"I had a chance to work in summer stock in New Jersey and had good parts lined up, but my father said no," said Ann Teal Bradley. "At the time, there were a lot of homosexuals in the theater, and in those days you didn't discuss gays—it was one of those unmentionable things—and my father was very opposed to my associating with people like that. He felt they were unhealthy. . . . I guess Nancy's parents thought she could handle herself."

Homosexuality was an unspoken fact of life in the all-female environment of Smith College, where people still whispered about Henrietta Bingham, the Louisville, Kentucky, newspaper heiress who had skipped to England in her freshman year with her English instructor, Mina Kirstein, to pursue a lesbian affair.

"There were rumors about those kinds of girls but just rumors," said Ann Teal Bradley. "It was one of those hush-hush things. Somebody might suddenly quit school, or leave, or commit suicide or something, and then you'd find out that she'd been a lesbian, but it was really very rare, very, very rare."

Other classmates remember homosexuality being prevalent on campus. "There was a lot of that at Smith, like at any girls' school," said Barbara Balensweig Wilk. "It wasn't something anyone talked about at the time, and most of it was not overt, but it was a time when women got crushes on women."

"It [lesbianism] was a tragic situation and, at that time, just out-and-out scandalous," said Juliette Harvey Guthrie.

In later years, students at Smith and other women's colleges used the term *four-year lesbians* to describe those who professed to be gay in college or had an affair with their best friend during school but after graduation became interested in men, married, and reared children.

"During the time Nancy and I were at Smith there was a lot of back-rubbing and hand-holding and hugging-your-best-friend kind of thing, but it was all very innocent," said Sally Gavin See. "I don't think there were any serious lesbian relationships in our class, but then, I don't know for sure."

Even so, a secret but romantic "best friends" relationship developed between Nancy Davis and a classmate who later became an avowed lesbian. The lesbian classmate was involved in the theater and very popular on campus. "They spent a lot of time together," said Barbara Balensweig Wilk.

"They were very wrapped up in drama," said Mary Heald Dickert.

Most Smith students found the college curriculum to be intellectually challenging but hardly daunting. "My definition of a 'Smithie' is a girl who knows she's intelligent, wants a good education, and makes the most of it later on in life," said the writer Madeline L'Engle, class of 1941.

The class of 1943 was no exception. Members prided themselves on picking rigorous academic majors and looked down on someone like Nancy Davis for choosing the "soft and easy route" of dramatic arts. "None of my friends majored in drama," said Amy Ward Beir. "It was not academically demanding enough, and it certainly didn't prepare you for life."

"The first two years at Smith we all had to take required basic subjects like language, math, science, history, and literature before we could begin our major, and we had to maintain good grades or else we couldn't participate in any campus productions," said Sally Gavin See. "That was tough for Nancy because she had a very hard time with her studies. I think she was pushed beyond her academic capacity, because her grades were not very good, which meant she couldn't be in any shows. You had to have good grades to do stuff like that, which is why she didn't star in anything until her junior and senior years. Once she started taking those easy drama courses she got A's and B's, which pulled up some of those early C's and D's."

Nancy admitted as much when she wrote about her college days at Smith. "I had a terrible time with science and math," she said. "My mind just did not seem to function correctly for these subjects. [Then] I majored in drama and did well."

Nancy's extracurricular activities were all social, like the Garden Party Committee, the Junior Prom Committee, and the Charity Ball Committee. "All very much in character, don't you think?" said Eleanor Terry Lincoln, the class dean.

Nancy is best remembered by her classmates as short (five feet, four inches), attractive, but chubby. "She was always worrying about her weight in college," said Sally Gavin See, "but it never seemed to fluctuate." When Nancy returned home after her first year at Smith weighing 150 pounds, Dr. Davis told her she had to reduce. So she went on a strict diet.

Despite her weight, Nancy was pretty. She had a flawless complexion; long, dark-brown hair; deep-set brown eyes; and a prominent nose. It was so prominent that eventually she had it reshaped by plastic surgery. She was described as "aloof," "cold," and "distant" by some of her classmates, but remembered by all for her extraordinary grooming and impeccable neatness.

Forty-six years later, one classmate still recalled the powder-blue quilted bathrobe trimmed with lace that Nancy wore to house meetings when everyone else breezed in wearing raincoats over flannel pajamas. "The rest of us were usually slobs, but not Nancy," she said. "I never saw her dressed less than perfectly—never!"

Another acquaintance recalled the maroon towels monogrammed with "Nancy" that she used at Smith for four years and then sold to an underclassman who shared the same first name. "She *sold* those used towels to

Nancy Keene; she didn't *give* them to her, even though she had used them for four years," said a housemate.

Generosity did not come naturally to Nancy, who had spent her early years wearing hand-me-downs, scrimping, and conserving. Her frugality, at times petty and thoughtless, became characteristic. She recycled gifts that she did not like—and kept an entire closet filled with presents she didn't want but that she could choose from when she needed to give someone a gift. In later years, she made sure that she got the presents she wanted by going into her favorite store before her birthday, making her selections, telling the saleswoman, and then sending her friends in to that store to shop. "It's much easier that way" was her matter-of-fact explanation.

Her intense ambition to be an actress was recalled vividly by her college classmates. "The minute the lights came on, Nancy came alive," said Barbara Balensweig Wilk. "She really wanted to be a star. There was no question about it, and when she wanted a part in a play, she went all out for it."

"She was a little pushy about trying to get into the 'in' clique," said Pat O'Brian Hayes.

"Being a star was her be-all and end-all," said Amy Ward Beir. "The driving force of her life."

"I didn't see very much of her because she was down at the theater most of the time," said Ruth Jeffers Wellington, class of 1945. "My recollections are not pleasant because she always seemed to be playing a role. Sort of posing and being on stage all the time. I guess that's why she spent so many hours in front of the bathroom mirror with her face creams and all. . . . I was an underclassman in Talbot, so I guess there was no reason for her to be friendly to me, but the thing I remember most is her aloofness. And her face creams."

Concentrating her charm on those she wanted to impress, Nancy bestowed her selective graciousness on the campus leaders at Smith, the drama professors who assigned the leading roles in student plays, and the wealthy girls from New York City who seemed so sophisticated to her. The rest of the student body didn't matter much.

"In college, Nancy was totally agreeable," said Mary Ann Guitar, editor of the student magazine and active in Bander-log, a Smith comedy troupe. "I mean, that was her entire identity. Just to giggle a lot and give everyone 'the gaze,' which was when she would look up at you adoringly. Everybody got 'the gaze' back then. And the perpetual giggle that made her so receptive, as if to say, 'Tell me more about yourself. I want to know all about you. I'm so boring and you're so wonderful.' That was the mechanism she used back then. Ole Nancy was a totally ingratiating human being at Smith, and I used to like sitting around with her in the coffee shops and at Wiggins Tavern having a few laughs. She was a great audience."

Throughout her life, Nancy worried about saying the right thing, fretting over what others might think as she emulated the daughters of the rich friends her mother was collecting. She was especially nervous about her debut on December 28, the date Edith had negotiated the year before with Miss Eliza Campbell, the social secretary who dictated when and how a Chicago debutante made her formal bow to society.

The date was the most prized of the debutante season because that was when the Princeton Triangle Club made its annual Christmas appearance in Chicago. The club's presence meant there were fifty more eligible young men in town than usual, assuring a debutante the most impressive stag line she could possibly have. Debutante mothers besieged Miss Campbell's office months in advance begging for that date, and in 1939, the social arbiter honored Mr. and Mrs. Hill Blackett, Sr., with the choice 11:00 P.M. slot for the extravagant ball they were throwing for their daughter. The Blackett debut was held at the Blackstone Hotel and featured Glenn Miller's band. Knowing she could never compete with such wealth, Edith gratefully settled for the hours of 4:00 to 7:00 P.M. so that she and Loyal could present a modest tea dance for Nancy at the Casino Club. But it would still be written up on the same society pages as the Blacketts' ball.

This was the era of the debut, when ambitious mothers and prosperous fathers wanted their daughters to be glamorous reincarnations of café society goddess Brenda Frazier, who had bowed in New York the year before at a $20,000 party covered by the press like a coronation.

In Chicago, the society pages of all four daily newspapers gave major coverage to "the season," which began in the summer with a swirl of garden parties, teas, and endless luncheons and culminated in a two-week spasm of balls during the Christmas holidays.

For many, "coming out" was an all-consuming job that required more elaborate preparations than a wedding, including caterers, musicians, florists, social secretaries, photographers, and a wardrobe as extensive as a trousseau. Just as a bride chose bridesmaids, a debutante chose assistants to pour tea or stand in the receiving line with her. Though Nancy was not asked to be an assistant as often as some of the more popular girls, her mother made sure that she was invited to the best parties by paying Miss Campbell $300 to be her "social coordinator."

Edith Davis drove herself to make sure that every detail of her daughter's debut was perfect. She sent out engraved invitations and borrowed elaborate sterling silver tea services from two friends, Mrs. Patrick A.

Valentine and Mrs. Robert J. Dunham, former actresses who, like Edith, had married well and settled in Chicago. As a favor to Edith, the two friends honored Nancy with dinner parties. Edith hired I. Newton Perry and his Yale University Orchestra for $3,500 to play at the tea dance, since she and the doctor could not afford one of the big-name bands. Perry was a fourth-generation Chicago boy, the son of a prominent banker. Edith invited Perry's sister, Sally, to be one of Nancy's twelve "pouring" assistants, along with some former classmates from Girls Latin. She also included Priscilla Blackett, whose father headed the powerful advertising agency that originated the radio soap operas in which Edith acted. Edith made do with yellow carnations for centerpieces, and she economized further by using the Casino Club's New Year's Eve decorations, thus conserving her budget for ushers who would make sure the Princeton stag line cut in on Nancy and the other debutantes as they were supposed to.

"Princeton guys were in great demand in those days," said John Farrington, Jr., class of 1942, "and you had to be on an approved list to get invited to the debutante parties. I remember Priscilla calling me and asking if I'd please escort a friend of hers named Nancy Davis, and I agreed. I showed up at their apartment on East Lake Shore Drive with an orchid and met this cute little bouncy roundfaced girl, who squealed and said I was the first boy to ever bring her an orchid. Whether she was telling the truth or not, I don't know, but that's what she said. We went to the Blackett garden party in the fall and then I saw her a couple of times after that and, of course, at her own debut."

For her debut, Nancy wore a white gown of mousseline de soie with a long-sleeved bodice of alternating silver lace that looked more matronly than demure. Her jewelry was a single strand of pearls that she had received from her parents, and she carried an old-fashioned bouquet of white bouvardia. Dr. and Mrs. Davis beamed proudly when she stepped up to the microphone to sing "Oh, You Crazy Moon" with the band.

"I don't want to take anything away from Nancy, but I've had better singers in my day," said Newton Perry. "She was certainly not Helen O'Connell, who was the singing rage at the time, but she was an attractive girl and entitled to sing at her own debut if she wanted to. Most debutantes didn't sing with the band, but Nancy loved to sing so she sang."

The underlying purpose of this formal bow to society was to ensure that the eligible daughters of prosperous parents met the most suitable men available, and from that standpoint, Chicago's 1939 debutante season was a thumping success for Nancy Davis. She later spent many weekends at Princeton visiting some of the men she met during that time.

One of those young men, Frank O. Birney, Jr., was killed in his senior year by a train at a junction near the Princeton railroad station. The story was that he was en route to New York City to see his half-sister and brother-in-law but missed his train and started walking down the railroad tracks. He had gone one-third of a mile when a train coming from the opposite direction struck and killed him. Few persons knew that Birney had actually committed suicide that Saturday evening because he was depressed about his grades and worried about flunking out of Princeton.

"I went to his room after we identified his clothes and I found the suicide note addressed to his mother and father in his wastebasket," said a close Princeton friend. "I took it and said nothing to any of the other guys, but I gave it to Frank's brother-in-law. Then we concocted a story for Frank's mother—he had been extraordinarily close to her—that he had been accidentally hit by a locomotive going seventy miles an hour engulfed in fog."

"Frank was an immensely talented guy who might well have become a star on Broadway or in Hollywood," said Richard E. Pate, his Princeton roommate. "He was active in the Triangle Club at Princeton, which produced Jimmy Stewart and Josh Logan. His parents and Dr. and Mrs. Davis were friends from Chicago, so he and Nancy were hometown chums and dated for a while. . . . She came to Princeton for dances on various weekends."

"They were both interested in theater," said Geoffrey Montgomery Talbot Jones, a Princeton friend who dated Gloria Vanderbilt at the time Frank Birney was dating Nancy.

Nancy's Talbot housemates, none of whom had ever met Frank Birney, remember her being at Smith the weekend she got the news of his death. A few days later, she left for Chicago for Christmas vacation and spent a great deal of time comforting Birney's mother.

"We had to bring the body home for the funeral right before Christmas, which was really rough on Frank's parents," said Richard Pate. "Nancy was almost constant in her attendance on Mrs. Birney during that time, and I would say that she as much as anyone made life halfway livable for the Birneys then."

In deep mourning by the time she returned to Smith in January, Nancy retold the tale of Frank Birney's death in gruesome detail. Years later, she wrote that Frank and she had planned to meet in New York that particular weekend and that she was waiting for him there when she received the telephone call reporting his death. She repeated this story so often over the years that by 1981 she had enlarged it into heroic proportions. "I had my first romance in college," she told Charlotte Curtis in *Ladies' Home Journal*. "He was killed in the war."

What she wrote in her autobiography about Frank Birney stunned some of his friends and her classmates: "We went together for about eighteen months . . . [and] talked a little bit about getting married, but it ended in tragedy before that ever happened."

She later spun the fiction for her daughter, Patti, who regurgitated it in her autobiographical novel. "My mother once told me the story of the time she waited and waited for a man," Patti wrote, "the man she planned to marry."

"They were never engaged, to my knowledge," said Daniel Stuckey, one of Frank Birney's Princeton roommates. "If it was an engagement, it certainly was not one that had been announced."

"It was a wonderful dramatic fantasy," said Sally Gavin See. "Nancy obviously had a need to create for herself some kind of romantic aura for whatever reason. You have to remember that we thought about men and sex in a very innocent way at that time. We used to sit around and talk about who was a virgin and who wasn't. Most of us were, of course, and the big question then was always: What if you don't get married, would you have sex anyway? I remember I said I didn't want to die curious.

"So you've got to put Nancy's Frank Birney fantasy in that kind of context. Also, she told us she was very late in developing sexually. She said she didn't start menstruating until she was sixteen years old, and her mother took her to a doctor to find out why she didn't get 'the pip,' as Nancy called it. Nancy was the first person I ever heard call her period 'the pip,' which I thought was very sophisticated at the time. That late sexual adjustment may be a clue to why she felt compelled to invent a romance . . . and go around the house all droopy and mopey. It was very theatrical."

Thirty-eight years later, in 1979, Nancy wrote that it took her a long time to get over Frank Birney's death. "I felt a deep loss then and a little scar still remains inside, but I learned that life goes on and you go on with it. I got back into college activities and eventually began to date again."

Within weeks, she was dating one of Frank Birney's Princeton suitemates. By that time, the shortage of men as well as a few other deprivations of wartime were being felt on the Smith campus. Days after the Japanese bombed Pearl Harbor, Smith's president summoned the student body to Greene Hall to say that there would no longer be maids to take care of the houses, and that the students had to assume the responsibilities of peeling potatoes, washing dishes, and making their own beds. Those who were offended by the prospect of such chores were told not to return to college after Christmas vacation.

"I don't know anyone who didn't come back," said Jean Struben Harris, class of 1945, "but Smith during the war was quite changed from its prewar self. The Waves [Women Accepted for Volunteer Emergency Service in the Naval Reserve] moved onto campus, and often marched [nine hundred of them at Smith] from place to place singing 'Anchors Aweigh,' and sometimes we all gathered in Greene and sang a descant while they sang the main part.

"Except for the brothers and beaus we kissed goodbye, that was about as close to the war as many of us got. We had occasional air raid practices and sat on the floor of the basement for long periods of time. And it was much harder to drive to Amherst and impossible to drive much farther away than that because of the gas shortage. We made up songs about the man shortage, but there were still quite a few of them around. I for one holed up in the library. Nancy obviously bypassed Yale and Harvard and saved herself for Eureka," an allusion to the college of Ronald Wilson Reagan.

In 1941, a group of talented students banded together to create a musical comedy satirizing their collegiate life, including skits about living for weekends and thinking only of men. They called themselves Bander-log, after Rudyard Kipling's monkey people, and their show was entitled *Ladies on the Loose.* Boys from Amherst took the male roles.

"That whole Bander-log crew was iconoclastic," said Sally Gavin See. "Each one—Mary Ann Guitar, Harriet Train Blake, Bobby Jones, Betty Cape—was outré in her own way. They were all out of the mainstream. Nancy, who was very much mainstream, was not part of the creative effort, but she did get a part."

The group rented a high school auditorium for two nights and charged students and parents, with the proceeds going to charity. Nancy was given a leading role and appeared on stage wearing a hat of bananas and spoofed Carmen Miranda.

"She could really belt out a song," recalled Ann Keyser Rawley, class of 1944. "Everyone was so shocked when this quiet girl stood up and started singing in her sultry, low register. She was quite good."

In her senior year, Nancy once again took center stage, this time as the singing lead in *The Factory Follies,* a song-and-dance revue. It was directed by Hallie Flanagan Davis, a high-voltage drama teacher from Vassar who had come to create Smith's first theater department. It was the first musical show staged by college students meant to entertain war workers. The factory workers dashed from their machines at lunch break to watch a chorus of pretty girls prance on stage, singing: "Make with the maximum, give with the brawn! Make with the maximum, smother that yawn!"

The morale-boosting show told the story of a rich glamour girl who complains of losing her butler and yacht because a war is going on and is branded a "shirker" until she becomes as committed to the war effort as everyone else. Nancy Davis, wearing a slinky black lace dress she borrowed, played the rich glamour girl, who sang: "Stop! I don't want to be a bottleneck / But I haven't got brawn, at least not that kind, / And working with brains just isn't my line."

After entertaining 5,000 workers in defense plants throughout New England, *Factory Follies* was staged for Smith's graduation ceremonies in the spring of 1943. Nancy's parents, however, were not there to see her perform because her father had been inducted into the Army Medical Corps and was serving in London, and her mother was prohibited from making the trip because of wartime restrictions on travel.

After graduating from Smith that year, Nancy never looked back. She skipped the class reunions, ignored the appeals for donations. She did not take part in alumnae activities or attend Smith Club events. Unlike her classmates, she snubbed her alma mater and never nourished the old school ties that are so much a part of Smith's strong tradition.

5

CHICAGO MAYOR EDWARD J. KELLY dispensed the spoils of 40,000 patronage jobs like the godfather doling out graft to gangsters, and Mrs. Loyal Davis was one of the first in line. With her husband serving in a medical unit overseas, she was hard-pressed to maintain her high-society standard of living. The radio soap operas had been dropped for lack of sponsorship and Edith was unable to pay the rent on her expensive apartment on East Lake Shore Drive. So she sublet the apartment and moved with her daughter into the less costly Drake Hotel. Through her friendship with the mayor, she got a $75-a-week job as commentator for the summer concerts in Grant Park. She also snagged a plum position on the city payroll for $2,141 a year, ostensibly as an undercover policewoman, but one who did not have to report to work—a no-show job. This was her payoff for directing the women's division of the Citizens Committee for Mayor Ed Kelly in 1943. Years later, instead of going to a bank for a loan, she simply went to "Big Ed" for the $25,000 she needed to build a retirement home in Scottsdale, Arizona. "The mayor took care of Edith," said Les Weinrott, "and she took care of him. There's no question about that."

During the war Edith worked closely with the mayor's wife, Margaret Kelly, who was her best friend. Together, they built the Chicago Servicemen's Center into one of the finest canteens in the United States. They recruited hundreds of pretty hostesses to distribute free cake, hot dogs, and movie tickets to soldiers on pass or waiting to be shipped out.

Edith volunteered at the center on a regular basis, becoming good friends with many of the young men.

On May 8, 1943, before moving into the Drake Hotel, she invited six sailors to her apartment to meet six smartly dressed young women as well as Chicago police captain Michael Naughton and Lieutenant Commander Carl Stockholm, the latter in charge of the Shore Patrol for the 9th Naval District. The enlisted men, all of whom were minors, were each given $3 spending money by Commander Stockholm and told to take the young women out to certain bars in the Loop area. Although underage, they were instructed to order drinks for themselves and their dates. After they were served, Captain Naughton and his forces would sweep in, raid the place, and arrest the bartenders and the owners, who automatically lost their liquor licenses.

Two weeks later, the suspects appeared in municipal court and pleaded entrapment, saying they had been set up. The charges were dropped after one of the sailors testified that the raids had indeed been planned in the apartment of a "Mrs. Davis on the North Lake Shore."

Curious reporters investigated the Mrs. Davis mentioned and found her listed on police payrolls as Edith L. Davis of 199 East Lake Shore Drive. Wondering if the undercover policewoman and the socially prominent doctor's wife were the same person, they called Edith.

"I have no comment to make," she said. "They told me not to talk."

"Whom do you mean by 'they'?"

"I'm sorry, I can't tell that. I don't know what the devil this is all about," she said, and hung up.

Another reporter rang her doorbell, and Edith answered with her hair in pin curls. She denied knowing anything. "It must be a mistake," she said, closing the door.

The reporter called back and Nancy answered the phone, saying her mother was "busy." She was not accustomed to this type of reporter, who was so unlike the genteel ladies on the society pages.

"What do you know about your mother's police activity?"

"I'm sure Mother never did any work like that," said Nancy. "It must be a mistake."

"Is your mother interested in social service work such as preventing liquor sales to minors?"

"Not that I know of," said Nancy.

"Does your mother disapprove of drinking in general?"

"Not that I know of," said Nancy.

"Well, how do you explain the mysterious coincidence of the policewoman named Edith L. Davis who lives at 199 Lake Shore Drive and your mother, who lives at the same address?"

"It must not be true," said Nancy.

The incident created a minor scandal in Chicago, where the story was splashed across the front pages for several days. "Is Mrs. Davis a Liquor Cop? She Won't Talk" screamed one headline. "Mrs. Davis, Socialite, Is a Policewoman" blared another.

In those days, the only women in the police department were the matrons at lockups, and they did not come from Chicago's Gold Coast or have daughters who were debutantes. Edith's neighbors on Lake Shore Drive were shocked that someone of her social standing would be so mercenary as to take taxpayers' money to set up bartenders and tavern owners while contributing to the delinquency of minors.

"[The Davises] were very politically minded," said Betty Shallberg Quely, whose family lived across the hall. "Her job was to keep track of prostitutes or something. . . . It was very shocking. I still can't believe she did it for money. I wouldn't have thought she would have had to do something like that. After all, her husband was a doctor."

Reporters hounded Mayor Kelly about the identity of the mysterious policewoman, but he shrugged it off, saying he didn't know what they were talking about. "Ask the police commissioner," he said. The commissioner told the reporters that he couldn't remember the first names of people on his force.

"Then how am I supposed to know?" said the mayor. "Besides, what difference does it make? Are all the affairs of the police department made public?"

The sergeant who headed the crime prevention bureau admitted that he had a policewoman on the rolls named Edith L. Davis who worked at the Chicago Servicemen's Center. "Among her duties is keeping kids away from the front door, keeping out unescorted and underage girls, [and] preventing petting in the center."

At a court hearing a few days later, the sailors were no longer available for questioning because, according to a petty officer, they had been transferred to "parts unknown." The judge ruled the arrests resulted from entrapment and dismissed the charges. Consequently, the liquor licenses were restored.

The city did not appeal and Edith kept her patronage job for four years. She resigned on May 24, 1946, and acknowledged her undercover role but sidestepped telling the truth.

"I guess I was listed on the police payrolls for the work I did for Mayor Kelly," she said. "I helped him with his radio programs, you know. I helped write, direct, and produce them."

"Did you ever do any active police work?" asked one reporter.

"Goodness, no. I'm not the type."

"What about the raids on saloons which sold liquor to minors?"

"You'll have to ask someone who was there," said Edith. "I wasn't. I've never been in those West Side saloons."

Nancy learned a painful lesson from the humiliating publicity surrounding her mother, and as a consequence she steered clear of all reporters who were not on the social beat. She also tried never to expose herself to public scrutiny. Though she would align herself with rich and powerful protectors throughout her life, she always made sure a layer of insulation shielded her from exposure. She refined the technique so well that by 1969, when she sought the help of a Mafia lawyer, the story made no newspapers and no one knew about her overture except trusted and beholden intermediaries.

Shortly before Edith's scandal hit the papers, Nancy was invited to join the Junior League of Chicago, a natural stepping-stone for a debutante on her way to marrying right and living well. Nancy seemed poised for both, especially when she became engaged to James Platt White, Jr., who had been graduated from Amherst in 1942.

Homeported in Chicago as a catapult officer on an aircraft carrier, "J.P." called Nancy Davis for a date, and the two began seeing each other regularly. She found her psychological twin in this man who was described by his classmates as she was described by hers: "impeccably neat," "beautifully groomed," "inordinately fond of dressing up," and "not much interested in athletics." Some of White's Chi Phi fraternity brothers remembered him as stuffy, pink-cheeked, and effeminate. "Not a man's man at all, if you know what I mean," said Dr. Morton Smith-Peterson, "and certainly not a frat man." Nancy, however, found J. P. White to be quite acceptable. Both brunettes, both interested in the theater, both the only children of strong-willed mothers, they seemed to have a lot in common.

Dr. and Mrs. Loyal Davis announced the engagement at a party in their apartment on June 24, 1944, two months after Loyal had returned from his army assignment as chief consultant on neurological surgery for European Theater Operations. The young man's parents arrived from Winchester, Massachusetts, carrying a large Tiffany diamond ring that they presented to Nancy on behalf of their son, who was on an aircraft carrier in the Pacific. The society pages of the Chicago and Boston papers reported the couple planned to be married at the end of the war. Within months, though, Nancy broke the engagement and returned the ring. Bored with selling clothes at Marshall Field's department store, she spent a few days in California with her parents visiting the Walter Hustons and came back determined to leave Chicago and pursue a career on stage.

"The engagement was one of those things that seemed glamorous and very romantic at the time," said Smith classmate Harline Ward Hurst. "They were good friends and normally would not ever have contracted a marriage or an engagement except that . . . well, Nancy was kind of blown away by the atmosphere at first."

"Jim was devastated when she called it off," said Bill Whorf, his Amherst roommate. "I think his mother may have had something to do with it, but I don't know for sure. . . . In any event, he never married."

"No, it wasn't his mother who broke things up," said Ward Patton III, another Amherst classmate. "I think Nancy just wanted to go on to better things. . . . She wanted to be a star and go into the movies. . . . It's true that Jim never married, but then some guys just aren't the marrying kind."

Her baby-faced fiancé never discussed the relationship because he and Nancy had made a pact not to talk. "All I can say is that she was a lovely, lovely girl. It was just one of those wartime things," he said. Nancy conceded only that she had made a mistake. "We were not meant to be married," she said.

The broken engagement marked the onset of sexual experimentation for Nancy.

"It's true that she became known around town as 'accessible,' " said Les Weinrott. "She was what men at that time thought of as available, which sounds a little better than promiscuous but means about the same thing."

One man Nancy saw on a regular basis was Dr. Daniel Ruge, her father's senior assistant at Passavant Hospital, who would one day become Ronald Reagan's White House physician. "He would call me and ask me to cover for him," said a resident at Passavant at the time. "Dan would say, 'I'm going to take Nancy over to the Esquire Theater,' and he'd sneak out for a couple of hours while I covered the house. What he did with her at that theater I don't know. He was too much of a gentleman to ever tell me, but that was a thing that was hot and heavy in 1945 for at least three months that I knew about."

Years later, Dr. Ruge denied any romantic involvement with Nancy Davis, saying, "I think someone is getting me confused with Clark Gable."

A few days before Nancy left for New York she ran into two male friends of her parents and shocked the two married men by her method of saying goodbye.

"Ben and I were walking down East Lake Shore Drive by the Drake Hotel," said one of the men. "We had just finished lunch when we saw Nancy, who came running over to us. She said she was leaving town and just wanted to say goodbye. She grabbed me first, kissed me hard on the

lips and plunged her tongue down my throat. Then she thrust herself at
Ben and did the same thing to him. Bye, bye, tra la, and off she skipped.
We were stunned, absolutely stunned by the whole thing. We felt so
shaken that we went back inside and had a drink to try to figure out what
the hell had happened. Here we were, both married men and close
friends of Nancy's parents. We were not the sort to molest our friends'
children and we certainly didn't expect to be molested by them. For
Nancy to kiss us that way was unclean, unhealthy, and symptomatic of
some sickness. Maybe it was just her rebellion over a broken engagement
to a feminine man, but Ben and I were shocked.

"We swore never to mention the incident again, but we made sure that
neither of us was ever alone with Nancy after that. . . . We were good
and shook by it for some time."

For the next few years, most of Nancy's closest relationships were with
homosexual men, both as friends and lovers. Homosexuality seemed to
envelop her world, and not simply because she worked in an artistic
arena. For the rest of her life she enjoyed platonic friendships with well-
dressed gay men who became her mentors in the arts, fashion, cuisine,
and interior design, shaping her taste and pointing her toward sophistication. She relished the cozy nature of these relationships, and at first she
was romantically attracted to some of these men. In 1946, when she got a
small part in *Lute Song,* she started an affair with one of the gay male
dancers in the show. Many years later, he confided that he was a homosexual who had slept with only three women in his life and that Nancy
was one of them.

Dolly Haas, who took over the lead in *Lute Song* from Mary Martin,
remembers Nancy and her homosexual lover coming into her dressing
room. "She was an enchanting, beautiful girl, and she and her young
man came to me one day," said the actress, who was married to caricatur-
ist Al Hirschfeld. "He was very interested in marrying her, and they
asked my opinion of marriage. I gave it a big boost."

Nancy's first job as an actress had come several months earlier as a
result of her mother's friendship with ZaSu Pitts, who got her hired for
the minor role of Alice in *Ramshackle Inn,* which was on tour and heading
for Broadway. "I grabbed the offer and joined the company in Detroit,
where the girl who had been playing the part was leaving," said Nancy,
who had three lines of dialogue. "It wasn't much but it was a start." The
play opened and closed in New York.

Within a few months, though, Nancy was back on Broadway, again
through the connections of her parents. This time she landed the non-
speaking part of Si-Tchum in *Lute Song* starring Yul Brynner and Mary

Martin, who had demanded that Nancy be given the role of her lady-in-waiting.

"She had been hired before I arrived as director," said John Houseman. "During the second or third week of rehearsal I suggested to the producer that Nancy was not physically convincing as a small Chinese handmaiden. He said, 'Talk to Mary [Martin],' and I did. Mary said, 'John, I have a very bad back and Nancy's father, Loyal Davis, is the greatest [neurosurgeon] in the U.S.A. We are not letting Nancy go!' And that was that."

Lute Song ran for five months on Broadway with critics raving about the magnificent sets and costumes but dismissing the play. Nancy's performance escaped appraisal. The minute the show closed, ZaSu Pitts was on the phone again, this time offering Nancy the minor role of Millicent in *Cordelia,* a play by George Batson, which had been tailored to the leading lady's comedic talents, but the show closed in New Haven.

Nancy returned to New York, her drama classes, and her Beekman Place apartment on 51st Street, which her friend Robert Fryer remembered as "impeccably done."

Financially supported by her family, Nancy liked living alone in Manhattan, where she had few friendships with other women, unless they were the older female friends of her parents, who functioned as surrogate mothers. In place of girlfriends her own age, she socialized with her family's theatrical friends. "The Hustons [Walter and Nan] had an apartment around the corner," she said. "Lillian Gish, another family friend, had one nearby. They often took me out to eat or to a show, or had me over to little parties. I used to go watch Spence [Spencer Tracy] rehearse for a play he was opening in, *The Rugged Path.*"

ZaSu swooped in again to rescue her with yet another touring role, this time as Susan Haggertt in *The Late Christopher Bean.* "Nicely sweetened without saccharin" was how the *Chicago Herald American* reviewed her performance.

One stop on that tour was the Olney Theater in Olney, Maryland, where Nancy played opposite James Karen, one of the company's resident actors.

"I don't think I ever said ten words to her offstage, and she less to me," he said. "Nancy was really quite prim and proper-seeming—very unlikely to pal around with raggle-taggle gypsies like us. In fact, we thought her snobby. Now, as the years have passed and I look back, she was probably in an awkward position—a young girl traveling with two older women, ZaSu Pitts and Zolia Talma, unable to play with the young kids in the resident company.

"Many of the folks in our audience were older grownups who well remembered the visiting stars like Ruth Chatterton, Leatrice Joy, John Carradine, Lenore Ulric, and ZaSu, who came to town and were paid $100 for one week's worth of performances. After a week, the stars left and went on to the next town. Audiences were curious to see how these actors, who were popular in the 1920s and 1930s, had aged. Some were happy, beautiful, and well-off financially; others were old, beaten-up, and broke, defeated by a hard profession. I was never sure about ZaSu's status, because she complained a lot publicly about Roosevelt's New Deal robbing her, but she seemed to be well-off. Nancy was very much under ZaSu's control. They lived together and dressed together and ate together. They never ever socialized with us or with any of the locals. They came to the theater, did their job, and then went back to their hotel in Washington."

At the end of the run, in late 1947, Nancy returned to New York, where she had a short affair with Alfred Drake, who was the king of Broadway musicals in the 1940s, starring in *Kismet; Kiss Me Kate;* and *Oklahoma!* Nancy was dazzled to be in his company, even briefly. Then she met Max Allentuck, general manager for Kermit Bloomgarden, the top producer in Manhattan, and began courting him vigorously, although some people felt her ambition exceeded her affection. "It had to be more professional than personal," said one man. "Max could get her parts. Other than that, he was forbidden fruit. How could she ever marry a Jewish man when the stepfather she adored was so anti-Semitic?" The question would arise again in Hollywood.

"Let's put it this way: She liked Max much more than he liked her," said Allentuck's secretary, who remembered Nancy Davis as "lovely looking and beautifully dressed in her suits and fur coats. She looked more like a society girl than a struggling actress.

"Sometimes, when she'd come around the office to take Max to lunch, he'd leave by the back door and she'd be stuck with me. So we'd go out to get a bite and I'd tell her to forget this tall, skinny, Jewish fellow and get out to Hollywood to meet some real men like Clark Gable. I knew that Spencer Tracy had fixed her up a couple times with Gable and, boy, was I impressed with that. I also knew her mother was good friends with Spencer Tracy—we were pretty impressed with that around the office, too—so I told her to use all those contacts and get out to the coast. I never thought she'd make it as an actress in New York anyway. She had aspirations, of course, but she wasn't making much headway. She was awfully nice, though. Not much humor, but awfully nice."

She had three dates with Clark Gable in New York and they led to phone calls from a parade of men passing through town, including Benjamin Thau, vice president of Loew's and head of casting for Metro-Goldwyn-Mayer. "Nancy was one of those girls whose phone number got handed around a lot," said writer Anne Edwards.

Unmarried at the time, the fifty-one-year-old Thau took the twenty-eight-year-old actress to see Spencer Tracy's play, *The Rugged Path,* and then to dinner afterward, where, as he recalled years later, he casually mentioned the possibility of a screen test in Hollywood.

When the MGM lion roared, Nancy jumped. She phoned her mother, who flew into action by calling Spencer Tracy to make sure the screen test came to pass. Tracy was more than happy now to reciprocate for the Davises' frequent hospitality by helping their daughter, which he did with incredible dispatch.

"Spencer was very grateful to Loyal Davis because Mrs. Tracy had taken their deaf son to him. He had told her there was no cure for nerve deafness," said Charles Williamson, executor of the George Cukor estate. "He said, 'You can either make a life for yourself or let this destroy you.' Mrs. Tracy turned her son's deafness into a cause by starting the John Tracy Clinic and devoting her life to working with the deaf. That's the reason Spencer Tracy went all out to get Nancy a screen test at MGM."

Tracy, one of Metro's biggest stars in 1949, called Dore Schary, the vice president in charge of production, to say that Nancy would be perfect for some of his films. "The girl knows how to look like she's really thinking when she's onstage," he said. Schary had been a close friend of Tracy's since 1938, when he wrote the Academy Award–winning script of *Boys' Town,* for which Tracy also won an Oscar. Schary quickly agreed to let Nancy test with Howard Keel in a scene from his new movie, *East Side, West Side.* Tracy then called George Cukor, MGM's most powerful director and a man renowned for working with women, to direct the scene. And he arranged for George Folsey, a superb cinematographer, especially skilled at photographing women, to do the camera work.

"With that kind of power behind her, the fix was in," said Gottfried Reinhardt, a former MGM producer. "All Nancy Davis had to do was show up for the screen test and not upchuck on camera. The contract was a foregone conclusion. After all, George Cukor was the studio's top director—an immensely influential man—and it was unheard of for him to do a screen test, especially for an unknown starlet. He did that as a favor to Spencer Tracy, who was his beloved friend. Tracy and Katharine Hepburn, who were having an affair, lived in the guest house on George Cukor's property and he directed their best movies together. He would never have said no to Spencer. Add to that Nancy's affair with Benny Thau, and she was a cinch to be signed by Metro."

Still, an immense amount of work was undertaken before Nancy signed a contract. "I prepared her for that screen test," said Lillian Burns Sidney, who coached Nancy in drama, voice, movement, deportment, dress, and makeup. "I don't like the title of drama coach, but I was in charge of all the young talent at MGM and I trained them. . . . I had to spend weeks with Nancy."

"I had told Lillian to give her extra special care because Benny had asked me to do the best I could with her," said Lucille Ryman Carroll, the former head of MGM's talent department. "I admit that bringing in someone like Nancy Davis was highly unusual for Benny Thau because he knew and I knew—everyone knew—that she would never be a star.

"The studio was only concerned with developing stars," Mrs. Carroll continued. "We did not care about producing good performers. A good performer does not make box office. Someone like Arthur Hill is a fine actor, but he does not make women's hearts flutter. Angela Lansbury is a fabulous actress, but she does not have the appeal that makes men want her. Now, we had Angela under contract because she worked all the time. If someone could work and earn their keep, we would renew her options, but that is not what we were looking for. We wanted *stars* like Ava and Liz and Lana who would make our box office bigger and our stock richer. That's what we cared most about.

"Nancy would qualify only for some of those girl-next-door roles in the B pictures that we were producing then, which really didn't matter. Dore Schary did a lot of them, and he liked her, but he should've been a rabbi. He was such a prude he didn't know what sex was. He's the reason that Marilyn Monroe was never signed by MGM. Dore couldn't see her sex appeal on screen. Besides, he didn't think sex was important on screen, whereas Louis B. Mayer felt that it was the only thing that mattered. Mayer said if you had sex appeal on screen and the right part, you could be a star. At the time Nancy came to the studio, he was letting Dore Schary run things, which is why Benny Thau felt that we could get away with signing her."

Nancy Davis became part of the world's largest and wealthiest moviemaking machine during Metro-Goldwyn-Mayer's silver jubilee year, when the studio was still boasting "more stars than there are in the heavens" and pointing proudly to Clark Gable, Spencer Tracy, Katharine Hepburn, Mickey Rooney, Fred Astaire, Ginger Rogers, Gene Kelly, Esther Williams, Judy Garland, Margaret O'Brien, Jimmy Stewart, Van Johnson, Ethel Barrymore, Lana Turner, Ava Gardner, June Allyson, Peter Lawford, Elizabeth Taylor, Gary Cooper, Errol Flynn, Frank Sinatra, and Lassie. Cowboys and comics were the money magnets of that era. The most popular stars of 1949 were Bing Crosby, Bob Hope, Abbott and Costello, John Wayne, and Gary Cooper.

"We were known as the Tiffany of movie studios," said Lucille Ryman Carroll. "MGM was the biggest and the best." Metro paid the largest salaries of any Hollywood studio, produced the biggest films, collected the most Academy Awards, and grossed the largest revenues. Within five years, the omnipotent studio would sputter and the star system collapse, but in 1949, the 178 acres of the MGM lot in Culver City contained 5,000 employees and 31 soundstages, plus a private zoo and a school for child stars.

Nancy Davis signed with Metro on March 2, 1949, for six months at $300 a week with twenty weeks guaranteed. She had that one option for six months at $300 and then an option escalating every year for six years if the studio renewed her contract, which would have taken her to 1956 at $1,250 a week. Her salary as a contract player paled beside the $1,000 a week that Lassie was making, but then the beautiful collie was top dog around the studio and known as "Greer Garson with fur." Nancy Davis was referred to snidely as "Benny's little protégée."

A week after Nancy signed her contract, she filled out the studio biography, listing her age as twenty-six rather than twenty-eight. "We rarely signed anyone over twenty-five years of age, so I think Benny told her to shave it a little," said Lucille Ryman Carroll. Stating that she was five feet four and weighted 117 pounds, Nancy said her childhood ambition was "to be an actress." Her favorite actors: Spencer Tracy, Walter Huston, Laurette Taylor, and her godmother, Alla Nazimova. She said she liked to sleep in "tailored nightgowns" with the "windows wide open." Asked about rules that govern her life, she wrote, "Do unto others as you would have them do unto you—I believe strongly in the law of retribution—you get back what you give." Any ambitions outside present career? "Sure." Greatest ambition is "to have successful happy marriage." Believe in hunches? "Yes." Any particular phobias? "Superficiality, vulgarity esp. in women, untidiness of mind and person—and cigars!" Any superstitions? "All of them and then some."

Nancy reported for work on March 7, 1949, and was immediately cast in *Shadow on the Wall* as Dr. Caroline Canford, a psychiatrist who must unlock the recollections of a terrified six-year-old girl who saw her mother murdered. All the child remembers is a shadow on the wall. Her scheming aunt (Ann Sothern) tries to keep the psychiatrist from finding out anything more specific about the shadow but confesses to the murder in the end.

"I made over seventy movies and that was not one of the best," said Ann Sothern forty years after the film was made. "I remember Nancy Davis as quite soft and pudgy and she looked like she'd had a nose job. Although she was pleasant enough, she seemed rather devious to me. I can't tell you exactly why. . . . It's just a feeling I had. Maybe it was because she was so ambitious. . . . She was a tough lady . . . who definitely knew where she wanted to go. . . .

"I came to MGM as a star making $100,000 a year and Nancy was just a little contract player who didn't make much of an impression on anyone at the studio. I never would have known her had we not been in the same film, and even then she didn't impress me much."

The difference between a contract player and a star was the difference between a mongrel and a thoroughbred. "In this town, the difference is everything," said former Hollywood columnist Dorothy Manners. "If your name goes above the title of a movie, you're a star. If your name goes below the title, you're a contract player, and that's all little Nancy ever was."

Most reviewers ignored Nancy's first screen performance, but not *Variety,* which said she gave "a standout performance as a child psychiatrist. . . . Actress definitely is a comer."

The day after filming was completed, Nancy started work on her second movie, *The Doctor and the Girl.* In an ironic piece of typecasting, she played the dutiful daughter of a prominent neurosurgeon (Charles Coburn). The critics just about ignored Nancy's bland performance, except for *Variety,* which said she "is to be favorably noted."

"She just wasn't star material," said producer Pandro Berman. "You have to have something quite wonderful to become a star, and Nancy didn't have that wonderful something. We did a lot of location shooting in New York for *The Doctor and the Girl,* and my good friend, Benny Thau, asked me to take Nancy to dinner while we were there, which I did as a favor to him. They were quite a romance then—people at the studio thought they might get married—and he helped her quite a bit to get into some of the pictures she did. She was always going up to his office because he was the top casting man at MGM.* If it hadn't been for my friendship with Benny, I wouldn't have paid a bit of attention to Nancy Davis. Not a bit."

"Benny took her to premieres and benefits and parties," said Lucille Ryman Carroll. "He also went with her to visit her parents in Scottsdale, Arizona, where they vacationed every year."

"At one point, he gave her a car—a Chevrolet as I recall," said publicist Rupert Allen.

"Their affair was a well-known, established fact at the studio," said Kathryn Grayson. "I think they were engaged for a time. . . ."

* See notes for Chapter 5.

"There's no question that Benny was in love with Nancy," said Lillian Burns Sidney.

A few years before he died, Benny Thau recalled his relationship with the young starlet. "You can say I helped her," he said. "Stars like Norma Shearer and Elizabeth Taylor—she couldn't compete with that. She was attractive, but not what you'd call beautiful. She's a very nice, behaved girl."

"Did you want to marry her?"

"I was friendly with her folks, and me being Jewish, I don't know."

"Did you think of marrying her?"

"I thought about it, but that's all I did."

"Because she was sleeping with Benny, we had to deal with her and cast her in our movies," said Gottfried Reinhardt, best known for producing *The Red Badge of Courage.*

"At MGM, the producer was the top man, not the director. It was the producers who made MGM great—maybe not artistically but commercially—and Metro was once the greatest entertainment empire that ever existed. We did the casting, and Benny Thau always made us cast the women he was sleeping with in our films. He couldn't fire us if we said no because we had long-term contracts, but we never wanted to alienate him. He was too powerful.

"I remember when I was preparing a picture and I got a call from him to come to his office. Benny was a very dour man who spoke in such a low voice that you could not understand him. Although he knew his business, he never said much and he didn't like me because I chain-smoked cigars, which he loathed. That day, though, he was smiling and very voluble. He even seemed to be enjoying my cigar.

" 'Why don't you take Nancy Davis for this film?' he said. Naturally, I did not say, 'You've got to be kidding,' although I thought that Nancy was a horrible actress and had no business being under contract to the studio, but because she was sleeping with Benny, we had to deal with her. Sidney Franklin, who was the top producer, had already turned her down, so Benny came after me. I said I'd think it over. I'd never make an enemy of this man for anything, but I'd also never cast Nancy Davis in any of my films. I never got back to Benny and so he palmed her off on Dore Schary, who had a bad back that was being doctored by Nancy's father, Loyal Davis. Now the combination of those two men is intriguing to contemplate because Dore was a liberal Democrat active in causes like the American Civil Liberties Union, the American Jewish Committee, and the Anti-Defamation League. Loyal Davis was a conservative Republican and a member of the John Birch Society, I think, who was supposed to be virulently anti-Semitic. But it shows you that Nancy had all the bases covered in the front office. She was sleeping with Benny Thau and her father was taking care of Dore Schary. What more could a starlet need?"

Dore Schary cast Nancy in the role she had tested for in *East Side, West Side,* which starred Barbara Stanwyck, Ava Gardner, and James Mason. It was a high-society drama about a marriage breaking up, leaving murder in its wake. Ava Gardner undulated across the screen as the luscious temptress who boasts that she need only crook a finger to make James Mason leave his wife, played by Barbara Stanwyck. Nancy Davis, who didn't show up on screen until halfway into the movie, was cast as the meddlesome friend who tells Barbara Stanwyck that her husband is having an affair.

By the time the film was released in 1950, Ava Gardner was being castigated in the press as a "home wrecker" for crooking her finger at Frank Sinatra, who came running as fast as he could. The couple created such a scandal with their love affair that they became front-page news across America. Even a U.S. Senate committee took notice of the publicity surrounding the romance, which it said hyped a movie that, to its thinking, celebrated infidelity in an era when illicit sex was publicly condemned.

The critics completely ignored the ordinary performance of Nancy Davis, but Nancy was still determined to be noticed. "That's all she talked about when she first started at MGM," said Arlene Sellers, a Hollywood lawyer. "We had lunch shortly after she arrived, and it was a long haul because Nancy said she wanted to be a big movie star more than anything else in the world. She talked about it constantly."

In Nancy's first interview with Louella Parsons, the Hollywood columnist, who knew Nancy was dating actor Robert Walker, asked whether there was any one man in her life. "Not yet," said Nancy. "I won't be trite and say I am married to my career, but that's pretty much the truth."

Although she later denied these career ambitions, saying she was never serious about becoming an actress, that "it was an amusing way of passing time until the right man came along," her co-workers at the studio remember differently.

"I recall Nancy Davis as being very pert and pretty and extremely ambitious," said Norman Panama, part of the (Melvin) Frank and Panama writing, directing, and producing team at MGM. "She was part of the B unit at the studio, the stock company that Dore Schary developed to make inexpensive pictures that weren't very good and didn't matter very much. She wasn't a bad actress, but she wasn't very good either. What I remember most is her table-hopping in the MGM commissary.

She was a good little politician going from table to table to better herself."

Richard Goldstone, who produced Nancy's last movie at MGM, *Talk
About a Stranger,* also remembered her in the studio commissary. "No
one every hopped much in the MGM commissary, unless they were finished with lunch and on their way out and they stopped by a table to say
hello. Nancy Davis stands out in my mind because of her systematic
table-hopping throughout lunch. She never sat with other starlets, and I
don't recall her at all friendly with any other women, just the male executives at MGM and the big male stars. She was socially ambitious and
could first-name a lot of the stars. She would hop over to Clark Gable's
table—she had gone out with him a couple of times, but who hadn't—
and then she'd hop over to Spencer Tracy's table. She'd hop from the
writers' table to the directors' table to the executives' tables. No other
starlet would have had the nerve. It was quite unusual for an unknown
little actress to do such a thing. She carefully selected her targets and
nothing would deter her. It was really something to see."

Nancy pursued romance in much the same way. Following her
penchant for weak men, she had begun dating MGM contract player
Robert Walker in 1949, shortly after he had been jailed for drunk driv-
ing. Dore Schary then sent the twice-divorced actor to the Menninger
Clinic in Topeka, Kansas, where he underwent treatment for alcoholism.
He returned in six months and talked openly of the experience, saying,
"If an actor can speak frankly of his solution to mental troubles, perhaps
it will encourage others to seek psychiatric help."

Nancy spent a great deal of time with Walker at his home in Pacific
Palisades and endeared herself to his two young sons from his first marriage to Jennifer Jones. Nancy picked out furniture for his house and
helped plan his trips with his children. "Peter Lawford and I once
dropped by Walker's place about four in the afternoon without calling
ahead like we should have," said producer Joe Naar. "Robert and Nancy
were going together at the time and when we arrived unannounced we
caught them off-guard. Nancy came out of the bathroom in a towel and
was very embarrassed to see us. We shouldn't have walked in on them
when we did; we were out of line. We had obviously interrupted a young
couple having a good time.

"The only way I can explain Nancy's attraction to Robert is to tell you
that he was very vulnerable. He was always so . . . he looked like he
needed taking care of, and I think women saw that in him and loved him
for it."

A few months after Robert Walker and Nancy broke up, he died at the age of thirty-two from an overdose of sodium amytal administered by his doctors.

Never losing sight of her greatest ambition, which was "to have a successful and happy marriage," Nancy jokingly showed a Metro co-worker a list of names that she had compiled of Hollywood's most eligible bachelors. The list contained the names of directors, producers, agents, and lawyers as well as actors. The top spot was occupied by the president of the Screen Actors Guild, Ronald Reagan, a B actor from Warner Bros. who had been divorced by Jane Wyman the previous year.

Nancy mentioned to Dore Schary that she would like to meet Reagan, and so Schary's wife, Miriam, arranged a small dinner party in the fall of 1949 and invited them both. Jill Schary Robinson recalled the evening, saying, "There was a lot of political talk and some arguments. Reagan made his [anti-Communist] views very clear. He was terribly articulate. Nancy listened to him attentively. She was sitting opposite him at the dinner table, and she kept smiling at him in agreement." As Schary's daughter recalled, the evening had an edge to it because her father considered Red-baiting a serious danger that was beginning to infect the movie industry by this time.

Reagan, under the code name T-10, had been an informant for the FBI from 1943 to 1947, secretly turning in the names of SAG members he felt were "subversive," "un-American," or "following the Communist party line."

Mrs. Schary had hoped that she could maneuver Reagan into driving Nancy home that evening, but the actor said he was scheduled to leave for New York early the next morning, so he left first, unaccompanied. He did not call Nancy afterward, but she called the Screen Actors Guild and, according to their official minutes, "indicated her willingness and desire to run for the board of directors [the following month in the annual November elections]." Still no call from Ronald Reagan. So Nancy devised another way to approach him, under the guise of seeking help.

On October 28, 1949, the *Hollywood Reporter* listed the names of those in the motion picture industry who had signed an amicus brief to the U.S. Supreme Court to reverse the conviction of Hollywood writers John Howard Lawson and Dalton Trumbo for refusing to disclose their political beliefs to the House Un-American Activities Committee. Among the 208 names listed was that of Nancy Davis, the wife of agent Jerry Davis, a liberal Democrat who abhorred the damage being caused by the blacklist.

Seeing her name appear as a supporter for convicted Communists was all that the MGM Nancy Davis needed. Filming *East Side, West Side* at the time, she approached her director, Mervyn LeRoy, and said she was worried because she was starting to receive Communist propaganda in the mail and would he please call the president of the Screen Actors Guild to straighten things out. He agreed to do so, and Nancy felt sure that Reagan finally would call her. She waited in her apartment all evening for the phone to ring.

Hearing nothing from him that night or the next, she asked LeRoy what had happened. The director said Reagan had called him back to say that there was another actress named Nancy Davis and that the MGM Nancy Davis should not worry; the Guild would stand behind her.

"I'd feel better if the Guild president would call me and explain it all to me," the conservative starlet told the MGM director.

Mervyn LeRoy then realized that Nancy Davis had her heart set on a face-to-face meeting with Ronald Reagan and not merely on clearing her name. So LeRoy decided to call him back.

"Ronnie, why don't you call her and see if you can help?" he said. "She's awfully cute, and you're a single boy now."

As SAG president, the thirty-eight-year-old actor was associating more and more with motion picture executives, and such a request from an important director of the most powerful studio in Hollywood was not to be ignored.

"That evening [November 15, 1949] I took up my post by the phone," said Nancy, "and this time it rang. Ronnie called to ask if I were free for dinner. I told him it was awfully short notice but I thought I could manage it. He told me it would have to be an early dinner because he had an early call on a film the following morning. I said that was best for me as I, too, had an early call. I didn't, of course, but a girl has to have some pride. He came on crutches. He had broken his leg in a charity baseball game. But he came anyway and took me to LaRue's for dinner. That was one of the popular places on the Sunset Strip when the Strip was still the place to go. . . . My name problem was quickly dismissed because, as Mervyn had already told me, Ronnie had discovered there were other Nancy Davises, so I had no problem. We talked about other things; well, like about a thousand other things."

Nancy said later that the date was "blinder for him than for me" and she "knew right away" that this was the man she wanted to marry. "I knew that being his wife was the role I wanted most," she said. And she would devote the next three years to getting it.

6

NANCY'S BIG CHANCE to see her name go above the title as a full-fledged star came on February 2, 1950, when Dore Schary summoned her to read for the part of Mary, the nice, middle-class, pregnant wife of Joe Smith, American, in *The Next Voice You Hear*.

The movie had been concocted by a man desperate to recapture the hordes of moviegoers who were staying home to watch television. The head of MGM thought that a low-budget film about God speaking platitudes over the radio to every part of the world "except behind the Iron Curtain" would inspire people to stampede movie theaters. Schary was determined to fly against three established axioms: "message" pictures drive people away from the movies, religion is box-office poison, and 60 percent of all tickets are bought to see bona fide, established, full-fledged stars. *The Next Voice You Hear* featured a religious message delivered by unknown actors without costumes or makeup.

"I felt that *Next Voice* might be outside the standard rules," Schary said. "Maybe we had such a strong and novel story that we could arouse the public's want-to-see on the angle of 'What's it about?' rather than 'Who's in it?'" He also believed that "in the present disturbed state of the world, a lot of people needed the assurance and comfort that this story could bring."

His only reservation was about taking his wife's advice to cast Nancy Davis in the female lead opposite James Whitmore. "This idea took a bit of getting used to," he admitted later. "This would be an exacting star role, and Nancy had had only three small parts in pictures." He couldn't bring himself to spend the money necessary to test her, but he did agree to let her read for the role.

During Hollywood's golden era—1920 to 1955—Metro-Goldwyn-Mayer catapulted more stars into the galaxy than any other Hollywood studio, but no one knew the exact formula for creating them. "We know *when* it happens, but beyond an elusive combination of the right person in the right vehicle, no one knows precisely *how* it happens," said former MGM director Richard Brooks. "When a starring role comes along, you don't exactly typecast, but you pick someone the audience will accept in the part; you assemble a great cast and crew; then you work like hell and hope magic happens. Once in a while it does."

Nancy Davis knew she had a chance at a starring role that could change her life; so she was understandably nervous as she went for her preliminary reading. She had recently tested so poorly that she lost the female lead in *Crisis* opposite Cary Grant.

"That *Crisis* test of Nancy's was the worst test I ever saw," said the movie's assistant director. "She had to wear a silk slip over her foundation and she was so fidgety about her girdle showing that she came through the camera flat."

Nancy walked into the MGM conference room with Schary, sat down next to James Whitmore, opened the script, and they began reading their lines aloud to director William Wellman. By the time they finished, Nancy had redeemed herself. "After a reading like this, a test would just be a waste of everybody's time," said Dore Schary.

"Nancy was so close to what the script described—a nice, quiet, well-behaved girl who wears a $12.95 maternity smock—that she was a perfect choice," said Charles "Cap" Palmer, who was on the set to write a book about the making of the movie, which MGM described in press releases as one of its most unusual and provocative productions of the year.

The part called for her to be the silent strength in her marriage, to quietly prompt her husband to say the right thing, a characteristic that she would carry into her own marriage.

"Since she had to be pregnant throughout the film and look like she had only a week to go before delivery, she spent time with a friend of hers who was soon going to have a baby so she'd know how to move," said Palmer. "She wore her wire hanger pregnancy pad during rehearsals and was beautiful to direct. She had ideas of her own, but she would do what she was told. She never argued; she never did the Dustin Hoffman bit of asking, 'What's your motivation?' and all that. . . . She and Jim got along fine, but they weren't close and they certainly didn't fraternize off the set."

Whitmore, who had trained at the Actors Studio in New York and been nominated for an Academy Award for his work as a supporting actor in *Battleground* the year before, worked with Nancy between takes, rehearsing and polishing. "It was the first starring role for both of us, and we worked intensely because both of us were very serious about our careers," he said. "Nancy was definitely not a frivolous person. When it came to her career, she was deadly earnest. She was delightful to work with, very affable, and had a good, hearty laugh. She'd throw her head back and just let loose from somewhere in the center of her being. But we didn't socialize off the set, and there was never any personal conversation about her boyfriends or anything like that. I do recall, though, that she held very strong political opinions which weren't exactly mine."

After three weeks of rehearsal and two weeks of filming, the set was struck; Nancy cracked open a bottle of champagne for the cast and Dore Schary presented her with a leather-bound script that he had inscribed on the fly leaf: "You'll never forget this picture, and I'll never forget you." The sneak preview of *The Next Voice You Hear* was held March 24, 1950, and the results were positive enough to persuade the studio to open it in Radio City Music Hall in Manhattan. Nancy was so thrilled to see her name on the New York marquee that she took a picture of it. "This I'll keep forever," she said.

"It was a big mistake to show that little movie about plain decent people in the huge cavernous hall of Radio City, which was so accustomed to extravaganzas," said James Whitmore many years later.

"It did very badly on first release because New York hated it," said Charles Palmer. "It closed after the first week."

The reviews were mixed, with most praising the good intentions of Dore Schary for producing a low-cost film with a religious message but dismissing the movie itself as insignificant. The *New Yorker* criticized it as "a meandering, maudlin affair." The *New York Times* was also unimpressed but praised James Whitmore as "hard to resist" and Nancy Davis as "cheerful and considerate as his heavily pregnant wife."

The movie won Nancy a Christopher Award for "creative work of spiritual significance," but it did not bring her stardom because she did not transcend the role. "She projected all the passion of a Good Humor ice cream—frozen, on a stick, and all vanilla," said Spencer Tracy.

"She never sparkled and seemed quite as young as, say, June Allyson," said Dore Schary. "She was more like a very nice, honest, thoroughly smart schoolteacher."

"She just didn't have that intangible star quality," said Charles Palmer.

"That aloneness, that apartness, that quality of disdain that characterizes a star."

The opinion that mattered most to her was delivered on September 12, 1950, the night of the premiere, by the man she had asked to escort her. "I told her to send her movie wardrobe to the cleaners and lose the ticket," said Ronald Reagan many years later, "but I also said she could go home and unpack, because she'd be around for quite a while."

This marked the first time that Ronald Reagan and Nancy Davis were photographed in public. Their picture appeared in movie magazines, which was important to Nancy, because she was frantically trying to compete with the ghost of Reagan's former wife, Jane Wyman. Heartbroken over his divorce, which became final on July 18, 1949, Reagan had spent the next year trying to win Wyman back by sending her flowers, giving her a poodle, and visiting her movie sets. He had even accompanied her to a few sessions with her psychiatrist, Dr. Ralph H. "Romy" Greenson. He told reporters he was still in love with his wife. "I believe we belong together," he said, "and that we will end our days together."

So devoted had he been to the moody, mercurial actress he had married in 1940 that when she started a love affair with Lew Ayres, her co-star in *Johnny Belinda,* he very publicly gave her permission for the marital transgression. "She is very intense, but she's been a wonderful wife and unsure because of that very thing," said Reagan. "The trouble is she hasn't learned to separate her work from her personal life. Right now, Jane needs very much to have a fling and I intend to let her have it."

But Jane Wyman had wanted much more than a fling; she wanted out of her marriage to "America's number one goody-two-shoes Mr. Nice Guy," as she put it. Her unutterable boredom was palpable to everyone around them. "Little Miss Button Nose," as Reagan so endearingly called her, had grown weary of her husband's talkathons.

"I used to visit them because Jane was such a good cook," said Ann Sheridan, who co-starred with Reagan in *Kings Row.* "On one occasion, Ronnie, a baseball nut, had heard a game on the radio and he gave us a play-by-play account. After the fourth inning, Jane said, 'Ronnie, please stop. Annie doesn't care about baseball.' But he went on for all nine innings." Reagan, who had been a play-by-play sportscaster for WHO Radio in Des Moines, Iowa, did not hear his wife's objection. She said that he was such a nonstop talker that he was making speeches in his sleep.

"I remember when I asked Ronnie some basic question and he answered me carefully, methodically," said June Allyson. "When he got through explaining something to me, Jane leaned over and said, 'Don't ask Ronnie what time it is because he will tell you how a watch is made.' "

Wyman told Gregory Peck that she had called it quits because "I just couldn't stand to watch that damn *Kings Row* one more time." Reagan had one of the second leads in the film and he insisted on showing it after every one of the couple's dinner parties since 1942. When reporter Jim Bacon asked her about Ronald Reagan as a lover, Wyman said, "He's about as good in bed as he was on the screen."

As his movie career faded ("I was the Errol Flynn of the B's," Reagan said), he became more interested in motion picture politics, and his impassioned devotion to the Screen Actors Guild produced glassy-eyed tedium in Jane Wyman, which occasionally led to fits of screaming rage. "I remember a SAG meeting when Ronnie as president was going on and on about something," said Rosemary DeCamp, a former board member. "Jane got so fed up listening to him that she stood up and shouted, 'Oh, for God's sake, Ronnie, shut up and go shit in your hat.' "

Nancy Davis was determined to soothe those wounds. She listened to Reagan's discourses as if enraptured; she watched his movies entranced; and she told him she so admired his work as president of the Screen Actors Guild that she, too, would like to be an active part of the organization. Flattered by her adulation, Reagan responded in July 1950 by proposing her to succeed Joan Caulfield on the board of directors.

SAG's official minutes show that after the motion was made and seconded, someone said that the MGM starlet wasn't important enough to be a board member. "The opinion was expressed that the Guild is in need at this time of 'name' strength on the board, and that Miss Davis will be of greater value after she has been in pictures for a longer time. The motion was thereafter defeated."

Nancy expressed such disappointment that Reagan asked Lee Bowman to propose her again when another opening came up. This time, the motion carried unanimously, and Nancy was appointed to the board for thirty days, until the November 1950 election, when her name was placed on the ballot. There were fourteen nominations, and ten of them were elected. Nancy Davis lost, but Reagan managed to get her appointed to fill the board vacancy left by Robert Ryan until November 1951, when she was finally elected to a three-year term. "We voted her in then," said Rosemary DeCamp, "but only as a favor to Ronnie."

Being on the board of directors of the Screen Actors Guild meant that Nancy would now see Reagan on a regular basis. Without those weekly Monday night meetings, the courtship might have foundered. Trying to forget his wife, Reagan began seeing several women, and for the next two years Nancy, much to her chagrin, was simply one of many, including Adele Jergens, Kay Stewart, Ruth Roman, Monica Lewis, Penny Edwards, Ann Sothern, Evelyn Knight, Dorothy Shay, Peggy Stewart, and Piper Laurie.

Most of them were at least ten years younger than he. They included Hollywood starlets, singers, models, and beauticians. Among the full-fledged stars were Patricia Neal, Doris Day, and Rhonda Fleming. Viveca Lindfors, his co-star in *Night Unto Night,* could not recall a single conversation with him of any substance, except on the subject of sex. "I remember him saying, 'Sex is best in the afternoon, after coming out of the shower,' and then he laughed his slightly embarrassed laugh," she said.

Reagan held a hearty sexual image of himself, which he did not feel was shown to proper advantage in *Dark Victory,* the movie starring Bette Davis and Humphrey Bogart in which he received fifth billing as the drunk dilettante hopelessly in love with Bette Davis. He said his big scene was badly acted because the homosexual director did not let him play it the way he wanted. "I actually believe he saw my part as a copy of his own life. I was playing, he told me, the kind of fellow who could sit in the girls' dressing room dishing the dirt while they went on dressing in front of me. I had no trouble seeing [the director] in that role, but for myself I want to think I can stroll through where the girls are short of clothes, and there will be a great scurrying about and taking to cover."

Reagan could not deal with a role that made him anything less than a masculine superhero. His taste in women ran to the same stereotype.

"Ronnie liked the big, outdoor, blond Pasadena Rose Bowl Parade queen type of California woman," said Doris Lilly, the author of *How to Marry a Millionaire.* "I know because I was one of them. I had a delightful little romance with him after his divorce. Intimately, he was nothing memorable, but he was an appealing-looking guy who was very, very sweet. I hate to say that he was weak—maybe a nicer word would be passive. . . . He loved to go out and be seen at all the nightclubs in those days, and he loved to drink, so we used to go out and get smashed. . . . He also loved the comedians, so we'd go to hear George Jessel and Sophie Tucker. . . . We went ice-skating in Westwood by the old veterans home . . . and I listened to all his stories. We had a great time for a while, but I was always going off to Europe and writing him from there. Then I'd go to California and he'd go to New York. He'd send me flowers and write me letters which were adorable because he was such a gent that he wouldn't spell out the words *damn* or *hell.* Instead, he'd write 'd——n' and 'h——ll.' "

His sexual references were not so oblique. "I'd like to be tossing off a 'short one' with you too," he wrote to her on April 28, 1948. "But if that is as far as your 'dreaming' goes—I just left you because I just dreamed us past the last drink (bar closed for the night)." Seven months later he wrote to say, "And another thing—your call interrupted *no* Sunday matinee (d——n it) I was just fogged over and sleepy."

Betty Underwood, a former Powers model, recalled her time with Ronald Reagan as "charming and delightful and very romantic," but Jacqueline Park, a former Warner Bros. starlet and later the mistress of Jack Warner, was humiliated by her affair with him. Thirty-nine years later, she said, "It's something I'd truly like to forget.

"After we were introduced by George Paley, a businessman in Hollywood, Ronnie called me at the Studio Club, where I was staying, and invited me to his house on Londonderry Drive above the Sunset Strip for a drink. I said I would take a cab but he said, 'You're only a block away from Sunset Boulevard. Why don't you take a bus and save your money?' Right then I knew he was cheap, but he was very attractive, so I got on the bus.

"He answered the door wearing one of those marvelous silk bathrobe things with an ascot that men used to wear in those days, and I think he was still suffering withdrawal pains from Jane Wyman. He was so in love with that woman that she had become an obsession with him. When she walked out on him, he couldn't function—couldn't go out of the house, couldn't work, couldn't cook, couldn't perform sexually. So it was tough for me in the beginning.

"He ordered dinner to be delivered from Chasen's, and we sat down to have a drink. He asked me to give him a massage, so I did. He kissed me and he held me and said, 'I really like you, kid,' but that was it. He had a couple more drinks and accidentally dropped his glass on the floor. He pointed to the shattered pieces and said, 'That is what's going to happen to your heart if you stay in this town. One way or the other—if you make it or you don't make it—this town will break your heart.' He kept pointing to the broken glass and saying, 'That's how your heart will look if you decide to stay here.' Dinner arrived, and afterward he said, 'Why don't you go home now and I'll give you a call again.' So I asked him for cab fare because it was late, but he said I had to take the bus because he didn't have any small change. 'All I have is big bills,' he said. I felt he had contempt for me because I didn't have any money but, thank God, I had enough for the bus. This routine went on for months and months, him calling me and me taking the bus to see him. I became great friends with the bus driver.

"Ronnie never took me out in public, never gave me a present, and never ever paid for a cab for me. He swore me to secrecy about our relationship and said I couldn't tell anybody at the studio about us. He did introduce me to his mother, Nelle, but he didn't say I was his lover. He said I was just a fan of his, which was true, I guess, because I was star-struck and in awe of him, but I felt there was more to the relationship than that because he always wanted to see me. I wasn't seeing anyone else at the time, but when I got pregnant I found out that our relationship didn't really mean anything at all to him.

"He said, 'You're what? Well, it's not from me. It's not mine. No sir, it's not mine.' He was awful. He said, 'I know how you Hollywood starlets play around with everybody and then you try to blame good people like me, but you can't get away with it. There's no proof that you've ever been with me. You're just going to have to work this one out for yourself. I don't want to be involved.' And then he hung up on me. I didn't know what to do. He was so powerful and I was just a nobody. I was afraid that if I pursued it, I'd lose my card in the Screen Actors Guild. So I called my friend Bentley Ryan and told him what had happened. He was outraged by Reagan's reaction, but he arranged for me to have an abortion and that, of course, was the end of my affair with the president of the Screen Actors Guild."

A series of women passed through Ronald Reagan's bedroom in those years, so many, in fact, that he later told Joe Santley, a publicist, that he once found himself in the Garden of Allah Hotel with a woman he didn't know. "I woke up one morning and I couldn't remember the name of the gal I was in bed with. I said, 'Hey, I gotta get a grip here.' "

So established was Reagan's reputation as a Hollywood swinger, spending $750 a month on nightclubs, that even the movie magazines of the era, which treated stars like demigods, took notice. "Never thought we'd come right out and call Ronnie Reagan a 'wolf,' but leave us face it," editorialized *Silver Screen* in May 1950. "Suddenly every glamour gal considers him a super-sexy escort for an evening. Even he admits he's missed a lot of fun and frolic and is out to make up for it. . . . Some say that torch for Jane Wyman is finally reduced to a feeble flame."

Aware of her competition, Nancy Davis was determined to outlast them all. Although she saw photographs in the fan magazines of Reagan dancing at Ciro's with Eileen Howe or dining at the Mocambo with Shirley Ballard or drinking at the Coconut Grove with Cookie Gordon, Nancy held on tenaciously, and worried more about the women he was seeing quietly, the ones he never took to nightclubs.

Nancy continued going to SAG board meetings every Monday night and managed to have dinner with Reagan afterward, either alone or with others. "She never said a word during those meetings, except to second all of Ronnie's motions," said Ann Doran, a former board member, "and she always sat there gazing at him with adoration." Such tenacity was not lost on Ronald Reagan's brother, Neil, who, upon meeting Nancy for the first time, observed to a friend, "It looks as if this one has her hooks in him good."

Maureen Reagan, who was ten years old at the time, remembers Nancy's elaborate efforts to woo her and her young brother, Michael, when they spent weekends with their father. In those days, Nancy was willing to do anything to gain favor with Ronald Reagan's children from his first marriage. She sang songs from *Call Me Madam* over and over with Maureen as they rode in the green Cadillac convertible that Jane Wyman had given Reagan for his thirty-seventh birthday. Nancy visited Maureen at her boarding school and whitewashed thousands of feet of redwood fence at Yearling Row, the 270-acre ranch that Reagan had bought in Malibu.

Michael, too, recalls how ingratiating Nancy was in those days. "I particularly liked Saturdays at the ranch because when Nancy came along she sat in the front seat of the car and I would sit on her lap. She would massage or tickle my back," he said.

Maureen and Michael came to realize that they were merely a conduit to their father's affection for Nancy, who later refused to have anything to do with them. "Those children—that was my courtship," she said thirty years later, barely able to contain her bitterness.

By 1951, her deep feelings for Ronald Reagan were evident to everyone around her. "She was a thirty-year-old woman unmarried but in love and so she started sleeping with him then," said Paula Raymond, a former MGM contract player. "We used to watch her go in and out of his apartment, and since Ronnie never closed the bedroom curtains, we could see a lot of what was going on. A love affair before marriage is not outrageous today, but back then when we all had morals clauses in our contracts, it was considered extremely risqué."

Reagan continued to see Nancy but not exclusively and certainly not consistently. Still, she made every moment count. In public, she never left his side. "I remember when I saw them at a gala at the Beverly Wilshire Hotel," said Mary Sinclair, a former actress at Paramount Studios. "I called to Nancy, whom I'd known in summer stock, 'Come over and talk to me.' And she said, 'What? And leave this great big wonderful man?' She refused to budge and would not come over to say hello to me. She just stood there looking up at Ronald Reagan with glazed apple eyes and holding on to him as if he was going to fall through the floor."

When they went out in public they frequently double-dated with June Allyson and Dick Powell. June Allyson said, "I remember telling Nancy, 'You have to marry Ronnie because he is just as wonderful as Richard.' She answered, 'I agree, but I think it's polite to wait until I'm asked.'"

The forty-one-year-old actor never asked because at the time he was deeply in love with an actress named Christine Larson who, despite her Wisconsin roots, looked very much like one of those big beautiful Rose Bowl queens that he so favored. It was Christine Larson, not Nancy Davis, who received Ronald Reagan's proposal of marriage in 1951, a proposal accompanied by a diamond wristwatch as an engagement present. The twenty-six-year-old actress decided to keep the watch but rejected the offer.

"Christine just wasn't that much in love with Ronald Reagan," said Jim Lewis, who attended religious meetings with Larson. "I think her big thing was with Gary Cooper. I knew her very well then; I was a neighbor and friend and we were both Bahais. She died several years ago."

"She was lovely," said the playwright O. Z. Whitehead, "and, like Reagan, I, too, wanted to marry her. She cared about art, music, theater, and her religious involvement in Bahai. Unfortunately for Ronnie, she was not at all interested in politics. That's one of the reasons they could never get married. As president of the Screen Actors Guild, his political activities made him unacceptable to someone like Christine, who was a devout Bahai. In our faith, you cannot be in politics because in politics you take sides and our beliefs don't subscribe to that. But Christine told me that Ronnie was very moved when she talked about Bahai to him.

"I think that's why when he became President of the United States he issued a public statement calling for a halt to the execution of Bahais in Iran. I firmly believe that was Christine working through him."

"I think she even took him to one of the Bahai firesides," said Jim Lewis.

Because Reagan's mother, Nelle, preached and prayed every day of her life ("Gramsie was a real Bible-thumper," said her granddaughter Maureen), and made her son go to Sunday school every week before church, and to Christian Endeavor class after church, and prayer meetings every Wednesday evening, Reagan was receptive to Christine Larson's religious commitment. As a Bahai, she believed Bahaullah to be the most recent in the line of Messengers of God, a line that included Abraham, Moses, Buddha, Zoroaster, Jesus, and Muhammad. One of the fundamental objectives of the Bahai faith is establishing world peace within the framework of a unified, spiritually enlightened new world order.

Christine Larson lived in a house on North Beverly Glen, a few miles from Nancy Davis's apartment on South Beverly Glen, which made it convenient for Reagan, who was seeing both women at the time.

One night, Nancy told him she was pregnant. He drove to Christine's house and, according to her best friend, Betty Laskey, told her what had happened and how trapped he felt. "He wondered if Nancy was tricking him into marriage."

A few evenings later, morose and alone, Reagan headed for Slapsie Maxie's on Wilshire Boulevard, one of his favorite Hollywood nightclubs. He arrived shortly before the 2:00 A.M. closing, spotted a big California blond starlet named Selene Walters, and asked to be introduced.

"Although I was with a date," she said, "Ronnie kept whispering in my ear, 'I'd like to call you. How can I get in touch with you? I want to see you.'

"To a kid starlet like me, being seen in public with a famous actor like Ronald Reagan, who was president of the Screen Actors Guild, would do wonders for my career, so I was delighted that he wanted to take me out. I was nineteen years old and so stupid that I didn't understand why he asked me if I lived alone and whether or not I had a roommate. I said I didn't, and I gave him my address and phone number, hoping that he would call me and take me someplace glamorous so we could be photographed together.

"Around three o'clock that morning he was ringing my doorbell and I was so angry because I didn't want to see him behind closed doors. I only wanted to go out in public with him, but he pushed his way inside and said he just had to see me. He forced me on the couch and I kept trying to keep a conversation going, saying stupid things like, 'Oh, tell me about your latest movie,' and 'How would you advise me to proceed with my career.' He didn't want to talk about that. He said, 'Oh, we'll talk about that another time. Another time. You're so beautiful. Let's just get to know each other.' He was so big I couldn't fight him off. It was the most pitched battle I've ever had and suddenly in a matter of seconds I lost. . . . They call it date rape today—I hate that word *rape*—but then I was so shocked and angry because he had spoiled everything. I told him, too, but he said, 'Oh, I just couldn't help myself. Don't worry about a thing. I'm going to call you and we're going to go out and then we'll talk some more about your career.' Needless to say, I had the shock of my life when I read the announcement a week later that he was going to be marrying Nancy Davis."

Christine Larson's best friend was not at all surprised by the story of Selene Walters. "The relationship with Christine was the most intense, but there were at least six others going on at the same time," Betty Laskey said. The woman she pitied most was the one Ronald Reagan reluctantly agreed to marry.

On February 20, 1952, with Nancy by his side, Ronald Reagan picked up the telephone and dialed Chicago. Edith Davis answered the phone, surprised by the strange male voice asking to speak to Dr. Loyal Davis. "I said, 'Who wants to speak to him,' and he said 'Ronald Reagan,' " she recalled. "I thought, 'What the hell's he doing calling Loyal?' I didn't know what it was for. I said, 'Just a moment.' I went in and said to Loyal, 'Ronald Reagan wants to speak to you.' And he said, 'Me?' And I said, 'Get to that phone 'cause I want to know what he wants.' Anyway, Loyal went to the phone. He said, 'That's interesting. Are you sure you can? Yes.' And they talked. [After he hung up] Loyal said to me, 'He wants to marry Nancy.' And I said, 'Oh, go on!' He said, 'No, I'm not kidding. He wants to marry Nancy.' And I said, 'That's very exciting, very exciting.' "

A few minutes later, the phone rang again. This time it was Nancy calling. Her mother answered and said, "Why in hell is that man calling your father for this?"

"We want to get married, but don't want to marry unless you and Daddy want me to," said Nancy.

"Of course," said Edith. "If he's a nice guy and you like him, then I'm sure he's all right."

"He is, you'll love him."

"Find out what you want for a wedding present. It can't be extravagant, but I want you to have what you want," said Edith.

Shortly thereafter, Nancy called back. "I'll tell you what we want," she said. "We want a camera that can take moving pictures and a screen that we can show them on, and that's all we want."

"Sold," said Edith, who soon ordered 350 engraved wedding announcements to send to all her friends.

The next day, the MGM publicity office issued a press release saying Nancy Davis would be marrying Ronald Reagan on March 4, 1952. It was the same leap year that cartoonist Al Capp finally let Daisy Mae marry Li'l Abner after an eighteen-year chase. The studio said the Reagans' ceremony would take place in California in a small church on the road to Phoenix, Arizona, where the couple planned a two-week honeymoon visiting the bride's parents, who would be arriving from Chicago. Actor William Holden and his wife, Brenda Marshall, were to be the best man and matron of honor.

This was the last announcement that MGM would make for its thirty-year-old starlet, because the studio was dropping her. The day before, the Metro publicity office tried to soften the blow by releasing a brief statement: "Nancy Davis has asked for and received her release from MGM. . . . The reason she gives is that there were no stories ready for her and she has outside offers."

In fact, the MGM legal files show that Nancy did everything she could to abort that announcement. Eager to have her contract renewed, she volunteered for a Movietime U.S.A. personal appearance tour, she posed for jewelry ads, she endorsed Quality Bakers of America so her photograph would appear on bread wrappers, she pushed Lux Flakes and Toilet Soap in national ads, she even appeared "free and without compensation" as an MGM representative at the annual meeting of the Community Chest at the Cathay Circle Theatre. All to no avail.

After the failure of *The Next Voice You Hear,* the curtain had started falling on her fledgling movie career, and she was used in many B-minus fillers, which ran with main features. Dore Schary did give her the role of a schoolteacher in his next flag-waving message film, but her little performance in *It's a Big Country* went unnoticed by reviewers.

"After that, I directed Nancy in *Night into Morning,* which she says is her favorite of all the films she made," said Fletcher Markle. "I found her to be a very gifted little actress. Of course, she was typecast for the role as a nice, sturdy war widow, but she had one big scene where she had to persuade Ray Milland not to commit suicide by jumping out a hotel window. She had an entire page of dialogue as she entered the hotel room, and I remember shooting it all in one take. She was very, very proud of herself for that, and I was proud of her, too."

But critics barely noticed. Nor did they pay much attention to her next low-budget film, *Shadow in the Sky,* with Ralph Meeker, James Whitmore, and Jean Hagen. By the time she was cast as George Murphy's wife in *Talk About a Stranger,* she knew she was finished.

"That was her last film at MGM and mine, too," said Murphy, who spent fifteen years at the studio before he became a U.S. senator. "After reading the script of that frightful picture, Nancy and I both realized that the studio wanted to get rid of us."

"Nancy Davis was so wooden that I couldn't do much with her in the film," said the director, David Bradley.

"Her performance was terrible," said the producer, Richard Goldstone, "but so was the movie. Neither was distinguished."

Nothing could save Nancy's contract at this point, not even her former lover, Benny Thau, who said, "She was an actress who wanted to make good in every way, but there were two hundred stars at MGM that she was competing with, and she was no Katharine Hepburn." Because she was no longer making her private visits to Thau's office every Saturday morning, no one felt obliged to rush to her rescue.

The studio's legal files contain an interoffice memo sent to the head office on January 31, 1952, asking about the possibility of renewing her contract. "I think we'll drop the option," wrote Al Corfino, a production executive. "Don't worry about it."

The departure of a contract player making $500 a week was barely noticed at the studio, where such stars as Elizabeth Taylor and Lassie reigned supreme at $5,000 a week each.

"Nancy Davis was merely a crumb at the banquet table of MGM," said Gottfried Reinhardt. "If it hadn't been for Benny Thau, no one would've ever known she was here. Why should we have noticed when she left?"

On February 29, 1952, Nancy Davis and Ronald Reagan applied for a marriage license. Although she was thirty, she gave her age as twenty-eight, a small deception she would maintain even with her husband-to-be. Four days later, they were married. She wore a gray wool suit with a white collar and cuffs; she carried white gloves and wore a small veiled hat of white flowers that fit close to her head. Ronald Reagan picked her up in his Cadillac convertible, and they drove to the Little Brown Church in the San Fernando Valley, a branch of the Hollywood Beverly Christian Church that Reagan and his mother attended. There they were met by the William Holdens and the minister, who performed a quick ceremony.

Ronald Reagan's mother, Nelle, was not among the wedding guests. He had moved her and his father, Jack, from Dixon, Illinois, to Hollywood in 1937, shortly after he signed with Warner Bros. After his father, an unsuccessful shoe salesman, died in 1941, Reagan visited his mother at least once a week and called her nearly every day. But he did not tell her about the wedding until after it had occurred. Nor did he invite his brother, Neil, and his sister-in-law, Bess, who lived nearby. He did not even invite his own children, eleven-year-old Maureen and seven-year-old Michael.

"I recall them talking about getting married," said Michael, "but the actual wedding was a surprise. They called Maureen and me at Chadwick [School] with the news. Looking back, the fact that my sister, Maureen, and I were not present at that wedding was a portent of things to come."

William Holden and his wife were barely speaking to each other on the day of the wedding, so they sat on opposite sides of the church, but Nancy was oblivious to their quarrel.

"I was so excited I went through the ceremony in a daze," she said. "Not only didn't I get a large formal wedding, as far as I can remember, I didn't get any wedding at all. I do recall getting a piece of wedding cake, which the Holdens had waiting for us at their home in the Toluca Lake area, argument or no argument. And, fortunately, they also had arranged for a photographer to be there, or we wouldn't even have had pictures of our wedding day. As much as I remember of that day, it was fine; I felt just fine about it."

Ronald Reagan was a reluctant bridegroom, as he admitted many years later. "The truth is, I did everything wrong, dating her off and on, continuing to volunteer for every Guild trip to New York—in short, doing everything which could have lost her if Someone up there hadn't been looking after me," he wrote in his autobiography. "In spite of my determination to remain footloose, in spite of my belief that the pattern of my life was all set and would continue without change, nature was trying to tell me something very important."

Two months after the Reagans were married nature nudged them into announcing the exceedingly obvious: The heir was apparent. Because of the stern moral climate of the times, they said the baby was due in December, which would be a socially acceptable nine months after the wedding. But the baby, Patricia Ann Reagan, was born October 21, 1952. And she weighed seven pounds. When his wife gave birth, Reagan was not with her in the hospital because he was with Christine Larson. In tears, he told her that he felt his life was ruined.

Though he had decided to do the right thing and marry Nancy, he kept on seeing the Wisconsin actress on the sly. Their affair ended shortly after Patti was born: One afternoon Reagan rang Christine's doorbell and a French actor answered wearing only a bath towel. "Ronnie was so angry he stormed off and that was that," said one of Christine's friends.

Nancy never admitted knowing about her husband's infidelity. All she ever said was how unhappy she was that he had not been with her in the hospital when their daughter was born. "When I was back in my room and the nurses brought me our baby for the first time, my first thought was that it was sad that Ronnie couldn't be there, because this was a moment meant to be shared by father and mother," she said.

Racked by guilt, Ronald Reagan finally began committing himself to his marriage. With the exception of a brief dalliance in 1968, he embraced fidelity as the path to marital happiness. In later years, he shared his feelings about monogamy with Dana Rohrabacher during an interview at Reagan's ranch.

Rohrabacher recalled: "He looked at me and said, 'I'd like to give you some advice.' It was as if it was some gift he wanted to give me, some insight that he'd learned and he knew would be very valuable for me to know. He asked me, 'Are you married?' I said I was. He said, 'Then let me give you just this advice, if nothing else: If you want to be a happy man, just don't ever cheat on your wife.' "

7

"I DON'T WANT TO DO ANYTHING else except be married," said the new Mrs. Ronald Reagan. "I just want to be Ronnie's wife." She knew that her husband believed his first marriage had been sundered by his wife's career. He had been publicly humiliated when Jane Wyman's star outshone his, when she obtained leading roles at Warner Bros. and he did not. The final indignity had come when Wyman won an Academy Award at a time when Ronald Reagan could barely get work. Nancy convinced her new husband that her career meant nothing to her. He needed to believe that, for his own was bottoming out.

"Her career and what would happen to it had entered my mind once or twice," he said, "and while I knew I'd be happier if the career ran second—way behind—I knew also I could never say 'give it up.' She was too good. . . . I shouldn't have worried—she was her mother's daughter and it was ingrained in her to simply say, 'If you try to make two careers work, one of them has to suffer.' She was fair. She said, 'Maybe some women can do it, but not for me.'"

Ronald Reagan's last film for Warner Bros. was *The Winning Team*, in which he portrayed Grover Cleveland Alexander, one of America's greatest baseball players, who secretly suffered from double vision and epilepsy. In an effort to help their new son-in-law, Dr. and Mrs. Loyal Davis threw a party in Chicago to preview the movie and, to ensure publicity, invited the widow of the pitcher. The party made the society pages of Chicago's newspapers, but that did little to impress Reagan's bosses, who let his contract lapse on January 28, 1952.

After forty-one films and fifteen years at Warner Bros., Ronald Reagan left the studio on his last day without so much as a farewell glass of champagne or a goodbye from the head of the studio. Nancy groused to her mother about this brush-off, and Edith called Frank Casey, the Warner Bros. representative in Chicago. "You tell that son of a bitch Jack Warner that he's the biggest bastard I ever heard of," she said. "He's a goddamned fool to let a star like Ronnie go."

Reagan had been complaining that his career had suffered because he had been forced by Warner Bros. to perform in mediocre films. So he became an independent agent and signed a five-picture contract with Universal Studios for $75,000 a film, saying he would not accept second-rate roles. Taking such a stand, he said, was the only way he could ever regain his stardom. After doing three films, he balked at the next film offered him, so Universal canceled his contract, depriving him of $150,000. After he married Nancy, he accepted a low-budget Western for $45,000, which finally put him at the bottom of the box office.

Nancy blamed his agents at Music Corporation of America (MCA) for her husband's failure to get good movie offers. "Marlon Brando gets everything," she said. Reagan blamed his role as president of the Screen Actors Guild, saying he had become too identified with the labor problems of Hollywood to be cast as a matinee idol. "They stop thinking of you as an actor. The image they have of you isn't associated with your last role, but with the guy who sat across the conference table beefing. And that's death," he said. So he resigned the SAG presidency in November 1952 but remained on the board of directors. Still, he didn't get any decent film offers.

"I went fourteen months and turned down half a million dollars' worth of films, not counting percentages," he said later. "It was tough."

The woman who "just wanted to be married" was also having trouble getting work until she was cast in *Donovan's Brain*. The script called for her to play the wife of a mad scientist who keeps the brain of a dead man alive and then becomes dominated by it. Nancy grabbed the part because she was to be paid $18,000 for six weeks' work. The low-budget science fiction film starring Lew Ayres was distributed by United Artists in 1953.

"The movie didn't turn out badly, but it was never a big sensation," said Ayres many years later. "Nancy Davis played my wife, and while she was never big enough to be considered my co-star, she was a very competent actress and very interested in her career."

Actually, Nancy was more concerned about her husband's career because they had very little money, having recently bought a three-bed-

room house on Amalfi Drive in Pacific Palisades. With a new wife and
child, plus support payments of $500 a month to Jane Wyman and mort-
gage payments on his $85,000 ranch in Malibu, Reagan was financially
strapped. His frustrated agents at MCA had almost exhausted all opportunities for the forty-two-year-old actor, who could no longer get starring
roles in feature films. He refused to lower himself to do television and
was ill-equipped to appear on the legitimate stage. All that was left for
the entertainer was Las Vegas. MCA finally found him two weeks of
nightclub work for $30,000.

"The idea scared the hell out of me," said Reagan, "[but] moneywise
the suggestion was a beauty."

He set up an appointment with his agents to discuss the proposal, and
that morning he consulted the syndicated newspaper column of his personal astrologer, Carroll Righter. "I looked and almost suspected an
MCA plot," Reagan said. "My word for the day read: 'This is a day to
listen to the advice of experts.' "

Clipping the item, the superstitious actor walked into the meeting and
without even saying hello, he asked his agents if they were experts.

"Well, I guess we—kind of are," they said.

"Let's get on with it then, and the first question is what do I do in a
nightclub?"

"How many benefits have you done?"

"Hundreds."

"What do you do at those benefits?"

"I always introduce the other acts."

"Right."

MCA then hired a young comedy writer by the name of John Bradford
to create a one-and-a-half-hour routine of acts for Ronald Reagan to introduce. Bradford, a former entertainer, had been a favorite of President
Harry Truman and went on to write for Frank Sinatra and Dinah Shore as
well as to provide Nixon jokes for John F. Kennedy during the 1960
presidential campaign.

"I was hired to cover Reagan's deficiencies, and at first I was scared to
death because I had never heard of a performer who couldn't sing or
dance doing a Vegas act before," said the writer. "So I met with Ron and
Nancy—she was always with him, always—to see what he could do. I
tried him out singing, and he was great; I gave him a sample monologue,
and his timing was perfect. He loved telling jokes in an Irish brogue, and
he was good at it, so I felt a little better. My wife and I then spent every
day for the next three weeks with the Reagans working on the act, and
Ron was terrific; he really knocked himself out because he was on his
uppers and needed the dough. I worked hard on the routine, too, be-

cause I liked him so much that I wanted him to be able to get a job out of it later.

"He was very political then—middle of the road, I'd say. I remember he wanted me to put a lot of tax jokes in the monologue because he'd just been hit with a whopping bill for back taxes and he hated the IRS. He said the Internal Revenue Service should be abolished. 'Everyone should pay ten percent of their income and that's it,' he said. He wanted to get rid of the department entirely and that was his own idea, not something that Nancy's father had indoctrinated him with."

Reagan suggested ending the nightclub act by reciting a poem entitled "The Definition of an Actor" by Irvin S. Cobb, which recounted the glories, sacrifices, and contributions of his profession. He asked that he be spotlighted center stage in a specially designed tuxedo which he insisted be made without pockets so he would look trim. In this poetic finale he said that actors weren't quite like doctors or lawyers because they didn't do regular work, but they did leave the world a better place in which to live. "There wasn't a dry eye in the house when he finished," said Bradford.

The writer designed an act consisting of the Continentals, a male quartet that had appeared at nightclubs like the Coconut Grove and Mocambo; the Blackburn Twins, a genteel song-and-dance act; and the Honey Brothers, a knockdown pratfall comedy team. "They did rough-and-tumble stuff which we referred to as 'blue' material in those days," Bradford said. "I cut out the blueness because I had Jack Armstrong, the squeaky clean all-American boy, doing the introduction, and there was no room for any type of Buddy Hackett bathroom humor."

The closest Reagan came to bad taste was a Dutch-accented routine he did in the beer garden. "Dutch because that was his nickname," said Bradford. Wearing a long apron advertising Pabst Blue Ribbon Beer with "Vos vils du haben?" written across it, Reagan was asked, "Vats zoo got under dere?"

"Underwear," he responded, scratching his crotch.

"Under dere," said one of the Honey Brothers.

"Ronnie loved the act and so did Nancy," said Bradford. "She attended every rehearsal and took notes like a secretary; she was that concerned. She was his amanuensis. She listened very carefully and made sure that Ronnie wasn't rolling the hoop on his lines or muffing his cues. She was totally involved in the act, and she was a great audience for him because she laughed at every one of his jokes. . . . The only time she got upset was when we tried out at the Statler Hotel in Los Angeles and Herman Hover, the fat booking agent from Ciro's, said, 'This act is going to bomb. What'll it cost for me to buy you out?' Nancy was furious, and so Ronnie held his ground. 'I'm not selling,' he said. 'I believe in the act and I'm doing it.' "

By then Reagan had converted the Continentals. "We expected to have to carry him," said Ben Cruz, one of the male singers. "At first he was rough as a cob, but then he really opened our eyes . . . by the end of the first week of rehearsals he was moving like the rest of us. He knew the choreography as well as we did. . . . Nancy would sit through all the rehearsals . . . some up to four hours long, and then all the shows, sipping nothing more than a glass of ice water."

The Reagans skidded into rhinestone gulch on February 24, 1954, for two weeks at the Last Frontier Hotel, complete with bosomy dancing girls in feather headdresses and an old-time baggy pants vaudeville routine of grown men racing around the stage smashing one another on the head with rolled-up newspapers. After watching, the critics deemed Reagan perfectly agreeable as a floor show emcee, but they worried about having "to suffer a retreating army of fading Hollywood stars."

Publicly, Reagan said the act was popular enough to generate offers from nightclubs around the country, but privately he realized that he had sunk to a new low. "When we got back home, we thought of it as just so many more weeks we'd bought that we could hold out in our waiting game," he wrote in his autobiography.

"Never again will I sell myself so short," he confided to his MCA agent.

MCA worked overtime for their unemployed client because they owed him a great deal. On July 14, 1952, Reagan, as president of the Screen Actors Guild, had signed a blanket waiver for the talent agency to engage in the unlimited production of television shows while *still* representing talent. SAG had granted a few very limited waivers to talent agencies wishing to produce motion pictures, but nothing like the waiver MCA acquired. The agency had recognized that filmed shows, particularly series, were bound to become a mainstay of television. Because the major movie studios were refusing to make films for television, MCA saw a lucrative vacuum and moved quickly to fill it. With SAG's blanket waiver, MCA became the biggest and most powerful packager of talent in America. The agency could create packaging companies that delivered complete shows to the networks for which they were paid and then load those shows with MCA talent—actors, writers, directors—from whom they collected additional money in commissions.

MCA had represented Reagan since 1940, shortly after he came to Hollywood. Within a few years, he had become an extremely valuable client to them because of his position as president of the Screen Actors Guild. Through this office, he developed close personal relationships with the agency, especially with Lew Wasserman, his agent, who shared his liberal politics at the time, as well as Taft Schrieber, and the founder of MCA, Dr. Jules Stein, a Chicago ophthalmologist who had started the business as a booking agency for musicians during the big-band era.

MCA now tried to convince him that after Las Vegas there was no place left to go but television, which was becoming the premier source of entertainment in America. Still, most Hollywood stars would have opened a vein before appearing on the dreaded small screen, which hosted Winky Dink, Sky King, Howdy Doody, Captain Video, and Hopalong Cassidy. But Ronald Reagan was no longer considered a star. The *Chicago Tribune/New York Daily News* syndicate described him as "one of [those] believed washed up by some industry heads." So, with limited options, he finally agreed to appear on a CBS dramatic anthology series and then on "The Priceless Gift" on NBC-TV.

In 1953, he appeared with Nancy as his wife in a half-hour dramatization called "First Born," the story of a young boy who resents his step-mother's efforts to convince him that she loves and wants him as her own son. It was an ironic role considering that the new Mrs. Reagan was now putting as much distance as she could between herself and her "difficult" eight-year-old stepson, Michael, the adopted child of her husband's first marriage. Although the Reagans received star billing, they were over-shadowed by Tommy Rettig, who played the young boy. Nancy was judged "competent" but Ronald Reagan was barely mentioned. Still, MCA managed to book nine more television appearances for him that year, plus two for Nancy.

By 1954, the age of television had arrived on thundering hooves. The TV dinner was introduced and the average family watched between four and five hours of television a day. More than 5,000 movie marquees across the country plunged into darkness as people stayed home to watch Ernie Kovacs and Milton Berle. Up to this time more than 50 percent of the population regularly went to the movies. In 1954, they stayed home to watch television. Hearts once pledged to Fred Astaire and Ginger Rogers now quickened to Lucy and Ricky and Fred and Ethel.

That year, MCA's Taft Schrieber, in charge of the agency's television production firm, Revue Productions, proposed Ronald Reagan as the pitchman for the "General Electric Theater," a weekly half-hour series to be shown on CBS-TV every Sunday at 9:00 P.M. The company interviewed several men for the role of host, including Edward Arnold and Walter Pidgeon, who was then president of the Screen Actors Guild. Kirk Douglas says the job fell to Reagan only by default.

"I was pitched on being the spokesman," said Douglas. "I didn't think, really, that I wanted to do it, but I wanted to hear their case. They made an eloquent address about me being part of the General Electric family. I turned it down."

Reagan believed he was the only person considered. "General Electric did a prodigious job of research on me before they signed me," he said. "It was gratifying to learn they considered me a better box-office bet than certain circles in Hollywood would admit."

For $125,000 a year, later raised to $150,000, "plus perquisites," he was eager to join the benign company of washed-up stars like Adolphe Menjou, Robert Montgomery, Gloria Swanson, and Gene Raymond, who introduced weekly dramas on television. He hosted the series, which followed the "Ed Sullivan Show" on Sunday nights, and took a leading role now and then, occasionally producing a show.

More than just a smiling presence on weekly television, Ronald Reagan became Mr. General Electric, the glorified corporate vendor who pushed the company slogan: "Progress is our most important product." He peddled it to the families watching television every week, to blue-collar workers in General Electric factories across the country, to local chambers of commerce, school boards, garden clubs, union halls, and Rotary meetings. He plugged it on promotional tours to city councils and to conventioneers. He hawked it to Shriners, to Masons, to Knights of Columbus. He marketed it to the Kiwanis, the Lions, the Elks, the American Legion—telling each that the corporate behemoth of General Electric was "as human as the corner grocer." So effective was he as an exalted front man that someone watching him deliver an institutional homily for the company's nuclear fusion plant said, "I really didn't need a submarine, but I've got one now."

As part of his contract, he had to tour the country for 10 weeks a year, visit 125 GE plants, meet 250,000 GE employees, and promote company products to the public—for which he received additional compensation. He sometimes made 14 speeches a day.

So grateful was Reagan to be a spokesman for big business that he adjusted his politics to fit the part and the liberal Democrat slowly metamorphosed into a conservative Republican. He railed against the domestic "Communist conspiracy," government regulation, high taxes, and federal interference with the private sector. When he spoke to labor leaders, he emphasized his five years of service as president of SAG while suggesting that General Electric was such a great company to work for that unions weren't necessary. While Reagan was selling factory workers on his labor credentials, GE's management was busting unions. The company was convicted of price-fixing and fined almost $1 million; three of its top executives were sent to prison.

Reagan adopted the Republican doctrine in denouncing the Tennessee

Valley Authority (TVA) as a socialistic freeloader that paid no taxes. The federally funded TVA provided electric power to the public at low rates private enterprise could not match. He suggested the government turn the TVA over to private owners. Reagan received a call from GE's advertising agency.

"Thought you'd like to know, Mr. Reagan, that GE does $50 million worth of business with TVA."

Chagrined, Reagan called Ralph Cordiner, president of General Electric. "What would you say if I said I could make my speech just as effectively without mentioning TVA?"

"Well, it would make my job easier," said the company executive.

Reagan, whose most captivating personality trait was his geniality, never mentioned the TVA again. He thrived on making speeches to GE workers, answering their questions about Hollywood, telling them about *Kings Row,* and autographing glossy photographs of himself. He said he felt reassured that "stars supposedly forgotten in Hollywood were still much beloved by the people."

"Ronnie cared deeply about the money he was making then and the financial security he was piling up," said Blaine Waller, a former production assistant who worked with Reagan on the "General Electric Theater." "We used to do most everything live in those days, so I'd have to tape the floors of the rehearsal hall on Mondays so the actors would not walk into tables once they started working with a set; we would do the dry blocking on Tuesdays and walk-throughs on Wednesdays. Reagan would sit with me every day and talk for hours, even though I was only twenty-five years old at the time and he was about forty-five. He was one of the nicest guys I ever met; he never showed any temperament and, because he was nearly blind without his glasses, he always had his lines memorized by the first day of rehearsal.

"He talked a lot about his marriage to Jane Wyman and said that it had ended because she cared too much about her career. His second marriage, he said, was perfect for him, and so was the GE job, because it was the most money he had ever made."

Reagan was paid for his company tours, received an additional fee for any show in which he acted, plus profit participation on episodes in which he had appeared after the show was in its fifth replay. Nancy, too, was given guaranteed compensation as a "supporting performer" in any scripts that were suited to her.

Determined to try to break Jane Wyman's record of having appeared in five movies with Ronald Reagan, Nancy accepted the film role of a promiscuous nurse in love with a submarine commander played by Reagan in *Hellcats of the Navy.* This 1957 Columbia Pictures release was to be their only feature film together, though they co-starred in four television dramas, two of which were on the "General Electric Theater."

The *New York Daily News* gave Nancy's *Hellcats* performance high marks for providing "subordinate romantic interest which does not get in the way of the film's primary offering—action." Reagan was shrugged off as "competent." Claustrophobic, he had a terrible time during the hours he spent cramped in the small conning tower of the submarine. He said he could not wait to get out after every take, and movie audiences felt the same way. The film had to be double-featured when it was shown and barely broke even at the box office.

A few months later, Nancy made her last feature film, fittingly titled *Crash Landing*. She played Gary Merrill's wife in an insipid story about passengers aboard a plane destined to crash into the ocean. The crash was averted in the film but not at the box office.

Still, Nancy Davis did not believe her movie career was over. Her husband, a bit more realistic about his prospects, blamed his role as Mr. General Electric. "I'm only on for a forty-five-second spot, but that makes me a television personality—and kills me off for movie offers," he said. The company compensated them with all-electric "perquisites" for the house he and Nancy were building at 1669 San Onofre Drive in the Upper Riviera section of Pacific Palisades overlooking the Santa Monica Mountains.

"It'll have everything electric, except a chair," he joked to newspaper reporters at the time.

On condition that they show the "all-electric home" for publicity purposes, GE equipped it free with the most sophisticated electronics of the day, including an intercom system in every room, a retractable canopy roof for indoor and outdoor dining, indirect overhead lighting, a film projection room, colored light wheels (pink, blue, yellow, and green) for the dining room dimmers, electronic opening and closing devices for the draperies, a heated swimming pool with underwater lights, an electric barbecue and rotisserie, electric hedge clippers, three television sets, two ranges, two ovens, three refrigerators, two freezers, a deluxe washing machine and dryer, heat lamps in the atrium, and an electric eye in the driveway. The eye's hidden red light could be seen from the road, indicating whether an intruder had crossed the concealed security sensors and entered the house.

Determined to live like a rich corporate wife, Nancy put a sign on the side door of the new house that said "Trade Entrance Only," and required her housekeeper to wear a uniform at all times. Like other housewives of the Eisenhower era, Nancy drove a wood-paneled station wagon and, to her young stepson, seemed to represent the all-American mom-mies he was seeing on television with their clean houses, sweet children, and spotless kitchens. Michael said that as a child he longed to be a part of his father's new family, but Nancy put as much distance as she could between him and that dream, concentrating instead on replacing him with something that Ronald Reagan's first wife could not produce—a son. Because of an astrological reading in 1952, Nancy had been convinced that her first pregnancy would produce that male heir. "For some reason, I had been sure I was going to have a boy," she wrote in her autobiography, not admitting her faith in the stars. For the next five years, she kept trying to get pregnant because she was astrologically assured of conceiving a boy "next time."

Reagan did not need to have this boy as much as his wife needed to produce it for him. "There was an extra room in the new house because Nancy had decided Patti should have a brother," he said. "Personally, I would have settled for the three of us . . . [but] I knew Patti would have that brother, because I couldn't say no to the Nancy who'd decided this. . . ."

After Nancy miscarried twice between 1953 and 1957, her obstetrician, Dr. Benbow Thompson, said she would have to stop working and stay in bed for three months while taking weekly hormone shots so the fetus would adhere to the uterine wall. Then she would have to restrict her activities for the duration of the pregnancy to carry to full term. Determined to have that baby boy, she followed her doctor's orders.

"I agreed because I had a lot of faith in him," she said. "He'd seen me through my first delivery and I wanted him to see me through my second. . . . It was difficult lying in bed . . . and it was hard to be careful with every movement I made the rest of the time. But it was also difficult keeping the baby, and every time I moved I thought I might lose him."

Despite a precarious pregnancy, Nancy continued to go with her husband to SAG board meetings. "So help me God, I think she was at a board meeting until the night before the baby was born," said Ann Doran. "She was so uncomfortable she could barely breathe and she had to sit there for hours without moving. I felt sorry for her and was amazed that just to be where he was, she was making herself so uncomfortable. I'd have stayed home and in bed, but she absolutely had to be where Ronnie was. The tie between the two of them was so strong by then that she did not leave his side and he didn't leave hers. I've never known two people who were so much one when they married. It was strange, very strange . . . as if she just submitted her whole soul to him."

A cesarean delivery was scheduled for May 20, 1958, and this time Nancy made sure her husband was present by having her mother and her best friend, actor Robert Taylor's wife, Ursula, accompany him to Cedars

of Lebanon Hospital early in the day. When Dr. Thompson delivered the
8½-pound baby, he held him up. "Look, Nancy," he said. "You got
your wish—it's a boy."

The baby, soon called Skipper, was named Ronald Prescott Reagan—
Ronald for his father and Prescott for his maternal grandmother, Edith
Prescott Luckett Davis, and Mrs. Barry Goldwater (Margaret Prescott
Johnson). The Goldwaters, Barry and his brother Bob and their wives,
had become close friends of Dr. and Mrs. Davis in Phoenix, and through
them with the Reagans. Ursula and Robert Taylor were chosen as god-
parents.

A disciple of Dr. Benjamin Spock, Nancy followed his suggestions in
preparing her six-year-old daughter for the arrival of her new sibling.
Nancy talked about the baby ahead of time so Patti could get used to the
idea gradually. Throughout her pregnancy, she let her daughter touch
her stomach to feel the baby move.

"Patti, who later became a real problem in the family, was overindulged with love as a small child," said Ursula Taylor. "Nancy gave a lot
of physical affection to her—hugging and kissing. They had a nanny for
quite some time, a British woman who first raised Patti and then little
Ron. Maybe Patti wasn't able to deal with having a baby brother. Maybe
there was too much love. I don't know."

"I remember that Patti was always a concern," said Jane Powell.
"Nancy would call me and we would talk about the problems we had
with our children and how we should handle them—'mom talk.' Patti
and Lindsay [her child] were about the same age. One time I invited
Patti to a Halloween party I gave for Lindsay. Patti was very unhappy.
She didn't like anything we were doing, any of the food, any of the
games, so I told her, 'Go on home.' And she did. That was Patti."

"The problems probably began with Patti's inception—the way Nancy
got pregnant, having to get married, then being forced to play out the lie
for her parents and the public by not gaining too much weight and showing too fast, and finally having to pretend that it was a premature birth,"
said a close friend. "On top of that, Nancy wanted a boy, but after an
excruciating delivery out popped Patti instead, and as Nancy has said
over and over, she was difficult from the very beginning. She said that
even as child, Patti was rebellious."

In her memoir, Nancy admitted her child-rearing problems with Patti.
"Sometimes after she had been fed she would lean over in her high chair
and throw up. That was lots of fun, as you can imagine. Once, when Patti
was around two, I was feeding her string beans. She held them in her
mouth, but simply refused to swallow them. I tried everything I could
think of, but nothing worked. Finally, I called the pediatrician. 'Don't

give in,' he said. 'Leave the room and get busy with something else and go back to her later.' An hour and a half passed, and by now it was past her nap time, but Patti was still sitting there with those damn beans in her mouth. When I came in, she looked up at me with a mischievous smile on her face and said, 'What I got in my mouth, Mommy!'

"When I called the doctor again, he said, 'Reach into her mouth and take out the beans.' This was a kid with a mind of her own. She was defiant, even angry, from the beginning. . . ." wrote the defiant, angry mother.

As intractable as her two-year-old, Nancy fought her daughter every step of the way. "Perhaps Patti was difficult because she sensed Nancy's resentment of her," said Jody Jacobs, former society editor of the *Los Angeles Times*, "plus the fact that she was born so soon after they were married. She was the child who kind of loused up Nancy's perfect little image—the image she wanted to present to the world."

Alarmed by her child's bouts of nonstop crying, Nancy called Chet Migden's wife for advice. "She used to call the house all the time because my wife was the knowledgeable one about children, having had twins a couple of years before the Reagans had their first child," said Migden, SAG's former assistant executive secretary. "She would call up Dina and say, 'My God, this kid is screaming. What do I do now?' "

Nancy talked frequently to friends about the difficulties she had experienced in delivering Patti, recalling bitterly the long, painful hours of labor she had had to endure. In later years, she told her daughter that she had been stubborn from the day she was born, so stubborn, in fact, that she wouldn't come out for eighteen hours.

"My mother told it this way," said Patti. "When she went into labor with me, the entire night and part of the following day passed, and there was still no progress. The doctors decided to do a cesarean section. What they found was that I had hooked my fingers around my mother's ribs, thwarting all her attempts to push me from her womb. I was in the eighth grade when I first saw a diagram of the female anatomy and realized the impossibility of what she described. The unborn infant would have had to punch through the uterine wall, shove the bladder out of the way, snake through the intestines, and clutch her fingers onto the muscle-ensheathed ribs."

Patti went home to confront her mother with the fairy-tale delivery, but Nancy remained unshaken. "She not only held to her story, she embellished it, telling me how I came out with abrasions on my poor little fingers," recalled her daughter. "As a last resort, I said, 'Could I have the phone number of the doctor who delivered me?' 'Well, you could,' she said, 'except that he's dead.'" Nancy's obstetrician, Dr. Thompson, had indeed died several years before.

Nancy frequently resorted to the hairbrush to discipline her daughter. "I remember when Patti would come running down the street to the neighbor's house, her face bruised and bleeding," said a friend. "She'd be crying: 'Help, help! She's doing it again.' Her mother had just smashed her in the face with a hairbrush because she hadn't done her homework or cleaned her room."

Years later, Patti talked about her tragic childhood. "I was very sensitive growing up," she said. "When I was eleven, I was taller than the other girls. I was more developed. I felt self-conscious about that. I felt ugly."

Her mother was equally traumatized by her daughter's budding sexuality. She tried to camouflage Patti's growing breasts by binding them in tight little-girl pinafores.

In an effort to keep herself thin and spare Patti the weight problems she herself had once suffered, Nancy refused to serve desserts, forbade sweets of any kind in the house, and prohibited Patti from trick-or-treating with her friends.

"I remember when we were in the fifth grade or so, Patti couldn't go trick-or-treating with us because she wasn't allowed to eat candy that came from other people," said Barbara Ling, a former neighbor from Pacific Palisades. "We all thought it was weird and very, very sad for Patti, but she didn't act like it was unusual at all. I remember Nancy as a real striking mom, though, one who always wore fashionable clothes, but we never went over to her house to play because I think she was one of those clean freaks who didn't want kids around."

Especially the children of Ronald Reagan's first marriage, who had felt estranged from the time she married their father. "Until then, Nancy had treated Maureen and me like her own kids," said Michael Reagan. "It soon became apparent that we were becoming less and less important in her life and Dad's."

Nancy never concealed her animosity toward Jane Wyman, who was equally disdainful toward Nancy. The antagonism between the two women agitated the children, but their father refused to acknowledge a problem until fourteen-year-old Michael was in such trouble at school that his psychiatrist suggested he be moved out of his mother's house and sent to live with his father.

"That was in 1959, when I was fourteen years old," said Michael, who was enrolled at Loyola High School in Los Angeles as a boarder, which was the only condition by which Nancy would agree to let him move into her home. He would not be there during the week, and on the weekends, Reagan promised to take him to the ranch. The Pacific Palisades home did not have an extra bedroom for him, so Michael was relegated to the living room couch, often having to wait until company left before he could go to sleep. He was assigned the guest bathroom off the hallway by the front door. A year later, Nancy decided to build a separate bedroom and bath for the nurse; Michael was moved to the daybed in the playroom between Patti's and Ron's bedrooms. When he asked his father why the nurse got the new bedroom and he didn't, Reagan said, "She's here all week and you're only here on weekends."

"I could be here all week, too, if I were a day student," said Michael. "Why can't Nancy drive me to school every morning and pick me up in the afternoon just like the other kids? It's only half an hour from home."

"She's too busy with Ron and Patti," said Reagan. "Don't you think it's enough that she has opened up her house to you and invited you in?"

That invitation had been the first time seven-year-old Patti had heard of a half-brother. At first, she had seemed quite pleased by his arrival. But Patti had been perplexed when his eighteen-year-old sister, Maureen, came to visit from Washington, D.C., where she was living.

"Did you know that Michael is my brother?" Patti asked Maureen the first time she met her.

"Yes, of course I know that," said Maureen. "And do you know what that makes you and me?"

"No, what?" said Patti.

"That makes you and me sisters."

Looking horrified, the little girl burst into tears and ran from the room screaming, "No, it doesn't! No, it doesn't!"

Maureen, Reagan's firstborn child, realized then that her father had never considered her a part of his new life. "Dad was quite embarrassed when he explained to me later that afternoon, 'Well, we just haven't gotten that far yet,' " she said. "They'd just gotten to Michael, and only after it was decided he would move in with them. It seems Patti was introduced to us siblings, or half-siblings, if you want to get technical, on a need-to-know basis, and until that time there had been no need for her to know any such thing about me."

Just as Nancy had done with her own father, she now denied the reality of her stepchildren, pushing them out of her mind—and her life—like bad dreams. The only way she knew to chart her future was to revise her past.

8

RONALD REAGAN WAS IMPRESSED by his wife's credentials—Girls Latin School, Smith College, the Junior League, a society debut, the elegant Casino Club. To Reagan, Nancy looked like an American aristocrat. Not being to the manner born himself, he could hardly be faulted for thinking he had acquired it in his marriage. He saw the luxurious apartment on East Lake Shore Drive, the mansion on Millionaires' Row in Scottsdale, the wealthy friends—the extraordinarily wealthy friends—who were frequently famous as well. What he couldn't know was the frenetic energy that had been focused on creating all that prosperity.

By the time Ronald Reagan met his mother-in-law, all traces of her previous life as a desperate actress teetering on disrepute had vanished. Only the patina of a theatrical background remained, burnished by such illustrious names as George M. Cohan and Francis X. Bushman. The impressionable Reagan saw the stunning results of a woman who had invented herself and created high-society respectability for her husband and her daughter.

But her genteel façade could never conceal the bawdy sense of humor that Reagan thoroughly enjoyed. He regularly traded dirty jokes with his mother-in-law and tried to top her filthy stories with filthier ones of his own. In public, though, he found Edith's profanity disconcerting, and so he and Nancy asked her not to swear so much in front of other people. "I'm always being told by them to watch my language," Edith said. "I guess no one had to remind Nelle Reagan."

Like her mother, Nancy, too, was creating her life, airbrushing her past as she went along. Very few remnants of Anne Frances Robbins ever seeped through the reconstruction. Her Hollywood friends knew nothing of her early life—not even Ronald Reagan knew everything. Nancy had planned to introduce him to her paternal grandmother when Nanee Robbins visited California in 1951, but the meeting never took place. Mrs. Robbins went to the Hollywood restaurant as planned, but while waiting for Nancy to arrive with Reagan, she had a heart attack. Her son, Kenneth, Nancy's father, flew to Los Angeles and took her back home. She recovered, but that was the last time Nancy ever tried to see her grandmother. When Nancy's wedding was set, Edith sent Nanee and Kenneth announcements, but Nancy never again got in touch with her father or grandmother, so neither one of them ever met Nancy's husband or any of the Reagan children.

When Nanee Robbins died in 1957 at the age of eighty-nine, Ken and his wife, Patsy, thought Nancy might want to know because she had been so close to her grandmother as a child, so they notified her. But Nancy sent neither flowers nor a note of condolence.

A few years later, her maternal aunt, Virginia Galbraith, died. Nancy did not go to this funeral either, even though Mrs. Galbraith had raised Nancy with her own child for the five years Edith had been on the road. "I think it was an election year when my mother died, and Nancy was too busy campaigning to come to the funeral," said Virginia Galbraith's daughter, Charlotte Ramage.

"After Nanee Robbins died, someone in our family called Nancy to ask if she could contribute some money so we could buy a headstone for the grave, but Nancy said she couldn't afford it," said her cousin Kathleen Young. "Reagan was working for General Electric at the time, making $150,000 a year, which was a staggering sum then, but Nancy said they didn't have any money. Nanee Robbins was buried in Pittsfield, Massachusetts, because our ancestors developed the town. But none of us could afford a gravestone, and her grave still looks so empty and forlorn without it.

"I could never understand why Nancy denied her grandmother the way she did. Nanee was nothing but good and kind and loving to her when she was growing up, and her own mother left her for all those years. Nanee truly loved Nancy because she was Ken's daughter and her only grandchild. Through the years, she saved all the newspaper clippings on Nancy's career in Hollywood and her marriage to Reagan. She [Nanee] was so proud of her.

"Ken and his wife had been living with Nanee in New Jersey because Ken's car dealership had failed and they had fallen on hard times. I remember that Edith and Loyal helped them out occasionally by sending care packages, but the old clothes they sent were torn and soiled and dirty. They should have been thrown away. It was very sad and so demeaning. They didn't even bother to clean or mend them beforehand. Ken and Patsy were humiliated, but they never said anything except 'thank you very much.'"

Nancy never addressed the subject of her father's misfortune. As far as she was concerned, he didn't exist; her family consisted only of her husband, her children, her mother, and Loyal Davis. So devoted was she to her stepfather that when Lillian Gish first met Ronald Reagan she knew that Nancy would fall in love with him because he was so like the doctor. "It will take," she told Nancy's mother, pointing out the striking similarities between the two men. "They even look alike."

Both men came out of strikingly similar backgrounds. Loyal Davis was born in Galesburg, Illinois (pop. 20,500), and attended Knox College on a scholarship. He understood the poor Midwestern roots of Ronald Reagan, who was born in Tampico, Illinois (pop. 1,276), was baptized in Galesburg, sixty miles away, grew up in Dixon (pop. 8,191), and worked as a dishwasher to pay his tuition at Eureka College.

Both were the small-town products of ambitious mothers who wanted their sons to cross over from the wrong side of the tracks and take their rightful places alongside the rich and famous. Pampered and indulged by these driving women, both men left home determined to succeed where their uneducated fathers had failed. Both later enjoyed their relative affluence and looked with reverence on the wealth and position they had achieved, which had eluded their working-class parents. Exasperatingly frugal, even cheap, both self-made men espoused conservative politics and resented paying taxes to support the less fortunate, their attitudes being "I've got mine. Now you get yours!" Both took exaggerated pride in their professions and savored the admiration of their peers; the pompous doctor perhaps demanded more respect than the genial actor, who simply needed to be liked by everyone. Still, there was an immediate rapport between the two of them.

Both had suffered public humiliation during their first divorces and been rescued by remarriage to women as strong and supportive as their mothers. Nelle Reagan, described by her son as "a frustrated actress," denied the painful reality of her past like her husband's alcoholism ("He's just a little tired right now"), cared about her clothes and her appearance, and gazed on her second son adoringly. As a child, Reagan had performed in church plays with his mother; as an adult, he accompanied her to church services regularly, even giving a percentage of his weekly income to her church for a while.

"If there was anyone behind Dutch, it was his mother," said his boyhood pal Edward O'Malley. "She was the guiding force in the family." Reagan's childhood friends and fraternity brothers remember how he courted his mother's approval. And as a paid-up member of Motion Picture Mothers, Nelle Reagan was proud of her son's accomplishments. Later in life, however, her Christian values were no longer his, and she was not impressed with money and success the way he was. After he moved her into a nursing home, Ronald Reagan transferred his need for motherly approval to his wife.

Nancy had consulted a few people to find a convalescent facility for her mother-in-law, but she wasn't too concerned with the amenities. The wife of an MCA agent recalled trying to give her a full report on various nursing homes in southern California. She detailed the services of each, type of nursing care, number of medical personnel, grounds, and recreational activities, but Nancy cut her off. "Just tell me which is the cheapest," she said. "After all, it's just Ronnie's mother."

The thin-planed face of his mother soon became the surgically lifted face of his wife. The same wide eyes, the careful smile, the adoring gaze. Both held strong, dogmatic beliefs. Nancy, who shared the same initials as Nelle Reagan, followed naturally in her doting wake, and Reagan, who grew up instructed by his mother to call her Nelle, soon began calling his wife Mommy. Nancy did not share Nelle's piety, and where her mother-in-law placed her faith in God, Nancy placed hers in astrology. Nelle Reagan studied the Bible; her daughter-in-law read tea leaves.

Reagan looked up to Loyal Davis as someone who had achieved all that was worthy in this world, who moved in a sphere where he was admired and befriended by people of influence such as director John Huston and Arizona senator Barry Goldwater. During their frequent visits with the Davises in Arizona, Reagan enjoyed being with their monied friends—actress Colleen Moore, one of the richest women in America; thoroughbred horse breeder Tom Chauncey, who was married to a Wrigley heiress; and Clare Boothe Luce, wife of the founder of *Time* magazine. Reagan was bowled over by these introductions. "He was a healthy normal guy who liked to saw wood," said Clare Boothe Luce. "Then he started to socialize with a better class. . . . People haven't liked to admit that the rich are often smarter and better."

By the time Reagan met Loyal Davis, the doctor's career was nearing its crest. He was chairman of the surgery department at Northwestern University and attending surgeon at Passavant Hospital. He would be elected an honorary fellow by the Royal College of Surgeons in England, receive an honorary fellowship to the Royal Academy College of Surgeons in Edinburgh, and be elected chairman of the board of regents of the American College of Surgeons, and president of the American College of Surgeons.

Despite his professional honors, Loyal Davis viewed his son-in-law with a tinge of envy, for Loyal had always aspired to be an actor. He once admitted resenting his friend Walter Huston, who made $75,000 for acting in the 1936 movie *Dodsworth* while Davis made only $500 for performing a prefrontal lobotomy. "I had more education than he; I could read aloud better than he. Given the opportunity, I could be Sam Dodsworth just as effectively as Walter had been and demand the same salary," said Dr. Davis. "I found myself looking at him critically, watching him to see what he had that I didn't."

He soon saw what it was when they read a scene from *Othello* and the Academy Award–winning actor immediately inhabited the character of the noble Moor of Venice while the doctor sounded pitiful and strained as Iago.

"Don't worry, kid," said Walter Huston afterward. "The first time I saw you operate, I thought I could do it, too."

When Dr. Davis performed surgery, he haughtily threw scalpels on the floor, hurled sponges at the nurses, and forbade talking. He expressed himself unhesitatingly, even to doctors, especially about doctors. He protested fee-splitting, the custom of doctors' paying other doctors for referring patients. His complaints so infuriated the medical establishment that some physicians circulated petitions charging him with unethical conduct, and tried to get the Chicago Medical Society to expel him. The charges were dropped, but Loyal Davis remained unfazed by the campaign against him. He never stopped criticizing medical misdeeds, especially by doctors who performed surgery they were not qualified to do.

He fought fixed-fee schedules in which each operation has a set price applicable to everyone. Instead, he said physicians should consult with patients and consider the patients' mortgages and other debts before setting a fee. He set up informal fee clinics for his interns and residents to teach them how to charge their patients, and campaigned for this concept years after it became obsolete. "I am opposed to the idea of a fee schedule," he said, "but I know I'm going to lose this fight."

Reagan, too, loved a lost cause, which he proved by lobbying Congress for a tax break for film stars. He said they had only five years at the most to make money and so should be taxed less than other professionals. "He went to Washington, D.C., to get a bill passed so that we would be taxed on a four-year aggregate basis instead of every year," said dancer-actor Gene Nelson. "Ronnie said it was only fair because the career span of actors and athletes is determined by age or deterioration or public opinion. He lost, of course."

Ronald Reagan admired his principled father-in-law in a way he never
did his own father, the itinerant shoe salesman, who was as insistent
about the New Deal principles of the Democratic party as Loyal Davis
was about medical ethics. In 1952, Reagan, still a nominal Democrat,
veered from his father's political party to support Dwight D. Eisenhower
for President. Reagan supported Ike again for reelection in 1956. He did
not need his father-in-law to tell him to rail against communism, high
taxes, and government intervention. Reagan had been doing that since
becoming president of the Screen Actors Guild. Still, by 1958, the conservative doctor's influence could be seen in Reagan's GE speeches, especially in the area of medical care for the aged. He talked a lot about
socialized medicine in England, comparing it to the widespread movement among Hollywood stars to leave the studio system to go out on
their own. "Some youngsters even think they do better that way," he
said. "It's like socialized medicine in England; the doctors working there
now are not the same as the men of medicine before socialization."

At Dr. Davis's urging, Reagan made a phonograph record the doctors
used in their battle against Medicaid. On it he said, "Medical care for the
aged is a foot in the door of a government takeover of all medicine."

Though Reagan's conservative politics were taking shape before he
met Loyal Davis, it was Davis who shaped his thinking on the issue of
abortion and ultimately changed the abortion laws in California in 1967.
It was also Dr. Davis who was primarily responsible for Ronald Reagan's
appointment of Sandra Day O'Connor, the first female justice, to the
U.S. Supreme Court in 1981.

Yet the doctor always played down his influence on Reagan. "When
he's asked my opinion, I've given it to him, that's all," he said. "I've
never had any cause or effect on his politics."

"What about your influence on Nancy?"

"She was never directed by me," he said. "She just did things properly."

When asked in 1980 why so many people believed that through the
influence of Nancy over her husband, the country saw the politics of Dr.
Loyal Davis, the physician paused.

"I don't know," he said. "I'm very pleased if that's correct."

"Make no mistake about it," said a colleague. "Loyal had a great deal
of influence over Ronald Reagan. I know because I was Loyal's assistant
for many years and then became his personal physician when he moved
to Arizona. I was there when he and Reagan talked, and I know how

Loyal shaped Reagan's conservative thinking and how he later got him started in politics."

The first political problem presented itself in 1959 when the Screen Actors Guild was girding for a possible strike over residual rights on films used by television. With SAG president Howard Keel declining to run for reelection because of a Broadway commitment, the nominating committee turned to Ronald Reagan and asked him to serve as president again. Nancy vehemently opposed the idea, believing that such a prominent role in explosive industry politics would harm his acting career and, more important, jeopardize his lucrative position with General Electric. For the past nine years, she had been attending regular SAG board meetings and was steeped in the politics of right-to-work issues for actors. She knew that the pending negotiations with producers would be acrimonious, so she told her husband to decline the honor, but he was conflicted. He loved his life in the velvet coffin of General Electric—"It's like subsidized retirement," he said—but he also relished being part of the action. He discussed the matter with his father-in-law as well as with MCA's Lew Wasserman, who assured him that his career would not be impaired. He then decided to accept the position. It was the first and last time he would go against his wife's political instincts.

After protracted negotiations with the studios had stalled, Reagan called a SAG strike, which turned Hollywood into a ghost town. Oddly, there were no pickets, no soup kitchens, no sheriff's deputies, and among the 14,000 guild members, there were no strikebreakers. Marilyn Monroe, Yves Montand, and Tony Randall walked off the set of *Let's Make Love* at 20th Century-Fox, and Fred Astaire, Debbie Reynolds, and Lilli Palmer gave up *The Pleasure of His Company* at Paramount. "It's so awful," said Clifton Webb. "Everything has stopped."

"This is no longer a matter of money or terms, but a question of principle," proclaimed an ad signed by Lauren Bacall, Bette Davis, Kirk Douglas, James Cagney, Bob Hope, Edward G. Robinson, Spencer Tracy, and Bing Crosby. "I don't know what the hell they're striking about," said John Wayne, forgetting that he, too, had signed the same ad.

The strike lasted seven weeks and, according to Reagan, cost actors $10 million in lost income and the studios $50 million in lost production. "It really didn't have to happen at all," he said later.

The settlement, signed April 18, 1960, still stirs ugly resentments in Hollywood, where many stars think that Reagan sold them out at the last minute on residuals. At the end of the strike, actors had won the right to collect residual payments for films made after 1948 when they were sold to television. But somewhere between that settlement and the signed contract, Reagan traded the residuals clause for a $2 million contribution to start the union's pension fund, although that amount was only half the producers' original offer.

"I was really pumping for actors' residuals, but the SAG board was not committed," said Gene Kelly, a former board member. "They were just too reticent. Reagan didn't pump for residuals at all. He was not committed to that. . . . And, yes, of course, there was some bitterness over that."

"I think Reagan sold us down the river," said actor Gary Merrill. "We were on a strike and . . . then all of a sudden it was called off because the studios said they would contribute so many millions of dollars to a pension fund. And I felt that Reagan kind of sold the idea to the union. I felt we should have held out for residuals of some kind on the sale of movies to TV."

At the next SAG meeting, an angry member accused Reagan of negotiating in bad faith because he was a union leader at the same time he represented management for General Electric. Reagan denied the charge while the member waved a piece of General Electric stationery with Reagan's name on the letterhead, setting off another rancorous debate. The next month, Reagan resigned the SAG presidency as well as his place on the board, citing his plans to become a producer with an interest in profits plus a 25 percent ownership interest in the films he made for General Electric. "I am hoping in the future this activity may extend to feature-length motion pictures," he said in his letter of resignation. Nancy, too, resigned her place on the board, still seething about the abuse that had been heaped on her husband during the strike.

Never part of Hollywood's select social circle, the Reagans became more alienated from the liberal Democrats who seemed to dominate society in the film colony.

"We were in constant contact during the strike," said Janet Leigh, "but afterward we never saw them again."

A few months before, the Reagans had refused to participate in the Hollywood salute to Soviet premier Nikita Khrushchev and his wife, Nina, at 20th Century-Fox studios. This unprecedented visit to America by a Soviet head of state brought out more than four hundred glamorous stars, including Frank Sinatra, Elizabeth Taylor, Eddie Fisher, Shelley Winters, Judy Garland, Shirley MacLaine, Juliet Prowse, Louis Jourdan, Maurice Chevalier, Cary Grant, Bob Hope, Richard Burton, Rita Hayworth, Gregory Peck, June Allyson, David Niven, and Marilyn Monroe, who whispered a sexy welcome to the Russian commissar. Rabid anti-Communists, the Reagans stayed away.

"I think all Democrats are Communists to Nancy Reagan," said the comedy writer Bob Schiller. "I'm exaggerating to make a point, of course, but not by much. I remember when we moved into the Reagans' neighborhood in Pacific Palisades, Nancy was furious at the woman down the street who had sold us one of her houses. Nancy said that she had ruined the neighborhood by selling to us, that we were Communists. I thought it was just because I had a beard, but I said, 'Ask Nancy if she thinks that Stalin lived this well,' because I live in a pretty nice house. Our neighbor said, 'She's serious. She claims she's seen it in writing that you and your wife are Communists.'

"That worried me a little, so I filed under Freedom of Information and got back our files, which showed that we were members of the Peace Action Council. I guess that translated into communism for Nancy. Later we were against the war in Vietnam, so that was probably further proof for her. She once drove by with her son when we were outside painting flowers on our garbage can. She was so shocked that she covered her kid's eyes and hid his face in her arms so he wouldn't see us do something so unconventional, I guess. . . . I'm sure she wasn't too pleased during the elections when we put the sign in our yard that said, 'Last Democrats Before Reagan.'"

Socializing in Hollywood broke down politically in those days, with Democrats partying with Democrats and the Reagans associating only with Republicans, a minority group that consisted of actors like Dick Powell, John Wayne, George Murphy, Robert Taylor, and Robert Montgomery, and a few producers like A. C. Lyles.

Since their marriage, Nancy Davis and Ronald Reagan had lost social standing in Hollywood; they were considered fading stars in a firmament dominated by such blazing meteors as Marlon Brando and Paul Newman. The Reagans still posed for photographs whenever they saw a camera, and occasionally their pictures appeared in movie magazines, but coverage of them was overshadowed by other Hollywood couples—Janet Leigh and Tony Curtis, June Allyson and Dick Powell, Esther Williams and Ben Gage, Sheila and Gordon MacRae.

"The Reagans were never invited to any of the big-shot Hollywood parties," said writer Philip Dunne. "There is a terrible caste system that operates out here, a sort of hierarchy among movie actors. It's regrettable but true. There are selective layers where A actors associate only with each other, and never with B actors like the Reagans. They were never included the way the Humphrey Bogarts and the Cary Grants were. They were not in the top rung of Hollywood society."

As contract players at their respective studios, neither Reagan ever enjoyed star billing, which affected their social standing in the film community. Reagan was never considered more than a second-string player to the Warner Bros. stars, most of whom dismissed him with contempt.

Once, when Humphrey Bogart was dragged into the studio's portrait gallery, he snarled, "For God's sake, don't make me look like Ronnie Reagan."

No one was more scornful than Frank Sinatra. "Frank couldn't stand the guy," said actor Brad Dexter, "just couldn't stand him."

"He hated him," said a woman who lived with songwriter Jimmy Van Heusen. "We'd be at some party, and if the Reagans arrived, Frank would snap his fingers and say, 'C'mon, Chester. We're leaving. I can't stand that fucking Ronnie. He's such a bore. Every time you get near the bastard, he makes a speech and he never knows what he's talking about. The trouble with Reagan is that no one would give him a job.' This happened time and time again because Frank could not abide being in the same room with the Reagans."

"It's true that Sinatra despised Ronnie almost as much as [he did] Richard Nixon," said Peter Lawford shortly before he died. "He said he thought he was a real right-wing John Birch Society nut—'dumb and dangerous,' he'd say, 'and so simpleminded.' He swore he'd move out of California if Reagan ever got elected to public office. 'I couldn't stand listening to his gee whiz, golly shucks crap,' Frank said. He couldn't stand Nancy Reagan either; he said she was a dope with fat ankles who could never make it as an actress. He took every opportunity he could in Las Vegas to change the words to 'The Lady Is a Tramp.' Instead of singing 'She hates California where it's cold and it's damp,' Frank would sing, 'She hates California, it's *Reagan* and damp . . . that's why the lady is a tramp.' "

Comedian Shecky Greene said Sinatra was vitriolic on the subject of Ronald Reagan. "We were all at a house in Miami watching Joey Bishop's show on television one night when Reagan came on to welcome Joey," he said. "Frank immediately got crazy and started screaming things and calling Reagan every name in the book. He hated the guy and cursed him out all night long."

Other Democrats dreaded seeing the Reagans, knowing they would be in for some kind of political harangue. "We got stuck with them once at a dinner party and it was awful," said Amanda Dunne, wife of Philip. "Nancy is so assessing—she always looks you up and down before she deigns to speak—and I'm afraid she hated me on sight because I don't dress up to her standards; that night I probably had on the wrong shoes or the wrong blouse or something because after scrutinizing me, she wouldn't say a word. Then when I got into the argument with Ronnie, she looked like she wanted to strangle me.

"Ronnie started off by bringing up Caryl Chessman, who had been convicted on several counts of kidnapping, robbery, and attempted rape against two young women, which carried the death penalty. Chessman had been on death row in San Quentin for twelve years, filing appeals and getting stays of execution. He was finally put to death in 1960, but the disposition of his case became the focus of a national debate over capital punishment, and a few weeks before he went to the electric chair Ronnie and I got into a big debate at Tom and Mary Frieberg's dinner party.

"Ronnie was all for the death penalty. 'I believe in an eye for an eye, and a tooth for a tooth, just like in the Bible,' he said over and over.

" 'But Chessman hasn't murdered anybody,' I said. 'He left the women in terrible shape but . . .'

" 'You don't know what you're talking about,' he said. 'He's a murderer and he deserves to die. There's no question but that he should be killed himself.'

"I tried again to explain that Chessman had not been convicted of murder, but Ronnie wouldn't listen. 'He's a murderer, he's a murderer,' he kept saying. Finally, Judge Lester Roth, who was sitting across from us, said, 'Ronnie, Amanda is right. Chessman has not been convicted of murder.'

"Ronnie was so taken aback by this correction from an appellate judge that he was speechless. I didn't want him to be publicly embarrassed like that so I quickly said, 'It's a tragedy really because one of the women is in a mental institution.' Ronnie rallied at that point. 'Well, then,' he said, 'she might just as well be dead.' Nancy, who was sitting a few seats away, glowered at me. I'd always been told that she was someone who should not be crossed, but I never paid any attention until that evening. Her face was pinched with hatred and I'm sure she wanted to kill me."

"The best way to describe Nancy's expression is to say that she looked like a basilisk [a fabled reptile whose breath and countenance were thought to be fatal]," said Philip Dunne. "I thought my sweet gentle wife was a goner for sure that night."

At no time was the social split in Hollywood more political than during the 1960 presidential campaign: Democrats like Frank Sinatra and his Rat Pack (Dean Martin, Sammy Davis, Jr., Peter Lawford, Joey Bishop, Shirley MacLaine, Lauren Bacall), plus Shelley Winters, Paul Newman, Joanne Woodward, Henry Fonda, Marlene Dietrich, Art Carney, Jo Stafford, Louie Prima, Judy Garland, Janet Leigh, Tony Curtis, and comedian Henry Morgan were lined up behind John F. Kennedy; Republicans like John Wayne, George Murphy, Irene Dunne, Helen Hayes, and the Reagans supported Richard M. Nixon. The Hollywoodization of politics reached its apogee with that election, which produced the postwar era's first "movie star" president, an event that would not be fully appreciated until a real movie star walked into the White House twenty years later. In 1961, Hollywood celebrities gravitated to John F. Kennedy, who was as thoroughly glamorous as any movie star. He, in turn, was naturally drawn to the hot sparkle of Hollywood and the allure of women like Gene Tierney, Marilyn Monroe, Grace Kelly, and Angie Dickinson. In the White House, Kennedy even subscribed to *Variety* to keep abreast of Hollywood news.

This Irish Catholic prince disturbed Reagan, who wrote to Richard Nixon after the Democratic National Convention in July of 1960 describing Kennedy's acceptance speech as a "frightening call to arms."

"Unfortunately, he is a powerful speaker with an appeal to the emotions," wrote Reagan. "He leaves little doubt that his idea of the 'challenging new world' is one in which the federal government will grow bigger and do more and, of course, spend more. . . . Shouldn't someone tag Mr. Kennedy's 'bold new imaginative' program with its proper age? Under the tousled boyish haircut it is still old Karl Marx—first launched a century ago. There is nothing new in the idea of a government being Big Brother to us all. Hitler called his 'State Socialism,' and way before him it was 'benevolent monarchy.' " Reagan then urged Nixon to choose Barry Goldwater as his running mate, saying, "I cannot support the ticket if it includes Rockefeller." He also offered to do anything to get out the Republican conservative vote during the fall campaign, and papers in the Nixon archives show that the candidate instructed his staff to "use him [Reagan] as a speaker whenever possible. He *used* to be a liberal."

So while Sinatra sang his heart out for John F. Kennedy, Ronald Reagan raised his mellifluous voice in praise of Richard M. Nixon, making more than two hundred speeches for the Republican ticket that fall. Reagan wanted to change his party affiliation and declare himself a Republican, but Nixon felt that he would be more effective campaigning as a Democrat for Nixon, so Reagan retained his registration until after the campaign. Nancy, an ardent conservative—"I've read the *National Review* since its first issue"—was so disgusted when Nixon lost the presidency by eighty-four electoral votes that she refused to watch the inauguration on television.

As a Republican, Reagan continued railing against Kennedy, waging a strenuous fight against the administration's medical care bill for the elderly. His phonograph record, "Ronald Reagan Speaks Out Against Socialized Medicine," underwritten by the American Medical Association, was distributed to doctors' wives, who were encouraged to write letters to Congress to oppose the legislation. Reagan warned them, "If you don't write these letters to your congressmen, one of these days you and I are going to spend our sunset years telling our children and our children's children what it once was like in America when men were free." Congress was swamped with mail, and tempers raged so on the issue that voting was postponed until 1963, when the bill was passed by a narrow margin.

Reagan continued mounting platforms to assail the Kennedy administration, castigating the President's program of federal aid to education as "the foot in the door to federal control," condemning farm subsidies as wasteful, and denouncing the social security system. He described unemployment insurance as "a prepaid vacation plan for freeloaders." He damned the progressive income tax, saying it would lead to a Communist takeover of America. "No country that collects one-third of a man's income has ever been able to hold off a socialist or Communist revolution. . . . It's a scheme by Karl Marx to eliminate the middle class."

He said political liberals like John F. Kennedy have one thing in common with "socialists and Communists—they all want to settle their problems by government action."

Reagan was obsessed by the specter of communism, telling 21,000 members of Rotary International that Communists had infiltrated Hollywood again. Otto Preminger had just announced that Dalton Trumbo, a previously blacklisted writer, had written the screenplay for *Exodus*. This encouraged Kirk Douglas to use Trumbo in 1960 for the script of *Spartacus*, the story of a Roman gladiator based on a book by Howard Fast, an avowed Communist. Reagan excoriated these "well-meaning but misguided" men for hiring "exponents of un-American philosophies."

Convinced that "Communists are crawling out of the rocks in Hollywood," Reagan participated in the Christian Anti-Communist Crusade rallies of Dr. Fred Schwarz, served on the advisory boards of right-wing organizations like the Young Americans for Freedom, managed Lloyd Wright's campaign to unseat Thomas Kuchel, the moderate Republican senator from California, and supported Congressman John Rousselot, a member of the John Birch Society.

With a Democrat in the White House, Reagan's speeches stirred right-wing Republicans, who were contributing more than $14 million a year to ultraconservative organizations. No one was more impressed by Reagan's convincing rhetoric than his conservative father-in-law. Sitting in the audience at the Phoenix Chamber of Commerce listening to Reagan fulminate about the "Red invasion," Loyal Davis decided that his son-in-law should seek elective office. But Reagan demurred, having declined opportunities to seek the U.S. Senate seat from California in 1962 as well as the governorship. Instead, he supported Richard Nixon in his losing gubernatorial campaign against Edmund "Pat" Brown.

Reagan had grown so politically strident that General Electric became uncomfortable about having a spokesman so strongly identified with the far right wing. A company executive approached him, suggesting that he confine his speeches to selling GE products, but Reagan balked, saying, "There's no way that I could go out now to an audience that is expecting the type of thing I've been doing for the last eight years and suddenly stand up and start selling them electric toasters. . . . Either I don't do the speeches at all for you, or we don't do the program; you get somebody else."

A few weeks later, in February of 1962, a U.S. marshal arrived on the set of the "General Electric Theater" and handed Reagan a subpoena to produce his tax records and those of his wife. He was ordered to appear before a federal grand jury to testify about the MCA waiver he had granted as president of the Screen Actors Guild. In investigating the monopoly of MCA, the Justice Department was looking into the possibility that Reagan had accepted payoffs for making the blanket waiver. No concrete proof was put forward to indict him, but to his embarrassment, the grand jury appearance was widely publicized.

Reagan swore that he had agreed to the waiver only because actors were having such a hard time getting work in 1952. "I felt they [MCA] filled a great gap in giving employment at a time when unemployment was quite heavy," he testified.

Within days, General Electric fired him, and he would not be employed again until his brother, an advertising executive with McCann Erickson, got him the job of introducing "Death Valley Days" for the show's sponsor two years later. On July 10, 1962, the Justice Department filed a civil suit against MCA for alleged antitrust violations, naming the Screen Actors Guild as a co-conspirator from the time Ronald Reagan was its president. The case never went to trial because MCA divested itself of its talent agency. Two months after that, the "General Electric Theater" went off the air.

Embittered by the experience, Reagan continued his political speechmaking full time, vilifying the Kennedy administration at every turn. While the far right despised the New Frontier, most of the country was enchanted by the aristocratic young President, the elegant First Lady, and their two adorable children, who scampered playfully around the Oval Office. America became besotted with the Kennedys, their pets, their touch football games, their White House state dinners. The country hungered for every detail about the bewitchingly beautiful people who splashed in the swimming pool at Hickory Hill, Robert Kennedy's house in McLean, Virginia, and sailed like royalty on the *Honey Fitz,* the President's yacht at Hyannisport. John F. Kennedy had cast his spell on the country, and only the far right seemed unmoved by his personal charm and Gaelic bouyancy.

On Friday, November 22, 1963, when the forty-six-year-old President of the United States was assassinated in Dallas, Texas, the lights went out for Americans. In the grip of hysterical grief, people rushed to their television sets, where they sat transfixed for the weekend, watching replays of Lyndon Johnson's swearing-in, of Jacqueline Kennedy's arrival at Andrews Air Force Base in her blood-spattered pink Chanel suit, of the flag-draped coffin lying in state under the dome of the U.S. Capitol, of the catafalque, the riderless black horse with boots turned backward as a sign that its fallen leader would ride no more, and the little boy who stepped forward to salute his father on his last ride to Arlington Cemetery.

"I was the only one in my family who sat in front of the television watching the entire aftermath of that assassination," said Patti Davis, who was eleven years old at the time.

Businesses and schools closed as the country sank into a miasma of mourning. Around the globe, flags were lowered to half-staff. Ships at sea cast wreaths overboard. In London, Sir Laurence Olivier interrupted a performance at the Old Vic to ask the audience to stand while the orchestra played "The Star-Spangled Banner." In Nairobi, Kenyan warriors held a tribal feast of lament. In West Berlin, thousands gathered with lighted candles. In Athens, rush-hour traffic came to a standstill, and in Moscow, Mrs. Nikita Khrushchev signed the book of mourning in the U.S. embassy with tears in her eyes.

In Hollywood, a personal memorial service was scheduled for Sunday evening in the home of Sam Goldwyn, Jr. One of the guests asked whether she could bring producer Frank McCarthy. He had invited her to attend a party that night at the Reagans' to which he had been invited weeks before.

"I'm sure the Reagans will cancel their party now because of the President's assassination, don't you think?" said the woman.

"Oh, I can't imagine that they won't," said McCarthy. "I'll call Nancy and find out."

Mrs. Reagan was quite surprised by his phone call. "My heavens," she said. "Why would we cancel our party just because John F. Kennedy died? Don't be silly. We'll expect to see you around seven P.M."

Feeling uncomfortable about attending a party that weekend, Frank McCarthy and his friend nevertheless rang the Reagans' doorbell at the appointed hour and were somewhat taken aback when Nancy answered.

"There's to be no discussion of you-know-what," she told them. "And I mean no discussion whatsoever."

They walked in and saw the stalwarts of Hollywood's right wing gathered around the bar drinking and celebrating. The sight of people like John Wayne and Robert Taylor and Ronald Reagan hoisting their glasses as if nothing had shaken their world unnerved the couple, who stayed only a few minutes before walking out.

Ironically, Kennedy, who had expected Barry Goldwater to run against him in 1964, had a speech in his suit pocket in Dallas that he never lived to deliver. The text differentiated between his centrism and what he saw as Goldwater's extremism. He scorned those who confused "rhetoric with reality," having said in an earlier speech: "They look suspiciously at their neighbors and their leaders. They call for a 'man on horseback' because they do not trust the people. They find treason in our churches, in our highest court, in our treatment of water. . . . Unwilling to face up to the danger from without [they] are convinced that the real danger is from within."

Reagan was one who remained convinced, and those convictions animated his political speech-making, which further endeared him to archconservatives like the used-car dealer Holmes Tuttle, the oilman Henry Salvatori, the steel magnate Earle Jorgensen, and the drugstore mogul Justin Dart, who beseeched Reagan to seek political office.

"Ronnie is always being asked to run for Congress, the Senate or governor," Nancy wrote to a friend in 1963. "I don't know that I'd like public life—but it might get me out of car pools."

As she pursued her career, her life then was as much casting calls as car pools. "I am one of an ever-increasing set of Hollywood women who are wives and mothers first—but a good movie part gets us back in makeup before the ink is dry on the contract," she said. She did a commercial for Crest toothpaste and appeared in fourteen television shows between 1953 and 1963, including the "Schlitz Playhouse of Stars," "Wagon Train," "The Dick Powell Show," and "Dick Powell's Zane Grey Theater."

"She used to drive Dick Powell nuts at Four Star Productions by calling all the time trying to get cast in one of his shows," said a former studio executive. "She was quite a noodge. I remember him coming in one day and saying, 'For God's sakes, give Nancy Reagan something so I can get her the hell off my back.' It was either that or get him an unlisted phone, because she was calling all the time. He was actually quite fond of her, but she was driving him crazy. I think we finally shoved her in some little guest star cameo for has-beens to give Dick a break!"

In her off-screen role as mother, Nancy was overly protective of both her children, Patti and Ron, whom she had enrolled in the John Thomas Dye School in Bel Air. A concerned parent, she was a member of the mothers club, ran the hot-dog concession at the annual school fair, and attended all school functions.

"When Patti would have her little friends to the house, Nancy would turn on the intercom system and eavesdrop," said Amanda Dunne. "I remember she overheard something that Patti and one of her pals had cooked up, and Nancy turned both little girls in to the principal, which seemed unnecessarily nasty for a mother to do."

Nancy also listened in on her son's telephone calls. "In 1969," recalled the mother of one of Ron's friends in grade school and high school, "the boys were on the phone talking to each other about what it would be like to smoke grass. The next day Ron told my son that his mother had been eavesdropping on their conversation. He knew, he said, because after they hung up, Nancy ransacked his room like a mad, crazy woman, ripping everything off the walls and pulling out drawers looking for grass."

With her husband traveling so much, the total responsibility for the children fell on Nancy, who frequently felt overwhelmed and could not handle it alone. "That's why she called my husband every single night of the week to complain about the children," said the former wife of the school's headmaster. "Usually it was about Patti, because she was always having trouble with her. Nancy wanted her daughter to be a Miss Junior America, but Patti, who was big for her age and rebellious, was not the type. My husband would have to go up to the house and tutor Patti all the time or play sports with Skipper, who was kind of a little wimp. There was always something. Every time I heard that phone ring at 6:30 P.M. I knew it was Nancy Reagan calling. She was so pushy and rude; she didn't care that we were in the middle of dinner or that my husband was working on his Ph.D. dissertation. She felt that she was the most important person in the world and he was just hired help. That's the way she treated him. She wasted so much of his time in those days, and he was just too nice to say he had other things to do."

As passionately partisan as her husband's, Nancy's politics dictated her children's friendships. Since Eric Douglas, the son of Anne and Kirk Douglas, was young Ron's best friend, Nancy frequently included Eric in the family's weekend trips. Shortly after the 1964 Republican convention, she was getting ready to drive the youngsters to the ranch. Weeks before, she had attended the convention in San Francisco with her husband to watch Barry Goldwater accept the party's nomination for President. The Reagans wanted "A Choice, Not an Echo," as their placards proclaimed. They returned home and plastered their car with bumper stickers.

"Eric was dropped off at the Reagans'," recalled Kirk Douglas. "As he went into the house with Nancy, he saw their station wagon in the driveway, with a Goldwater bumper sticker. Eric said, 'Boooo, Goldwater,' echoing a sentiment he'd heard in our household.

"Nancy was incensed. She called us immediately. 'You come right up here and take this boy.' Eric was crying. He didn't know what the hell he'd said. We had to send somebody to bring him back."

Left with the Reagans' maid, the five-year-old child could not stop crying. When he was picked up, he was still crying—forty-five minutes later. "Nancy had just dumped him and taken off for the ranch," said Anne Douglas. "It was quite traumatic for Eric, and I'm sure she wouldn't do it again, but she is very, very faithful and loyal to not only her friends and her husband but also to the Republican party. I guess that's why she reacted the way she did.

"I tried later to reconcile things with her, but she wouldn't let her son speak to Eric for quite some time, and it was a good few years before she'd speak to Kirk and me again. When I called her to try to straighten things out, she said, 'It's very sad that you are influencing the children at this early age in politics,' or something like that. It was very hard on Eric because he and Ronny were best friends, and he couldn't understand why the friendship suddenly had to be interrupted. We tried to explain that what makes this country great is that everybody can express an opinion and it's not necessary that you have the same political opinions as your friends, but that if you have different opinions, you can still be friends. I'm afraid that my five-year-old did not understand it all at the time."

A few years later, the Douglases and Reagans saw each other and finally began speaking, but the truce did not last through the evening. "I was dancing with Nancy at the house of David May of the May Company department store chain," said Kirk Douglas. "Nancy was a wonderful dancer. Still is. Somebody brought up politics. Remembering the incident with Eric, I figured I'd tread lightly. I said, 'Nancy, I'm not in politics. Although I'm a registered Democrat, I vote for who I think is the best man. If I thought a Republican was the best man, I'd vote for him. For example, I would vote for Rockefeller as President.' Nancy's eyes flared. She turned on her heel and walked away. I was stunned. I knew how Eric felt."

Gore Vidal said he recognized that fervent partisanship in Nancy Reagan the first time he saw her, at the 1964 Republican convention in San Francisco. She was sitting with her husband in the Cow Palace listening to former President Eisenhower deliver a speech attacking the press. "First, there was her furious glare when someone created a diversion during Ike's aria," he said. "She turned, lip curled, in Bacchanalish rage, huge unblinking eyes afire with a passion to kill the enemy so palpably at hand —or so it looked to me. For all I know, she might have been trying out new contact lenses. In any case, I had barely heard of Nancy then. Even so, I said to myself: There is a lot of rage in this little lady."

As co-chairman of California Republicans for Goldwater in 1964, Ronald Reagan campaigned strenuously throughout the state, delivering his standard speech, "A Time for Choosing," which never failed to produce a standing ovation. Reagan recruited his brother, Neil, to look at Goldwater's television commercials. "We took on the Goldwater assignment and I traveled with the senator for sixty-five days on the campaign plane," recalled Neil "Moon" Reagan.

IN YOUR HEART YOU KNOW HE'S RIGHT thundered the Goldwater billboards.

EXTREME RIGHT countered Lyndon Johnson's posters.

Capitalizing on Goldwater's comment about using tactical nuclear weapons in a crisis, the Democrats ran their devastating "Daisy Girl" television commercial on September 7, 1964. It showed a small child pulling the petals off a daisy and counting them as the idyllic picture dissolved into a mushroom cloud. An H-bomb horror show. The suggestion of nuclear annihilation was terrifying.

"In Your Heart You Know He Might" now dogged the Arizona senator, as even conservative Republican newspapers rushed to endorse Lyndon Johnson for President. Gallup polls showed him trailing Johnson 65 percent to 29 percent, and Goldwater was plagued by retorts to his slogan, particularly "In Your Guts, You Know He's Nuts."

In desperation, the California Goldwater group decided to buy one half hour on the CBS network to telecast Ronald Reagan's standard speech, but Goldwater's top aides objected, saying the speech was wildeyed and too extreme. The candidate himself called Reagan and asked him to withdraw, but Reagan suggested he listen to the speech before making up his mind. Neil Reagan made arrangements for Goldwater to hear the audio portion in a control booth in Washington, D.C. "After it was all through, Barry came out and said, 'What the hell's wrong with that?' So Ronald gave the speech," said his brother.

On October 27, 1964, one week before the election, the genial actor so familiar to television viewers from eight years with the "General Electric Theater" looked into the camera and spoke reassuringly to America, invoking honor, patriotism, and all that a democracy holds dear. He barely mentioned Barry Goldwater's name.

"You and I have a rendezvous with destiny," he concluded. "We can preserve for our children this, the last best hope of man on earth, or we can sentence them to take the first step into a thousand years of darkness. If we fail, at least let our children, and our children's children, say of us, we justified our brief moment here. We did all that could be done."

David Broder of the *Washington Post* called the speech "the most successful national political debut since William Jennings Bryan electrified the 1896 Democratic convention with the 'Cross of Gold' speech." *Time* magazine praised it as "the one bright spot in a dismal campaign." Nancy Reagan said it raised over $8 million in campaign contributions; the figure was closer to $1 million, but all the Republican money in the country could not buy Barry Goldwater a victory that year. He lost to Lyndon Johnson in what was then the greatest landslide in presidential election history. The Democrats carried forty-four states and the District of Columbia, plus Reagan's state of California. They won twenty-eight of thirty-five senatorial seats, giving them a majority in the Senate, and by picking up forty-one congressional seats, they gained a better than two-thirds majority in the House of Representatives. They also reigned supreme in the statehouses, with thirty-three governors to only seventeen for the Republicans.

Nancy Reagan was stupefied by the results. "We didn't expect it to be as lopsided as it was," she said. "Other people may have expected it, but we didn't."

9

THE CONVULSIONS OF THE SIXTIES smashed into conventional society with shattering force, leaving in their wake long-haired hippies, psychedelic trips, love-ins, draft dodgers, peace marches, and flower children turning on and dropping out. Opposed to U.S. involvement in Vietnam, the disaffected young wanted to make love, not war. Campuses from Berkeley to Columbia erupted, ghettos burned, and Negroes demanded to be called blacks. The era of sex, drugs, and rock 'n' roll became the most turbulent decade of the twentieth century, and perhaps the most cataclysmic, producing political assassinations and national funerals.

Among the casualties of the decade were wayward adolescents like sixteen-year-old Michael Reagan, who in 1961 couldn't seem to get on a firm footing with anyone, including his divorced parents and his rigid stepmother, who resented his living in her home. He had attended six grade schools before moving in with the Reagans to start high school at Loyola in Los Angeles. His grades there were poor, which only worsened the strained relations at home.

"When Nancy got ahold of my bad report card, she verbally ripped into me, concluding with, 'You're not living up to the Reagan name or image, and unless you start shaping up, it would be best for you to change your name and leave the house,'" he said.

" 'Fine,' I said, 'why don't you just tell me the name I was born with so at least when I walk out the door I'll know what name to use.'

" 'Okay, Mr. Reagan, I'll do just that.' "

A week later, Nancy confronted her stepson with the information that his given name was John I. Flaugher and that he was born out of wedlock, his father an army sergeant who went overseas and never returned.

Michael said he was rocked by the heartless way he received the news, especially from a woman who had been abandoned as a child and later adopted. "I guess I expected Nancy to be more sympathetic," he said years later.

The moment his father came home from a business trip, Nancy told him what had happened and Reagan called his son in.

"How could you pressure Nancy into going down and finding out your real name?" he asked. "It was wrong of you, and you should apologize to her."

"Wait a minute," said Michael. "I want to tell you my side of the story."

"I don't need to hear your side," Reagan said. "I've heard the story. You're wrong. Nancy is right."

From that moment Michael's days on San Onofre Drive were numbered. A few months later, he was shipped off to the Judson School in Phoenix, Arizona.

"That place was filled with a lot of kids whose parents really didn't have time for them," said Charis Webb, one of Michael's classmates. "Some kids coped with that and some didn't. Michael made a career out of talking about how much his parents ignored him."

He was never disappointed. "I remember at Christmas," Webb said, "the Reagans did not come to the airport to pick him up, so we gave Michael a ride home, and then we had to pick him up when vacation was over. I went to the house once during that time and had dinner with them—just Michael, me and Nancy and his father. It was awful. The Reagans were so cold; they didn't even speak to us. They just talked to each other."

Even with Michael away at school, tension still crackled in the Reagan household as Nancy fought with her adolescent daughter, who felt like the family outcast and begged for professional help. "There was so much emotion in our family," Patti said years later. "Everyone would sort of fly off the handle at things." Patti wanted to avoid these emotional scenes, so the youngster asked her parents if she could see a psychiatrist.

"They wouldn't let me because it was something you were ashamed of, that you wouldn't tell any of your friends about. So it wasn't acceptable at all. But as soon as I had any money at all, I did go," she said.

Before that, though, she, too, was shipped off to boarding school. At the age of thirteen, Patti was sent to the Orme School in Phoenix, so that she, like Michael, would be close to Dr. and Mrs. Davis, who could function as surrogate parents on weekends.

The Reagans went to see their daughter for Thanksgiving vacation in 1965, but the visit was explosive. "I'll never forget the shock on their faces when they arrived," said Patti. "I was going through my Julie Christie–Beatles period. My hair was parted *way* over on one side, hanging in my face. I had on thick, black eye makeup and white lipstick, and my skirt was so short and tight I could hardly walk. Mom and Dad gasped as they walked to meet me, so I decided to go for broke.

" 'As long as you're getting upset about everything,' I said, 'how about this!' I had just gotten my ears pierced, but the earring was so tiny my father could hardly see it. He just sort of squinted in amusement and then said, 'Just do us a favor, okay? Before you have your appendix taken out, will you let us know?' My mother didn't pull the earrings off, but she had a fit. She went and sat in the car."

The disputes between mother and daughter went deeper than mere cosmetics; they arose from strong differences in values. "It was kind of everything," said Patti. "I always felt I was very strange. I didn't quite understand why I was in this family. . . . My parents liked nice things. They had wealthy friends. And I wanted to go join the circus."

Wealthy friends like Holmes Tuttle, Henry Salvatori, and Cy Rubel had already formed an organization called "The Friends of Ronald Reagan" to raise $100,000, which was to be spent by December 31, 1965. The purpose was to test Reagan's political appeal throughout the state. These men saw in Reagan a standard-bearer for their own political philosophy, and they wanted to run him for governor against the incumbent, Edmund "Pat" Brown. They promised Reagan financial support, plus the professional management of Spencer–Roberts & Associates, a political consulting firm that would arrange speaking engagements, write news releases, tutor him on issues, and tone down his archconservative image. They also brought in two behavioral psychologists to reprogram him to psychologically appeal to voters throughout the state. They also hired Neil Reagan to handle advertising. "I knew how to sell him," he said. "I sold Dutch not as my brother but like a piece of soap." His brother, in turn, promised to stump the state for the six-month trial period and decide by the end of the year.

"Holmes Tuttle and I raised about $20,000," said Henry Salvatori, "so Ronnie could go up and down California giving speeches. Wherever he went, he was well received."

Reagan was not without political ambitions. In 1952, he had confided his aspirations to Virginia Mayo, his co-star in *She's Working Her Way Through College.*

"He told me that his first stop would be Sacramento, then Washington," recalled Mayo. Ten years later, in a letter to his daughter Maureen, who had written to express concern about the liberal direction of the country, Reagan responded, "Well, if we're talking about what I could do, Mermie, I could be President."

He enjoyed speaking on conservative issues to appreciative audiences. But by his own admission he was lazy, and an exhaustive campaign from one end of the eight-hundred-mile state to the other was not appealing to someone like Reagan who was so deathly afraid of flying that he refused to get on an airplane. Further, he did not relish being buffeted by a bitterly riven Republican party still recovering from the Goldwater debacle, and he worried about the money he would lose by having to quit his job as host for "Death Valley Days."

But Nancy had already made up her mind. Having been promised by Holmes Tuttle that they would be taken care of financially, she was determined that her husband pursue this opportunity. She recognized his telegenic appeal, and after studying the polls, she, like Tuttle and Salvatori, was convinced he could win.

She knew that the Muchmore political poll had Reagan as the favorite gubernatorial candidate of one-third of the 3 million registered Republicans in the state. Further, the election of George Murphy to the U.S. Senate by the largest plurality ever garnered by a politician in California had broken the taboo against actors holding public office. So she was convinced that Ronnie could easily become the next governor of California. Now she had to convince him. She coaxed and flattered and cajoled; finally, she enlisted the aid of her stepfather.

At home during Christmas vacation, Michael Reagan overheard an argument between his father and Nancy. "I was in the guest bathroom. They were in the driveway, where they often went for private discussions," he said. "Nancy was telling Dad that . . . her stepfather was willing to raise $200,000 in campaign money if Dad agreed to run. Personally, I don't think Dad ever had really strong ambitions to be a politician, but Mommy—his name for Nancy—prodded him."

"It was a difficult decision to make," Nancy admitted later. "It was not a decision Ronnie made alone obviously, and we had several sleepless nights . . . [but] it was a great chance in our lives."

On January 4, 1966, Ronald Reagan, fifty-four, formally announced his candidacy for the Republican gubernatorial nomination in an elaborately staged television appearance. It was followed by a press conference and a reception for 6,000 supporters. He adroitly turned all his perceived negatives into positives by saying that he was simply a citizen politician out to get rid of the boys in the back of the smoke-filled room.

None of his children attended the press conference, but standing at his side was his pretty forty-six-year-old wife, who had recently had plastic surgery to lift her eyes for this very occasion.

The reaction in Hollywood to Reagan's announcement ranged from stunned disbelief to hilarity. Jack Warner could not comprehend the casting. Remembering Jimmy Stewart as the star of *Mr. Smith Goes to Washington* and Ronald Reagan as the B actor who usually lost the girl and ended up as the perennial pal, Warner said, "No. No. No. You've got it all wrong. Jimmy Stewart for governor. Ronald Reagan for best friend." Gleeful Democrats handed out bumper stickers that read: "Elizabeth Taylor for H.E.W."

Even Governor Brown laughed. "I thought it was a joke," he said many years later. "I really felt that running a motion picture actor—and one who was not a grade-A actor at that—was so funny I didn't regard Ronald Reagan as a strong candidate."

The two-term governor always got a laugh when he said, "This is what I was doing for you while my opponent was making *Bedtime for Bonzo*." He even told a class of schoolchildren, "I'm running against an actor, and you know who shot Lincoln, don't cha?"

The former television host of "Death Valley Days" responded with éclat. When a reporter asked, "Will you give Governor Brown equal TV time?" Reagan responded, "Well, sure, our audience is accustomed to seeing both ends of the horse."

During the primary, Governor Brown concentrated his fire on George Christopher, the former Republican mayor of San Francisco, who was Reagan's major opponent. Heavy-set and swarthy, Christopher, who had been defeated twice for statewide office, was effective in small groups but clumsy on television. He rumbled like a thundercloud while Ronald Reagan radiated sunshine. "You look at him and you can smell cornfields and new hay and you can hear a little brook running over the rocks," wrote columnist Jimmy Breslin of the actor's appeal.

In an effort to heal the divisions within his party, Reagan refused to attack other Republicans. Instead, he concentrated on the incumbent, ridiculing him with one-liners. "Keeping up with Governor Brown's promises is like reading *Playboy* while your wife turns the pages." Asked to name the best quality of his opponent, Reagan said, "I think Governor Brown is probably a good family man. God knows, he's put all his relatives on the public payrolls."

Audiences howled their appreciation and applauded Reagan throughout the state. They gave him standing ovations each time he promised "to clean up the mess at Berkeley," where he said the students were staging "sexual orgies so vile I cannot describe them to you." Understandably, Reagan was enjoying his role as the celebrated underdog. So much so that he finally agreed to start flying instead of taking trains, which meant even more speaking dates.

"When we first met him, he knew practically nothing about California," said Dr. Stanley Plog, one of the two behavioral psychologists hired to make him palatable to voters. "He was clipping articles from newspapers himself. He did not have a secretary. He was organizing all of his speeches. He had no background information of his own. I can remember once, I was in his house working with him on the campaign on some issue, and he put the books down suddenly and said, 'Damn. Wouldn't it be fun to be running now for the presidency? Wouldn't that be great?' "

On June 20, 1966, Reagan won the Republican primary by a two-to-one ratio, 1,417,623 votes to 675,683. "That night Ronnie asked me, 'Do you think there will ever be another night like this?' " recalled his wife. "I told him I was sure of it."

And she would do all she could to make it happen. With two troublesome teenagers away at boarding schools, and a housekeeper to take care of her eight-year-old son at home, Nancy now concentrated all her energies on her husband's campaign, sometimes to the dismay of his political staff. She called the Los Angeles headquarters so often that one morning the switchboard operator, forgetting to close the incoming-call switch, announced, "That bitch is on the phone again!" Mrs. Reagan heard the remark, and for a few days, at least, her morning calls ceased.

"We were at our headquarters on Wilshire," said one campaign staffer. "We had just put up this sign and the next morning I get a call from Nancy. 'The color of the sign is terrible,' she says. 'It's ugly. It's just not Ronnie.' So I ask, 'Well, what colors are Ronnie?' She insisted we paint it over, and Ron even got on and asked that we do it to please her."

At first, Nancy said she was "too timid" to give speeches, but she soon overcame her reticence enough to tell reporters what she thought was wrong with the political climate in Washington, D.C. "We are being governed by a dictatorship," she said. By October, the polls showed Reagan to be a sure winner, so she scorched Governor Brown for seeking a third term. "No man should have that much power that long," said Nancy. "It's not good. It's not right." She called her husband's candidacy more than a mere quest for office. "It's a crusade, a real crusade," she said fervently.

Conservative movie stars like Pat Boone, Edgar Bergen, Chuck Connors, James Cagney, Bing Crosby, Roy Rogers, and Cesar Romero signed full-page ads proclaiming that "California needs a governor like Ronald Reagan."

A few days later, another full-page ad appeared throughout the state

sponsored by Republicans, Democrats, and Independents in the entertainment industry who supported Governor Brown. "We respect Ronald
Reagan as a veteran member of our industry. . . . But we believe very
strongly that the skills an actor brings to his profession are NOT the skills
of government. We have no reason to doubt that Mr. Reagan might, after
serving an appropriate apprenticeship, acquire the knowledge to serve in
public office. But we question, very seriously, the wisdom of permitting
him to begin this learning process in California's highest elective office
where the safety and solvency of 19½ million people are at stake. Fortunately, we have a governor who has shown us that he can administer
California's complex affairs calmly and skillfully."

The ad was signed by 147 people, including Steve Allen, Ben Gazzara,
Peter Falk, Norman Lear, Carl Reiner, Jill St. John, and Frank Sinatra.

Six weeks before the election in late September 1966, a white policeman in San Francisco's Hunters Point section shot a black teenager. The
young black man had stolen a car and was trying to get away. Residents
in the black neighborhood rioted. They looted, burned, and rampaged.
By midnight, Governor Brown called out the National Guard. The episode at Hunters Point so inflamed racial divisiveness that Reagan's opposition to the Voting Rights Act of 1964 no longer made any difference to
"the forgotten American" of his speeches, "the man in the suburbs working sixty hours a week to support his family and being taxed heavily for
the benefit of someone else." The white backlash benefited Reagan, who
had recently posed for *Look* magazine standing next to a statue of a
painted black jockey with large white lips that welcomed visitors to his
Malibu ranch.

A few weeks later, a very sure, almost smug, Nancy Reagan told a
press conference, "I think we have reason to be optimistic." Ever superstitious, she quickly amended herself. "But as Ronnie says, he talked to
'President' Tom Dewey and he told him not to get too confident," she
said, referring to the 1948 presidential election when overconfident
Republicans predicted Dewey would beat Harry S Truman.

On election day, November 8, 1966, Ronald Reagan declared, "This
is the beginning of the longest day of my life." He jokingly told reporters who accompanied him and Nancy to the polling place near their
Pacific Palisades home, "Rain or shine, we've got to get out the vote.
This campaign is a crusade and the other side is going to be voting
tombstones, empty lots and warehouses."

Early that evening, guests began arriving at the Brentwood home of
Sylvia and Irving Wallace to watch the election returns. They expected a
long night, but Reagan took an early lead and less than two hours later
was declared the winner, with an enormous margin of 993,739 votes.

"Mickey and Paul Ziffren had called earlier in the day to see if they could bring their houseguest, the political journalist Theodore H. White, to the party," said Irving Wallace. "He came and sat transfixed in front of the television set watching Ronald Reagan win. We gave him his own chair because he said he wanted to be by himself and make notes on Reagan. 'Why bother?' I said. 'He's just a broken-down actor running for governor. No one gives a damn about him.' But Teddy disagreed. 'No, he's going to be President someday,' he said. I thought he'd gone over the edge with that one, but he was convinced that by winning the governorship of the most populous state in the Union, Reagan eventually would win the presidency."

A few days before the election Nancy had wanted to see the governor's mansion in Sacramento, so Thomas Reed, one of Reagan's aides, drove her past the large Victorian mansion at 16th and H streets in the busy commercial section of the state capital. The nineteenth-century mansion had once been home to the muckraking journalist Lincoln Steffens.

"She was singularly unimpressed," said Reed, enumerating her objections: the American Legion hall next door, the seedy motels nearby, and across the street the neon-lighted gasoline stations.

"It's a firetrap and an eyesore," said Nancy, who returned to Los Angeles determined not to live in the mansion. She immediately called Holmes Tuttle to complain, something she would do regularly whenever she felt that she and her husband were being put upon because of the sacrifices they had made to go into public service. She told Tuttle the worst part of winning the governorship was the terrible monetary deprivation they would suffer now that Ronnie's salary would be reduced from $100,000 to $44,000 a year. She said that it wasn't fair, having to sell their ranch because they could not afford to pay the property taxes, and then having to live in a house that was not fit for habitation.

"Please, Nancy, give it a chance," said Tuttle. "Other governors and their families have been very happy there."

Nancy was not to be placated, but she agreed to return to Sacramento in mid-November for an official tour of the mansion. Her guide was Mrs. Edmund Brown, who took pride in showing off the eighty-nine-year-old residence where California's governors had lived since 1903. She ushered Nancy into the first-floor music room, decorated in pale pink and featuring overstuffed purple velvet chairs and long purple velvet draperies. "We loved living in this house," said Bernice Brown, pointing out the seven bedrooms and bathrooms.

"Oh, I'm sure you did," said Nancy.

"My son, Jerry, studied for the bar exam in that third-floor bedroom."

"Oh, I see," said Nancy.

"The house has eight marble fireplaces, but safety regulations forbid us from firing any of them up."

"Oh, my," said Nancy.

As they moved from room to room followed by reporters, Nancy smiled wanly. "Of course, it's old, but it will be just fine," she said. "I'm sure I can fix it up to make it attractive and livable, but I have been worrying since I heard it called a firetrap. I'm also concerned about my son finding playmates here in the center of the city."

Marian Darmsted of the *Sacramento Bee* was struck by the patronizing manner of the governor-elect's wife. "I got the impression that Nancy felt she was far superior to Bernice Brown," she said years later. "She acted as if she was above it all. I wondered at the time if she did not feel ill at ease and was simply using this overbearing attitude to cover up her insecurity. Maybe that's just the way she is. Then again, Sacramento might have been a little hick-townish compared with the Hollywood glamour she liked so much."

As soon as Nancy left the three-story wooden mansion, she went straight to the airport for a flight back to Los Angeles by chartered plane. The *Bee* reporter accompanied her to the Sacramento airport, and Nancy, who was still angry about that newspaper's vigorous opposition to her husband during the campaign, berated Darmsted for working for "that terrible rag which ran those vicious cartoons and told all those lies about Ronnie."

"Nancy really let poor Marian have it with both barrels," recalled Martin Smith, the *Bee*'s former managing editor. "She was probably in a foul mood after seeing the governor's mansion and then mad that she had to share her car with a reporter whose newspaper had been so rough on them during the campaign. Nancy hated the *Bee* so much that she refused to let the governor subscribe to the paper at home. He couldn't operate effectively with the legislature without reading the most important paper in the state capital every day, so he had to read it at the office."

Both Reagans were so incensed by the newspaper's endorsement of Governor Brown that they could hardly bring themselves to be civil to *Bee* reporters after the election. "I had to go to their house in Pacific Palisades the day after Christmas to do a photo story," said Jim Wrightson, a former reporter, "and I'll never forget standing out in the howling wind with the photographer and not getting so much as a hello or Happy Holidays or won't-you-have-a-cup-of-coffee from the Reagans. I certainly didn't expect to be welcomed as a long lost relative, but their reception was so rude and cold I never forgot it."

The only reporter Nancy Reagan valued at the time was Jody Jacobs, who wrote for *Women's Wear Daily* and later became society editor of the

Los Angeles Times. She represented the audience that Nancy cared about most, so Jacobs, a charming woman who was never unkind, received unprecedented access.

When Nancy got home from touring the governor's mansion, she immediately called Holmes Tuttle again and started crying. She wept about everything from "the dark, creepy hallways" and "china milk-pitcher lamps" to "the potted plants still wrapped in aluminum foil." She said it was the gloomiest house she had ever seen and she didn't see how anyone could expect her to leave her beautiful home in Pacific Palisades to live in a slum in Sacramento. "Ronnie will be miserable," she warned. Tuttle listened patiently and said he was sure they could reach a satisfactory arrangement after the inauguration. Somewhat mollified, Nancy hung up. Her next phone call was to *Women's Wear Daily* offering an exclusive interview.

"I remember I went to the Pacific Palisades house because Nancy wanted to talk about her inaugural wardrobe and her plans for the gala," said Jody Jacobs. "She said confidentially how much she despised the mansion, and what a godawful firetrap it was with bathrooms that looked like they belonged in a prison, and fireplaces that wouldn't work, but, of course, I couldn't quote her on any of that. She didn't mind going on the record, though, to make a snide remark about Governor and Mrs. Brown having separate bedrooms; she said that she and Ronnie would share the same bedroom, of course, and turn the second one into a sitting room. It was a small but gratuitous comment."

Much as Nancy hated the governor's mansion, she wanted to move in early, so she told her secretary to relay her plans to Mrs. Brown, hoping that the governor's wife would offer to move out ahead of schedule. "I remember that very well," said Bernice Brown many years later. "Her secretary called my secretary and asked if we would move out Friday. Mrs. Reagan wanted to host a preinaugural luncheon in the mansion on Sunday, December 31, and they needed extra time so state workers could come in to wash windows and wax floors and all that. I was surprised by the request, but it was not a great problem. We agreed to move a few days early, and we left in such a hurry that I did leave some things behind. Mrs. Reagan had them sent to me."

Publicly diplomatic, the governor-elect's wife told *Women's Wear Daily* that while the governor's mansion was typically Victorian, "I could be happy anywhere if my husband and children are with me." A disingenuous comment considering that Nancy had not spoken to her stepdaughter in five years, except to call and ask if Maureen's husband, a captain in the Marine Corps, could get Michael Reagan shipped off to Vietnam. No longer speaking to Michael, she had cut him off financially for getting bad grades. She had told him he would have to get a job and support himself if he wanted a college education; at nineteen, he quit school and started doing manual labor for $3 an hour while taking college courses on the side. He soon quit school altogether and, like the rest of the Reagan children, never earned a college degree. Nancy no longer considered Maureen or Michael part of her family, and she did not want either of them publicly associated with their father. During the campaign, she had insisted that her husband's biography be released to the press stating that "Ronald Reagan is married to the former Nancy Davis and they have two children, Patti and Ron." No Maureen. No Michael.

She was also barely speaking to Patti, who remained away at her Arizona boarding school. Many years later, Patti recalled how her views were rejected and belittled by her parents from the time she was an adolescent. "It was like living under a dictatorship," she said. "What bothered me didn't bother other people in the family. The common comeback was, 'Where did you hear that?' And about half the time I couldn't remember and didn't think I had heard it anyplace. . . . I don't think it was a good way to raise a child."

"Poor Patti! She was indeed the outcast," said Jody Jacobs. "Nancy never talked about her, never referred to her. Instead, it was always 'The Skipper this' and 'The Skipper that.' Young Ron was obviously the favorite child, and Nancy was so overly protective of him that even he felt smothered at times. She worried about him if he wasn't home at four o'clock every afternoon, and that was her way to get out of her political duties. She said she simply had to be home for her young son."

The only child now in her care, eight-year-old Ron told anyone who asked that he was not going to go into politics like his father when he grew up.

"I was only a kid at the time, but I remember saying that I thought politics was corrupt and sleazy," he said many years later. "I was exposed to the machinery of politics when I was little, watching my father run, and it seemed like there were too many unhealthy guys in wrinkled suits that smelled like cigars."

Oddly, the Reagans decreed that the swearing-in would be held at 12:01 A.M., January 2, 1967. "Every seventh year, New Year's Day falls on a Sunday," Nancy said. "Then the Rose Bowl game and parade are postponed until Monday. Usually, the inaugural is on January 2, but we don't want to take away from the excitement of the Rose Bowl. So Ronnie will be sworn in on midnight of the first. Then everybody can enjoy the game and parade the next day."

No governor in the history of California had ever chosen to take the oath of office in the middle of the night, but the Reagans were acting on advice from an astrologer, who said that this was the most propitious time. The Reagans, believing that the elements control destiny, insisted on that time. "When the decision was made to do it at this hour, we had our reasons," Ronald Reagan said.

Governor Brown, who thought the hour was preposterous, simply shrugged his shoulders. "My only guess is that it's because he believes in astrology," he said.

California astrologers concurred. In San Francisco, Gavin Chester Arthur, an astrologer and grandson of the twenty-first President of the United States, said Jupiter, the sign of kings and the symbol of prosperity and fame, would be high in the sky at the moment of the inauguration. "I truly suspect that Reagan was advised by an astrologer because no better time could be picked," he said.

"It's not just a coincidence," said Louise Huebner, a Los Angeles astrologer.

"It was common knowledge that the Reagans used astrologers, and it was no big deal," said Wendy Goodwin, a San Diego astrologer.

At the time, Reagan's aides hurried to deny his reliance on the zodiac. Most of them did not know then that Reagan and his wife were devoted clients of Los Angeles astrologer Carroll Righter and secret devotees of seer Jeane Dixon. The executive secretary to the governor-elect said, "He does not believe in astrology. He is not guided by the stars, nor do we intend to have stargazers in the administration."

But Reagan, who admitted to believing in flying saucers, and even swore that he had seen a few unidentified flying objects, did little to dispel doubts about his belief in the supernatural. "The law prescribes that at midnight it is the end of the present administration," he said. "I hate to be a pessimist, but accidents may happen. I don't want anything to interfere."

"I just thought it was a great publicity stunt and a way to say he wanted to get right down to business without wasting any time," said Lyn Nofziger, Reagan's former press secretary. "I didn't pay any attention to all that astrological crap."

On January 1, 1967, the Reagans waited out the final hours before the midnight ceremony at a private dinner party for forty people hosted by Marion and Earle Jorgensen at the Firehouse restaurant in Sacramento. They were surrounded by the monied circle that had made the evening possible: Dr. and Mrs. Loyal Davis, Virginia and Holmes Tuttle, Grace and Henry Salvatori, Jean and William French Smith, Betsy and Alfred Bloomingdale, Harriet and Armand Deutsch. Ronald Reagan raised his glass to toast his wealthy benefactors, "At the risk of sounding just a bit partisan, let me point out that my administration makes no bones about being business-oriented." Shortly after 11:00 P.M., the party began moving toward their limousines for the ride to the capitol, where they would be among the 150 people invited to witness the private swearing-in ceremony in the rotunda. The official inauguration for the public at large would take place three days later, when the governor gave his speech on the west steps of the state capitol.

Shortly before midnight, the Reagans walked into the rotunda in the glare of blinding lights from thirty-two television cameras. At 12:01 A.M.,they joined the rest of the gubernatorial party on a small wooden platform. A minute later, chamber singers in an arc around the balcony sang "America, the Beautiful," their voices reverberating stirringly under the 247-foot-high dome of the old building. Then Senator George Murphy stepped forward to administer the oath of office to Robert H. Finch, the forty-year-old Los Angeles lawyer who had been elected lieutenant governor.

At 12:11 A.M., Associate Justice Marshall F. McComb of the California State Supreme Court, a frequent dissenter from the court's liberal decisions, administered the oath of office to a westward-facing Ronald Reagan, who officially became California's thirty-third governor at 12:16 A.M.

A few months later, an English witch, Sybil Leek, was standing on the deck of a Dutch ocean liner sailing to the United States. A pleated chiffon scarf wrapped around her brown, frizzy hair billowed in the wind like a swirling sorcerer's hat. Rocking her hulking frame back and forth in gold sandals with red ties looped between fleshy toes, she was an unforgettable sight to the other passengers—all 275 pounds of her. Green mascara dripped from her eyes, snake bracelets curled up her chunky arms, and a crystal pendant heaved up and down on her enormous bosom. The high priestess of world witchcraft, as she referred to herself, was traveling with a young niece and a live snake.

"She was the weirdest woman I ever saw in my life," said Virginia Lehman, one of the passengers. "She introduced herself as a witch and said she was head of the European witches' coven. She talked casually about casting spells, incantations, goats' feet, herbal brews, and the Devil. She said she followed only white witchcraft—that is, witchcraft for good, not evil. She was very much against black magic and selling your soul to the Devil for money. She said she had recently moved from England and was now living in southern California. My daughter and I were absolutely fascinated, so we stood there talking to her for a long time.

"She asked me if I had ever heard of Ronald Reagan, who had been elected governor of California."

" 'Sure,' I said.

" 'I'm his astrologer,' said the witch.

" 'Really?'

" 'I'm the one who told him he had to be inaugurated right after midnight facing west in a part of the capitol that had never been used for a swearing-in before.'

" 'You mean the television actor?'

" 'Mark my words,' said the witch. 'You're going to hear a great deal about him in the future. He's going to be a very important man.'

"I didn't pay much attention to that part of the conversation, because I wasn't a big Ronald Reagan fan and I wasn't from California, so I could not have cared less that the governor believed in witchcraft. I was more interested in what Sybil Leek was feeding her snake."

10

THE WOMAN NANCY REAGAN MOST ADMIRED in the world was the
soignée wife of the founder, president, and chief executive officer of
Diners Club. "Betsy Bloomingdale was her idol, her goddess," said journalist Jody Jacobs. "She was everything Nancy wanted to be."

It was Betsy who introduced Nancy to Adolfo, her little knit suit designer; to Monsieur Marc, her New York hairdresser; to Ted Graber, her
Beverly Hills decorator; to Jerry Zipkin, her New York walker. Betsy
bought her luggage at T. Anthony in Manhattan, so that's where Nancy
bought hers. Betsy went to George Masters in Los Angeles for makeup,
so that's where Nancy went. Betsy went to Julius to get her hair done, so
Nancy did, too. Betsy wore one-shoulder gowns by Galanos, so Nancy
started wearing them, although she had to buy hers on sale. Betsy mixed
oriental objects with traditional furnishings and so, on a much less grand
scale, did Nancy. Betsy got Nancy into the Colleagues, a select group of
Los Angeles women who raise money for charity, and she paved Nancy's
way onto the best-dressed list, where Betsy was a perennial. Alfred
Bloomingdale frequently joked that it had cost him $500,000 to put his
wife on the best-dressed list because he had had to hire two publicists—
Serge Obolensky and Earl Blackwell—to promote her in all the society
columns. As a result, Betsy was often mentioned by Suzy and Eugenia
Shepherd and appeared regularly in *Women's Wear Daily.*

Socially connected to everyone from the Newhouses of New York to
the de Ravenals of Paris, Betsy Bloomingdale epitomized elegance to

Nancy. The two women had met while picking up their children from summer camp. Since then, they had become almost inseparable, talking on the phone at least once a day and lunching frequently at the Bistro in Beverly Hills. Betsy's husband, a Democrat who had once supported Governor Pat Brown, became a Republican for Ronald Reagan, one of his unofficial advisers, and one of his biggest contributors.

Nancy was entranced by her friend's sumptuous life: of servants, chefs, chauffeurs, interior designers, florists, couturiers, and antique dealers. Betsy wore cashmere trenchcoats with mink collars and cuffs; her 18-karat gold belt was decorated with fifty carved emeralds from David Webb, one of the finest jewelers in America; her three-acre garden brimmed with the rarest orchids in southern California, and her kitchen produced cuisine worthy of connoisseurs. In addition to a Los Angeles mansion in affluent Holmby Hills, the Bloomingdales owned an apartment in New York City and a pied-à-terre in Paris.

Nothing summed up Betsy Bloomingdale better than her own words to *W,* the biweekly fashion bible, during a national energy crisis in the 1970s. She said she was simply a conscientious citizen trying to do her part. "I ask my servants not to turn on the self-cleaning oven until after seven in the evening. We must all do little things and big things to conserve energy." She probably never understood why her statement produced such derisive laughter.

In a world where money alone conferred social standing, Betsy Bloomingdale reigned supreme, and it was to this shrine of affluence that Nancy Reagan genuflected. The newly minted riches of the Bloomingdales and the rest of the arrivistes around the Reagans helped Nancy bury her proletarian roots and assume a more elegant, aristocratic façade. She told reporters she couldn't possibly shop in Sacramento. "Here everything is scaled down for these Valley farm women." Nor could she conceive of going to a beauty salon in the state capital. "No one in Sacramento can do hair," she said. Such a worshiper of luxury could hardly be expected to lower herself to endure the thumping radiators and leaky faucets of the governor's mansion.

"Mansion is hardly the description I'd use," Nancy corrected a reporter. "Residence is more like it."

Because young Ron could not transfer schools until the end of January, he and his mother commuted from Los Angeles every weekend to be with the governor in the state capital. Nancy insisted on keeping their house in Pacific Palisades, where she kept her housekeeper on duty and everything in readiness for their regular trips to southern California. "Thank heavens we can escape to Beverly Hills on the weekends," she said. Each week, on the housekeeper's day off, she ordered one of the governor's aides to travel 377 miles to feed their dog.

Thirty-three days after her husband had been sworn in as governor, the first lady of California had had enough of the mansion's purple velvet chairs. She said she couldn't stand them another minute, and he agreed, promising to announce their pending departure the next morning.

"Yes, we're considering moving out and letting the governor's mansion proceed to become a historical monument as planned," said the governor at a press conference. "A group of citizens desire[s] to build and present the state with a new governor's residence. We're wide open, and we're considering finding an interim place if such construction is to start."

Nancy sat quietly on the sidelines, motioning for Lyn Nofziger, the governor's director of communications, to tell reporters that the two reasons for moving were the hazards of traffic and fire to their son's safety. Still, the announcement drew criticism to the governor, who had been elected for promising to cut down on government spending.

Nine days later, at 2:30 on Friday afternoon, a fire alarm mysteriously went off inside the executive mansion and sent the household help scurrying and Nancy running into the street clutching the hand of her eight-year-old son. No one directly accused the governor's wife of triggering the alarm, but fire department officials said they could not rule out the possibility of "someone" intentionally pulling the lever. The incident gave Nancy the excuse she needed to announce what she had been planning secretly for weeks.

"I'm going house hunting," she said. "This place is just not safe. . . . It backs up on the American Legion Hall where I swear there are vile orgies every night. I said to Ronnie, 'I can't let my children live there!' "

Within days she found a "tastefully furnished" house in the fashionable Sierra Oaks section of Sacramento. The house was owned by a Republican couple willing to lease it and all their possessions to the Reagans. Captivated by the lovely antiques, Nancy wanted to move in right away, but the governor's staff felt that the dining room was too small for entertaining state legislators, which they insisted the governor had to do if he wanted any legislation passed. Knowing that a small dining room would appeal mightily to Mrs. Reagan, who had no intention of entertaining legislators, the staff persuaded Governor Reagan to reject the house for security reasons. He agreed, knowing he could not tell his wife the real reason. "It's simply a matter of security," he told her. "The residence has no fencing in front and no facilities for guards."

Nancy continued her search for the ideal residence-in-exile and finally found it in a two-story Tudor house with six bedrooms and bathrooms. It stood on an acre of land in a stately old neighborhood two and a half miles from the capitol. Containing 6,700 square feet, the house had an outdoor swimming pool, a pool house, sculptured gardens, and a large recreation room with a pool table and electric train. "It's a place that Ronnie can be very comfortable in and the Skipper will enjoy immensely," she said.

At first, few legislators ever saw the inside of the house. Instead, when Nancy was forced to entertain them, she held a large party in the backyard and insisted that everyone stay outside. When several legislative wives headed toward the house in search of a bathroom, she lunged at them, barring their entry. "You can't go in," she said, directing them to a poolside cabana, where they had to stand in a long line. "We felt we weren't welcome," said one woman. "We could come to the party but not come inside her house."

"That's true," said Jody Jacobs. "Nancy just hated those legislative wives. She said they were all fat and messy. She thought they were too provincial, not sophisticated enough for her. I remember Nancy Reynolds, her press secretary, having such a rough time getting her to show up for anything official that included the wives. Nancy Reagan said she didn't want them around. She imported her friends from Los Angeles instead."

At the insistence of the governor's staff, the poolside parties for the legislators and their families became an annual affair. For one party, Nancy hired a mariachi band to play while her husband handed out autographed pictures of himself. At 9:45 P.M., she began sending signals that the party was over, and within half an hour she had cleared everyone out.

Lou Cannon, then a reporter with the *San Jose Mercury-News,* recalled a press party the governor and his wife held for reporters at which Nancy started looking at her watch as the appointed hour for the end of the event drew near. "Finally, she said to an aide, 'C'mon, it's time to get rid of them.' Reagan, oblivious to this concern, was telling old movie stories to reporters in the garden."

Eventually, Nancy was convinced that inviting legislators and their spouses to a small dinner party would be advantageous to her husband, so she began extending invitations on a marathon basis, twice a week, until all 119 members of both the senate and assembly, plus their spouses, had sat at the governor's table. And if they ever offended her husband, they could expect to hear from her. Each dinner party was precisely planned and organized to the last detail.

"The pattern never varies," said Yvonne Brathwaite, former assemblywoman from Los Angeles. "We are allowed so much time for a before-dinner drink, so much time to consume some canapés. Always dinner is buffet style. Always Mrs. Reagan is warm and affable. After dinner, we always go downstairs to play with Skipper's electric trains. Always we shoot a little pool. It is a faithful picture of a man and his family at home. To some, it is very appealing."

While waiting for the new governor's mansion to be built, Reagan decided to economize by using Governor Brown's leftover letterhead stationery. He also insisted that he and his wife pay the rent on the interim house for the sake of good politics. Nancy balked. "I can't believe we had to rent it with our own money," she complained to reporter George Christy. "Wouldn't you think that the state would provide a residence for the governor and his family? When I go to other states and see how the governors live, I'm embarrassed; we're an important and powerful state, and deserve an official residence."

The Reagans signed a two-year lease on the house. When the lease was up, the owner asked them to move because he wanted to sell the house. Once again, Nancy called Holmes Tuttle in tears, so the Tuttles, Bloomingdales, Jorgensens, Salvatoris, and Deutsches bought the house for $150,000. They made $40,000 worth of improvements and leased it back to the Reagans for $1,250 a month so they wouldn't have to move out. "We just did it to help the governor out," said Henry Salvatori. "We didn't get anything out of it."

Actually, Mr. Salvatori profited handsomely from having his friend as governor when Ronald Reagan proposed legislation that exempted oil rigs from being taxed as property. The L.A. County Assessor labeled the bill a "blatant piece of special interest legislation that set the pattern for the entire Reagan administration," but oilmen like Henry Salvatori were ecstatic.

Nancy Reagan could not stand having to pay her own way, even for a few months, and she did not let up on the subject until the state took over the payments on the house in June 1971. In addition, the state government paid $10,000 a month for upkeep on the property, plus $14,804 a year in gardening expenses, causing some legislators to complain about taxpayers' money protecting the personal investment of the governor's millionaire friends. Even with the state picking up the tab, Nancy continued to whine that she needed furniture. Her fund-raising drive to build a new governor's mansion had been stymied by controversy, but she decided to plunge ahead anyway and, oblivious to political ramifications, solicited donations of antiques that she could use until the new mansion was built. She claimed the donations were all her friends' idea.

"They asked if they could donate furniture to the state since the house needed furnishing," she said. "Mrs. Reese Milner [Ginny] donated my

1.

Edith and Ken Robbins with their only child, Anne Frances,
born July 6, 1921.

2.

Nancy Reagan with her mother, Edith.

Nancy (far right) with her
aunt, Virginia Galbraith,
and her cousin Charlotte
at the Galbraiths' home in
Bethesda, Maryland.

Nancy with her aunt,
Virginia, and her cousin
Charlotte.

3.

4.

Nancy with her father,
Ken Robbins, at Niagara
Falls in 1930.

5.

6.

*Dr. Loyal
Davis in
1960.*

7.   *Nancy Davis (fourth from left) with her field hockey team at Girls Latin
School in Chicago.*

8.

This photo of Nancy Davis appeared in her Smith College yearbook, class of 1943.

9.

Nancy Davis as a student at Smith College in The Factory Follies, singing "Make with the Maximum" to entertain factory workers.

Ronald Reagan in one of his posed publicity shots at Warner Bros.

11.

Jane Wyman with her Oscar for best actress in 1948 for her leading role in Johnny Belinda.

Actress Christine Larson, the woman Ronald Reagan proposed to before he agreed to marry Nancy.

Alla Nazimova, godmother to Nancy Davis, talking to George Cukor, one of MGM's top directors.

13.

14.

ZaSu Pitts, one of Edith Luckett's close friends. She made sure that Nancy Davis was cast in some of her touring plays.

Benny Thau, the MGM executive in charge of contract players, whose affair with Nancy Davis launched her career at MGM.

15.

MGM still of starlet *Nancy Davis.*

16.

Gary Gray, Lillian Bronson, James Whitmore, and Nancy Davis in The Next Voice You Hear.

17.

favorite piece—an antique French Regency fruitwood secretary [worth $2,800]—and the Alfred Bloomingdales contributed a mahogany dining table that can seat twenty-four [worth $3,500]. The Earle Jorgensens donated two Queen Anne armchairs and ten side chairs [worth $3,000] and Mrs. Howard Ahmanson loaned eight paintings [valued at $5,750]. The furniture [total worth $17,865] belongs to the state, not to us, but wouldn't you know that some politicians tried to make a brouhaha of it?"

Once she acquired enough furniture for her house, Nancy started acquiring for her husband's office. "I just didn't like the look of the place," she said. "It didn't look like the office of the governor of California should look."

Rooting through a basement at Sutter's Fort, part of a state historic park, she found pictures, engravings, and documents from the gold-rush days of California, appropriated them, and meticulously supervised while state workers hung them on the walls of Reagan's office. She swooped through the capitol, ordering state carpenters to lay yards of bright red carpet in the corridors, rip out the old burnished leather walls ("dark, horrible, shabby") and replace them with beige burlap ("modern, classy"), to install new red and white draperies, reupholster couches, replace tables, and throw out chairs.

"I'm just a frustrated decorator," she said. "Having a pretty place to work in is important to a man." When secretaries saw her coming, they groaned. She issued orders that no one could leave a coffee cup on a desk, ashtrays had to be emptied after every cigarette, and women could not wear pants to work—only skirts and dresses. "It's part of the overall decor," she said.

One visitor described the governor's office as "Hearst Colonial," likening it to the garish interior of William Randolph Hearst's castle in San Simeon. But Nancy was proud of her work right down to the apothecary jar on the governor's desk that she kept filled with hard candies. "I feel strongly about giving historical meaning to my husband's offices," she said. "So if anyone has any early California furniture he wants to loan . . ."

She tried her best to emulate Jacqueline Kennedy, who brought style to the White House by acquiring valuable antiques, but unlike Mrs. Kennedy, Nancy made her requests for furnishings sound like demands, as though expensive antiques and a new governor's mansion were her personal due.

"If everyone in the state contributed 10 cents toward a fund, a house could be bought, furnished, and taken care of," she said. "You know, when Vice President and Mrs. Agnew came to stay with us, they had to use our daughter Patti's bathroom down the hall. Not that they complained, but it's all so Mickey Mouse, when you can't look after world figures properly. We wouldn't dream of inviting European dignitaries to stay with us; it'd be too embarrassing. So we put them up at local hotels, which are all right, but isn't it nicer if we can invite them to the governor's residence? It's more personal and makes a better impression."

Political criticism of Nancy's acquisitiveness reached such a pitch that she called a press conference to explain why she solicited $125,000 in furnishings for the governor's residence. Angry and defensive, she said that a proper home, furnishings, and a professional decorator were beyond the financial means of the Reagans. "We didn't improve our income by changing professions," she told the assembled reporters. She said she was embarrassed that the state had not replaced the ninety-year-old governor's mansion, now a state museum, and that a new governor's mansion should be the first order of business. "California is too great a state to let this go on any longer," she said, adding that the state should buy the house in which she and the governor were living and let them live there rent-free. She also said she had done a wonderful job collecting antiques. "Frankly, I am very proud of what I've done. I wanted to get a good start collecting things for the mansion, having them donated to the state, the same as they did for the White House. The people who donated to the White House received a pat on the back. The people who donated things here deserve the same thanks."

The antiques never found a permanent home and languished in a dusty state warehouse after the Reagans left Sacramento. Nancy pushed the new executive mansion to completion, leaving as her legacy a 25,000-square-foot house of thirty-one rooms built on eleven acres of oak and olive trees overlooking the American River outside Sacramento. She supervised the plans for this sprawling mausoleum of stale yellow concrete blocks and bulletproof windows. The building cost $1.4 million, not including the property, which was donated by the governor's rich friends. Nancy's plans included a pool with integrated fountains, a Jacuzzi, three courtyards, an outdoor tiled barbecue, and a tennis court. She insisted the kitchen countertops be lower than standard height to accommodate her "petite stature." She approved every feature for the grand ballroom, the first lady's room, the governor's master suite, the Cinderella suite, the honeymoon suite, and the California suite. Built in 1974, the house has never been occupied by a governor. Reagan's successor, Edmund "Jerry" Brown, refused to live in the mansion, declaring it a "garish, expensive Taj Mahal" that was desecrating the sacred burial grounds of Indians.

From 1975 until it was put up for sale in 1984, the state of California paid $1,000 a month for caretakers to live in the empty monstrosity, polishing the bulletproof windows and feeding the guard dogs behind the eight-foot chain-link fence. The hulking structure stands like an empty supermarket, unwanted and unoccupied, a monument to Nancy Reagan's taste.

The first lady of California saw herself as more than just a governor's wife. She was married to the man many people were talking about for President in 1968, and his national stature became hers. "A woman, I would hope, would be a help to her husband no matter what he does," she told a Smith College alumnae publication. "Of course, the more successful he is, the more important her role becomes." Consequently, she eschewed the parochial projects and ceremonial duties of other governors' wives, choosing instead more important visibility. She did insist on certain perquisites, such as a cook, a maid, a personal secretary, a car and driver, plus personalized license plates for the car she traveled in. Michael Deaver, the governor's aide, ordered the plates for her, and then canceled them, thinking that everyone would recognize the NDR initials and start harassing her wherever she went. A month later, when Nancy had not received the personalized license plates, she called Verne Orr, the director of the Department of Motor Vehicles, who recalled the conversation:

" 'Hello, Verne, this is Nancy.'

" 'Yes, Mrs. Reagan.'

" 'How is my license plate coming?'

" 'Mrs. Reagan, I am sorry but I was told to stop it.'

"There was a long pause on the other end.

" 'Verne, whose car is it?'

" 'It's yours, Mrs. Reagan.'

" 'I want that license plate,' she said, hanging up the phone.

"You can bet that Nancy Reagan got her license plates as fast as I could get Folsom Prison to make them up," said Verne Orr.

The first lady accepted an appointment by her husband to the California Arts Commission, but later resigned because she didn't have time to attend any meetings. "She was probably too busy getting a tan so she'd look good in her photographs," said an aide. During those years, Nancy spent hours sitting by the pool sunbathing. When Paul Healy, a national political correspondent, visited the governor's office, Reagan, without calling ahead, decided to take him home for lunch to meet Nancy. Walking into the house, he yelled "Mommy," and Nancy called for him to come upstairs. "He bounded back down a minute later to explain that Nancy had been sunbathing and at the moment was wearing oil, hair curlers and not much else," wrote the journalist. "He suggested returning to meet her later in the day."

As first lady of California, Nancy agreed to be honorary chairman of the California Christmas Seal campaign, and to meet the March of Dimes poster child because all she had to do was pose for pictures. More or less ignoring the local media, she concentrated instead on getting coverage in such national publications as *Look, Ladies' Home Journal,* and, of course, *Women's Wear Daily.*

When *Life* magazine wanted to do a fashion layout, the photographer asked Nancy to pose in the state senate chamber. She eagerly agreed, having no compunction about breaking up the proceedings of a legislative session. "I just came to have my picture taken," she told the startled senators. "I hope I didn't interrupt your carryings-on." Shuffling uncomfortably, the senators graciously recessed so the governor's wife could pose on the rostrum in her new clothes.

"I was surprised by what a sharp businesswoman she was," recalled Stanley Gordon, who produced a feature on Nancy for *Look* magazine. "I had called to say that we wanted to photograph her in color and she said, 'That will be fine but you'll have to pay for it.' She made us agree to fly her hairdresser up from Los Angeles and pay all his expenses. 'It costs me money every time I'm photographed,' she said. 'I have to look my best and I'm just not going to go to that expense anymore unless the magazines pay for it.' It took a certain amount of audacity to talk that way to a publication that was there to give her publicity, but she didn't back down and so we paid for the transportation to and from Sacramento for her Hollywood hairdresser and whatever his fee was. In all my years in the business, I've never had anyone else demand that sort of financial accommodation, not even the most famous movie stars."

The writer Jack Star, senior editor of *Look* and head of its Chicago bureau, was also put through his paces by the governor's wife. "Invited to have a drink with them at home, I was trying to establish some rapport with the Reagans, who seemed suspicious of a hatchet job," he said. "I mentioned to Nancy that in Chicago I had known her father, Dr. Loyal Davis, who was chief of neurosurgery at Northwestern University Medical school. My claim was more or less true since I had met the good doctor once or twice in the course of doing some medical stories. She leapt on me.

" 'You were a *friend* of *my* father's?' she asked. 'Well, I was just about to call him.' She dialed his number in Phoenix, where he was now living. " 'Dad?' she said. 'I've got an old "friend" of yours here, Jack Star of Chicago,' and she handed me the phone. I chatted for a moment or two with the doctor, who, naturally, was mystified by the whole matter.

There isn't any doubt in my mind that Nancy was being malicious, or at least very suspicious when she put me on the phone with her father. The whole point of the call seemed to be to show me that she could see through me."

The *Look* photographer was also put through his paces. "Nancy liked to be shot with celebrities, preferably men putting their arms around her," recalled Stanley Tretick. "I could never figure it out; I guess it made her feel loved by the movie stars who never gave her a tumble when she was a starlet. She had learned the softening effects of being shot with kids, especially handicapped kids, and she's the master of the long smile. She can hold a full-toothed, flash-frozen smile longer than anyone I've ever seen. I photographed her on a hospital visit where she hugged a little kid for so long that the kid got squirmy and peed all over her shoes, but Nancy wouldn't let go of him. She never stopped smiling until I stopped clicking."

Writer Joan Didion visited Nancy during her first year as governor's wife and was given a tour of the new residence on 45th Street, where glossy white matchbooks were displayed that read EXECUTIVE MANSION. She, too, noticed Nancy Reagan's ability to contrive a cinematic smile for the cameras. Her withering article, entitled "Pretty Nancy," appeared in the *Saturday Evening Post* and showed the onetime actress "playing out some middle-class American woman's daydream circa 1948." The most devastating part of the piece came when the writer described Skipper's arrival home from school, which she had been told was the high point of Nancy's day. The little boy did not rush in to say hello to his mother. In fact, he tried to sneak out unobserved. Nancy intercepted him, though, and forced a very brief appearance:

"Come in for just a minute, Ronnie."
"Lo," he says, appearing in the doorway.
"How's Chuck's cold?" Nancy Reagan asks.
"Chuck doesn't have a cold."
"Chuck doesn't have a cold?"
"No. Bruce has braces."
"Bruce has braces," Nancy Reagan repeats.
"Bye," the Skipper says.
"Bye," I say.
Nancy Reagan smiles radiantly at me. . . . "I don't believe in being an absentee mother," she says to me. "I just don't."

Nancy never recovered her equilibrium after Joan Didion's article. From then on, she nursed a grudge against the writer, telling friends that Miss

Didion had been "mean, unfriendly and deceptive." When Nancy wrote
her memoirs more than twenty years later, she recalled vividly her anger
and humiliation at being depicted as a relentlessly smiling mannequin. "I
thought we were getting along fine together," she said of the writer.
"Maybe it would have been better if I snarled a bit." By that time, she
was blaming her bad press on the women who wrote about her, suggesting they were envious of her youthful good looks and pretty clothes.
"One reason may be that some women aren't all that crazy about a
woman who wears a size four, and who seems to have no trouble staying
slim."

Others also saw in Nancy Reagan the cold smile of a calculating autom-
aton. "I met her shortly after her husband became governor and her
discussions about her daughter and son were so remote and so alien that I
was shocked," said Lenore Hershey, the former editor of *McCall's* and
the *Ladies' Home Journal.* "She wasn't really a mother, and she certainly
wasn't involved with her children at all, particularly her daughter. I
found it quite scary."

But reporters in general seemed fascinated by the chic first lady, and
frequently compared her to Jacqueline Kennedy, whose cool glamour
had retooled the image of the political wife. They were especially en-
grossed by the public spectacle of the Reagans' marriage—her rapt gaze,
his proclamations of eternal love, and their long passionate embraces
when one or the other left a room. "My life began when I married
Ronnie," Nancy repeatedly told the press. "I think I would have died if I
hadn't married him. . . . He is my hero." Reagan responded in kind. "I
can't imagine my life without her," he would say for the next twenty
years. "Obviously, I'm very much in love with her."

Curiosity about the California governor's wife grew in direct proportion to speculation about her husband's political ambitions. "The interest
in her is tremendous. She seems to fascinate people," said Warren
Steibel, television producer for William F. Buckley's "Firing Line," who
made an hour-long documentary in 1967 entitled "Nancy: First Lady of
California." "What I set out to do was give an honest picture of what it's
like to be a governor's wife—the pains, the pleasures, the delights. The
point was to produce a portrait of what Nancy Reagan was really like."

For seven days Steibel's cameras followed the first lady on her rounds,
capturing her as she stalked the carpenters in the corridors of the state
capitol, where she ordered them to hang pictures according to her specifications. "I said I wanted it hung *there,*" she snapped. "No, over *here.*
Put that one there . . . I said *there.*"

"What came through was a very strong, demanding woman who knew
exactly what she wanted and got it," said Steibel. "She was very eager to

do this film and was just great to work with. She was not given prior approval, but she did ask to see the film beforehand, and as a matter of courtesy I showed it to her the day I delivered it to NBC. She loved it."

Before filming, the producer interviewed Nancy in the living room of her Pacific Palisades home, and asked her about her career in Hollywood and some of the movies she had made. "Oh, my goodness, I don't remember any of them," she said. He didn't comprehend the disingenuousness of her response until she left to take a telephone call. He glanced at the bookcase: Eleven large leatherbound scrapbooks were prominently displayed, one for each of the movies that Nancy Davis had made as a starlet.

Following Nancy and Betsy Bloomingdale to the Reagans' former ranch in Malibu, Steibel's cameras unintentionally showed the governor's wife in another round of incessant poor-mouthing as she told her best friend how much she missed the place that the Reagans had been "forced to sell" when they moved to Sacramento. She neglected to mention that the sale of the Malibu ranch for $1.9 million to 20th Century-Fox had for the first time made the Reagans millionaires.

"I remember that during the campaign the longing to get out in the country and breathe the fresh air became almost an ache at times," she said to a background of Rachmaninoff. The camera filmed the petite first lady standing on her toes tearfully stroking the nose of her horse, saying, "I miss you . . . I miss you." From there, Nancy and Betsy got back into the limousine and were driven to the Los Angeles salon of their favorite couturier, James Galanos, where Nancy could not hide her adoration of couture. "She was mad for clothes and I still can see her fairly salivating over all those red dresses," said the producer, who filmed her trying on a dramatic gown with jeweled flowers that cost $1,500. She convinced Galanos that he would get more than his money's worth in publicity if she wore his design in public, so he sold it to her at half-price.

The cameras followed the governor's wife back to Sacramento, where she showed the old governor's mansion to the wives of the governors of Arizona and Oregon. This was the first and only time she had returned to the residence, which she now referred to as "that hideous place."

"Yeah, I know how she hated it, but on camera she was all smiles and very gracious," said the producer. "Of course, it was all staged and measured and carefully considered. I didn't realize how much of an actress she was until we got to the end of the program. I asked her to walk on the beach and do a voice-over of some lines I had written about loving America from sea to shining sea.

" 'Oh, I couldn't read those lines,' she said.

" 'Why not? Why don't you just try it?' I said.

" 'Oh, I just couldn't,' she said. 'These aren't my words. Why don't you leave them. I'll rewrite something myself and we can finish tomorrow.' "

The producer and his crew returned the next day expecting to film the governor's wife reading her revised words. "I couldn't believe it when she read exactly what I had written," said Steibel. "That's when I understood that she was an actress and had needed time to rehearse her lines but couldn't be direct enough to say so. I had wanted to capture something spontaneous, but I couldn't because there was no spontaneity in Nancy. She was always on, always coiffed, always scripted, always playing a part. You never get a real person with her because there isn't one there. It's sad."

The documentary was shown throughout California and in other parts of the country as interest in Ronald Reagan's political future grew.

Nancy publicly scoffed at speculation about her husband's 1968 presidential ambitions. "Our plans don't go any further than Sacramento," she said over and over. Privately, though, she knew how entranced Reagan was by the prospect of higher office. Two months into his governorship, he had announced that he would be a favorite son candidate at the 1968 Republican National Convention, ostensibly to avoid a primary that could split the party. "The Republicans have an excellent chance to win the presidency, Vietnam War or no Vietnam War," he said, "regardless of who the candidate is."

"That's the reason I signed on with him," said Lyn Nofziger many years later. "I wanted Ronald Reagan to be President in 1968, and that's what I was working toward."

Barry Goldwater had talked at length with Reagan during this period, and he later told Vice President Hubert Humphrey about their conversation. Humphrey wrote a confidential memo to President Johnson dated August 23, 1967, about the conversation: "He [Goldwater] tells me that Reagan . . . will not take second spot on a Rockefeller ticket. He said he told Reagan that this was not his time and that Reagan shouldn't kid himself into believing that he could beat Lyndon Johnson. Goldwater said he told Reagan that the same little old ladies in tennis shoes that used to cheer and clap for him did the same thing for Bob Taft and Tom Dewey [both of whom were defeated for President]. In other words, don't be fooled by the enthusiastic response of a handful of hard-core conservative Republicans. He also told me that he didn't think Reagan was ready for the Presidency."

The governor would soon prove Barry Goldwater right. Reagan's reaction to the public disclosure of a homosexual scandal within his administration nearly destroyed him politically. A blind item in *Newsweek* (October 30, 1967) reported that a "top GOP presidential prospect has a potentially sordid scandal on his hands. Private investigators he hired found evidence that two of his aides had committed homosexual acts. The men are no longer working for the GOP leader, but the whole story may surface any day." Nancy Reagan called Lyn Nofziger and told him to "do something" to keep the story from being further publicized, but Nofziger knew that was impossible. He had been part of the small group months before that had confronted the governor with evidence that the two aides, both married with children, had been involved in homosexual activity, some of which involved boys under the age of eighteen.

Professing shock, the governor summoned the men and told them they were out. No charges were pressed, and the men resigned quietly. But the scandal affected others on the governor's staff, including another of his aides, who was suspected of being part of the secret homosexual ring and quickly married. The governor's bodyguard, Art Van Court, who had conducted the private investigation, was subsequently appointed a federal marshal.

"The governor thought that that was the end of it," said Nofziger, "but I knew the story would eventually surface because too many people knew about it. So I decided to lance the boil by leaking it to a few selected journalists and getting it out in the open so we could get it behind us. I knew that was the only way Reagan would ever have a chance to be President. Better it surface in 1967 than to have it come out in the middle of a campaign."

Nancy Reagan never appreciated that political logic; she could not be convinced that the story would have become public with or without Nofziger's intervention. Besides, the messy appearance of the roly-poly aide, who smoked cigars and considered ties an affectation, riled her so much that she could not stand being in his presence. Now she blamed Nofziger for the Drew Pearson column that broke the rancid news in the *New York Post.* The syndicated columnist reported that "a homosexual ring had been operating out of Governor Reagan's office" for six months with his full knowledge and that the governor did not act until pressured by aides into firing the men. The columnist alleged that Art Van Court had a tape recording "of a sex orgy which had taken place at a cabin near Lake Tahoe, leased by two members of Reagan's staff."

The scandal of homosexuality frightened newspaper editors in those days, and many refused to reprint the Pearson column for fear of libel. But the story became national news when Governor Reagan denied everything and called the columnist a liar.

Reagan was bombarded by questions at his weekly press conference about why he was denying what Nofziger had already confirmed, and

Reagan slammed his fist on the lectern and yelled at reporters. He said he refused to identify the two men who had been fired because innocent wives and children were affected. "Now if there is a credibility gap . . . because I refuse to participate in trying to destroy human beings with no factual evidence . . . then there is a credibility gap."

The scandal scorched the governor and singed his administration. A poll by Mervin D. Field showed that 36 percent of California voters thought Reagan's reputation would be harmed by his handling of the episode.

The Reagans immediately adopted a censorious public stance toward homosexuality. He condemned it as "an abomination in the eyes of the Lord," and she denounced it as a "sickness" and an "abnormality." Yet privately they continued to patronize their astrologer, Carroll Righter, a homosexual, and to socialize with a homosexual male couple who were frequently invited to the Bloomingdales' dinner parties. Nancy maintained close relationships with Truman Capote, Roy Cohn, and Jerry Zipkin, who once lived with Somerset Maugham; she depended on homosexual men like her hairdresser and interior decorator to define her style and execute her taste. The governor enjoyed telling homosexual jokes and would act them out with a lisping voice and exaggerated limp-wrist gestures. He would take mincing little steps, swing his hips, and act swishy. Truman Capote visited Reagan's office a few months after the scandal broke to plead for the men on California's death row. The governor joked about the homosexual ring within his administration. Turning to an aide, he said, "Perhaps we should trawl Truman through the halls to see if there are any of them left."

Editorials across the country questioned Reagan's integrity and criticized him for lying. The *Washington Star* viewed him as "the fallen knight" and said "the black mark on Reagan's record is not that he hired such men, or that he was slow in firing them. Where he stumbled was in his histrionic denial and in calling Drew Pearson a liar when he must have known that Pearson's article was factually correct. The motivation of this extraordinary performance is not easily discerned. It was, in any event, a serious error of judgment in Reagan's first real test under pressure. And it must inevitably raise very real doubts about his personal dedication to the truth and his fitness for the high office to which he so obviously aspires."

Such public humiliation of her husband was more than Nancy Reagan could stand. She demanded that Lyn Nofziger be fired on the spot. The governor refused. So she turned to his kitchen cabinet, sending them all the adverse columns and editorials. She then telephoned each one, begging him to call Reagan to demand Nofziger's firing. Most of the men

did as the governor's wife asked them to do, but Reagan remained resolute. Nofziger was his only staff member with national political experience, and the governor needed him. Finally, Lyn Nofziger approached
Reagan himself and offered to resign.

"Nancy is unhappy, and she's telling people she wants me out," he
said.

"No, she isn't doing that, Lyn."

"Well, Governor, she is."

"I want you to stay."

"Governor, I can't be effective for you if your wife continues like
this."

"It's not going on, but if it is going on, it won't go on anymore," said
Reagan. "Please. I want you to stay."

"I will stay until after the convention because I want to be part of the
effort toward the presidency, but that's it."

Nancy reluctantly stopped trying to orchestrate Nofziger's firing, but
she didn't speak to him for the next five months.

Publicly, Governor Reagan denied he was launching a presidential
drive as he made fund-raising trips to Iowa, Kansas, Texas, Illinois, and
Ohio. At the Republican governors conference in Washington, D.C.,
Nancy Reagan told reporters she was under enormous pressure from
conference delegates to urge her husband to announce his candidacy,
although the GOP front-runners were Richard Nixon and Nelson
Rockefeller.

Governor Reagan accepted a Chubb Fellowship for four days of lecturing at Yale University in the winter of 1967 in hopes of improving his
tarnished image. He wanted to convince the powerful Eastern establishment that he was not some homophobic Hollywood cowboy who rode
into the statehouse on a slap and a smile. Nancy, of course, accompanied
him on the trip and took a few hours off to visit Smith College, her first
trip there since graduation in 1943. "This is where my heart is," she said
as she toured the campus.

"One of my friends was showing Mrs. Reagan around and unfortunately brought her to her old room on the second floor of Talbot House,
which was quite messy and filled with a bunch of us smoking and playing
bridge in our underwear," said Kate Beardsley, class of 1970. "All I care
to say about her reaction is that she was not a terribly polite person."

Nancy was even more distressed when she saw the new Center for the
Performing Arts a few blocks away. She later wrote her impressions for
the Smith alumnae newsletter:

"I did all those things that you shouldn't do like going back to your
old house and your old room. They showed me the new theatre building,

which is fabulous and I said it was, but I then had to follow it by saying that I hoped that they would tell all of their students who were really seriously thinking of going into the theatre that they would never find anything like that in the professional theatre, that the only place they had to go from there was down. And somehow I think that's all backwards. I think you should work up instead of down. I don't think it should all be handed to you in college, this fancy a package. It was pointed out with great pride that now they had a system whereby you don't have to bend down to paint the scenery. You just stand there and this thing rolls by and you put your brush out and it's painted. God forbid, you should bend down or reach up. I know that sounds marvelous but I'm not sure it is. I don't really believe in making the campuses quite this plush."

Some of Nancy's classmates were disappointed by her comments. "I don't understand the Cinderella attitude Nancy has about herself," said Mary Ann Guitar, "but I guess it's a typical ideology of her and her group: 'I had it rough so I don't want to make it nice for anyone else. Let them work as hard as I had to work. I'm entitled to everything I've got because I really worked for it. You welfare mothers don't work so you're not entitled.' It's very odd, indeed."

In New Haven, Connecticut, a two-hour drive from Smith's campus in Northampton, Massachusetts, Governor Reagan was receiving a much more enthusiastic response as he sat on a desk at Yale conducting a class in American history. He disarmed the Ivy League students by saying that he had never taught anything before, except swimming and Sunday school. They all laughed, gave him a standing ovation, and rushed to shake his hand afterward. In a later press conference, though, he was hit with a few hostile questions.

"Should homosexuals be barred from holding public office?"

"It's a tragic illness," said the governor. "Yes, I do think that homosexuality should remain illegal."

"Do you feel that homosexuals have any place in government?"

"Well, perhaps in the Department of Parks and Recreation," he said, touching off a tirade from department workers in California who branded his remarks as "tasteless, undignified, and crude."

"That trip was really tough for the Reagans," recalled Susan Granger, the daughter of Armand and Harriet Deutsch. "My husband and I were living in New Haven at the time, and Nancy called to say that they would be staying at Timothy Dwight College. I invited her to lunch and to come on my radio show, but she said that she was to be entertained by the master of the college and his wife. But then the wife was so horrid to her that she called me back and said she would have time to spend with me after all.

"Apparently, when the Reagans arrived, they were shown to their room, where the professor's wife had stacked all this filthy, virulent, anti-Reagan reading material on their bed stands. Nancy said that when the governor was picked up for his first appearance on campus, the professor's wife turned to her and said, 'Well, Mrs. Movie Star, I'm sure you have a lot of plans of your own, and I do, too, so I will see you later.' With that, she waltzed out of the room and left poor Nancy sitting there with all those horrid books.

"So she [Nancy] called me, and we had lunch together; then I interviewed her on my radio show. That evening my husband and I went over to join them and the professor [the master] and his wife for drinks before Ronnie's big dinner speech. There were just the six of us. The professor said, 'What would you like to drink, Governor?'

" 'I'll have a vodka martini,' said Ronnie.

" 'Sorry, Governor. At Yale we make our martinis with gin.'

" 'I'm sure that's the way a martini should be made, but I'm allergic to gin, so I'd like vodka, please.'

" 'Yes, but at Yale we drink only gin martinis.'

"My husband was so incensed by this rudeness that he jumped up and said, 'Look, Governor, I'll make it for you myself,' and he did. There had been tremendous controversy over inviting Ronald Reagan on campus, and the hosting professor and his wife were obviously part of the liberal faculty that did not want the Reagans there. The whole school did not feel this way, but there was enough animosity to make things uncomfortable. The Reagans were great, though, very charming and nice the whole time. Nancy rose above it completely, saying, 'Look, it's important for Ronnie to be a Chubb Fellow at Yale, and I'll be as gracious as I have to be for that.' And she was."

Ever since the homosexual scandal, the governor's wife had become fiercely protective of her husband's image, which led to her becoming quietly but intimately involved in his official business. Behind the scenes, she became a key player in the affairs of state, and to accomplish this, she worked closely with her best friend's husband, Alfred Bloomingdale, a former theatrical producer whose grandfather had founded the department store bearing his name. During the time she had tried to get Lyn Nofziger fired, she was on the phone to Bloomingdale every day. He had told her that he had a telephone on his desk at work that he alone answered; only his wife and children had the private number. He told Nancy to call him anytime on that phone with any problem concerning the governor.

"That began the daily 'I-have-a-problem' calls from the governor's wife," said Bloomingdale's former executive assistant, Sheldon Davis.

"She called Alfred every morning and throughout the day, and they discussed how to get things done for Ronnie, especially things that were a little messy or had to be handled delicately through back channels. They talked about everything, from getting legislation passed to handling the California Board of Regents to dodging the recall movement that was launched against the governor.

"Both Nancy and Betsy were consumed by how they and their husbands appeared in the press," said Davis. "Anytime Alfred was described as Al, Betsy was on the horn yelling at me. 'I want this stopped immediately, Shelly,' she'd say. 'I won't have it. The name Al is disgusting. It makes him sound like he's still in show business. I just won't have it.' "

Nancy monitored her husband's press just as closely, and whenever she was displeased she telephoned him in the office. One of the governor's aides heard her call to complain about the militant Eldridge Cleaver, who had uttered profanities about Reagan when the governor tried—and failed—to prevent the black activist from lecturing at the University of California at Berkeley. "But honey, I can't have him arrested just because he says those things," he was heard explaining to his wife.

During an abortive recall movement in 1968, caused by Reagan's controversial cutbacks in health and education expenditures, Nancy became inflamed when she saw the bumper stickers that said, REAGAN FOR PRESIDENT—SHARE THE BURDEN; IMPEACH BONZO AND HIS CO-STAR; and JANE WYMAN WAS RIGHT!

"She was on the phone every hour of the day trying to get Alfred to figure out a way to get people with those bumper stickers arrested and thrown in jail," Davis said with a laugh as he recalled Bloomingdale's efforts to calm the first lady.

When the state's finance director made a statement in Los Angeles contradicting what the governor had said in Sacramento, Nancy called her husband, who was talking with a reporter at the time.

"It's my wife," said the governor when he took the call. "Yes, dear. Yes, dear. . . . No, dear, I don't think he was being insubordinate. . . . It's just when I say something in Sacramento and he says something in Los Angeles, we'll have to get together."

After hanging up, the governor said to the reporter, "She bleeds pretty good. Sometimes I come home and find she's pretty sore about something I laugh off. It's much harder on them [wives] than it is on us—there's no way for them to fight back."

Nancy worked behind the scenes. "Usually by getting someone like Alfred to do her dirty work," said Davis. "She was always hollering about some hippie who'd just called the governor a pig.

"In the beginning, some of the longest discussions between Nancy and

Alfred centered on Ronnie's covert grab for the presidential nomination in 1968. He wanted it, and Alfred wanted him to have it, but no one could admit publicly what we were all doing privately to bring it about."

Three of the governor's kitchen cabinet—William Wilson, Earle Jorgensen, and Bloomingdale—had managed to get themselves elected as delegates to the Republican National Convention, where they were part of the delegate bloc pledged to Reagan as a favorite son. Although Richard Nixon seemed to be assured the nomination, Reagan's eighty-six delegates hoped for a deadlocked convention so they could declare themselves and perhaps swing the convention to their candidate. They had hired F. Clifton White, the political consultant who had choreographed the Draft Goldwater movement in 1964, to plan Reagan's preconvention maneuverings.

While declaring himself a noncandidate and hiding under the façade of favorite son, the California governor went to seventeen states looking for delegates. When asked why her husband would undertake such an itinerary if he wasn't running for President, his wife said, "Oh, Ronnie just likes to make speeches."

Alfred Bloomingdale understood the power of packaging and presentation. He told Nancy that her husband had to go to the Republican convention in Miami looking like a winner. He said he would hire someone to help her plan some strategic entertaining of the press and some of the undecided delegates, and he would pay the costs. He also chartered a plane to fly the Reagans to Florida, while Betsy Bloomingdale and Betty Wilson, the wife of Bill Wilson, paid for their Beverly Hills hairdresser to be on duty for Nancy as well.

"I was Alfred's guy in Miami that year," said John Monahan, "and at his direction I worked closely with Nancy Reagan to find a yacht decorated by Carleton Varney which would be the appropriate place for her to host her various luncheons. I recall her as a pleasant-looking lady who was very polite and did not show one bead of perspiration in the middle of August in Florida. She was firm with service people but ladylike, and she definitely knew what she wanted."

"I found her to be a royal pain," said former FBI agent Clarence Newton, who handled some of Governor Reagan's security detail at the convention. "I was supposed to accompany her to a luncheon because we had been told there was going to be a lot of disruptive hippies and demonstrators—remember, this was the height of the Vietnam War protests—so I met Nancy in front of the Fontainbleu Hotel, where people were pushing in from all sides. I got in front of her and she grabbed the back of my coat and said, 'Okay, broadback, let's go,' as if I was some kind of hired gorilla who was supposed to part the waters for her."

As her husband courted delegates, Nancy made the political rounds of women's luncheons, always making herself available to the press, careful never to say anything controversial and to recite only scripted, practiced lines. At one point, she was asked about Vietnam and she smiled. "I don't talk about political matters," she said. "That's not my department."

"If you don't want to answer the questions, Mrs. Reagan, why did you come?"

The color drained from Nancy's face. She looked directly at her questioner and replied evenly, "I thought you wanted to know about me."

At the time, Charlotte Curtis of the *New York Times* thought Nancy was hostile. Years later she said she believed that Nancy was actually terrified.

The governor's wife continued answering reporters' questions with the pat little answers she had developed to give away nothing. "When Ronnie and I made the decision to go into politics, it cost us many sleepless nights," she said. "We knew it meant giving up all privacy and not gaining financially—and that certainly is true. But we both felt strongly there had to be a change and we felt we had to make the decision we made."

Hungry for a story, the reporters wanted to know what she thought about the possibility of her husband's becoming Vice President if Nelson Rockefeller were to get the nomination.

Nancy despised the liberal multimillionaire governor of New York, but she smiled sweetly. "My husband is not a candidate for Vice President," she said. "He feels he can implement his philosophy and ideas more as governor of California than as Vice President, and I certainly agree with that."

"How do you feel about becoming First Lady of America?"

"I know nobody believes me, but I really have never thought about living in the White House," she said. "I think the governor's mansion in California looks twice as good."

Maggie Savoy of the *Los Angeles Times* gasped at this comment from the woman who had publicly run down the state's executive residence.

Nancy recognized that her husband's quest could not possibly be rewarded at this convention. As a noncandidate, he had rounded up nearly one-quarter of the GOP primary votes in Nebraska and Oregon, making for a committed delegate count of about 200, but he was a long way from becoming a serious challenger to Nixon, who was assured 700 delegate votes on the first ballot and needed only 667 to win. Not even Alfred Bloomingdale, with all his millions, could transform a little groundswell for Reagan into a tidal wave. So the next day, Nancy called a press conference to say that her husband was not a candidate for the Republican presidential nomination. Then she left to get her hair done.

A half hour later, Governor Reagan called a press conference and unknowingly contradicted his wife by announcing that he was indeed a candidate for President.

"Oh, no," she said, sinking into a chair when she heard the news. "Well, how about that. . . . I am surprised, completely surprised, but . . . but . . . I'm very glad if that's what he wants to do. It's just that no woman would want the man she loves in the presidency. It's so tremendous, so awesome a job. . . ."

The next night, Nancy walked into the convention hall with her parents to watch the demonstration for her husband after he was nominated.

On the way home, Governor Reagan shrugged off his embarrassing loss at the convention. "How can you lose when you can go back to being governor of California?" he said. "I'm not exactly unemployed, you know." Figuring that Nixon would win the White House that year and hold it for two terms, Reagan had already decided to run for reelection to the statehouse in 1970, thus putting himself in a much better position for the presidency in 1976.

Pledging total support for the Republican ticket, Reagan made speeches on behalf of Nixon and his running mate, Spiro Agnew, who would become a close personal friend. During the campaign, Reagan met an eighteen-year-old girl.

"It was a brief meeting but it was very sweet," said Patricia Taylor, who later dedicated a book of her poetry to Reagan.

"I was in California at a party in Studio City in October of 1968," she said. "I was the youngest person at the party, and I had had a fight with my boyfriend. I went outside to sulk by the swimming pool, and that's where I met Ronnie. He had come in with two or three other men. He had a drink in his hand and he started talking to me. He asked what I was doing outside, because it was very chilly. I told him I was upset with my boyfriend. He was trying to be nice to me and I was feeling awfully sorry for myself. He wanted to comfort me and I let him. One thing led to another. He led me back in the house through a doorway that led up to a loft bedroom and we laid down to make love. He was very gentle and very passionate. He was no prude. I didn't realize he was the governor then. Being eighteen, I guess I was more interested in myself, you know? But he was great. Just great."

As a married man, the fifty-seven-year-old governor was not known to play around. "He liked to look at women—no doubt about that—but if he did anything about it, he was very discreet," said a former top aide. "There were rumors about an affair with his young private secretary, Helene von Damm, but as soon as Nancy got wind of it, she refused to let Helene travel with him anymore, and that was the end of that."

A few years later, reflecting on the sanctity of marriage vows, Governor Reagan wrote a letter to his son Michael on the eve of his wedding, saying: "Some men feel their masculinity can only be proven if they play out in their own life all the locker-room stories, smugly confident that what a wife doesn't know won't hurt her. The truth is, somehow, way down inside, without her ever finding lipstick on the collar or catching a man in the flimsy excuse of where he was till 3 A.M., the wife does know, and with that knowing some of the magic of this relationship disappears. . . . Any man can find a twerp here and there who will go along with cheating and it doesn't take all that much manhood. . . . If you truly love a girl, you shouldn't ever want her to feel, when she sees you greet a secretary, or a girl you both know, that humiliation of wondering if she was someone who caused you to be late coming home, nor should you want any other woman to be able to meet your wife and know she was smiling behind her eyes as she looked at her, the woman you love, remembering this was the woman you rejected even momentarily for her favors."

Returning to Sacramento after the 1968 convention, the governor's vigilant wife resumed her daily phone calls to Alfred Bloomingdale. "She called Alfred every single day, at least once or twice, when Ronnie was governor," said Sheldon Davis. "She even sent the governor in to see Alfred a few times when he was fighting the Board of Regents of the University of California. Usually, when Nancy called, there was some sort of crisis; sometimes she'd need Alfred's advice about getting legislation passed, or getting something defeated that Ronnie didn't want to go through. She called about student demonstrators, and how to get Ronnie a better image in the press because he was being attacked as antistudent and antieducation. Nancy and Alfred were in constant communication every day of the week—we used to laugh about how the two of them were running the state of California—and then they saw each other socially on the weekends, when they talked some more.

"I remember Alfred coming into the office one Monday morning and laughing his head off about a small dinner party the Bloomingdales had given on Saturday night. The Reagans were there, the Bloomingdales, the Jack Bennys, and the George Burnses, I think; I forget who else was there. Anyway, they were all sitting around the dining room table eating Betsy's famous peach ice cream for dessert and talking about drugs and the problems with the kids on campuses. Someone said, 'What's the big deal with this marijuana stuff anyway? What the hell is it?' Nobody knew anything about it, except what they had read or heard from their children. So Alfred went upstairs and got a joint that he had bought that afternoon from a hooker. He took it down to them, lit it, and passed it around so everyone could take a few toots. Within five minutes they all started giggling but claimed they didn't feel a thing and said they couldn't see what the big deal was. Alfred said it was so funny to watch Jack Benny and then the governor and his wife smoking pot. He laughed like hell every time he talked about it."

On another weekend, the Reagans and the Bloomingdales attended the opening night of the Mark Taper Forum in the Los Angeles Music Center. The evening's presentation was *The Devils* by John Whiting, a drama based on Aldous Huxley's nonfiction *The Devils of Loudun,* a study of witchcraft and debauchery in a church and nunnery in seventeenth-century France.

"The play deals with a libertine priest who got into trouble with authorities because of his loose sexual behavior and a nun who had erotic fantasies about this priest and suffered from hysteria," said Gordon Davidson, artistic director of the Mark Taper Forum. "The play also deals with the violent way the community responds to these two people who did not follow accepted codes of behavior. In the end, the priest is hanged.

"It was quite controversial. The conservative Catholic segment of Los Angeles was up in arms, the Board of Supervisors threatened to set up a censorship board, and on opening night Governor and Mrs. Reagan walked out in the middle of the play with their friends, the Bloomingdales. The irony of Alfred Bloomingdale's taking such a high moral stand was not fully appreciated at the time. Only in retrospect, when you know about the sadomasochistic games he played—riding piggyback and then whipping Vicki Morgan, his mistress of so many years—does his righteousness that evening seem amusing."

Nancy Reagan had long ignored the gamy side of the man who was now her fixer. She needed him to solve many problems for the governor, including the crisis that hit California in late December 1969 when employees at every racetrack in the state went on strike, costing the treasury $300,000 a day. Racetrack revenues brought $60 million to California's coffers in 1969, and profits were expected to exceed $65 million in 1970.

When her husband couldn't bring about an agreement by the end of January, Nancy began to worry. She knew he couldn't raise taxes to cover the lost revenue because he'd already hit the state with the highest income tax ever levied. So she called Alfred Bloomingdale, who she knew had ties to organized crime.

"She was desperate," said a former Bloomingdale aide. "She said, 'You've got to do something—and fast.' I was in the room when that call came, and I heard Alfred's side of the conversation and part of hers. She

said, 'I want that strike settled, and I don't care how.' When Mrs. Reagan
told Alfred to go to Sidney Korshak if he had to, I nearly fell over.''

Long accused of having ties to the Mafia, Korshak is a Los Angeles
labor lawyer who does not have a law office, a staff, stationery, business
cards, or a listed telephone. All he needs are his negotiating skills, which
are enhanced by the menacing aura of the Mafia.

"As soon as Alfred got off the phone with Nancy, I was sent to see
Korshak at Associated Booking Corporation in Beverly Hills—in a room
with no windows, no name on the door, no listed address. I walked in
and told him that someone wanted the strike settled. He asked me who,
and I told him about Mrs. Reagan's call to Bloomingdale. I said Nancy
and the governor were very upset about the strike and what it was costing the state. I said they were desperate to get it settled. He listened. He
smiled, and then he said, 'All right. The strike will be settled by Monday.
On one condition.'

" 'What's that, Sidney?'

" 'Just let the governor and his wife know who did it.'

" 'No problem,' I said.

"I then went back to see Alfred, whose Diners Club office was on the
seventh floor of 1801 Avenue of the Stars, and told him about my meeting. It was Friday afternoon. He called Nancy and said that thanks to
Sidney Korshak the strike would be settled by Monday. And I'll be
damned if the union pickets didn't suddenly disappear and the deadlock
that had gripped both sides for twenty-eight days didn't miraculously
melt away, and lo and behold, if it wasn't post time exactly when Sidney
Korshak had promised it would be. I don't know if he ever collected on
that favor because I never asked. But since then I've always thought of
Nancy Reagan as the female version of the Godfather because she's certainly a woman who knows how to get things done without leaving any
fingerprints!''

11

THE CURTSYING LESSONS began shortly after President Nixon appointed Walter Annenberg ambassador to the Court of St. James's. "The girls," as Nancy Reagan called her little clique, hoped to go to London to meet the Queen now that their friends, the Annenbergs, were so perfectly situated. But unaccustomed to meeting royalty, "the girls" fretted about the proper protocol over lunch at Harriet Deutsch's house.

"Those women were in a dither about what to wear and what to say and whether to curtsy to Queen Elizabeth or not," recalled KNBC-TV reporter Linda Douglas, who was then married to Steve Deutsch, Harriet's (and Armand's) son. "They were all rich enough to wear $1,000 suits by Galanos, but they didn't know the first thing about breeding, so they spent three hours practicing their curtsies. It was a scream. The first hour they all did deep bows from the waist; the second hour they did what they called the Jackie Kennedy dip, which is what she did when Prince Philip came to the White House to pay his respects following the assassination of President Kennedy. The third hour they rehearsed little knee-bend curtsies before deciding that that's what they should do. They didn't know that Americans aren't supposed to bow to foreign dignitaries." As it turned out, they needn't have bothered. They never met the Queen.

"The girls," all wives of self-made business tycoons who swore political allegiance to Ronald Reagan, were not to the manner born. Nor were they schooled in the niceties of old-family decorum. Most were former actresses and divorced models who acquired their taste from their interior decorators—who studiously tutored them in fine furniture and good food, the superficial marks of cultivation—and their style from fashion designers accustomed to making mutton look like lamb.

"She runs a great house" was the supreme compliment for any of these women whose grandiose homes were their testaments to the world, and who judged one another by the efficiency of their servants. Behind their gleaming front doors, though, lurked a commonness that might have barred them in better circles.

"People who don't come from much money and then go into a social milieu higher than they are accustomed to are sometimes nervous about acting right," said Ellen Pollon, a Gucci saleswoman in Beverly Hills. "They do nothing at all so they won't make mistakes, and that's why Nancy Reagan is so rigid. She's really not very sophisticated. She didn't always know how to act around Europeans. The same with Harriet Deutsch, who was once a salesgirl, and poor Betsy Bloomingdale, who wore her tiara to a ball before the royal wedding in 1981. Everyone knows you don't wear a tiara or crown in front of royalty."

Most of "the girls" were married to fast-buck, brash, self-made millionaires who earned their money in the get-rich-quick areas—nursing homes, used cars, oil, and gas—not in the professions of law, medicine, and banking. Such wealth might not have been acceptable to the Cabots of Boston, but it made little difference in the social circles of Beverly Hills.

Some of the husbands, like Alfred Bloomingdale and Reese Milner, kept mistresses on the side, and these secret liaisons eventually became public scandals. Bloomingdale died of lung cancer in 1982, and his death led to the unraveling of his sordid private life. His mistress, Vicki Morgan, made public his perverted sexual practices when Betsy cut off the $18,000-a-month allowance he had been paying. So the mistress sued the wife. The Bloomingdale name was muddied again a few months later when Vicki was murdered by her roommate, a homosexual who beat her to death with a baseball bat.

Several years before, Reese Milner was indicted for hiring two ex-convicts to torture, rob, and murder his mistress. He had commissioned the thugs to use a bolt cutter to cut off one of the woman's fingers because she had bitten off one of his fingers. Milner was sentenced to one to five years in prison for the assault, which also included robbery and mayhem.

When Walter Annenberg was selected to be ambassador to Great Britain, he was elevated to the ranks of his socially prominent predecessors—John Adams, Winthrop Aldrich, and David Bruce. In this position of international influence and prestige, the Jewish publisher could finally rise above the underworld reputation of his father, Moses ("Moe"), who made $6 million a year running a racetrack wire for bookies. The elder Annenberg was convicted of income-tax evasion. Sentenced to three years in prison, he served one year before he died of a brain tumor. His son spent the rest of his life trying to give the family dignity by making sizable donations to charity.

"The girls" were edified by the Annenbergs' spending more than $1 million to refurbish Winfield House, the stately London residence of the American ambassador. These women, who cared passionately about accoutrements, sat transfixed when Leonore Annenberg returned to Los Angeles and related every trifling detail about installing new gilded walls, Louis XV chandeliers, imported Portuguese needlepoint rugs, lotus-patterned Lowestoft china, and Ming chests. The eighteenth-century Chinese wallpaper taken from a great hall at Trinity College, Dublin, was sent to New York for gilding and cleaning, to Hong Kong for repairs, and back to New York for antiquing and pressing before the precious strips were applied to the drawing room. "The girls" could hardly wait to see the results.

When the Reagans went to London in November 1969, where the governor was to address the Institute of Directors in Royal Albert Hall, they became the Annenbergs' first houseguests. The Bloomingdales accompanied the Reagans, but they stayed at Claridge's.

"Nancy Reynolds and I also went on that trip," said Jody Jacobs, "and the entire way over on the plane we talked about doing my *Women's Wear Daily* interview with Nancy Reagan in the embassy residence, but once Lee Annenberg got wind of that, she took me aside and said that she had spent too much time and effort on the house to have anyone but herself be the first one interviewed there. When Nancy Reynolds and I told that to Nancy Reagan, she just shrugged and said, 'It figures.' "

This was Nancy Reagan's first trip to Europe since she was twelve years old, when she had been taken by her parents to see Josephine Baker in Paris. Miss Baker's barefoot and topless dancing had so shocked Loyal Davis that he left the show during intermission, taking his wife and daughter with him. Reagan's only trip abroad had been in 1948 when Warner Bros. sent him to London to make *The Hasty Heart.*

Now, the fifty-eight-year-old governor and his forty-eight-year-old wife were traveling on diplomatic passports with the blessing of the President of the United States. The month before, they had flown in a presidential jet to the Philippines with Patti and Ron to represent Richard Nixon at the opening of the Cultural Center on Manila Bay. That was the beginning of their close friendship with Ferdinand and Imelda Marcos, who through the years would give Nancy thousands of dollars' worth of clothing and jewelry. "That didn't stop Nancy from making fun of Imelda later by telling us about all the billboards she had seen which said: 'This new road comes to you via the generosity of your First Lady,'" said a friend. Nancy also complained about cockroaches in the Malacañang Palace bedroom where they stayed. "The Reagans called for one of [the] Marcoses' servants, who came running in with a big spray can and killed the roach," said Mike Deaver, one of the governor's aides. "'Don't worry about it,' the servant said, 'they just come from the kitchen.' Somehow that didn't make the Reagans feel any better."

No such indignities had to be endured on the nine-day trip to London and Paris in the winter of 1969, although Nancy later mentioned a banging window sash or shutter that flapped and kept her awake at night. And Governor Reagan complained about the embassy servants being *too* efficient and swooping in to wash his underwear before he had a chance to do it himself.

As it turned out, the highlight of that trip for Nancy was the time the Reagans spent in Paris with the Bloomingdales, who arranged for a tour of Versailles with curator Gerald Van der Kemp's special guide, Madame Erlich ("When she talked about Marie Antoinette and Louis XVI walking out of separate rooms for their wedding, I could see them," said Nancy). Betsy Bloomingdale took her to the House of Dior ("They'll file my measurements so I can order by mail," said Nancy), and arranged for her to have her hair done by Alexandre, the Parisian hairdresser made famous by the Duchess of Windsor ("Can you believe that I actually had to rebrush it afterwards at the hotel myself? And there were dogs everywhere, and everyone was shouting. I don't do so well under those conditions"). The pièce de résistance at the Van der Kemp dinner party was meeting the Duchess herself. That meant more than the possibility of meeting the Queen of England, for to Nancy Reagan the vacuous Wallis Warfield Simpson symbolized the height of class.

Nancy and Betsy had spent hours gossiping about the rarefied lives of the Duke and Duchess, how they dressed for dinner every night of their lives, how their servants unrolled their toilet paper and cut it into prepared squares for them, how their kitchen boy sorted their salad leaves and matched them for size, how footmen wearing navy blue uniforms served their pug dogs meals in silver bowls.

"The Duchess was the star of the evening," Nancy told *Women's Wear Daily,* "the absolute star. . . . Her yellow Givenchy dress over pants was so beautiful even Ronnie mentioned it. . . . It's not just that she looks so good. It's her charm and the way she has of making you feel you're the most important person in the world when she's talking to you.

. . . And the Duke of Windsor . . . oh, he was wonderful. . . . He told Ronnie, 'I'm completely behind what you stand for.' Since the Duke is in agreement with Ronnie, do you think he'd come to America and campaign for him?''

Most political wives would not want the public support of a man who had once socialized with Adolf Hitler and then admitted that he had been taken in by the Nazi leader. But Nancy was captivated by the Windsors.

The governor had not yet announced his intention to run for reelection, but the decision to do so had been made by both Reagans. As much as they hated living in Sacramento during the week—"It's a Democratic city," said Nancy—they relished their positions of power, the governor as much as the governor's wife, and recognized that without the office their lives would be deflated and devoid of glamour.

Winning a second term seemed to be a foregone conclusion for Reagan. He was running against the big-bellied, cigar-chomping speaker of the state assembly, Democrat Jesse Unruh. He had been described as the century's most important state legislator and was famous for his proclamation that "Money is the mother's milk of politics." A raffish, backroom politician, the assemblyman could hardly compete against the trim, sun-bronzed movie star governor who looked ten years younger than his age. Even after dieting off ninety pounds, Unruh still could not shed his startling resemblance to "Big Daddy," the corpulent patriarch in Tennessee Williams's *Cat on a Hot Tin Roof.*

Unruh railed against Reagan for higher taxes, sky-rocketing welfare costs, increased crime and violent disorders on campus, saying all those problems had worsened during his four years as governor. But Unruh had no money for newspaper advertising, billboards, television, or radio and could not get his message across. The governor was rolling to victory on a hefty bankroll of $1.8 million, with the kitchen cabinet working overtime to keep the coffers full.

"I was approached by Grace Salvatori to donate to Reagan's reelection in 1970," recalled Mary Bogdonovich Dexter, an heiress to the Starkist Foods fortune. "I had contributed $25,000 to Richard Nixon's presidential campaign in 1968 because of Grace, and so she invited me to a private reception at the Century-Plaza Hotel to meet the Reagans. She took me to their suite, where we had to wait our turn to go in for a one-on-one meeting. It was like going to confession. Jack Warner of Warner Bros. was ahead of us, and when he came out, we went in. Grace walked in front of me to talk to Nancy. She told her that I was an important person for the Reagans to know, but before she could finish, Nancy cut her off, and asked, 'Well, just how rich *is* she?'

"Grace was terribly embarrassed to have me overhear that comment, and mumbled something about my father being the founder of Starkist. I walked over then, extended my hand, and introduced myself. I complimented Mrs. Reagan on the Persian turquoise-and-diamond earrings she was wearing—I had a similar pair with a matching necklace, bracelet, and brooch at home—and then I left. I never contributed a dime to Ronald Reagan because of his ill-bred wife and her rudeness, and I never will."

But thousands of dollars did roll in to the Reagan reelection campaign, and leading the list was Dr. Loyal Davis's $1,000 contribution, followed by $2,500 each from the tire company executive Leonard Firestone; Henry Salvatori; Holmes Tuttle; Taft Schrieber, Reagan's former agent at MCA; Jack Warner; Art Linkletter; and Roy Disney.

The biggest contributor turned out to be a liberal Democrat who had hated the Reagans so much he would leave any room they entered. Frank Sinatra quickly redirected his enmity when the only other option was Jesse Unruh, a Kennedy disciple who had refused to support Hubert Humphrey, Sinatra's beloved friend and candidate for President in 1968, at the Democratic National Convention. "Unruh hurt my man badly in Chicago," said Sinatra. "In fact, he hurt the whole Democratic party. Humphrey didn't lose. His people lost for him."

Suddenly, Ronald Reagan no longer struck Sinatra as "boring and stupid." Subscribing to the old proverb that "Revenge is a dish best eaten cold," Sinatra decided to announce his support for the conservative Republican. In addition, he would be co-chairman of Democrats for Reagan and stage benefits throughout the state that would raise more than $500,000 for the campaign.

After being assured of Sinatra's goodwill by the Annenbergs and the Deutsches, Reagan asked Sinatra to work for his reelection and was almost as jubilant as Nancy when the singer agreed to do so. A public statement was drafted by the Reagan campaign staff and the announcement on July 9, 1970, was carried as a major news story. "Sinatra Explodes Political Bomb," said a headline in the *Los Angeles Times.*

"I have been and will continue to be a registered Democrat [but] it is my duty as a citizen to put aside partisan considerations when I think the other party's candidate is clearly the outstanding candidate for the office," said Sinatra's statement. "Those who do not know Governor Reagan and me, as we have known each other for more than 20 years, may be surprised by this announcement. However . . . we share the same desires for the welfare of the people of the state of California and the nation."

Reactions to the Sinatra defection were swift.

Stunned, Jesse Unruh said, "You've got to be kidding."

"I can't believe it," said former governor Edmund "Pat" Brown.

"Frank has always been a good Democrat and one of my strongest supporters. He knows the tragedy of the Reagan administration, and maybe we can get him to change his mind."

"It's a shock," said comedian Joey Bishop, once a member of Sinatra's Rat Pack.

"It figures," said Peter Lawford, a Kennedy in-law.

The *Hollywood Citizen-News* ran an editorial saying that although Frank Sinatra was a great entertainer and his politics were his own business, "we can't help but feel sorrow that he chooses to lend his support to a man whose accomplishments as governor preclude a second term."

The *Los Angeles Times* disagreed and endorsed Reagan for reelection despite what it called "our acknowledged disagreements with the Governor."

"I don't agree with everything Reagan does, and I told him so," said Sinatra. "But what do you do? It's better than not voting. I told Reagan that. I feel we have the right to make a choice, and I took Reagan. By the same token, if Reagan ran for President against Humphrey, I'd come out for Humphrey. I'll say one thing: Reagan believes what he does. He's a very honest guy. Now Nixon scares me. He's running the country into the ground. I wouldn't be surprised if they dump him in '72."

But a reporter asked Sinatra, "How can you support a man who just withdrew $10 million in welfare aid for California's aged, blind, and disabled?"

"Did Reagan do that? Did he really do that?" asked Sinatra.

"He certainly did."

"Well, I suppose you don't withdraw your support for a candidate over one issue, but I'll look into it. And you can bet I'll speak to him about it."

During this time, the Internal Revenue Service was conducting an investigation at Caesars Palace in Las Vegas into the relationship between the entertainment industry and the Mafia. Frank Sinatra was among the targets of IRS surveillance. During the graveyard shift on September 6, 1970, the undercover agent working in the cashier's cage watched as one of Sinatra's entourage approached the window with a pile of black chips and walked away with $7,500 in cash. The agent had been watching Sinatra carefully for weeks because the singer was cashing in chips that had not been deducted from his salary and were not paid for by his winnings. To make matters worse, he was bragging that when he performed at Caesars and then sat down to gamble, he attracted so much big money that the casino profited enough so that his markers didn't need to be repaid.

Sinatra kept cashing in his chips throughout the night until the IRS agent finally summoned the manager, Sanford Waterman, who confronted Frank and demanded $10,000 in cash.

"That's when the trouble started, and Frank called Waterman a kike and Sandy called him a son of a bitch guinea," said the IRS undercover agent. "They went back and forth like that in front of a big crowd of people, including three security guards, until Sandy whipped out his pistol and popped it between Sinatra's eyeballs. . . . Sinatra laughed and called him a crazy Hebe. He said he'd never work at Caesars again and walked out."

The next day the district attorney said he was going to call Frank in for a little talk to ask him about his ties to the Mafia. "One remark he supposedly made to Waterman as he was going out the door was, 'The mob will take care of you,' " the DA said. "I wanted to ask him about who owned the nightclubs where he sang in the early days, who started him on his way, and his friendships with the underworld."

The Las Vegas sheriff was equally outraged. "I'm tired of him intimidating waiters, waitresses, and starting fires and throwing pies," he said. "He gets away with too much. He's through picking on the little people in this town. Why the owners of the hotels put up with this is what I plan to find out."

None of this negative publicity seemed to matter to Ronald Reagan. When reporters asked him about the incident at Caesars Palace, he stoutly defended his new friend. "Why don't you fellows ask me about the good things he's done, like Richmond, Indiana," he said, alluding to the benefit Sinatra and Jerry Lewis had staged to educate the nine children of the former police chief Dan A. Mitrione, who had been kidnapped and killed in Uruguay by Tupamaro leftist guerrillas.

Sinatra campaigned in earnest for the governor, performing at fundraisers up and down the state, singing his silky ballads for $125-a-plate audiences and raising $90,000 in one night. In a ballroom of the San Francisco Hilton, he mesmerized 2,500 Reagan supporters, and the governor bounced up on stage at the end of the show to express his thanks.

"Most people believe that politics is a game of quid pro quo," said Reagan. "But I want to assure you that following Frank's endorsement of me, it is only the sheerest coincidence that there is going to be a freeway run right through the lobby of Caesars Palace."

Nancy clapped like an enchanted ingenue. Her infatuation with Sinatra was obvious. Even the governor's staff noticed how she took every opportunity to be in his presence and how she flushed with excitement whenever he entered the room. Her crush was mentioned in the *Sacramento Bee,* which noted that "the singer has been a longtime favorite of Mrs. Reagan." The flirtation continued for months, but no one took it seriously until Sinatra flew to Chicago and Nancy followed him a few days later. Her top aide later admitted making private arrangements for her, ostensibly to visit her parents when she was actually with Sinatra in his suite at the Ambassador East.

The affair, which continued for years, was not out of character for Sinatra, who was unmarried at the time. He was accustomed to taking the wives of his friends for his own pleasure. Nancy Reagan was not the first wife, nor would she be the last. In that sense, Frank Sinatra acted like a dog marking his territory.

Still, the relationship with Sinatra proved invaluable for Ronald Reagan because the singer raised thousands of dollars for the reelection campaign, and he was always available to perform personal acts of philanthropy for the governor. "We sent all the requests for money to Sinatra," said Nancy Reynolds, "and he always responded. One letter from a disabled woman on welfare who lived in Palm Desert said that all she wanted was enough money to give her son a nice Christmas. The governor sent the letter to Sinatra, and he went out and bought all sorts of things, including a big red bicycle, and delivered them personally to the woman's house. He knocked on the door and said that Governor Reagan had told him of her plight. He gave her all the toys and food, wished her a Merry Christmas, and left. He told us that what he loved most was that the lady didn't even recognize him."

Sinatra also opened social doors for the Reagans that would otherwise have remained closed to them. In 1970, he prevailed upon the grande dame of Hollywood society, Edith Mayer Goetz, the daughter of MGM's Louis B. Mayer, to hold a dinner party in honor of the Reagans. As a loyal Democrat, she was reluctant to do that, but agreed as a favor for Sinatra, inviting the Reagans and their friends to her home in Holmby Hills. Having been told that the governor liked fish, she had instructed her chef to prepare a special sole mousse for him, but that evening she was distressed to see that when the waiter presented the platter to him, Reagan took only the gelatinous bits, no fish.

"Ronnie, I thought you liked fish," she said.

"Oh, I do. I love it."

"Well, then," she said, pointing to the platter, "why don't you take some?"

Realizing his faux pas, Reagan helped himself to the sole. Years later, Nancy Reagan copied Edie Goetz's dinner menu for her first private party in the White House.

Sinatra profited as much as Reagan from their new association, for he was once again traveling in the company of political power. "One key to Frank is that he relishes power. He revels in it more than any public figure I can think of," said writer Tommy Thompson. "Perhaps his reasoning now is that because he has occupied for so long a time the summit position in show business, this entitles him to sit as an equal at the table of other kings—those of industry, medicine, politics, government. His evolution from a passionate liberal to querulous conservative is not hard to explain."

But outrage in Hollywood's liberal community over Sinatra's political about-face continued to grow, and he continued to reassure people of his political affiliation. "I'm an Italian Democrat all the way," he said. "On that score, I could never change." To prove his point, he announced that he was supporting Edmund "Jerry" Brown, Jr., for secretary of state in California and John Tunney, another California Democrat, for the U.S. Senate against Ronald Reagan's good friend George Murphy. But he then endorsed Republican John Lindsay for mayor of New York City and contributed $10,000 to New York Republican governor Nelson Rockefeller's reelection campaign.

Those who were not totally confused by Sinatra's political allegiances assumed that he supported Ronald Reagan, a man he once despised, simply because he had been rejected by the Kennedys and Unruh was a devoted Kennedy man. It was no secret that in 1960 Sinatra had spent many thousands of dollars renovating his Palm Springs compound because he was convinced that his home on Wonder Palms Road would become the Western White House for John F. Kennedy, and would serve as a vacation retreat for the President when he came to Palm Springs. He had built a heliport and a large new guest house with a dining room capable of seating forty, had put up a flagpole for the presidential flag, and installed an extensive communications system for the White House operators.

Yet when President Kennedy came to the desert he ignored the man who had staged his inaugural gala and raised so much money for his campaign. Attorney General Robert F. Kennedy was waging an all-out war against organized crime at the time, and he had refused to let his brother stain the presidency by staying in Sinatra's house, which had also provided hospitality to Mafiosi like Sam Giancana, Johnny Roselli, Mickey Cohen, Johnny Formosa, and Joe Fischetti. Instead, Kennedy stayed at the home of Bing Crosby, the other singer of the era, who was a Republican. To Sinatra, the public humiliation was excruciating.

"The excuse given was security—that the Secret Service thought Crosby's place afforded better protection—but Frank didn't buy that for a minute," said Peter Lawford many years later. "He was livid. He called Bobby every name in the book, and then rang me up and reamed me out again. He was quite unreasonable, irrational really. His valet told me later that when he got off the phone, he went outside with a sledge-hammer and started chopping up the concrete landing pad of his heliport. He was in a frenzy."

Steve Allen published an open letter to Sinatra on September 7, 1970, asking how a lifelong liberal could suddenly support one of the leading exponents of conservatism. How could a crusader for civil rights like Frank Sinatra lend his name to a man like Ronald Reagan, who had said of America's blacks in 1962 that "They're eating each other for lunch"? Allen listed the governor's reactionary positions on prison reform, medical care for the aged, farm labor, hunger, the generation gap, taxes, campus unrest, antiwar demonstrators, education, consumer interests, capital punishment, and mental health; then he begged Sinatra to set aside his "Sicilian vengeance" and return to the Democratic fold.

He ended his letter with, "Only a few thousand people may read this letter, Frank. I offer you access to a few million if you'd like to visit my TV show and explain your position."

Sinatra did not respond, but the governor's wife did. She sought out reporters to denounce Steve Allen's criticisms. "Lord, yes, I have strong feelings, especially at this point in the campaign," she said. "I went into this one thinking that because I'd been through it before I wouldn't get so mad and upset. But that's not true. . . . This campaign has been dirty. . . . It started on a low plane . . . and now it's gone into an area I deeply resent—questioning my husband's integrity."

She was incensed by Unruh's attack on Reagan as a rich man's governor and the tool of the "half hidden millionaires" who had financed his campaigns and bought his house in Sacramento. She was infuriated when Unruh recalled the homosexual scandal in her husband's administration by posing for a picture with two young women and announcing, "We used to have a saying in Sacramento in those days. Prove you're straight and take a girl to lunch."

Her anger, usually controlled in public, was clear as she took a swipe at Jesse Unruh. "Do you know he took six weeks' vacation in Europe while the legislature was in budget sessions? Ronnie had seven days off this summer. It doesn't really seem fair."

Then, with dervishlike energy, she began making the luncheon rounds of Republican women's clubs throughout the state to expound her own political philosophy, "which is Ronnie's, too, of course."

Eschewing formal speeches, she confined herself to demure question-and-answer sessions in which she lectured her listeners on the evils of dirty movies, women's lib, and the fashion rage of hotpants. Pornography so inflamed her sensibilities that she winced whenever the subject was broached.

"Pornography is pornography, what is there to see?" she would ask
with irritation. "How curious can you be? Unless, of course, you're interested in becoming a voyeur, which I'm not. I'm appalled and ashamed of
the motion picture industry today. Movies are attempting to destroy
something that's supposed to be the most beautiful thing a man and
woman can have by making it cheap and common. It's what you don't see
that's attractive. What they're showing is animals."

After one of these scoldings, the student body president of Mills College stood up to object. She said that she believed it was better for young
people to be able to see sex in movies and read explicit books than
sneaking behind the barn to learn about life. Mrs. Reagan smiled coldly.
"I can't agree with you," she said to the young woman. Without raising
her voice, she communicated her anger, and the subject was quickly
dropped.

In public, Nancy managed to keep her temper in check. "Blowing my
cool wouldn't help Ronnie very much, now would it?" she asked. "The
main thing I want to do is help my husband."

She dismissed feminists demanding equal rights as "silly women's libbers" who don't know their place. "They're just ridiculous," she said. "I
really believe a woman's real happiness is found in the home with her
husband and children. That doesn't mean they should not have interests,
but they should be done in the framework of marriage, not in competition with marriage. That's where I think the women's libbers are in for
trouble. God made men and women different, and they have different
needs. . . . I think a woman gets more if she acts feminine."

The author of *The Feminine Mystique* was not amused. "Nancy is like
Madame Chiang Kai-shek, doing it the old way through the man," said
Betty Friedan. "We were at Smith together, and I remember then that
she was one of the few women in college who was serious about a career.
But when she got married, she decided to pursue power through her
husband. It's a disgrace the way she has betrayed her own sex."

Years later, Nancy Reagan refused to endorse the Equal Rights
Amendment, which caused Betty Ford to say, "I think when Nancy met
Ronnie that was it as far as her own life was concerned. She just fell apart
at the seams." Later, the former First Lady explained, "What I meant was
that I couldn't understand how a woman [like Nancy], who had had a
professional life, could show so little interest in working women. I didn't
understand how she could be against the ERA."

As loving wife and supportive helpmate, Nancy appeared less threatening to men, especially to her husband and the men surrounding him,
most of whom never fully took her measure. Petite, almost fragile, she
elicited their protection, which enabled her to accomplish her goals more

effectively. She even flirted at times and said she couldn't understand why a feminist as pretty as Gloria Steinem had to be so confrontational. "I happen to have heard Gloria on a TV interview in Sacramento, and the man introduced her as being attractive, which she is," said Nancy. "But Gloria didn't like it. Well, what is the matter with that? It's gotten like these women hate men or something. . . . I don't get that. I like all the things about being a woman. I like being taken care of. I like strong men. I want somebody to be the leader. I like the feeling of being protected."

Beneath the feminine façade, though, she did not hide her strong opinions on the issues of the day. She was as consumed by politics as was her husband, and rattled off bureaucratese like an insider as she berated the Nixon administration for "F.A.P.," the acronym for their ill-fated federal Family Assistance Plan. "The President ended up trying to adopt my husband's welfare reform plan," she said, launching into a diatribe against welfare recipients. "Somebody has got to get a handle on welfare because it's breaking us. The system is bogged down by too many social workers and too much staff that's not needed."

She said that on a recent trip to New York, where she and the governor stayed in a suite in the Waldorf Towers, she had read that a welfare family had been housed in the same hotel. "I was shocked and I think the people of New York should be shocked, too. There must be somewhere else to put these people."

The first lady appeared so imperious that she became the target of ridicule. One comedian always got a laugh by saying: "Somebody asked Nancy Reagan if she understood poor people. She said, 'Only if they speak slowly.'"

A practical joker within the county welfare department in Fresno, California, sent a letter to the governor's wife informing her that she did not qualify for public assistance and so her name was being removed from the county's food stamp program. Unlike her husband, Nancy had never cultivated the sense of humor to shrug off such incidents.

A passionate believer in capital punishment, she described herself as "outraged" by the U.S. Supreme Court decision outlawing the death penalty in 1972. "I feel a little less safe today," she told a Ladies Day luncheon at the Lodi, California, Rotary Club. "Capital punishment is a deterrent to crime. I'm sure most people in California are as upset as we are. I don't think they [the justices] were legally in a position to do that. They changed the constitution, and nobody has authority to do that but the legislature and the people."

She worked the telephone for weeks gathering supporters, collecting signatures, and circulating petitions to place the death penalty on the ballot for the next election. Nancy, like her husband, continued her public support for capital punishment until 1976 when the Supreme Court upheld the constitutionality of executions.

She also joined Attorney General Evelle Younger in launching a campaign to require mandatory prison sentences for persons who commit certain crimes. "Everybody nowadays, particularly women, are concerned about crime and violence," she said at a press conference. "We all need protection from dangerous criminals, and this initiative offers that protection."

Representing a conservative minority at the time, both Reagans supported U.S. involvement in Vietnam and held a private dinner and reception for South Vietnam president Nguyen Van Thieu and his wife at the Beverly Wilshire Hotel in Los Angeles. The Reagans were repelled by the sight of long-haired demonstrators protesting the war, including Jane Fonda and her husband, Tom Hayden, who stood outside the hotel boycotting the dinner. Zsa Zsa Gabor, one of the first guests to arrive, told newsmen, "Tell Jane Fonda what a dope she is." Mrs. Reagan smiled her approval.

The bellicose governor, whose military experience as an army captain did not extend beyond the borders of Hollywood, where he made documentaries during World War II, advocated full-scale bombing of North Vietnam. "We could pave the whole country and put parking stripes on it and still be home by Christmas," he said more than once. Consequently, he was dogged by antiwar demonstrators wherever he went, especially on college campuses. There he called for disciplinary action against students and faculty taking part in such demonstrations. He struck back at hippies carrying MAKE LOVE, NOT WAR signs by saying, "Trouble is, they don't look like they are capable of doing either." When a long-haired student raised his hand to ask a question at Claremont College, Reagan called on him by saying, "This young lady over here." For a moment the 1,800 students sat in shocked silence and then burst into laughter as Reagan apologized, saying the light was so dim he couldn't see that his questioner was male. Later he said, "The fellow had a haircut like Tarzan, he walked like Jane and smelled like Cheetah." Hounded by protesters, his good humor failed him on one occasion when he became so angry at student militants that he thrust out his middle finger as he was leaving a Board of Regents meeting on the Berkeley campus. The photograph of him giving the finger ran on the front page of the *Signal* newspaper in Newhall, California.

Reagan enjoyed these confrontations with students, and when he was running for President he reminisced with one of his Secret Service agents about his prowess in dealing with protesters.

"He and I would collect wood at his place in California and he'd tell me macho stories about when he was governor," said former Secret Service agent Marty Venker. "How he really kicked ass when those hippies were storming the campus buildings."

"I really became alarmed hearing my parents during the Vietnam War say, 'Just go and bomb the country,' " said Patti Davis many years later. "I was in high school at the time, but I knew that people were getting killed for something that most of the country wasn't even sure about. That really opened my eyes a lot."

Nancy would not tolerate views unlike her own, especially in her own household, so Patti never actively protested the war in Vietnam and learned to stop expressing her doubts. "I always got in a bad situation when I did, so I decided I would just keep my mouth shut," she said. Years later, influenced by her idol Jane Fonda, she learned to speak out. That enraged her mother, who despised everything that Jane Fonda represented. Nancy regarded the peace movement in the United States as a fifth column and the antiwar demonstrators as saboteurs. "They help the enemy rather than us," she said.

On October 15, 1970, the day of the Moratorium in Washington, D.C., one of the largest antiwar demonstrations ever held, the governor's wife issued a press release inviting television cameras to accompany her as she made her rounds at Letterman Army Hospital in San Francisco visiting soldiers wounded in Vietnam.

"It's a symbolic visit," she said. "I want the boys here to know there are a lot of people in California who are grateful to them."

Three years later, the Reagans invited California's returning prisoners of war to an all-American chicken and apple pie buffet in their honor. "California had more prisoners than any other state. So my husband and I decided to have two dinners up in Sacramento for POWs from the northern part of the state and two more dinners at our Los Angeles home for men from southern California," she said. "It was the most marvelous experience. Just to be around them made you proud to be an American. They told such moving stories about their prison experiences."

Throughout the reelection campaign of 1970, Nancy spoke out on the issue of abortion, defining the intent of the law her husband had signed in 1967. She said the California statute permitted abortions only if there is "true and legitimate" fear that having a baby would gravely impair the mother's physical or mental health. She condemned doctors who had been using that mental health provision to perform abortions on anyone who asked.

"I think that's been very abused. . . . That's not what my husband meant," she said. "I do not believe in abortion at will. I do not believe

that if a woman just wants to have an abortion she should. . . . I do
believe if you have an abortion you are committing murder."

Although Nancy maintained this posture publicly throughout her husband's political career so as not to antagonize his conservative right-to-
life constituency, she deviated privately when her own daughter needed
an abortion. Upset by Patti's out-of-wedlock pregnancy by a man she
heartily disapproved of, Nancy ran to her friends for comfort and confided her distress to top aides. "Patti reputedly had several abortions,"
said one of Mrs. Reagan's secretaries. "Helene von Damm and Mike
Deaver told me and they knew all about them."

"My mother told me about Patti's abortions," said the daughter of one
of Nancy's closest friends. "Nancy had to rush her off to Dr. Leon
["Red"] Krohn once for surgery on a botched-up job. Nancy said later
she didn't think her daughter would ever be able to have children because of that."

Patti has never publicly acknowledged the abortions her mother told
others about, but she is pro-choice about a woman's right to have an
abortion. In *Home Front,* her autobiographical novel, she devoted five
pages to a graphic description of an illegal abortion. The abortion in her
novel took place in 1968, the year in which Patti was sixteen. She told
Ms. magazine: "Two girls I knew had abortions. One crossed the border
to Mexico, to a strange house in an empty field. She was scared to death.
It was so badly done that later she had to have an ovary removed. The
other girl was left with so much scar tissue that she couldn't have children. It's important to remember what illegal abortion was really like."

With the governor and his wife speaking out on the public issues that
mattered to them—sex, drugs, abortion, and the war in Vietnam—the
polls showed Reagan losing his huge lead. By the middle of October
1970, Jesse Unruh had almost caught up as more and more blue-collar
Democrats began returning to the fold. On election day, Nancy was
beside herself.

Ever superstitious, she insisted that her husband play golf that day with
Holmes Tuttle exactly as he had done in 1966 when he was first elected
governor. She planned for them to eat dinner with Earle and Marion
Jorgensen that night and requested that Mrs. Jorgensen invite the same
guests, hire the same help, and serve the same food—chicken curry—she
had in 1966. Nancy needed all her "good omens" in place, plus the
reassurances of her astrologers. Still, she waited nervously for the election results.

By the time dessert was being served she learned that her husband had
won. He was elected to a second term with 3,439,664 votes and 52.9
percent of the total to 2,933,607 votes for Jesse Unruh. The Democrat

had spent $1,207,000, or 42 cents a vote. The governor had spent $3,550,000, or 98 cents a vote—more than twice as much.

Turning to the man who had raised the most money for him, Reagan asked Frank Sinatra to oversee his inaugural gala. In 1962, Sinatra had done the same for Governor Pat Brown. That year, Sinatra and his Rat Pack had stomped on stage in Sacramento to tell the celebrating Democrats how fortunate they were. "Just think," Sinatra had said. "If Dick Nixon had won, you'd be sitting here listening to Roy Rogers and Ronald Reagan."

Now the political chameleon would be singing for another governor— "my governor," as Sinatra now called him.

12

FIVE MONTHS into her husband's second term, the first lady's vaunted reserve cracked wide open. "I'm so angry," she said as she threw her first public tantrum. "Politics is such a dirty field. It's just a dirty business. My friends told me it would be this way, but I never believed them until now. . . . I hope my husband will never seek public office again."

What triggered her anger was the public reaction to the governor's admission that he, a millionaire, had not paid any state income tax for 1970. That made a mockery of his electioneering slogan: "Everyone should pay taxes and taxes should hurt." A reporter for the *Sacramento Bee*, trying to confirm a tip, had asked the governor during a press conference whether he had paid any state taxes for 1970. Reagan admitted that he had not. His refusal to release his financial records, list his holdings, or disclose his net worth only fed the outrage.

The governor said he did not have to pay taxes because of business reverses, but he refused to say what those business reverses were, and bawled out reporters for asking. He accused them of trying to make him look as if he had done something wrong. He said they were trying to invade his privacy. When they asked him to clarify the status of his federal taxes, he snapped, "Why should I have to clarify the status?" But then they asked him to differentiate between his insistence on the privacy of his personal fortune and a bill he had endorsed that would throw open the tax returns of welfare recipients to the state welfare department. Red-faced, Reagan said those were two different situations and couldn't possibly be compared.

The *New York Times* reported that the Democratic leader of the California state senate said, "It's very easy to say 'taxes should hurt' when you're not paying your fair share." The *New Yorker* published a cartoon of two bums sitting on a park bench, one saying to the other: "I dreamed Ronald Reagan was a panhandler and I wasn't, and I refused to give him a dime, and I gave him a lecture to boot."

When the *Los Angeles Times* ran an article on the governor's tax problems and on the loopholes he could take advantage of as a rancher, Reagan responded in a petulant letter to the editor. "By the way," he wrote, "when the roll is called up yonder, do you think not paying a tax you don't owe will rate as many demerits as receiving stolen property and selling it for profit? Maybe that is oversimplification, but somehow, in my mind, it applies to the [New York] *Times* and the purloined [Pentagon] papers."

"Nancy came into Gucci on Rodeo Drive the day [the news] broke in the papers and she was so upset she started crying," recalled Carlo Celoni, the former manager of the Beverly Hills store.

Nancy instructed her staff to arrange an appearance on a television talk show in Sacramento so she could air her grievances. Her press aide gently suggested that this might not be the occasion to complain again about the Reagans having had to pay rent on the house they were living in. Nancy agreed to confine herself to the tax matter.

"We did pay taxes," she insisted on the air. "We paid a federal tax. We paid $14,000 in property taxes. We paid over $91,000 in state income taxes since we've been in Sacramento. That's a lot of money. We've never avoided taxes. We've never taken advantage of anything."

She let the interviewer know that Ronald Reagan's decision to run for governor in 1966 was by "mutual agreement," that any future career decisions by her husband would also be by "mutual agreement," and that at this time she was not prepared to approve his seeking public office again. "I don't think I'd be for it," she said. "It really is going to take me a long time to get my equilibrium back." Seven years later, she was still carrying on about the *Sacramento Bee* reporter who broke the story. "What that girl did was illegal, getting our tax records," she told Nan Nichols of the *Bee* in 1977. "It would have been illegal for her to get at your tax records. But, of course, no one in the press picked up on that."

Neither the governor nor his wife seemed to grasp the ethical responsibility of an elected official to be publicly accountable, especially in financial matters. Governor Reagan spurned the suggestion of turning over his assets to a trustee for the duration of his governorship so as to avoid suspicion of his being influenced in his official actions by his private financial interests. At his wife's insistence, he steadfastly refused to release his tax returns or to issue a public financial statement. Even after the polls showed that 72 percent of the state agreed that reporters had a right to ask about such matters, he would not answer their questions.

The *Sacramento Bee* investigated the governor's finances and alleged that he had paid minimal taxes, averaging only $1,000 a year on more than $50,000-a-year earnings in the first four years he was in office. Reagan asserted the newspaper story was another invasion of his privacy, and he again refused to comment.

His popularity plummeted as all but the most impassioned conservatives deserted him, shrinking his hard-core support to a mere 25 percent of the voters. "He's on a real decline," poll-taker Mervin Field told *Newsweek* in a story entitled "Ronald Reagan's Slow Fade." "It's going to be very hard for him to replenish his popularity," Field said.

The magazine reported that the governor, shaken by his deteriorating image, was hiding from the public by rushing home from work every night to spend quiet evenings with his wife and son, and tripping off for weekends with old movie cronies such as John Wayne and Bob Hope.

Nancy went on the attack. She sent a letter to the editor of *Newsweek,* a letter her staff rewrote several times: "Your clocks and mine must be set differently," she wrote. "According to mine, my husband usually gets home around 7:00 or 7:30. But if *Newsweek* says it's 5:00, it must be so and I'll re-set mine immediately.

"Also according to my date book, we have seen Bob Hope and John Wayne approximately six times in the last six years, and have yet to spend a weekend with either one, although we do consider them good friends.

"I can see I have a lot in store for me—long, leisurely weekends with Duke and Robert, and a husband who rushes home to me early. I think I should thank you for the life I never knew I had."

Nancy was striking back at anything that might threaten her husband's political position and thereby endanger their way of life. After four years in the statehouse, she and the governor had become addicted to their trappings of power. He relished his security detail and traveled with as many hefty bodyguards as he could get the government to pay for. She, like the Queen of England, assigned an aide to carry her purse. To accommodate themselves and their entourage when traveling, the Reagans leased a jet plane for $525 an hour. He charged $25,000 for every speech he made out of state, plus first-class expenses, and she took her hairdresser with her on all trips. They required their daughter, Patti, to make a debut in Los Angeles, despite her reluctance, because they wanted to be accepted by that segment of society which prizes such rituals.

They ordered an elaborate coat of arms purporting to trace Reagan's descent from Hibernian aristocrats only to learn that it was a fake. In a panic, they contacted Captain Adolf Karlovsky of the International Academy of Heraldry in Switzerland, and he gently explained that their coat of arms belonged to another Irish family, unrelated to them. He offered to devise a new Reagan crest with a modern coat of arms, as legitimate under Swiss law as if it had existed for centuries. The Reagans eagerly provided him with a tape-recorded interview describing their families, interests, and hobbies from which Karlovsky fashioned a crest featuring a bear, the state seal and flag of California, a horse, and an actor's mask. Underneath, the motto read: Facta Non Verba. ("Deeds. Not Words.")

To see the world at taxpayer expense, they asked the White House to send them abroad as official emissaries. The presidential papers of Richard Nixon indicate the staff's initial resistance to dispatching the California governor as a special envoy "because he is inexperienced in foreign affairs and hence not the appropriate person for such a mission," so Nixon made sure the trips were mostly ceremonial. In 1971, the Reagans toured the Far East on behalf of the President; in 1972, they spent three weeks in Europe, visiting Copenhagen, Brussels, Paris, Madrid, Rome, London, and Dublin; in 1973, they traveled to Australia, New Zealand, and Singapore. Each time they requested diplomatic passports, a White House plane, Secret Service protection, and presidential letters of introduction to all heads of state.

"Reagan was always asking for those trips," recalled John D. Ehrlichman, assistant to the President for domestic affairs, "and it was not unusual for Nixon to let him go. That was the way the President appeased the right wing of the party."

Richard Nixon believed in keeping his friends close to him and his enemies even closer. Since Ronald Reagan's abortive attempt for the 1968 Republican nomination, Reagan had been heralded as *the* conservative contender for the White House, and so he fell into the enemy column. Nixon spent a great deal of time courting him with invitations to the Western White House at San Clemente and to state dinners in Washington, D.C. The Reagans were also invited to Tricia Nixon's wedding in 1971, which was held in the White House on the same day as the wedding of Reagan's son Michael, which was held in Hawaii. The Reagans did not attend either wedding.

For his reelection in 1972, the President needed to keep the glamorous governor very much on his side in order to carry the state of California. After the election, Nixon invited the Reagans to Washington for his second inaugural, and the President-elect, grateful for Reagan's support during the campaign, arranged for them to have a lovely suite at the Madison Hotel, where a huge bouquet of roses awaited their arrival. "During the inaugural I shared a room with Nancy Reynolds at the Madison," said a friend, "and every night we'd go to the Reagans' suite and have a good gossip with Nancy Reagan, who would be in her quilted robe. We were there when the Reagans arrived in Washington. Nancy Reagan went into the suite and inspected the roses Nixon had sent and then told the governor that there were a couple of dead ones in the bouquet. He said, 'What did you expect?' "

The flowers had been intended more for Nancy Reagan than for her husband because Nixon, before many other people, recognized her as the power in the marriage. He told an aide a few years later, "Nancy Reagan runs Ronald Reagan. She's a very strong woman, and, if you make her angry, you're never going to pull this guy into camp. . . . You just can't afford to alienate Nancy Reagan, because she's the guy's chief adviser. I'm telling you, Nancy Reagan's a bitch, a demanding one, and he listens to her."

Nixon made sure that trips were mostly ceremonial. In 1971 the Reagans toured the Far East on behalf of the President. In 1972, they spent three

Nancy had become so taken with her role as first lady of California that in 1972 she agreed to do a weekly newspaper column for the *Sacramento Union* that would provide a forum for her political pronouncements. She used the eight-hundred-word column in question-and-answer form to defend her husband against criticism of being "unfeeling and unsympathetic." She said he was "a man who performs warm and compassionate deeds each day that are unknown to the public." She harangued against X-rated films, saying she would never go to see one even if it received awards. She denounced what she called the loose morality of unmarried couples living together and having children. She condemned the legalization of marijuana, predicting it would lead to reefers in vending machines and billboards proclaiming "Fly higher with Brand X." She advised seventeen-year-olds to delay marriage and said eighteen-year-olds should be taught to love freedom and be willing to fight for it.

"I think the family unit is the strength and backbone of our country, and I think the downgrading of it—whether intentional or unintentional —is extremely frightening," she wrote.

At the time of these declarations, Patti, who had started college at Northwestern University, got into a fracas that involved the campus police. "It was quite a scandal at the time, and one that Nancy and Ronnie totally absented themselves from," said Les Weinrott. "It was just another parenting problem that got dumped on the grandparents because I think Nancy was too busy raising hell about Ronnie's tax problem at the time to pay attention to her child. I remember Edith called me from Arizona and instructed me to keep the incident out of the press, but it was too late for that. Patti and a black man had exchanged words . . . and the confrontation became ugly. It was in the *Chicago Tribune* and all over the Evanston papers. I told Edith the story was too big to suppress, so Loyal, who graduated from Northwestern and practiced at the hospital there, flew in from Phoenix to take care of things.''

On the evening of February 19, 1971, Patti had been sitting at the information booth of Allison Hall at Northwestern. She was talking to a friend when a man approached with a box containing several pairs of hotpants for two women in the dormitory who modeled for his store. Patti asked him what was in the box.

"I said it was something to show the girls," said Larry Alexander, owner of the Tan-Yer-Hyde Boutique in Evanston and the brother of an alderman there. "Then I asked her what her name was."

"Snow White," Patti told the black man.

He asked her whether she would like to try on a pair of hotpants, and they began arguing. Patti claimed he was "abusive and offensive in his language" and called the security guard, who told Alexander to leave. He refused, so Patti called the Evanston police, who charged him with criminal trespass. He was released on $1,000 bond pending a court appearance. The next day, the *Tribune,* Chicago's largest newspaper, carried the squabble on page one under the headline: "Reagan's Daughter in Hotpants Hassle."

Loyal Davis soon showed up, and within two days, he had brought Patti and Alexander together to denounce the press coverage they had received. "The incident was completely blown out of proportion," said Patti. "The press coverage made me look as though I overreacted and as though [Larry] was abusive—neither is true." About the hotpants, a fashion statement her mother detested, she said, "I think they'd be fine in the spring, or summer, but not in the winter." Alexander said with a smile, "I think she'd look good in them anytime."

After the academic year, Patti transferred to the University of Southern California, where she began a major in drama. She dropped out after her junior year and began playing the guitar. She took her mother's maiden name in 1974, becoming Patti Davis, so she could distance herself from the politics associated with the Reagan name.

"I can certainly understand that," said Nancy's second cousin Marian Robinson. "I was so embarrassed by Nancy's politics and those of her husband that I never let it be known that we were related.

"I had written to Nancy when Reagan was first elected governor. My letter was not congratulatory but concerned about what Governor Reagan may—and indeed did—do to higher education in California. My letter was formal, but I did mention the family connection, which, you will note, she did not."

Nancy's handwritten response to her cousin, whose father and Nancy's father were brought up together in Pittsfield, Massachusetts, did not mention the time the two young women had spent together as children. Nor did Nancy mention Marian's trip to Hollywood in 1949 when Nancy had introduced her to Ronald Reagan.

Not acknowledging their family relationship, or her cousin's position as professor of literature at San Jose State College, Nancy addressed her merely as "Mrs. Robinson" and proceeded to list her own and her husband's educational credentials, while omitting the name of Eureka College, Reagan's alma mater.

Dear Mrs. Robinson—

Thank you for your letter of congratulations to us following the election.

As far as the University of California goes I think it might be helpful if you knew a little of my background and that of my husband's [sic]. I'm a graduate of Smith College and was raised in an academic atmosphere. Loyal Davis was Professor of Surgery for over thirty years at Northwestern Medical School. He retired two years ago and became Professor Emeritus. He is a past President of the American Surgical Association and the American College of Surgeons to which he was a regent for thirteen years and chairman of the Board of Regents. He is the editor of the oldest and most respected medical journal in our country, Surgery, Gynecology and Obstetrics, and is the recipient of two honorary degrees—one from the Royal College of Surgeons in London and the other from Edinburgh.

My husband got his degree in economics and sociology after working his way thru [sic] college. He is on the board of trustees of that college and has an honorary degree from it. He is also a member of the Board for Fundamental Education.

I think from the above you can see that both of us have a very deep belief in promoting and maintaining excellent educational surroundings and opportunities in all universities and keep [sic] them free from any political interference.

Sincerely,
Nancy Reagan

Professor Robinson was so appalled by the letter from her cousin that she never replied. "Nancy is a dreadful woman without a thought in her head," she said years later. "A frozen face. Every family has a black sheep; mine just happens to be famous."

Nancy so disliked being reminded that she was the natural daughter of Kenneth Robbins that she refused to respond to anyone on his side of the family. She had written off her father and his relatives years before when she had persuaded Loyal Davis to adopt her. From that point on, her natural father did not exist, except to receive a printed Christmas card each year from Governor and Mrs. Ronald Reagan.

"Nancy would not even respond in 1972 when Ken was in ill health and dying," said Kathleen Young, another cousin. "I was beside myself at the time, because he would send me these terribly sad letters after his wife died, saying how lonely he was and how sick he'd become. One letter, which had tearstains on the bottom of the stationery, said, 'I'm so lonely I could die.' I was broke at the time and could not go to him, so I tried to reach Nancy, knowing how much it would have meant to Ken to hear from her.

"I called the governor's office in Sacramento and left very detailed messages with her secretary about who I was and why I was calling, but she never returned any of my calls. Then I phoned Loyal and Edith in Arizona to say that Ken was sick and dying and I needed to reach Nancy so that we could decide what to do for him. I was only Ken's niece. Nancy was his daughter, and I thought she'd want to help him in some way.

"Loyal bawled me out for calling and said Nancy had enough to do as the governor's wife and wanted nothing whatsoever to do with this kind of thing. He was so mean and nasty I started crying. I felt so bad. I didn't have the money to go to Ken and comfort him, but I knew that Nancy and Ronnie Reagan did. I wanted Loyal and Edith to tell Nancy how sick her father was. She was his only child, and I thought she'd want to know."

Almost blind in one eye, Kenneth Robbins, seventy-seven, suffered from phlebitis and respiratory problems. He died on February 2, 1972, in New Jersey's Newton Memorial Hospital without ever hearing from his only child. His short obituary in the *New Jersey Herald* included: "He was a retired auto dealer who had served in the Army during World War I. He is survived by several nieces and nephews." No mention was made of his daughter, Nancy Reagan.

• • •

"Ken died of a broken heart," said Kathleen Young. "He left everything
to me because Nancy had virtually ignored him, except for those cold
official Christmas cards. He knew that she was not interested in him, but
he never stopped loving her and always carried her picture in his wallet.
Since he had nothing but old papers and photographs, most of which
were of Nancy as a child and a young woman, plus $20,000, I guess he
decided to leave it all to me because I was the closest thing he had to a
family."

Showing no remorse over her father's death, Nancy never contacted
his lawyer or any of his survivors. "She hated her real father," said her
stepson, Michael Reagan. "She once told me that it upset her every time
people referred to her as the adopted child of Dr. Loyal Davis because
she always thought of him as her father."

Nancy admitted as much many years later. "Kenneth Robbins was my
father, but I somehow never could think of him that way. I've never
talked about him because Dr. Davis is the only father I've ever known. I
didn't want to hurt my real father. . . . If I were pressed, the things I
would have to say wouldn't have been kind—and I was terribly fond of
my grandmother, his mother. I just never saw any point to it."

In her memoir, published in 1989, she says that her father was graduated from Princeton. The university, though, has no record that Kenneth
Robbins ever enrolled, attended, or graduated. The only basis for her
assertion is a photograph of Ken Robbins wearing a sweater decorated
with a large *P.* "I assumed it stood for Princeton and I was wrong, but
that's what I told a reporter a few years ago," said Kathleen Young. "My
assumption was published in the *Los Angeles Times* and that's where Nancy
picked up the information, I'm sure." In her book, Nancy recounts a
disturbing childhood visit with her father during which she claims that he
made a disparaging remark about her mother. "This enraged me to the
point where I screamed at him that I wanted to leave," she wrote. "He
got upset and locked me in the bathroom. I was terrified, and I suddenly
felt as if I were with strangers.

"His wife felt terrible and wrote a letter of apology to Mother, but
there were no more visits. And to this day I can't stand to be in a locked
room. Years later, when Ronnie and I were staying in a hotel suite during
a campaign trip, I had to ask him to unlock the bedroom door. He
couldn't understand why, until I explained that the memory of being
locked in that bathroom had never entirely disappeared."

Her cousins do not believe the bathroom story. "I can't imagine dear,
sweet Ken ever doing something like that," said Marian Robinson. "It's
entirely out of character for him."

"I can't call Nancy a liar, because I wasn't there when she visited

Ken," said Kathleen Young, "but that doesn't sound anything like the wonderful, gentle man I knew all my life." Mrs. Young's home in Redondo Beach, California, is full of loving family memorabilia. Nancy's living room was filled with silver-framed photographs of Barry Goldwater, Dwight D. Eisenhower, Richard Nixon, and Ferdinand and Imelda Marcos. They—not family members —were given pride of place atop the grand piano in the Reagans' home.

"I have trouble reconciling Nancy's inhumane treatment of her dying father with all her public pronouncements about the sanctity of the family," said one of her cousins.

Both women questioned Nancy's public commitment to the Foster Grandparents Program, a federally financed project started during the Democratic administration of President Lyndon Johnson that united volunteers over the age of sixty with hospitalized children. Nancy Reagan had been impressed with the project during a visit to Pacific State Hospital and had become its champion throughout California, extending its reach to all state hospitals. "I think we have tended to forget about the elderly in this country and what they can contribute," she said.

Senior citizens serving as foster grandparents received a small, hourly stipend, a hot meal, and $1 each day for transportation to state hospitals. They spent up to four hours daily caring for foster grandchildren who were mentally ill or handicapped.

"Children in state hospitals, they need an extra amount of love and attention, more than any hospital can provide," said Nancy. "On the other hand, the elderly, some are very, very sad. They feel they aren't needed or wanted and they have so much love to give. This program matches up the two. Also deaf children are involved and juvenile delinquents, who, by and large, have never known what grandparents are."

Toward the end of Reagan's second term in Sacramento, Nancy Reynolds suggested that her boss hold a picnic at the executive residence for twenty-five foster grandparents and their foster grandchildren. Nancy Reagan embraced the idea and dispatched her aide to make the arrangements, which featured entertainment by a clown, a puppeteer, and an accordionist. The Reagans gave everyone a small gift.

"I only wish that all our grandparents and their children could be with us today," Nancy told reporters. "I dearly love each of these wonderful men and women and boys and girls. This program is the finest example I know where both sides benefit. These special children get the extra love and attention they need and want while our older senior citizens can enjoy a sense of giving and being needed. The hours I have spent with these people in this program have enriched my life many times over."

Endearing photographs of the governor's wife embracing mentally retarded and handicapped children appeared in newspapers throughout the state, but Kathleen Young and Marian Robinson remained skeptical, having never seen such pictures of Nancy with her own children and stepchildren. They viewed her activity with Foster Grandparents as cheap political posturing.

"Perhaps it's easier for her to offer periodic spurts of affection to total strangers than to give sustained love to her own family," said Kathleen Young.

Her relations were so ruptured within her own family during the time Reagan was governor that Nancy no longer spoke to her stepchildren. When Maureen and Michael wanted to speak to their father, they had to call his office, and their calls were rarely put through. Nancy had disowned her twenty-three-year-old daughter, Patti, for moving in with Bernie Leadon, a rock musician with the Eagles, and she had sent her seventeen-year-old son, Ron, away to boarding school, where she communicated with him through his teachers. The dean of students at the Webb School in Claremont, California, remembers the incessant phone calls he received from Mrs. Reagan while her son was a high school student.

"She would call about anything that she felt wasn't right," said Roy Bergesen. "She would worry about anything. She was very concerned about drugs even then and was very alert to drugs on the campus. She didn't miss much. She's pretty sharp that way. If she felt a teacher or a class or his dorm wasn't right, she'd call and say so. . . . It was far better for Ron to be in boarding school. No one could have survived at his home. She was not used to being countermanded."

A typical phone call occurred shortly before one of Ron's scheduled visits with his parents.

"My son's coming home for the weekend, and to avoid a fight with his father, could you get him to cut his hair?" Nancy asked.

"I can't make him, Mrs. Reagan. His hair conforms to the rules," said the dean.

"But he sees his father so infrequently, I'd really like it to be a pleasant visit."

Finally, the dean agreed to ask Ron whether he would consider a haircut for the sake of family peace, but the teenager balked.

"You can't make me," he said. "I know the rules."

"Your mother would like to avoid an argument."

"Absolutely not," he said.

Ron kept his hair long and defied his mother each time she tried to get him to cut it. Maribe Nowell, who lived across the street from the Reagans, heard his screams each time Nancy confronted him. "Leave me alone!" he would yell. "All I want is to be left alone."

Years later, Ron admitted that his occasional drug use also strained relations with his mother. When she was asked whether her children had ever had a drug problem, she replied, "Experiment, yes; a problem, no."

"Moms don't really like to talk about that kind of stuff," said Ron. "I never had a huge . . . I never had a drug problem, depending, of course, on what you call a problem. If smoking a joint some night is a problem. . . . None of us were ever heavily into coke or heroin or anything like that. We experimented but never with heroin. I mean, we were growing up in the seventies. You give a try to just about anything that comes your way."

His sister, Patti, also admitted taking drugs, but said she quit smoking marijuana "because it makes you forget things—like where you live."

In December 1974, Ron was expelled from Webb. "They threw me out halfway through my junior year," he said. "I was too much of a troublemaker. Too prankish. My mother was mortified. . . . She thought my life was over. But my father had a good sense of humor about that sort of thing. He took it with a little more grace."

Living at home with his parents in Pacific Palisades, Ron enrolled at Harvard, a private prep school in Los Angeles. Right away he warned his teachers about the persistent phone calls they would soon be receiving from his mother, especially during the dinner hour.

John West, the first black teacher hired by the school, had persuaded Harvard's administration to let him teach a dance class as an alternative to physical education. Only four boys signed up, but Ron was one of them, and he was quickly taken with the prospect of becoming a dancer. Soon, West was peppered with calls from Nancy Reagan.

"I wasn't the favorite teacher in their household," he said. "Ron always wanted to step out of himself and try something new, but his parents wouldn't let him. The boys always used to ask him, 'What are your parents going to say about this?' Ron respected his father always. He'd be more vocal about his mother. They'd have a falling out, and he'd pack up and go stay with his sister [Patti] for a while. Ron needed space. All he wanted was to be accepted as himself."

Away from school, Ron spent most of his time at his best friend's house. "I can still see him sitting at our breakfast table with his long hair and his dirty old overcoat from the Salvation Army that Nancy hated so much," said his best friend's mother. "Ron was just going through one of the stages that all kids go through, but Nancy wanted to control him completely. . . . It was almost a sickness with her. She had to know what he was doing all the time, where he was going, who he would be seeing. She was so controlling that Ron was intimidated and spent as much time at our house as he could get away with."

Nancy was so consumed with her husband's political career that she had little interest in anything else. Well before the end of Reagan's second term as governor, she was determined that he seek the presidency in 1976. Life as the first lady of California had been sweeter than anything she had ever known, and she now thrived on the high-wire act of politics as much as he did. She realized that she had married a man with extraordinary speaking skills, who was telegenic in an age when television was determining elections. Like a jockey with a thoroughbred steed, she wanted to ride her horse to victory.

She sat in on the presidential planning sessions during 1974 with press secretary Lyn Nofziger, who had returned to the Reagan camp, pollster Richard Wirthlin, and political operative John Sears, who would become the campaign manager. She encouraged Michael Deaver and Peter Hannaford to leave their families in northern California and move to Los Angeles to start a political consulting firm with Reagan as their main client. She wanted to ensure that her husband would remain a formidable presence on the national political scene while making a great deal of money writing, speaking, and broadcasting. So Deaver and Hannaford lived together during the week in a one-bedroom apartment in Brentwood and on weekends commuted to their families in the north.

Reagan had already announced that he would not seek a third term as governor, but Nancy let everyone know that he would stay active in politics. In 1972, she told the press, "My husband is very concerned as to the direction the Republican party takes, not only in California, but in the country, and he certainly wants to have a voice in that determination."

In 1973, she said, "He's not going to sit on the sidelines in politics."

In 1974, Frank Sinatra was performing at Republican fund-raisers for Reagan, singing: "Nancy's beam is like a lighthouse. She sees her husband in the White House."

During this time, Richard Nixon was sinking into the morass of Watergate, and Ronald Reagan was vigorously defending him. Reagan claimed the Watergate conspirators were "not criminals at heart," and that the congressional investigators looking into the crime were doing the work of a "lynch mob." Nancy, on the other hand, deplored the break-in as "a stupid, stupid, immoral, illegal thing to do." She said she felt very sorry for Nixon but blamed him for depressing people's spirits. "There's nothing to uplift us and it's all contributed to a tremendous cynicism among the American people," she said. "People are generally upset, disturbed, depressed. They feel anchorless and hurt. And the trouble is, there's no way to get away from it all. There's no relief. . . . I wish they'd bring an impeachment motion and get it over with and done. There's relief in decision."

The U.S. Supreme Court forced Nixon to surrender tape recordings that left no doubt he had tried to obstruct justice. He spared himself the humiliation of impeachment by resigning on August 8, 1974—the first President ever to do so. Ten months before, Spiro Agnew had resigned in disgrace over crimes committed while he was governor of Maryland, and Nixon had named House Minority Leader Gerald Ford as his Vice President. Ford now was sworn in as the thirty-eighth President of the United States, and he selected Nelson Rockefeller to be his Vice President. A month later, Ford granted Nixon a full, free, and absolute pardon, which Ronald Reagan completely supported.

By naming the liberal New York governor as his Vice President, Gerald Ford alienated the conservatives of his party, and Nancy Reagan became more convinced than ever that 1976 was her husband's time to run for President. But Ronald Reagan was not fully persuaded. Too many of his advisers were cautioning him against challenging an incumbent Republican President who was struggling to pull his party together after the disgrace of Watergate. Stalwart Reagan supporters such as political consultant Stuart Spencer, Taft Schrieber of MCA, and Henry Salvatori, the head of the Reagan kitchen cabinet, supported President Ford, but Nancy pushed hard in the other direction, dismissing Ford as a "bumbler, nothing more than a congressman who never proved himself in a statewide election and just by luck became a caretaker President." She told her husband they had everything in place to run and had to take advantage of the opportunity now. Reagan had lined up a daily five-minute syndicated radio show, a newspaper column, and lucrative speaking engagements to keep him in the political forefront, but he questioned the timing. So Nancy consulted the stars.

She had been quite impressed at first with Jeane Dixon, the Washington, D.C., soothsayer who had predicted in 1956 that a Democrat would win the 1960 election but be assassinated or die in office "though not necessarily in his first term." Nancy had insisted that her husband meet privately with Mrs. Dixon whenever he went to Washington, and each time he sat down with the seer at a secret session in the Mayflower Hotel, she promised him that he would eventually live in the White House. He always returned to Sacramento fortified by these visits.

"I worked for Jeane Dixon during those years and I remember all the

times she met with Governor Reagan," said Alice Braemer. "He was
never on her official schedule, because she did not want people to know
how deeply involved in astrology the Reagans were. Nancy, too. Mrs.
Dixon flew out to California to attend a big luncheon, and she and Mrs.
Reagan had their picture taken with their arms around each other."

Besides predicting the White House in their future, Jeane Dixon had
endeared herself to the Reagans on two counts: she shared their conservative politics, and she never charged them. "Reagan and his wife,
Nancy, were good-time buddies," she said. "They come to my speeches.
I've made suggestions [over the years] and things like that, but I don't
think it's right to say he formally consults me. I bump into him from time
to time. Sometimes I write him a letter or two. We exchange Christmas
cards. Of course, I have a long list of suggestions for him, but he makes
up his own mind. I'm not considered one of his advisers, but I advise
him."

Nancy Reynolds became so fascinated listening to the Reagans discuss
Jeane Dixon and her astrological predictions that she asked the governor's Washington office to make an appointment for her. When she met
Mrs. Dixon at the Mayflower Hotel for breakfast, the astrologer asked to
order for her, saying, "I know exactly what you like." She then proceeded to order rich, heavy foods that Reynolds hated and never ate.
Naturally, the governor's aide became a little dubious of Dixon's powers
of clairvoyance, but such a miscue did not shake Nancy Reagan's confidence. She remained dependent on the stargazer despite Dixon's predictions that Russia would be the first nation to put a man on the moon, that
Walter Reuther would run for President, and that the third world war
would begin in 1958 over the Chinese islands of Quemoy and Matsu.

But her illusions ended when Jeane Dixon refused to prophesy a Reagan White House in 1976.

"I don't see you as President yet," the astrologer told Reagan. "I see
you here at an official desk in California, and because you're at that desk
some right things happen in Washington, but you're not there to do
them."

So Nancy went shopping for another astrologer—one who would tell
her what she wanted to hear. Television talk show host Merv Griffin, who
felt that he and Nancy enjoyed a special karma because they shared the
same birthday, had introduced her to Joan Quigley, a stargazer from San
Francisco. But Quigley, too, saw no Reagan presidency in the immediate
stars. "I did a little bit on his 1976 campaign," she said, "but I knew it
wouldn't work out."

Finally, Nancy called the Reagans' Hollywood astrologer, Carroll
Righter, who described himself as "gregarious Aquarius." Among his

clients he counted Marlene Dietrich, Cary Grant, Grace Kelly, Arlene Dahl, Lana Turner, Peter Lawford, Dick Powell, Glenn Ford, and Susan Hayward—many of whom would not think of signing a contract, making a trip, or getting married without first consulting the dapper little man who kept the charts of his favorite clients by his bedside so he could handle their late-night calls. "They need me here," he said. "Just like they need a doctor."

As governor, Ronald Reagan had issued an official proclamation of appreciation to Carroll Righter, which Righter framed and hung in his front office. The governor publicly acknowledged his interest in astrology, especially that practiced by Righter, who frequently visited the Reagans at home and at their ranch. "Nancy and I have been very close friends of Carroll, so we're always interested in what [his column] has to say. We get a kick out of reading it every morning. . . ."

Righter's zodiac parties, each honoring clients whose birthdays fell during the month, were famous in Hollywood. "All the stars were there —Rhonda Fleming, Hedy Lamarr, Betty Grable," said Arlene Dahl. "Fish were swimming around in his pool for the Pisces party, he rented a live lion for my Leo party, and he lined up sets of twins for the Gemini party." He served astrologically appropriate food, such as meat and potatoes for Moon Children, lemon pie for the tart tastes of Aries people, and hot red peppers for passionate Scorpios. Righter invited 500 guests each month for 150 months, and photographs from his files show that the Reagans were regulars.

Righter also conducted weekly Tuesday night astrology classes, which Nancy Reagan attended regularly in the fifties and early sixties. She became an expert at doing astrological transits and conjunctions. Maureen Reagan, who later became a regular in Righter's night-school classes, considered becoming an astrology teacher.

"Our offices were in Carroll's Los Angeles home at 1801 N. Curzon, above Hollywood Boulevard, which is where he usually saw Nancy," Carroll Righter's personal secretary said. "He told me that she had called —she always made her appointments under the name of Nancy Davis, although Carroll called her 'Moon Child'—and for me to keep an eye out and meet her in the entry hall. So I was standing at the door of Harmony Hall waiting for her when the chauffeured red Datsun pulled up and the driver—a man in a black suit—opened the backseat door for her. She got out disguised in sunglasses with a kerchief wrapped around her head. It was kind of comical. I opened the door just before she rang the bell. She said, 'I'm Nancy Davis.' I think she really thought that I didn't know she was the governor's wife. Naturally, I didn't say anything. I led her into Carroll's living room, where he always met with his clients.

"It was quite a long session, and at one point he summoned me to bring tea. I took it in to them and when I left he did not close the door completely, so I could hear them talking. Nancy was whining in a thin little voice. 'Why must we wait? Why can't we go now?' Carroll would give her his answer, but she didn't want to hear it so she kept pressing him. 'Why can't we? Why? Why? Why?'

"After she left, Carroll was so tired he collapsed in his chair. 'She wears me out,' he said. 'And I swear that voice of hers is going to drive me crazy one of these days.' Carroll told me that Mrs. Reagan wanted her husband to run for President in 1976, but he [Righter] had told her the timing wasn't right. 'I told her that it wasn't a good period astrologically for Ronnie in the public eye, but she won't accept it,' he said. 'She just won't accept it. Poor Nancy. She's a Moon Child and she's dominated by her home and her husband. She is determined to make him go for it. I tried to tell her that it won't turn out well, but she won't listen. I said there is a better time coming, but she wants to go now.' "

The predictions of recalcitrant astrologers would not stop the warrior queen from crowning her passive king. "She wanted it more than he did," said Gene Nelson, the dancer-actor-director who lived with Maureen Reagan from 1975 through 1978. "Ronnie was happy with his little radio show and his syndicated newspaper column. He was making $200,000 a year, and he said he felt more effective doing that than running for President. There was no one to dispute him, which is a comfortable position for a man who hates confrontation. But after eight years as the governor's wife, Nancy had had a taste of power, and she wanted more. So she pushed and pushed and pushed him until the poor bastard finally caved in and agreed to make a run for it."

13

BETTY FORD BURST INTO THE PUBLIC EYE like a cork popping out of a champagne bottle. Full of effervescence, she bubbled and sparkled as she became one of the country's most popular First Ladies, bringing small-town warmth to the cavernous White House, which under the Nixons during Watergate was as gloomy as a graveyard. Speaking openly about the breast cancer that led to her mastectomy in 1974, she radiated the same kind of honesty and decency that her husband was trying to restore to the presidency.

Surprisingly forthright for a politician's wife, she supported the Equal Rights Amendment and the U.S. Supreme Court decision legalizing abortion, even though her husband opposed both. "I do not believe that being First Lady should prevent me from expressing my ideas," she said. "Why should my husband's ideas, or yours, prevent us from being ourselves?" Following a televised interview in which the President outlined his conservative views on abortion, she sent him a message on a slip of paper: "Baloney! This is not going to do you a bit of good." Just before signing an executive order establishing a National Commission on the Observance of International Women's Year, he turned to the First Lady with a smile. "Before I sign this, Betty," he said, "if you have any words of wisdom or encouragement, you are welcome to speak." Mrs. Ford laughed. "I just want to congratulate you, Mr. President," she said. "I am glad to see you have come a long, long way."

At the end of the year, *Newsweek* featured the pretty fifty-seven-year-old First Lady on the cover as "Woman of the Year." *Time* chose her as "Man of the Year," one of only eleven women so honored. A *Good Housekeeping* poll found her to be the most admired woman in America. Across the country, Democrats as well as Republicans were sporting buttons that read: BETTY FORD'S HUSBAND FOR PRESIDENT.

Newsweek ran a cover story on Ronald Reagan entitled "Ready on the Right" in March 1975, which described him as "the most kinetic single presence in American political life." President Ford invited the Reagans to dinner in Palm Springs a few weeks later in hopes of dissuading the former governor from a debilitating intraparty challenge. The ploy did not work.

Betty Ford said that by the end of the evening she and her husband knew without even speaking to each other that Reagan was going to run against him. As disturbed as she was by this challenge to her husband's presidency, she was even more disgusted by the challenger's wife.

"She's a cold fish," said Betty Ford. "Nancy could not have been colder. Then the flashbulbs went off, and she smiled and kissed me— suddenly an old friend. I couldn't get over that. Off camera—ice. On camera—warmth."

Nancy, in turn, was appalled by what she described as Betty Ford's "spaciness" after one or two drinks. Although unacknowledged at the time, the First Lady had developed a crippling dependency on painkillers for arthritis in her neck. When the prescribed drugs were mixed with alcohol, they rendered her less than coherent. Even after she publicly faced her addiction and committed herself to a sanitarium to dry out, Nancy remained critical.

"Betty parades her alcoholism like a Medal of Honor," she said. "Why is she overcoming the problem when she shouldn't have it in the first place?"

The differences between the two women became strikingly clear when Mrs. Ford appeared on "60 Minutes" and said she wouldn't be surprised if her eighteen-year-old daughter was having an affair, and suggested that under some circumstances sex before marriage might prevent divorce.

Nancy Reagan was outraged. With the righteousness of a public scold, she proclaimed her revulsion at this kind of "new morality." So determined was she to speak out on the issue that she soon had a speech drafted and distributed to the press for her appearance at the Women's Republican Club of Grosse Pointe, Michigan. "I am disturbed about the growing immorality," she said. "Our sons and daughters are told not [only] that it's all right to break our rules of morality, but that there should be no rules at all. . . . The young people on our campuses are told to be 'cool' and 'with it,' that they should have no 'hang-ups' about sex and premarital living arrangements. . . . I believe it is time the great majority of us said, 'Enough already—stop.' "

At the time she was making these pious declarations, the problems of premarital sex were sitting on her own front porch. Her twenty-three-year-old daughter, Patti, was living with Bernie Leadon, guitarist for the Eagles, one of the most popular rock bands of the era. Like other disaffected young people of that time, the couple, both college drop-outs, had long hair and wore blue jeans, boots, and black leather jackets. They smoked marijuana openly. Together they wrote "I Wish You Peace," which the Eagles recorded for their album *One of These Nights.* Years later, the Eagles' drummer, Don Henley, disparaged the song as "smarmy cocktail music" and said the composition was "certainly not something the Eagles are proud of, and came about solely as a result of the Patti Davis–Bernie Leadon 'love relationship.' "

"Ronnie and I were very much opposed to that relationship," Nancy said. "You have to remember that we come from a different generation, and the idea of living together without being married was foreign to us. During Patti's years with Bernie, we had virtually no contact. It wasn't because she was living with a rock musician, although the Eagles were not exactly a mother's dream. . . . It was that they were living together, which we just couldn't accept."

"It was very hard for Nancy because she has very definite principles of what is right and what is wrong, and she sticks by those principles," said her best friend, Betsy Bloomingdale. "There was a separation of a couple of years, a period when Nancy and Patti were not all that friendly."

Ron, too, became a problem for his mother when, in 1975, at the age of seventeen he started an affair with Kris Harmon Nelson. She was thirty years old and the wife of Ricky Nelson, one of the country's leading rock and roll singers, and the son of Ozzie and Harriet Nelson, television's most wholesome family. Ron had met Kris Nelson while skiing and was so taken with the pretty blonde that, despite her marriage and her four children, he called and asked her to come to his home for dinner when his parents were out of town. Curious and adventurous, she accepted. He made elaborate preparations for the evening, telling the Reagans' longtime housekeeper to prepare and serve the meal with wines he had selected from his father's extensive wine cellar. That night he answered the door wearing a dramatic silk smoking jacket. After dinner he read his favorite poetry to Kris, who was so moved by the "sensitive and romantic" recitation that she willingly became Ron's first sexual experience—in his parents' bed.

Hours later, when she awoke and began scrambling for her clothes, she accidentally hit the alarm button, which brought the Secret Service men storming into the bedroom. The agents had been assigned to guard all announced and unannounced presidential candidates and their families. Despite young Reagan's protests, Kris was pinned to the wall and questioned rigorously. The agents finally let her go but kept her driver's license and reported the incident to the Reagans when they returned the next day.

Shocked by what they were told, Ron's parents forbade him from ever seeing Kris again. "What would people say?" said his mother, quite beside herself. "Her youngest child is only one year old, and she has children who are almost as old as you are."

Michael Reagan learned about the incident a few days later when his father called him.

"Nancy and I came back from a trip a little early, and we caught your brother," Reagan told his son.

"Caught my brother doing what?" asked Michael.

"There was a young lady in the house for the weekend," said Reagan. "Ron had the cook making breakfast for them in bed and preparing candlelight dinners. And he wasn't using his room; he was using our room and our bed!"

Michael started to laugh. "Well, Dad, there's good news and bad news."

"What do you mean?"

"The bad news is that you came home early and you caught him. The good news is that you found out he isn't gay."

There was a moment of silence on Reagan's end of the line. Finally, he said, "I hadn't thought of it that way, but you're absolutely right. I guess it is a blessing. Thanks, Mike. I must tell Nancy."

Nancy was not amused. A few weeks later, she was having lunch at the Bistro in Beverly Hills with some of "the girls" when she saw Kris Nelson enter the restaurant. Unfortunately for Mrs. Nelson, she had to pass Nancy's table to get to her own. As Kris walked by, she smiled politely at "the girls," some of whom were friends of her famous parents, football great Tom Harmon and former actress Elise Knox. When the young woman passed behind Mrs. Reagan's chair, Nancy grabbed her arm and yanked her down to the table. "Leave my son alone," she said. "Do you hear me? Leave him alone." Thoroughly shaken, the younger woman stumbled to her table. A few minutes later, she left the restaurant.

Despite his mother's objections, Ron continued the affair through his senior year in high school—and after. He even appeared with his married lover on a television program where both of them talked about the problem of dealing with their instantly recognizable last names. As children of famous parents, both said they enjoyed their celebrity status.

Many years after Ricky Nelson was killed in a plane crash and Kris was married to Mark Tinker, Nancy wrote about her son's love affair in her memoirs, unnecessarily disclosing to the world what only a few people had known. "For several years, Ron was romantically involved with a significantly older woman from a show business family who had a teenage daughter of her own," she wrote. "I was heartsick when I learned about it, because I believed she was robbing him of his wonderful teenage years. But there was nothing I could do about it. Their relationship ended while Ron was at Yale, when she dropped him."

Meanwhile, Nancy's thirty-four-year-old stepdaughter, Maureen, twice divorced, was living with Gene Nelson, a Hollywood contemporary of her sixty-four-year-old father.

"Nancy and Ron did not approve of our relationship at all," said Nelson, who had danced in such films as *Lullaby of Broadway, So This Is Paris,* and *Oklahoma.* "They never said anything to me, of course, but Maureen told me how upset they were about our sleeping together, especially when we traveled in public, which we did all the time promoting the Equal Rights Amendment.

"When I first met Maureen, she was a pain-racked lady who did not deserve the rotten things that had happened to her in life. Her mother, Jane Wyman, had virtually abandoned her and Michael as children, throwing them both into boarding schools when they were five years old so she could pursue her career without interruption, which is all she ever really cared about anyway. When she did deign to speak to them, she was so laceratingly brutal that they were usually in tears. Jane's got a razor-sharp tongue that can wound and destroy. She's like Bette Davis and Joan Crawford, always playing the grande dame.

"Nancy was not much better. She said she never considered Maureen her daughter, so Maureen had no right to think of herself that way. Nancy refused to see or speak to her for years on end and held so tightly to Ronald Reagan that there was never any room for Maureen, who virtually had no father whatsoever. Maureen told me that when Nancy married Ronnie she had laid down the law by saying that he had to leave his past life behind. She said she would give him children but that she wanted no part of his children from Jane Wyman. I can't describe to you how Maureen would cry at night. She would sob her heart out saying she couldn't understand how they allowed themselves to separate from their children the way they did. She said it was cruel and unnatural for parents to act like that, and I had to agree with her. Maureen and Michael grew

up without anyone who ever cared about them, which is probably why
they turned out the way they did.

"Maureen has a helluva temper and is impatient, vindictive, and dis-
trusting, but she's a brilliant woman, a great political tactician, and can be
a lot of fun. Mike is just a boob. So stupid. The epitome of a good-time-
Charlie conventioneer, slapping everyone on the back and telling dumb
jokes. I guess that's why he was a good salesman, but Maureen was
constantly having to tell him how to behave in public. He later claimed
to have been sexually abused as a child, and I don't deny that he was.
He's not smart enough to invent a story like that for sympathy, and
something obviously happened to him early on to screw him up.

"Maureen had had two disastrous marriages and divorces by the time
she was twenty-six years old. She'd never finished college and couldn't
make it as an actress. She'd lost a very good shot at being a talk show
hostess on NBC-TV, although she was terrific on the air and better than
anyone I've ever seen on the network. But her last name was Reagan,
and in an industry of liberal Democrats, that didn't get her very far. By
the time I met her, she was very, very fat, and although she lost weight
and started looking great after a while, it was still a miserable, desperate
time for her. Her only goal in life then was to unite her family emotionally. She said that she had never had a mother or a father, and she wanted
that more than anything else in the world. So she set about trying to heal
the family wounds just as Nancy and Ronnie were gearing up for the big
race in 1976. Knowing Nancy as well as she did, Maureen felt that she
would be receptive to such an overture then, because she would not want
the public image of an estranged family. The first step was getting us
invited to dinner at the Pacific Palisades house on San Onofre Drive.

"God! What a night that was. Ronnie answered the door and immediately started playing the drunk scene in *She's Working Her Way Through
College,* the Warner Bros. movie we had been in together in 1952. He
was a lousy drunk, but he started his routine the minute he opened the
door. He didn't even say hello to Maureen, but she pretended not to
notice. That's how desperate she was to be accepted. It had taken her
weeks, but she had finally accomplished the monumental feat of being
invited for a social evening with her parents, and she didn't want to blow
it. She was smart enough not to try to be alone with her father but to
share the evening with both of them.

"I felt that Nancy was not in the least sincere that night, except when
she talked to Ronnie. Then she would reach out and touch him as if to
show squatters' rights: This was her property, and no one else was allowed to claim it, or even touch it, including his daughter. Nancy and
Ronnie were very lovey-dovey throughout the evening. Unnecessarily

so, I thought, but I guess she wanted to make sure that Maureen got the message."

Reagan's daughter chose to rise above her stepmother's possessiveness to accomplish her long-term goal of establishing family ties. Her reward was an invitation to help paint the tiny adobe cabin on the 688-acre ranch that the Reagans had recently bought in the Santa Ynez Mountains above Santa Barbara. "We went up there and Maureen offered to do anything she could for her father's presidential campaign, despite real political disagreements with him, especially on the subject of the Equal Rights Amendment," said Nelson. "She came right out and asked him why he was so against women, and I think that Ronnie was actually afraid of her. I know it sounds silly, but he was intimidated by her knowledge of the issues and her arguing skills. She quoted the Bible to him about 'men and their chattels' and he was so dumbfounded that he couldn't say a word. Nancy, of course, was furious with Maureen for bringing up the subject and putting her father on the defensive. I quickly jumped in and tried to jolly things up by joking around with Nancy. At one point I think I put my arm around her. She was always surprised anytime I made a spontaneous show of affection, but Maureen just loved it. 'Keep it up,' she'd whisper. 'Soften her up. Break her down. Miss Ice Cube. Break her down.' "

With Gene Nelson's support, Maureen tried to bring about a reconciliation between Nancy and Patti. "She [Maureen] was on the phone to both of them for hours, calling them back and forth, trying everything she could think of to make peace between them," he said. "Nancy talked about Patti's 'stupid bearded hippie boyfriend' all the time. She kept saying, 'Patti is nothing but a damn hippie. That's all she is. A damn hippie.' But she finally agreed to let Maureen set up a meeting between them in the den of the Pacific Palisades house to see if they couldn't work things out. Maureen was ecstatic thinking she could bring them together and at last have a happy family to be a part of, but the meeting didn't accomplish much. There was no sensitivity or love or longing on Nancy's part to be close to her daughters. She cared only about the public image of appearing close for political reasons. Patti was the first person to see through her mother, and she wanted no part of her or that kind of family. Maureen, on the other hand, was desperate for any kind of family."

By the fall of 1975, Nancy had finally broken her husband's resistance to a presidential campaign. With his ambition now matching hers, Reagan was ready to declare himself publicly. On Halloween, Nancy called a family conference so that he could tell his children before telling the country. Patti was not invited, but Maureen came with Michael and his fiancée, Colleen Sterns. Ron joined them without saying a word.

Everyone knew from reading the newspapers what was coming, so this family announcement was no surprise. Earlier in the evening Michael had approached his father to say he hoped his father's running for President would bring the family closer together. Reagan looked at him quizzically. "But the family *is* close," he said. At that point, Nancy walked into the room and asked what they were talking about.

"I said I hoped Dad's running for President would bring about a rebirth of family closeness," said Michael.

"I wouldn't count on it," she said.

The Reagans walked into their living room and directed the children to the couch. The Reagans, taking the two chairs facing the children, sat like a king and queen addressing their subjects. Impersonally, Reagan told his children that he was entering the presidential race. He said if he didn't run, he'd always feel like the player who sat on the bench and never got into the game.

"At every hotel and airport I see 'Reagan for President' placards," he said. "But you know what really gets to me? When I check into a hotel, the bellmen who carry my bags ask me why I don't run for President. 'We need you,' they say. And as I walk out of my room in the morning, the chambermaids stop me to shake my hand and say they like me and want me to run for President. It doesn't matter where I go; it's always the same. So the grass-roots response is out there, and I feel I have a good chance to win if I run for President."

But not everyone in Reagan's own living room was pleased. Nancy beamed and Maureen, Michael, and Colleen applauded the decision but Ron sat sullenly.

"I think Ron was disappointed because there hadn't been more discussion of this decision in advance," said Nancy later. "He just sat there silently. Looking back on it, I think he was probably right—that we should have found more time to talk about this as a family."

This first family conference made thirty-one-year-old Michael Reagan hope for a closer family. He was going to be married again in a few days, and he wanted his father to be present. His one-year marriage to Pamela Putnam had ended in divorce in 1972 when his pregnant wife announced that she was leaving him. The Reagans had refused to attend that wedding, but they would attend this one.

On the evening of November 7, 1975, Jane Wyman, looking every inch the glamorous movie star, arrived at the church in Anaheim, California, wearing a gold lamé gown and cuddling a poodle wearing a matching gold nugget. "I had never seen her so beautiful," recalled Michael, who paced anxiously waiting for his father and Nancy to arrive. They were a half hour late when they finally walked in, and he was startled to see Ron with them. "I had not invited him or Patti because I did not feel that close to them, and I felt the feeling was mutual," he said.

Knowing how much Nancy Reagan and Jane Wyman despised each other, Michael cringed after the ceremony when the photographer asked for the mother and father of the bridegroom to step forward for pictures. "Uh-oh, I thought. If Dad and Nancy got up, my mother would be upset. If Mom got up, Nancy would be upset. I looked at my parents, who hadn't spoken with each other for years, certain my marriage—only minutes old —was going to cause problems. . . . You could have heard a pin drop. Nancy was looking at Dad, who continued staring straight ahead. For a moment I thought we were going to need an NFL referee to keep track of the penalty phase of the wedding.

"After what seemed like an eternity, Mom stood up, looked directly at Nancy, and said, 'Nancy, don't worry about a thing. Ron and I have had our pictures taken together before. If you'd like to join us, fine. Now, Ron, come on. The photographer's waiting. Let's get our pictures taken.' " Relieved that the uncomfortable impasse had been broken by someone else, the paterfamilias walked to the altar, where he meekly posed for pictures flanked by his two hostile empresses. Thirteen days later, he announced his intention to become the leader of the free world.

Reagan had phoned President Ford to inform him of his plans, and the President tried once again to dissuade him, saying such a race would be divisive and damaging to the party, but Reagan disagreed. "How can you challenge an incumbent President of your own party and *not* be divisive?" asked Ford, exasperated. Reagan said he would abide by the Eleventh Commandment, the motto of the California Republican party: "Thou Shalt Not Speak Ill of Other Republicans." Disgusted, President Ford hung up.

A few minutes later Reagan arrived at the National Press Club in Washington, D. C., to make his announcement. It was one of the few times in recent political history that a man declared himself for the presidency without being surrounded by his loving family. Only his wife was standing by his side as he told reporters that he wanted to clean up the mess in the nation's capital. The press listened respectfully but did not take the former governor too seriously despite his high standing in the polls. After all, no Republican President had been denied his party's renomination in one hundred years and none had been challenged within his own party since Teddy Roosevelt did so in 1912 against William Howard Taft, and Roosevelt lost.

Reagan began his presidential campaign minutes after that press conference of November 20, 1975. He and Nancy toured the crucial primary states of Florida, New Hampshire, North Carolina, Illinois, and

California. And for the next eight months, they flew around the country, barnstorming states to try to win enough delegates to arrive at the convention unchallenged.

"That's when it really started," said a former employee of Deaver & Hannaford. "Mrs. R, as we called her, had always been difficult, but during the 1976 presidential campaign she became so impossible she left scars on all of us. When the office phone rang, we all tried not to be the one to answer for fear it was her calling. You could walk into the room and tell without asking that she was on the phone just by looking at the pained expression on the other person's face. All of us tried to route those calls directly to Mike Deaver because by that time he had become bound to her by some invisible cord. When she yanked, he jumped. He was her hatchet man, the guy who did her dirty work at every turn.

"During the campaign, if you saw Mike Deaver running down the hall, you knew that Mrs. R wanted someone fired. If you saw him sweating, you knew that Mrs. R wanted someone tossed off the plane. If he was biting his fingernails, that was a sign that Mrs. R wanted something unspeakable done to someone for something which usually had to do with appearances, because that's all that really mattered to her."

Mike Deaver thrived in his role as a worker bee for the queen, but his honeyfugling soon earned him the disparaging nicknames of "Nancy's Nancy" and "Lord of the Chamber Pot."

"I remember in New Hampshire, Mrs. R was walking the precinct with a young volunteer who absolutely idolized Ronald Reagan," said a campaign aide. "It was right before the primary and someone asked her an inconsequential question. She didn't know the answer, so she turned to the volunteer. The poor kid didn't know the answer either, but because Nancy felt he made her look stupid in public, she told Deaver to fire him. She didn't understand that you couldn't fire a volunteer, especially one who worked night and day, but Mike said he'd do it, so we hid the kid in another part of the campaign where he'd never be seen by the candidate's wife again.

"If the governor made a mistake and got into trouble by answering a hypothetical question, which he did all the time, Nancy never blamed him for being stupid; it was always someone else's fault. Whoever didn't prepare him properly to answer the question—that person had to go. During the campaign, he was asked a question about Rhodesia, and he said something about sending in U. S. troops, which made headlines. This gave Stu Spencer, who had switched his allegiance from Reagan to Ford, the ammunition for that warmongering commercial he ran in New Hampshire, saying: 'Governor Reagan couldn't start a war, but President Reagan could.' Nancy went crazy. She couldn't fire Stu because he was working for Jerry Ford, but she didn't speak to him again for four years, and none of the rest of us were allowed to speak to him either."

Then there was the speech in which Reagan proposed a systematic transfer of authority and resources to the states to reduce federal spending, he claimed, by $90 billion. With that savings, he promised everything short of sunny days and starry nights, swearing it would be possible to balance the federal budget, make a $5 billion payment on the national debt and cut federal taxes for every American by 13 percent. His staff released a list of the specific programs to be cut from the budget to achieve this $90 billion miracle and the Ford campaign pounced, claiming the plan would demolish Social Security, throw old people out in the snow, and send welfare recipients traipsing from state to state to get the biggest handout.

"Jeffrey Bell of the Washington office wrote that speech," said a former Deaver & Hannaford employee. "It was approved and amended by the governor, but when it blew up in his face, Nancy said Bell had to go, and so he was quickly sent into the ozone. Mrs. R was a terror, but the governor was great. He's kind, caring, compassionate—everything she is not."

Staff members spent hours speculating about the "good" governor and his "bad" wife, wondering how someone as warm and passive as Ronald Reagan could be devoted to someone as cold and abrasive as Nancy. "They must have signed a pact with the Devil so that he would always be the good guy and she would be the bitch," said one former top aide, suggesting that the forged bond between the Reagans lay deeply rooted in their childhoods. The lonely little girl who had been abandoned by her mother for so many years reached out to the young boy whose alcoholic father moved his family seventeen times in eighteen years. Both these forlorn children grew up gravitating to the make-believe world of acting and moved to Hollywood where fantasy could blot out all pain and deprivation. Finding each other in the Hollywood heap, neither ever became a star of the first magnitude. They invested all their fantasies in their marriage, which gave each of them a protective husk. "She allows him to remain remote, emotionally unengaged from people, and above the fray," said the former aide. "Being able to protect him from confrontation and steer his direction gives her life purpose. . . . I don't know how else to explain it."

"Appearances were everything to Mrs. R," said a former Deaver & Hannaford employee. "How things looked, what people thought—everything was sacrificed to that, starting with her daughter, Patti, whom the Reagans considered a nonperson in the 1976 campaign. She didn't exist, and we were not allowed to mention her name. If a reporter asked

Mrs. R a question about Patti, like where she was or why she wasn't campaigning like the other kids, she would lie—just outright lie—and say that Patti was traveling or working on her career or something. She wouldn't tell the truth and say that she'd disowned her daughter for being a 'hippie brat' and living with a long-haired rock and roll singer.''

''It was not just that she had disowned her child,'' said John Sears, the campaign manager. ''When I broached the subject of Patti, Nancy said, 'We don't know where Patti is. She'll turn up sometime, we hope, but we don't know when.' The kids were constantly trying to get their parents' attention. They couldn't get it unless they did what they were told, and they were having none of that. They liked their father, but he was not calling the shots.''

The thirty-nine-year-old campaign manager understood at once who held the power in the Reagans' marriage, and he became close enough to the candidate's wife to gain her confidence. She, in turn, was taken by his shrewdness. ''John Sears was urbane and articulate,'' she said, ''and he knew as much about politics as anyone I had ever met. I loved having lunch with him because he was bright, knowledgeable, and fascinating to listen to.''

During those lunches, Sears came to know a highly intelligent woman whom he later described as a good student of people, someone who had developed keen antennae, because she always suspected the worst in everyone.

''She was especially bright about her husband,'' said Sears. ''She knew Ronald Reagan better than anyone, and for that reason she was a great help to me during the campaign. She knew how Reagan would respond in an unfamiliar situation. She knew that he couldn't be worked full time, that he needed his naps, needed to have a few days off to get recharged. She knew that he was better later in the day and not early in the morning. But beyond this, she had insights into other people which probably came from the lonely childhood she had. Growing up sad and always an outsider, she was unlike happy youngsters, who were enjoying their life. Nancy was always frightened and standing off to the side watching what was happening around her.

''She told me that she felt much more comfortable with men than she did with women,'' Sears said. ''She felt that men were smarter, more accomplished, and she much preferred their company to that of women. She said she had a great deal of trouble making friends with women. She had difficulty trusting anyone, but especially women.''

Nancy did not include her years of friendship with ''the girls'' in her discussions with Sears, and yet even within this closed group of female friends, there were definite gradations of trust. Nancy felt closer to Betsy

Bloomingdale than she did to Harriet Deutsch, Leonore Annenberg, or Marion Jorgensen. Because she did not like Justin Dart, she kept a certain distance between herself and Jane Dart.

"Being as insecure as she was, Nancy was anxious to be thought well of by others, and I'd have to say that she was probably the most impatient woman I've ever met in my life," said Sears. "She told me how angry she used to get at Patti when the child was two years old and refused to eat her beans. 'She'd just hold those damn beans in her mouth for hours and I'd get so mad I'd walk out of the room,' Nancy would say. Now *that's* impatient. She blamed Patti for their ruptured relationship and said that it was Patti's fault. 'She won't be the way she should be so that I can be close to her. That isn't my fault; it's her fault.'

"Nancy's total dependence on astrology is part of her insecurity," continued Sears. "I knew about the tea leaves and the fortune-tellers and all the rest of that rot because Deaver told me about them. He said Reagan had started with astrologers early in his Hollywood career and then Nancy got into it.

"Those grave insecurities of hers go back to her early childhood and the fact that she never had a relationship with her real father. She said that she was deathly afraid that she would be at some public event during the 1976 presidential campaign and be accosted by a strange man who would come up to her and say, 'I'm your father.' That bothered her very much, and I would try to comfort her by saying, 'Well, you've been in public life now almost ten years and it's never happened, so I wouldn't worry too much.'" Sears could not explain why Nancy told him this when she knew that her father had been dead for three years.

"Maybe it's part of the fantasy," he said, explaining that both Reagans were obsessed with illusions and appearances. "It wasn't just Nancy. Reagan himself insisted on always looking good. That was his first priority. He wouldn't do something unless he looked good doing it, and Nancy aided and abetted him in this obsession. In that way, they reinforced each other."

Mike Deaver, too, believed that appearances governed Ronald Reagan. Deaver related his experience at a church banquet in the Midwest, where big bowls of country gravy had been served. "When we got back into the car, Reagan mentioned how much he had enjoyed the meal. I said, 'Yeah, I did something I hadn't done in years. I dipped some bread in that bowl of gravy.' A wistful look crossed his face. 'You know, I wanted to do that, but I was afraid it wouldn't look too good.'"

Ronald Reagan never wanted to be seen as unpleasant. "He never crossed anybody," said Henry Salvatori. "He never raised his voice or said anything bad about a person, that he left to his wife. . . . He was just like a good-looking little puppy."

"As the second son of an alcoholic, Ronald Reagan grew up being a people-pleaser," said John Sears. "He did not cause trouble around him, did not make waves. The first son, Neil, became responsible, stood up to things, and was unafraid of confrontation, but Ronald Reagan was not that way. He was nice to everyone so he could get along without any more traumas than those being visited upon him by his drunken father. That's how he coped. He survived his pain by being nice. That's why he refused to make any decisions. Decisions are tough and they can offend people on occasion. So Reagan refused to make any. The key to him was that he never got mad and never did anything to make anyone get mad at him. He could not tolerate being seen getting mad, and Nancy didn't want him to be seen that way either. That's what I meant by their reinforcement of each other.

"Once, when the Reagans were in Washington, Senator Paul Laxalt [as former governor of Nevada, he was a close friend of Reagan] and I were with them in their suite at the Madison Hotel. Laxalt and I were disagreeing about some campaign strategy and we were discussing it ardently. We were not violent and we certainly did not feel angry toward each other, but we were heated over the issue and we were going at it in front of them. Reagan was starting to get mad and so Nancy suddenly burst into tears to keep us from seeing her husband unfold in rage. She used it as a diversionary tactic. We were all so stunned by her hysteria that Paul and I stopped talking and Reagan stopped getting mad. Nancy just sobbed. Then she wiped her eyes. 'Ronnie and I better get some sleep now,' she said. 'We'll see you tomorrow.'

"Laxalt and I left the suite, and he turned to me. 'God, I didn't think we were so terrible as to bring all of that on, did you?' he said.

" 'No,' I said. 'I didn't.' And we weren't. That was just Nancy's way of intervening for her husband, to protect his fantasy of himself and make sure that no one saw him lose control and get mad."

The vision of how she wanted things to appear frequently led Nancy to varying degrees of dissimulation. Years later, she coyly admitted to a "little lie" about accepting free clothes from designers but only after she was caught. Usually her little lies were directed toward enhancing the image she had of herself or her husband.

Striving always to present Ronald Reagan as virile and youthful, she said that until 1981 he had never been in the hospital, except for a broken leg in 1947. Actually, in 1967, while governor, Reagan had been hospitalized for a prostatectomy, but Nancy, squeamish about the nature of the operation, told reporters at the time that it was minor surgery for kidney stones. "I knew it was prostate because I had one at the same time, and Ron and I talked to each other from our hospital beds," said former senator George Murphy.

Nancy never mentioned the ten scrambling years she spent in New York and Hollywood chasing her dream of being a movie star. She dismissed her acting career as "nothing more than a stopgap in my life" lest she appear too driving and ambitious for a politician's devoted wife. "My being an actress was so short-lived and really meant so little to me that it's like talking about another life," she said over and over again. "It all seems so hazy to me now."

Discussing the horse her daughter, Patti, had boarded at the Orme School in Arizona, Nancy wrote, "Her psychiatrist had suggested that it might be good for her to have something of her own to take care of, so we gave her a horse." Patti disputed her mother's version. "No, that's not true," she said. "I never saw a psychiatrist in high school—I don't know where she came up with that—and I'd had a horse all my life."

While Nancy's detractors considered her little lies deceitful, her admirers rationalized them as her way of protecting her husband. "Take the issue of the governor and his naps," said a former Deaver & Hannaford employee. "Everyone on staff in 1976 knew that Ronald Reagan, who was sixty-five years old then, had to take afternoon naps and could not be overscheduled or else he would blow it. Mrs. R was sensitive about the age issue, especially after President Ford's crack that 'Ronald Reagan isn't old—he's just prematurely orange.' That kind of stuff drove her crazy, so she'd always say that the governor never took naps. Now that's a lie, but it's coming from a wife trying to promote her sixty-five-year-old husband, who politically cannot afford to appear old. Is that so bad?"

"Nancy is a lot tougher than the image America has of her," said Stu Spencer. "Nancy is ambitious, very ambitious."

"She was tough, tougher than he was, no question about it," said David Keene, who organized the Southern states for the Reagan campaign. "I was in Florida with her and it was going so bad there that I pulled her aside and tried to be reassuring. 'Don't worry,' I said. 'It will work out in the end.' She looked me dead in the eye and said, 'For your sake, you better hope it does.' After that I stayed away from her to the extent that I could."

Minutes before Reagan was to deliver a speech in Tallahassee, Keene, who was standing offstage with the candidate and his wife, said, "Well, Governor, you have two options: You can either go out there and follow the Eleventh Commandment and lose your ass, or you can kick the shit out of Jerry Ford and win." Nancy looked at David Keene with a new-found respect. "That's the kind of talk I like to hear," she said. Her husband then bounded out to the podium and lambasted President Ford, the President's foreign policy, and the President's Secretary of State, Henry Kissinger.

The steely tenacity of the candidate's wife became obvious to the other side when the Reagans fought the Fords in Iowa. "There were thirty-seven GOP delegates at stake, and the question was, who was going to get nineteen and who was going to get eighteen," said Peter Sorum, chief advance man for Betty Ford. "I not only wanted Ford to win the most delegates, but I wanted his wife to get credit for promoting Republican unity coming out of the convention. At the last minute, the President was unable to attend a large delegate rally so he sent Betty in his place. I knew the Reagans would be there, sitting in front of the stage eating a box lunch to try to demonstrate that they were part of the Iowa community. I also knew that Ronald Reagan, who is one of the most decent human beings on the face of the earth, would never turn his back on kids. So I decided to stage Mrs. Ford's entrance with children. I told her she was to follow me and not to touch anyone but Ronald Reagan, and when she got to him she was to extend her hand in unity.

"I lined up the networks and the still cameras, and when we hit the hall, I cued the band and released the kids just as Mrs. Ford entered. They came running up to her as we walked down the aisle to where the Reagans were sitting. The children jumped up and down, and Betty extended her hand to Ronald Reagan, who stood up like a gentleman and accepted the gesture. Betty looked at Nancy Reagan to shake her hand as well, but Nancy refused. She knew exactly what I had done, although her dear old husband probably never figured it out.

"Minutes later, she [Nancy] sent her principal advance man over to me to ask for my name. 'I'm nobody,' I said. 'Well, Mr. Nobody, Mrs. Reagan wants you to know that when we win the White House, you will never serve in our administration.' I laughed and thought nothing more about it. I knew I had 'em. I got the nineteen delegate votes for Ford, the front pages of the next day's papers for Betty, plus twenty seconds on the evening news featuring the First Lady as the party conciliator. It was terrific!"

Trudging through the snowbanks of New Hampshire and the cornfields of Illinois, Reagan banged away at "the dead hand of federal interference in our daily lives" while his wife campaigned on her own schedule, answering the questions of students in Wisconsin, tobacco farmers in North Carolina, and senior citizens in Florida.

"My teacher wants to know why Mr. Reagan campaigns on foreign policy instead of domestic issues," asked a high school student.

"Presidents do deal with foreign affairs and people everywhere keep asking my husband about defense, about détente, about Panama. And we don't turn over and play dead for a little dictator down there when he says to. That's the only way to avoid war."

"What would you be doing with your life today if you hadn't married Ronald Reagan?"

"I don't know what I'd do," she said. "Kill myself!"

"What do you think about the Supreme Court?"

"I think there should be a mandatory retirement age for the court's justices."

"Who would your husband appoint as Secretary of State?" asked one senior citizen.

"I can assure you it would not be Henry Kissinger."

"Could you vote for a homosexual?"

"No, I don't think I could," said Nancy. "In order to hold office, you have to be a terribly strong man emotionally. No, I don't think I could."

"Do you not consider a homosexual as emotionally stable as a heterosexual?"

"No, I don't think he would be as strong," she said.

The Sears strategy had been predicated on Reagan's winning in New Hampshire, which would supposedly guarantee victories in the early primary states, garnering enough delegates for the candidate to roll to an easy triumph by summer. "We feel we can win the nomination before we get to the convention," Lyn Nofziger told reporters. "And with the nomination he can cakewalk to the White House."

Within a month, Ronald Reagan looked like he was finished. Suffering five stinging defeats in a row in New Hampshire, Massachusetts, Vermont, Florida, and Illinois, he had been slammed to his knees. His campaign was defeated, his staff demoralized, and his coffers bankrupt. "We were roughly $2 million in debt," recalled Martin Anderson, Reagan's issues adviser, "and none of the senior staff had been paid for weeks."

The power structure of the Republican party turned on Reagan in full force. The National Republican Conference of Mayors called on him to withdraw, and eleven of twelve former chairmen of the Republican National Committee endorsed President Ford. The Republican governors then delivered the final humiliating blow by calling on their former colleague to quit the race for the good of the country.

With the North Carolina primary only days away and the polls showing President Ford winning by seventeen points, everyone assumed this would be Ronald Reagan's last primary, the one that would destroy his presidential candidacy. "For Reagan, the real question ought not to be *whether* to bow out, but *when,*" editorialized the *Los Angeles Times.* A few days later, his campaign manager, John Sears, without telling Reagan, met secretly with Ford's campaign chairman to discuss the inevitable withdrawal.

Then a supporter from Texas offered to lend the campaign $100,000 for national television time to run Reagan's speech thrashing President Ford and Secretary of State Kissinger on national defense.

"What we can do, Governor, is basically forget all that has happened up to now, borrow the $100,000, and gamble everything on one last appeal to the voters," said John Sears. "But you should understand, it's very much of a long shot."

Suddenly the cautious, indecisive candidate became a reckless gambler. "OK, we'll do it," said Reagan. "Borrow the $100,000. And run the national defense piece on national television. I'm taking this all the way to the convention in Kansas City, and I'm going even if I lose every damn primary between now and then."

Later, he tried to appear sanguine about the primaries still facing him, and he told the press he would be pleased if he ran a close race in North Carolina, which the *New York Times* interpreted as a concession. The next day's paper ran just such a headline: "Reagan Virtually Concedes Defeat in North Carolina."

Expecting to lose, the candidate and his wife did not remain in the state on the evening of the primary but flew to Wisconsin, where Reagan delivered a speech to a group of conservationists.

The North Carolina returns started coming in midway through the evening and flabbergasted his staff, who could hardly believe their candidate was carrying the state. So accustomed had Reagan become to losing primaries that he did not declare victory until the final vote was tallied the next day. Then the jubilant candidate said he was packing his bags for the GOP convention. He went on to win the Texas primary as well as Nebraska and California and Missouri while conceding Michigan, Ohio, New York, and New Jersey. Neither he nor President Ford had the 1,130 delegate votes needed for nomination.

That's when Reagan began learning the real definition of power, and it was a lesson never forgotten by his wife. "President Ford took full advantage of his office," she said bitterly. "He brought dozens of uncommitted delegates to the White House for lunches, cocktails, meetings, and dinners. He invited an entire state delegation to have lunch with him. He invited the chairman of the Mississippi delegation to a state dinner for Queen Elizabeth, and Mississippi was the largest uncommitted delegation attending the convention. Over the July 4 weekend, he invited seven uncommitted delegates to watch the tall ships sail into New York Harbor from the flight deck of an aircraft carrier. . . . I was furious. The White

House stands for something more important than partisan politics and uncommitted delegates—or at least it should."

Further enraging her were the comments of her old family friend Barry Goldwater, whom her husband had defended against charges of extremism in 1964 in a stirring television speech that galvanized conservatives and launched his own political career. The Arizona senator had not only declared his support for President Ford in 1976, but had added insult to injury by criticizing Reagan's stand on the Panama Canal. Reagan had said, "We bought it, we paid for it, it's ours, and we aren't going to give it away to some tinhorn dictator!" Goldwater said Reagan's view sprang from "a surprisingly dangerous state of mind" that could "needlessly lead this country into open military conflict."

Nancy Reagan could barely speak. "I feel as if I have been stabbed," she told reporters at a news conference in Sacramento. "I was surprised, hurt. Of course, everyone knows what my husband did in 1964 for him [Goldwater]. I feel as if I've been doubly stabbed because our families have been such good friends. I would have felt better if he had called my husband on the phone."

One person who did go ahead and phone was Nancy's mother, Edith Davis, as hot-tempered and foul-mouthed as ever. And the man she phoned was Barry Goldwater. In a blast of obscenity, she pronounced her neighbor and good friend persona non grata.

"You are a fucking horse's ass for doing this to Ronnie," she screamed at Goldwater, "and you'll never walk into my house again. Do you hear me? You goddamned asshole."

"It was many years before Edie [Edith] forgave him," said Robert Goldwater, the senator's brother, "but she finally came around. It was a long time coming, but she certainly forgave Barry before Nancy ever did."

The strain of the campaign had exhausted the Reagans, and they retired to their ranch to get ready for the Republican convention in August. "When 2:00 P.M. arrived, no matter how busy his staff was, Reagan would lie down at the pool with his sun reflector," Secret Service man Marty Venker said. "That might seem like a vain, sissy thing to do, but Reagan had this cowboy way of describing it. He said he was getting 'a coat of tan.'"

Nancy was still miffed over the perquisites that President Ford was doling out. "I could ask [the uncommitted delegates] to the ranch for a barbecue, but it isn't the same as having dinner at the White House with the Queen of England," she said. John Sears convinced her that the most effective move would be for the governor to phone all 136 uncommitted delegates. Reagan balked, but Nancy insisted, and like a dutiful secretary, she placed every call herself, saying: "Governor Ronald Reagan is calling from his ranch in California and would like to speak to you about the convention. Please hold the line for the governor."

The personal phone calls did nothing to change the delegate count in Reagan's favor, and by the middle of July, President Ford looked as if he had the nomination cinched. The Reagan camp needed to stave off the public perception of defeat before Reagan got to the convention. So John Sears boldly approached Senator Richard Schweiker of Pennsylvania, a liberal Republican, to see whether he would allow his name to be submitted as Reagan's running mate before the convention. Sears approached Schweiker without first talking to Ronald Reagan, but he had, of course, discussed the matter with Nancy, implying that Schweiker could deliver Pennsylvania's ninety-six uncommitted delegates.

"That in itself shows you how little John Sears thought of the candidate," said a top campaign aide, "but much as I resented him for his contemptuous attitude toward Reagan, I have to say that announcing Schweiker as the vice presidential choice was a brilliant move in that it kept us alive and in the race when we were almost written off."

Henry Hyde, a conservative Republican congressman from Illinois, disagreed. "It's like a farmer selling his cow," he said, "to buy a milking machine."

The decision to select Schweiker as running mate was easily sold to Ronald Reagan by Sears, who suggested bringing the senator and his wife to Los Angeles for a few days before making the announcement.

"I had to get them to agree to spend a little time together beforehand so they'd know something about each other," he said. "So we flew the Schweikers in from Pennsylvania and the Reagans invited them to lunch at their house in Pacific Palisades. I remember that it was paramount that Justin Dart and Holmes Tuttle be there to meet them as well.

" 'We have to do this, John,' Nancy said to me. 'It won't change anything, of course. You understand that, but we've got to have them here so they can think they have okayed the decision.' "

Nancy's sop to the kitchen cabinet was not lost on the political strategist. "It was very smart on her part," said Sears, who respected her intelligence more than her husband's.

After lunch, Nancy, who had been put off by the Pennsylvania senator's preference for striped polyester pants, a white short-sleeved nylon shirt, and a wide, garish tie, took Sears aside. "Does he always dress that way?" she asked anxiously. "Can't something be done?"

Sears reassured her that Schweiker would undoubtedly dress better on the campaign trail—"I'm afraid he had no place to go but up in that department"—but more important than his taste in clothes, said the campaign manager, was the political strength Schweiker would bring to Ronald Reagan.

"John believed that a Reagan-Schweiker ticket would be hard to beat in November, and I believe he was right," Nancy said many years later. "But when Ronnie announced that he had chosen Schweiker, conservative Republicans were furious. They saw Schweiker as too liberal, as another Rockefeller, and they felt that in choosing him, Ronnie had betrayed the cause. . . . As always, some of Ronnie's supporters insisted on putting ideological purity ahead of victory."

By this time, Nancy had learned Machiavelli's message: Principles count for nothing in politics and winning is everything. She lived by this precept now, discarding friends and embracing enemies, all in an effort to obtain the elusive prize—making her husband President.

After nine months, twenty primaries, and $13 million spent trying to win the GOP nomination, the Reagans arrived in Kansas City for the convention on August 16, 1976. Their chartered plane disgorged their entire staff with the exception of one woman whom Nancy had left at the airport in California, refusing to let her on board because she was having an affair with a Secret Service agent. In addition to the staff, the Reagans were accompanied by Nancy's hairdresser, Julius; Nancy's best friend, Betsy Bloomingdale; Nancy's New York armpiece, Jerome Zipkin; and three of the Reagans' four children. Michael Reagan was there with his wife, Colleen. Eighteen-year-old Ron, who had taken a semester off from high school to work for his father, attended without his married lover, and Maureen Reagan arrived with Gene Nelson, who was carrying his own movie camera to record the event. Patti, still unmarried and living with Bernie Leadon, was not invited.

The Reagans and their entourage were besieged by reporters clamoring for stories, and everyone, including Betsy Bloomingdale, gave interviews extolling the candidate's virtues and those of his wife. "Nancy does things quietly," she said. "I think she'd be a First Lady more in the Jackie Kennedy mold. She'd lend a certain graciousness. They both have that certain kind of education and breeding, and that quiet reserve." Weeks later, Mrs. Bloomingdale was not so accessible to reporters. She had pleaded guilty to altering a customs invoice, claiming two Christian Dior gowns cost $518.68 when they had cost $13,880—a federal offense. The judge fined her $5,000 and rebuked her, saying she "deserved the contempt of society which has served you so well."

The presence of people like Mrs. Bloomingdale and Mr. Zipkin in the Reagan family box at the Kemper Arena disturbed the strenuously working Reagan aides. "I needed ten seats in that box so that I could bring in people from the uncommitted delegations every twenty minutes to sit with the Reagans and schmooze, which might have changed the delegate count," said one staff man, "but Nancy refused, saying she needed the seats for her friends. She was so adamant about getting society people into her box that she ignored the people who could do something politically for her husband. No wonder he came in second."

Nancy's arrival at the convention caused pandemonium among the conservative delegates, who jumped to their feet screaming and stomping and chanting, "We want Reagan. We want Reagan." The eruption of applause halted proceedings for ten minutes as the candidate's petite wife in a startling red dress waved and smiled, acknowledging the cheers. Betty Ford watched impassively.

"We have friends on both sides of the aisle," Betty Ford said later. "Always have. There shouldn't be any feeling of bitterness just because you're running against each other. But damn it all, Nancy Reagan was tough from the beginning. She's a queen bee and expects to be treated that way!"

First Lady Betty Ford still smarted over Reagan's intraparty challenge to her husband. She blamed him for causing the President to squander his energies in a bitter primary fight. "Personally, I think it should have been uncontested," she said. "Jerry has done such a good job in the last two years. To fight is very bad, very bad for the party; it has built up animosities. The Democrats somehow always are able to go away from a convention and make up, join forces. The Republican party has a history of 'If my man doesn't get in, I'm just going home and sit on my hands.' We've got to have unity in the party."

The next night, Mrs. Ford whipped the convention into a screeching frenzy when she appeared in an electric yellow dress and took her place in the Ford family box with singer Tony Orlando. Determined not to let Mrs. Ford have the spotlight to herself, Nancy arrived minutes later, thereby throwing the horn-blowing Reagan delegates into a deafening contest with the foot-stamping Ford delegates. The band played "California, Here I Come" as the Reaganites clapped and chanted and waved their banners. Then the band, which like everything else at the convention was controlled by the Ford forces, swung into the "Michigan Fight Song."

"Nancy still seemed to be getting more applause," said Peter Sorum, the advance man for Betty Ford, "so I signaled the band to stand playing 'Tie a Yellow Ribbon 'Round the Old Oak Tree,' which was Tony Orlando's theme song. He got up, put his arm around Mrs. Ford, and started dancing in the aisle with her, and the place went nuts, absolutely nuts. The front page of the next day's *New York Times* carried the headline: 'Betty Ford Bests Nancy Reagan on Applause Scale.'"

"Nancy was enraged by Betty Ford's performance that night," recalled Gene Nelson, who was sitting with her in the Reagan family box. "She was sputtering, she was so mad. She said it was a deliberate attempt to upstage her. Of course, she knew by then that Ronnie had lost, and she was quite distressed. That night there had been a preliminary vote on a Reagan proposal which showed that we didn't have the muscle to win. That's when Nancy knew it was over, and she's such a driven woman, so very ambitious, that the loss was harder on her than it was on Ronnie."

Before the crucial delegate roll call the next night, Reagan told his family what had become obvious. "I know all of you have worked very hard, but I don't have enough delegates to get the nomination," he said. "I'm just not going to get the job done. I'm truly sorry you all have to see this, but I'm glad we are all here together as a family."

Before leaving for the convention floor, Nancy, who was standing by the fireplace in their suite at the Alameda Plaza Hotel, poured champagne. "She toasted Dad," recalled Michael Reagan, "and then spoke directly to him, her voice cracking with emotion. I don't remember her words verbatim, but I had the impression that she was trying to take the burden of Dad's loss onto her shoulders and, somehow, accept the blame and pain for his failure. . . . She apologized to Dad for pushing him into the first political failure of his life, but she did it because she loved him and no matter what happened they still had each other. . . . She hugged him and I heard Dad say, 'I love you, too, Mommy.' "

Reagan turned to the rest of the room. "The long ride is over," he said. Mike Deaver spoke up quietly, suggesting that Reagan might want to thank Richard Schweiker for all he had done. Reagan quickly corrected his oversight and told the Pennsylvania senator that it had taken courage for him to join up. "Well," said Schweiker, who had been unable to deliver his state's uncommitted delegation, "the country is the loser."

Nancy told everyone to dry their eyes. "We are going to walk into that convention center with our heads up," she said. And they did, leaving behind the candidate, who was not scheduled to appear until the following night. That's when President Ford would accept the nomination by acclamation and beckon Reagan and his wife to join him on stage, setting off another thunderous ovation that shook the convention hall.

Their final day in Kansas City the Reagans headed for the red-wallpapered ballroom that had been rented for their victory celebration; the defeated candidate wanted to thank his loyal supporters. On the way, they ran into Clarke Reed, the Mississippi conservative whose defection to Ford might have cost Reagan the nomination. "Governor," said the delegate, weeping, "I made the biggest mistake of my life."

"It's all right, we all make mistakes," said Reagan, his anger melting. Nancy refused to speak and quickly turned away as if to block out the repugnant sight of the little man who had caused them such unhappiness.

In the ballroom, Reagan greeted his campaign workers and pepped them up with a hint he'd run again in 1980. "Nancy and I, we aren't going to go back and sit in our rocking chairs and say that's all for us," he said. "Don't get cynical, because look at yourselves and what you were willing to do, and recognize that there are millions and millions of Americans out there that want what you want, that want it to be as we do, who want it to be a shining city on a hill. . . . You just stay in there. The cause is there and the cause will prevail, because it's right."

He then turned to his wife, who was choking back tears, and gestured for her to take the microphone. "I can't," she whispered, lowering her head so the cameras wouldn't catch her crying. She turned her back to the crowd and faced the red wallpaper, struggling for composure. The crowd shifted uncomfortably for several minutes and Reagan made no move toward her. He just stared ahead sadly. Finally, she recovered, and turned around, smiling wanly. She said later that the only pleasure she took from Kansas City was seeing a hand-painted sign at the airport: GOODBYE REPUBLICANS. YOU PICKED THE WRONG MAN. On the plane home she said she could hardly wait until the 1980 election.

The animosity between the Reagans and Fords could not be overcome in time for the general election, so President Ford had to campaign against the former governor of Georgia, Jimmy Carter, without the full support of the Republican party. Whenever Reagan was asked to campaign for Ford, he pleaded the press of previous commitments. He stumped for conservative Republican congressional candidates in the Western states and praised the GOP platform at every turn, but never the GOP President. Reagan even refused to travel with Ford through California during the last week of the campaign.

On election day, the Reagans went to the polls, but abstained from voting for President. Jimmy Carter won and Nancy confided to a friend that she was relieved. "At least," she said, "I'll never have to see another one of those damn 'Keep Betty Ford in the White House' buttons again as long as I live."

14

THE REAGANS HAD BEEN LOOKING FORWARD to spending Thanksgiving 1976 with William F. Buckley, Jr., and his wife, Pat, at their family estate in Sharon, Connecticut. The conservative editor in chief of the *National Review* had been an ardent political supporter and close personal friend of the Reagans for many years. A graduate of Yale University, he had exercised the prerogative of a famous alumnus by getting eighteen-year-old Ron Reagan accepted for admission. Ron's parents had been so enthralled by the prospect of having their youngest child attend an Ivy League school that despite his resistance they had insisted that he enroll.

"When Ron first said he was going to Yale, he said he was going because his parents wanted him to," said John West, his high school dance teacher at the Harvard School in Los Angeles. "But he said that he knew he wouldn't finish. He threatened to flunk himself out because they wouldn't respect his wishes. . . . Ron did not want to follow [in] the footsteps that his parents had already laid out for him. It wasn't so much his dad as his mom. She was the one who was basically determining where he ought to go and what he ought to do."

On the night before Thanksgiving, two months after he had started college, Ron met his parents in New York City and dropped his bomb: He told them he was quitting Yale that weekend to become a ballet dancer. His father gasped, his mother shrieked, but he remained adamant, refusing even to consider finishing his first semester. He said most

ballet students begin dancing seriously by the age of fourteen; at eighteen, he felt there wasn't a moment to lose, including December and
January. The next day, the parents and their errant son arrived in Connecticut to spend the weekend with the Buckleys.

"Just before lunch, Nancy had drawn Pat aside while Ron Sr. took me
into another room, and each of us was told of their awful experience the
night before," recalled William F. Buckley, Jr. "Their son had arrived in
New York on Wednesday night to announce that he had decided to leave
Yale and study ballet! Such a decision is not easily received in any household. In this household, it was received with true shock.

" 'Who am I to object?' the father said to me, pacing the floor of the
music room. 'I mean, *I* ought to know about show business, and the
ballet is great stuff. But so few people make it. And pulling out of college
. . . in the middle of a semester . . .' Reagan does not act excited, but
one can sense when he is excited. He was thinking out loud. He paused.
And then said he was determined that his son should finish out the semester, because that way his record at Yale would be clean 'if he comes out
of it—you know, if he doesn't make it.' "

By the time the Reagans flew home to California, they were so overwrought about their son that they could talk of nothing else. They
begged him to change his mind, but he wouldn't, so Nancy played her
trump card. "Decide what you want to be and if it's medical school or
law school, we'll be happy to pay everything," she said. "But if it's
dance, we won't support you." Ron said he didn't care about their
money; he would support himself. The argument ended when he
stormed out of the house and went to stay with his sister, Patti. The next
day his father called Gene Nelson.

"I need to talk with you. Meet me downstairs in the restaurant of my
office building [Deaver & Hannaford] at 4:00 P.M., " Nelson recalled
Reagan saying.

"I met him and he started right in. He said, 'I don't know how to
handle the situation with Ron and I don't mean to cast aspersions on you
as a dancer, but there are so many homosexuals in dance that it is largely
looked upon with disdain. Male dancers. You know what I mean. Huh?'

" 'I said I knew what he meant, but he couldn't blame it on dance. I got
through it and I'm not gay. It does not necessarily follow that if Ron
wants to dance, he's going to end up being homosexual. I did say that it
was late to start dancing at the age of eighteen, but it was not impossible.
I told him that it was wrong for him and Nancy to withhold their support
because of Ron's dedication to dance. I said: Even if it's a phase he's
going through, it can't hurt him. The learning of dance will never do

your boy any harm. The homosexual thing that bothers you so much, well, Ronnie, you're just going to have to gamble on your son." Making that leap of faith was not easy for Ronald Reagan. Yet according to his son's high school dance teacher, he need not have worried so much about his child's sexual preferences. "Ron had an active sex life as a teenager. That was pretty common knowledge," said John West, who knew about his student's love affair with Kris Harmon Nelson. "I was aware of that relationship and there was never any question about it being just an experiment to see if he liked girls or whatever. I mean it was clear that he was quote unquote normal."

Still, the public image of his son as a ballet dancer troubled Reagan, who prided himself on his rugged demeanor as a horseback-riding he-man. He remained defensive about Ron's choice of a career, even after Ron was awarded a scholarship by the Joffrey II Company, the training troupe for the Joffrey Ballet in New York. Photographs of his delicately featured son in a leotard and tights leaping gracefully made him uncomfortable. He refused to attend Ron's debut with the Joffrey II dancers in 1980, and it would be another year before he could bring himself to watch his son perform. He strained awkwardly when answering questions about Ron's dancing career. "How could I say no?" he asked one reporter. "As he said to me, nobody said 'no' when I wanted to be an actor." To another he said, "He's all man—we made sure of that." The thought of being publicly ridiculed over his children, whom he could not control, was discomforting.

As governor of California, Reagan had been criticized for sending his daughter Patti to an out-of-state school, and he had reacted immediately, moving to withdraw her to stop the carping. "I remember when he called me," said Charles Orme, owner of the Orme School in Mayer, Arizona. "He said he would have to bring Patti home and put her in school in California. I said I certainly regretted that because we'd like her to carry on with us and he said he would, too, but he was under political pressure. Apparently, Patti, who had a fairly strong will, objected so strenuously that she was able to prevail in the end."

Now Reagan was faced with the specter of his son entering the field of ballet. He kept reiterating to friends his desire that Ron put his efforts into something more substantial, less frivolous. In frustration, he called his son Michael and asked what he should do.

"I almost said, 'Buy him a tutu,' but thought better of it," recalled Michael Reagan. "I knew that Ron's choice of a profession did not fit in any way with the Reagan image. Most of the public who supported Dad perceived male ballet dancers as gay. But I was flattered that Dad was seeking my advice about my younger brother, and I was kind of glad Ron was on the hot seat. . . . For once it was Nancy's own child who wasn't reflecting well on Dad [and not me]."

It was Nancy, according to Gene Nelson, who was most agitated about Ron's decision to dance. Though she had many homosexual friends and former colleagues, she could not stomach the thought of her son being perceived as one.

She became especially alarmed when Ron went out drinking with a group of young men and ended the evening by doing a striptease. She learned later that private photographs of her son had been taken.

"Ronnie told me that Nancy was distraught about the situation," said Gene Nelson. "She didn't want her boy dancing with homosexuals. She was more of a bigot about the homosexual thing than Ronnie was. Ronnie was picking and choosing his words carefully when he was talking to me, of course, because you don't call up a dancer and say, 'You guys are all fags and I don't want my son to be a fag.' But he still got the message across loud and clear. It was totally friendly. I felt he was really hurt at having to make this judgment, but Nancy was so concerned about the sexual orientation of her son that he said he had to do something.

"After our talk, I strongly recommended that he and Nancy support their son, financially and emotionally. I said I would call a friend of mine, who runs the Stanley Holden Dance Center, to audition Ron to see if he had any potential. Stanley auditioned him and called me back, saying, 'I'm quite surprised. He has talent but no matter how hard he studies and works, he's too old to become a premier dancer. Still, he could possibly become a partner in a ballet dance company. Possibly. And that is a worthy career in itself.' Stanley got the impression from Ron that he was determined to prove himself as a dancer, to prove to his mother and father that he could do it.

"I called Ronnie back and told him about Stanley's evaluation. Holden had been apprised of the family situation, the problem with money, and the parents' intention to withhold it. So Stanley gave Ron a job at the desk of the Dance Center to pay for his lessons. Maureen persuaded Ronnie and Nancy to pay for his apartment. I lobbied for it, too, and Stanley did his part by giving his professional evaluation. To help Ron, we all pleaded with his parents to be supportive, but they refused."

Ron helped to support himself through a series of odd jobs, all of which he said he hated, such as selling menswear at I. Magnin. "I got the job because my mother knew the president of the store," he said.

At the same time they were coping with the shame of a ballet-dancing son, the Reagans were trying to position themselves for another run at the presidency. Nancy implied as much when she talked to *Women's Wear Daily* six weeks after Jimmy Carter was elected: "I am going to help

Ronnie, where I can, restructure the Republican party. People are tired of politicians. There has to be a new breed of person in government. Carter is an unknown; I hope he does well for this country, but we will need another voice, and we will need new leaders, leaders with more spiritual sensitivity and an ability to make the tough decisions when necessary."

To ensure that her husband would be considered just such a leader, the Reagans invested $1.5 million left over from 1976 campaign contributions in a political action committee, Citizens for the Republic (CFTR). It was run by Lyn Nofziger and aimed at Reagan's zealous constituency, the ideologues whom Nancy Reagan would later dismiss as rigid "jump-off-the-cliff-with-the-flag-flying conservatives." To these true believers, Reagan preached his gospel in regular newsletters, attacking the Panama Canal treaty, Communist Russia, and the deficiencies of the Carter administration. He made speeches on behalf of conservative congressional candidates supported by the CFTR and addressed any group willing to pay his $25,000 fee plus first-class expenses. He continued his radio broadcasts and his weekly newspaper column, all geared to keeping his voice raised as the preeminent Republican spokesman opposing the Democratic President. He held regular staff meetings that, according to Peter Hannaford, were structured "to review the performance of the Carter administration and the state of the Republican party." He conferred with his personal pollster, Richard Wirthlin, examining the polls like a gypsy reading tea leaves.

The most important decision facing the undeclared candidate was choosing a campaign manager. Reagan had given his word to many conservatives around the country that he would not put John Sears in charge again. Sears's selection of liberal Richard Schweiker as Reagan's running mate in 1976 still rankled the right wing.

"Imagine their reaction if they had known my first choice was Nelson Rockefeller," said Sears fourteen years later, still convinced that a Reagan-Rockefeller ticket would have won the White House in 1976. "The only problem was that there were too many advisers around Rockefeller who would've persuaded him not to take the offer. Left to his own devices, I'm sure he would've said yes, and it would've been a winning ticket, but because he would've been talked out of it, I decided on Schweiker instead."

Such calculation was more than Reagan's impassioned followers could stomach. They did not trust Sears, the smooth-talking Washington lawyer.

But Mike Deaver, Reagan's top aide, was so impressed with Sears and his contacts within the Eastern press establishment that he argued strenuously in his favor, saying that the next presidential campaign could not be won without him.

"Sears was no ideologue," said Deaver. "He was at heart a brain for hire who wanted to play on a winning team. And those were terms I understood."

So did Nancy Reagan, and she and Deaver teamed up to convince her husband. Sears was invited to the Reagans' ranch above Santa Barbara, where they discussed strategy for the 1980 campaign. He outlined how he would present the candidate as the GOP front-runner in a field that was highly likely to include George Bush, Senators Howard H. Baker, Jr., and Robert Dole, Congressmen John Anderson and Philip Crane, and former Texas governor John Connally. By the end of the day, Ronald Reagan was running for President and John Patrick Sears was once again in charge of the campaign.

This time around, though, Sears insisted on complete control. Having convinced the Nancy Reagan–Mike Deaver axis that a less conservative-sounding Reagan would be more palatable to voters, Sears was determined to tie a moderate ribbon around his candidate. This was abhorrent to the right-wing California stalwarts surrounding Reagan. Sears didn't trust any of them, so he began trying to get rid of them. He started by complaining about Lyn Nofziger, who was in charge of fund-raising, saying that his harvest netted only 50 cents for every dollar spent. Sears easily convinced Nancy, who had long ago tried to get rid of the bedraggled aide, that Nofziger was ineffective at emptying other people's pockets. With her help, Sears obtained the candidate's permission to fire Nofziger. Mike Deaver was chosen to swing the ax on the former press secretary who had been one of Reagan's first and most devoted aides.

Nofziger bitterly told Deaver that Sears would eventually turn on the ax-wielder himself and then on Ed Meese, Reagan's top policy man, until Sears had gotten rid of all the Californians who wanted Reagan to be Reagan. Within six months, Nofziger looked more prescient than Nostradamus.

From 1976 through 1979, the firm of Deaver & Hannaford continued representing "the Governor," as they respectfully referred to him, arranging his speaking dates, orchestrating his press coverage, and advancing his trips, especially the foreign trips that he took with Nancy, which included trips to England, France, Germany, Japan, Taiwan, Hong Kong, and to Iran to visit the Shah, their "dear friend" on the Peacock Throne.

The Reagan account naturally included handling Mrs. R as well, which meant hours of slavish attention to the imperial packaging of the candidate's wife. A simple interview request was treated like a petition for a royal audience. After an initial phone call in which the interviewer was interviewed—How much of Mrs. Reagan's time is required? Is an hour enough? When will the piece appear? Will it be syndicated? Who will take the photographs?—the request had to be submitted in writing to the public relations firm, where it was scrutinized by Mike Deaver and Peter Hannaford for possible "problem areas," such as the reporter's liberal bias or hidden agenda. The two men, always fidgety when it came to Mrs. R and the press, especially female reporters, still flinched remembering Joan Didion's interview in Sacramento for the *Saturday Evening Post*. A repeat of her "Pretty Nancy" piece and they would lose their biggest client. Consequently, all requests for interviews with Mrs. R were examined microscopically.

If the publication was too influential to ignore, like the *Los Angeles Times*, or too important to the candidate's wife, like *Women's Wear Daily* or *Town & Country*, the request was then submitted in writing to Nancy, with the added written recommendation of Mike Deaver. If Mrs. R agreed to the interview, the reporter was invited to the Westwood offices of Deaver & Hannaford, where he or she was presented with a biographical sheet listing Mrs. Reagan's awards and accomplishments beginning with the Foster Grandparents Program and ending with her "fashionable distinction of ten years on the best-dressed list." Then someone would discreetly phone the Pacific Palisades house to see whether it was safe to send the reporter ahead. Only after the all-clear signal was sounded by the Reagan housekeeper was the reporter given directions on how to find San Onofre Drive.

These reporters invariably left the Reagan home feeling they should receive hardship pay for trying to extract information from a woman who was too guarded to give them good copy. "As an interview subject, Nancy Reagan speaks only when spoken to," said Nan Nichols of the *Sacramento Bee*. "Polite and smiling throughout, she volunteers nothing. She seems to weigh every response before giving it voice. She is gun-shy, she explains, having not always been treated kindly by the press since her husband turned from acting to politics."

"She just drove me nuts," said Nancy Collins, formerly of *Women's Wear Daily*. "She sits there with her legs glued together, her hands all white knuckles, teeth grinding, and that face just a mask—no animation, no laughter, no spontaneity, nothing. She was awful, just awful."

Her lack of responsiveness toward the distaff press was no less galling than her rudeness. Louise Sweeney of the *Christian Science Monitor* was kept waiting at a maid's entrance for more than an hour when she arrived to interview Mrs. Reagan for a campaign story in Florida, and Susan Stamberg of National Public Radio stood in the rain for thirty minutes in Virginia before she was ushered into a back bedroom to wait for another half hour for her interview. "Finally, I was allowed to go into the living room to wait, and after twenty minutes or so Mrs. Reagan made her entrance. She walked toward me, but before saying hello, she stopped at least four times to empty every ashtray along the way."

Nancy played to the heavyweights of the press corps, ignoring the daily newspaper peons, while reserving her charms for powerful media men like the late Frank Reynolds, anchor of ABC-TV's "World News Tonight," the conservative columnist George F. Will, and Mike Wallace of CBS-TV's "60 Minutes," a friend of her mother's from their radio days in Chicago. As for the female press contingent, only society writers like Betty Beale and Aileen Mehle, who wrote under the byline "Suzy," were considered acceptable. As was Liz Smith, the gossip columnist of the *New York Daily News*, who endeared herself in the late eighties by phoning and reading her columns to Mrs. Reagan, letting her rewrite the Reagan items in their entirety. Liz then would phone her editors around the country, instructing them to insert Mrs. Reagan's changes.

"For the most part, though, Nancy didn't like women reporters at all," said Laurence Barrett of *Time* magazine. "She much preferred male journalists."

More than anything else about Nancy Reagan, it was "the gaze"—the lights-are-all-out look she beamed on her husband whenever he made a speech—that soured the stomachs of many reporters.

"It puts you in mind of the lowly oxen in the manger," wrote Elgy Gillespie in England's *Today*.

"It's transfixed adoration more appropriate to a witness of the Virgin Birth," wrote Lou Cannon in the *Washington Post*.

Time magazine described it as "prima facie evidence of a Goody Two-Shoes phoniness," and Calvin Trillin satirically suggested in the *Nation* that it might set back progress in Jordan and prompt a lead editorial in that country's official newspaper that it was "the best argument we in the Muslim world have seen for the reinstitution of the veil."

Needing to create the fantasy of a publicly adoring wife, Nancy resented such criticism. When a television interviewer said, "And now, Mrs. Reagan, tell us about your famous 'gaze,'" her tight little smile turned mean.

"Gays?" she said coldly.

"Your 'gaze,' the way you look at your husband whenever he gives a speech."

"Well, what am I supposed to do?" she snapped crossly. "Count the house?"

With that she yanked off her microphone and stormed out of the studio, sliding into her waiting car with her chief of staff, Peter McCoy, and rolling her eyes heavenward.

Most reporters assumed that Ronald Reagan's devoted wife was simply time-traveling back to "The Donna Reed Show," where marriage was a sitcom of perfection. They did not understand that "the gaze" was a personal stratagem that had been developed by a pathetically insecure child to ingratiate herself with others—and had been used with remarkable success over the years. "I have a picture of my mother looking at my father [Loyal Davis] in just the same way," said Nancy. Now that she needed to charm a nation of voters for her husband, "the gaze" would become a clever campaign device to counteract Rosalynn Carter's public image as a First Lady who insisted on attending cabinet meetings ("I never ask questions. I sit in to listen and learn," Rosalynn said. "That way I can speak intelligently when I travel around the country"). Tagged "the Steel Magnolia," Mrs. Carter frequently acted as a surrogate President, and Nancy, who deplored such obviousness in a woman, used Mrs. Carter's co-presidency to her advantage, always professing great shock at Rosalynn's wifely arrogation of power. "I'm certainly not going to sit in on cabinet meetings," Nancy said archly. "That may suit Mrs. Carter, but it's just not my style."

Beneath such synthetic self-effacement lurked ambition that craved recognition of its own. "Nancy wanted more for herself than any woman I've ever known," said John Sears. "She was driven to be acknowledged. She had to be somebody, and Ronald Reagan was the vehicle."

The ego hidden behind the selfless wife surfaced during the campaign with the publication of her 219-page autobiography, which she had insisted be entitled *Nancy.*

"No other title would do," said Julia Knickerbocker, former publicity director of William Morrow and Company. "Others were suggested, but she was adamant. . . . I've blocked most of the details of publishing that book because she was so loathsome to work with."

"She wanted it to be her book," said one of the editors. "She even cut much of the original copy about Ronald Reagan and fought to get his photograph removed from the back of the jacket cover, but was finally overruled on that. . . . The book was all sweetness and light, and we had this strange feeling that she did not want to be upstaged by Ronnie. We had to say to her, 'Look, we're publishing this book because you're the wife of a presidential candidate.' "

Writer Bill Libby, who tape-recorded Nancy's reminiscences for the book, was embarrassed by the final product. Nancy went through ten rewrites, cutting all but the most perfunctory references to her children and refusing to say her son was a ballet dancer. "Let's leave it that he was artistic," she said.

"I was not entirely happy with what she was willing to leave in, but it was her book, not mine," said Libby. "I think there's more to her than shows in there—good as well as bad."

In the end, Nancy refused to divulge her date of birth or mention Jane Wyman's name. Instead, she produced the life story of a woman who felt an affinity for artifice, and reading it was like slogging through Winnie the Pooh's honeypot. She papered her pain with a tissue of lies. She said her childhood years, in which her mother left her, letting her grow up with her aunt and uncle in Bethesda, Maryland, were "good old times in the good old days, a peaceful time in a peaceful place, when we ate ice cream in the summer and slid down a snowy hill in the winter." She said in the book that she had not seen her real father since her early teens, although she had visited him years later. She barely mentioned Nanee Robbins or her cousins.

Nancy carefully omitted all the heartache along the way: her struggle to get adopted and her campaign to get Ronald Reagan to marry her. She didn't deal with the pregnancy that finally forced that marriage, or the trials of raising her children in the sixties and dealing with their abortions, their drugs, their lovers. The purpose of the book was, after all, to promote herself as a personality with "strict moral standards" and, in the process, help get her husband elected President.

That effort began in earnest for the Reagans in March 1979, although the candidate would not formally declare himself for eight more months. This time, though, everyone around them had the feeling that they were finally at the right station, about to board the right train, and that only a catastrophic collision could derail the locomotive heading toward the White House. The pressure to avoid such a collision would eventually take its toll on the candidate's wife, who more than once stood in her bra and slip, her face slathered with cold cream, her hair in rollers, screeching at Peter McCoy.

"Yes, it happened more than once, but we were operating out of tight quarters during that campaign, which was a pressure cooker," said Mc-Coy, who was also known as "the Purser" because he had to carry Nancy's pocketbook whenever she wished. "These trips were hard on her. She's very disciplined on the campaign trail, but she was working on six hours' sleep. She was doing her own makeup. There's a time when she looks bad."

Gearing up for the press scrutiny of the 1980 campaign, Nancy insisted on presenting the public with a picture of an enraptured wife and her hearth-loving family, and she managed it on November 13, 1979, when Ronald Reagan announced his intention to seek the presidency: The photograph showed Mrs. Reagan flanked by four children smiling in various degrees. Bringing those children together for the presidential announcement was considered quite a feat by those who knew the Reagans well.

"Thank God it was a short announcement," said John Sears.

"The kids are all strange and crazy out of neglect," said Peter McCoy. "They're relatively unproductive, and it's certainly not from being overindulged or showered with too much love. I think it's more from having parents who should never have had children. Nancy and Ronald Reagan just didn't need kids; their lives were complete with each other."

Patti, twenty-seven, no longer living with Bernie Leadon, was struggling to become an actress, a singer, and a songwriter. She had been welcomed back into her mother's presence for her father's presidential announcement, but Patti would not campaign for him because she said she hated politics. Maureen, thirty-eight, whose live-in relationship with Gene Nelson had recently ended, was now considered suitable enough for public presentation. Ron, twenty-one, had improved only marginally in Nancy's eyes after he substituted a love affair with an unmarried woman only seven years his senior for his previous one with a married woman thirteen years older than he. His career as a ballet dancer still troubled her. "She was worried that the press, with the presidential election [coming], would think they had a flighty son flitting around," said thirty-four-year-old Michael Reagan. As for Michael, he who had been the most problematical of the children was now the one who seemed most respectable, with a wife, a child, and a steady job. Still, this did nothing to endear him to his father and stepmother.

With Patti and Ron refusing to campaign, Maureen and Michael volunteered to represent the family, much to the dismay of Nancy, whose relationship with both stepchildren had disintegrated since the 1976 campaign. At a birthday party Maureen gave for her poodle, Barnae—attended by, among others, her mother, Jane Wyman, her brother Michael, and Robert Scheer of the *Los Angeles Times,* who was writing a profile of Reagan—someone pointed out that if Maureen's father was elected President, Barnae would become First Dog.

"No, that position is already taken," said Maureen.

"Yeah, it sure is," said Michael. Together they chorused: "Nancy is First Dog!"

Nancy had delivered a smiling family for public consumption, but she could not camouflage the dissension within the Reagan campaign: John

Sears was no longer speaking to Mike Deaver, and Deaver, who had refused to attend the announcement ceremony in New York, was not speaking to Sears.

"A campaign is like an orchestra," said Sears many years later. "Everyone has to sit in a chair. And everyone has to play the same music. From my point of view, Deaver was having trouble sitting in a chair and playing."

On Thanksgiving Day, Nancy called Deaver and asked him to come to the Pacific Palisades house for a meeting. When he arrived she steered him into the bedroom, but he saw Reagan sitting in the living room with John Sears and his top two campaign aides, Jim Lake and Charles Black. "What's this?" he asked.

"We're just finishing up a few things," said Nancy. "It will only be another five minutes or so."

Deaver sat in the bedroom for twenty minutes before he summoned the courage to venture into the living room. "What's going on?" he asked.

"Mike, the fellows here have been telling me about the way you're running the fund-raising efforts, and we're losing money," said Reagan. "As a matter of fact, they tell me I have to pay $30,000 a month to lease my space in your office building."

Deaver insisted the complaints against him were baseless and an excuse by John Sears to seize total control, an accusation Sears denied. Reagan started to get angry, and Nancy burst into tears. But Sears did not flinch. He demanded that Reagan make a decision "for once" about whether he wanted to continue with Deaver at the controls or to allow Sears to run the campaign with Lake and Black. This brought Nancy up short.

"Yes, honey," she said finally. "You're going to have to make a choice."

Before Reagan could respond, Deaver spoke up.

"No, Governor," he said. "You don't have to make that choice. I'll resign." With that he walked to the front door with Reagan following, agitated. The candidate returned to the living room furious that his weakness as a decision-maker had been exposed.

"The biggest man here just left the room," he said. "He was willing to accommodate and compromise, and you bastards wouldn't."

The next day, campaign aides were so incredulous that the Reagans' most faithful adjutant had been banished that one brave soul approached Mrs. Reagan about the matter. "I know you're upset," Nancy said, "but Mike's departure is for the good of the campaign. Besides, he has personal problems he has to work out."

"I knew then that staff was staff and friends were friends—and you

could never be both," said the aide. "No matter how many years you
worked for the Reagans or how closely. Joe Holmes, a longtime Rea-
ganite, finally set me straight. He said:
   " 'You have to understand that this is the beginning of the biggest
movie the Reagans will ever star in and all of us are bit players. If you
ever leave, all they'll have to do is call Central Casting and a new guy will
be brought in to take your place.' He was right, of course, which I found
out after working for them for over ten years."
   Two months later, when Reagan lost the Iowa caucus and his status as
the Republican front-runner was damaged, the countdown began against
John Sears. "From that point on, his days were numbered," said David
Keene. "Nancy would never forgive him for her husband's loss in Iowa
to George Bush, whom she abhorred for ridiculing Reagan's tax cuts as
'voodoo economics.' "
   Some thought the countdown had begun the month before in Florida,
when Nancy arrived to campaign and found orders from Sears's office
instructing her not to speak to the press. "Nancy exploded," said former
Florida campaign director Pat Hillings. "She really decided from then on
she'd get John Sears. . . ."

   The Reagan campaign was in tatters heading into the New Hampshire
primary—broke, demoralized, and desperate. "I felt the campaign was
lost," said Paul Laxalt, campaign chairman. Nancy tried to accompany
her husband as often as she could. Afraid of violence, she pulled him
away from autograph hunters at every stop and the loquacious pols who
took up too much of his time. "Smile, honey, smile," she would whisper
as he got ready to tape a television interview. She coached him behind
the scenes. "She hears Dad, and she comes back and has a discussion with
him, like maybe, 'Don't talk about your percentages so much,' " said
Michael Reagan. Without ever dropping "the gaze," she managed to
save him from countless embarrassing remarks and impolitic comments.
   At a press conference, Reagan said "a marijuana cigarette probably is
several times the cancer hazard for lung and throat cancer that a tobacco
cigarette is."
   "But a person doesn't have to smoke as many marijuana cigarettes to
get the desired effect," said a reporter.
   Nancy poked her husband. "You wouldn't know," she whispered.
   "I wouldn't know," said Ronald Reagan.
   Nancy did not hesitate to assert herself if her husband seemed threatened, as in the case of a female reporter who demanded to know why he
did not support the proposed Equal Rights Amendment. "May I speak to

that?" Mrs. Reagan said, stepping firmly between her husband and the microphone.

Occasionally, she would take the microphone away from him to improve on his response, as she did in Jaffrey, New Hampshire. "Her husband had been asked a cream-puff question by a supporter who wanted to know what Reagan would do about drugs if he were elected President," recalled Martin Smith, political editor of the *Sacramento Bee.* "The trouble with such imprecise questions is that they encourage imprecise answers, and Reagan's reply wandered everywhere without saying very much beyond suggesting that the federal government might launch an advertising campaign on the dangers of drugs.

"She listened as attentively as only Nancy Reagan can appear to when her husband is speaking, but when he finished, she took the unusual step of taking the microphone to improve upon his answer. She really did improve on it, too, giving a more sensible as well as a more philosophically conservative reply. She said that the proper exercise of parental authority, not the government, is the key line of defense against the misuse of drugs by children. Parents had to learn to say no and to make it stick, for the long-term good of their children, even at the risk of temporarily alienating them.

"She then apologized for speaking up, explaining, 'I feel so strongly about this I would love to be somewhere where I could do something about it.' " She received a resounding round of applause and probably delivered the Jaffrey parental vote.

But in Chicago a few days later she alienated the black vote. She was representing her husband at a fund-raiser, and he called from out of town over a phone hook-up to speak to his supporters. Over the microphone, she gushed, "Oh, Ronnie, I wish you could be here to see all these beautiful white people." She hesitated a moment, paled slightly, and quickly backtracked. "Beautiful black and white people, I mean." Later she apologized to a reporter. "I'm so sorry. I didn't mean it." Reagan's Illinois campaign manager tried to protect her, saying, "Well, she didn't mean that, she was talking to her husband about the white snow and that's how she got mixed up."

Campaigning without his wife in New Hampshire, Reagan committed a blunder of his own by telling an ethnic joke his son Michael had told him:

"How do you tell who the Polish fellow is at a cockfight? He's the one with the duck.

"How do you tell who the Italian is at the cockfight? He's the one who bets on the duck.

"How do you know the Mafia was there? The duck wins."

Listening to him repeat the joke to reporters, Ed Meese said, "There goes Connecticut."

The press reported the joke, causing a minor uproar among Connecticut's Poles and Italians, forcing Reagan to explain himself. He said he had been "stiffed" by the press. He had told the joke only to illustrate the kind of anecdote politicians should never tell.

Separated from each other, the Reagans were prone to such gaffes. The difference was that he usually laughed his off while she always blamed hers on someone else. This time they both accused the press of "inflating" his ethnic joke and "misinterpreting" her racial slight.

"No one loved a good ethnic or homosexual joke more than Ronald Reagan," said one of his top aides. "I remember in New York when we went to visit Vernon Jordan, former head of the National Urban League, who was in the Cornell Medical Center recuperating from a shooting attempt. En route to the hospital, Reagan told one of his favorite black jokes and laughed like hell telling it:

" 'A black guy walks into a bar with a parrot on his shoulder. He sits down at the bar and orders a drink. Before long, the bartender, who is quite curious, approaches them and asks, 'Where did you get him?' The parrot answers, 'In Africa!' ' "

A few days later, on the campaign plane, Reagan and the telephone advance man, George Gatchel, improvised one of their homosexual vaudeville routines for the amusement of the inner circle.

Spotting a copy of *The Washingtonian* magazine, which had superimposed a picture of Reagan's head atop the sweat-glistening body of a male bodybuilder, Gatchel held the photograph out to Reagan and winked, feigning delight.

"Oooooh, when you get all greased up like that, Ronnie, it just turns me on sooooo much."

Reagan took his cue and smiled primly, flicked his wrist, and put his hands on his hips.

"Ooooooh, Georgie, don't say that. You know I can't control myself."

"Don't get him started, Gatchel," said one aide, knowing Reagan's proclivity for the homosexual vamp, but the candidate continued swiveling his hips and taking mincing steps until Nancy, terrified that the press might see her husband, jumped up and closed the curtains between the two sections of the plane. She spent the next fifteen minutes trying to calm things down long enough to discuss the political situation that lay ahead of them.

• • •

Reagan had refused to debate in Iowa, but now that he was coming into
New Hampshire as a loser, Nancy told him he had no choice. So he
challenged George Bush to a debate, and the *Nashua Telegraph* agreed to
sponsor it. Two days before the event, the Federal Election Commission
ruled that the paper's sponsorship amounted to an illegal campaign contribution, so Reagan offered to split the $3,500 cost with Bush, but Bush
said no. John Sears then announced that the Reagan campaign would pay
for everything and began calling the other candidates to participate, despite rules stipulating that only Bush and Reagan could take part. That
evening the other candidates, Congressman John Anderson and Philip
Crane of Illinois, Senator Howard Baker of Tennessee, and Senator Robert Dole of Kansas, showed up at the debate site, and George Bush,
trying to protect his front-runner status, said he would not take part in an
open debate. Without Bush, Reagan considered backing out, but Nancy
argued against it.

"No," she said. "You should all go out."

So Reagan walked on stage and took his seat on the podium with the
four other candidates—still excluded by the debate rules—standing behind him. Bush, now feeling ambushed, came out, sat down, and stared
straight ahead. The audience of 2,500 started hollering for a free-for-all.
The publisher of the *Nashua Telegraph* tried to quiet them, but he was
booed. Reagan then tried to explain why he wanted the other candidates
to participate.

"Mr. Reagan is out of order," said the newspaper's editor, Jon Breen,
banging his gavel. "Turn his microphone off."

With theatrical flourish, Reagan grabbed the microphone in front of
him. "I paid for this microphone, Mr. Green," he exploded, mangling
the editor's name in the process.

Nancy jumped to her feet, shouting, "You tell him, honey, you tell
him!"

Reagan captured the crowd, most of whom did not recognize the
words as a direct steal from Spencer Tracy in *State of the Union,* who, as a
Republican presidential candidate, had commanded, "Don't you shut me
off, I'm paying for this broadcast!"

The former movie star cowboy glowed like Destry the night he rode
again. He knew from the ringing applause that he had just delivered his
best performance, which was later confirmed by one of his aides, who
said, "There were cells in Reagan's body that hadn't seen blood for
years. He was terrific!" The *Boston Globe* concurred: "At a high school in
Nashua, the Gipper grabbed the brass ring."

Rejuvenated, Reagan began campaigning with the energy of a raven-
ous underdog. Going into Iowa, reporters had made jokes about the

Ronald Reagan doll that, when wound, ran for forty-five minutes before it collapsed to take a nap. Now he went twenty-one days straight, amazing everyone around him.

He was invigorated by his days on the stump, but he dreaded the nights, when he had to return to the hotel and face the internal combustion among his top aides. Fractiousness dominated the campaign as John Sears, who had gotten rid of Nofziger, Deaver, and economic adviser Martin Anderson, now trained his sights on Ed Meese, who had always been viewed by Reagan loyalists as the heart and soul of their candidate.

"No other man could think and talk as much like Ronald Reagan as Ed," said Meese's top aide, "but Sears and his men had cut him off from the campaign's operations, and the isolation had taken its toll. He began drinking too much wine on campaign flights back to California, and his briefcase overflowed with unread position papers. Sears finally threatened Reagan a few days before the New Hampshire primary. Either he fire Meese or Sears and his men would leave.

"As on all overnight stops, I had a hotel room adjoining the Reagans', since I was constantly at their call. On this night, only a flimsy door separated my room from theirs, and I jumped at the sound of Reagan's raised voice. 'You dirty rotten bastards,' he was yelling, 'this is the same speech you made when I agreed to let Mike Deaver go!' I cupped my ear to the door so I could hear their response, but it was overwhelmed by another burst from Reagan: 'I'll be goddamned if I'll stand by and see Ed run out of this campaign!'

"Reagan's voice was so loud, and the doors so thin, that I immediately worried whether staffers passing in the hall could hear. I opened my door and peered outside. Only the Secret Service agent was there, and when he saw me he silently clapped his hands, signaling his support for what Reagan was saying. I nodded to him, relieved there was no one else there, and stepped back into my room, cupping my ear again to listen to the argument on the other side of the wall."

Reagan kept railing at John Sears. "You got Deaver, but by God, you're not going to get Ed Meese! You guys have forced me to the wall."

"Governor, this is your campaign," said Sears. "You have to do what you need to do. But I can't stay under these conditions."

Nancy, who had been sitting quietly with her husband, was afraid he was losing control. She broke in to calm him down. "Ronnie rarely loses his temper," she said later, "but he certainly was angry that night. . . . I was sure he was going to hit John, so I took his arm and said, 'It's late, and I think we should all get some sleep.' "

The alliance between John Sears and Ronald Reagan had never been made in heaven. The campaign manager could barely disguise his contempt for the passive candidate who refused to make decisions, and Reagan could not abide Sears because he never looked him in the eye. "He looks you in the tie instead," he said.

So Nancy decided to step in, and with deliberation worthy of Messalina, the Roman empress who executed anyone who thwarted her desires, she plotted the evisceration of John Sears and his two lieutenants. She called her former hatchet man, Mike Deaver, and said the campaign was in trouble. Deaver, who was thrilled to hear from her after eight months of silence, suggested that she consult William P. Clark, Reagan's onetime executive secretary and later his appointee to the California State Supreme Court. She called and asked Clark whether he would please take over as Reagan's chief of staff.

"Doesn't the governor already have a chief of staff?" asked Clark.

"That's our problem," said Nancy. "We've got two of them."

Clark agreed to meet with the Reagans, but he was loath to leave the bench and Reagan did not want to pressure him. Nancy then suggested William J. Casey, the former chairman of the Securities and Exchange Commission, whom the Reagans had met only once previously, at a fundraising dinner in New York. Reagan liked the idea and called him immediately. Casey agreed to come on board and straighten out the campaign finances.

All that remained was to inform John Sears. Nancy, still in communication with Sears under the guise of trying to mend things, suggested to her husband that he summon Sears, hand him a letter of resignation, and ask him to sign it. Instead, the letter became a press release stating that Sears had decided to return to his law practice in Washington, D. C., and that Jim Lake and Charles Black were leaving with him.

Nancy credits her husband with the timing of the presentation. "It was Ronnie's idea to let them go on the day of the New Hampshire primary, before the returns were in," she said. "In case we lost, he didn't want John to think that was the reason he was fired. And if we won, he didn't want John to think he was ungrateful."

On primary afternoon, February 26, 1980, Reagan summoned Sears, Lake, and Black to his third-floor suite in the Holiday Inn in Manchester, where he was sitting with Nancy and William Casey. Reagan handed Sears the press release, which Sears read and passed to Lake and Black.

"Well, John?" said Nancy from across the room. "Well?"

"I'm not surprised," Sears said with a shrug.

"The hell with this," said Charles Black, turning the press release over without reading it. "I quit."

The three men walked out of the room and Nancy followed them, saying, "I'm so sorry things turned out this way. I hope we won't be

Ronald Reagan and Nancy Davis in Hollywood during their two-and-a-half-year courtship.

18.

19.

Nancy Davis and Ronald Reagan in Hellcats of the Navy, 1957.

Nancy Davis and Ronald Reagan after applying for their marriage license in Los Angeles.

Ronald and Nancy Reagan on their wedding day, with William Holden and Brenda Marshall (a.k.a. Ardis Holden).

22.

Ronald and Nancy Reagan with their children: Patti, age five and a half, and Ronald Prescott, age one month.

Young Ron ("Skipper") talking with his mother.

23.

24.

*Jeane Dixon, the Reagans'
Washington astrologer.*

25.

*Carroll Righter, the Reagans'
astrologer in California.*

26.

*Joan Quigley, Nancy Reagan's San Francisco
astrologer.*

27.

*Governor Ronald Reagan with his administrative assistant, Paul
Beck, and his press secretary, Lyn Nofziger, in Sacramento.*

28.   *The Reagans and the Bushes
      watching election returns in 1984.*

29.

*Dr. and Mrs. Loyal Davis arriving
in Washington, D.C., for the 1981
inaugural.*

The First Lady tries to get her husband dancing at his seventieth birthday party in February 1981.

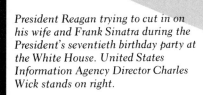

President Reagan trying to cut in on his wife and Frank Sinatra during the President's seventieth birthday party at the White House. United States Information Agency Director Charles Wick stands on right.

31.

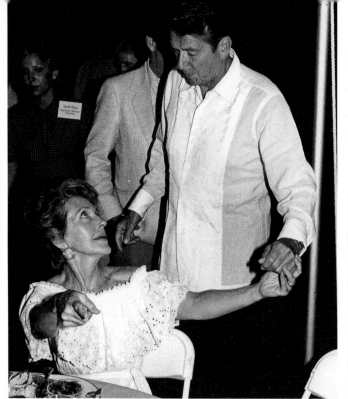

Nancy Reagan directing her husband in the fall of 1980 at Wexford, the house Jackie Kennedy built in Middleburg, Virginia.

32.

33.

Nancy Reagan instructs campaign manager William Casey, who later became director of the Central Intelligence Agency.

enemies." She added in a louder voice, "Please don't do anything that you will regret later."

Sears told her that he and his comrades would have to protect their professional reputations—an effort they began two days later with a press conference in Washington, D. C.

Minutes after the resignations were announced, the press questioned Reagan; Nancy was at his side.

"Where did the pressure come from to fire Sears?" a reporter asked. Reagan stood speechless. Nancy nudged him.

"From you," she prompted.

"From me," he said.

Hours later, Ronald Reagan overturned George Bush by taking the New Hampshire primary two to one, a victory that reestablished him as the Republican front-runner. The Democrats seemed immobilized. Three months earlier, Iran had seized fifty-two Americans, who were still being held hostage. Jimmy Carter had not been able to secure their release. Every night on television, people saw footage of rabid Iranian throngs burning the American flag, defiling the American embassy, and terrorizing U. S. citizens.

Reagan fed the national frustration over American inaction by threatening swift retribution against acts of international terrorism and deriding Carter as a disgraceful President. "I wouldn't stand there and do nothing," he said. Nancy joined in, "I don't know what Carter is," she said, "but he's not a strong leader."

By spring, the Reagan train looked like it was Hallelujah-bound, and with John Sears gone, the deposed Californians began returning to the campaign. One by one they came back—first Mike Deaver, then Martin Anderson, Lyn Nofziger, and, finally, Stu Spencer. But they had learned that they were expendable, and that their faithful service over the years was not reciprocated with total loyalty. They came back because they wanted to be part of a winning team. Within five years, some of them would lose all they had spent a lifetime building, and most would realize again, with pain and humiliation, that their relationship with the Reagans was based on expediency: staff was staff, friends were friends.

Two months before the victory train pulled into the Republican convention, one of the few friendships cherished by the candidate and his wife cast a small shadow across their happy horizon. Frank Sinatra, who had endeared himself to the Reagans by campaigning throughout 1980 and staging fund-raisers that netted more than $250,000, submitted Reagan's name to Nevada officials as a character reference for a gambling license. Sinatra had lost his original license in 1963 for entertaining Chicago's Mafia chieftain Sam Giancana at the Cal-Neva Lodge, and now—sixteen years later—he said he wanted to restore his reputation.

"I called Ed Meese the minute I heard the news and told him that Frank Sinatra's closeness to Reagan was going to do nothing but bode ill because the guy's been controlled by hoodlums for years," said Clarence Newton, a former FBI agent. "Meese said, 'But he's never been indicted.' I said, 'Oh, Christ, Ed, you sound like a defense attorney, not a prosecutor.' I tried to warn them, but Sinatra was giving them a hell of a lot of money at the time from doing benefits, so what I had to say fell on deaf ears."

"I was with Newt when he made that call," recalled William Roemer, the former FBI agent in charge of investigating organized crime in Chicago. "He told Meese how wrong it would be for Reagan to be a witness for Sinatra at his hearing before the Las Vegas gaming control board, but Meese didn't seem to be the least bit interested."

In fact, Meese was more than a little concerned about what the FBI agent had told him, and he quickly scheduled an appointment to talk to the Reagans about their friend who was so closely tied to the Mafia. But Meese might just as well have suggested the Reagans give all their money to the poor as to advise caution about Frank Sinatra. They chose not to listen to what they called "those terrible Mafia rumors." Nancy Reagan was particularly adamant on the subject. She demonstrated her disdain for Ed Meese's advice a few days later by inviting Sinatra and his wife to be special guests in the Reagan box at the Republican National Convention in Detroit. So when Ronald Reagan accepted the presidential nomination, Nancy watched from the box, sitting next to her honored guests, the Sinatras.

She had told her mother how impressed she was by the money Sinatra had raised for the Reagan campaign, plus the $1.3 million he had raised for the Desert Hospital in Palm Springs. Edith Davis, who was helping raise money for a small Catholic church in Phoenix, decided Sinatra needed God's blessing.

"She came in to see me," said Father John Doran, "and said, 'You probably think that Frank Sinatra is a son of a bitch, and he is, but he's done a lot of good for a hospital in Palm Springs, so I want you to say a mass for him. Do you think your hands will burn, if you do?'

"I said I didn't think so," said the priest, "and so as a favor to Edith, I said a mass for Frank Sinatra."

15

MIKE WALLACE WAS EXPECTED. As the CBS television correspondent later told colleagues, when he walked up to the house of Dr. and Mrs. Loyal Davis in Scottsdale's Biltmore Estates, the eighty-four-year-old physician was standing in the front door of his Arizona home. Next to the distinguished doctor was his little white-haired wife.

"Hey, Mike, how the fuck are you?" she hollered.

Wallace laughed, as he always did at Edith Davis, but this time even he was a bit startled as she lifted her dress over her head to show him her recent surgical scars.

"Look at what those fucking cocksuckers did to me," she shrieked.

Nancy's mother, ninety-two years old, had fallen the year before in Chicago and broken her hip. She had not completely recovered and still required the use of a wheelchair on occasion. But more worrisome to her friends was the mental slippage they had begun to notice. Her strange behavior had not alarmed anyone at first because she'd always been uninhibited, but what was once delightfully outlandish had disintegrated into the embarrassingly grotesque.

"As a matter of fact, when she was at the height of her mental instability, I used to have to take her blood pressure sidesaddle because she'd always go for the crotch," said one of her Arizona physicians. "I'm sure she had Alzheimer's disease, although the only way you make a definite diagnosis is to do a brain biopsy, and we were never given an opportunity to do that."

Dr. Daniel Ruge, the White House physician from 1981 to 1984 and a close personal friend of the Davises, disagrees. "I don't think Edie had Alzheimer's," he said. "It was senility—nothing more than that."

"The First Lady's staff knew that Edith Davis had Alzheimer's," said one of Mrs. Reagan's secretaries. Edith's friends concurred.

"I remember when I took her to high tea at the Plaza Hotel in New York in the late seventies, she took out her dentures and put them on the table," said Les Weinrott, her friend from Chicago. "Once around with that kind of thing was enough for me. The next time she did it, I said, 'Deedle, this isn't the kind of behavior one would expect of the First Families of Virginia.' She said, 'Oh, fuck you, Lestah. They're my fucking dentures, and I can do what I fucking want with them.' When we went to visit her in Arizona a few months later, she was fine for a couple of minutes but then started yelling at me about something, and Loyal quickly wheeled her out of the room. I realize now that that was probably the onset of her Alzheimer's, which he had recognized instantly, but the rest of us didn't understand for many years. It's a shame that Nancy covered it up the way she did, because she could've done a great deal of good for other families victimized by the disease by going public with it."

"It wasn't just the Alzheimer's," said Patti Davis later. "It was also a series of little strokes."

Although Edith Davis would live for seven more years, in 1980 her vitality was so diminished by age and disease that she no longer radiated the joy she once had. "She got less mellow as she got older," recalled Patti, who, as an adolescent, had been the beneficiary of her grandmother's love and attention. "I remember as a kid when we went to the grocery store once and I sneaked some grapes. She said, 'Hurry up and eat those so I don't have to pay for them.' "

During the time Patti had attended the Orme School in Arizona, her grandmother had functioned as her mother, who was playing the role of absentee parent—the same role Edie had played in Nancy's childhood.

"All communications with the Reagans were copied to Mrs. Davis, and it was she, not the parents, who stepped in when there were school crises for Patti," said Allan Hilton, formerly dean of admissions at Orme. "The Davises visited far more often than did the Reagans, and Patti spent many weekends with her grandparents in Scottsdale.

"There was always a major Parents Weekend at school in conjunction with the Thanksgiving holiday weekend. All the parents were invited to come down. There was a big rodeo the kids would participate in and a big Thanksgiving dinner at the school. The parents would come on Thanksgiving and then on Friday there would be a Parents Day and the families that came would take the kids down to Phoenix and spend the weekend. . . . I don't remember the Reagans ever coming for Parents Day. I'll bet they didn't come more than once or twice, if at all. . . . All the kids who didn't have their parents there were always upset and felt their mother and father thought other obligations were more important [because] so many events of the weekend were to show the kids off to their parents."

Patti was among those children without parents to show off for, but her grandparents were always there for her, as they were for Michael Reagan. When he had to repeat his junior year of high school, Loyal Davis got him into the Judson School in Arizona. Although Nancy could not abide Ronald Reagan's adopted son, her mother warmly embraced the troubled youngster, inviting him for weekends, staying in touch with his teachers, even attending his baseball games.

"My first time up at bat with two men on base, I heard Dee Dee yell, 'You better hit a home run, you little son of a bitch,' " he recalled. "When I graduated from high school, she gave me a gold signet ring that I cherish to this day."

On her good days, Edith Davis was thrilled by the prospect of her son-in-law's accepting his party's nomination and disgusted at Patti and Ron for refusing to campaign for him. Edith had done her part by nudging everyone she met "to get off your goddamned asses and give Ronnie some money so he can become President." Now immobilized by old age and disease, she would not be able to accompany him to the GOP convention.

Traveling by themselves on a chartered jet, the Reagans arrived in Detroit on July 14, 1980, to be crowned by the most conservative GOP convention since 1964. For the first time in forty years, the Republican platform renounced support for women's equal rights and endorsed a "human life" plank that prohibited almost all abortions.

Public opinion polls showed Reagan with a clear lead over President Carter. The only suspense awaiting the delegates was the identity of the man their nominee would anoint as his running mate.

Nancy's heart beat for Paul Laxalt, the handsome Nevada senator who had been Reagan's friend since their days as neighboring governors. But her head recognized the choice as foolish because the Western conservative brought nothing to the ticket that Ronald Reagan did not already have, except for the specter of his having dealt with Nevada's natural resource—organized crime. Viscerally opposed to George Bush, Nancy would not even discuss him as a possible vice-presidential choice, and

closed the subject by pointing out that he was for the Equal Rights
Amendment and his wife was pro-choice, two positions that the Reagans
opposed. Some campaign strategists suggested that Bush on the ticket
could help blunt the appeal of the Independent presidential candidate
John Anderson to moderate Republicans, Independents, and dissatisfied
Democrats, but Nancy was not convinced that Bush could carry water
outside his own wading pool. "He's never won a statewide election," she
said, "and he didn't even beat Ronnie in the Texas primary." She resented his not dropping out of the race sooner; she felt he could have
saved her husband the wear and tear and expense of a prolonged campaign when the outcome, according to her, was already a foregone conclusion. She had conveniently forgotten that Bush had beat Reagan in
some key primary states, including Iowa, Massachusetts, Connecticut,
Pennsylvania, Michigan, and Delaware, and that Bush still had a strong
political organization in the industrial Northeast and Midwest, where
Reagan was weak. Despite Bush's stunning array of public service credentials, Nancy dismissed him as "a bit whiney," saying, "He just
doesn't have what it takes."

Her main concern at the time was her husband's fixation with making
Gerald Ford his running mate and selling the ticket as a "co-presidency."

"I thought the whole idea was ridiculous," she said. "I didn't see how
a former President—any President—could come back to the White
House in the number-two spot. It would be awkward for both men, and
impractical, and I couldn't understand why that wasn't obvious to everybody. 'It can't be done,' I told Ronnie. 'It would be a dual presidency. It
just won't work.' "

With the polls predicting Reagan-Ford as a "dream ticket," her husband wasn't listening to her. When he asked her to intercede with Betty
Ford, she indulged him long enough to place a call to Mrs. Ford about
the prospect of their husbands running the country together, then glee-
fully reported that Betty, now contentedly retired, did not like the idea
of returning to politics.

Still, the two men and their staffs continued discussing the notion for
three days and nights, as if it were a serious, workable proposal, until
Ford came to his senses and said no. Then, despite his wife's tears, Reagan bowed to political reality and called the man who had ridiculed him
throughout the primary season. He had had doubts about Bush from the
time of the New Hampshire primary debate when Reagan had grabbed
the microphone and Bush had sat stonily silent. "I'm wary of a man who
freezes under pressure," Reagan had said. "George froze that night. That
haunts me." Now, though, he rose above his reservations and picked up
the telephone.

"Hello, George, this is Ron Reagan," he said. There was a pause. "I'd like to go over to the convention and announce that you're my choice for Vice President . . . if that's all right with you."

"I'd be honored, Governor."

"Fine. I'll head over to the convention, then we'll get together in the morning."

That night, Reagan's name was placed in nomination and he broke tradition by appearing at the Joe Louis Arena to make his announcement. But until that moment, the evening belonged to Nancy Reagan.

Sitting center stage as the star of her own featured presentation, the pretty, fifty-nine-year-old wife of the Republican standard-bearer held court in the family box—the cynosure of whirring television cameras and doting delegates. Her aides ushered celebrities to her side, where they paid homage for twenty minutes before being whisked out of camera range and replaced by other notables.

The seating around Mrs. Reagan had been precisely planned by Peter McCoy and Michael Deaver. "She was in the center frame of the television cameras at all times, and we controlled who would sit directly in front and in back of her and on either side," said McCoy, who conceded those choice seats were not wasted on family members. "A great deal of time went into this because Nancy knew she would be the center of attention, and she wanted things to look right on television."

McCoy and Deaver were accustomed to the exacting demands of the candidate's wife. Earlier in the campaign, she had given them a checklist of 106 items for advance men to carry on every Reagan stop, specifying that staff members' hotel rooms must be at least one floor away from those occupied by reporters. She also specified that the Reagans be given the hotel's full restaurant menu, not just the abbreviated room-service version. She liked to receive a complimentary box of chocolates from the hotel's public relations director so she would have candy to distribute to reporters on the plane. She insisted on a full complement of newspapers for herself at every stop, the local papers as well as the *New York Times,* the *Washington Post,* the *Los Angeles Times,* and, of course, *Women's Wear Daily.*

Nancy spent hours on the details of her wardrobe for the Republican convention. For the nomination night she had chosen a custom-made $950 Adolfo dress of pale apricot crepe de chine and had instructed the Cuban-born designer to cut the armholes high and to secure the waist with a snug unseen belt so that she could wave graciously to the crowd without worrying about the dress riding up when she waved. That evening as she raised her arms to acknowledge her standing ovation, she looked as perfectly groomed as a little Dresden doll.

The irony of Metro-Goldwyn-Mayer's former contract player commanding the key light was brought home to television viewers when a former MGM queen rolled onto the screen looking like a zeppelin caricature of her former self. Elizabeth Taylor, once heralded as "the most beautiful woman in the world," had married John Warner of Virginia, her sixth husband, in 1976; and two years later had helped make him a U.S. senator. In the process, she had transformed herself into a nominal Republican, though still pro-choice on abortion and pro-Equal Rights Amendment, and had ballooned into obesity. At the convention, she plopped down next to Nancy Reagan, a constant dieter who deliberately chewed each morsel of food thirty-two times before swallowing. The one-time starlet whispered to the former movie queen, "Did you ever think that you and I would be sitting here tonight?" The two former "Metro girls" giggled and chatted through a speech by NAACP executive director Benjamin Hooks and then Liz Taylor, once the highest-paid movie star in America, was yanked off camera to make room for Nancy Kissinger, who, twenty minutes later, was scooted away to make room for Tobin Armstrong, husband of former ambassador Anne Armstrong—all satellites orbiting Nancy Reagan's sun.

Around 10:00 P.M. word flew through the aisles that Ronald Reagan was going to be making a triumphal entrance to announce his running mate. Nancy yielded center stage and returned to her supporting role of adoring wife as she took her place alongside her husband at the podium. While he told the convention that his toughest rival, George Bush, would now become his running mate, she looked vulnerable and lost, unable to hold back her tears. Senator Paul Laxalt wrapped his arm around her thin shoulders trying to comfort her, but she still couldn't smile. She hated the thought of George Bush on the ticket. "She looked like a little girl who had just lost her favorite Raggedy Ann doll: sad, disappointed, almost crushed," reported the *Washington Post.*

The next morning, when the Bushes walked into the living room of the Reagans' suite at the Renaissance Center Plaza, the governor was waiting for them, but Nancy hung back and waited in the bedroom for a few minutes. Barbara Bush walked toward Reagan with her arms outstretched. "Governor, let me promise you one thing: We're going to work our tails off for you." Reagan was disarmed by her frankness. Without embarrassment, she had acknowledged the past differences between her husband and Ronald Reagan, and their reservations about each other, but she also reassured the presidential candidate that from this day forward he need never worry again about choosing George Bush as his running mate. To underscore the point, the Bushes immediately dropped their support of the ERA and changed their position on abortion to be in accord with the Reagans.

Mrs. Bush would have a more difficult time charming the candidate's wife, for Nancy Reagan was not as easily beguiled as her husband, and already disliked the silver-haired aristocrat who was so sure of her place in the world. But Barbara Bush was undeterred; she was determined to take the high road. The next day, when a reporter asked why Nancy Reagan could not stand her, she gracefully deflected the question.

"Is it your earthy directness?" the reporter asked.

"Why, that's silly," said Barbara Bush, laughing lightly. "We've only met twice. And from what I've seen of Nancy so far, I like her and she likes me. Furthermore, I think she's ravishingly beautiful. When we were with them, I could hardly take my eyes off her . . . and she's been just darling to us. If anything, I think she's just shy."

"People say there is a big difference between you and Mrs. Reagan. Can you describe the difference?"

"Why, yes," said Barbara. "Nancy is a size four, and I'm a size forty-four."

The differences between the two women would become more pronounced a decade later, but even in 1980, they had little in common. Although both had gone to Smith College—Nancy class of 1943, Barbara class of 1947—Barbara dropped out to get married. Both came from families where Eleanor Roosevelt was reviled, and both had married men they revered, but these were not similarities that would make them friends. Temperamentally, the two women were incompatible.

Nevertheless, it was in a public show of unity that the two couples left Detroit the next day for a rally in Houston, the city that George Bush, born in Milton, Massachusetts, now called his hometown. "We all flew to Houston to have lunch with George and Barbara Bush and their son Jeb," recalled Maureen Reagan. "All of us, that is, except Ron and Patti —Ron was on tour with the Joffrey II Ballet Company and Patti was busy with whatever it was she was busy with."

Michael Reagan, accompanied by his wife, Colleen, and their two-year-old son, Cameron, sat two rows behind his father and stepmother on the plane to Texas. During the flight, Michael walked his young son up the aisle, hoping to be noticed by his father. Seeing his grandson, Reagan looked up and held out his arms to the little boy.

"Cameron, come here," he said, and began bouncing him up and down and singing to him.

Irritated by the interruption, Nancy shot a hard look at her husband. "Not now, Ronnie," she said.

Reagan immediately handed the child back to Michael without another word.

When they arrived at the Bush home, George Bush swooped Cameron up to his shoulders and promised to show him all his grandchildren's toys. He marched him into a playroom where he dumped out everything from the cupboards for the youngster to play with.

"I thought then and still do that George Bush is one of the nicest men I have ever met," said Michael Reagan many years later.

Barbara Bush started the luncheon by saying grace, but, seconds into her blessing, Cameron came barreling into the room pulling a jangling toy he had discovered in the playroom.

"Nancy seemed embarrassed by the interruption," said Maureen, "but Barbara paused in the middle of her blessing and said, 'Don't worry, this happens all the time.' "

Following the hot shrimp luncheon, the two families headed for Houston's opulent Galleria II mall. More than 3,000 people were waiting impatiently to welcome the Republican nominee and his running mate, stomping, clapping, and whistling louder for the bottom of the ticket than the top, a fact not lost on the press.

From Houston, the Reagans headed for Los Angeles, where Nancy stepped forward to address the crowd welcoming them at the airport. "It certainly is nicer coming home now than it was four years ago, when Ronnie was defeated. But I don't want to get carried away with the euphoria of the moment," she said. "It's nice, but there is a lot to be done."

The first chore facing the Reagans was releasing their 1979 income tax return, which they had resisted as long as they could. Throughout his political career, Reagan had adamantly refused to make any kind of financial disclosure, maintaining that his money was his own business and a matter of privacy, but now he had no choice since President Carter had made his tax returns available.

At the last possible minute, Reagan's office released his twenty-three-page tax return. It portrayed a prosperous man with a net worth of more than $3 million, including $515,878 in income derived primarily from speeches to bankers, egg producers, Taiwanese businessmen, insulation contractors, highway lobbyists, and truck stop operators. For each speech, he had charged at least $10,000. He even charged for making personal appearances at GOP fund-raising events, a fact that angered some Republicans.

"He was running for President and charging us for it," said H. G. Taylor, Republican chairman of Macon County, Illinois. It was the only time in Taylor's thirty years in politics that he'd known a party figure insisting on being paid to campaign for himself.

Reagan often talked about growing up in a family so poor that they sometimes had to live for a week on a 10-cent soup bone and some throwaway calves' liver cadged from the butcher "for our cat." Yet he campaigned on the premise that more of the burden of caring for the poor should be borne by private charity rather than the federal government. He was not a man disposed to private philanthropy. Although his adjusted gross income was $227,968 he gave only $3,089 to charity, slightly more than one percent. When he was publicly criticized for billing the United Way for appearing at a fund-raising drive, he reluctantly gave back half the fee. He charged his daughter Maureen $481 in interest on money she had borrowed to help Gene Nelson recuperate from a heart attack. Although Reagan had received $7 million in federal campaign funds during the 1980 primaries, and another $29.4 million for the fall campaign, he and Nancy had not even checked off the box on their return giving $1 each for federal elections.

The Reagans now found themselves in an uncomfortable position: To the poor, they had to defend themselves against being considered rich, but with the rich they felt poor. They acted defensive about their status as millionaires when Tom Brokaw interviewed them for "The Today Show" in the fall of 1980.

"You are very prosperous, upper middle class."

"Are we?" exclaimed Nancy Reagan.

"I think by most standards, wouldn't you say that's fair?" said Brokaw. "I don't mean that to denigrate your position. I think most people would be happy to trade places."

"I think it has been exaggerated," said Nancy, wearing a $950 suit.

"You do?"

"A bit," said Ronald Reagan. "In other words, if we don't do this, I— we cannot sit back and retire and be inactive. I will have to continue doing what I was doing before I became a candidate."

"You mean if you don't go ahead . . . it's not only that you want to be President, you need the job—is what you're saying?" said Brokaw.

"Something like that," said Nancy Reagan.

"There are some that pay better," said Ronald Reagan.

"I understand . . . that you would not use the word *wealthy* then to describe yourselves?"

"*No,*" said Nancy Reagan.

"The way I think of it is, I think of it as someone who's independent and therefore doesn't have to add to what they have or . . . ," said Reagan.

"But I've seen a net worth at, what, $3 million. I don't want to dwell on this unduly, but the fact is that by most standards that is pretty wealthy," persisted Brokaw.

"No, that's very much exaggerated," said Reagan.

"I think we are dwelling on this," said Nancy.

"Well, one of the reasons that I want to ask about it is that you are now concentrating on blue-collar, working-class, ethnic neighborhoods of the Northeast, and it just does strike me as a kind of ironic marriage here, of the candidate and the background with the kind of constituency that you find."

"Do you know anything about his background?" snapped Nancy.

"I know about his background, yes, indeed," said Brokaw. "I know about his background, but I'm just saying that the kind of life that you now have, and . . . and the kind of identification that you have with those groups, I'm just wondering if you are always at ease, or if you're struck by that from time to time."

"Sure . . . oh, yes, that's not . . . that's not a fair judgment or statement," said Nancy. "The wonderful part about our country is that you can work hard and better yourself, which is what Ronnie did, but that doesn't mean that you forget all those times that went before when you were earning, when you were starting to work at fourteen at 35 cents an hour."

Having hit an exposed nerve, Brokaw allowed the couple to change the subject to what Ronald Reagan as President could do to help forgotten Americans build their "shining city on the hill."

On her separate campaign schedule, Nancy also tried to appeal to low-income voters by attacking court-ordered school busing as a fraudulent, wasteful remedy that creates more problems than it solves in achieving desegregation.

"There's something phony about busing, and I think children know it," she said in Cleveland, Ohio. "It just doesn't make sense for a child to have to get up at five in the morning and travel across town to go to school. I think it sets up more problems than it solves. All the black people I talk with feel the same way. I would rather see the money spent on busing be used to upgrade schools."

She went on to say that busing would not help break barriers against job discrimination for future generations. "We've made a lot of progress in that area already," she said.

In his acceptance speech at the Democratic National Convention, Jimmy Carter had defined the presidential campaign of 1980 as "a stark choice between two men, two parties, two sharply different pictures of what America is and what the world is. . . . It's a choice between two futures."

But the present under the Carter administration was one of double-digit inflation, a gasoline shortage that reminded frustrated Americans of their dependency on foreign oil, and the lingering hostage crisis in Iran. It was a present that did not leave much promise for the future, except the realization that things could get much worse. And he predicted dire tomorrows of dwindling supplies, shared sacrifices, and poorer lives. On top of this, he warned his countrymen of a "crisis of confidence . . . that strikes at the very heart and soul of our national will."

Like an Old Testament prophet, Carter preached austerity to the American people while Ronald Reagan bounced happily on the scene promising to rescue them from their lassitude and to make them proud to wave their flag again. "I find no national malaise," he said. "I find nothing wrong with the American people." He sold them their patriotic dream of themselves as living in the greatest country on earth. He reinforced their fantasies by telling them that he could "make America great again." He made them stand tall in their own eyes and revived their hope for a better tomorrow. And they believed him; after all, his was the voice of General Electric that once persuaded America to believe "Progress Is Our Most Important Product."

Now he was telling ordinary Americans that they were "heroes" who had never shirked history's call. "Any nation that sees softness in our prosperity or disunity . . . let them understand that we will put aside in a moment the fruits of our prosperity and the luxury of our disagreements if the cause is a safe and peaceful future for our children." For Americans in 1980, the shriveled face of the Ayatollah of Iran epitomized the evil of Adolf Hitler, and Ronald Reagan represented John Wayne winning World War II.

Americans wanted to believe that they would never have to bow to terrorism again, never have to sit by impotently watching their flag set afire by Shiite Muslims, their countrymen seized and tortured by sects whose names they couldn't pronounce and held captive in hellholes they couldn't find on the map. "I believe that this administration's foreign policy helped create the entire situation," said Ronald Reagan. "And I think the fact that the hostages have been held there that long is a humiliation and disgrace to this country." Like an Old West cowboy with his six-shooters firing silver bullets, Ronald Reagan promised to gallop to America's rescue, even with the wagons surrounded.

While President Carter took people to the abyss of reality and made them confront their fears, Reagan cheerily tapped into their enduring dream of a better world.

"Are you better off than you were four years ago?" he asked in his closing statement during the presidential debates. "Is it easier for you to go and buy things in the stores than it was four years ago? Is there more or less unemployment in the country than there was four years ago? Is America as respected throughout the world as it was?" If the answer was no, the vote was yes for Reagan.

Carter retaliated in a Chicago speech by saying that his opponent was trying to divide the country in two. He said Reagan had promised not to introduce the fifty-two American hostages into the campaign, and he had broken that promise by using the tragedy for his own political gain. He lambasted Reagan's foreign policy ideas as "naive," and claimed that Reagan had advocated measures that could move the nation closer to nuclear war.

Before Reagan could begin to form a response, Nancy jumped right in. "Carter is waging a vicious and cruel campaign," she said, her voice quivering with anger. "I'm offended when he tried to portray my husband as a warmonger, as a man who would throw the elderly out on the street and cut off their Social Security when, in fact, he never said anything of the kind at any time. That's a cruel thing to do. It's cruel to the people. It's cruel to my husband. I deeply, deeply resent it as a wife and a mother and a woman."

Nancy was motivated by fear as much as anger, for she had read a Gallup poll on October 25, 1980, that showed President Carter favored by 41 percent of the country, Reagan by 40 percent, Independent John Anderson by 10 percent, with 9 percent undecided. Among those considered likely to vote, Reagan had a 42 percent to 39 percent lead over the President, but that was too close for his wife. She was prepared to do anything to put herself and her husband where they both had longed to be ever since he first ran for President in 1968.

She had been in daily contact with her astrologer, Joan Quigley, who carefully charted the days between August and the November election. "I sent a written report of what Reagan should watch out for during that time," said Quigley. "I told him not to make any pronouncement on foreign policy on August 19. That was the day he made the comment about recognizing Taiwan instead of China. . . . He was perceived [as] inexperienced in foreign policy and he made a bad mistake on that day. I had underlined it in red on my written report, so from then on people in the campaign began to pay real attention to what I was saying."

The astrologer also told Nancy that the stars were propitious for her to defend her husband against attacks, so Nancy had sprung into action and grabbed the spotlight, appearing on "Good Morning America" the day after President Carter's speech.

"I'm mad, yes, I am, and if you think I'm mad, you should hear my children," she told David Hartman. "You almost have to tie them down, they're so mad.

"The picture [Carter] has tried to create of my husband is absolutely untrue. . . . Anything to prevent conversation about the record," she said with exasperation in her voice. "It seems to me that the issues in this campaign are Mr. Carter's record, and those are the issues that should be discussed. . . . Why is our country regarded in the way it is by our friends overseas, who don't know if we're their friends or we're not their friends. Why our men have been taken hostage. Why they're left to sit there in Iran. And why, if you plan a rescue mission,* why can't you plan it well? I think even I would know better than the way it was planned. And we lost eight boys."

She accused President Carter of using scare tactics, because "that's the most effective weapon that there is, particularly with women. Why, you scare them and they think that their sons are going to maybe go to war, that's a very powerful weapon and a very unfair weapon. You just don't fight like that. Campaigning is very character-revealing. How you choose to fight your battles is very character-revealing. . . . I don't like the way Jimmy Carter campaigns."

She insisted that the Reagan campaign feature her in a sixty-second commercial to run on national television nine days before the election, registering her outrage at the President's accusations. The media plan, which had been set for weeks, was to focus entirely on inflation and the economy. "That's what we intend to talk about," said Peter Daily, the Los Angeles advertising executive who was Reagan's media advisor. "Inflation is the principal issue. It's the most graphic demonstration of a failed presidency. If Carter doesn't want to talk about it, we will."

But when the candidate's wife persisted in making her own commercial, Daily quickly rearranged the schedule to accommodate her. "She is really upset about the way Carter has attacked her husband," he said, proclaiming her television spot "dynamite."

* In April 1980, President Carter had ordered a team of commandos to rescue the hostages in the U.S. embassy in Tehran. Six C-130 transport planes and six RH-53 helicopters carrying ninety commandos had landed in an Iranian desert on a remote landing strip. The hydraulic system of one of the helicopters broke on landing, and the craft could not fly. The team commander said the rescue could not be made with the remaining helicopters. President Carter agreed to the recall of the rescue team, but one of the helicopters struck a transport plane while it was refueling. Eight Americans were killed in the fire and explosions that followed, and four others were badly burned. The commandos left Iran in the remaining planes. President Carter went on television, disclosed the attempted rescue and its failure, and took full responsibility for the tragedy.

She introduced her commercial by saying, "I don't often speak out in campaigns, but I think this campaign now has gotten to the point and the level where I have to say something." She then sailed into Carter. The next day she gave interviews to the *Washington Post* and the Associated Press, denouncing the President for assailing her husband and predicting that the President would somehow pay for such a campaign tactic. "I am a big believer that eventually everything comes back to you," she said. "You get back what you give out."

She herself soon felt the smack of payback when Judy Bachrach wrote a column in the *Washington Star* objecting to Nancy's ritual of "forcing" chocolates down the throats of reporters traveling on the Reagan campaign plane. Diabetics demurred and the overweight tried to, but she persisted in her disastrous routine.

Her press relations had become so strained that one of her p.r. people suggested she hand out the chocolates, thinking such hospitality might engender goodwill and possibly good press. "People were always giving us boxes of candy, and since Ronnie and I don't eat candy (I prefer cookies while Ronnie sticks to jelly beans), I would give them away," said Nancy later. "It was all done in good fun, and it never entered my mind that anyone would think I was forcing it on them. When [Judy Bachrach] wrote a column saying that unless you ate your candy, you wouldn't get an interview with Ronnie, I was so hurt and embarrassed that I never wanted to go down that aisle again. But . . . I did—with a sign around my neck that said: TAKE ONE OR ELSE!"

Unamused, the columnist wrote: "The first thing that becomes apparent is that she, herself, detests the performance of this little function, executes it dutifully but with the cool menace of a potentially vengeful robot, since it brings her into contact with the press she hates with a very pointed loathing. Like any devotee of brinkmanship, Nancy Reagan knows that through this series of cruel and artful confrontations she has put the press on the defensive and terrorized them into abject subjugation; the cynic might conclude that is the main reason she persists in a ritual both parties dread. The offering of the chocolates seems such a hospitable, generous act that it turns rejection, no matter how valid, into assault, it places the burden of innocence on the victim, and rectitude becomes the natural portion of the persistent and implacable intruder."

The column cast the candidate's wife as Lady Macbeth, being "far cleverer and more ruthless than her husband." It ended with a paragraph that proved particularly painful:

Nancy, it must be pointed out, never eats her own chocolates. "I am a size 4," she admits to all admirers of her tiny waist, beneath which, like a charming play with third-act trouble, a pair of piano legs taper with unhappy abruptness. Her smile is conciliatory. "I am," she says, "a hot bread freak."

"God, that column devastated her," recalled Michael Evans, the Reagan photographer. "She cried and cried and literally got sick over the piece. Nancy has always been sensitive about her shapeless legs and heavy ankles, and when that column was published she took to her bed for two days. I spent two hours each day letting her cry on my shoulder, trying to tell her it was nonsense to even think about, but she was inconsolable."

Nancy read the column on the plane and stayed in her bedroom, sobbing. She refused to come out once during the flight. Reagan was beside himself with anger but unable to do anything to alleviate his wife's pain. Campaign aides such as David Fischer were seen trying to comfort her, but to no avail. Martin Anderson accosted Bachrach in fury, and Lyn Nofziger ordered her off the plane at the next stop for the duration of the campaign, but nothing could make Nancy feel any better about herself.

"Unfortunately, she saw herself in terms of what others wrote about her," said one Reagan aide. "The vain things in life were so important to her—her clothes, her appearance. Those were the things that mattered most to her, which is why that column nearly killed her."

Hurt and humiliated, the candidate's wife wanted to strike back at the reporter, and to do so, she enlisted her trusty aide, Nancy Reynolds, a lobbyist for Bendix Corporation in Washington, D.C., who had taken a leave of absence to work in the Reagan campaign.

"After talking to Mrs. Reagan on the phone, Nancy Reynolds came into my office and said, 'Have you got a bunch of people who can write letters to the editor protesting that column?'" recalled an aide. "I said, 'Sure,' and she told me, 'Get 'em on it right now.' I really didn't see how that kind of a dirty trick would help the campaign in general or the candidate's wife in particular, so I indulged in a few days of creative inactivity. Every time Nancy Reynolds came in and asked me how the letters project was going, I said, 'Full steam ahead,' and never did a damn thing about it."

Later that day, Lou Cannon of the *Washington Post* sat down to interview Ronald Reagan, who asked him to turn off his tape recorder. "He was distraught," recalled Cannon. "He was really very unhappy about that column and asked me what he could do about it. I basically commiserated with him, because it was a nasty piece of business designed to make Nancy feel bad, which it certainly succeeded in doing. But I said there wasn't much anybody could do about it. Interestingly enough, I had had a very critical story about Reagan in the paper that morning, but he didn't care about that. All he cared about was what the 'piano legs' column had done to his wife."

Up to this point, the Reagan campaign had been obsessed with the possibility that President Carter would achieve release of the American hostages, bring them home to a national celebration, and walk off with the election. "One of the things we had concluded early was that a Reagan victory would be nearly impossible if the hostages were released before the election," said Michael Deaver. "There was nothing we could do about it. We did, however, begin talking up the idea in August of an 'October surprise.' This had the effect of making anything Carter did before election day seem calculating and political. Still, there is no doubt in my mind that the euphoria of the hostage release would have rolled over the land like a tidal wave. Carter would have been a hero, and many of the complaints against him forgotten. He would have won."

To prevent such a victory, the Reagan campaign secretly set up its own intelligence unit, headed by William Casey, and tried to penetrate Carter's National Security Council (NSC) to obtain inside information on the administration's negotiations with Iran.

On October 2, 1980, a mysterious Iranian met three Reagan campaign officials at the L'Enfant Plaza Hotel in Washington, D.C., to discuss release of the hostages. White House aides suspected this meeting led Reagan forces to make a preelection deal with Iran at a secret meeting in Paris on October 19. The suspicion was that the Reaganites told Iran not to release the hostages until after election day and, in exchange, promised that once Reagan took office, he would resume the sale of U.S. arms to Iran. Carter's former director of the Central Intelligence Agency, Stansfield Turner, believes this haunting scenario did take place, but it was never proved.

"No question about it," said Carter's White House press secretary, Jody Powell. "My theory is that the Reagan campaign made an overture to Iran regarding the release of the hostages; they cut a deal. I don't know that for a fact, but I would bet my life on it."

In any event, by election day, it was obvious that the hostages were still not on their way home.

But most pollsters did not forecast the electoral landslide of November 4, 1980. Among the very few who did foresee the one-sided election was President Carter's pollster, Patrick Cadell. He advised Carter to call the Mayflower Moving Company the day before the election.

In Los Angeles, the Reagans, relying on the forecasts of their astrologers and of their conservative pollster, expected to be in for a long night, but it was one they planned carefully with their superstitions in mind. Dinner would be at the home of Earle and Marion Jorgensen, where they would join the same friends who were with them in 1966 when Reagan was first elected governor and again in 1970 when he was reelected. They would be served the same menu of chicken curry and California white wine that they had had on those election nights served by the same people who had catered previously. The Reagans felt lucky in repeating the rituals of these previous victories, and the Jorgensens were only too happy to humor them. After dinner, "the group," which consisted of the Tuttles, the Bloomingdales, the Darts, the Deutsches, the Wilsons, the Smiths, Charlie and Mary Jane Wick, and various offspring, would watch the early returns and then go to Reagan's campaign headquarters at the Century Plaza Hotel later in the evening for what they confidently predicted would be a victory speech. "I still expected we'd be in for a long night as we waited for the votes to come in," said Nancy.

At 5:08 P.M., Pacific time, as they began getting ready for the evening, the Reagans turned up their bedroom television set so they could hear the news in their large pink bathroom. At 5:15 P.M., Nancy heard John Chancellor on NBC-TV predict that Reagan was going to win in a landslide. Leaping out of the tub, she threw a towel around herself and started banging on her husband's shower door. He jumped out, grabbed a towel, and ran to the television set. "And there we stood, dripping wet, wearing nothing but our towels, as we heard that Ronnie had just been elected," she recalled.

President Carter called at 6:01 P.M. (9:01 Eastern time) to congratulate Reagan on his victory and less than an hour later, the President publicly conceded his loss on television. At 7:01 P.M., Pacific time (10:01 Eastern time), he sent a White House telegram to the Pacific Palisades house:

Dear Governor Reagan:

It is now apparent that the American people have chosen you as the next president. I congratulate you and I pledge to you our fullest support and cooperation in bringing about an orderly transition of government in the weeks ahead. My best wishes are with you and your family as you undertake the responsibilities that lie before you.

Jimmy Carter

"We were all surprised because no one in the history of presidential politics had ever conceded while voters were still at the polls," said

Michael Reagan. "Everybody had expected Dad to win by a large margin, but the results were staggering. He carried forty-four of fifty states, receiving more votes [43,899,248] than Carter [35,481,435] and Anderson [5,719,437] combined."

When the motorcade of limousines pulled away from the Jorgensen home, the Reagans were in the lead car smiling and waving, followed by the Wicks, who had taken a year off to move to Washington, D.C., to set up the Reagan for President headquarters. Now, clearly savoring the victory, Mrs. Wick stood up on the seat of her limousine to wave out of the roof of the car while Betsy Bloomingdale followed in another limousine waving out of her window.

By the time the Reagans and their friends arrived at the Century Plaza Hotel, where the campaign staff had reserved two penthouse suites, it was obvious that Mrs. Reagan wanted to be alone with her husband. "We put up checkpoints on the floor below and just tried to restrict access up to the penthouse floor because it became a madhouse," recalled Peter McCoy. "I got the very real sense that Nancy and the governor would have liked to have spent thirty minutes all alone. I don't think she wanted to share him at that moment in time with all of the other guests and people. They were in the bedroom watching the state-by-state results, just the two of them, when I came in to tell the governor to come and say hello to somebody. I could read it in her eyes, 'Doesn't this ever end?' Picking up on that I began misdirecting people away from their suite so they could spend a little more time together. I was hardly endearing myself to some of their closest friends, but I had read Nancy's eyes and some of these people think they have a special right of access all the time; I just hope they later understood."

A few miles away, the Democratic friends of television producer Al Burton began gathering in his Coldwater Canyon home to watch the election returns. As the Reagan landslide registered, guests whooped and hollered when they were told that one of the actors present had once been intimate with an unknown starlet named Nancy Davis when she had appeared in *The Late Christopher Bean* at the Olney Theater in Olney, Maryland, in 1947.

"We all got hysterical watching Jimmy Karen dance around the room that night," recalled writer Elizabeth Forsythe Hailey. "He jumped up and down, singing at the top of his lungs: 'I fucked the First Lady to sets and music during summer stock. I fucked the First Lady to sets and music during summer stock.' That little piece of information certainly gave us a new insight into the prim and prissy Nancy Reagan we all thought we knew so well!"

16

THE REAGANS OPPOSED GOVERNMENTAL HANDOUTS to the needy, but Nancy encouraged fancy handouts—for herself. She had come to expect it. As first lady of California, she had persuaded merchants to sell to her at wholesale prices simply for the prestige of serving the governor's wife.

"During that time, she would go to Saks Fifth Avenue two times a year to see the Adolfo collections," said Oscar de Lavin, who worked for the Cuban-born designer for twenty-five years. "She would take the style numbers off the models and then call Adolfo in New York to order ten to twelve items directly from him so she could get things wholesale, which was just above cost or approximately fifty percent less than the retail price. If she had ordered directly from Saks, she would've had to pay full price. And Nancy Reagan would never pay full price for anything, if she could help it."

Before her husband was elected governor, Mrs. Reagan shopped at Amelia Grey, an elegant dress shop in Beverly Hills, where the salespeople remember her as "a very cheap shopper" who would insist on buying the small sample sizes at a cut rate.

"She was always romancing Amelia," said Laura Young, a saleswoman. "She was like a little worm who crawls under your skin. She'd come into the shop and head directly for Mrs. Grey's office in the back, where she would be cutesy and sweet and tell her all the gossip. She'd only let Mrs. Grey wait on her, or if she was busy, then maybe Mrs. Grey's sister helped her. Amelia wouldn't give her anything for free, of course, but she did let her buy at cost sometimes, and she would tell her about the upcoming sales."

If retailers didn't offer their discounts up front, Nancy did not hesitate to ask for them. She felt entitled to these adjustments as a fair exchange for the visibility she brought to the merchandise. In England, the royal family bestows a warrant on tradesmen who earn their patronage, and this coveted insignia is imprinted on the products. In America, the counterpart of the royal warrant is publicity, and Nancy made the most of it.

She had grown accustomed to these deals after General Electric had equipped her Pacific Palisades house in 1956, making it a national model for all-electric living. In exchange for receiving $100,000 in electrical appliances, she opened her front door to reporters and photographers whenever requested so that General Electric could receive the publicity dividend on their investment.

She also relied on the Reagan kitchen cabinet for similar abatements. "Nancy never hesitated to call and ask for a favor," said Henry Salvatori. Not only had the kitchen cabinet bought and furnished the Sacramento house they had then rented to the Reagans, but they had given the state of California eleven acres on which to build Nancy the $1.4 million governor's mansion she wanted.

Every year, on July 6, "the girls" gathered at The Bistro in Beverly Hills to celebrate Nancy's birthday. There they presented her with one important (i.e., expensive) gift that she could not or would not buy for herself. One birthday brought her three beautiful Martin Van Schaak bags ($1,650 apiece), among the costliest purses in the world. On another birthday, "the girls" gave her a stunning set of coral jewelry. The following year, she was given a heavy 18-karat gold chain from which dangled a gold-encrusted lion with diamond eyes.

"Another birthday, we gave her a pair of gold earrings from Van Cleef & Arpels with interchangeable hoops," said a friend who attended regularly. "We gave her one or two extra hoops and then Ronnie gave her diamond-studded ones for Christmas."

"The girls" had begun the annual rite of celebrating Nancy Reagan's birthday back in 1966 after she became first lady of California. Some years, the birthday luncheon was followed by a dinner party at Chasen's in Los Angeles that husbands were allowed to attend. Then the William Wilsons began staging an annual Western party at their ranch in honor of the birthday; it was later moved to the Reagans' ranch near Santa Barbara. However the birthday was celebrated, the gifts to Nancy from her wealthy friends were always impressive.

She rarely reciprocated this generosity. "We never received a gift from

Nancy in all the years we knew her," said Henry Salvatori, "but what the hell. We didn't expect any."

"Nancy, I think, is one of those people who find it more divine to receive than to give," said Peter McCoy. "This bothered some people, but that was the price they paid for admission into her inner circle. Of course, they never said anything to her about it, but several of the husbands were sensitive about being used."

Nancy's penchant for frugality was applied to the services of her L.A. and D.C. astrologers, her hairdresser, and her interior decorator, all of whom worked for her free. An exception was her San Francisco astrologer, Joan Quigley, who charged $3,000 a month after Nancy moved into the White House.

She was very clever about getting the financial accommodations she desired. Because she was interested in Bulgari jewelry, she invited Nicola Bulgari, who ran the family's North American operation, to the Reagans' Pacific Palisades home in 1977. That invitation produced a cache of gifts for her: a solid gold coin necklace and a Bulgari watch, which were worth $25,000. Later came a substantial collection of costly jewelry from Bulgari, some lent for public occasions, others given by the international jeweler who understood the value of his gems being publicly displayed on the right person in the right place.

The publicist for London Lair, a chic boutique in Beverly Hills, made frequent trips to Mrs. Reagan's home with trays of expensive items so Nancy could select gifts for her friends. These costly trinkets were *given* to Nancy Reagan because of her position as first lady of California and because the recipients would be women who lived to acquire and accumulate, and would display their valuables to good effect.

"Nancy never bought gifts for her friends," said Carlo Celoni, the former manager of Gucci in Beverly Hills. "She was not a great one for spending. . . . She was very careful about how she spent money. If she got a birthday present she didn't like, she'd always bring it in to us and we'd credit it to her account for when she wanted to buy something for herself. We did that a lot for her."

A New York City fashion reporter was enlisted to get Mary Chess Tuberose perfume for Nancy when the company discontinued the scent. "I finally called some executive at the corporate headquarters and told them that their Tuberose was the favorite perfume of the California governor's wife and that she was quite upset because she couldn't find it anymore. Naturally, they shipped her tons of the stuff for free," said the reporter.

"Free—that's the key word with Nancy Reagan," said Hollywood hairdresser George Masters. "I've been working with her on and off for over twenty years, and I've never charged her, and she's never paid. Never. She's the greatest manipulator of any woman I've ever met. The first time I did her hair I knew that she never paid, and I wanted her to know that I knew. Because she's a politician's wife, she feels she has prestige to bestow, and in exchange for that prestige, she should not be charged for services. In a business sense, she was a loss leader. She had a swarm of women buzzing around her like bumblebees, but I didn't get any more business because of her, but that's okay. I was always booked with more than I could handle so I turned her over to my assistant, Julius Bengtsson."

The assistant, a former ballet dancer, soon became the master, and like the master, his services to Mrs. Reagan also were free, or else paid for by "the girls," who subsidized his trips to the Republican National Conventions in 1968, 1972, 1976, and 1980 to do her hair.

"Nancy never paid Julius when she was the governor's wife and she never paid him when she was the President's wife either," said Joanne Carson, Johnny Carson's former wife, who was one of the hairdresser's private clients.

Now that she was going into the White House and having "to live on only $200,000 a year," the salary of the President of the United States, Nancy Reagan told Julius that he had to make an accommodation with Clairol to underwrite his expenses as her personal hairdresser. In return for her using Clairol products, she expected Clairol to provide whatever was needed to set up a beauty salon in the White House.

The Clairol company agreed and signed Julius to a $20,000-a-year contract to fly to Washington every three weeks to color Mrs. Reagan's hair. The color was publicized as "a combination of Miss Clairol Moon Gold and Miss Clairol Chestnut." The payoff for Clairol, of course, was an unabashed commercial that carried the imprimatur of the White House, an endorsement worth far more than $20,000 a year. Whenever he visited the White House to color the First Lady's hair, Julius also dyed the President's gray roots, which he had been doing secretly since 1968.

"Nancy never gave Julius a cent," said Joanne Carson, to whom the hairdresser confided this story, "and so when he went to Washington to do her hair, he cashed in his first-class ticket and flew tourist so he'd have some money. She let him stay at the White House, of course, but that didn't cost her anything, and when she took him on all those official trips abroad, the taxpayers footed the bill, not Nancy Reagan."

Nancy was comfortable having other people pay her bills. Although she and her husband were millionaires, she never felt rich. "She was always poor-mouthing," said a member of her senior staff. "She cried so easily. 'Oh, we just can't afford it. Ronnie and I don't have that kind of money. We've been in public service so long we haven't had a chance to build a nest egg for our old age and now our old age is here.' Then the tears would spill and the friends would open up their purses."

Having profited handsomely from people eager to be of service to her as the governor's wife, Nancy Reagan as First Lady of the land could look forward to hordes of shopkeepers and hustling vendors willing to bow and scrape for her patronage.

The first to receive her favor after the 1980 election was Gucci. The store in Beverly Hills was closed on November 24 to all other customers while the wife of the President-elect spent two hours selecting her booty.

"Nancy always wanted to shop privately, so we would close the store for her so she could get clothes and things whenever she wanted," said Carlo Celoni. "She refused to take the things free after the White House. She said she had to take them all before the inauguration. Up to that time, we would give her everything gratis. I was invited to both inaugurations."

"I've been helping Nancy Reagan since 1966 when her husband became governor," said Celoni. "They did not have major money, and I guess that's why she never gave us gifts at Christmas like her friends did. I was pleased to help her, though. After all, she was the state's first lady. It was so exciting to have the governor's wife shop in our store. . . . She had tremendous naïveté. She would stand in front of the mirror and we would tell her what we thought. She'd say, 'Do you think this looks good on me? Do you really think so?' We had to assure her over and over that it did."

Although Nancy ate sparingly, she had a passion for sweets, which Celoni catered to. "She loved chocolate," he said, "so I'd have chocolate-covered strawberries when she came in and she'd eat every one of them. Nancy is a Libra and I'm a Gemini. We're both air signs, so we got along very well together. Of course, I knew of her devotion to astrology. She talked about it all the time.

"When she came in after the presidential election, I gave her a black silk egg purse [$600], a miniature beige calf bag with bamboo handle—style 0633—the $650 one that Jackie Onassis made famous in America, so, of course, it was a favorite of Nancy's, too—plus a dressy daytime black lizard bag [$650], and a white evening bag accented with our double G [$850] to go with the white Galanos gown she planned to wear to the inaugural balls."

After presenting the purses, Celoni summoned his assistant, Ellen Pollon, to bring in the clothes: a herringbone topcoat with a plush leather collar ($1,500), a silk afternoon dress in fuchsia and gold with a gold belt and matching shoes ($2,000), a two-piece multicolored silk dress ($575), several gabardine skirts ($350 apiece) and matching silk blouses ($350 apiece), a black and gold silk blouse ($350), a leather jacket ($1,000), seven ties for Ronald Reagan ($35 apiece), several pairs of women's shoes ($200 apiece), and a pair of white satin pumps decorated with rhinestones to wear to the inaugural ball ($350).

"She made a big point of saying she had to take the free merchandise *before* she got into the White House because she couldn't do it afterward," recalled Pollon. "So she came in several times between the election and the inauguration to load up. She posed in all the outfits we gave her so we could photograph her. . . . She wore the coat when she flew to Washington after the election, and we saw her on the national news that night wearing Gucci, so I guess it was worth it. Stories about her so-called shopping spree also appeared in *Women's Wear Daily,* the *Los Angeles Times,* and the *Los Angeles Herald-Examiner,* not mentioning, of course, that everything was free. After she was in the White House, she wore only American designers in public, so we didn't do much business with her. I guess that's why she took all she could from us beforehand."

Her decision to wear only American designers as First Lady opened a cornucopia for Nancy. During her eight years in the White House, she would accept designer goods worth more than $1 million. Had she paid full price, her inaugural wardrobe would have cost $46,000. As First Lady, she paid nothing, and was never shy about asking for whatever she wanted. If she wanted a red alligator handbag to take on a trip, she simply called Judith Lieber and asked her to send her best little $2,500 purse to the White House. The designer always complied by sending not one but usually three of the bags, and Nancy usually kept all of them.

"Free clothes rolled in here all the time," said a White House photographer. "Bill Blass showed up regularly with armloads of suits and dresses and gowns. He and the First Lady would take them into her dressing room and that was the end of that."

Mrs. Reagan's obsession with acquiring and possessing eventually led to the kind of excess practiced only by women like Imelda Marcos and Leona Helmsley. Blind to the legal ramifications of accepting expensive gifts without declaring them as taxable income, Nancy lied about her acquisitions for several years until she was finally investigated by the Internal Revenue Service.

The designer with whom she became most closely identified was Adolfo, who specialized in the little Chanel-style bouclé knit suits and dresses that she had been wearing since 1967. "We first met Mrs. Reagan through Betsy Bloomingdale," recalled Oscar de Lavin, the former Adolfo executive. "That was when she was the governor's wife. She wasn't all that nice then, but she got even worse as she got more powerful. Believe it or not, Leona Helmsley was nicer than Nancy Reagan. As the governor's wife, Nancy got everything wholesale, but after the White House, it was all free. There was never a bill sent to her once she became First Lady. Never. Everything was free, which meant about $50,000 to $100,000 worth of clothes a year.

"Adolfo made both her inaugural outfits. The first one was a red coat, and dress and hat—about $3,000 retail. The second was a blue dress, coat, and hat. Then she got anywhere from ten to eighteen pieces from every collection, twice a year, plus all the jewelry and purses and hats she wanted. Adolfo always had to make lists of what she should wear with what so she would know how to coordinate everything. Otherwise, she'd wear the wrong things. He knew her taste perfectly, so he would select for her, and either he or I would deliver the clothes to her in the White House. She was never billed for this expense. She would send a White House limousine to pick us up at the airport and take us to the White House. Adolfo paid for me to fly to D.C., but he never charged Nancy Reagan for the expense. She was not charged for anything after she [*sic*] became President.

"Nancy Reagan was the only one to ever get Adolfo clothes for free. Sometimes he'd loan dresses to society ladies for an evening, or sell to them wholesale, but he never gave anyone anything free before. Not even Barbara Walters, who paid wholesale, and she was on national television. But Adolfo said it was worth it to him to give Nancy Reagan everything for free because he got great publicity from her wearing his clothes, and increased his sales as a result. For example, after Nancy went into the White House, Adolfo sales at Saks Fifth Avenue in Palm Beach alone went from $100,000 a season to $385,000 in 1981, and it was like that all over the country—in Dallas and Houston, Texas, in New York, Chicago, Los Angeles—all over.

"After the White House, Nancy didn't visit the shop much. We had her mannequin, so we could alter everything perfectly, but she liked to come to New York and have Adolfo go to the Carlyle with a model and fit her there. Before that, she'd come into the shop with that awful Jerry Zipkin person, who just drove Adolfo crazy. Right after the presidential election, when she came to New York, she was trying on dresses, and Jerry Zipkin screamed and flapped his arms: 'Nancy, take it off. I don't like it. Quick. Take it off. Off! Off! Off!' She immediately took the dress off and refused to get it. Adolfo was furious at Jerry Zipkin, and extra furious at me because I was sitting at the desk with my eyes down and my ears out like Dumbo. I heard everything, which humbled Adolfo because we grew up together in Cuba. I've known him all my life."

The designer gave everything in his spring and fall collections to the

First Lady, plus whatever she wanted custom-designed. In the beginning, he delivered the clothes to the White House himself. Once he arrived carrying six wardrobe bags filled with suits. The guard at the gate took the bags for the First Lady and tipped Adolfo a dollar, thinking he was the deliveryman.

When Nancy visited Adolfo's shop to select her inaugural outfit, she made the designer show her photographs of everything he had ever designed for the Duchess of Windsor, Nancy's exemplar of elegance. From Adolfo's photographs, she selected the red coat and dress outfit with a braided doughnut hat.

While the President-elect's wife was visiting designers' showrooms in New York selecting her free clothes, American couturier James Galanos was in California working on the $25,000 satin gown that he, too, would give Mrs. Reagan to wear to the inaugural balls. Later, she would present it to the First Ladies Hall in the Smithsonian's Museum of American History.

Ever superstitious, Nancy had asked Galanos to design a white one-shoulder sheath, as he had for the first gubernatorial inaugural in Sacramento.

Expecting a Reagan victory, the designer had bought the white satin material in France in July 1980. Shortly after the November election, he presented Nancy with a simple design overlaid with lace and outlined with a fern motif of embroidered crystal and chalk beads with raised bugle beads. It had required painstaking handstitching by six Portuguese women working around the clock for six weeks.

"I wanted Nancy to really look glamorous," said Galanos, a Democrat who never let politics get in the way of business. "She's representing the highest office in the country, in the world. . . . I just wanted her to look elegant and in keeping with the new formality."

After the election, the prospective First Lady gave interviews in which she said she intended to restore to the White House some of the traditional customs dispensed with by the Carters, such as the playing of "Hail to the Chief" each time the President made an official entrance, white tie and tails, diplomatic receptions, a ceremonial color guard for state visits, dancing after state dinners, and the serving of hard liquor.

"There will be a return of dignity," said Nancy Reagan, as if the Carters had been jugheads in blue jeans who prodded cattle through the halls. The comments from people around her were equally insulting.

"This will not be a Coca-Cola and ketchup White House," snipped Monsieur Marc, Nancy's New York hairdresser.

"We are finally going to see some real style in Washington," said Julius, Nancy's California hairdresser.

"Say goodbye to 'Grits 'n' Fritz,' " crowed *Women's Wear Daily,* referring to the Southern President and his Vice President, who was nicknamed "Fritz."

"Style is not a word you can use for the Carter administration," sniffed designer Oscar de la Renta. "I had heard so much about the Southern way of entertaining—Scarlett O'Hara, etcetera—but it wasn't evident at the White House. The luster is gone. It's such a bore to have Amy Carter at every dinner party, especially when you've made an effort to go out and buy an expensive dress, thinking you're going to sit next to Mr. So and So. It's a letdown. The Reagans are going to bring back the kind of style the White House should have."

Still in awe of the Eastern establishment, the newly elected Reagans were determined to court social acceptability in a way the Carters never did. Self-conscious about being perceived as California nouveau riche, the President-elect and his wife longed to be part of the ruling class exemplified by such mandarins as Katharine Graham, publisher of the *Washington Post,* and New York philanthropist Brooke Astor. To this end, Nancy Reynolds, the Reagans' Washington representative, worked overtime arranging appropriate dinner parties in the Reagans' honor. The parties were heavily covered by the nation's top newspapers, making the Reagans' arrival in Washington rival the triumphal reentry march of Radames into the Pharaoh's court.

Showing just how determined they were to befriend Washington's establishment and differentiate themselves from the people of Plains, Georgia, the Reagans sent telegrams to the city's elite two weeks after the election, inviting them to a dinner party at the F Street Club. This extraordinary invitation from a President-elect warranted a front-page story in the *New York Times,* which was headlined: "Reagan Asks for a First Waltz and Wins Hearts in the Capital."

"We want to avoid Jimmy Carter's fatal mistake," said Michael Deaver. "He never met the power brokers in this city. He never had any real friends here. Governor Reagan feels he not only wants to know them, but that he needs them to get this place working again."

Like Nancy Reynolds, George F. Will, described by the *New York Times* as "a political columnist turned unofficial social director for Mr. Reagan," expended a great deal of energy introducing the President-elect and his wife to the people in Washington, D.C., he considered crucial to their social success: trial lawyer Edward Bennett Williams, the AFL-CIO chief Lane Kirkland, *Washington Post* editorial page editor Meg Greenfield, former Democratic National Committee chairman Robert Strauss, and Evangeline Bruce, widow of David Bruce, former ambassador to the Court of St. James's.

"It was through George Will that Brooke Astor offered to give a party for the Reagans in New York in December that was very exclusive and quite delightful," said Jewell Jackson McCabe, president of the National Coalition of 100 Black Women. "I think the Reagans were as impressed to be with the Douglas Dillons as the Dillons were to be with the newly elected President and his wife."

Being honored by the queen of New York society conferred the social certification that Nancy Reagan had been aspiring to all her life. Breathless over Mrs. Astor's pink and turquoise Park Avenue dining room, the monogrammed crystal emblazoned with the Astor family crest, the orchids from the Astor greenhouse, the gilded finger bowls from the Astor vault, and the hostess's diamond and pearl earrings that were so heavy that during dinner they fell off her ears into her bodice, Nancy called Betsy Bloomingdale the next morning to relate every detail of the evening.

"Nancy carried on forever about the food," said another friend, who also received a phone call the next morning. "Quite impressed that Brooke had served spaghetti and mushrooms as a first course."

Nancy telephoned *Women's Wear Daily* to say the appetizer was "the best I've ever tasted." But Mrs. Reagan's newly appointed press secretary, Robin Orr, unintentionally embarrassed her boss when she told the press that the Reagans had dined on "cold cuts," which made the dinner sound like carry-out from a Seventh Avenue deli.

Knowing the dinner was off-limits to the press, Nancy talked freely to her table companions. She complained that she had to wait seven days too long to move into the executive mansion. Tom Brokaw, a guest at the dinner, later told Jane Pauley, who told the rest of the country on "The Today Show" the next morning: "Mrs. Reagan wonders why the Carters don't just move into Blair House the week before the inauguration so she can have the White House ready for Ronnie as soon as he takes the oath of office."

Nancy later denied ever saying such a thing, but Mrs. Edmund "Pat" Brown told reporters that, in 1967, she, too, had been asked to move out of the governor's mansion in Sacramento so the Reagans could move in before he took the official oath.

"If Nancy did it once, maybe she did it twice," said Bernice Brown. "My experience with her does lend credence to the story, doesn't it?"

When Mrs. Carter did not offer to move out early, Nancy, unable to hide her impatience, told a reporter that she might consider moving out of the White House before the end of the Reagan presidency to give their successors time to move in. Nancy's comment was widely interpreted as a broad hint for the outgoing Carters to pack up and leave.

The traditional tour of the White House for the future First Lady, conducted on November 20, 1980, had been especially uncomfortable for Rosalynn Carter, who was still smarting from her husband's humiliating defeat.

"It was awkward, totally awkward," recalled Mary Finch Hoyt, Mrs. Carter's press secretary. "I felt so protective of Rosalynn at that point, having somebody just come into your house and open up your closets, which is exactly what happened. . . . After all, Mrs. Carter was still First Lady, and the White House was still her home."

Another Carter aide was shocked to hear Mrs. Reagan say, "Where are the closets? Betty Ford says you've got some great closets around here. That's what I'd like to see first. The closets."

"Mrs. Carter was cordial," continued Mary Hoyt, "but it was difficult for her, especially when she tried to describe the history of some of the rooms and all Nancy Reagan wanted to know about was the closet space. Mrs. Carter was quite shocked by that. Later she said, 'All she cared about was the closets. That's all she cared about. Closets. Closets. Closets.' I think that was the point where Rosalynn turned the tour over to the chief usher, Rex Scouten, who finished escorting Mrs. Reagan through the state rooms. Then Mrs. Reagan insisted on coming back two more times with her decorator, Ted Graber, to go over the floor plans and check out the closets again. They came once while the Carters were at Camp David."

In briefing the press later, Robin Orr said Mrs. Reagan had been shown everything "except for two of the kids' rooms, which Mrs. Carter said weren't tidy enough to be seen." Orr referred to Rex Scouten, the esteemed chief usher of the White House, as a "super, super butler." Mrs. Reagan learned to her chagrin that that was a disrespectful description of the elegant man who was charged with the full responsibility of running the executive mansion, its extensive grounds, and its 150 employees.

"The White House would fall down around the President's ears without the chief usher," said Mary Finch Hoyt, rushing in to rescue her successor.

"The atmosphere on that tour between Mrs. Carter and Mrs. Reagan was strained because there had been so much animosity beforehand," said Hoyt, referring not just to the campaign rhetoric but to the remarks made by the Reagans' twenty-two-year-old son. The week before, Ron had said he would not shake hands with President Carter on Inauguration Day because he felt Carter had the morals of a snake.

"I will never forgive the way he called my father a racist and a warmonger over and over again," Ron said. "Carter would have sold his mother to get reelected. . . . My father is the most honorable man who has ever been elected President. I don't want to take anything away from Abraham Lincoln, but my father has the potential to be the greatest President there ever was. . . . I have no affection or respect for Mr. Carter. I think he's a real rat."

The comment seemed out of character for a young man reared by political parents and especially tasteless coming on the heels of his father's resounding victory over Jimmy Carter. But young Ron Reagan had no apologies to offer. "If something pisses me off, I do something about it," he said.

During the campaign, Ron had been incensed when Gore Vidal had appeared on television talking about Ronald Reagan's dyed hair. "He was . . . going on and on about this so-called cut-rate dye job of my father's when my father has *never* dyed his hair," said Ron. "It just pissed me off unbelievably. The next day, I fired off a telegram to Gore Vidal that said something like, 'If you're talking about cut-rate dye jobs, why don't you talk about your cut-rate lobotomy?' I just figured, F—— 'im. Did I sign my name? You bet. Ron Reagan."

Shortly after the election, the young ballet dancer was asked by a *Washington Post* reporter if he was homosexual. Ron dismissed the question by saying, "I find that amusing more than anything else. I think it's kind of irrelevant." But he later complained to Marie Brenner of *New York* magazine.

"It's laughable, isn't it?" he said. "I mean, I just can't believe the level of stupidity of reporters in this town. Until people brought the subject up —and believe me, at least they have the sense to seem embarrassed about it when they do—I never even thought about it. The idea that anyone would think dancing is effeminate. I'll tell you this: It's a lot more athletic than playing baseball."

A few days after the reporter's inquisition, Ron Reagan and Doria Palmieri, his twenty-nine-year-old roommate, walked into New York's City Hall and were married by a state supreme court justice. The bride wore a black sweater, black slacks, and red cowboy boots. The twenty-two-year-old bridegroom wore a red sweatshirt, blue jeans, and tennis shoes. The two witnesses were Ron's best friend, Calvin Williford, and Secret Service agent Lane McNitt. No one else was invited.

"I just knew with all the places we would be going and the people we would be seeing, it would be a lot easier for us if we were married," said Ron. "Besides, marriage is nothing romantic to me. That's not where our romance comes from. What is a wedding anyway but a $7 license and somebody asking you if you have the clap?"

Minutes after the 10:30 A.M. ceremony, Ron phoned his parents in

California, where it was 7:30 A.M. His father answered the phone and said his mother was sleeping.

"Dad, it's Ron," young Reagan said.

"Hi, how're you doing? What's happening?"

"Oh, I just got married."

There was a pause at the California end of the line.

"Yeah? Anyone I know?"

"Yes, it was Doria, of course," Ron said.

"I'm only kidding," said his father. "Your mother and I wish you every happiness and the best of luck. We'll talk to you later today. Congratulations."

Nancy burst into tears when her husband gave her the news. Years later, she admitted her feelings about Doria Palmieri, the daughter of an Italian house painter. "I didn't particularly like Doria then," she said. "I guess I was thinking back to Ron's other relationship [with Kris Harmon Nelson], and because Doria, too, was older, I was afraid this one would come to the same disastrous end, and Ron would wind up being hurt."

Managing to pull herself together before she met reporters outside the house, Nancy told them she was not disappointed in the least that she and her husband were not invited to the wedding. "That's the way Ron wanted it," she said. "His father and I had a small wedding. The main thing is that Ron is happy."

In the six weeks since the election, the burnished image of America's future First Lady was beginning to show a few smudges. Johnny Carson referred to her in his monologues on "The Tonight Show" as "the Evita of Bel Air" or "Nancita." The press reported her extravagant inaugural wardrobe, her intemperate suggestion that the Carters move out of the White House so she could start redecorating, her refusal to disavow her son's comments about President Carter's having the morals of a snake, and then her own statement to reporters about setting an example in the White House to bring about "a return to a higher sense of morality."

One of the bigger blemishes occurred a few days after John Lennon of the Beatles was murdered by a deranged fan in New York City. Given that death, Helen Thomas of United Press International (UPI), who was interviewing Nancy, asked about her opposition to gun control. The future First Lady said that despite Lennon's assassination she, like her husband, would continue to oppose gun control because she felt that otherwise the "wrong persons" would get guns. She did not explain what she meant. Instead, she said, she favored stiffer penalties for criminals who use guns.

"I have a little gun," she volunteered. "My husband showed me how to shoot it. . . . It's a tiny little gun. Ronnie was away a lot, you know. He was out speaking a lot and I was alone in the house." She then laughed and said she probably wouldn't need her gun now that she was going to be living in the White House with Secret Service protection. She said she never used the weapon anyway, and didn't even know what kind of gun it was. "It's just a tiny little gun. I don't know anything about it."

Sitting in on the interview were Nancy Reynolds, who was directing the transition staff, and Robin Orr, the newly appointed press secretary.

"Well, I'm sure I know what the papers will carry tomorrow," said Nancy Reynolds.

Mrs. Reagan looked puzzled. "Lots of people have guns," she said, not comprehending that her "tiny little gun" comment following the violent deaths of John Lennon and Washington, D.C., cardiologist Michael Halberstam, who was shot by a burglar, might appear callous and insensitive.

The UPI story was sent around the world and appeared under headlines like "Pistol-Packin' Nancy Keeps a Gun in Her Bedroll" and "Don't Worry, Nancy, D.C. Will Be Disarming." One angry columnist asked if a "tiny little gun" shoots "itsy-bitsy bullets that leave you just a little bit dead?" Suddenly the wife of the President-elect looked like Calamity Jane. Five days later, Robin Orr, who had been unable to protect her boss from herself, was fired.

"Nancy Reynolds and I were both in the room during the 'tiny gun interview,'" she explained. "What could we have said? She answered the question . . . and Nancy Reynolds is certainly a more seasoned Washington person than I am. What either of us could have done at that particular juncture, I don't know. To me, however, I must admit, it didn't seem that bad."

After twenty-eight days on the job as the future First Lady's press secretary, Robin Orr, former society editor of the *Oakland Tribune,* was sent back home. "Nancy Reynolds, who had essentially hired me, said that Jim Baker [Reagan's new chief of staff] did not think I was right for the job," she said. "He wanted to put Sheila Patton in because she was supposedly schooled in Washington politics. So they appointed me to be director of the International Communications Agency reception center in San Francisco, which was quite a coveted spot. I flew there on Air Force One with Nancy Reagan and she was very sweet to me. She felt terrible about what had happened . . . but, no, I never heard from her again after that."

Nancy Reynolds and Michael Deaver placed a hurry-up call to Letitia

Baldrige in New York City to help recruit the right staff for Mrs. Reagan. The former White House social secretary to Jacqueline Kennedy agreed to come to Washington to advise Deaver and Reynolds as they tried to hire people qualified to operate the East Wing of the White House.

The Reagans' biggest gaffe had blue eyes. Frank Sinatra had been one of the first persons Ronald Reagan had called after winning the presidency. The President-elect had asked the singer to host his inaugural gala, as he had once done for John F. Kennedy. Sinatra, delighted to finally have a U.S. President he could call his own, accepted eagerly.

But the appointment—the first Ronald Reagan made after his election —drew wide coverage, setting off rumors that the singer might be made U.S. ambassador to Italy. This drew scathing commentaries from Italian newspapers.

"Sinatra is welcome at any time for a singing engagement or to make a movie. But not in any other capacity," editorialized *La Stampa,* the respected Turin daily. "If the American government thinks of Italy as the land of mandolins and La Cosa Nostra, then Sinatra would be the appropriate choice."

For Sinatra's sixty-fifth birthday on December 12, 1980, his wife gave a surprise party in Rancho Mirage, California. The Reagans could not attend because they had to be in Washington for Katharine Graham's dinner party in their honor the night before and for Nancy's third tour of the Carter White House the next day. However, most of the Reagans' closest friends were on hand to honor Sinatra, including Betty and Bill Wilson, Marion and Earle Jorgensen, Harriet and Armand Deutsch, Leonore and Walter Annenberg, and Jean and William French Smith, the last-named being Reagan's personal lawyer, whom he had nominated to be U.S. Attorney General. It was Smith who had assured the Nevada Gaming Control Board of Ronald Reagan's high opinion of Sinatra. "The governor finds him to be an honorable person who is extremely charitable and loyal," Smith had told the board.

Also attending the birthday party that evening was Sidney Korshak, husband of Barbara Sinatra's best friend. This meant that Smith, scheduled to become the nation's highest law enforcement officer, shared a social evening with the Mafia's lawyer at a party honoring a man associated with organized crime.

A reporter called Smith's office in Los Angeles to inquire about his relationship to Korshak. Through a spokesman, the Attorney General-designate denied knowing the Mafia lawyer and said he "had never met him and wouldn't recognize him if he saw him on the street. . . . If he talked to Korshak [at the party], it was purely accidental."

The Reagans had socialized with Sidney Korshak on many occasions, including Frank Sinatra's wedding to Barbara Marx in 1976 and during a Sinatra anniversary party in the summer of 1980. And, of course, Nancy had dealt with the Mafia lawyer through Alfred Bloomingdale, when she was trying to get California's racetrack strike settled during her husband's first term as governor.

During the 1980 presidential campaign, the scandal-ridden International Brotherhood of Teamsters had been the first major union to endorse Reagan, and Allen Friedman, a former Teamster official and Jackie Presser's uncle, claimed that he had given Ed Meese a suitcase full of money for Reagan. Shortly after the election, Reagan showed his gratitude by appointing Teamster president Jackie Presser as a senior adviser to his economic affairs transition group. Government officials were stunned. Attorney General Benjamin Civiletti said he couldn't understand "how anyone trying to develop a new government could conceive of making this selection."

"The involvement of the designee for attorney general in the rehabilitation of the reputation of a man [Sinatra] obviously proud to be close to notorious hoodlums," wrote William Safire in the *New York Times*, "is the first deliberate affront to the propriety of the Reagan administration."

The Pulitzer Prize–winning columnist went on: "Let birthday-party goer Smith review the FBI's Sinatra file. Then let him tell the Senate to what extent he thinks it proper for a friend of mobsters to profit from being a chum of the chief executive and of the man who runs the Department of Justice."

Outraged, William French Smith described the birthday party as a "civic function" and called Safire's column "scurrilous . . . just absolutely scurrilous."

A few days later, when Safire asked the President-elect about Sinatra's gangland connections, Reagan responded genially: "We've heard those things about Frank for years. We just hope none of them are true."

Hordes of Ronald Reagan's wealthy supporters stormed the nation's capital to celebrate the triumph of a politician and a cause they had supported since 1966. They came to crown the first conservative President in fifty years. They displayed what was to become the hallmark of the Reagan era: bright, shiny, new, noisy wealth that is most often seen in long limousines, rustling furs, ornate gowns, and jewels the size of cow droppings. Their celebration continued during the four days and 103 parties of the inaugural. Distracted in their dash from one party to the next, some women forgot their minks on the Washington Metro and left cashmere coats unclaimed in hotel checkrooms. Such lavish consumption alongside the high unemployment, homelessness, rampant inflation, and economic anxiety plaguing the country in 1980 dismayed at least one Reagan conservative.

"When you've got to pay $2,000 for a limousine for four days, $7 to park and $2.50 to check your coat, at a time when most people in this country just can't hack it, that's ostentatious," said Senator Barry Goldwater.

But nothing epitomized the Reagan era more than what was called "the Frank Sinatra Gala." Televised live from the Capital Centre, a sports arena in Landover, Maryland, the two-and-a-half-hour show raised over $5 million for Ronald Reagan's $10 million inaugural, the most expensive in the nation's history.

On January 19, 1981, more than 20,000 people jammed the Capital Centre, after paying $2,000 to $10,000 for an inaugural box. They watched Rich Little do imitations of the President-elect and Donny Osmond run around the stage shouting "Go Ronnie go, go, go Ronnie go, go Ronnie be good." The Reagans arrived by helicopter with Julius, the hairdresser, so he could apply a last-minute touch-up to Nancy's coiffure.

The host, Francis Albert Sinatra, wearing a $2,500 custom-made tuxedo, escorted the President-elect and his wife to their blue velour thrones a few feet from the stage, where they sat like potentates. Nancy was in a $3,000 black velvet Bill Blass dress, which was free. Her husband was wearing one of his black $35 ties from Gucci, also free. They watched Johnny Carson as master of ceremonies introduce Bob Hope, Ethel Merman, Mel Tillis, Debbie Boone, Grace Bumbry, Charlie Pride, Jimmy Stewart, Charlton Heston, and Ben Vereen—all of whom Sinatra had described as "the greatest talents America could offer to any audience."

The critics disagreed.

"It looked like a cross between Dial-a-Joke and 'Hee-Haw,' " said Rex Reed in the *New York Daily News*. "I feel America is the greatest country in the world, and the greatest talents in our country should have been up there proving it. Instead, we got a parade of jerks, clowns, and no-talent mediocrities that made you look forward to the brassiere and toilet-cleaner commercials. Except for the Metropolitan Opera's Grace Bumbry, the show had nothing to offer anyone with intelligence or a respect for quality."

"For a celebration and cross-section of American bad taste it was not all-inclusive, but not for lack of trying," said Tom Shales in the *Washington Post*. He dismissed the gala as "a tacky combination of a Hollywood awards show, a Kiwanis club talent contest, and a telethon stocked with fewer greats than near-greats and even more pure mediocrities."

The performance of Ben Vereen, who appeared in painted-on black-face with bubbled white lips, jolted Mike Royko of the *Chicago Sun-Times*. "For sophistication," he wrote, "it would be hard to top having a shuffling, grimacing, bulging-eyed black man in bum's clothing come out and do a minstrel routine in which he appeared to be brain-damaged," he wrote. "You just don't see that kind of sophisticated entertainment any-more—not since Step'n Fetchit died, and no other black actor came along who could so hilariously portray the dim-witted, gape-mouthed, obsequi-ous black stereotype. It's possible that this performance offended some black viewers, but it probably made many of the rich Republicans in the audience yearn for the days when you could get good domestic help."

Toward the end of the program, Sinatra approached the Reagans' thrones and, reading from index cards, said, "I should like to do some-thing special for our new First Lady. This is one of my favorite songs, and we've had just a little change in the lyrics. And I hope you'll like this, Nancy."

Then, to the tune of "Nancy with the Smiling Face," the song that Jimmy Van Heusen had written to honor the birth of Sinatra's first child, the singer looked directly at Ronald Reagan's wife and sang with an intimacy that was unsettling to some in the audience:

> . . . *I'm so pleased that our First Lady's Nancy,*
> *Also pleased that I'm sort of a chum,*
> *Bet the eight years all will be fancy,*
> *As fancy as they come. . . .*
> *Nancy, Nancy, Nancy with the Reagan face.*

By the last verse, Nancy's eyes were brimming, and when Sinatra fin-ished, she blew him a loving kiss.

The next day at noon, Ronald Wilson Reagan was sworn in as the fortieth President of the United States. At sixty-nine, he was the oldest man ever to be inaugurated. He had specified that semiformal attire would be the appropriate dress for the occasion, so most men on the podium appeared in gray stroller jackets or club coats rather than morn-ing coats. They did not wear the customary plain or pleated-front white shirts with studs, dove gray vests, striped gray trousers, striped gray four-in-hand ties, black socks, and black oxford shoes. Dark gray suits had been recommended for women, and Nancy, sensitive to criticisms of opulence, had ruled out fur coats on the podium.

The Reagans' family and friends sat with them overlooking the West Front of the Capitol, the first time in history that a President took the oath of office facing the Washington Monument and the Lincoln Memorial. Joining them were Ron and Doria Reagan; Patti Davis; Michael Reagan, his wife, Colleen, and their son, Cameron; Maureen Reagan and her fiance, Dennis Revell; Ronald's brother, Neil, and his wife, Bess; Nancy's parents, Dr. and Mrs. Loyal Davis; her stepbrother, Dr. Richard Davis, his wife, Patricia, and their children, Anne and Geoffrey; the Reagans' housekeeper, Ann Allman; their decorator, Ted Graber; their driver from Sacramento, Barney Barnett; Michael Deaver; and Nancy Reynolds. The only Reagan intimate left out was Frank Sinatra, but moments before the President-elect appeared, he barged up the steps to take his place on the platform.

"Sinatra had not been invited to stand on the steps with the President and First Lady, but he bulldozed his way in anyway and took someone else's place," said a White House photographer. "He didn't have an authorized ticket, but he balled through, ramming past the Secret Service and the capital police. No one had the nerve to stop him. No one!"

The highlight of the day came after the inauguration ceremony. As the new President was eating lunch with congressional leaders, he received the news that everyone had been waiting for: the 52 hostages held in Iran for 444 days had been released. Former President Carter received the news while on his way to Andrews Air Force Base, Maryland, for the flight back to Georgia. When he heard it on the phone in his car, he turned to Walter Mondale and the two men wept.

That evening, in her free $25,000 Galanos gown and a pair of $480,000 diamond earrings "on loan" from Harry Winston, Nancy Reagan set off with her husband to dance at their ten inaugural balls.

"She insisted we get them to every one and then to the Kennedy Center so they could dance with all the Californians and still be back to the White House by a reasonable hour," said Peter Sorum, in charge of presidential transportation for the evening. "It was a killer, but I managed to get them to everything and home in bed by 12:18 A.M."

The most important party as far as Nancy was concerned was scheduled for February 6, 1981, to mark the President's seventieth birthday. This was to be a surprise for Ronald Reagan from his wife, although she was not paying for the event. Nancy had been told that the President and First Lady are charged for every private meal they eat in the White House, plus all incidentals, such as dry cleaning, toothpaste, and toiletries as well as all meals for guests unless on official business. Claiming she could not afford to pay for her husband's party, she turned to "the group," eight of whom—the Annenbergs, Wilsons, Jorgensens, and Deutsches—took over the expenses.

But it was Nancy's party to plan and she did: slaving over every detail from the green moiré tablecloths down to the eggshell-colored initials RWR on the twelve birthday cakes of vanilla sponge soaked in raspberry brandy, which would be carried in by White House chefs in big white hats and served at each of the twelve tables. In place of seventy candles, she specified a jumping white horse of spun sugar to decorate the biggest cake. She specified that the East Room be filled with lighted ficus trees surrounded by tulips, lilies, and jonquils to give the effect of a spring garden, and that the six-piece orchestra of Billy Wilson play as late as the Reagans wished to dance.

She limited the guest list to 120 people, and deliberated over whom to invite. She deleted people she did not like, such as George Bush, Lyn Nofziger, Helene von Damm, and the Salvatoris, but when it was pointed out to her that the President would notice their absence, she reluctantly reinstated them. Only Maureen Reagan among the children was invited, but without her fiancé because Nancy would not let them sleep together in the White House until they were married. Nancy did let her decorator and his male lover share the Lincoln Bedroom, but that was because the decorator was donating his services to redecorating the White House.

She summoned her manicurist from Los Angeles for an emergency one-and-a-half-hour session before the party, and the manicurist, who also had donated her services, made arrangements for the First Lady to have a manicure every week—free. "I'm a Republican and I'd like to do it as a public service," said the manicurist, who was not included on the guest list. But Nancy did invite her Hollywood hairdresser.

With the exception of Vice President Bush, Defense Secretary Caspar Weinberger, Attorney General Smith, and CIA director William Casey, Nancy did not invite any members of the cabinet. Most of the guests were California friends who, in addition to "the group" and "the girls," included Elizabeth Taylor, who wore the most spectacular rubies at the party, the Frank Sinatras, Jimmy Stewarts, and Irene Dunne, who, as one of Reagan's favorite old-time movie stars, had the place of honor next to him at the President's table. At the First Lady's table, Nancy had placed Frank Sinatra on her right.

"We had to be on hand, of course, to take pictures throughout the night," recalled Michael Evans, the chief White House photographer, "and ordinarily nothing could be released until it was first approved by Mrs. Reagan. Every White House photo of the First Lady had to be approved by her, and if it wasn't approved, it had to be destroyed. Those were her orders. Other photos had to be approved by Mike Deaver or Jim Baker. But this particular evening was an exception because it was going to be so late and neither Deaver nor Baker wanted to be awakened at 3:00 A.M., and they certainly didn't want me waking up Mrs. Reagan at that hour, so Deaver told me to go ahead and make the decision myself, which I did."

The White House photograph released to the press after the President's birthday party was most revealing of Nancy Reagan as she danced with Frank Sinatra, his arm wrapped around her back, pressing her closely to him. The President was caught with a perplexed look on his face as he put his hand on his wife's arm to cut in. Sinatra was smiling jauntily over his shoulder at the President, but the First Lady looked as if she had been awakened from a dreamy trance. And she seemed peeved that her husband was interrupting her dance with the man she adoringly referred to as Francis Albert.

"The picture was picked up all over the world, but not just because it was a good photograph," said Michael Evans. "At the time, Sinatra was involved with a grand jury investigation into the Westchester [New York] Premier Theater scandal and also was scheduled to go before the Las Vegas Gaming Commission to try to get back the license he'd lost years before because of consorting with gangsters. I really didn't think of any of that when I decided to release the photo. It just happened to be the best one of the evening."

But when Michael Deaver saw the picture the next day, he exploded. Roaring into Evans's office, he started screaming at the photographer. "You dumb son of a bitch! You goddamned stupid idiot! Why did you release a picture of the First Lady with Frank Sinatra, of all people? You know damn well that he is mobbed up to the eyeballs. You know about his Mafia connections. What the hell is wrong with you?"

The close friendship between the singer and the First Lady had concerned people close to the President for some time.

"It was those private 'lunches' in the family quarters that were the most troublesome," said one presidential assistant, shaking his head. "Sinatra's name was never on the First Lady's schedule, and he was always brought in the back way, but I still worried about the press picking it up."

"We always knew better than to ever interrupt those private 'luncheons,' " said a member of Mrs. Reagan's White House staff. "The family quarters were off limits to everyone during that time. You could feel the air charge when he was around her. She played the music low, all his songs, of course, which she played in her bedroom day and night. She scheduled their private lunches in the solarium and fussed over the menu and the flowers. . . . Few people knew when he was up there. She usually would arrange those 'lunches' when the President was out of town, and they'd last from about 12:30 to 3:30 or 4:00 P.M. Sinatra came to the gate and Muffie Brandon [White House social secretary] would escort him up there. Then she would get lost immediately. All calls were put on hold. We were under strict instructions not to disturb. No matter what. When the First Lady was with Frank Sinatra, she was not to be disturbed. For anything. And that included a call from the President himself."

17

THE FIRST LADY'S STAFF was frantic. The President had been in office only thirty days and already his wife was acting like a Marie Antoinette windup doll, leaving her imperial mark on the White House.

During an interview she said that what pleased her most about her first month in Washington had been redecorating the second and third floors of the White House, which are never open to the public.

"I love to do tables [and arrange centerpieces for parties], but the White House needs some more china," she said. "There hasn't been any china bought for the White House since the Johnsons, and that's the one with the state flowers on it. It's very pretty, but . . ."

The First Lady was determined to have a set of state china in her own name as part of her White House legacy. She had been "horrified" by all the chips and cracks she spotted in the Wilson, Roosevelt, Eisenhower, Truman, and Johnson plates in the White House cupboards, which contained over 10,000 pieces of china when she moved in. Most distressing to the rigid Los Angeles hostess, who preferred wall-to-wall carpeting, finger bowls, and dishes that matched, was that she could not seat a state dinner without mixing the china patterns. This was unacceptable in her opinion for entertaining royalty, even though the Queen of England herself mixed various china patterns. Three days after Nancy Reagan moved into the White House she instructed Rex Scouten to call the Lenox China Company in New Jersey.

"He called and said Mrs. Reagan was interested in a quote on the price of new china for the White House," said Robert Sullivan, Lenox vice president. "This was at 3:00 P.M. and then he said, 'Can I have a quote by five o'clock?' "

Unruffled by the estimate of $1,000 a place setting, the First Lady began a series of meetings with Lenox representatives to design 220 place settings of seven different styles of plates as well as finger bowls, cereal bowls, berry bowls, ramekins, and cocktail cups used specifically to hold sauce for shrimp. She specified a raised 24-karat gold presidential seal in the middle of every plate, which required hours of artisan work because each had to be handcrafted. Displeased with the color samples she saw, she went to the next meeting wearing a red dress to show the Lenox people exactly what shade of red she wanted.

"She had a very positive idea of the color of red and the look she wanted to achieve," said Charles Solt, chief of design. "She was very concerned that the china have the dignity and formality necessary for the White House."

She ordered wide scarlet borders with double rings of gold etching, specified the size of the teacup handles, ordered deep gravy wells, and a 24-karat gold lattice design on the service plates. She needed more than fifteen meetings before the design was executed to her satisfaction.

"She was very interested in every detail, every piece," said Robert Sullivan. "The emphasis was on elegance, on great style in the classic sense of that phrase. . . . I think she was having fun. In fact, I think one of the things she enjoyed most as First Lady was choosing this new service."

Having designed her own set of state china, which would be displayed in the White House collection in a special room established by Edith Galt Wilson, the second wife of President Woodrow Wilson, the new First Lady now decided she needed personal china as well, so she began another series of secret meetings with representatives of the Boehm Studios in Trenton, New Jersey. With these people, she designed a 264-piece set of hand-painted porcelain named "Nancy," with 24-karat gold double-banded teacups monogrammed NDR. No two plates were alike, and each piece carried the presidential seal plus the inscription on the bottom: "Designed for the First Lady of the United States of America, Mrs. Ronald W. Reagan."

Unfortunately for her, the First Lady announced the acquisition of her $209,508 state china on the same day the President cut school lunches and declared that ketchup would be counted as a vegetable in the federally subsidized program.

The outcry was deafening as editorials across the country lacerated the Reagans for their insensitivity to the poor. An Oliphant cartoon featured a destitute couple sitting at a bare table eating off tin plates. The husband is holding a newspaper with the headline: "First Lady Orders New China For White House—$1,000 A Place Setting." The wife, in a torn housedress, is glancing at the headline.

"Oh, really? What pattern?" she asks.

The little penguin in the corner says: "This is what we call our 'American Dream Truly Needy Series.'"

The President, who had acknowledged accepting a pair of $1,000 cowboy boots as a gift a few days before, quickly rescinded the ketchup-as-vegetable decree and then tried to defend his wife's china purchase. He said all 4,372 pieces had been donated by the Knapp Foundation of Maryland and "did not cost taxpayers a cent." In fact, the U.S. Treasury pays indirectly for half of such a tax-deductible donation.

Nancy was so shocked by the criticism that when her personal china arrived a few months later, she refused to accept the $100,000 order. She instructed Rex Scouten to call Helen Boehm and tell her that she had exactly one hour to get the china out of the White House.

"There was no way we could send anyone down from Trenton that fast, so I called an old friend, Bill Marriott, Sr., and asked for help. He sent his chauffeur over to the White House to pick it up," said Boehm. "I put them in a safe, where they've been ever since."

A few days later, Mrs. Reagan's social secretary complained to the Associated Press that the White House was having a "terrible tablecloth crisis" and had no money to resolve it.

Mrs. Reagan's interior decorator, Ted Graber, said the average price of decorating one good room in a house, not including art and antiques, was $50,000. That announcement generated news stories estimating that the First Lady's redecoration of the White House would cost over $3 million.

Not so, said the First Lady, who proudly disclosed that she had already equipped the White House beauty salon with thousands of dollars' worth of free furnishings, fabrics, and cosmetics from the beauty industry. Donations for the renovation included a $3,700 Peruvian rug, a $400 salmon-colored Louis XV lounge chair, a $346.65 shampoo bowl with temperature controls, two hair dryers valued at a total of $1,200, a $720 white leather chair, a $230 manicurist's stool, $1,800 worth of red and green glazed chintz draperies and wallcoverings from Clarence House, and $300 worth of lipsticks, eye shadows, creams and foundations donated by Redken Laboratories.

Anger swept across the country like a tidal wave and engulfed the First Lady. Everyone from the political right to the left expressed disgust.

The archconservative newspaper publisher William Loeb wrote a

front-page editorial in the *Manchester Union-Leader* saying that while the
President cuts federal programs and asks Americans to sacrifice, Nancy
must not live as if "money grows on trees." "The shrieks of radical
Democrats that your husband Ron's program is favoring the rich and
against the poor is at the moment not having any general success," Loeb
wrote. "But if you keep this lifestyle, it will, because it gives the impression of a modern-day Marie Antoinette living very high on the hog regardless of how other people are having to get along on much less."

The liberal *Washington Monthly* magazine bated: "So, Nancy, maybe
it's true. Maybe we're all born irredeemably greedy and selfish. But can't
you be just a little hypocritical? Can't you just *pretend* you care about
something in life besides handbags and hors d'oeuvres?"

The President's staff jumped in to save things. Behind her back they
dismissed her as "Mommy," "the Missus," and "the Hairdo with Anxiety," but they still worried that she might damage the President's economic recovery program. So they went into damage control: The Reagans would not use the congressional appropriation of $50,000 to
redecorate their private quarters in the White House. Instead, they
would return the money to the Treasury and raise the necessary funds
from private donations. At the same time, the President announced that
cabinet officers would not be allowed to redecorate their offices, and
government workers would have to cut back on equipment purchases
and all travel vouchers.

Reporters asked why the cabinet was forbidden to redecorate even as
the First Lady was planning to spend $822,640 redecorating the family
quarters. "There's a difference between a place where you live and a
place where you work," explained White House press secretary James
Brady lamely. As the issue simmered, her $50,000-a-room decorator was
flying back and forth to California on Air Force One at taxpayers' expense.

The President also imposed a freeze on all federal hiring, saying that
this was part of his campaign to bring the runaway budget under control.
"I view the implementation of these orders as critical. The American
people are determined to have action on the economic problems that we
face," he said.

The First Lady did nothing to mitigate the damage to her image. When
she received a letter from a Chicago woman criticizing the President's
budget cut of aid to handicapped children, Nancy responded like a
movie queen patronizing one of her fans. She sent a photograph of herself plus a copy of the Reagans' "favorite" recipe for artichoke and
crabmeat casserole.

When another media barrage was aimed at the free-spending First

Lady, her staff responded by directing that no more photographs be sent out without approval. Then they issued a new "favorite recipe": macaroni and cheese.

In a scathing series, "The Woman Who Would Be Queen," the *Los Angeles Herald-Examiner* described the President's wife as a frivolous social climber with more political ambition than Lady Macbeth. The *New York Times* reprinted a cartoon of her flouncing into breakfast wearing a fur stole, swirling gown, and ropes of jewels with a cigarette holder in one hand and a martini glass in the other. The President glances up from his comic book.

"Nancy! The inauguration's over. You can put on your bathrobe now. . . ."

"This *is* my bathrobe!" she says.

Anxious to present the First Lady as a serious woman interested in substantive issues, the White House issued a media advisory that she would meet the press on February 9, 1981, to introduce her East Wing staff and disclose her plans to promote Foster Grandparents, the program she had been involved with in California when her husband was governor.

The one hundred reporters assembled in the White House family theater waited fifteen minutes for Nancy to arrive for her first official appearance. They were surprised when she elected to be announced like the President, with a sonorous voice over the loudspeaker proclaiming: "The First Lady of the United States." She walked up to the microphone, said a few tittery words, and introduced her chief of staff, her press secretary, and her social secretary.

The event had been orchestrated to give Nancy a cause as worthy as those of her predecessors, each of whom had been committed to specific projects: Lady Bird Johnson to beautification, Pat Nixon to volunteerism, Betty Ford to women's rights, Rosalynn Carter to mental health. But Nancy Reagan had been so uncomfortable in talking about her commitment to the Foster Grandparents program that she rebuked Helen Thomas for breaking the rules with a question.

"You're not going to let your husband cut the program out, are you?" asked the UPI reporter.

"This is not a press conference, Helen," said the First Lady sternly. "But no, I'm not. Nor would he want to." (The Reagan administration would propose no new funding for the program and actively oppose increases proposed by the National Association of Foster Grandparent Program Directors.)

"What a joke that briefing was," said Julia Malone, then White House correspondent for the *Christian Science Monitor*. "Mrs. Reagan herded us into a narrow briefing room, put her staff in front and the press in the back. She refused to answer questions or allow photographers to take pictures, and she displayed absolutely no sensitivity to the roomful of professional working women. She introduced Peter McCoy as her chief of staff by giggling and saying, 'Here is my token male.' He stood up, giggled, and said, 'Oh, gosh.' Then he sat down, while she made it clear she was much too busy unpacking boxes upstairs to stay with us. 'I'm just a little nester,' she said, and after twelve minutes she disappeared. She left us to watch a little movie on Foster Grandparents for the next twenty minutes.''

The First Lady's staff knew the press briefing had failed miserably when it became fodder for one of Johnny Carson's monologues a few nights after the event.

''I read in the paper that Nancy Reagan recently met with the press, although reporters were forbidden to ask any questions,'' said the comedian on ''The Tonight Show.'' ''A couple of questions slipped by, though. One was about Mrs. Reagan's religion, which we all know is Christian Dior, and her favorite junk food, which is caviar. Someone questioned her about foreign policy and whether or not she favored Red China. She said she did, but not with yellow tablecloths.''

Reacting to the ridicule, the First Lady's staff announced that Mrs. Reagan would go horseback riding the next day with retarded children in Rock Creek Park, accompanied by Effi Barry, the black wife of the black mayor of Washington, D.C.

In July of 1981, around the time of the First Lady's birthday, her senior staff dreamed up yet another idea for improving her image.

''There had been no positive press coverage of Mrs. Reagan in months,'' said one of her top aides, ''so we decided to give ourselves a break by giving the Washington, D.C., black kids a refurbished pool. If we had to do something that cost money which would help Nancy, there was always a short list of loving friends who would pony up. Whatever we needed in terms of dollars would be provided by the Bloomingdales and Deutsches and Wilsons and Darts.''

''The group'' raised $3,800 to repair the indoor swimming pool at the D.C. Center for Therapeutic Recreation. The First Lady attended the ribbon-cutting ceremony at the pool and said the refurbishment in her name was the best birthday present she could think of.

She joined the board of Wolf Trap and even donated $25,000 to its performing arts program from the White House redecoration fund, but none of this kept her from slipping in the opinion polls. By the end of the year, nearly one-quarter of the American people had an unfavorable opinion of her, with a substantial majority saying she cared less about the plight of the underprivileged than any First Lady of the twentieth century.

The East Wing staff next tried to compensate for her bad press by arranging "Lady Bountiful outings," as one of them called the public relations junkets they dreamed up. For every newspaper picture of Nancy wearing her $25,000 Maximillian mink coat, they tried to get her photographed hugging a handicapped child, "preferably black." Each time she was reported wearing a new $950 Adolfo suit, or lunching in New York at Le Cirque with Jerry Zipkin, now referred to in the press as the First Fop, they sent her on a hospital tour.

Following the Reagans' first state visit to Canada, it was reported that the First Lady had taken her hairdresser, Julius. She thought that he could travel free on Air Force One; she did not realize that the laws governing such travel expenditures for nongovernment employees stipulate that she herself or the Republican National Committee had to reimburse the government. A first-class commercial round-trip ticket on that route would have cost $260.50. Nancy refused to pay. Instead, she sent the bill to the Republican National Committee, saying it was a political expense.

She had said that she was doing her part to fight inflation. "We're doing the things that all people are doing right now. You're just pulling in. You have to," she told NBC-TV. "We tightened our belt in many ways." She cited the sale of their California home, which they put on the market at $1.9 million and sold a year later for $1 million. "We're selling our home in Pacific Palisades, which we dearly love . . . [but] even with my husband's annual salary of $200,000, we're not making any money here and we're not spending as much money."

The staff groaned upon hearing that, because the average American worker made only $10,491 a year. They hurriedly arranged a highly publicized trip to St. Ann's Infant and Maternity Home in Hyattsville, Maryland, so she could be photographed visiting the unwanted and neglected youngsters there, most of whom were black. Because ten foster grandparents also worked there for $2 an hour, the staff thought this would be an excellent opportunity for her to demonstrate commitment to her project.

The next day's newspapers carried photographs of Nancy kissing babies, hugging toddlers, and being knocked off her feet by an exuberant five-year-old. Weeks later, Nancy visited the pediatrics ward of Howard University Hospital, where photographers were positioned to take her picture with little black children who were trotted out like props. When the photographers complained they couldn't see her clearly, the former actress changed angles, stooping to the floor to hug and kiss the children.

Despite the positive publicity such photographs brought her, she resisted most of these outings during her first few months in the White House, and railed at her staff for scheduling them.

"She called me after an event with inner-city children and gave me hell," said one senior aide. "I had tried to create an event to humanize her and soften her image, but she said it was hot, boring, and dull, plus she was surrounded by hordes of black children. She was fit to be tied. The fact that her photograph ran on the wire services and appeared in the *Washington Post* and the *New York Times* was lost on her."

Nancy much preferred staying upstairs with her decorator discussing their plans for the $822,000 renovation of the living quarters and supervising the installation of all the extra closets she wanted. She had her own government-paid wardrobe mistress in Anita Costello, who organized her wardrobe with plastic-covered tags listing the designer, the color, and the occasion the outfit had been worn so that she would not wear the same outfit twice in the same company.

Back in February, when confronted with the Reagans' first state dinner, in honor of British prime minister Margaret Thatcher, the First Lady had spent every day trying to transform the executive mansion into Buckingham Palace. "I wanted the White House to look as beautiful as possible, so we worked right down to the wire," she said. "We made it— almost. But two antique chairs that were being repaired were not yet ready, so Ted [Graber] and I placed two old chairs in front of the grand piano, hoping no one would turn them around to expose the stuffing coming out of the backs.

"The menu for the dinner had been planned down to the tiniest detail, and we even held a dress rehearsal in advance. As a result, tiny little potatoes and mushrooms were added to the vegetables accompanying the rack of lamb, and the sauce for the Grand Marnier soufflé was eliminated."

Never before had a First Lady subjected the White House chef to auditions and tastings and run-throughs the way Nancy Reagan did. The chef, Henry Haller, an Alsatian, had been hired by President Johnson in 1966.

"All of her taste was dictated by her interior decorator, and the two of them drove Henry crazy telling him how to do his job," said a former member of her staff. "Having been cooking superbly for Presidents for twenty years, the executive chef of the White House was suddenly being ordered around his kitchen by the First Lady's interior decorator, who would prance in and say, 'We put the pear half there with the lettuce leaf here, and we put the dessert cookie here with the little doily there.' "

Demanding tastings before every state dinner, the First Lady and her decorator were served a sample meal that they critiqued in writing, sending their copious notes back to the kitchen. Chef Haller blanched over Nancy's Beverly Hills way of doing things, but he dutifully posted her critiques for his staff, and reluctantly followed her dictates. The juxtaposition of julienne carrots to slivered mushrooms and how much parsley perched on the plate were the criteria by which Nancy Reagan judged the chef's efforts. Polaroid pictures had to be taken of the dishes the First Lady approved so the staff would know exactly how she wanted the food presented.

The same obsessive woman who would spend an entire day deliberating the amount of nutmeg to be shaved into a chicken velouté sauce seemed oblivious to the havoc she was wreaking on herself. "I really haven't changed my habits that much," she said. "I'm just being myself." Perplexed by the censure she was drawing, she did not understand that her excruciating attention to the details of social fripperies exposed her to criticism in an era when the President's wife was expected to be more than a mere hostess. Not since Mary Todd Lincoln had the White House had such an extravagant mistress, and like Mrs. Lincoln, Nancy Reagan blamed the press for all her problems.

"She was hurt and puzzled," said Elaine Crispen, personal secretary to the First Lady during the first Reagan term. "I can remember her saying, 'Why does this happen? Why do the media dislike me so much?' "

"The press made me sound so terrible," said the First Lady a few months after moving into the White House. "And it started before I even got there. I never got half a chance. They wrote things that were so . . . so unbelievable. They knew none of those things were true, but they went ahead and printed them anyway. It was pretty mean."

One of the most searing indictments came in the early months from the pen of Garry B. Trudeau in a "Doonesbury" comic strip that satirized the First Lady's image with trenchant humor. Trudeau featured Mark Slackmeyer, the strip's radio host, interviewing the White House social secretary:

"A stroke of good luck, campers! We have on the line Miss Muffie Brandon, White House topsider and today's WBBY preppy profile! Muffie, I understand you're helping Mrs. Reagan start an exciting new outreach program! Could you tell us about it?"

"I'd love to, Mark. . . . Recently, the First Lady has been very caught up in the new mood of volunteerism. Even though the Reagans give literally hundreds of dollars annually to charity, this year she wanted to do more!"

"Did she have a cause in mind?"

"Yes, she knew she wanted to work with overprivileged kids.

Because of constant changes in values, Mrs. Reagan feels young preppies today are confused about which designers to go to, how much to spend on china, and other painful dilemmas. Mrs. Reagan was afraid that without guidance, many of these youngsters might never make the social register. So she decided to enlist the help of some of her oldest and dearest friends from Smith College, taste-makers all!"

"And that's how the Foster Grandpreppy program was born?"

"Right. She felt these kids could be saved from a life of faux pas."

Seizing on the Smith College connection between the First Lady (class of 1943) and her social secretary (class of 1957), Mike Deaver dispatched Muffie Brandon to Northampton, Massachusetts, to talk to the college president about awarding their distinguished alumna an honorary degree. Deaver felt the degree would confer a measure of much-needed prestige.

Jill Ker Conway, the president of Smith and a prominent historian and author, gently explained that this kind of tribute from the college was reserved for graduates of accomplishment, such as Mary Rogers, founder of the Maryknoll Sisters; Barbara Polk Washburn, the first woman to climb Mt. McKinley; and Marjorie Fine Kowles, first inspector general of the Department of Labor.

"We don't give honorary degrees for basking in a husband's reflected glory," she said.

"But she's the First Lady of the United States," said Muffie.

"A position she holds by virtue of her husband's accomplishments, not her own," responded Conway.

"Oh, God. If they only knew," said Mike Deaver later. "If they only knew."

Mrs. Reagan was so incensed by this slight from her college that she declined to attend her fortieth class reunion in 1983, made no financial contribution to the endowment fund, and refused to invite the Washington, D.C., alumnae chapter to tea at the White House. In the past, other First Ladies, including Lady Bird Johnson and Pat Nixon, had extended this invitation to "Smithies."

The White House kept knocking on the door of Smith College as members of Nancy's staff made pilgrimages to Northampton to plead for that honorary degree. But the answer, delivered politely but firmly each time, was no. At one point, the college offered to honor Mrs. Reagan with a tea or a formal reception, but she wanted the honorary degree or nothing. The White House even lobbied Smith's board of trustees, but the vote remained negative.

"I tried for seven years to get Nancy Reagan an honorary degree from Smith, but the board always refused, probably because they couldn't stand her husband's politics," said trustee J. Roger Friedman, president of Lebhar-Friedman, Inc.

In 1985, the pursuit became public when *Time* reported how much Mrs. Reagan wanted the honorary degree, and how Smith had resisted conferring it. The college then issued a statement: "Smith has considered a number of ways it might honor Mrs. Reagan but has made no decision. The matter is still under review."

By the time the college decided to invite Mrs. Reagan to address a convocation ceremony and receive an honorary degree, she was no longer in the White House. The honor had already been bestowed on her successor, Barbara Bush (class of 1947), and she hadn't even been graduated from Smith, having left after her freshman year to get married. Nancy Reagan was so furious at her alma mater for denying her the honor when she was First Lady that when it was finally offered in 1990, she just said no.

Without that coveted honorary degree, her White House staff kept falling back on the "Lady Bountiful outings," which were not always well received by the First Lady, who much preferred socializing with her friends. She would willingly pose for a picture with the March of Dimes poster child in the White House, but she did not like having to leave the executive mansion unless it was for one of the small Georgetown luncheons that Letitia Baldrige had arranged to introduce her to Washington society.

"She preferred dressing up and going out at night to the Kennedy Center or something like that, and she lived for her trips to New York to socialize with Brooke Astor and Gloria Vanderbilt," said one of her secretaries.

The Reagans had made their first trip to New York City as a presidential couple on March 14, 1981, to see their twenty-two-year-old son make his debut at the Metropolitan Opera House. Accompanied by the Bloomingdales and Saudi Arabian ambassador Faisal Alhegelan and his wife, they had sat in the presidential box. Each with a pair of binoculars, they watched Ron Reagan perform in a ballet ensemble. What they saw, according to the *New York Times,* was "a talented dancer who has worked very hard and who has done extremely well for a late starter."

During intermission, the First Lady sprang to her son's side, wrapped her arms around his neck, kissed him fully on the mouth, and told him how proud she was. Her husband stood back a few feet looking slightly discomfited by his wife's show of affection but full of praise for his son.

"We all tend to be a little cynical about the human race, even about ourselves," said the President. "Then you see something this way and say, 'Any creature that can do anything that beautiful, he must be remarkable.'"

"That trip to New York was a big occasion for us, too," said Frances Borden, who was then public relations director of the Waldorf-Astoria, "because we once again had a President who knew how to live and wanted to go first class. Jimmy Carter, who carried his own luggage and stayed in people's homes, had been very disappointing. With Reagan, we now had a President who wanted to stay in a luxury hotel, particularly in the presidential suite.

"So we had several meetings to decide on what amenities we should offer the Reagans. We selected luxurious rose-colored towels with her monogram in beige, beige towels for him monogrammed in brown. We had monogrammed toothbrush glasses, a crystal box with gold filigree trim for tissues, Imari bowls in the suite—that sort of thing. We even had white linen placemats with dainty, scalloped borders for Mrs. Reagan's breakfast when we were told she preferred mats to tablecloths. As a little amenity, the food and beverage director suggested we get a Baccarat crystal jar for jelly beans, since that was the President's favorite candy, so we sent someone to Baccarat to buy a beautiful crystal container for about $150."

The afternoon of the ballet, Mrs. Reagan, who had not spoken to her son or daughter-in-law since they had married four months before, got ready to visit them in their Greenwich Village apartment.

"As she's leaving the hotel," said Frances Borden, "she looked around the room and said, 'Oh, dear. I didn't buy them a gift.' Taking a look at the Baccarat crystal jar, she said, 'Do you mind?' Then she whisks it up and waltzes out the door with our $150 amenity. It was at that point that I suggested we use plastic jelly bean jars for any future visits by the Reagans."

Four nights later, the presidential couple made their first appearance at the John F. Kennedy Center for the Performing Arts in Washington, D.C., to attend the stage debut of Elizabeth Taylor, who was playing Regina in Lillian Hellman's play *The Little Foxes*. Afterward, the Reagans went backstage to congratulate the cast and the playwright.

Preceding her husband, Nancy made her way down the line of actors, graciously shaking hands and telling them how much she enjoyed their performances. When she got to Maureen Stapleton, who had once been married to producer Max Allentuck, she paused momentarily. Stapleton was an indirect link to the promiscuous past she had put firmly behind her. Forcing a smile, she quickly extended her hand to the actress.

"Hello, Maureen," she said.

"Hello, Nancy."

As the President and First Lady moved down the line, Lillian Hellman turned to Stapleton with a shocked expression on her face, and a voice full of reproach.

"You *know* her. You actually *know* her," she said.

Stapleton shrugged.

"You *know* her. *She* said, 'Hello, Maureen,' and *you* said, 'Hello, Nancy.'"

"She used to be an actress. I'm an actress. Actresses call each other by their first names."

The playwright, who despised the politics of Ronald Reagan and his wife, could not believe that her dear friend, a liberal Democrat, could have anything in common with the President's marzipan wife. Hellman pushed Maureen on the subject until Stapleton finally blurted:

"I *don't* know her," she said. "I just know Max fucked her."

All carping at Nancy stopped at 2:35 P.M. Monday, March 30, 1981, when six bullets from the revolver of a deranged young man blasted the President and five of his aides as they were leaving the Washington Hilton Hotel after a luncheon speech to 3,500 AFL-CIO union members. One bullet ricocheted off the President's armor-plated black Lincoln limousine, entered his left side, bounced off the seventh rib, punctured and collapsed a lung, and lodged in the spongy tissue an inch from his heart. Another round hit press secretary Jim Brady, penetrating his brain, leaving him sprawled on the sidewalk in a pool of blood. D.C. policeman Thomas Delahanty was shot in the neck. Secret Service agent Timothy McCarthy turned to face the gunfire while remaining upright, as he had been rigorously trained to do, and took a bullet meant for the President in his chest. Michael Deaver, who was able to duck for cover behind the fender of the armored limousine, escaped unscathed.

Upon hearing the firecracker pops, Dennis McCarthy, one of the Secret Service agents accompanying the President, dived for the assailant and landed on his back as the last shot was fired. Jerry Parr, another agent, instinctively shoved the President inside the car and fell on top of him to protect him. He ordered the motorcade to proceed directly to the White House while he ran his hands up and down Reagan's body checking for bullet holes. Finding none, he radioed the Secret Service command post at the White House with the first report of the incident: Shots had been fired but "Rawhide" (the President's code name) was unhurt.

In pain, Reagan cursed him. "You son of a bitch. You broke my ribs."

Parr now saw that the President was coughing up oxygenated blood.

"Get to George Washington Hospital immediately," Parr barked.

Swerving to reverse its course, the limousine arrived at the hospital minutes later. The agents sprung out prepared to carry Reagan inside, but the seventy-year-old President, although barely able to breathe, refused their help. For himself and for the office he represented, he needed to be seen walking in on his own power.

Weak and disoriented from the sudden loss of blood, he nevertheless told the Secret Service to let him walk into the hospital alone and unassisted. He knew the television image of a wounded, helpless President would diminish him and throw the country into a panic. Only when he was safely beyond the press and the cameras did he gasp for air and crumble to the floor.

"His eyes rolled upward and his knees started to buckle," said Roberto Hernandez, a paramedic. "I thought we were losing him."

"I can't catch my breath," the President rasped to Kathy Paul, the twenty-eight-year-old emergency room nurse who ran to his side.

She grabbed his arm and with Hernandez's help strapped him onto a stretcher.

"I feel so bad," he said, gasping for air.

Thinking he was having a heart attack, the nurse began cutting his shirt and ripping off his blue and white pin-striped suit. Two minutes later, the President was near shock with a dangerously low systolic pressure. The reading hovered between 50 and 60; normal is considered 130.

"I can't breathe," the President repeated. "I can't breathe."

Three IV lines were pushed into his arms to force fluid and blood into his system, boosting his blood volume. Within four minutes, his blood pressure registered 78.

Outside, the ambulance carrying Jim Brady pulled up to the emergency room entrance with sirens screaming. The ground-floor corridor of George Washington Hospital was now teeming with doctors racing to the trauma unit and nurses and orderlies scurrying back and forth. Presidential aides, terrified that they had lost their commander in chief, looked frightened as they arrived at the hospital to set up a communications unit. The cacophony was deafening as reporters, trying to find out what was happening, shouted questions but were drowned out by the hospital's blaring loudspeaker and the squawk of police walkie-talkies. Inside the emergency room, the air became suffocatingly hot as the crowd of people swelled.

Standing at the far end of the President's stretcher was the tall, quiet figure of Daniel Ruge, who had been selected by Loyal Davis to be White House physician; as such, he always accompanied the President. A widely known and respected neurosurgeon who had worked with Davis in Chicago, Dr. Ruge tried to reassure the President, who had been stripped naked for emergency life-saving procedures. Not knowing yet that the bullet had penetrated the chest cavity, Dr. Ruge thought Reagan might have suffered cardiac arrest as a result of being shot. He quickly answered the attending doctors' questions about the President's health: his blood type (O positive), his allergies (adhesive tape and sulfa drugs), his previous medical history (prostatectomy fifteen years ago).

Six blocks away at the White House, Mrs. Reagan had just returned from a Georgetown luncheon at the home of Lucy and Michael Ainslie (president of the National Trust for Historic Preservation) and was sitting in the third-floor solarium with Ted Graber and Rex Scouten. The head of her Secret Service detail appeared and motioned for her to come to him.

"There's been a shooting at the hotel," George Opfer explained. "Some people were wounded, but your husband wasn't hit. Everybody's at the hospital. It's best if you stay here. It's a madhouse over there. The President is fine. They'll be bringing him back. There's no need for you to go."

Mrs. Reagan insisted on being taken to the hospital at once, so agent Opfer radioed ahead that he would be bringing "Rainbow" (the First Lady's code name) through the emergency entrance. Mike Deaver was standing outside waiting for her.

"He's been hit," said Deaver.

"But they told me he wasn't hit."

Rushing past reporters, photographers, policemen, and onlookers, she demanded to see her husband.

"You can't," said Deaver. "Not yet. They're working on him."

"Mike," she pleaded. "They don't know how it is with us. He has to know I'm here!"

Sensing she was on the verge of hysteria, Deaver steered her to an office to be with John Simpson, the head of the Secret Service, while Deaver ran to find out when she could be taken in to see her husband.

"They put me in a tiny room, tiny little room, really tiny," she recalled later. "There was a desk, no examining table, no windows. It was really tiny and hot. There were so many people running back and forth in the halls, and police and doctors and a lot of noise, a lot of people shouting, 'Get back, get back out of the way.' My main thing was, I just wanted to see Ronnie."

The blood-spattered doctors did not want Mrs. Reagan to see how desperately they were fighting to save her husband's life, so they told Deaver he could not bring her into the emergency room. He reported back to her that it would just be a matter of minutes.

She was insistent. "I want to see my husband," she said.

"The doctors say just as soon as he's cleaned up and stabilized," said Deaver.

By the time the First Lady was taken into the emergency room, the doctors knew they had to operate at once to remove the bullet and they began prepping the President for emergency surgery. There was not even time for the First Lady to give her written consent, so she agreed orally.

The President, ashen-faced, with tubes in his chest and his arms, was breathing laboriously through an oxygen mask. Seeing his wife, he lowered the mask and through blood-caked lips he whispered Jack Dempsey's line after losing the world heavyweight title to Gene Tunney.

"Honey, I forgot to duck."

Shocked by the sight of her robust husband caught in the twilight between life and death, she was unable to hold back her tears as she leaned over and kissed him. "Please don't try to talk," she said.

She would replay that scene over and over in the weeks to follow as she assumed the role of her husband's ferocious protector. "To people close to her, she would say, 'I saw him lying naked with strangers looking down at his naked body and watching the life ebb from him, and as a doctor's daughter I knew that he was dying,' " recalled former presidential assistant Bill Henkel. "She wanted us to feel the genuine emotion that she felt about him and why she was so determined to protect him, no matter what."

The fifth American President struck by gunfire and the only one to survive, Ronald Reagan was wheeled into surgery at 3:41 P.M., accompanied by John Simpson. The First Lady was escorted back to the tiny room that was now crowded with several presidential aides and Senator Paul Laxalt. They sat with her as she watched replays of the shooting on television and learned that her husband's assailant was twenty-six-year-old John Hinckley, an alienated young man who had become obsessed with movie actress Jodie Foster. Two hours before he shot the President, Hinckley had written Foster a letter, expressing his love:

Jody, I would abandon this idea of getting Reagan in a second if I could only win your heart and live out the rest of my life with you. . . . . The reason I'm going ahead with this attempt now is because I just cannot wait any longer to impress you. I've got to do something now to make you understand in no uncertain terms that I am doing all of this for your sake.

(Fifteen months later, at the end of a seven-week trial, a federal jury would find John Hinckley not guilty by reason of insanity, and the judge would commit him to St. Elizabeth's Hospital, a mental institution in Washington, D.C.)

Standing in front of George Washington Hospital that showery March afternoon was the rumpled but comforting figure of Lyn Nofziger, who calmly relayed bulletins to the press on the President's progress, reporting all of Reagan's one-liners to reporters to reassure Americans that their fallen leader was not lost.

"As he went into surgery, he looked around at the doctors and said, 'I hope you people are all Republicans.' One surgeon assured him, 'Today, we're all Republicans, Mr. President.' When he saw Mike Deaver, Ed Meese, and Jim Baker, who went in to talk with him beforehand, he said, 'Who's minding the store?' "

Within the hospital, Deaver and David Fischer opened a line to the White House, where they were in contact with assistant press secretary Larry Speakes, who was dealing with reporters in the briefing room.

"It was wall-to-wall people, bedlam reigned, and everyone was shouting questions," recalled Speakes. "Someone asked if U.S. forces were on any increased alert. My answer, 'Not that I am aware of,' is a standard press secretary reply."

Secretary of State Alexander Haig and other cabinet members and aides were in the Situation Room watching Speakes on television. Hearing the standard press secretary reply, Haig shot out of his chair.

"What's *he* doing there? We've got to straighten this out," said the Secretary of State. The next exchange on TV aroused him further.

"Who's running the government right now?" asked a reporter. "If the President goes into surgery and goes under anesthesia, would Vice President Bush become acting President at that moment or under what circumstances would he?"

"I cannot answer that question at this time," said Speakes.

Bursting through the door of the Situation Room, the Secretary of State bounded up the stairs to the press room and practically shouldered the press secretary aside as he made his way to the lectern. Wild-eyed, shaky, and out of breath, Haig informed reporters that the President was on the operating table and the Vice President was on his way back from Texas.

"There are absolutely no alert measures that are necessary at this time that we're contemplating," he added, intending to clear up any doubt that Speakes might have created.

"Who is making the decisions for the government right now?" a reporter asked.

Sounding like Dr. Strangelove, the Secretary of State dealt with the question of presidential succession inaccurately.

"Constitutionally, gentlemen, you have the President, the Vice President, and the Secretary of State in that order [according to the law, the Speaker of the House and the President pro tem of the Senate, as elected officials, outrank the Secretary of State], and should the President decide that he wants to transfer the helm to the Vice President, he will do so. He has not done that. As of now, I am in control here, in the White House, pending return of the Vice President, and in close touch with him. If something came up, I would check with him, of course."

At the hospital, Dr. Ruge opened a phone line to Scottsdale, Arizona, to give Dr. and Mrs. Loyal Davis regular updates. The White House physician was so deeply concerned about the President's condition that he did not think of calling for a temporary transfer of executive power, as described in the Twenty-fifth Amendment, although he carried a copy of the amendment in his little black bag. Years later, he admitted the amendment should have been put into effect as the President went into surgery.

"I think we made a mistake in not invoking the Twenty-fifth Amendment, no doubt about it, because Mr. Reagan could not communicate with the people a President is supposed to communicate with," he said. "If ever there was a time to use it, that was it. This was not a cold or diarrhea. . . . But it never occurred to me then."

Sitting with Dr. and Mrs. Loyal Davis in the den of their Biltmore Estates home in Arizona was their personal physician who feared that the couple might not survive the stressful news of the shooting.

"I was at the house all afternoon because I thought one of them would surely collapse," said the doctor, "but they held up pretty well, all things considered. Dan Ruge, who was my chief at Northwestern, called us from the emergency room every fifteen minutes or so and we knew that the assassination attempt was much more serious than the country ever knew. Reagan was so close to death it was unbelievable. It was touch and go for a while. . . . We almost lost him."

That night, the anguished First Lady wrote in her diary: "Nothing can happen to my Ronnie. My life would be over." Racked with guilt because she was not with her husband that afternoon, she could barely eat or sleep for weeks afterward, and suffered a severe depression that did not abate for months.

"Every time I think about him in the back of that car without me . . ." she sobbed to Nancy Reynolds over the telephone days later. She added that for the rest of her life she would always feel a little guilty about not being with him as he was leaving the Hilton Hotel "that afternoon." Unable to say the words *shooting* or *assassination attempt,* the First Lady referred only to "March thirtieth" or "the thing that happened to Ronnie," as if euphemisms could eradicate her pain. Once her husband was out of the hospital, she never discussed the shooting with him, and never referred to it in his presence.

"Suddenly she realized that the man she'd spent years with could die, and she could be left alone," her son, Ron, said later. "She responded with shock, followed by depression."

Ron and Doria had received the news of the shooting from their Secret Service agents in a coffee shop in Lincoln, Nebraska, where the Joffrey II ballet was performing. The couple had immediately chartered a plane for Washington.

In Los Angeles, the agents guarding the President's other children made arrangements for Maureen Reagan and her fiancé, Dennis Revell, Michael Reagan and his wife, Colleen, and Patti Davis to fly to Washington on an Air Force cargo jet that landed at Andrews Air Force base at 5:30 A.M., March 31.

"We stayed at the White House and rose early the next morning for breakfast with Nancy Reynolds," said Michael Reagan. "She told us that although Patti and Ron were at the hospital, we wouldn't be allowed to see Dad until later. This, of course, infuriated Maureen and me. . . . [Later] we went to where Dad was recovering from surgery. Patti and Ron were already in his room when we arrived, but Maureen and I were told he was too weak to see us, too. When Patti and Ron came out of the room, they walked by us without a word. . . . Maureen and I were fuming, beset by the old jealousy."

The shooting brought no healing dimension to the splintered family members. Though Nancy drew close to her son and embraced her daughter during the hours in which no one knew the President's fate, the same crisis seemed to put further distance between her and her stepchildren. She was, to use her own word, "furious" at Michael for embarrassing the President with his business dealings a few weeks before. Michael had sent out letters soliciting contracts from the Air Force and referring to "my father's leadership at the White House." He also had been accused of felony violations in California for soliciting investors in a fraudulent stock scheme and for spending money invested by others in a company he operated out of his home that exploited the potential of gasohol. Months later, he was cleared of all these charges, but not before they were played out in excruciating detail in the press.

Maureen, too, had alienated the First Lady by announcing her candidacy for the U.S. Senate seat from California, and by making her father look coldly indifferent for not endorsing her, while she had given her all in each of his presidential campaigns. His public explanation was that as President he couldn't get involved in Republican primary contests. He said he would only support the GOP nominee. Maureen did not receive the Republican nomination.

Within twenty-four hours, all of the Reagan children left Washington, giving up their places beside the First Lady to Frank Sinatra, who had flown in from California with his wife. The next afternoon, Sinatra visited Nancy alone at the White House. He told reporters, "I just came to see if I could be helpful to the family in any way," adding that he had not seen Reagan in the hospital and did not expect to. "It would be an imposition to see him at this time." That night, at Pisces, a private club in Georgetown, he proudly quoted to friends Mrs. Reagan's first words upon seeing him: "Frank! Thank God you're here. There's finally someone I can tell my dirty stories to!"

Sinatra returned to Washington the following month to be the surprise entertainer for the Congressional Club luncheon in Nancy's honor. He sang for more than half an hour and directed all of his songs to the head table where the beaming First Lady sat, obviously enthralled.

The President's convalescence began on April 11, 1981, when he left the hospital to return to the White House, where he, too, suffered a bout of depression as he struggled with the realization that he was not universally loved, a crippling blow to a man who had spent his entire life being a people pleaser.

"For quite a time afterward, there was a certain sadness," said Senator Paul Laxalt. "It wasn't just the physical pain. I think that he was deeply hurt, emotionally, that this could happen to him, that someone would do this to him. Of course, he would never talk about this to us."

Patti Davis saw the change in her father as well, describing it as something "beautiful and frightening" in his eyes.

Pale, disoriented, and in great pain, the President was unable to conduct business upon his return to the White House, and the few aides allowed to see him in the third-floor solarium where he recuperated were shocked by his appearance and his dependence on a breathing apparatus they assumed was for oxygen.

"What he had was an instrument that he blew into to make his lungs expand," said Dr. Ruge. "It was not a respirator, but a Respirex with little balls in it that he had to blow into to rehabilitate his lungs."

The First Lady barely left the White House during the coming weeks so that she could oversee her husband's convalescence and monitor the number of people who came to see him. She had already established her power base in the Oval Office through Mike Deaver, who controlled access to the President and reported all scheduled visitors to her in advance.

"The First Lady knew ahead of time who was going to see the President each day, and why," said a former Deaver aide. "If there was someone she did not want him seeing, she told Mike to scratch the name, and he scratched the name. That's the way she operated as the power behind the throne. Not even the President knew that she was overseeing things this way. It was a little more difficult for her after 1985, when Deaver left the White House, but she still managed."

There were no long, private "luncheons" with Sinatra while the President was recuperating in the White House, but Sinatra continued to function as the First Lady's official entertainment czar, choosing the performers for White House state dinners. He also volunteered to record "To Love a Child" to help promote a book by that title that was ghostwritten in Nancy Reagan's name. The book's proceeds were to go to the Foster Grandparents Program, in another effort to give her a positive public image.

Sinatra even went on the Larry King radio show to defend the First Lady. "She's had such a bum rap," he said. "The china was a terrible misrepresentation. The china was given by citizens. She didn't buy it with our . . . tax money . . . and what's wrong with having pretty china in the White House? What's wrong with having a White House that's the most wonderful capital building in the world? Nothing wrong with that at all. When she first came to town . . . she got a bad going-over by the press, which doesn't surprise me . . . [Nancy] is a very classy lady. She's quite shy, contrary to what is said about her . . . she is warm and fun. She has a great sense of humor and giggles and she's just great . . . just great."

Sinatra was so determined to help the First Lady that he engineered the Scopus award of the American Friends of Hebrew University for her, and it was presented at a gala in her honor. The event raised money for one hundred three-year scholarships for students of different faiths at the university in Jerusalem. Some proceeds also were for the proposed Nancy Reagan Plaza designed to front the Frank Sinatra International Student Center on the university campus. Nancy would reciprocate the singer's generosity by making sure that he received a lifetime achievement award from the Kennedy Center in 1983. The President, too, rewarded the singer. In 1986, when he no longer faced reelection and therefore had no fear of political ramifications from bestowing the nation's highest civilian honor on a man connected to organized crime, Reagan gave Frank Sinatra the Medal of Freedom.

"There was a terrible outcry when the President gave him that award," recalled Shirley Watkins, one of Mrs. Reagan's secretaries. "I had to answer a lot of the calls that came in from people saying he [Sinatra] was a crook and a member of the Mafia. There was so much mail about it that the White House had to come up with a form letter to be sent out. A report was finally sent to the Reagans about it."

The First Lady ignored it. "Others in the business had gotten the same medal—Greg Peck, Danny Kaye, gosh, who else? Jimmy Cagney," she said. "Frank deserved it for all the charity work he does—many things that people don't know about. If you're in a position to give old friends what they deserve, then why not? Old friendships are important to me. None of us has that many years left to build up those kind[s] of friendships, you know."

As enamored as she was with the singer, the First Lady was also concerned with her image, so she would flinch whenever Sinatra insulted the media people that she was trying to cultivate, like Barbara Walters. He frequently made fun of "Baabaa Waawaa," ridiculing her lisp: "Did you ever listen to that broad? She says 'too-too twain' and 'I wuv a wabbit.' She needs diction lessons." Upon meeting Katharine Graham, owner of the Washington Post Company, he said her newspaper was a rag and so were her clothes. The gossip columnist Liz Smith, who lives openly with a woman in New York, got the Sinatra treatment as "Lez" Smith: "Most girls want to make it with Burt Reynolds, but old Lez, she wants to make it with Debbie Reynolds."

During her husband's recuperation, the First Lady kept his visitors to a minimum, barring even the Vice President. "Like everything else, he needs rest and I think Mrs. Reagan is determined to see that he gets it," said George Bush at the time. "And well she should."

As for Jim Brady, the man who had almost died and was left permanently brain-damaged, Nancy refused to invite him to any White House social functions. Only when she found out that she was going to be publicly criticized in a biography of Brady for such callous disregard did he receive an invitation. She supported keeping him on full salary as White House press secretary, although his deputy, Larry Speakes, had taken over the job. But Brady's slack-jawed presence and occasional wailing made her uncomfortable to be around him. Emotionally, it was too painful a reminder of what had happened to her husband.

Nancy had visited Sarah Brady in the hospital on the day of the assassination attempt and the two women had sat together as their husbands underwent surgery. A few weeks later, they both attended a large dinner and were seated at the same table. Nancy, still rattled by the shooting, monopolized the conversation by talking about how much *she* had suffered when the President was shot and how *she* had not yet recovered her equilibrium. She seemed oblivious to Sarah Brady, whose husband was still in critical condition.

The First Lady received a copy of the President's daily schedule plus the packet of press clippings assembled each day by the White House press office, which she read religiously. Days after Reagan returned to the White House, she saw a story about a student at the University of Pennsylvania who had written a column in the school newspaper saying he hoped the President would die of his gunshot wounds. Infuriated, she called Attorney General William French Smith and demanded that the student be prosecuted. Smith told her that he could do nothing because the student's inflammatory column did not violate the law.

"That's when she would start calling Mike and demand that he do something like bad-mouth the kid to the press," said a former Deaver aide. "She had a legitimate reason to be outraged by the student's column, I suppose, but she wouldn't understand why he couldn't be arrested. She just couldn't stand any kind of criticism whatsoever."

The First Lady saw advice columnist Ann Landers on a Washington, D.C., television show criticizing the Reagan administration for contributing to the unemployment problem by slashing job-training funds. That evening the two women met in a receiving line.

"I saw you on TV this morning," said Nancy, "and I'd like you to know that you are not up on things." She told the columnist about the President's Job Training Partnership Act, and sent her more information the next day. Ann Landers later wrote a column extolling the legislation.

Congressman Thomas Downey (D-N.Y.) was one of the first to feel the long wrathful arm of the First Lady. He objected to her refusal to let a Boy Scout group from his district tour the White House on a special pass, a privilege accorded all members of Congress for their constituents. The congressman told the press that Mrs. Reagan's office had said she discouraged special tours by children because they could not appreciate the artwork and rugs in the White House, and consequently she felt they didn't deserve anything more than a quick public tour. The morning the President's wife read those comments in her daily White House news summary, she saw to it that the congressman lost all special group tours for his constituents. He was even denied the weekly passes that every congressional office automatically receives.

"The congressman owes the First Lady an apology over his personal attacks," Mike Deaver told the *New York Daily News.* "There is great unfairness in involving Mrs. Reagan, of attacking her with press releases, when there is no reason." The First Lady's maître d' left no doubt that the tours would not be reinstated until an apology was offered. The congressman, a member of the House Ways and Means Committee, refused, charging a political vendetta by the White House, which he said was guilty of pettiness and breathtaking stupidity. His requests for constituent tours continued to be denied for eight more weeks, until he finally worked out an accommodation with the First Lady. In the end, neither side apologized, but there emerged from the fray one member of Congress who fully comprehended the power behind Ronald Reagan's throne.

It would take the rest of Washington several years to recognize the First Lady's astonishing influence within her husband's administration. Nancy-inspired firings and forced resignations started in January 1982 with national security director Richard Allen, for accepting money on her behalf from a Japanese magazine for an interview, and continued with:

First Lady's chief of staff Peter McCoy in January 1982 for not changing her negative public image;

Assistant to the President Joe Canzeri in February 1982 for double-billing two expense-account dinners to the White House and the Republican National Committee, and accepting a below-market home loan from banking friends;

Secretary of State Alexander Haig in July 1982 for being too excitable and always demanding priority seating on Air Force One;

U.S. ambassador to Great Britain John Louis in 1983 for being absent from London during the Falklands War;

White House photographer Karl Schoumacher in May 1983 for double-exposing a roll of film containing photos of Frank Sinatra that Nancy had wanted to give to the *Washington Post;*

Secretary of Interior James Watt in October 1983 for being too politically conservative and for banning the Beach Boys from singing on the Mall;

First Lady's speech writer Mona Charen in 1985 for not being subservient enough;

Secretary of Interior William P. Clark in February 1985 for being too politically conservative and not acceptable to the First Lady and Mike Deaver;

U.S. ambassador to Austria Helene von Damm in August 1985 for too much cleavage and too many husbands;

Press secretary Jennifer Hirshberg in September 1985 for being too pretty and drawing more press coverage than the First Lady;

Secretary of Health and Human Services Margaret Heckler in December 1985 for a messy divorce;

First Lady's third chief of staff Lee Verstandig in February 1986, after only four weeks on the job, for not being able to handle the Mommy account;

White House curator Clement Conger in April 1986 for not being deferential enough;

U.S. ambassador to the Holy See William A. Wilson in May 1986 for embarrassing the administration by flying to Libya to privately negotiate with Muammar Qaddafi;

U.S. ambassador to Spain Thomas Enders in August 1986 for having a wife who had been less than polite about the First Lady, according to Jerry Zipkin, although Mrs. Enders denied it;

First Lady's projects director Ken Barun in September 1986 for being too self-promoting;

CIA director William Casey in February 1987 for not taking the fall for the President on Iran-Contra;

Chief of staff Donald Regan in February 1987 for not being deferential at all;

White House photographer Terry Arthur in July 1987 for referring to Mrs. Reagan's advance team in Venice as "Nancy's Navy";

White House director of photographic services Billie B. Shaddix in July 1987 for not being competent enough by the First Lady's standards;

White House chef Jon Hill in January 1988 for not fully appreciating the First Lady's incessant food tastings.

Only after the contentious resignation of White House chief of staff Regan in 1987 did people begin to suspect the fine hand of the First Lady. Up to then, Nancy Reagan had managed to hide behind her pose as the President's devoted wife, someone who cared nothing about policy.

"Quite the contrary," said Paul Weyrich, the conservative Republican president of the Free Congress Foundation. "Mrs. Reagan cared so much about policy that she got heavily involved in everything from the administration's public stand on abortion to the signing of the Intermediate-Range Nuclear Forces (INF) Treaty. The American people never understood that by electing Ronald Reagan they were getting two Presidents— the man they elected and the woman he married. In the end, it would be the First Lady who would undo national security matters and change members of the cabinet, not the President.

"In my view, if we're going to have a First Lady who is going to be determining policy in the way that Nancy Reagan clearly did, then the public has the right to know this and calculate it into their decision on who to vote for. I actually proposed in 1988 that we have the wives run with the husbands so that we would never have another Nancy Reagan again. Rosalynn Carter was bad enough attending cabinet meetings, and Betty Ford tried to get Jerry cranked up on the ERA, but even those women had limits. Neither had a foreign policy of her own like Nancy Reagan, whose liberal views on issues such as aid to the Contras and a pardon for Oliver North [she opposed both] ran at cross-purposes with the conservative views of her husband.

"In dealing with the Reagan White House, you had to have a three-part strategy for every policy question posed. First, you had to have a strategy to reach the President, and one to reach the chiefs of staff because they acted as the President half the time because he was not engaged in much of what went on in his administration. And then you had to have a strategy to reach and neutralize Nancy so that she didn't undo whatever it was you were proposing."

During her husband's convalescence, which lasted eight months, the First Lady canceled most of her official schedule, except when Prince Charles visited Washington in May and New York in June. She entertained him in the White House and flew to New York the following month to have lunch with him on Malcolm Forbes's yacht and attend the Royal Ballet at the Metropolitan Opera House. Ever since she met the Prince of Wales in 1976 at the Annenbergs' estate in Palm Springs, she had been in awe of him. Her best friend said the feeling was mutual. "Prince Charles is absolutely cuckoo about Nancy Reagan," said Betsy Bloomingdale.

On one of her trips to London as First Lady, Nancy stayed at Winfield House with the American ambassador, Charles Price, and his wife, Carol. Mrs. Price mentioned that Prince Charles had been invited for tea the following day. Minutes before his arrival, Nancy told the ambassador's wife that she was not to answer the door, nor was she to take tea with the Prince. Mrs. Price was shocked.

"I can't do that," she said. "It would be a diplomatic slap in the face if I didn't greet His Majesty."

"I will greet him myself," said Nancy Reagan, who insisted that the ambassador's wife remain upstairs while she greeted the Prince and entertained him alone downstairs.

The Prince's visit to Washington occurred on May 1, 1981, just five weeks after the President was shot. Mrs. Reagan planned a private dinner party for him in the White House living quarters.

"It was just a fun little group she put together," recalled her staff director, Peter McCoy, who attended with his wife, Kacey, a Doheny heiress from Los Angeles. Other guests included Jerry Zipkin; Betsy Bloomingdale; Ted Graber; James Galanos; Audrey Hepburn and Robert Wolders, the man Hepburn lived with; songwriter Sammy Cahn; television actress Shelley Hack; former editor of *Vogue* Diana Vreeland; former ambassador Walter Annenberg and his wife, Lee, the latter now U.S. chief of protocol; the Cary Grants; the William F. Buckleys; the Paul Mellons; and London banker Robin Hambro and his wife, friends of the Prince.

The guest list was designed to showcase the cream in the Reagans' social register, but a writer for the *New Republic* was unimpressed. "Don't they know any writers (other than Buckley), artists, scientists or even politicians?"

Nancy had begun her plans for the party two months before, when she called Bobby Short to ask him to entertain. "The evening was exactly the way Mrs. Reagan had said it would be when she telephoned me back in March," he said. "For the honored guest, she wanted to arrange a small dinner party with some close and amusing friends. Would I come and play? Of course, of course, I said."

Consumed with her desire to impress the Prince, the First Lady had fretted over the dessert for that evening, and made the White House chef redo it five times until the brown-sugar feathers on the ice cream crown looked exactly like the royal insignia. It was then placed atop a red, white, and blue concoction of sherbet to become what the menu called a "Crown of Sorbet Prince of Wales." She had the Marine Guard greet guests upon arrival, lead them into the Grand Foyer, which she had banked with red, white, and blue flowers to match the dessert and to complement the American flag and the Union Jack on display that evening. She specified that the Marine Corps string quartet be situated at the top of the Grand Staircase and play show tunes as people entered. She told the President to stand outside the door of the yellow oval room to greet people and steer them inside, where she was standing to the right of the guest of honor.

Upon being introduced to His Royal Highness, Diana Vreeland dropped to her knees in a deep curtsy, as did nearly everyone else, including Lee Annenberg; the day before she had been criticized for making the same curtsy to the Prince in public. Photographs of her inappropriate greeting had appeared in newspapers around the country, sparking disapproving stories about an American paying obeisance to a British royal. The chief of protocol, who carries the title of ambassador, worried that her action might have embarrassed the President, but when she approached him at the dinner party to apologize, he would not hear her out.

"You did exactly the right thing," said President Reagan, earning her loyalty forever.

Walter and Leonore Annenberg had been close to the British royal family ever since they represented the United States at the Court of St. James's, and so they had been among the first to be invited to the royal wedding of Prince Charles and Lady Diana Spencer that was to take place in July. When an invitation was extended to the President and his wife, Nancy Reagan was determined to attend, although her husband's staff decided that the royal nuptials should not be the occasion of his first foreign trip as President. The First Lady had refused to leave her convalescent husband's side to attend Maureen Reagan's wedding in California in April 1981, but she thought him well enough to leave now for the royal wedding. She talked of nothing else for months beforehand.

"I'm very happy and flattered to be asked, and I am excited at the prospect of being present at such a historic and romantic occasion," she said when the White House announced that she would be going. She spent weeks planning her wardrobe, discussing details of what she should wear with Adolfo and Galanos, both of whom produced special designs for the trip (gratis). She summoned the Bulgari representative to the White House so that she could "borrow" jewelry for each of her outfits. It included a matched set of diamond and ruby earrings, ring, and necklace; a pearl choker centered with a large carnelian intaglio, dating from the second century; a necklace of pale sapphires; and to wear to the Queen's gala at Buckingham Palace, a pair of $880,000 diamond earrings (not until the matter became public did she return the jewelry). Feeling she still did not have enough jewelry, she dispatched her chief of staff to New York to "borrow" additional gems from Harry Winston.

"For six weeks beforehand," said a former top aide, "she was on the phone every day to the British embassy discussing the protocol of that visit, how she should be introduced to royalty, whether she should curtsy, when she should stand, how she should sit, what she should wear, what kind of wedding present she should bring, when did she have to wear a hat, and who her chaperones should be."

The First Lady was concerned about where she would sit at the wedding, and after weeks of negotiation she was placed in the sixth row behind the crowned heads of Europe and the King of Tonga. She was flanked by the President of Iceland, Vigdis Finnbogadottir, and the Vice President of Nigeria, Alex Ekwueme.

"Nancy had not been invited to the private ball for Charles and Diana before the wedding, and she was wild about it," recalled a member of her staff. "Lee Annenberg had to call the Queen to get the First Lady included. The Annenbergs had been invited, of course, but Nancy had not. This was a dance for the kids and their friends. No other heads of state were invited, but Nancy wanted to be there, and Lee finally got her in at the very last minute."

The former royal clerk, Malcolm Barker, claims that Queen Elizabeth felt the American First Lady's reach was extending well beyond her rank, and at one point referred to her as "that damned woman."

"It was kind of an intimidating experience for Nancy," admitted her chief of staff, recalling that Mrs. Reagan had never met the Queen of England before. "We had to fly to London to advance everything so Mrs. Reagan would be at ease and not worry about how to dress and what to do. She did not want to find herself in a situation she'd never been in before. For example, on the last day, she was invited to a formal luncheon by Britain's prime minister Margaret Thatcher at the Bank of England, and it turned out that there had been no one appointed to greet her when she arrived and no one to tell her where she would be sitting. That was just unacceptable; she would have had to wander in by herself and hope that someone noticed her. Those are the kinds of things you find out when you advance a trip, and because we had advanced that one so thoroughly we knew that someone would have to escort Mrs. Reagan to that lunch and be with her."

Those costly advance trips financed by U.S. taxpayers became a necessity for the socially insecure First Lady, who insisted that her staff make on-site inspection trips for all her travels, domestic and foreign, so that every minute could be scripted, right down to putting masking tape on the floors to position her for photographs. The First Lady's White House staff went to great lengths trying to meet her exacting demands. When she called her chief of staff to check on the weather so she would know what to wear, Jim Rosebush would not simply give her the day's temperature. He had to leave his office on the second floor of the White House and go outside so he could more accurately describe the feel of the temperature. Mrs. Reagan's fanatical attention to detail was such that she frequently sent her wardrobe with the second or third advance team so they could make sure that the colors she planned to wear would not clash with the setting in which she was to be photographed.

In the White House, the demands of the First Lady were interpreted as crucial to the presidency.

"A happy Mrs. Reagan meant a happy President," said Bill Henkel, head of the White House advance team. "We had to anticipate *all* her needs and have the right candy in her suite, the right flowers, all the little touches. And God forbid if you were traveling on a Monday before some of the national magazines had been delivered. No matter where we ended up, those magazines had to be there. Sometimes that required extraordinary arrangements, but we did whatever it cost to get Mrs. Reagan those magazines. On several occasions we had to have a military plane fly those damn magazines from Washington to California or to London or to wherever Mrs. Reagan was just so she'd have them on Monday.

"For the royal wedding, her advance team, ever conscious of her public image, scheduled a photo opportunity for her at the Spastics Society Centre to receive a red, white, and blue bouquet from a thirteen-year-old child confined to a wheelchair.

"We had to do stuff like that so the trip wouldn't look like one long week of parties, which is really all it was," said a member of her staff.

Having announced that she would not curtsy to the Queen, or reveal what she planned to wear to the wedding ("We do not want to compete with the bride," said her press secretary), America's First Lady arrived in London on July 24, 1981, with sixteen pistol-packing security agents, four hat boxes, twenty dresses, her wedding present (a $75,000 Steuben glass bowl that she said "only cost taxpayers $8,000"), and an entourage that included her three top aides, her secretary, her hairdresser (Julius), a nurse, a White House photographer, a State Department liaison officer, thirteen reporters, and her official chaperones, Betsy and Alfred Bloomingdale.

Chatting to reporters on the plane about how excited she was to be going to London, she had said, "When am I ever going to see anything like this again? I've never been to a polo match. I've never been to Buckingham Palace, well, the whole thing. I've never been to a royal wedding."

Betsy Bloomingdale was just as excited. "I grew up in Hollywood, so Gregory Peck and his sort are nothing special," she said. "But this—this kind of greatness is what's special to me."

Miffed by Mrs. Reagan's decision not to curtsy, and her elaborate entourage, the British press went to work on her. The *Guardian* reported the arrival of "the one-time starlet of such B-films as 'The Next Voice You Hear' (1950) and 'Hellcats of the Navy' (1957)." The *Times* of London ridiculed her for squeezing "more engagements into the week before the royal wedding than Alice's white rabbit."

The British Broadcasting Company (BBC) mocked her for roaring in to Prince Charles's polo match at Tidworth, Hampshire, with a long motorcade of shiny black limousines with dark-tinted windows led by police motorcycles and a helicopter circling overhead—while the Queen herself drove King Constantine, the exiled monarch of Greece, in her little green Vauxhall station wagon with her Corgis in the backseat. A

Nancy Reagan and Henry Kissinger discuss campaign strategy before the November 1980 presidential election.

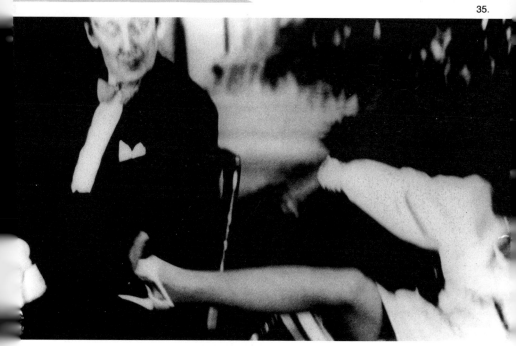

First Lady Nancy Reagan falling off her chair in the East Room of the White House as pianist Vladimir Horowitz looks on, October 5, 1986.

Two of "the girls," Mrs. Earle Jorgensen (Marion) and Mrs. Norman Sprague (Earleen), talking to the First Lady.

Helene von Damm, former personal secretary to Ronald Reagan, who appointed her ambassador to Austria in 1983.

Nancy Clark Reynolds, who worked for Governor Reagan in Sacramento and later became Nancy Reagan's unofficial adviser.

Another one of "the girls," Mrs. Armand Deutsch (Harriet).

The ambassadors
Annenberg—Leonore,
chief of protocol in the
Reagan White House, and
her husband, Walter,
Nixon's envoy to the Court
of St. James's in England.

Betsy Bloomingdale, Nancy's
best friend and fashion mentor,
with her husband, Alfred
Bloomingdale, a member of
Reagan's kitchen cabinet.

40.

42.

41.

Jean Smith and her husband, William
French Smith, Ronald Reagan's personal
attorney and secretary of the kitchen cabinet
during the gubernatorial years. Smith later
became attorney general of the United
States.

43.

Michael Reagan, the son of Jane Wyman and Ronald Reagan, adopted in 1945.

Ronald Reagan being kissed by his eldest daughter, Maureen.

44.

President Reagan looking on as the First Lady kisses her favorite child, after his debut performance at the Joffrey II Ballet in 1981.

45.

46.

First Lady Nancy Reagan (Secret Service code name: Rainbow) arrives at George Washington University Hospital to join her husband (code name: Rawhide) shortly after the assassination attempt.

47.

President Ronald Reagan leaving George Washington University Hospital to return to the White House, clutching his wife's hand, as his daughter Patti clings to his arm.

SUNDAY	MONDAY	TUESDAY	WEDNESDAY	THURSDAY
(P) - President * - Away from WH ** - First Lady's Event t - Tentative r - Remarks		**1** 11:30am Pvt. appt. 2:30pm Pvt. appt.	**2** 11:00am Pvt. appt. 2:45pm Staff meeting	**3** FYI (P) To Ohio 12:30pm Pvt. luncheon
		**8** 9:00am Pvt. appt. 10:00am (P) Arriv. Cere. for P.M. Lee of Singapore 11:00am DAR Pin 6:15pm Pvt. appt. 7:15pm (P) State Dinner Events **BLACK-TIE**	**9** 11:00am Pvt. appt. 2:45pm* Depart f/pvt appt. Aft. Return WH	**10** 11:15pm Pvt. appt. 12:00pm Partnership Annouc. 12:30pm* Depart f/Pvt. Lunch Aft. Return WH
		15 FYI (P) To Idaho and Wisconsin	**16** 9:20am* Depart f/pvt. appt. Aft. Return WH	**17** Bob & Goldie Arthur's Anniversary 11:30am Pvt. appt. 4:00pm Pvt. appt. 7:30pm* (P) Dropby Republican Governor's Asson. dinner
20 11:00pm* Depart WH 1:15pm* Arrive New York 1:45pm* Arrive Theater 2:15pm* Depart Theater 2:30pm* Arrive hotel 3:00pm* Intv. w/Good mor. Am. 3:15pm* Intv. w/NBC News 5:30pm* Pvt. appt. 6:30pm** Depart f/Salute to Mary Martin **BLACK TIE** (r) **ON NEW YORK**	**21** Patti Davis' B-Day 8:15am* Pvt. appt. 8:55am** Depart f/FL Meeting (r) 1:00pm** FL Luncheon 3:00pm* Return to Hotel **ON NEW YORK**	**22** 10:30am* Pvt. appt. 12:15pm Pvt. appt. 12:40pm** Depart for Mrs. Perez de Cuellar luncheon 3:05pm* Return to hotel **ON NEW YORK**	**23** FYI (P) To New York 11:00am** Pvt. appt. 1:00pm** Pvt. Luncheon 7:00pm* (P) UN Reception 8:45pm (P) Pvt. Dinner **ON NEW YORK**	**24** United Nation's Day 9:00am* Pvt. appt. 10:20am* (P) Depart f/Pres. UN Speech 3:00pm* (P) Attend 40th Anniv. Ceremony 7:30pm* (P) Recept. f/Allies **ON NEW YORK**
27 Return to WH	**28** 10:00am Pvt. appt.	**29** 11:30am Pvt. appt. 11:50am* Depart f/pvt appt 12:00pm* Pvt appt Aft. Return WH 4:00pm Pvt. appt.	**30** C. Z. Wick's B-Day 11:00am Pvt. appt. On Dep. Photo Op. w/Lab School 12:00pm** Girl Scouts Drug Luncheon (r) 4:00pm* (P) Pvt. tour at National Gallery	**31** Halloween 11:30am Staff Meeting 1:30pm Pvt. appt. 2:30pm Tour and Reception f/British Lenders

The personal White House schedule of First Lady Nancy Reagan for October 1985.

National Security Adviser Richard Allen, Deputy Chief of Staff Michael Deaver, and Presidential Counselor Edwin Meese III.

50.

FRIDAY	SATURDAY
4	**5**
3:20pm• Depart for Andrews to meet (P) 4:00pm• (P) To Camp David Approx.	
ON CAMP DAVID	ON: CAMP DAVID
11	**12** Charles Wick's B-Day FYI Fall Garden Tour
12:00pm Pvt. appt. 1:30pm• (P) To Camp David	
ON: CAMP DAVID	ON: CAMP DAVID
18	**19** Anne Allman's B-Day
12:00pm Birthday Party/Foster Grandparents (r) 2:00pm (P) Ronald Reagan Library Found Meeting	11:00am Pvt. appt 7:00pm Pvt. appt. 8:00pm• (P) Depart f/Italian Amer. Found. Dinner BLACK-TIE
25 FYI (P) To Bilaterals	**26**
12:00pm• (P) Depart Hotel f/Camp David 2:10pm (P) Arrive Camp David	
ON CAMP DAVID	ON: CAMP DAVID

51.

(Top right) First Lady Nancy Reagan hugs a child at a Foster Grandparents Program at the Columbia–Presbyterian Medical Center in New York City.

Gridiron member Charles McDowell with First Lady Nancy Reagan after her performance of "Secondhand Rose" at the Gridiron Dinner of 1982.

52.

53.

Nancy Reagan with her good friend Katharine Graham, chairman of the board of the Washington Post Company.

54.

Nancy finally meets her idol, Jacqueline Kennedy Onassis, at a fundraiser for the John F. Kennedy Memorial Library in 1985.

BBC television crew filmed the arrival of Her Majesty, wearing oxfords, heavy argyles, and a scarf tied around her head like a peasant's babushka. Minutes later, the cameras caught Mrs. Reagan and her entourage roaring up. The First Lady stepped out in her bright red and white $1,200 Adolfo suit, accompanied by a contingent of security guards and aides. The BBC commentator told his audience that the ground was soggy from the previous day's rain and, noting the First Lady's lacquered appearance, said her high heels were sinking into the grass.

"I do hope we won't lose her," he said. "Or . . . oh, dear . . . I hope she doesn't fall and break her hair."

The next day, Nancy was scheduled to lay a wreath on the grave of the Unknown American Serviceman in the American chapel of St. Paul's Cathedral. Despite a police escort of four motorcycles, her convoy of eight cars took an hour to travel three miles from the U.S. ambassador's residence in Regent's Park, where she was staying, to the cathedral. She arrived a half hour late, keeping the dean of St. Paul's waiting, as she did the Queen Mother the following day. She told the dean that she could allot only fifteen minutes for a brisk tour of the cathedral because she simply could not be late for luncheon with Princess Margaret. Later, the dean briefed the ushers on the dignitaries to be seated at the royal wedding, and said, "We all know foreigners are difficult to deal with. Having shown Mrs. Reagan around St. Paul's, I know this for a fact."

Derided by the British press for trying to appear more regal than royalty, Nancy Reagan also embarrassed many Americans, including her cousin Kathleen Young.

"If Nancy had ever cared anything about the family background of her real father, she would've known that her ancestor Robert John Ayres (her great-great-great-great-grandfather) had married Anne Weston in St. Bride's Church on Fleet Street in London on December 20, 1814. If she had gone there to see the plaque commemorating the event instead of to all those king-and-queen parties, the British might have taken her more seriously or at least been a little more respectful."

"The royal wedding was handled very badly," admitted a member of Mrs. Reagan's senior White House staff. "Careening through the streets of London with sirens blowing and horns blaring. Peter McCoy, Joe Canzeri, and the Secret Service are to blame for that. The British press went wild writing about the gauche and vulgar Americans who had stampeded their country."

By the time the President's wife left London to return home, her imperious image was so firmly established that any further Lady Bountiful outings with handicapped children seemed hopeless. On both sides of the Atlantic, "Queen Nancy" postcards popped up, showing her wearing a crown and holding a scepter. To salvage the First Lady's public image would take a brain trust of two presidential aides, twenty-five members of the East Wing staff, the White House pollster—and one astrologer.

18

ALWAYS FEARFUL OF JOSTLING CROWDS and jumpy about possible attackers, Nancy Reagan had become even more preoccupied with security after her husband's shooting. She was fitted for a bulletproof slip, which she wore when she had to accompany the President and sit on an exposed dais. She insisted that he wear a lead-lined vest or his armored raincoat in public and both readily acceded to such Secret Service recommendations for tighter security as adding more agents to their details and not announcing their schedules in advance. So that he was no longer visible from the street, large canvas awnings with flaps were thrown across the entrance to any building the President entered.

"It was a simple change, but just seeing that piece of cloth was a big comfort to me," said his wife.

The Reagans agreed to blocking all traffic on East Executive Avenue between the White House and the Treasury Department and throwing up a concrete wall of bollards around the executive mansion to keep any terrorists from crashing through the fence with truckloads of bombs. Within two years, a concrete landscape would encase 1600 Pennsylvania Avenue, marring the once graceful view with squat columns linked by thick black chains.

Presidential security reached exaggerated proportions the day Air Force One was heading for Forbes Field in Topeka, Kansas, where Reagan was going to speak at Alf Landon's hundredth birthday. On the ground, airport authorities working in cooperation with the Secret Service were trying to secure the area so that nothing would disrupt the safety and decorum of the welcoming ceremony for the President and the First Lady.

Two dogs were mating some 2,000 feet from Runway 31, where the President was scheduled to land, and the Secret Service aboard Air Force One radioed orders that the animals had to be removed. Two airport security officials went out to the runway with welding gloves, and walloped the dogs five or six times in an effort to separate them, but the animals remained locked in copulation. The security officers retreated, but returned minutes later with a rifle. According to a witness, they shot the dogs, shoved them into plastic bags, threw the bags on a flatbed truck, drove them to the edge of the airfield and shoved them into an incinerator.

Not for a minute was the President or First Lady in any danger from the coupling animals, but the deputy director of the Metropolitan Topeka Airport Authority justified killing them by saying that he was responding to a Secret Service "freeze" on all unauthorized activity within a security perimeter.

"We could not guarantee that the dogs would not break free and run into the runway," he said. "All this second-guessing about what should've been done seems to show more concern for the dogs' lives than for human life. We didn't have time to debate the issue."

The Reagans, who had never been regular churchgoers, used the excuse of "presidential security" to get out of going to church on Sunday; they said the Secret Service provisions were just too onerous to subject other churchgoers to them.

"If it was known in advance that we were coming, everybody had to go through a metal detector, which just didn't seem right," said Nancy Reagan. "But if we showed up unexpectedly, the congregants were so busy watching us that they didn't pay attention to the service. That didn't seem right either, so we rarely went to church during our years in Washington." Apparently, it never occurred to the presidential couple to invite clergy to the White House or Camp David to hold services there as other Presidents had done. The Reagans' unfamiliarity with church ritual had struck Mike Deaver during the 1980 campaign when he escorted them to an Episcopal service in Virginia.

As they were starting toward the altar to receive communion, Nancy Reagan grabbed Deaver's arm.

"Mike," she whispered. "Are those people drinking out of the same cup?"

"It's all right. They'll come by with the wafers first. Then, when the chalice reaches you, dip the bread in the cup, and that is perfectly all right. You won't have to put your lips to the cup."

Reagan, who was practically deaf, strained to hear the instructions.

"What? What?" he said.

"Ron, just do exactly as I do," directed his wife.

The tray of wafers was passed and Nancy picked up a square of bread, dipped it in the chalice of wine, and accidentally dropped it. She looked at Deaver in horror.

Oblivious to what had happened, Reagan did exactly as his wife had instructed him and picked up a square of bread, dipped it in the chalice, and dropped it in the wine.

"I watched the minister move on, shaking his head, staring at these blobs of gunk floating in his wine," said Deaver.

President and Mrs. Reagan relied on the Secret Service to chart all their movements in concert with the decisions of their astrologer, Joan Quigley, who, by consulting the stars, dictated when to leave the White House and when to land Air Force One. She sent computerized spreadsheets to the First Lady every three months, which Mrs. Reagan passed on to Mike Deaver, who used them to draw up the President's travel schedule.

Aside from security, the Reagans used the Secret Service assigned to their children for surveillance of their activities. That way the Reagans would know what their children were doing at all times and with whom. The First Lady, more than the President, used this personal spying system; she would check the agents' daily logs and chronicles to learn where Ron and Patti and Maureen and Michael were on any given day.

Ron was the first one to put a stop to this parental scrutiny by discontinuing his Secret Service protection in 1981, despite his mother's strenuous objections.

"It's hard to imagine what it's like being watched and followed by guys carrying Uzis around all the time," he said. "Or to come back from a trip and find out they've been in your home and didn't really think to mention it to you. . . . My wife and I decided we'd rather die than live like that."

Patti was the next one to confront the issue when her mother phoned in a white fury about her sleeping with singer/actor Kris Kristofferson.

"You should be ashamed of yourself," Nancy said to her startled daughter. "Absolutely ashamed for spending the night with someone who is so much in the public eye and could embarrass our family."

Patti, who had grown up with her mother's eavesdropping on her and her playmates through the house intercom system, knew immediately that the information had come from her Secret Service detail. She confronted them that evening.

"I think I have a constitutional right to my own privacy," she said, "and that includes who I sleep with. The only way my mother could've known about me and Kristofferson was through you guys, and I want it stopped right now. I don't want you reporting to her anymore, and if you continue to do so, I'll take steps to see that you are stopped."

The agents, obviously nervous and uncomfortable, hung their heads and kept quiet. A few months later, Patti dismissed her Secret Service detail.

Michael Reagan was also victimized by the Secret Service agents guarding him and his family. His agents reported to the President and First Lady that he had been observed "stealing" a candy bar, a T-shirt, a bottle of Binaca mouthwash, and a small bottle of liquor from a flight attendant's airline tray. The Reagans accepted the Secret Service reports at face value, and never bothered to get Michael's side of the story, which was that the agents had not seen him purchase the items in question. Believing the Secret Service reports, the Reagans did not speak to Michael for the next three years, and refused to invite him to the White House or include him in any family functions.

He was unaware of his alleged transgressions until the head of his detail accused him of kleptomania. Michael denied the charges and asked for a meeting with his father. Michael explained everything to the Reverend Donn Moomaw, pastor of Bel Air Presbyterian Church in Los Angeles. He asked the clergyman to accompany him to the family meeting where Moomaw presented Michael's case. The Reagans listened, and after a long silence, the President said, "I'm sorry. I guess it's all a misunderstanding."

"Why is it you believe me when the pastor says I am innocent," asked his son, "but when I tell you, you don't accept it?"

"Because the Secret Service saved my life, and I trust them more than you because your past history leaves a lot to be desired."

Michael demanded that his father get a letter from the Secret Service apologizing and exonerating him from their allegations of thievery. The President agreed, and his son received the letter six months later, but not in time to spend the first White House Christmas with the President and First Lady. That year, Michael and his family were excluded for the holidays, as was Maureen, who was gearing up for the California senate race against her father's wishes. So, in 1981, only Patti and Ron and Doria received invitations to Washington, and then for only two days.

. . .

The Reagans planned to spend the holidays much as they had done in California: They had reserved Christmas Eve for dinner with their friends Charles and Mary Jane Wick at their house, and had invited the Wicks and their five children for Christmas dinner with them and whichever Reagan children were currently in favor. But the holiday traditions were played out in the nation's capital amidst a sprinkling of snow and a jittery battalion of security agents on alert against a Libyan hit squad that had reportedly threatened the President's life. As a consequence, the First Lady refused to leave the White House to do her Christmas shopping.

"I'm doing it all by catalogue this year," she told reporters.

Not known for her generosity, Nancy's gift-giving took bizarre, even eccentric turns, according to her friends, relatives, and employees. They were well aware that their presents usually came from the discarded heap of free samples and rejects accumulated by the Reagans over the years.

"She's got this closet in the White House, and none of us are ever allowed to see it," said Maureen Reagan. "She squirrels things away in this closet. Later, things come out of it. When my husband moved . . . she said, 'Does he need a coffee maker?'

"I said, 'Well, yeah, I think so.'

"Rummage, rummage, rummage. We heard this sound, and all of a sudden, out comes a coffee maker."

Maureen's wedding present of thirty-six pewter swizzle sticks topped by tiny elephants came from the closet, which housed all the elephant presents pushed on the Reagans by enthusiastic Republicans over the years.

"Each year," said a presidential aide, "my Christmas tie or sweater smelled of mothballs, which meant that the gift originally had been sent to the President, discarded by the First Lady as not good enough, and stashed in her recycling plant to be palmed off on someone like me for Christmas. The first couple of times it happened I was hurt and insulted, but after a while you learn to accept it. We laughed every year when Dennis LaBlanc [deputy director of special support services in the White House], who was Reagan's ranch friend, got the Vin Scully athletic stuff. Vin, the Dodger baseball announcer, was a neighbor of the Reagans in Pacific Palisades, and each year he sends Reagan some kind of jock present, which Mrs. Reagan automatically recycles to Dennis."

"One Christmas," said one of the First Lady's secretaries, "Barbara Bush sent a sprayed white vine wreath to Mrs. Reagan at the White House, and she immediately put someone else's name on it, told me to gift wrap it and send it off to one of her friends in California."

No one was spared from Nancy Reagan's recycling—neither her children nor her closest friends. She gave Julius, her hairdresser, an $800 jacket from Mr. Guy in Beverly Hills that had been sent to Ronald Reagan. She didn't like it, and neither did Julius. He returned it for a store credit. As a house-warming present, she gave Nancy Reynolds a cheap acrylic blanket that had been given to the Reagans during the campaign and was later thrown into "the closet." "It couldn't have cost more than $25," said Reynolds. Even the First Lady's grandson wound up with a gift from the Reagans that they hadn't bought. When Cameron, the son of Michael Reagan, visited the White House during the inauguration in January, the toddler was clutching his teddy bear. Several months later, back home in California, Cameron received a package, gift-wrapped, on his third birthday. The card read: "Happy Birthday to our grandson. Love, Grandma and Grandpa." The gift: Cameron's own lost teddy bear.

"I guess Dad and Nancy saw the bear at the White House and didn't know it had already been given to Cameron. So they had it wrapped and sent to him as a birthday gift," said Michael Reagan.

The thrifty First Lady was thoughtful in remembering the birthdays and anniversaries of her friends and relatives, which she recorded on her private calendar. In February, she noted the sixth as "RR B-day," the fourteenth as "Adolfo B-day," and the twentieth as the birthdays of Leonore Annenberg and Gloria Vanderbilt; in December, she wrote on the twelfth "Frank Sinatra's B-day" and on the eighteenth "Jerry Zipkin's B-day." The birthdays of all "the girls" were recorded and remembered as well as those of their husbands, plus the wedding anniversaries of every couple in "the group." She also remembered the birthdays of her facialist, Suzanne Zada, her florist, David Jones, and her decorator Ted Graber, whose cards were always addressed "Dear Cancerian" or "Dear Cancer Twin" as he and Nancy shared the same astrological sign.

The First Lady liked to be publicly acknowledged for her thoughtfulness and frequently instructed her press secretary to call reporters about her gift-giving. "I remember when the Reagans' godchild, Tessa Taylor [daughter of Ursula and Robert Taylor], called me," said Jody Jacobs of the *Los Angeles Times*. "She said Nancy Reagan's press secretary had told her to call and say that Nancy had given her a wedding present of coral, pearl and diamond earrings with a matching ring. That was probably one of the few presents Tessa had ever received from Nancy Reagan, but I dutifully wrote it up."

"When Sheila [Tate], the First Lady's press secretary, was getting married in 1981," recalled a former White House aide, "I suggested that she might want to send a wedding present. Nancy said, 'Take care of it.' So I went to a shop in Georgetown, bought a long, sterling silver serving spoon, and had it engraved to Sheila and her husband from President and

Mrs. Reagan with the date of their wedding. I later submitted the bill for $200 or so, but I was never reimbursed. I didn't pursue the matter, because I didn't want to make an issue of it. I know Mrs. Reagan hates to pay for things and feels that others should always pay her way like her rich friends do."

Though recycling took care of most of the presents to her family and friends, the Republican National Committee paid for the First Lady's Christmas gifts to her East Wing staff, buying the letter openers, pens, mint trays, and pill boxes imprinted with her signature. She also ordered two hundred plastic compacts containing lip gloss and sunscreen that she specified be made with her signature embossed on the lids, also paid for by the Republican National Committee. She ordered Plexiglas etchings of the White House carved with her signature, and for state gifts she frequently gave a silver box engraved with her signature, such as the one she presented to Danielle Mitterrand, wife of the French president.

"She loved to give presents which had her name on them written in that dyslectic handwriting of hers," said one of her secretaries, exaggerating about Mrs. Reagan's strange penmanship.

She also liked to give autographed photographs of herself to friends like columnist George F. Will, who framed his eight-by-ten color photo of the First Lady in a glittery gown. He displays it on a table in his office. She wrote in her schoolgirl scrawl: "And the little girl grew up and began going out to lunch with a well-known columnist in Washington. Rest is history. LOVE."

"Each Christmas we would go up to the solarium or the family dining room for a staff party, which was the only time most of us ever saw Mrs. Reagan, because with the exception of her senior staff, who saw her every couple of weeks or so, she was very isolated from the rest of us," said Shirley Watkins, who worked for the First Lady for four years and saw her in the East Wing only three times.

"The staff Christmas party routine was always the same. Mrs. Reagan would keep us waiting for fifteen or twenty minutes in the family quarters, and then she'd walk in with her chief of staff, say 'Hello, everyone,' and go directly to the windows. If the drapes were open, she'd close them, and say, 'There is too much sun.' If the drapes were closed, she'd open them, and say, 'There is not enough sun.' That was the first thing she always did. She was very cold and distant to all of us, a terrible hostess, really, who acted like 'Let's hurry and get this over with.' Cookies and coffee would be served, and she'd say, 'Help yourselves,' and then go talk to her social secretary. That would take maybe ten minutes or so. Then we would all sit down, and someone would wheel in a bunch of presents, which were placed in front of her. She'd pick up each gift, read the name on the card which the White House calligraphers had written, and look around for the person to step forward. It was very embarrassing because she didn't know any of us by name. She only knew her chief of staff, her press secretary, her social secretary, and her personal secretary. The rest of us might just as well have been illegal aliens.

"We'd step forward, take our pro forma little gift from the First Lady, sit down next to her, and get our picture taken. She would smile for the camera but never say a personal word. As soon as she had passed out all the presents and posed with everyone, we were sent back to our offices feeling dreadful for imposing on her time. We all talked about it afterward and couldn't believe that she didn't even know her own staff and made no effort to learn our names. Each year it was the same thing, with the Christmas party lasting about a half hour and all of us feeling terrible later."

Though the First Lady gave gifts paid for by the Republican National Committee, her staff of twenty-five always contributed their own money to buy her a lovely gift. One year it was a piece of Lowestoft china on a Lucite stand designed by Jeffrey Bigelow; another year it was a small impressionist painting by Frederick McDuff that had been commissioned by Mrs. Reagan's chief of staff. For her birthday, it was a piece of expensive Mark Cross luggage, and always a staff party with cookies, which were her favorite treat.

"Those birthday parties for the First Lady made me shudder," recalled Shirley Watkins. "I remember one where we all had to bring salads. Mrs. Reagan was standing next to me, looking like she didn't know which salad to choose. Trying to make conversation, I said I had just sampled Elaine's salad and found it quite delicious. Mrs. Reagan froze me out. She didn't say a word, but the anger in her eyes said, 'How dare you have the effrontery to speak to me, you filthy peasant.' She did not put people at ease at all, and her attitude was the same as at the staff Christmas parties: 'Let's hurry and get this dreadful ordeal over with.'"

Given the First Lady's fondness for entertaining, some staffers felt that she was comfortable only with the White House social secretary, a position first held by Muffie Brandon, who was succeeded by Gahl Hodges, and then Linda Faulkner.

"I remember the first year after the Christmas party in the family quarters, Mrs. Reagan beckoned Muffie over and opened a drawer from which she took out a silver Estée Lauder solid-perfume container," recalled an aide. "It was one of the free samples that Estée had given to the First Lady. She handed it to Muffie and said, 'Merry Christmas.' No, it was not gift-wrapped, and yes, it was a free sample. But Muffie took it and responded gratefully. And why not? She was the only one I ever saw who got a little something extra from Mrs. Reagan."

But Yetta Galiber, the executive director of the Christmas Store in Washington, D.C., which distributes toys to the neediest children in the nation's capital, has a very different picture of the First Lady.

"I had invited Mrs. Reagan to attend one year," she said, "because I thought her presence would give us publicity and make the community understand the importance of the Christmas Store, which gives poor, handicapped children play money to actually buy toys. Hundreds of children attend every year, and many are so severely disabled that we have to separate them in wheelchairs so they won't get hurt. I was stunned when Mrs. Reagan walked in, because she headed directly for those kids and touched every single one of them. Some are so physically disfigured, like the hydrocephalics, that they have been abandoned by their parents. Others are mentally retarded and have lost muscle control, so they drool and gurgle. A few don't have arms and legs.

"I've had volunteers who come in and can't deal with the deformities; they back away from the kids, or else break down and start crying. I always have to caution them not to do that, but Mrs. Reagan never flinched. She went directly to those children and touched every one of them as if she actually loved their disabilities. She wasn't just doing that for the television cameras either. Her touch was genuine, and I was quite surprised by what I saw. I didn't expect it at all."

A member of the First Lady's senior staff also noticed this ability to embrace physical deformity without recoiling, which seemed incongruous in someone as fastidious as Nancy Reagan.

"I can't explain why, but she always headed for the burn wards in hospitals, where the charred victims were not at all grotesque to her, although they were to everyone else," said the aide. "I thought maybe this was a projection of Nancy['s] reaching out to hold the ugly part of herself. Perhaps the unwanted child who was Anne Frances Robbins sees herself in these isolated, scarred children, who are so ugly as to be frightening and unloved by their own families. Holding them seems to give her the love she never had as an unwanted child, who was abandoned by her mother for the first five years of her childhood. She would reject this out of hand, of course, because she can't explain that part of herself which she has buried, but I think it accounts for the extreme insecurity that lies deep inside of her, and continues to govern her life.

"Her mother was a bawdy, racy, lively woman who told dirty jokes and laughed uproariously. Her only daughter is shy, timid, and basically inarticulate. Unlike the mother, spontaneity is not part of the daughter's nature because it's too dangerous, and might put her out of control. To this day, Nancy still stutters. She does not have words to convey her thoughts, so people think she's stupid, but it's not that. She's simply too frightened to try to be anything other than the 'perfect decorum' image she's programmed for herself. That's what her whole life is about, and it's the only thing that makes her feel secure. I'm not sure she really feels anything, though. She certainly does not have strong love feelings. . . . Something is missing from deep inside this woman, which is why she's so extremely acquisitive. She loves getting presents and needs to fill herself up with things so that she feels loved, but because of that hole deep inside herself she can never be satiated. So her life becomes a pathetic cycle of taking and getting and acquiring in an effort to feel loved and accepted, even momentarily."

"Where you or I would be turned off by a mongoloid or a guy who had both of his legs broken, she's able to cope," said Mike Deaver.

Other Reagan staffers were not so sympathetic toward the First Lady, feeling she was cold and calculating, nothing more than a reflection of her rich, vacuous friends. "No matter how many years you worked for the Reagans, staff was always staff, and nothing more than hired help," said one aide. "This became abundantly clear the first Christmas Eve in Washington when we had to accompany them to the Wicks' for dinner."

A puffed-up little man (five foot seven) who made millions off a string of poorly run nursing homes, Charles Z. Wick had made his presence felt in Washington during the inauguration when he defended the wealth being flaunted by the Reagan crowd as comforting to the nation's poor in the same way that Hollywood films brought glamour to the masses during the Depression.

After the President appointed Wick director of the United States Information Agency, he doled out several USIA jobs to the children of his Hollywood friends. He jolted the Senate Foreign Relations Committee by testifying about his trip to Africa: "Some of them have marvelous minds, those black people over there."

He created a furor when he secretly tape-recorded his phone calls to reporters ("I barely escaped that one," he said later), and he caused another uproar by nonchalantly charging the government $31,700 for a home-security system. As a close friend of the Reagans, though, he bounced around Washington with immunity.

Specializing in double entendre humor, he once rattled a woman at a Washington dinner party by whispering, "In my ear. That's my favorite place." She looked at him askance as he rolled into his routine of Las Vegas one-liners and juvenile jokes. "Hey, did ya hear the one about the dog who was lost? The owner posted a notice that the dog was lame in one leg, blind in both eyes, suffering from rabies and distemper, and answered to the name of Lucky. Ha-ha-ha-ha."

His wife, Mary Jane, functioned as Mrs. Reagan's best friend in Washington and the financial conduit to her astrologer, Joan Quigley. It was Mary Jane who paid Quigley $3,000 a month to read the Reagans' charts and Nancy reimbursed her friend, one of the few times she actually paid for services rendered. The purpose of the bookkeeping charade was to conceal the First Lady's use of astrology.

"The Wicks were rich, and Mary Jane, like Nancy Reagan, made a point of subtly conveying this fact to those of us a notch beneath her station," said one of the seven persons who accompanied the Reagans to the Wicks' Watergate apartment for dinner on Christmas Eve.

"We [members of the White House staff] were whisked into a back bedroom of the apartment, cloistered away from the celebrations taking place in the other rooms. We chatted and watched television while the Reagans and Wicks sang Christmas carols, ate a sumptuous dinner, and exchanged gifts.

"Early in the evening, the door to the bedroom opened and one of the Wick girls, an elegantly dressed woman in her mid-twenties, looked in. She took stock of our plight and asked if we'd like to have some hors d'oeuvres. The cooks, she said, had prepared some marvelous shrimp. None of us had eaten, so we gladly accepted her offer. But twenty minutes passed, and there was no food. She appeared again and asked if we still wanted some shrimp. We told her that we were starving and would very much like some. Another twenty minutes passed, and she came back. This time, she laughingly asked if we still wanted shrimp, or if we'd prefer a steak dinner instead. It finally dawned on us that she had no intention of ever giving us any food.

"All of us had been yanked away from our families for the evening, so the joke didn't seem too funny. Neither the Reagans nor the Wicks cared about the dismal Christmas Eve we had to endure on their account, which surprised me. Finally, the President's military aide sent one of the White House drivers to Burger King for hamburgers and french fries. Later that night, as the President and First Lady were leaving, I happened to pass by the Wicks' kitchen. There stood platters of uneaten food, one or two mounds of shrimp, heaps of sirloin and a counterful of pies that had not even been touched."

During the 1981 holidays, Nancy Reagan wrote an article reflecting on her Christmases, past and present. "When you are a child the only thing that you're thinking of is whether Santa Claus will come, and whether he will bring what you asked for," she wrote. "As you get older you are more aware of the true meaning of Christmas and how it brings out the nicest, kindest, gentlest qualities in people, qualities you wish would continue all year long."

The weekend the article appeared, the Reagans were at Camp David with their retinue, which always included their Secret Service details, the White House physician, the President's military aide, a White House press secretary, a White House photographer, and David Fischer. Fischer had worked as Ronald Reagan's personal assistant since 1975 and now served in the White House as special assistant to the President.

On this particular weekend, Fischer had brought his wife and two young children, Tiffany, five, and Lindsay, three, to the presidential retreat in Maryland's Catoctin Mountains to see the Christmas decorations. The children were enraptured by the large tree standing in the center of the living room in Laurel, the main staff lodge, and they kept gazing at the lights and touching the decorations. Their father mentioned that there was only one other Christmas tree at Camp David and that was in Aspen, the cabin where the President and First Lady stayed. The little girls begged to see it, so Fischer promised them that he would ask the President the next day if it would be possible.

"Shortly after Reagan had delivered his Saturday morning radio address, he and Nancy were walking toward their cabin when we ran into Dave and his kids," recalled one of the aides in the presidential party.

" 'Would it be okay if the girls stuck their noses in to see your Christmas tree?' Fischer asked the Reagans. 'They are so excited.'

"Mrs. Reagan refused. 'Well,' she said. 'The one in Laurel is very similar to the one we have.'

"Dave was so stunned by her remark that he stopped dead in his tracks; he looked as if he had been slapped in the face. She kept on walking, oblivious to her cruelty, and so did the rest of us, but we were all terribly embarrassed by what she had said, especially the President, who called Dave later in the afternoon to say that he could come to Aspen anytime and to please bring the children with him. He didn't, of course, and I don't blame him."

The Reagans ended their first year in the White House by flying to Palm Springs, where they spent New Year's Eve at the Annenbergs' estate for their annual black-tie dinner dance. The guests included "the group," plus Sandra Day O'Connor, whom Dr. Loyal Davis had recommended be the President's first appointment to the Supreme Court as the first woman to sit on the bench. Three members of the cabinet were invited: Secretary of State and Mrs. Alexander Haig, Secretary of Defense and Mrs. Caspar Weinberger, Secretary of the Treasury and Mrs. Donald Regan; and from the President's personal staff, William Clark, Mike Deaver, and Helene von Damm. The Frank Sinatras, who had been married at the Annenberg estate in 1976 and lived a few miles away, also attended. Sinatra spent the entire evening talking with the First Lady, which so angered Barbara Sinatra that she would not accept another New Year's Eve invitation from the Annenbergs.

Relations between Mrs. Reagan and Mrs. Sinatra had always been strained. "Barbara is such a tough woman," said Charles Wick. "The First Lady did not like her at all. She's too tough. Just too tough."

"We had a terrible time dealing with the Mrs. Reagan–Frank Sinatra business at state dinners," said a White House social aide. "She [Nancy] always insisted on seating him next to her, and putting Mrs. Sinatra in outer Mongolia. The White House social secretary would diplomatically try to rearrange things, but Mrs. Reagan would not hear of it. She wanted Frank Sinatra sitting next to her, no matter how bad it looked."

At the state dinner for the president of Sri Lanka, protocol called for the visiting head of state to be seated to her right, so she sat Sinatra *a sinistra* (to her left).

"She spent the entire evening talking to Frank Sinatra, and aside from a cordial 'pass-the-peas' type of comment to President Jayewardene now and then, she virtually ignored the guest of honor," said a woman who sat at Mrs. Reagan's table. "She was totally consumed by Sinatra and paid as little attention to the poor Sri Lanka president as she did to the waiter serving the wine. It was quite incredible."

After ringing in the new year with the Annenbergs, the Reagans returned to Washington, where the First Lady was determined to put 1981 behind her.

"That first year was the worst of my life," she said. "Everything I did was misunderstood and ridiculed. I sometimes had the feeling that if it was raining outside, it was probably my fault."

"Nancy Reagan's first year in the White House was a disaster," said Elaine Crispen, personal secretary to the First Lady for four years and later her press secretary. "I don't know what we were doing that first year. I guess we were still in awe, lost, wandering the corridors of the White House, looking at our pretty new passes."

The First Lady blamed her naive staff for her poor public image and Peter McCoy was forced to resign as her chief of staff at the end of the year. At one of his last senior staff meetings, McCoy made a suggestion that the First Lady haughtily dismissed. "I wish I could pull a shade down in front of your face," she said in front of everyone. That kind of public humiliation was characteristic of Nancy Reagan.

The management of the Century Plaza Hotel in Los Angeles also experienced the First Lady's wrath. In 1981, during a jewelers' convention, the Reagans were forced to wait for a few hours in a lesser penthouse because the president of the jewelers' association, who had booked the Presidential Suite a year in advance, had not left. Nancy summoned a hotel official to her room and while onlookers cringed, she upbraided the man with a public tongue-lashing in the hallway. "We'd get better treatment," she said, "if my husband were a diamond dealer."

Michael Deaver recruited James S. Rosebush, a delicately handsome man, to deal with "the image problem." So far, all the queen's horses and all the queen's men hadn't put the Humpty Dumpty queen together again.

The first business facing Rosebush was the sensitive matter of the undeclared, unpaid-for wardrobe that the First Lady had been stockpiling ever since her husband took office.

At the end of the year, when the White House lawyer explained the laws governing disclosure, she asked incredulously, "Does this mean I have to declare my clothes?"

"What clothes?"

"My clothes from Adolfo, Bill Blass, Oscar, and Jimmy [Galanos]."

The room fell silent as it dawned on everyone that she had been accepting hundreds of thousands of dollars in designer goods. Having always operated on the basis of my-celebrity-brings-the-best-kind-of-exposure-for-your-free-clothes, Nancy Reagan had no compunction about accepting her wardrobe from her favorite designers. In the past, many First Ladies had accepted clothes at wholesale price, but none had ever gone to the extreme of taking everything and paying nothing!

"I think it's fair to say that we saw it as a potential public relations problem," understated one administration official.

"I was up in the living quarters with Mrs. Reagan in the pale green office with the flower prints on the wall when Jim Baker came bounding in to give her hell," recalled a member of the First Lady's senior staff. "He was furious. 'Goddamnit, Nancy,' he yelled. 'It's got to stop and it's got to stop right now. This is going to be an embarrassment to the President.'

" 'Oh, Jim, I will, I will,' she said.

" 'Nancy, I'm serious. It's over. Do you hear me?'

" 'Yes, Jim, I hear you,' she said."

White House lawyers gingerly pointed out to the Reagans that if the clothes—at least $50,000 in Adolfo suits, dresses, and gowns; $22,000 in Jean Louis designs; plus thousand of dollars more from Galanos, Bill Blass, Oscar de la Renta, and David Hayes—had been given as gifts, they had to be reported as taxable income at their retail value. The 1978

Ethics in Government Act requires high-ranking government officials and their spouses to report any gifts they have received worth more than $35.

If the designers merely "lent" their clothes to the First Lady, the clothes would not be considered taxable income, but a loan presupposes temporary use on condition of return, and Mrs. Reagan had had no intention of returning anything.

Several days of meetings and telephone calls, followed by late-into-the-night discussions among various White House lawyers, presidential aides, members of the East Wing staff, and the First Lady, eventually produced the solution: an announcement that the clothes were "loans" from designers and would "after one or two wearings" be given to museums such as the Smithsonian Institution, the Brooklyn Museum, the Western Reserve Historical Society, and the Boston Museum of Fine Arts.

"I was called by Sheila Tate [First Lady's press secretary] sometime in January of 1982 and asked if I would oversee a program for disposing of some of Mrs. Reagan's beautiful clothes by giving them to museums on a rotating basis," said Anne Keagy, former head of the Parsons School of Design in New York. "Although I think it came about because of the tax situation, I thought it was a wonderful idea, so I agreed to administer the project for Mrs. Reagan."

At an awards dinner of the Council of Fashion Designers of America, held in the Great Hall of the New York Public Library, Mrs. Keagy disclosed details of the museum program from a telegram sent in the name of the First Lady.

"This is being done to encourage the American fashion industry, which Mrs. Reagan feels is the best in the world," said Sheila Tate. "We really are rather pleased with this. Its significance is both historical and educational."

Tate acted astonished when someone wondered whether this plan was not just a ploy to avoid declaring the clothes as gifts, which would mean the Reagans would have to pay additional taxes. "Oh, no, not at all," she said with a straight face.

Mrs. Reagan called all her designers before the program was announced, and they all promised to support her publicly.

"I consider it an honor to give the First Lady clothes," Adolfo told reporters.

"I think anything she does is valid, and what she's doing for fashion is wonderful," said David Hayes.

"All this fuss is much ado about nothing," said Oscar de la Renta.

"I think the museum plan is a great idea," said Bill Blass.

Not all agreed. Geoffrey Beene, not one of her designers, wondered who would be selecting the clothes to be donated and whether they would be of museum quality. When told that Mrs. Reagan would choose the garments she wanted to donate, he said that her wearing the clothes and then donating them had the overtones of a commercial. "They also claim she's helping to 'rescue' the American fashion industry, but I didn't know that it was in such dire straits," he said.

"I think the program will enhance only Nancy Reagan and those designers involved," said Ralph Lauren. "I don't think it will benefit the entire industry. It would certainly not be representative of the total look of the seventies and eighties."

During the next nine months, Mrs. Reagan selected fifteen outfits that she was willing to part with and sent them all by private courier to Mrs. Keagy in New York at taxpayer expense. "I received six Adolfo, five Bill Blass, two David Hayes, one Jean Louis, and one Galanos," she said. "I never heard another word from the First Lady after October of 1982, and I never received another outfit. I retired shortly thereafter, and as far as I know the program was quietly discontinued."

After Mrs. Keagy's retirement, columnists, cartoonists, and commentators condemned Nancy's cavernous closets and the clever scheme hatched to avoid the tax consequences of stuffing them for free.

"It is using one's office for personal gain," said Sheldon Cohen, a Democrat and former commissioner of the Internal Revenue Service. "An IRS agent is forbidden from even taking a free lunch. Is a free dress less than a lunch? These people don't understand that maybe you shouldn't do something like this. It is more a question of taste than anything else. It smacks of favoritism and gives the appearance of privilege to a certain group. You can bet your life that the designer who provides the gowns will be invited to the White House regularly. . . ."

Without question, the free dresses provided an "open sesame" to the Reagan White House. Invitations to state dinners went often to Adolfo, Galanos, Bill Blass, Oscar de la Renta, and Carolyne Roehm. But the names of Geoffrey Beene and Ralph Lauren never appeared on the invitation lists.

After a month of unrelenting criticism, including the editorial admonition of the New York Times to abandon the plan of accepting loans and gifts of clothes, the First Lady capitulated. She hoisted a white flag and announced that she would no longer amass haute couture because it was "misunderstood."

"The First Lady will discontinue accepting clothes from American designers," said her press secretary, "but she will continue to donate her own clothes to museums because she believes that the clothing of any particular era is a visual story of the people of that period."

Mrs. Reagan's press secretary told reporters that the First Lady had returned an expensive handbag and belt to their designer, Judith Lieber. The designer was surprised to receive them. The bag and belt had been sent as birthday gifts six months before. The items were accompanied by a note from Mrs. Reagan, saying that she was not wearing them and felt that someone else might use them more. Lieber, noted for her jeweled, gold-plated evening bags, offered to send one of her trademark cat bags. "Mrs. Reagan said, 'I don't like cats—I hate cats,' " Lieber recalled.

The First Lady's press secretary also told reporters that Mrs. Reagan had returned the "borrowed" Bulgari jewels she had worn to the royal wedding in London.

Figuring she had mollified public opinion, the First Lady turned around and started all over again, accepting free clothes just as she had previously, only now she began doing it discreetly.

"Adolfo told us not to deliver the free clothes to Washington so much after that," said Oscar de Lavin. "Instead, Nancy came to New York and got them there, and then she was fitted at her hotel. Adolfo kept giving her everything free and she kept taking it. She didn't get caught again until 1987."

Occasionally, a designer would arrange with a Washington department store to deliver free clothes to the White House, as was done on June 17, 1985, when Mrs. Reagan accepted an evening gown as a gift from designer Carolyne Roehm, who was rewarded with an invitation to the state dinner for the prime minister of India. The next morning, a picture in *The Washington Post* showed Mrs. Reagan wearing the $6,000 two-piece green and white ensemble. The dress had been delivered through Garfinckel's, a Washington department store, and picked up by Mrs. Reagan's social secretary, Gahl Hodges, who had slipped it past White House security with the help of an assistant. The woman at Garfinckel's who handled the matter had attended a state dinner on April 18, 1985.

"All packages for the President and First Lady must first go through the White House Usher's Office, but Gahl got the dress by Rex Scouten [the usher] without having to declare it as a gift, and he was real upset about it," said Shirley Watkins. "He felt that if someone found out about the expensive gown coming into the White House that way, he would be part of something unethical."

East Wing staff members did not delude themselves—they knew they still had a problem. At the bottom of public opinion polls, Nancy Reagan was being blamed for everything from harming her husband's legislative program to causing many women to quit the Republican party.

"It's hard to think of a First Lady who has been so damaging, but Mrs. Reagan . . . crystallizes an important criticism of this administration: its supposed bias toward the rich," said the political analyst William Schneider. "She is the image of the suburban matron who spends her time shopping and having lunch."

In *Ms.* magazine, Gloria Steinem described her as "the rare woman who can perform the miracle of having no interests at all."

Judy Mann in the *Washington Post* said Nancy Reagan was cold, uninvolved, uncaring. "She has been someone who is far more interested in being socially chic than socially useful."

Everyone around the President was trying to think of ways to give the First Lady a cause outside her closets. Public relations specialists were commissioned by the Republican National Committee to "strategize." And the senior staff of the East Wing spent months working with Mike Deaver, Richard Wirthlin, the White House pollster, and Dr. Carlton Turner, director of the White House Drug Abuse Policy Office, to "formulate" a serious showcase for the First Lady so she could pursue her interest in combating drugs.

"We felt, at least I did, that if Nancy Reagan became better known, the real Nancy Reagan became better known, she would be much better liked, that she would provide some political leverage and strong support to the presidency," said Wirthlin.

Deaver worried about "positioning" the First Lady in the fight against drugs, as did Sheila Tate, who told the syndicated Hearst columnist Marianne Means that the staff felt it was dangerous to get the First Lady involved in a public service project that could be such a liability. "There are many groups with questionable motives, such as Scientology," she said. "We've met with some organizations, but it's difficult to know what approach to take. Does the First Lady also protest marijuana? Do we want to use her that way?"

At first, Mrs. Reagan wanted to align herself with Hollywood celebrities to fight the drug problem, so her staff started talking with the producer Robert Evans, whose movies include *The Godfather, Urban Cowboy, Love Story,* and *Chinatown.* But when Evans pleaded guilty in New York to possession of cocaine, the White House quickly pulled back. "That was a close call," said one aide. "It showed us how much we still had to learn."

The First Lady was frustrated. "When I was dining with her," said Margaret Truman, "she kept asking my luncheon partner, commentator

David Brinkley, how she could improve her image. She really had a tough time with the press and couldn't understand the reason for it."

Finally, she called her astrologer. "I'm getting a terrible press. It's so unfair," she told Joan Quigley. "I want to be loved. . . . I'm really a very nice person. Can you tell me what to do?"

The San Francisco astrologer agreed to help. Quigley told the First Lady that if she followed her advice, based on the positions of the stars and planets, she would transform her own image.

"I told her she must get involved in a volunteer project and then play down all her privileged social connections," said Quigley. "I said there would be absolutely no articles in fashionable magazines, or at least no interviews granted to them. That was the hardest thing for her—to give that up."

After four months of preparation, the First Lady's drug-abuse program was launched with a two-day trip to Florida and Texas in February 1982 to visit prevention and treatment programs. Local press coverage from the trip drew praise for the First Lady from the directors of the programs she visited.

"Super! Fabulous!" said Sheila Tate of the reaction to Mrs. Reagan. "Everybody is focusing on the issue and the problem and that's exactly what we wanted them to do." The press secretary made sure that when the First Lady went to New York City to attend the Metropolitan Museum of Art opening for "The Vatican Collections: The Papacy and Art" that she was not photographed looking at any nude sculptures. At the National Gallery of Art in Washington, D.C., Tate would not let photographers take pictures of Mrs. Reagan in her expensive designer gown with Bunny Mellon at a white-tie dinner. Following the astrologer's advice to grant only interviews that would enhance the new image, Tate saw to it that Mrs. Reagan did not answer certain questions from reporters.

"When I was a correspondent for Westinghouse, I went to the White House to interview Nancy Reagan as they were getting ready to launch her on the drug crusade," said Patricia Sagon. "God, the ground rules for that interview were incredible. I couldn't ask any questions about her family, her clothes, the White House china, and nothing personal. All questions had to be about the impending drug crusade. Sheila Tate sat in on the interview, and when I strayed off the drug questions and asked something else, Nancy would look at Sheila and refuse to talk. Sheila then threatened to pull the plug on our camera lights. She was a real tough cookie, and I'm sure she was following Mrs. Reagan's instructions. She had to sit in on every interview because Nancy didn't know what she was talking about."

Marianne Means was struck by the way the First Lady tried to camouflage her ignorance. "I went to the White House to interview her, and she walked in with three-by-five cards hidden in her hands," said the columnist. "She slipped them under her seat when she sat down. I saw them and she saw me seeing them. 'Oh, these are just to jog my memory,' she said."

In the next seven years, the First Lady would travel more than 100,000 miles, visit 64 U.S. cities and 8 foreign countries, and spawn 3,400 Just Say No clubs. On every visit she made to drug rehabilitation centers, she listened to the young people tell their horrific stories of addiction. She cried as they related how they had run away from their families and bartered their bodies for drugs. She listened wide-eyed to their searing stories of squalor, crime, and degradation: "I started getting high on PAM cooking spray as a kid" . . . "I tried to kill my little sister by luring her into a pit of broken glass" . . . "I swiped my father's bottle of Thunderbird and chugged it down" . . . "I watched my mother spoon dope into balloons to sell." The First Lady clapped as they recited the triumph of their recovery. She ended each session by standing up and saying, "I am so very proud of all of you." And she always cried when she delivered her remarks. "I was under orders from her chief of staff to write maudlin stories for her," said one of the First Lady's speech writers, "because she wanted to choke up and weep in every speech. So I would make up the most outrageously tear-jerking junk, and like the actress she was, Nancy would deliver it and always, without fail, sob and cry on cue."

Even after years of exposure and education in the field of drug abuse, Nancy Reagan never quite shed her judgmental attitudes. During a tour of Via Avanta House, a drug recovery center in Pacoima, California, she listened to twenty-six women tell their stories. She interrupted only once, when one of them said, "I have six children, three of them drug babies." "Six!" exclaimed Mrs. Reagan incredulously as if the woman was a brood mare. "Six?"

After reading a cover story in *The Washingtonian* magazine by Nancy Whittier Dudley about her million-dollar drug habit and how she kicked it, the First Lady invited the young woman to the White House for tea. The recovering addict, a tall, beautiful blonde, had grown up in an affluent home in Washington, D.C., where Walter Lippmann frequently came to dinner. She had been educated at the best schools. At the age of thirty-three, she was as stunning as a movie star. And she was the only drug addict Mrs. Reagan had ever invited to the White House. She was ushered into the living quarters for her private audience with the First Lady a few days after the magazine article appeared.

"Well, you've certainly been through it all, haven't you?" said Mrs. Reagan.

"Yes, I've been through a lot," said the young woman, who had written about her involvement with drug dealers, her arrest, and her two-year rehabilitation.

"Tell me, did you prostitute yourself?"

"I . . . I . . . well, I . . . I guess . . . I prostituted myself spiritually," said the woman, who was angered by the prurient question.

In the beginning, reporters viewed the First Lady as a porcelain princess venturing into the arena of drug abuse simply because she needed to transform her frivolous image. But on the night of March 27, 1982, Nancy Reagan disarmed the Washington press corps.

At the annual Gridiron Dinner, which brings together the most influential people in the nation's capital, an elite group of journalists puts on a show that lampoons politicians. For more than a century, the Gridiron has roasted the nation's leaders with vaudeville skits. Although it "may singe," as their motto puts it, "it never burns." By tradition, a leading politician from each party responds with a humorous speech, and the President of the United States always gets the last word. And even if he has been roasted, he also gets toasted by the six hundred guests in black tie. Lyndon Johnson, who felt unjustly ridiculed by the group, dismissed the annual dinner as "about as much fun as throwing cow shit at the village idiot." In contrast, Ronald Reagan called it "the most elegant lynching I have ever seen."

Knowing that the First Lady would be a butt of parody that evening, members of her staff approached the club to ask whether Mrs. Reagan might take part in the show. The cast for that night's show had planned a song to the tune of "Secondhand Rose" restyled to "Secondhand Clothes," a slap at the First Lady over her wardrobe, so costly yet cost-free. When the club learned that Mrs. Reagan was willing to take part, they invited her to come on stage to take a poke at the press. She wisely declined, but she was convinced by her staff that a self-deprecating song making fun of herself would do wonders for her in front of some of America's most influential people.

"She was terrified at first, but we got [presidential speech writer] Landon Parvin to write a spoof song for her, and sent a piano player up to the family quarters every day for a couple of months to rehearse her," said a senior staff aide. "By the night of the Gridiron, she was still scared, but she did a smashing job."

That evening, she accompanied her husband to the Capital Hilton and

took her place on the dais with Vice President and Mrs. Bush, Soviet
ambassador Anatoly Dobrynin, nine other ambassadors, four Supreme
Court justices, and most of the cabinet. She sat facing a crowd that she
knew contained many who were hostile to her. Midway through the
show, a reporter, dressed like the First Lady, belted out a song.

> *Secondhand clothes.*
> *I give my secondhand clothes*
> *To museum collections and traveling shows.*
> *They were oh-so-happy that they got 'em.*
> *Won't notice they were ragged at the bottom.*
> *Good-by, you old, worn-out mess.*
> *I never wear a frock more than once.*
> *Calvin Klein, Adolfo, Ralph Lauren,*
> *   and Bill Blass.*
> *Ronald Reagan's mama's going strictly*
> *   First Class.*
> *Rodeo Drive. I sure miss Rodeo Drive*
> *   in frumpy Washington.*
> *Secondhand rings.*
> *Donate those old, used-up things.*
> *Designers deduct 'em.*
> *We're living like kings.*
> *So what if Ronnie's cutting back on welfare?*
> *I'll still wear a tiara in my coiffed hair.*

Nancy abruptly left the table in the middle of the song, causing many
people to think that she was stalking out. Her husband assumed she had
gone to the rest room. Minutes later, she poked her head through a
clothes rack on stage and said to the orchestra leader, "Let me see that
score."

As the crowd looked at the slight figure wearing yellow Donald Duck
boots, a white feather boa, strings of pop-it beads, a floppy plumed hat,
and a red and yellow Hawaiian skirt held together with safety pins, people fell silent for an instant. Then they gasped when they realized that
this was the First Lady. People jumped to their feet and started to ap-
plaud, and Nancy Reagan, who loved to sing, swung into her lyrics:

> *Secondhand clothes,*
> *I'm wearing secondhand clothes.*
> *They're all the thing in spring fashion shows.*
> *Even my new trench coat with fur collar,*

Ronnie bought for ten cents on the dollar.
The china is the only thing that's new.
Even though they tell me that I'm no longer queen,
Did Ronnie have to buy me that new sewing machine?
Secondhand clothes, secondhand clothes,
I sure hope Ed Meese sews.

"People were shocked," said Sheila Tate.

"No one thought that Mrs. Reagan had any slapstick, any self-mockery in her," said Hedrick Smith of the *New York Times*.

"It was one of the most astute moves I've seen in a long time," said Virginia governor Charles Robb.

"In a league with William Jennings Bryan's 'Cross of Gold' speech," said Daniel Boorstin, librarian of Congress.

The First Lady rewarded the cheering crowd with an encore. Then she dropped a plate that had been painted to look like her White House china, and as it shattered all over the stage, she kicked up her yellow rubber boots and took her final bow.

The next day's *Washington Post* carried the story with a headline that read: "First Lady Steals Show at Annual Gridiron Dinner." The thundering applause she received that night soon reflected itself in rising polls as well as positive press coverage. The public learned that the First Lady had enough of a sense of humor to laugh at herself. So, for once, Nancy Reagan had the last laugh.

19

THE WHITE HOUSE ANNOUNCED that the First Lady was leaving for Arizona in mid-August 1982 to see her father, hospitalized that week with congestive heart failure. The public saw a worried daughter hurrying to the bedside of her beloved father, who was eighty-five years old. But those with Loyal Davis had a far different view of Nancy Reagan.

"When she was here she spent most of the time in overalls in the garage of her parents' home crating the silver and china that she wanted," said her father's doctor. "She spent only a few minutes at the hospital with Loyal. The rest of the time she was with the family attorney."

Months before, the Davises' family physician had phoned Nancy at the White House to say that he was very concerned about her parents' being left alone on the weekends with only a maid. He said they no longer could take care of themselves. He felt that in addition to the nurse they had during the week, they needed a nurse for the weekends.

"When I asked her about getting the extra nursing care," said the doctor, "Nancy said, 'Are you willing to pay for it? If you want to put a nurse on, then *you'll* have to pay for it.' "

Since Mrs. Reagan would not pay for the nursing care, the doctor called the Davises' close friend Colleen Moore. The former movie star, still one of the wealthiest women in America, told him not to worry, and a nurse appeared at the Davises' home the next weekend.

By the time Nancy arrived in Arizona in mid-August, her relations with her parents' physician were strained. The doctor, who had been a student of Loyal Davis's in Chicago, was losing a friend and a mentor. He dreaded another dispute with the First Lady, but he had promised her father that he could die at home, and now he wanted to honor that last request. He met Nancy at the hospital and talked to her about moving the dying man back home. Nancy would not hear of it.

"That is what your father wanted and I promised him," said the doctor.

"What right have you to promise anything to my father?" she said.

"I have the right as his doctor." The physician then produced a letter Dr. Davis had given him a few months before, stating his last wishes for himself and his wife. Although Loyal Davis had professed to be an atheist and anti-Catholic as well, he requested that the Reverend John P. Doran, a Catholic priest, preside at his funeral at Greenwood Memorial Park, which he stipulated must be a "very brief service" for only fifty guests. He specified cremation for himself as well as his wife, who would outlive him by five years, barely cognizant, confined to a wheelchair with round-the-clock nurses. Edith had helped Father Doran raise money for his church, so Dr. Davis left instructions that when she died, her funeral was to be held in St. Thomas the Apostle Roman Catholic Church in Scottsdale.

"At the time," said the physician, "I asked Loyal why he was giving me the letter. And he said, 'Because I don't trust Nancy.' His exact words."

Now, when the physician wanted to send Loyal Davis home, Mrs. Reagan insisted he resign the case and turn over his medical records to the family attorney. Several days later, her father died—at Scottsdale Memorial Hospital.

Her stepbrother, Richard Davis, the son of Loyal's first marriage, quarreled with Nancy so bitterly that he did not go to his father's memorial service.

"The two of them got into a loud argument at the family home the evening before Dr. Davis's memorial service," recalled Larry Speakes, the acting White House press secretary, who had accompanied the President to Arizona to attend the service. "Although we heard of the spat between the two, we never knew what caused it."

"They fought about two things," said the family physician: "the disposition of the immediate physical assets of the house—dishes, flatware, silverware—and the fact that Nancy had arranged with the Biltmore to have a buffet afterward. Also, he was furious that I was invited, but that was in Loyal's will. Richard and I had been classmates and we got along reasonably well, but we had a falling-out toward the end when I wanted to call in another cardiologist for his father. He said to me on the phone,

'Listen, you son of a bitch, let him die.' This was really something. Nobody in that family was talking to each other. Nobody. And particularly that last scene—I'll always remember the funeral—Nancy did not talk to any of her children. They stayed in one corner of the room, completely away from her. Completely away from her. The only guy with any warmth was Ronald Reagan."

The President approached the physician after the service for a personal talk. "First, he said, 'I want to thank you for everything you did for Loyal,' which is something, considering Nancy never thanked me once in the ten years that I took care of her parents. I never even got so much as a Christmas card from her. But that's Nancy. . . . Her husband is different. He asked me about Loyal's final days, and I told him how much his telephone call a few weeks before had meant to his father-in-law.

"I had stopped by to see Loyal right after the President had called. He said that the President had told him that it was his faith in God that had saved his life after the assassination attempt. Loyal was supposedly a nonbeliever, but at the very end he asked me to call a priest to his bed. I did, but I left the room when he came in, so I don't know if Loyal converted at the last minute or not. I told this all to the President, and he started to cry. I mean, he sat there with tears streaming down his face. This was the man Loyal Davis had converted from a florid Democrat to a Republican. And make no mistake about who converted Reagan."

Weeks before, the President had tried to convert his father-in-law to the healing balm of faith by writing him a seven-page letter setting forth St. Thomas Aquinas's arguments for the existence of God. He urged the doctor to make his peace before he died, and after the funeral Reagan approached Father Doran for reassurance that his father-in-law had made his peace with God.

"I'm sure he did, Mr. President, I'm sure he did," said the priest, who had been summoned from retirement in Santa Barbara, California, to fly to Scottsdale a few days before.

"I was working in the garden at the time and unavailable by phone," said the priest. "All of a sudden the California Highway Patrol came motorcycling up with sirens and flashing red lights to say that the White House was trying to reach me. It was Nancy calling to say that her father was approaching death and would I please come immediately. I did, of course, and when I got there, Loyal was in a coma, but he came out of it when I started talking to him. We talked about death because it was facing him. Nancy was in the room and she was crying. 'Oh, Bapa, Bapa, don't leave me, don't leave me,' she said over and over."

Distraught over her father's death, Nancy was unable to sleep. At 3:00

A.M. the next night, she called Chicago and spoke to Les Weinrott, who had been close to her parents for so many years.

"I've never seen anyone die before, Les," she said. "I sat with him and watched him die. I was there. I watched him die."

She talked for forty-five minutes, telling him about the funeral, which her chief of staff had arranged to her specifications, including white-on-white flowers and the 140 straw fans from Pier One that she felt the congregants needed to deal with the desert's scorching 112-degree heat. She said she had found a morocco leather box in Loyal's dresser with all his studs and cufflinks, so she took it downstairs to give to her stepbrother, but he was gone.

"Nancy was so upset by this she had to unload on someone who knew the family," said Weinrott. "We talked about Richard's not attending the funeral, and I tried to explain that he was so dominated by his father all his life and they had such a tormented relationship that it was probably too much for him, which is why he walked out. I said what I could to console her. She kept saying that it was the first time she had ever seen anyone die. She also told me that Edie was completely out of it and for me to stop bothering with the weekly package of Chicago newspaper clippings that I'd been sending her ever since they'd moved to Arizona. That was sad, too."

Six months later, Nancy sold her parents' home and moved her mother into an apartment in the Cloisters in the Biltmore Estates, where she lived until her death in 1987.

At sixty-three years of age, Nancy Reagan had never experienced a death that mattered more to her. The closest she had come was in college when a boyfriend committed suicide and in 1969 when actor Robert Taylor died of lung cancer. Then she had flown from Sacramento to Los Angeles to stay with Taylor's widow. "She was wonderful," said Ursula Taylor Schacker. "She made herself totally available to help me along. She practically took over my life for me."

Now Nancy was trying to provide the same kind of support for Betsy Bloomingdale, whose husband had died in Los Angeles the day after Loyal Davis. His illness had led to Nancy's shuttling between California and Arizona. Standing behind her friend at this time was the most principled act of loyalty that she had ever displayed, for she was aligning herself with someone whose husband had dragged his family into a lurid scandal of sadomasochistic sex, drugs, prostitutes, and, eventually, murder—all made public in a series of lawsuits filed by Bloomingdale's mistress.

FBI files disclosed that Alfred Schiffer Bloomingdale had been investigated in connection with Las Vegas Mafia figures in the late 1960s, and that in 1969, he had paid $5,000 in blackmail because of his habit of beating up prostitutes. One report in his FBI file revealed:

Al Bloomingdale is a family man, but not the ordinary sort. At about 43 years of age, he lives with his wife and children in an appropriate house in Bel Air. His principal interest is the internationally famous Diners Club, of which he is president.

There is another facit [sic] to Bloomingdale. He likes girls. In fact, in another circle of society he is known as quite a playboy—ready, willing and able to accept the services of high-priced Hollywood prostitutes. This story is not just fancy—it is substantial information from a man who for many years was connected in the bail bond business with the notorious Izzy Glasser, at one time a henchman of Mickey Cohen, and is verified in part by Bloomingdale himself.

Because of his mistress and his ties to the Mafia, Bloomingdale could not be named as ambassador to France, the position he wanted most. Instead, Reagan appointed him to the President's Foreign Intelligence Advisory Board, which consisted of a small elite group of prominent citizens—including Henry Kissinger, Edward Bennett Williams, and Clare Boothe Luce—who would assess the performance of the nation's various intelligence and counterintelligence agencies.

The appalling details of Bloomingdale's debauchery became public in 1982 after his wife discovered that he had been keeping a mistress for twelve years—to the bountiful tune of $18,000 a month. Although he was near death, Mrs. Bloomingdale summoned her lawyers and had them draw up a new will converting all his assets into a Bloomingdale Family Trust with herself as sole executor. She made him sign the new will on July 25, 1982, days before he died. Once in charge of her husband's financial organization, she stopped all payments to mistress Vicki Morgan.

The mistress retaliated with a $10 million lawsuit claiming that she had been promised lifetime support. She elucidated in detail some of "the benefits" and "the happiness" she had provided Bloomingdale over the years.

"When we'd go to the apartment that we had on La Cienega," she testified in her deposition,

it got to the point, "So, Vicki doesn't like it; then, Vicki, darling, you beat the women. And . . . if they don't call me 'Master,' hit

them harder," but . . . I'm not kidding when I say that the eyes
got glazed . . . and . . . he'd stand there and watch the girls get
on the floor and crawl. . . . He'd have these girls crawl on the
floor and he'd sit on their back . . . and drool.

Refusing to settle one cent on her husband's mistress, Betsy Bloomingdale instead let that deposition be made public. A blizzard of sensational
newspaper articles followed, pitting an implacable wife against a rapa-
cious mistress. The public followed avidly as the two women fought over
the fortune of a desiccated old man dying of cancer. The disease had
devoured his esophagus, a result of his smoking three packs of cigarettes
a day for forty years.

On Friday, August 20, 1982, at 10:05 P.M., Alfred Bloomingdale died
at St. John's Hospital, where he had been registered under an assumed
name. His wife, who had stopped by earlier in the day, was at a dinner
party. It was after 1:00 A.M. when she returned home and found the
hospital's message. Within twelve hours she had consigned her husband's
body to a $200 wooden coffin. The graveside service at Holy Cross
Cemetery—born a Jew, Bloomingdale had converted to Catholicism to
marry Betsy—lasted ten minutes. The ceremony was attended by his
widow, his three children, and his four grandchildren. No one told his
brother about the death, so he did not learn of it until two days later,
when the news became public. The will was filed within the week.

"She buried him like a dog," cried his mistress. "Like a dog. I went to
the cemetery and I found there was not one flower on the grave, except
what I put there. When I saw that, I was shocked."

Incensed by the way her lover had been unceremoniously laid to rest,
Vicki Morgan granted her first interview to the *Los Angeles Herald-Examiner.* She told a reporter that Betsy Bloomingdale had known of her
husband's extramarital affair for many years.

"Nancy told her about me eleven years ago when she saw Alfred and
me together," she said.

"Nancy who?"

"Nancy Reagan," she said. "Alfred and I were apparently out to lunch
together, and Nancy saw us. And within a week or two, Betsy and her
daughter saw Alfred drop me off at the hairdresser. . . ."

Vicki Morgan asserted that Alfred's wife had forced him to change his
will at the last minute. "Betsy Bloomingdale eventually locked herself in
the room with him and made the nurses leave and was in there for over
four hours with that [man] and he's not strong. . . . Betsy did say to
someone that she'd make him mentally incompetent by the time she was
through with him."

Shortly before Bloomingdale died, presidential assistant Morgan Mason invited the mistress's lawyer, Marvin Mitchelson, to Washington, where they discussed the lawsuit. "I voiced my opinion that it was an unfortunate situation," said Mason, the son of actor James Mason and Hollywood gossip columnist Pamela Mason. "The guy is deceased now. I felt it was kind of a sad thing for Betsy to have to deal with."

Although Mason was acting on his own, his meeting with Mitchelson was interpreted in the press as a summons on behalf of the Reagans. Upon reading the story, the First Lady called Mike Deaver and instructed him to deny that the White House was trying to bring pressure on anyone in this matter. Then she called Morgan Mason and told him to mind his own business. "Just remember," she said. "Betsy's still my friend."

This was exceptional loyalty from a woman who had disowned her daughter for "living in sin" with a rock star, and spurned her ballet-dancing son because people might think he was homosexual. Ordinarily, Nancy Reagan put as much distance between herself and potential scandal as she could. When Congressman Tom Evans (R-Del.) was publicly involved in an extramarital affair and lost his congressional seat, she stopped speaking to him. "She even cut us off her Christmas card list," said the former congressman. When Barbara Bush told her about a secretary on her staff who was having an affair with a married U.S. senator, the First Lady fired the secretary. "I was totally devastated by her cruelty," said the former White House secretary. "I was very much in love with the senator, who was separated from his wife at the time, but I was willing to stop seeing him because I needed my job and I loved the work I was doing for Mrs. Reagan. But she had me locked out of my office the day she learned about it. . . . I felt I was being punished for some terrible crime. . . . I went into the hospital for depression and it was one year before I could work again."

Nancy Reagan was so skittish about appearances that she refused to allow an unescorted divorced woman to share the presidential box with her and the President at the Kennedy Center. "I had arranged for the Reagans to attend the opening night of the Dance Theatre of Harlem, and I was supposed to sit with them, but Mrs. Reagan was very upset that I was divorced at the time," said Jackie Rush. "She didn't want me sitting with them alone, so she arranged for Congressman Sonny Montgomery [D-Miss.] to be my escort. She couldn't stand the thought of an unattached, divorced woman sitting with them in public."

Despite Nancy Reagan's excessive concern about propriety, she stood firmly beside her friend Betsy. As the sex-for-hire suit made its sordid way through the court system, the mistress threatened to write an exposé about the Reagan kitchen cabinet. She had already introduced into evidence photographs of herself on trips with Bloomingdale; proof that he had gotten her a job in the Reagan for President headquarters; documentation that the two of them occasionally lunched with Ed Meese and Justin Dart; and invitations to the Reagan inauguration, during which Bloomingdale had her tucked away in a Washington, D.C., hotel so she would be available whenever he could break away from his wife.

In September 1982, a California judge dismissed most of Vicki Morgan's lawsuit seeking lifetime support. However, he let go to trial the part of the lawsuit dealing with the legal contracts that Bloomingdale had signed, promising her $10,000 a month for two years plus her half of his interest in a nationwide pizza chain. Betsy's lawyer filed an appeal.

Five months later, the California State Supreme Court ruled against Vicki Morgan. It said she could not sue the Bloomingdale estate because the deceased held no financial interest in the pizza chain. Facing economic ruin now, she no longer had the will to fight. She tried to take her life with an overdose of sleeping pills. She was rescued by a friend and lived four more months, until the night of July 7, 1983, when she was bludgeoned to death in her rented apartment with a baseball bat by a deranged homosexual.

"I was sitting with Nancy in the private quarters of the White House having coffee and cinnamon toast when she got that news," recalled a friend. "The phone rang, and Nancy said, 'That's funny, because I told them to hold all calls.' She picked up the phone and said, 'Well, Elaine, tell her I'll call her back.' She returned to me and sat down, saying that it was Betsy calling, and she would talk to her later. In a half hour, the phone rang again, and this time she was a bit sharp with Elaine. 'I told you I didn't want to take any calls,' she said, but Elaine must've said it was urgent because she said, 'Well, put her on.' Then she said, 'Bets . . . oh, my God,' and there was lots of silence. Finally, she said, 'I'll call you back later.'

"She sat down and said, 'That woman's been killed, Vicki Morgan.'

"How terrible."

" 'Yes, I guess that will dredge up all that stuff now,' she said, looking pretty upset. 'You know, people say that I saw her with Alfred, but I never did. I didn't know anything about her.' "

There were rumors about what happened to the exposé Vicki Morgan was supposedly working on and the alleged sex tapes that purportedly showed her cavorting with Bloomingdale and other members of the Reagan kitchen cabinet. But her exposé was never written, and her sex tapes, if they existed, never surfaced. Her mother pursued the remaining part of her lawsuit, and eventually won $200,000 from the Bloomingdale estate.

Throughout the scandal, the First Lady stayed in daily telephone contact with her best friend and even allowed the White House to announce the "little dinner" Betsy gave for her in Los Angeles in January 1983. "Not only did she hold my hand all the way through the illness, but she even went to see Alfred in the hospital," said Betsy Bloomingdale. "And she was *most* supportive through the other problem."

Nancy made sure that Betsy was invited to all the parties that mattered most to them, which meant anything involving European royalty, especially British royalty. Nancy and Betsy were on the phone daily discussing the festivities surrounding the visit of Queen Elizabeth II and Prince Philip to the United States in February 1983, which was going to include a few hours with the Reagans at their Santa Barbara ranch. "She was frantic about that [part of the] visit," recalled Betsy. "She told me, 'Thank God, they're not going to stay the night.' It *really* is a little ranch house with a guest bedroom about as big as a minute and a bathroom you can hardly turn around in."

The Queen's impending nine-day trip to the west coast of the United States, the first time she had ever visited that part of the country, threw the First Lady into a turmoil for months. She wanted to reciprocate the hospitality that she and her husband had received at Windsor Castle in June 1982, the first time a U.S. President had been so honored since World War II. "I don't think I'll ever have such an experience in my whole life," Nancy had said of her stay in the Queen's castle. "They [Queen Elizabeth and the royal family] are so warm, so easy. All of them have such a wonderful sense of humor."

After the scathing press Nancy had received in Britain during the royal wedding in 1981, she had been apprehensive about returning to England in 1982. So Mike Deaver and Jim Rosebush made three advance trips to pave the way for her new image, sending her off to visit children in cancer wards and drug rehabilitation centers at every stop. Still, the British press noted that she arrived with eighteen suitcases and Julius, the hairdresser, in tow, refused once again to curtsy to the Queen, and wore the $880,000 diamond earrings that she had "borrowed" from Harry Winston.

Now that the Queen was coming to the United States and sailing up the Pacific coast on the royal yacht, *Britannia,* the First Lady was eager to make the visit as grand as possible. So she dispatched Mike Deaver and Jim Rosebush to work out all the details: scheduling a party for the royal couple in San Diego, a state dinner in San Francisco, and a Hollywood extravaganza at 20th Century-Fox under the direction of Frank Sinatra.

The Queen, in turn, invited the Reagans to celebrate their thirty-first wedding anniversary on board the *Britannia.* "Nancy was ecstatic," said a member of her White House social staff. "This was almost better than staying at Windsor Castle, because this was the Queen of England coming to America and paying homage to the Reagans on her royal yacht, which is the size of a destroyer and the largest private yacht in the world. A visitation from the Lord Himself would not have meant more to her than that invitation from the Queen. All the President cared about was taking Her Majesty horseback riding at the ranch, but the First Lady wanted to show her off up and down the coast. God! We had to work overtime for months on that one!"

Fierce storms and torrential rains battered California the day the royal couple arrived in Los Angeles, drenching the area and giving rise to tornado warnings. As a result, much of their schedule was washed out, with the exception of the royal visit to the Reagans' ranch.

"Because of the weather, they had an extra night in their Los Angeles schedule, so we arranged a dinner for the Queen and Prince Philip at Trader Vic's," recalled a White House aide. "They had not been to a restaurant in seventeen years, but they agreed to come, and we had a wonderful time with them. Just their royal traveling staff and a few of us from the White House. Prince Philip had never seen a fortune cookie before, and everyone laughed when he opened his and read the fortune aloud: 'You will marry a very rich person.' The Queen laughed harder than anyone."

Frank Sinatra had been working for months to create a spectacular dinner gala for the British monarch that would reflect grandly on the First Lady.

Under the tin roof of the "M*A*S*H" television soundstage at 20th Century-Fox, set designer Walter Scott was trying to create what he called a "lovely Hollywood-style garden" with fiberglass statues, painted backdrops of the sky, three hundred live trees, ferns and azaleas, a statue of Bacchus left over from filming *The Robe,* and a twenty-four-foot-high fountain from the set of *Hello, Dolly.* Meanwhile, Nancy worked on the invitation list. She discarded five drafts until she was completely satisfied she had the right five hundred people. Guests included the entire British contingent of the movie colony, although Elton John seemed more impressed with seeing Jimmy Stewart than with meeting the Queen of England, and Roddy McDowell paid homage only to Bette Davis. "She's *our* queen," he said breathlessly. "The girls" and "the group" turned out in full force for Her Majesty, as did the First Lady's decorator, her hairdresser, her florist, and her couturier, James Galanos.

"Mrs. R even invited her daughter, Patti Davis, and fixed her up with John Ziffren [son of attorney Paul Ziffren] for the evening, but Patti showed up in a nubby denim skirt and a fringed shawl, so that was the last White House invitation she ever got," said one of the First Lady's secretaries.

Several days before the gala, Sinatra threatened to walk off the job: He had learned that the Queen was having a private anniversary dinner for the Reagans the next night on board the *Britannia,* and he had not been invited. He browbeat his wife into calling the White House to talk to Mike Deaver, who said there was nothing he could do because the guest list was the Queen's. Mrs. Sinatra was adamant, so Deaver relented and called Buckingham Palace, reluctantly.

"We have a very difficult situation here," he said, "and I do hope you won't think us too presumptuous, but if it would be possible to receive Mr. Sinatra on the yacht, we'd be most grateful."

The palace declined to extend the invitation. Having dealt with Deaver the year before when he advanced the Reagans' trip to Windsor Castle, the royal adjutants were not impressed with the White House image-meister. He had ruffled royal feathers on that visit by suggesting that the shrubbery surrounding Windsor Castle be backlighted so the President would look better in his television footage with the Queen. Deaver had also suggested that, for maximum pictorial effect, the Queen should know exactly where she was going to ride when she appeared on horseback with the President. And he added that it would be nice if Mrs. Reagan could be filmed having breakfast with Her Majesty in her private quarters at the castle. Palace officials had taken the White House deputy chief of staff aside and gently admonished him, explaining that the Queen of England was not accustomed to being told where to ride for maximum pictorial effect, nor to eat her morning meal in front of television cameras.

After Deaver's request for a royal invitation for Frank Sinatra fell on deaf ears, the singer once again threatened to pull out as producer of Mrs. Reagan's royal dinner. Frantic, Deaver begged Walter Annenberg to intercede, and only then did Elizabeth II assent to adding the Sinatras to her shipboard party.

With the exception of Patti Davis and Roy Rogers, both of whom wore cowboy boots, Hollywood gussied up in taffeta and tassels for the gala. The Queen wore a diamond tiara and a long chiffon dress embroidered with orange California poppies in honor of the state she was visiting. Following in her royal wake was the erect figure of her consort, the Duke of Edinburgh. Together, they walked down the red-carpeted aisle of the studio soundstage with Nancy Reagan, who had arrived without the President. She was wearing a $10,000 purple and gold gown she had "borrowed" from Galanos but never returned. The Queen and the First Lady waved to guests being held back by velvet ropes, each turning genteelly from side to side to acknowledge their subjects. As they glided down the aisle to the head table, the First Lady stayed abreast of the Queen, with the royal hips brushing the common hips ever so lightly as the two women swayed from side to side, waving to the crowd.

The combined social pressure from the White House and Buckingham Palace seemed to overwhelm Sinatra, who nervously stumbled over his lines. He even neglected to welcome the Queen. He then compounded his faux pas by singing off-key, forgetting the words to his song, and throwing kisses to the First Lady. Teaming up with Perry Como to sing a duet, he tried to be funny by saying, "Welcome to the Italian Hour," but Tommy Lasorda of the Dodgers seemed to be the only one in the audience who laughed.

George Burns, then eighty-seven years old, creaked onto the stage to tell a string of off-color jokes in the presence of the Queen, who tried to smile gamely.

"If a director wants me to cry, I think of my sex life," said the comedian, puffing his cigar. "If he wants me to laugh, I think of my sex life. I must be a great actor, because this morning, after taking a shower, I took a look at myself and I laughed and cried at the same time." All five hundred pairs of eyes slid sideways to see whether the Queen was laughing. She was not.

"The evening was a disaster—an absolute disaster," said one of the White House social aides. "Frank put on the worst Las Vegas variety show, completely lacking in style and taste, and Mrs. Reagan was humiliated. She was very upset with him, very irritated. . . . The menu was seafood, which the Queen had expressly asked not to be served, plus sticky, cold chicken pot pies and sour wines. The valets ran out of umbrellas, and then Frank violated all protocol by leaving before the Queen did. I guess he knew that he had blown it and just wanted to get away as fast as he could."

The First Lady was beside herself when she read the British reviews of her Sinatra-staged evening in honor of the royal couple.

"Queen's Trip In Turmoil" headlined the London *Evening Standard.*

"Snub For Yanks" said the *Daily Star,* because the Queen had not been introduced to Hollywood luminaries like Bette Davis, Fred Astaire, and Jimmy Stewart.

The *Daily Mail* gave Nancy a dressing-down for wearing purple and gold, the colors traditionally associated with royalty.

Describing Sinatra's voice as "rasping and flat," the *Manchester Guardian* pronounced the evening extremely tedious: "Overall, it was not exactly an exhilarating performance."

Even British stars agreed. "It was so boring, I almost fell asleep," said Elton John.

"A bit dour," said Julie Andrews.

When Dudley Moore and Anthony Newley were asked what they thought of the show, they collapsed into each other's arms in stage laughter.

"It was the usual Hollywood cattle call, rather dull in many ways," said Pamela Mason.

The U.S. media featured daily stories on the Queen's trip. The evening news shows, newspapers, and newsweeklies showed the First Lady's spindly body dancing attendance on the short, matronly Queen in her clunky heels and mumsy dresses. The stern visage of Prince Philip was barely glimpsed in the background. The President joined them in San Francisco for a state dinner at the M. H. deYoung Museum in the heart of Golden Gate Park, where he and the Queen toasted their friendship and the close alliance between their two countries.

To blunt the First Lady's royal-visit press coverage, the White House issued a media advisory that when the Queen left California, Mrs. Reagan would remain behind to tape an appearance on the television comedy series "Diff'rent Strokes," urging children to shun drugs. A few days later, she hosted "The Chemical People," a two-part series on public television documenting teenage drug and alcohol abuse. She also cohosted "Good Morning America" with David Hartman one day when the morning talk show devoted two hours to drug abuse.

"The hard statistics, not to mention the touching personal stories I've heard, make it clear to me that we must educate ourselves and others about drug abuse—its symptoms, its dangers, and its treatments," said the First Lady.

She was so conscious of her antidrug image that she canceled plans to see her friend Mary Martin in *Legends* at the Kennedy Center when she was told the play contained a scene with people eating hashish brownies.

A hard-liner, the First Lady believed drug lyrics should be censored and drug paraphernalia shops should be outlawed. She encouraged children to call the police on their dope-smoking parents. She favored drug testing for everyone, including public officials, and she endorsed rigid rehabilitation programs like Toughlove and Straight. Vehemently opposed to legalizing drugs of any kind, she condemned casual users as "accomplices to murder" and called for the death penalty for pushers.

"Each of us has a responsibility to be intolerant of drug use anywhere, anytime, by anybody, and to force the drug issue to the point that it may make others uncomfortable and ourselves unpopular," she said. "We must create an atmosphere of intolerance for drug use in this country." Striking out at the motion picture industry, she accused Hollywood of forsaking its moral responsibility to children by glamorizing drugs and making them look like fun. Without mentioning names, she denounced the movie *9 to 5* in which three working women—played by Dolly Parton, Lily Tomlin, and Jane Fonda—get hilariously high on marijuana. And she pounded pop star Madonna for glamorizing drugs in the film *Desperately Seeking Susan.*

The motion picture industry responded with a series of public service announcements (PSAs), a testament to the First Lady's growing influence as the country's number one antidrug crusader. The Hollywood producer Jerry Weintraub called the White House to explain the concept of eleven PSAs he envisioned. Featuring Hollywood stars, the trailers would precede films appealing to young audiences. He offered the First Lady a chance to appear in one and choose her own co-star. She eagerly accepted and chose Paul Newman. But Newman, who had been speaking out against drug abuse since his son, Scott, died of an overdose in 1978, declined the honor, saying he did not support the policies of the Reagan administration. The First Lady's second choice was Clint Eastwood, who readily accepted.

Together, the *Dirty Harry* star and the First Lady filmed a forty-second antidrug message ("Don't ever try it. The thrill can kill"), which was to be shown as a preview before *Jaws, the Revenge* and *Superman IV*. "These trailers will reach millions of young people, and I'm sure they'll have an effect," said Mrs. Reagan at a White House theater premiere of the series, which included spots by Rosanna Arquette, James Woods, Rae Dawn Chong, Dudley Moore, Pee-wee Herman, Bette Midler, Roy Scheider, and Olivia Newton-John.

"If it wasn't royalty or her rich friends, it was movie stars. That's what mattered most to Mrs. Reagan," said Shirley Watkins. "She didn't want to get involved with anybody else. She always wanted to be on television and would go out of her way to do a sitcom like 'Diff'rent Strokes' because the viewing audience was 28 million. She would extend herself for the celebrity success stories like that of the pretty girl on the cover of *The Washingtonian* who wrote about her addiction and rehabilitation, and the ballet dancer Gelsey Kirkland, a former cocaine addict, because she [Nancy Reagan] got press coverage out of meeting with them. She would write letters to celebrities, as she did to Ethel Kennedy when her son was arrested on heroin charges, but the desperate little people who called the White House for her help got nothing.

"Someone sent us a letter about a little boy dying of muscular dystrophy who had two wishes he wanted fulfilled before he died. As an adopted child, he was longing to meet his twin sister, from whom he'd been separated at birth, but his natural mother would not permit it, so I thought the least we could do was grant his second wish, which was to meet the First Lady. I asked Jack Courtemanche, who became Mrs. Reagan's chief of staff in 1986, if we could arrange a quick photo op some weekend before the Reagans left for Camp David. He said, 'Absolutely not. The First Lady doesn't want her picture taken with some drooly kid on a respirator. It's too disgusting.'

"Jack told me to stick to pushing her image in the field of drug abuse, so I did. When [the] Reverend Richard Halverson, chaplain of the U.S. Senate, approached me with a letter saying the Senate wives had expressed an interest in getting involved with Mrs. Reagan in some personal, grass-roots, get-your-hands-dirty work in the slums of Washington, D.C., I approached Jack again, but he said, 'Absolutely not—Mrs. Reagan wouldn't think of doing that kind of thing, and besides, the Senate wives have no business getting involved in the First Lady's cause.' I told the chaplain we had hit a dead-end street on that one.

"Parents who called wanting to know where to send their addicted kids for rehabilitation, for financial assistance, or for encouragement were cut off. We were instructed to tell them that Mrs. Reagan had a campaign, not a program, and could not get personally involved in their problems.

"Yet when Jim Rosebush had been chief of staff, he kept saying he wanted us to make Mrs. Reagan go down in history looking better than Eleanor Roosevelt, the most beloved First Lady of the twentieth century. We worked hard at fostering that image, and we tried to make it appear that Mrs. Reagan cared about people, but it was such a fraud. We spent more man-hours declining requests for her help than it would've taken to do a good deed in her name. It was crazy and so frustrating. We wouldn't have spent any more time sending some of the requests to the senators and congressmen who represented those people than we did saying no in letters that took hours to compose so that Mrs. Reagan looked like she had some kind of human compassion. We could've genuinely helped some of those people while giving her the Eleanor Roosevelt image she cared about so much. After a while I became so frustrated that I started acting on my own and sending the requests to friends of mine in Congress who might be able to help, which was the reason I went to work for Nancy Reagan in the first place—to help people. I thought the White House was the ultimate place of service in America, and that as First Lady, Mrs. Reagan was in a powerful position to do good. And she could've done so much for so many if she had wanted to. Sometimes she got as many as a hundred calls a day, and the volume of mail was stupendous, but there was no personal involvement on her part. She didn't care, and we could not always manufacture a caring attitude for her because she would not take the time to be that kind of First Lady. Mothers desperate about their children on drugs would call and ask if Mrs. Reagan would send them a letter or make a phone call to encourage them. I tried once to get her to make that kind of phone call and almost got fired for 'bothering' her. She had been on the phone with Betsy Bloomingdale.''

By means of a withering stare and stone-cold silence, the First Lady let people know when she was being bothered, and few on the staff would risk being flash-frozen.

"I remember when she was told that Bess Truman had died," recalled another aide. "She turned to Jim Rosebush and said, 'Now don't expect me to go to *that* funeral,' and he started to sweat. Finally, he said, 'I do expect you to go to that funeral because last month you went to Monaco and sat with Princess Diana at the funeral of Princess Grace, and so if you don't go to Independence, Missouri, for Mrs. Truman's funeral, it looks like all you care about is European royalty and international glitz.'

"That took real courage for Rosebush because no one dared to disagree with Mrs. Reagan. She looked at him for a few seconds as if she expected him to withdraw his words and apologize, but he didn't, so she said, 'Well, I'll think about it.' Then she called Mike Deaver, and he must've agreed that it was a good idea or else he told her that Betty Ford and Rosalynn Carter were going to the funeral, so she had no choice, but she called Rosebush back and said, very begrudgingly, 'All right. I'll go.'

"The White House had already announced that the First Lady wouldn't be attending the funeral but would be represented by the Vice President's wife. So now we had to concoct a little lie and say that she decided to postpone dental surgery and rearrange her schedule because she wanted to pay her last respects to Mrs. Truman. Of course, she didn't want to go to the funeral at all, but she went because she was afraid of how she'd be ragged by the press if she didn't.''

Having been mocked in Great Britain for traveling with her hairdresser, the First Lady did not list Julius's name on the manifest of Air Force One, and when reporters started calling Jerry Zipkin the "First Fop," she kept his name off publicized guest lists, which was her way of dealing with press criticism.

"Once I got a suicidal call from a father who had telephoned the First Lady in desperation," said Shirley Watkins. "His wife had been killed by a drunk driver, and he had two teenage daughters who couldn't function without their mother. He felt his life was over. As a minister's wife, I don't ignore threats of suicide, so I wanted to get this man's name and address and keep him on the phone, but people on the staff kept telling me to hang up—'Get rid of him. Hurry up. What's in it for you?' We'd been instructed to get people off the phone as soon as possible, but this was not a kook call. This was someone who needed help, but before I could get his name, one of Mrs. Reagan's secretaries got so irritated with me for talking to the man that she picked up the phone and deliberately disconnected the line. I was heartsick about it, and to this day I still don't know whether or not that poor soul took his life, because he never called back.

"He might've been an excellent candidate for one of the Great American Family Awards dreamed up in 1983 to honor outstanding families who enhance the quality of daily life in their communities. The families were flown to Washington courtesy of some airline, put up free in a hotel, and given a dinner and taken sightseeing. Then they were brought to the White House, where Mrs. Reagan would give them their awards. The White House calligraphers had to make toe cards for her every time she appeared in public so she would know where to stand. Then she read a little speech off her five-by-seven cards about how much her own family meant to her—she had to have everything written out for her in advance —and sometimes she'd cry a little bit when she said that. Then she'd pose for pictures with the winners, who would be served refreshments afterward with their guests, but she would never stay and mingle with the families. Actually, the annual event was more a public relations tool to enhance her image than anything else because she was the honorary chairman every year, and all the local television stations showed up to cover their local families getting an award from Mrs. Reagan at the White House. All the public ever saw was a lovely smiling actress on stage acting the role of a First Lady who was honoring the backbone of America. They didn't see behind the scenes.

"The ceremony was arranged every July with K. Wayne Scott of the American Family Society, but in 1987 the White House would not give him confirmation, and by June he was frantic because traveling arrangements had to be made for the families, many of whom have lots of foster children. He called me and I told him to call Mrs. Reagan's chief of staff and say that if the White House could not confirm, that he'd call Mrs. Bush and have the event at the Vice President's house. I knew *that* would bring them around faster than anything because Mrs. Reagan couldn't stand Mrs. Bush, who was a very warm and caring person. We were always supposed to be on guard that Mrs. Bush didn't outshine Mrs. Reagan or invade her territory in any way. I remember several times when Jim Rosebush called Susan Porter Rose, Mrs. Bush's chief of staff, to say that he didn't want Mrs. Bush attending some political event because Mrs. Reagan wasn't going to be there and he didn't think it would look right for the Vice President's wife to be in attendance when the President's wife was not.

"That kind of dissension was prevalent on Mrs. Reagan's staff, which was full of rivalries, back-stabbing, and petty jealousies. Sheila Tate couldn't stand Jim Rosebush and he couldn't stand Mike Deaver, and nobody liked anybody very much. There was constant turmoil, immense self-promotion, and a great deal of turnover. I worked for three different chiefs of staff, three different social secretaries, and when I left four years later only five people working for Mrs. Reagan had been there when I was first hired. There was no loyalty because everyone was out for himself. I guess that kind of thing filters down from the top, which is probably another reason why Nancy Reagan could never acquire the beloved status of Eleanor Roosevelt."

Outside the White House, the First Lady's rehabilitated image proved quite effective as the honors and awards rolled in, extolling what they described as her compassion and humanity. The executive director of Second Genesis, a nonprofit residential drug-and-alcohol treatment program, praised her as a "national treasure" for her leadership in the fight against drug abuse. The Salvation Army of Greater New York honored her with its annual Citation of Merit. The Red Cross International Service Committee gave her a medallion. The United Service Organization of Metropolitan Washington made her their annual Woman of the Year. Phoenix House, a residential drug rehabilitation center for teenagers, presented her with a special award for fighting drug abuse. Pepperdine University in Los Angeles gave her an honorary doctorate for her commitment to public service.

The days and weeks spent courting the press had paid huge dividends for the First Lady.

"We made every effort to have Mrs. [Katharine] Graham and Meg Greenfield get to know Nancy Reagan better," said Nancy Reynolds.

The effort the First Lady put into her private lunches with Mrs. Graham, the chairman of the board of the Washington Post Company, and Miss Greenfield, the editor of the *Washington Post*'s editorial page, was not wasted. When Nancy sponsored the First Ladies Conference on Drug Abuse, which brought together the wives of the leaders of seventeen foreign countries to publicize the global nature of drug abuse, it paid off handsomely: The *Post,* one of the most influential newspapers in the country, praised her effusively:

> Nancy Reagan has done something extremely right. She has
> thrown herself into the fight against drug abuse with vigor and intel-

ligence. If she had been shopping for a worthy cause, she might have picked a homier, more heartwarming or more photogenic one. Instead, she picked a relatively ungainly and untended one where her particular contribution could be of special value: to display a personal commitment and to use the public's, the media's and even the bureaucracy's inevitable interest in her to draw others to the cause. The conference that Mrs. Reagan is running is a good illustration of her work. . . . Does it make a difference in the end? How can it not make a difference for the idea to spread that drug abuse compels the alarm and the informed attention of responsible women like these. . . . For using the resources of her position to increase [personal warmth and shared purpose], Mrs. Reagan deserves gratitude.

Even before that laudatory editorial appeared, the word had seeped into the newsroom of the *Washington Post* that Nancy Reagan was lunching frequently with Katharine Graham, and *Post* reporters got the message.

"It suddenly became clear we were not to take swipes at Nancy Reagan," said Lee Lescaze, who covered the White House for the *Washington Post*. "I was never told specifically to do or not do stories . . . but we were aware of those private lunches, and what followed was a kind of atmosphere of: enough is enough; she's not running the country."

20

THE POOR BOY FROM BAKERSFIELD, CALIFORNIA, had traveled a long way from his childhood dream of becoming an Episcopal priest, and there were some who felt that Mike Deaver had sold his soul to the Devil. Until 1984, the deputy chief of staff of the White House dominated the circles swirling around the First Lady as surely as Rasputin had controlled the czarina. The holy man of Russia finally fell at the hands of noblemen, while Deaver annihilated himself. His downfall was caused by a scandal of his own making, resulting from greed and arrogance that would send him tumbling from millions to bankruptcy.

The power emanating from what Harry S Truman once called "the great whited sepulcher of ambitions and reputations" had enticed the forty-two-year-old White House aide when he arrived in Washington in 1981. As the gargoyle guarding the door for Nancy, he held the kitchen cabinet at bay, telling Holmes Tuttle that the President was too busy to see him, blocking Justin Dart from the Oval Office on Nancy's orders, and even, on occasion, barring Walter Annenberg. He intercepted requests for speaking engagements and invitations from leading conservatives, such as William F. Buckley, and pursued instead the First Lady's priorities: movie stars, socialites, and royalty.

"All of that would have been tolerable, I suppose—silly, but tolerable —had the son of a bitch not courted Ronald Reagan's political enemies as well," said archconservative Paul Weyrich, viewing Deaver from his own perspective. "Thanks to Deaver and the First Lady, it was liberals and

Democrats who got invited to the White House by the first conservative President in fifty years, not the people who put him there."

The Republicans invited to state dinners and private parties in the family quarters of the White House were often liberal members of the party, such as David Rockefeller and Henry Kissinger. And other guests included such liberal Democrats as Katharine Graham.

"Mike wanted in with that liberal group of people," said a former Deaver aide. "They were the power elite, the society people that he wanted to associate with. Mike loved Katharine Graham. He used to tell me, 'She is the best friend we have in Washington.' He was so enamored with her as the publisher of the *Washington Post* that no one could make him see that her newspaper was not too kind to the President. Mike didn't care. He just wanted to go to her parties."

The son of a gas station owner who lived on the poor edge of the Mojave Desert, Deaver became a social mountaineer. In Washington, he was assiduously courted for his access to power; there he was no longer a mere house servant. For the first time in all his years with the Reagans, he experienced the rush of receiving his own engraved ecru invitations. To maintain equal footing with his betters, he became as obsequious as Uriah Heep, all thin lips and crocodile smile; with his lessers, he was as heartless as Scrooge. Political conservatives gnashed their teeth over the people he and the First Lady selected for presidential honors.

"A White House ceremony for the Robert F. Kennedy Medal? Inviting Ethel Kennedy to a state dinner? Refusing to attend the twenty-fifth anniversary party for the *National Review,* but showing up at Ted Kennedy's house for a fund-raiser for the John F. Kennedy Library? C'mon," said one conservative Republican. "This was done because Nancy and Deaver wanted to be accepted by the ruling class, which, unfortunately, in Washington is dominated by Kennedy Democrats. Deaver even got Warren Beatty invited to the White House for a dinner and a private screening of *Reds,* his movie glorifying communism, and Warren Beatty was an active supporter of George McGovern and Gary Hart."

In 1983, the Reagans paid homage to the legacy of the Kennedys by allowing the South Lawn of the White House to be used for a benefit for the Special Olympics. "I gather even Jack Kennedy would not allow that," said the First Lady proudly. The Reagans also invited the family and friends of Robert F. Kennedy to the White House Rose Garden to present the senator's widow with a medal Congress had authorized in 1978 "in recognition of the distinguished and dedicated service which her late husband gave to the government and to the people of the United States." The medal took two years to make and was not delivered to the White House until the fall of 1980 when Jimmy Carter was President.

"When we found out that it hadn't been given when it *should* have been given, well . . ." sniffed the First Lady, leaving no doubt that the Reagans were righting a grievous wrong committed by the Carters.

Nancy extended several White House invitations to Jacqueline Kennedy Onassis, who had accepted only once since her husband's assassination, and that was during the Nixon administration. Mrs. Reagan tried in June of 1981 by inviting her to the Ethel Kennedy presentation of the medal in the Rose Garden, but the former First Lady declined. Instead, she was represented by her children.

"Nancy wanted to get Jackie to the White House in the worst way possible, but Jackie would never come," said a member of Mrs. Reagan's senior staff. "She invited her to tea, dinner, lunch, anything. She wanted to rub up against that. Bad."

Nancy Reagan had tried to emulate the former First Lady's style from the minute she moved into the White House. She had started by consulting Letitia Baldrige, the Kennedys' former social secretary, who suggested she hire Muffie Brandon as White House social secretary. That set off reverberations in the personnel office.

"Helene von Damm, who was in charge of ideological purity in the early days, went to the mat over that appointment," recalled one of the First Lady's secretaries. "She went to see Nancy and said, 'No, no, absolutely not. Brandon is a Kennedy liberal Democrat and she doesn't deserve to be the social secretary of *our* White House.' But Mrs. Reagan, who hoped that some of the Kennedy panache would rub off on her, paid no attention. Muffie was up for membership in the Women's National Democratic Club at the time, so when Mrs. Reagan gave her the appointment, she [Nancy] asked her to withdraw her name so she wouldn't upset any of the 'extra-chromosome conservatives,' as Nancy called them, who were acting 'so silly,' as she said, about the appointment. Muffie quickly withdrew her name and didn't join the Women's National Democratic Club, but Helene was still incensed."

In November 1981, the First Lady extended another invitation to Mrs. Onassis when the Reagans invited Rose Kennedy, ninety-two years old, to visit the White House, but again Mrs. Onassis said no. The Kennedy matriarch accepted, though, saying she was honored by the invitation. She arrived with her son Ted to thank the President for presenting the Robert F. Kennedy medal five months earlier. In appreciation, she gave him the handwritten notes from a speech that John F. Kennedy had delivered to the National Football Foundation.

In 1983, J. Bernard West, the former White House usher who served under six presidents, including John F. Kennedy, died, and Jacqueline Kennedy Onassis called Mrs. Reagan's chief of staff to ask whether the

President would allow West to be buried in Arlington National Cemetery. Unless the White House recommends otherwise, Arlington accepts only career military people, their spouses, or recipients of military awards, and West did not qualify.

"When Jim Rosebush told Nancy that Mrs. Onassis had called him about the White House usher, Nancy went a little nuts," said an aide. "'Well, why would she call you?' she said. 'Why didn't she call me?' Rosebush handled the matter, but Mrs. Reagan called Mrs. Onassis back and said she would be more than happy to make all the arrangements. Then she quickly leaked it to the press that Jackie had called her."

Mrs. Reagan's press secretary quoted her as saying that she and Mrs. Onassis talked for ten minutes. "They both expressed an interest in meeting each other," said Sheila Tate breathlessly. "Mrs. Reagan said, 'We called each other Jackie and Nancy, even though we've never met. We feel like we know each other.'"

The First Lady had to endure a long wait before meeting the predecessor she so admired. A year later, the two children of John F. Kennedy called to invite the President and Mrs. Reagan to attend a fund-raiser for their father's library. Knowing Jackie would be there, Nancy accepted instantly. On that evening, at Senator Edward Kennedy's home in McLean, Virginia, Nancy and Jackie posed for a photograph. A high point came when President Reagan delivered a stirring speech, describing John F. Kennedy as a man whose magic had captured the country.

"And when he died, when that comet disappeared over the continent, a whole nation grieved and would not forget. A tailor in New York put a sign on the door—Closed Due to a Death in the Family," said the President. Reagan and his wife had thrown a cocktail party in their Pacific Palisades home the weekend of Kennedy's death. Now President Reagan wanted to close the distance between himself and the Democrat who had lived in the White House for a thousand days. So as the oldest man to be elected President of the United States, Reagan praised the youngest to his family and friends, saying that Kennedy's time was too short, but as a man of hope and history who personified the spirit of his times, his legacy would live forever.

With tears in her eyes, Jacqueline Kennedy Onassis approached Reagan after his speech, and, touching his arm, said in her breathy voice, "Mr. President, nobody ever captured him like that. That was Jack."

Nancy Reagan beamed. Nothing better exemplified the synergy of her marriage than that particular moment when her husband made possible her sweetest fantasy. And nobody understood better than Mike Deaver. He knew that the feat could never have been accomplished without

Nancy's wifely ambition, which drove her husband to open the doors she longed to walk through.

Deaver was not a political ideologue who had signed on with Ronald Reagan because of commitment to conservative politics. He was part of the inner circle because he had made himself indispensable to Mrs. Reagan, who worked her will through his accommodating manner. Together, they presided over the White House, dictating the President's schedule, shaping his policies, and choosing his personnel, including his ambassadors. Together, they rewarded their friends and punished their enemies.

"Once Nancy got rid of Helene von Damm as ambassador to Austria, she put Henry Grunwald in because he was married to a New York socialite friend of hers, and when Grunwald left Vienna, Ronald Lauder got the post because he was the son of her good friend Estée Lauder," recalled a former Deaver aide. "She appointed Lee Annenberg as chief of protocol, but then made Deaver get rid of her when Lee became too important. Henry Salvatori, who wanted to be ambassador to Italy, didn't have a chance because Nancy couldn't stand him, and so, of course, Deaver couldn't stand him either, despite the millions he had contributed to Reagan's political career over the years. With an eye toward his future, Deaver made Joseph Reed III the ambassador to Morocco as a favor to David Rockefeller; he put Greg Newell in as assistant secretary of state and he wasn't even a college graduate, but he was young and pretty; he appointed Richard Burt to be ambassador to West Germany and made liberal Republican Drew Lewis special envoy to Canada to work on the problem of acid rain. These were just some of the people he later used to launch his own business when he left the White House."

The First Lady and her Mr. Fix-it spent hours discussing various guest lists, dispensing White House invitations to those they deemed worthy. Hollywood's right wing was represented by Charlton Heston, Efrem Zimbalist, Jr., Pat Boone, and Buddy Ebsen, along with such aging alums from Metro-Goldwyn-Mayer as Ginger Rogers, Ann Miller, Ernest Borgnine, Debbie Reynolds, Eva Gabor, Esther Williams, and June Allyson. Television sitcom and soap opera stars were included—Henry Winkler of "Happy Days," Michael J. Fox of "Family Ties," Joan Collins of "Dynasty," Michele Lee of "Knots Landing," Linda Gray of "Dallas," Don Johnson of "Miami Vice."

"The only celebrity to turn the Reagans down was Bill Cosby, who said that since he did not agree with the President politically, he would not accept his social invitation," said Shirley Watkins. Gregory Peck, a liberal Democrat, attended a Reagan state dinner in 1984, but was never asked back after he opposed the President's nomination of Judge Robert

Bork to the Supreme Court and recorded television spots opposing Senate confirmation.

"I came to the conclusion that having that guy on the Supreme Court would be the beginning of turning back civil rights—and I felt it was time to step up to bat," said Peck. "I don't think it was my spots that defeated him. What gave them so much importance was when Marlin Fitzwater [White House press secretary] said publicly that President Reagan regarded me as a 'former friend.'"

Other names, such as Jessica and Henry Catto, were never even considered for a state dinner list because the First Lady automatically crossed them off. "They don't rank," she said of the multimillionaire couple, who were fervent supporters of George Bush. "We don't need them." Required to invite the Vice President and his wife to all state dinners, she refused to include their friends and vetoed all suggestions to invite the Bush children as well. She also refused to invite her own children. One exception: Maureen Reagan, who was rewarded with several invitations after her work in the 1984 reelection campaign. That was a turnaround from 1980, when Maureen and her fiancé, Dennis Revell, were prohibited from riding in the same car as the Reagans, and the First Lady wanted to exclude Revell from inaugural photos. Mrs. Reagan disliked inviting journalists to state dinners but was told that inviting one or two White House correspondents was mandatory, so she reluctantly agreed, but barred their spouses. "Why waste two seats?" she said. Reporters objected so strenuously to being treated like scullery maids that she rescinded her order. She wanted to cross off Danny Kaye's name from the Queen's Hollywood gala but was restrained by palace aides, who pointed out Her Majesty's affection for the comedian.

After she got to the White House, Nancy Reagan put as much distance as possible between herself and the Californians—except for "the girls," who had helped launch her husband's career. "She considered [the other Californians] social boobs," said one of her social secretaries. "She was more interested in flying to New York and having lunch at Le Cirque with Gloria Vanderbilt and Brooke Astor than socializing with Ursula Meese or Joan Clark." Nancy never treated the wives of Ed Meese and William Clark as friends during their eight years together in Sacramento, and the distance became even more pronounced in Washington, D.C. The wives were never invited to the White House family quarters. Their husbands saw the upstairs of the White House only when they delivered papers to the President.

Surprisingly, few among the kitchen cabinet were invited to White House state dinners, the most coveted invitation in America. Of the eighty dinners held by the Reagans in their eight years, the William

French Smiths attended three, the Justin Darts two, and the Henry Salvatoris only one. That compared feebly with the thirty-six attended by the Michael Deavers and the Jim Bakers. When the guest lists were submitted, the First Lady regularly crossed off the Holmes Tuttles. "Later. We'll have them later," she would say as she struck them in favor of one of her dress designers.

"The Tuttles had not been invited to the White House, except for one state dinner [Australia, June 30, 1981], and they only got that invitation because Lee Annenberg called and demanded it at the last minute," said a Tuttle relative. "They were invited to the President's seventy-fifth birthday party, but that was it, and they probably contributed more money over the years to Ronald Reagan's political career than anyone else. They helped buy the Reagans three houses—the house in Sacramento, the house in Bel Air, and the White House, but Nancy never once said thank you."

Mrs. Reagan felt her obligations to the Tuttles had been discharged when their son, Robert, was put in charge of White House personnel, and his wife, Donna, was made undersecretary of commerce for travel and tourism. "Putting his son . . . into the White House was a sop to Holmes, but every single one of those personnel appointments went upstairs to Nancy, so Bob Tuttle had no power whatsoever," said a member of Mrs. Reagan's senior staff. "He simply rubber-stamped all her approvals and rejected all her rejects."

A few years before Holmes Tuttle's death in 1989, the wealthy eighty-four-year-old automobile dealer speculated on the odious treatment he and his wife received from the First Lady. "Years ago [after she behaved badly], I took Nancy out for a long walk in 1976 at the ranch and said, 'Oh, Nancy, you can't behave this way. You simply cannot,' " he said. " 'Oh, Holmes, I'm so sorry,' she said, but she always resented me telling her this, and we paid for it through the years. But at least we got Ronnie to be President, and that's all that really mattered."

"We despaired over the White House guest lists because they were filled with people who were invited solely to attain social prestige for Nancy Reagan or enhance Michael Deaver's future job prospects," said Faith Whittlesey, former ambassador to Switzerland, who earlier had worked in the White House. "There was never a feeling that we should invite people to show our appreciation for what they had contributed to Ronald Reagan, or for building a future, lasting political coalition as he headed toward the reelection campaign. I remember one Columbus Day, we wanted to have the President celebrate with the Knights of Columbus and the Sons of Italy, but they weren't fashionable enough for the Nancy Reagan–Mike Deaver–Jim Baker axis, which preferred surrounding the

President with Italian movie stars and Italian dress designers, which is exactly what happened."

With the power he derived from the First Lady, Deaver ruled his White House fiefdom like a little despot, denying gymnasium privileges, parking places, and passes to the White House mess to "extra-chromosome conservatives" who he felt were too partisan. In advancing trips for the Reagans, he roamed the world in the President's airplane, traveling as regally as the chief executive himself. "I was with him on a lot of those trips," said a Deaver aide, "and when we'd land, Mike would make the staff get off the back of the plane while he got off the front alone just like the President. He bought whatever he wanted at great discounts and flew all the stuff back at taxpayers' expense on military planes. In Hong Kong, he met Y. K. Powell, the rich shipowner, and so because of Mike, Powell went to three state dinners and was in and out of the Oval Office frequently. Powell even brought his own camera crew to film himself with the President. Reagan got mad at one point and said, 'How many times do I have to meet with this guy, Mike?' Deaver held private wine tastings with Bill Plante, the White House correspondent for CBS, in his office to select the best vintages for all the state dinners, and he used the White House tennis courts to cater to CBS-TV executives and other people who became his clients once he left the White House."

Early in the administration, the pudgy Deaver became as obsessed with dieting and exercise as was the First Lady, who had taken off ten pounds in the fall of 1983 to try to reduce the size of her legs. When people noticed the weight loss, she attributed it to worrying about the assassination attempt on her husband in 1981 and her father's death in 1982, but that was not true.

"Mrs. Reagan was obsessed about her legs and constantly dieted to try to reduce their size," said one of her doctors at Bethesda Naval Hospital. "After she lost ten pounds and went from 115 to 105, she told me, 'I've tried everything but there's nothing I can do about them. I exercise and diet constantly.' I can tell you that she does diet constantly. She's anorectic. So much so that the White House doctors were worried stiff about her. The only reason she was dieting was to lose those heavy legs, but she couldn't do it, although she religiously rode her exercise bicycle every morning while watching the news. You'll never see her in a bathing suit. She's too self-conscious about her thighs and her calves."

The First Lady starved herself into dizziness that caused her to topple over. Her falls—at the 1984 Republican convention, in a hotel room during the 1984 campaign, during a photo session with Archbishop John O'Connor in 1984, on the steps of the President's helicopter in 1985, off the East Room stage of the White House in 1986, putting a log on the fire at Camp David in 1986, on the red carpet at the Vatican in 1987—caused speculation. "I wondered if she was on some kind of medication," said one of her senior staff. "She always had so much energy that I thought maybe she was on amphetamines to curb her appetite."

Deaver became as fixated as the First Lady on the subject of weight, and together they frequently went on dieting binges. Attempting to curry favor with the deputy chief of staff, several White House aides scrambled to work out with him in the White House gym.

"I witnessed this ritual once and nearly got sick," recalled a presidential assistant. "I had gone to the executive gym for a shower and shave before going to a Christmas party, and Deaver was in there with Bob DeProspero, head of the Secret Service presidential protective division, working out with weights. After my shower, I walked into the dressing room to shave, and Mike was standing in front of the mirror, completely naked. He turned to me, pointed to the muscle on the back of his arm, and asked what it was called. I told him it was his tricep. He rubbed it for a moment, complaining that it hurt. He turned to DeProspero and yelled, 'This muscle really hurts!' Patronizingly, Bob said, 'You must've had a good workout, Mike.'

"Deaver continued staring at his body in the mirror while he primped, flexing his triceps every few seconds as if to confirm the workout had been a success. He had been using the weights for two years and had lost fifty pounds, but I thought he looked worse than when he started because he was kind of thin and spindly-looking . . . but he always bragged that when she first met him, Jacqueline Kennedy Onassis had said, 'Oh, you look so svelte. Like a young Fred Astaire.' He claimed that Angie Dickinson put her hand on his leg, too, but I always found that hard to believe."

One of the men who accompanied Deaver on his ritualistic forays to the gymnasium was Bill Sittman, who had worked at the State Department doing advance work for Jimmy Carter. "That in itself made a lot of political people in the White House crazy, because he didn't seem to be a Reagan Republican, but Mike didn't care. He made him an assistant to the President, and the two of them became great buddies," said a Deaver aide. "In fact, he and Sittman were so close that Mike took up cigarettes because Sittman smoked. He started wearing Polo cologne because Sittman wore it, and then he got the same kind of tortoiseshell glasses that Bill had. On the road, they had rooms next to each other and they watched videos together all the time. They were so inseparable that the Secret Service made sick jokes about it."

Deaver complained he could no longer support his family on his White House salary of $72,000, but he ordered a $90,000 Bosendorfer, the ultimate in pianos, to be air-freighted from Austria and drove a $50,000

Jaguar. Convinced that the President would be resoundingly reelected, he and Sittman decided to resign after the second inaugural and start their own political consulting business. "Everybody in this town is out to make a buck," Deaver said.

While the rest of the White House was gearing up for the 1984 campaign, the Reagans acted coy about whether the President would seek reelection. During a fit of pique in her first year in the White House, the First Lady had said she had no interest in a second term. "Let's just finish up the first four years and all go back to California," she said. She changed her mind once she climbed off the bottom of the popularity polls. After the midterm election in 1982, she and the President decided they would run again despite the loss of Republican congressional seats, the recession, the rise in unemployment, and the polls showing that if Reagan ran under prevailing conditions, just about any Democrat could beat him. During 1983, the First Lady cross-examined the President's political operatives to reassure herself that her husband could be reelected. "How *is* it out there?" she would ask. "Can he win or not?"

In October 1983, the President signed documents authorizing formation of a reelection committee but decided to delay the announcement as long as possible. And to pinpoint the right time for the announcement, the Reagans relied on the divination of their astrologer, Joan Quigley.

"They wanted to make the announcement in early December, but I did not like the astrological indications for December of 1983," said the astrologer. "I persuaded them to wait until the end of January 1984, when I had found a time as near to perfect for entering a contest as any I have seen in all the many years I've practiced astrology. The chart was not only superb in itself, it accorded with the President's horoscope so amazingly that I felt if he declared his intention to run at the time I chose, he was a cinch to win the election."

The astrologer selected 10:55 P.M., just before the late night news, on Sunday, January 29, 1984, as the perfect time. That morning, the First Lady, still playing the coquette, decided to heighten the suspense by issuing an ambiguous statement from the White House: "It was a mutual decision. I support him fully. I'm very proud of him and all he has accomplished in a very short space of time."

That evening, she sat in the Oval Office with Maureen Reagan and her husband, Dennis Revell, Chief of Staff Jim Baker, and presidential speech writer Ken Khachigian, who had followed the Reagans' directive by writing a statement that would milk the suspense until the very end.

"It's been nearly three years since I first spoke to you from this room," the President said solemnly. "Tonight I'm here for a different reason. I've come to a difficult personal decision as to whether or not I should seek reelection." He recounted the mess he had inherited from Jimmy Carter, the wonders he had wrought, the dreams he held for the future. Then he looked into the camera with avuncular ease and asked the country for its continued support so that he and Vice President Bush could serve the public for another four years.

"All the usual suspects signed on for that last roundup, with Laxalt theoretically in charge and Stu Spencer actually running things in concert with Mrs. Reagan," said one political operative. "The first thing we had to do was bolster the President's foreign policy posture after the October [1983] bombing in Beirut, where 241 Americans were killed. He pulled the marines out of Lebanon after that, but the Democrats were already squealing about the number of U.S. casualties. The President sent troops to Grenada [1983] to topple the Marxist government there, so we planned the man-of-peace trip to China in April of 1984—his first to an 'evil empire' country—and then sent him off to the economic summit in London in June, to Ireland to do his bit in Ballyporeen—after all, there are 40 million Irish-Americans who can vote—and then to Normandy [June 1984] for the fortieth anniversary of D-Day, where he could stir souls by saluting 'the boys of Point de Hoc' . . . the men who took the cliffs."

The First Lady accompanied the President on all the trips, but now she was "kept under wraps" so there would not be a repeat of the unfavorable press coverage she had received before, especially in England.

The U.S. embassy staff in Ireland was dumbfounded when the imperial First Lady arrived with her personal dresser and *two* hairdressers in tow "in case one got sick."

"Advancing a trip that included the First Lady was always hard, because you had to have the right kind of suite, all the right magazines, and all the flowers that she liked, but the biggest requirement was providing enough working space for Julius, her damn hairdresser," said presidential assistant Bill Henkel. "That queen was the biggest pain in the ass in terms of his requirements, and he bedeviled me for years about everything. The amount of energy and anticipation we spent figuring out how to keep Julius happy is something that I'm not exactly proud of, but it had to be done because a happy hairdresser meant a happy First Lady, which meant a happy President. Since Julius was not charging the First Lady for his services, he expected to be treated well, and if he wasn't, God help us all!"

Mike Deaver, who advanced the trips, insisted on $300,000 worth of "painting and prettying up" in Ireland. His painting directive included Reagan's ancestral Town of the Little Potatoes, better known as Ballyporeen, which Deaver specified be decorated with the Irish tricolor and

the Stars and Stripes as well as a network of stiles and stairways to make
sure that the Reagans, who would visit for two hours and fifteen minutes,
saw only approved step dancers. Deaver directed that the twenty-eight-
inch-high bed in the Ashford Castle Hotel, where the Reagans would
stay in County Mayo, be lowered by four inches. In Dublin, he arranged
for the First Lady to unveil a portrait of her late stepfather, who had been
inducted into the Royal College of Surgeons there.

In Galway, he persuaded the National University of Ireland to confer
an honorary doctorate on the President. But the results were not as
anticipated. Many of the people who had been honored previously by the
university met to burn their parchments publicly in protest against Reagan. The angry crowd of demonstrators included Nancy Reagan's second
cousin.

"I demonstrated against Reagan because I considered him to be the
most frightening man ever to hold the presidency," said Marian Robinson, who was a visiting professor at University College, Galway, at the
time. "I am appalled and terrified by his foreign policy and especially his
stand on nuclear warfare. . . . Nancy is a dreadful woman without a
thought in her head. A frozen face . . . but her husband is just terrifying . . . because he lives in this kind of make-believe B-movie world.
The idea of giving Ronald Reagan a degree of any kind is ludicrous
because, whatever he is, he's no intellectual."

In England, Deaver tried to make sure that the President's meeting
with summit leaders would not be overshadowed by press coverage of
his wife's social schedule with members of the royal family, so he allowed
the First Lady only one public event—a trip to the London Zoo, where
he wanted her photographed with "underprivileged" children. This he
hoped would balance her visit with Princess Diana at the palace the day
before. Nancy had given a birthday present to the two-year-old heir to
the British throne—a two-foot-high rocking horse with a silver plaque
that read: "To Prince William of Wales from the President of the United
States and Mrs. Reagan, June 21, 1984." The year before, she had sent
the year-old prince a Chippendale chair with a needlepoint seat done by a
member of her staff. That gift also carried a silver plaque bearing greet-
ings from the Reagans.

The underprivileged children at the zoo received brown-bag lunches
from the First Lady with a chicken leg, potato chips, a piece of fruit, and a
Coke.

"It was all so bloody patronizing," said John Shephard, one of the
nursery school teachers involved in finding the appropriate children.
"We were told Mrs. Reagan wanted to get some orphans to pose with,

but we don't really have any orphanages anymore. It was just one big electioneering stunt."

The forty-one children bused in from the borough of Southwark were dazzled by the First Lady with all the American flags waving around her, the crackling Secret Service walkie-talkies, the whirring of photographers' motorized cameras, the bustling newspaper reporters with tape recorders, and the television correspondents with their boisterous camera crews.

"Oh, she is a queen. She is in charge of America," said nine-year-old Jason Tomkins of Boucher School, Bermondsey. "It is great to meet her."

"She's going to run for President," said another awestruck child.

The reelection campaign was very much on the President's mind. He tried to bring a White House photographer to his lunch with the Queen at Buckingham Palace. "No, this is a private occasion," said Her Majesty, refusing to be drawn into the presidential campaign.

The Democratic convention would not take place until July, but months before that, the politically astute First Lady had picked Walter Mondale as the nominee. In October 1983, polls had shown that if Senator John Glenn (D-Ohio) were nominated, he would beat Ronald Reagan, but Nancy had said the former astronaut would never get the nomination because he was "too boring."

"The one guy who shook her up was Gary Hart," recalled John Roberts of the President's reelection staff. "He looked like a comer in some of the early primaries, and until Mondale knocked him off, Nancy was scared to death because she said he was young, handsome, and Kennedy-esque."

She was not too worried about the "jowly" man from Minnesota because he had been Jimmy Carter's Vice President for four years, but when Mondale picked Geraldine Ferraro as his running mate, Nancy agonized that the Democrats would capture the female vote.

Stu Spencer tried to dissuade both Reagans from watching the Democratic convention in San Francisco, knowing they would not react well to the bashing they were sure to receive, but Nancy could not help herself. She sat riveted to the television set every evening. Hearing Jesse Jackson say that Franklin Delano Roosevelt in a wheelchair was better than Ronald Reagan on a horse made her blood boil. She got furious at Tip O'Neill's ridicule and became splenetic listening to Teddy Kennedy. She called Senator Laxalt the next day. "Did you *hear* all that?" she asked, fulminating about the "string of cheap shots at Ronnie," especially the remark Kennedy made about the President's summoning his helicopter. "All he has to do is push a little button. I just hope it's the right button," Kennedy had said. The First Lady ranted about the "inexcusable" remark, but the President dismissed the Massachusetts senator as a carnival barker and said he did not consider Ferraro worthy of competition. "She steps on her own lines," he said. "She can't wait for the applause moment."

The eloquent governor of New York was another matter. Listening to Mario Cuomo's vigorous keynote address incensed Ronald Reagan. It was he who called Laxalt the next day. "He was really out there kicking my brains in last night," said the President, who felt he had been accused of everything from gross stupidity to killing nuns in Central America.

The First Lady was more troubled by Mondale's acceptance speech. "I had never heard the word *family* mentioned so often," she said. Most hurtful to her were the insinuations that she and her husband were not the loving parents that they had represented themselves to be. One humorist said that Mike Deaver was so close to the Reagans that he was often described as being like a son to them—"something that has never been said of any of their own children."

Although she and the President had not spoken kindly to Michael Reagan in three years and had yet to see their new grandchild, who was sixteen months old, she still resented criticism suggesting that they were cold and uncaring about their family. Because of that, and because it was an election year, she decided not to ignore her daughter Patti's wedding in California in August. Initially, Nancy had refused to announce the engagement of the thirty-one-year-old woman to her twenty-five-year-old live-in yoga instructor, hoping that they would break up and he would move out of her Santa Monica apartment. So the couple made their own announcement by posing for *People* magazine in body-revealing bathing suits and saying they did not want to have children.

"I'm not looking forward to jumping into fatherhood," said the fiancé, Paul Grilley. And Patti chimed in, "I've never had a particularly strong desire to have a baby," adding that she might like to adopt a child someday.

The tension of Nancy's relationship with her daughter had not subsided with age or distance. They continued to wrangle over everything, including Patti's politics, which were outspokenly liberal. Like her idol, Jane Fonda, Patti believed in a woman's right to abortion, said her mother was "silly" to advocate arresting marijuana users, and campaigned fervently against her father's military buildup, even appearing at antinuclear rallies to voice her opposition. The first time she had done this her mother had issued a statement from the White House saying she felt Patti had been used.

"I don't know what her motives were in saying that," said Patti. "The most visible group at that time was the Alliance for Survival, and *I* called *them*. I don't feel I've been used by anyone. I have very strong opinions, and if I choose to speak out on those opinions, I will."

Hoping to engage her father in a talk with an impassioned but knowledgeable antinuclear activist, Patti had invited Dr. Helen Caldicott to Washington to meet the President on December 6, 1982. The night before, Reagan left a letter on his daughter's pillow at the White House.

"Patti, I think we should keep this a personal visit," he wrote. "I won't be saying anything to the press about it and I don't think you or the Dr. should either. That way they can't get into any stories about family disagreements, etc."

The meeting disappointed all the participants.

"It was a disaster, just a disaster," Patti admitted many years later. "I realized afterward that there could never be any way to communicate with him on these issues and that I had to give up the illusion and stop trying."

Dr. Caldicott, an Australian pediatrician who had been affiliated with the Harvard Medical School, had been shocked by her meeting with the President. "He said the Russians were evil, godless Communists. . . . He quoted some material saying the nuclear freeze movement was orchestrated by Russia and that we were KGB dupes. I looked at him and said, 'That's from the *Reader's Digest.*' He shook his head and said, 'No, it's not; it's from my intelligence files.' " Dr. Caldicott later found the material in the *Reader's Digest.*

Angry at the young physician, Reagan refused to shake her hand when she left, which embarrassed Patti.

"She was very ashamed of her father's rudeness," said her agent, Dolores Robinson. "Then Nancy got mad at Patti for upsetting her father. It took them quite a while to get things back on track again."

Five months later, Caldicott delivered the commencement address at the University of Massachusetts and accused the President of believing that the United States could engage in a nuclear war with the Soviet Union and win. Nancy showed the newspaper story to the President, who again wrote to Patti:

. . . As you know her words about my believing we could win a nuclear war were never part of that visit in December. (I don't believe such a thing.) So her speech is a complete falsehood both as to having a conversation with me at all and as to the subject of the supposed conversation.

It isn't easy to learn we've misplaced our faith & trust in someone. I know. I've had that experience once with someone I thought was my closest friend. But when it happens we must be prepared to accept it & not shut our eyes to the truth.

There was a time in ancient days when a messenger bringing bad news was put to death. I hope you won't call for my execution. I'm afraid the Dr. is so carried away by her cause she subscribes to the belief that the end justifies the means. Such a belief if widespread would mean the end of civilization. Love Dad.

Patti was not looking forward to her father's reelection campaign. "I wish he wouldn't run," she said. "I wish he'd go live on the ranch." Much as she loved him, she said, she would not campaign for him, nor would she ever vote for him. "I never have. I'm a registered Democrat," she would acknowledge in 1989.

But now, saying that all she had ever wanted Ronald Reagan to be was a father, she asked him to give her away in marriage. She surprised everyone by choosing a fairly traditional wedding ceremony and wearing a white gown and a veil. She had a bridal shower and, at her mother's suggestion, registered for china and silver.

Insisting that hers was to be a "private" wedding, she said that meant no press, no politicians, no celebrities. "I certainly don't want a Prince Charles and Lady Diana sort of wedding and I can't think of anything worse than getting married at the White House. I just don't feel particularly comfortable there." She chose the garden of the Bel-Air Hotel for the ceremony.

Taken aback by her daughter's comments, Nancy recovered quickly by saying, "I think a wedding should be what the bride wants it to be." However, the full-page photograph in *People* of Patti wearing a skimpy bathing suit and an ankle bracelet and doing a back bend with her fiancé, who wore only a little Speedo bikini, so offended the First Lady's sensibilities that she immediately took over the wedding preparations. She dictated the menu, ordered the flowers, and made arrangements with the Reverend Donn Moomaw to perform the service. She summoned White House press secretary Larry Speakes and instructed him on how she wanted things handled for the event, telling him to ban reporters from the Bel-Air Hotel on the day of the ceremony.

"Mrs. Reagan and I discussed when she should send out the invitations for the August wedding, who was on the guest list, and where the wedding was going to be," said Speakes. "She wanted to be sure that it would be depicted as a family wedding with Patti's friends, instead of a grand state occasion with the princess getting married, which is what happened when Johnson and Nixon had daughters get married while they were in the White House. Patti didn't fit the image of a princess at all."

Still concerned about the public reaction to her daughter's comments, the First Lady told her staff to issue a fact sheet on how much the gala White House weddings of Alice Roosevelt, Luci Baines Johnson, and Tricia Nixon had cost. Pointing out that eight sons and daughters of Presidents or Presidents-elect had been married outside the White House, the fact sheet added gratuitously that seven of those marriages were later "dissolved by divorce." By 1990, Patti Davis's would become the eighth.

By June, the First Lady's press secretary was briefing reporters, saying that the guest list would be confined to 130 people who were important to Patti, but not divulging the names of Norman Cousins, a holistic health advocate, and Harold Willens, a leader of the nuclear freeze initiative. Instead, she cited the Reagans' Pacific Palisades housekeeper, Ann Allman; the former California state trooper who drove Reagan as governor and now worked on the ranch, Barney Barnett; Patti's godmother, Colleen Moore; Patti's dentist, Paul Schick; and A. C. Lyles, the Paramount producer who was the first family friend to visit Patti in the hospital after she was born. Lyles told a member of Mrs. Reagan's staff how over the years he had tried, with little success, to get Patti work playing her guitar in wine pubs. "It's very hard," he said, "because she can't sing."

Mrs. Reagan insisted that "the group" be invited to the wedding, which meant sending invitations to the Annenbergs, Deutsches, Jorgensens, Tuttles, Salvatoris, Smiths, Wilsons, and Betsy Bloomingdale. Her own family was more problematical. Ron Reagan was invited, as was his wife, Doria, who was one of Patti's two attendants, but Maureen and Michael Reagan were not included, although the First Lady told her press secretary to say that they and their spouses had been invited but could not attend. No one had thought to invite the Neil Reagans, which Nancy learned to her embarrassment when she telephoned her brother-in-law on July 1.

"Nancy had called to speak about the wedding," said Neil Reagan, "and when I told her we hadn't been invited, there was dead silence. Since then, we've gotten our invitations. I guess some aide is now walking around with fried hair."

The Reagans were on vacation at their Santa Barbara ranch two weeks before the wedding, so the First Lady sent her social secretary, Gahl Hodges, to Los Angeles to oversee the preparations that she had set in motion.

"I remember there was a big problem over who would pay for Gahl's expenses," said Shirley Watkins. "The White House lawyer said that the wedding was not a presidential activity, so the taxpayers should not have to pay for it. But Mrs. Reagan argued that Gahl had to be there because she needed someone to make sure the wedding was orchestrated perfectly. I think in the end she made the Republican National Committee pay for Gahl. When Gahl came back, she had nothing favorable to say about the groom. She described Paul Grilley as a 'spacey, off-the-wall, yoga-type person,' and said that Mrs. Reagan wasn't happy at all about the marriage but was very cordial to the Grilleys and did all she could to make it nice for them."

"The wedding went off without a hitch, although the press wasn't too happy about being banned from the hotel at the Reagans' insistence," recalled Larry Speakes.

"My mom said the wedding was terrible," said the child of one of the Reagans' closest friends, "but they all agreed that the yoga instructor was better than the rock musician. Everyone in 'the group' has kids they care about and talk about and socialize with, except for the Reagans. Their kids are never, and I mean never, included in anything like the rest of us. I haven't seen Patti since she was a little girl, Ron's never around, and Maureen and Michael don't count because Nancy doesn't consider them her children. I'm over the age of thirty and I can't remember a time when Nancy was not having problems with Patti. She [Nancy] was always talking about what a problem Patti was. My parents and their friends have said that the greatest heartache for the Reagans will be that they will never have any grandchildren. It's just understood or assumed, and quietly whispered, that Ron Jr. is gay and Patti, as we were told years ago, can't have children as a result of her abortions. So in a sense that wedding was bittersweet for everyone."

A week later, the Reagans flew to Dallas for the Republican National Convention, where the starlet and the B actor would finally achieve top movie billing for the first time in their lives.

Two gauzy films, produced by Phil Dusenberry, co-creator of *The Natural* with Robert Redford, were shown to introduce the President and First Lady to the convention. The $450,000 cinematic paean to the President was so touching that the first time he saw the eighteen-minute film tribute, he cried. But the First Lady was not moved by her celluloid homage, which she saw before the convention. On the contrary, she summoned the campaign managers to the family quarters of the White House and lectured them for an hour on the deficiencies of her movie, demanding that it be reshot and lengthened from six minutes to twelve minutes. Two staffers later objected, saying that it would not be fitting to give the President's wife almost as long a salute as the President had.

"That's what the First Lady wants," said Mike Deaver.

After a week of delicate negotiations, a compromise was struck for an eight-and-a-half-minute film followed by Frank Sinatra singing "Nancy with the Smiling Face." Sinatra's song served as background music for the President, who said, "Everywhere we go, Nancy makes the world a little better. I can't imagine life without her." The film then showed the couple strolling hand-in-hand toward the sun-dappled woods on their ranch. As they were walking out of view, their backs to the camera, Mrs. Reagan lifted her leg playfully and kicked her husband in the rear. That split-second kick in the keister, to borrow the President's word, unwittingly revealed the essence of the Reagans' marriage.

Nancy Reagan had been figuratively booting her husband's rear end for years, but always behind the scenes—and out of camera range. She recently had instructed his top aides to prepare complete scripts for the President so he would know exactly what to say during meetings. The scripts, written on four-by-five index cards, were labeled "suggested talking points," but they were explicit: "Let me start by saying thanks to all of you for coming today." When the President met Senate Majority Leader Robert C. Byrd and other senators who had returned from a trip overseas, his cue card read: "Bob, I appreciate you and your colleagues coming down today." Among the suggested talking points: "Bob, I want to thank you especially for undertaking this and for handling your discussions over there so effectively." And then, leaving nothing to chance, the President was directed to say: (1) "I want to thank all of you for your input." (2) "Can you tell me more about your efforts?" (3) "God bless you all."

The First Lady's efforts had become more overt because she sensed something that most people would not admit for many years: Ronald Reagan seemed to be mentally slipping. He was less alert, more obviously disengaged. He greeted Sugar Ray Leonard and Mrs. Leonard as "Sugar Ray and Mrs. Ray," he called Chairman Doe of Liberia "Chairman Moe," referred to Senator Don Nickles as "Don Rickles," Paul H. Nitze as "Ed Nitze," poet Emma Lazarus as "Emmett Lazarus," and greeted HUD Secretary Samuel Pierce as "Mr. Mayor." Most embarrassing to Nancy was the White House dinner when the President intro-

duced the Prince of Wales and "his lovely lady, Princess David." The
ballerina sitting next to Sir Peter Ustinov gasped.

"What? Did he *really* say Princess David?"

"Don't worry," whispered Ustinov. "He's just thinking of next weekend at Camp Diana."

At first, Nancy attributed these lapses to his deafness or his fatigue
from being overscheduled. Some of the lapses were minor, like the recent political rally at which she had to point out where the American flag
was. A few were attributable to ignorance, like his comment to the National Religious Broadcasters Annual Convention in which he tried to
ingratiate himself with Jews by noting one of their religious holidays. "In
December, I would see the huge menorah celebrating the Passover season in Lafayette Park," he said, substituting Passover for Hanukkah.

Other lapses were more frightening, such as when reporters had asked
him at the ranch what he was doing about U.S.-Soviet talks on space
weapons, and how he planned to negotiate with the Russians. He paused
and gestured but was unable to speak, as if the gears of his brain had
locked. He stared straight ahead, looking confused and uncomprehend-
ing. The First Lady, standing next to him, leaned in close and, barely
moving her lips, whispered, "Tell them we're doing everything we can."

"We're doing everything we can," echoed the President.

This was far from the first prompting that Nancy Reagan had had to
give her husband, but it was the first to be picked up by television cameras. Shown on the national news, it made the seventy-three-year-old
President look like an old man teetering on senility.

Back during the last week of the 1980 campaign, when reporters asked
Reagan if he expected to win, he said, "You know me. I'm too superstitious to answer anything like that." But Nancy nudged him and whispered, "Cautiously optimistic," and so he quickly echoed her. "Yes, I'm
cautiously optimistic."

Sometimes, though, he was too cautious for her. During a television
interview on the White House lawn on July 19, 1983, he was asked
whether he would fire the culprits who had stolen the papers Carter used
to prepare for his 1980 debates with Reagan. Reagan hesitated and stammered, "Well . . . I . . . ." Standing next to him, the First Lady repeatedly and emphatically nodded, leaving no question that there would be
full-scale firings if anyone was caught.

One weekend, as he was returning from Camp David, the President
was asked about the situation in Tehran, where passengers of a hijacked
Kuwaiti airliner were being held hostage. The President hesitated, obviously at a loss for words. The First Lady prompted him, "Nothing new
on Iran, no." So the President told reporters, "No, nothing new." Mrs.

Reagan later told her press secretary that the President couldn't hear the question.

Nancy was always concerned about the President's image. In the fall of 1983, during a picture-taking session at the ranch, the President was romping with Patti's frisky mutt, Freebo, in a playful tug-of-war over a ball. The photographer focused his lens, but the First Lady jumped in front of the camera.

"Don't!" she told her husband.

"Why not?"

"Because it may look like you're being mean to the dog."

The President dutifully dropped the ball.

Now, in 1984, facing the last important political challenge of his life, Ronald Reagan was uninvolved and uninterested in the campaign, and so the First Lady took over. For weeks she had been treating convention staff members as if they were inmates weaving brooms. She hectored them about what they should do and when they should do it, who should be given the convention spotlight, who should be allowed on the platform, and for how long. She invited Joan Rivers to the convention to entertain 2,000 women because she thought the comedienne's risqué humor would show that Republicans were not stuffy. Determined to demonstrate that the GOP had not abandoned blacks, Nancy saw to it that Pearl Bailey was invited, and urged that Roosevelt Grier, former football player and a Robert Kennedy Democrat, be booked on morning television shows to talk about his born-again Christian conversion to her drug-abuse campaign.

After the convention, she became obsessive about the campaign, so much so that campaign manager Ed Rollins dreaded hearing the telephone ring, fearing it would be Mrs. Reagan with yet another demand.

"One day she called him fourteen times," said a Rollins aide, "and he was almost in tears."

Again the First Lady phoned, this time asking why there was no campaign office in Beverly Hills.

"Beverly Hills?" said Rollins, incredulous.

"My friends in Beverly Hills want to volunteer for the campaign, and they can't find an office there. I don't think that's very smart, do you?"

"Mrs. Reagan, we felt that we could carry Beverly Hills without opening a campaign office there, and we wanted to spend the money in other places, like [Mondale's home state of] Minnesota, where we could possibly get one more state in our column if we allocate the funds carefully."

Dead silence on the other end of the line. Rollins got the message. He assured her that an office would be opened immediately for her friends in Beverly Hills. Later, he complained that the $1 million spent to appease the First Lady had probably cost the President Minnesota, which Mondale won by only 3,761 votes.

The first time Rollins tried to reassure Nancy by citing polls showing the President could not possibly lose the election, she laced into him for being lazy, complacent, and overconfident. The next time, he took the polls to her that showed Ronald Reagan at the peak of his popularity with Americans for restoring the economy and bolstering military defense. "For your sake, you better be right," she said menacingly. "You better be right."

A month later, the First Lady read a California press poll showing only four percentage points between the President and Mondale; again, she called Rollins, this time in a panic. He told her the poll was wrong, but she would not believe him. "That damn poll cost me another million dollars," said Rollins, "because the First Lady demanded emergency phone banks and door-to-door canvassing."

Nancy summoned Rollins to the White House with Mike Deaver and campaign aides Lee Atwater and Stuart Spencer; she interrogated Rollins at length. The campaign manager knew better than to respond, so he sat silently taking her abuse. As they were leaving, Spencer whispered, "She smelled fear all over you, Rollins!"

Stu Spencer's time came a few days later when Geraldine Ferraro questioned Ronald Reagan's Christianity. Leaving church in Elmore, Minnesota, Ferraro had been confronted by an antiabortion protester carrying a placard asking: "What kind of Catholic are you?" A reporter had asked the Democratic vice presidential candidate how she felt about the sign.

"Who is anyone to judge whether or not I am a good Catholic?" she said. "If you take a look at the policies of the administration when it comes to budget policies and concern and fairness for others, the President walks around calling himself a good Christian. I don't for one minute believe it, because his policies are terribly unfair; they are discriminatory, and they have hurt a lot of people in the country."

Within seconds, the First Lady, who was watching Ferraro on television, was on the phone to Spencer. "I want you to get that woman any way you can," she said. "You get her! Do you hear me?"

Spencer hung up and turned to his aide. "What've ya got on Ferraro? Let's get going. We've got a customer."

"We then mounted a very serious effort to look into every public record we could lay our hands on pertaining to Ferraro's family business," recalled the aide. "All the FEC [Federal Election Commission] records from her past campaigns, who her contributors were. We went as deep into her background as we could, and probably the best story we developed was that her mother and father did not have a nickel-and-dime store like she said, but ran a nightclub in Newburgh, New York, where her father had been arrested for numbers running. She was only nine years old at the time and probably didn't know what had happened, but we gave the story to the *New York Post* and they printed it full page. That's the story that made her cry when she read it on the campaign plane."

The story also reported that on the morning Ferraro's father was supposed to appear in court, he dropped dead. His death notice had been altered at the request of the undertaker, leading to what the newspaper called a "mystery."

On the Phil Donahue show, Ferraro said that her family's background had been unfairly explored. Watching the show in Chicago with a reporter, Mrs. Reagan scoffed. "They've gone into all our pasts," she said. She blamed Donahue for stirring audience sympathy for the vice presidential candidate. "You're in no doubt as to how Phil Donahue is going to vote," she said. "Phil is a Democrat, and it's a very biased show."

The First Lady's demands remained so intrusive throughout the campaign that she had people running in all directions to do her bidding, bumping into one another trying to satisfy her.

"I remember when we were in Michigan, she called me and said her jewelry box was missing," said an aide. "I said I would call Air Force One, the usher's office, the Secret Service, and the military aides to check on it for her. Seconds later, I saw Ed Hickey running off to call the White House operators. Next her Secret Service man, George Opfer, came charging out to radio Washington. Then Elaine Crispen and Jane Erkenbeck rushed in to work the phones. Suddenly, the whole White House switchboard was jammed and no calls were coming in because the First Lady had appropriated all the lines to try to locate her jewelry box, and no other business could be done. That's how Nancy operates. She involves everyone because she trusts no one, and by pitting us all against each other she just might end up with her jewelry box on *her* time schedule, which is always *right now!*"

Her happy-go-lucky husband was content to bounce along from city to city, bashing the liberal Democratic ticket, while remaining aloof from the friction she was creating around him. Soon, though, even he noticed the trouble she was causing on Air Force One, but never one to confront a problem, he did nothing.

"He simply hid behind his newspaper," said an aide. "I think he was as afraid of her as we were. Things got so bad that Deaver finally approached the President, but Reagan refused to come out from behind his newspaper. So Deaver sent for Stu Spencer, which is like calling in the marines. Stu has no fear and nothing to lose.

" 'Goddamnit, Ron, Nancy's on a fucking tear. You've got to do something,' Spencer said, but the President still would not lower his paper.

" 'Yo, Ron,' said Spencer, rattling the newspaper. 'This is serious. You've got to get your wife off this plane before everyone goes for the parachutes.' Finally, the President peeked out.

" 'You do it,' he said, putting the newspaper in front of his face again.

"So Spencer went to Nancy and told her that she was such a valuable campaigner on her own that she was wasted traveling with the President. 'You've become such a powerful force in this country through your drug-abuse campaign that we need you campaigning on your own schedule so the Reagan magic can be spread around, and reach more voters.' She bought it, of course, and we gave her a separate schedule. That's when she insisted on having Frank Sinatra accompany her to various fund-raisers. It cost the Republican National Committee $500 a month to hire Joe Canzeri simply to babysit Frank Sinatra to accompany the First Lady, but at least we got her out of the President's hair."

The First Lady's anger spilled over on everyone, even the fair-haired Deaver, who broke down late one night in California. Drunk and sobbing, he told her that he could no longer put in twenty-hour days.

"I'm cracking up," he said. "My marriage is suffering and my wife'll leave me if I don't get out. . . . I don't know what I'm doing anymore."

Mrs. Reagan, wrapped in a bathrobe, looked at him.

"Well, Mike," she said, "if Carolyn can't keep up with us, leave her."

Days later, the First Lady almost came unhinged watching the first presidential debate on national television. Her husband seemed to self-destruct. His telegenic gifts were crushed under a raft of incoherent sentences, incorrect statistics, and rambling, disjointed statements. He said in that Louisville debate there was "no connection" between the deficit and interest rates, and he attributed the guarantee of "life, liberty and the pursuit of happiness" to the Constitution, rather than the Declaration of Independence. He once again trundled out his old "There you go again" one-liner, just like the prosecuting attorney in Otto Preminger's *Anatomy of a Murder;* the retort had worked effectively when he debated Carter in 1980, but now Mondale turned it against him. Reagan then cited a "Democratic governor" of California who had signed a bill into law requiring that a man who abuses a pregnant woman so as to cause the death of her unborn child shall be charged with murder. The "Democratic governor" was a Republican: Reagan.

Worse than the inaccuracies sputtered by the seventy-three year old President was his pathetic, head-bobbing, bumbling performance. He looked as if he had been stricken with Parkinson's disease. It terrified the First Lady, who knew that 125 million Americans would watch the two presidential debates and probably vote accordingly. Recognizing that Reagan had, in his own words "blown it," she bawled out his senior staff, blaming them for "overloading" him with statistics and "brutalizing" him with facts and figures.

"What have you done to my husband?" she demanded of Mike Deaver, who was as flabbergasted by the President's doddering performance as everyone else.

While the First Lady blamed the President's aides for his poor performance, the Reagans' astrologer blamed herself—for choosing the wrong time and place. "I really goofed in my choice for the first debate," said Joan Quigley. "It was the only time I failed the Reagans or gave them less than excellent advice. My choice for that debate, instead of emphasizing Mondale's lack of charisma, as I had intended, livened Mondale up and gave him pizzazz. My choice for the second debate, however, ensured that Ronnie would emerge victorious."

After the Gallup poll for *Newsweek* showed that 54 percent of the American public thought Mondale had won the first debate and only 35 percent gave it to Reagan, the First Lady took over preparations for the second debate. She instructed Deaver at excruciating length, and he dutifully instructed Jim Baker, Dick Darman, and David Stockman that their exhaustive statistic-laden rehearsals in the family theater of the White House were over. The First Lady said she would allow them "only a few meetings" at Camp David to prep the President, and these had to be "positive, lighthearted stroking sessions" preceded and followed by "lots of jokes."

"You have to build him up, boost his ego, tell him all the good things he did," she said.

Behind his back, the President's top advisers ridiculed him for being inept and complained that he had no agenda for a second term. But they assumed that voters would be gullible enough to support him on the strength of stage-managed appearances, a test of which took place during the second presidential debate October 21, 1984, in Kansas City.

Coddled according to the First Lady's explicit instructions, and charged by stirring music that she had arranged to greet his arrival, Ronald Reagan walked away from this debate as the hands-down winner.

The President was ready and when one of the reporters raised the dreaded subject of his age, suggesting he might not be competent enough to retain the highest office in the land.

Anticipating that question, the President had rehearsed his spontaneity. "I will not make age an issue of this campaign," he said with a twinkle in his eye. "I am not going to exploit, for political purposes, my opponent's youth and inexperience." Even Mondale laughed.

The First Lady later stepped onstage to take a bow for her behind-the-scenes manipulation. When a reporter asked her whether she felt she had made any substantive changes in preparation for the second debate, she smiled and said, "Well, the second one was better, wasn't it?"

Still refusing to accept any of the polls showing that Reagan would win, she fretted that the campaign staff was not doing enough, and pushed them daily to do more. In an attempt to woo FDR Democrats, she saluted Eleanor Roosevelt on the centennial of her birth with a luncheon at the White House. She invited the three surviving Roosevelt sons, two of whom, James and Elliott, promised publicly to vote for Reagan.

The Democratic presidential candidate resented this "grave-robbing" gesture. "You don't honor Eleanor Roosevelt by cozying up to racists in South Africa and dictators in Latin America," said Mondale. "You honor her by standing up for human rights everywhere in the world."

Feminist leaders picketed the White House, calling the Reagan administration's policies on civil rights and women's rights "an affront" to Eleanor Roosevelt's memory. The President's self-styled feminist, Maureen Reagan, watched the women demonstrate up and down Pennsylvania Avenue. She got angry.

"Those people out there are never going to get into this house," she said, "and that's why they're upset."

The First Lady praised Eleanor Roosevelt as "a truly great American lady who always seemed larger than life to me." Reading from her three-by-five index cards, Mrs. Reagan said: "No person's problem was too small to attract her attention—and today we can only guess at the scale of her generosity because so much of what she did was without fanfare and in secret. . . . You couldn't help but be a fan, whether you were a Republican or a Democrat didn't make any difference. But I wasn't politically involved at that time—politics never entered my mind until my husband and now—three more weeks, four more years."

The salute to Eleanor Roosevelt played well on the evening news but did not win over the *Washington Post* editorial page. The newspaper enthusiastically endorsed Mondale for President a few days later, praising him as "a serious, steady, bright, decent, qualified man who wants to be President and who should be."

That endorsement, which appeared on October 29, 1984, stunned the First Lady. After so many personal lunches with Katharine Graham, Nancy took it as a personal affront to read the newspaper's assessment of her husband as "maddeningly indulged and overpraised" and a man who, "by all evidence, genuinely does not understand the instability into which he has led the American economy."

But the *Post* had as much effect on the 1984 election as the placard-carrying feminists who had picketed the White House. No one paid any attention. Most Americans felt good about themselves and their country, which is why Ronald Reagan swept into office on November 6 with forty-nine states in his column, representing almost all categories of voters: young, middle aged, and elderly; low, middle, and high income; Protestant and Roman Catholic; professional and blue collar. And women, too, who voted in overwhelming numbers for the President. They did so despite his stand against abortion, child care, and the Equal Rights Amendment.

The landslide did not inspire either the President or the First Lady to be magnanimous in victory. The President refused to salute his opponent, and the First Lady vowed to get even with her enemies.

"We've swallowed enough and taken enough," she said after the election night victory party in the Tower of the Century Plaza Hotel. "From now on, we're going to do it our way."

The first to feel her bile was the chairman of the board of the Washington Post Company. For the next eight months, Nancy would not speak to Katharine Graham. Finally, in July of 1985, Mike Deaver, who had left the White House but was still advising the First Lady, urged her to make up. He said she must let bygones be bygones because the *Washington Post* was too powerful to have as an enemy. So Nancy accepted an invitation from Meg Greenfield to lunch with her and Katharine Graham at Greenfield's house in Georgetown. Later, at Deaver's suggestion, Mrs. Graham invited the First Lady to join the Deavers at her home on Martha's Vineyard. Nancy, ecstatic, accepted immediately. But her decision to go irritated her chief of staff.

"You can't just take an air force plane and personnel to Martha's Vineyard because you want to spend two days at Kay Graham's house," said Jim Rosebush. "At least, let me set up a drug event in Boston, Massachusetts, so you can legitimize the plane for official business." Mrs. Reagan agreed, reluctantly.

"I had advised Kay not to invite a bunch of Republicans Nancy already knew," said Deaver, "but to invite people she wouldn't otherwise meet. Kay outdid herself."

The guest list included Jackie Onassis, who had a house on the Vineyard; Meg Greenfield; Mike Wallace; Warren Buffet, the billionaire CEO of Berkshire Hathaway; Walter Cronkite; Ruth Gordon and Garson Kanin; Beverly Sills and her husband, Peter Greenough; Margaret Jay, the former wife of British ambassador Peter Jay; Carter's Secretary of

State, Cyrus Vance; Kennedy's Secretary of Defense, Bob McNamara; attorney Edward Bennett Williams; Anne Buchwald, the wife of humorist Art Buchwald; William Styron; Henry Grunwald, whom Nancy had made U.S. ambassador to Austria, and his wife, Louise Melhado.

"Jackie and I were at the same table," Nancy Reagan wrote in her diary that evening, "and I invited her to the White House [again] to see the changes. She said she prefers not to return to Washington, but if she changes her mind she'll let me know."

That was the last invitation the First Lady extended to Jacqueline Kennedy Onassis. "They did not become soul sisters," said Deaver. "Nancy had always respected and liked her, once was in awe of her, and welcomed the chance to see her under quiet circumstances at the Vineyard. At one point, Jackie said, referring to the press snipping, 'You're going to be there [the White House] a long time; you might as well get used to it.'

"Her respect for John Kennedy's widow has not lessened," said Deaver, "but I think the awe is gone, a reflection more of Nancy Reagan's new public confidence than anything else." Still, he admitted how thrilled the First Lady had been to socialize with Katharine Graham's friends on Martha's Vineyard. These were the people whose social acceptance she craved. "Nancy always wanted to know what these people were like and what they said," he recalled. "She was the little girl with her nose pressed up against the candy-store window."

21

THE BIG BRIGHT RONALD REAGAN BALLOON bobbing along the American skyline began leaking air in 1985. The first pinprick was the loss of Jim Baker as White House chief of staff after the inaugural. He switched jobs with Secretary of the Treasury Donald Regan. The exchange, which was Regan's idea, was blessed by Mike Deaver, approved by Nancy Reagan, and finally accepted by the President, who was the last to know.

The First Lady wanted the entire cabinet to submit their resignations at the start of the second term, but the President resisted.

"Nixon did it," she argued. "He requested written resignations from all his top appointees the day after his reelection."

"And look what happened to his second term," said the President.

Reagan knew his wife was trying to get rid of some of his favorite people: presidential counselor Ed Meese, who, having barely survived a bruising inquiry into his personal finances, was to be appointed Attorney General; Secretary of the Interior William Clark, whom she deemed too conservative; and Secretary of Labor Raymond Donovan, who was under a federal grand jury investigation in New York. She also wanted to dump Secretary of Defense Caspar Weinberger, who she felt was "too militaristic"; Secretary of Health and Human Services Margaret Heckler, who was going through a messy divorce; and Office of Management and Budget director David Stockman, for stating openly that Reagan's economic policies would never work. But the President turned off both of his hearing aids and asked all his appointees to stay in place.

Clark and Stockman soon resigned, as did Donovan, who was indicted but later acquitted. Meese went to the Justice Department and Weinberger remained at the Pentagon.

"You see, I don't win them all," she said, trying to downplay her influence on her husband.

In the midst of the reshuffling, Deaver was trying to cushion the First Lady for his May 1985 departure from the White House. He started by sharing some of his "Mommy" responsibilities with presidential assistant William Henkel, who was in charge of the White House advance team.

"Mike had to have someone inside the White House to get his ticket punched to get out of there," said Henkel, "so my relationship with the First Lady began in January of 1985 when he started the process of making me him in her eyes, especially with regard to scheduling, which meant having to tell me about the astrologer."

The disclosure that the President and First Lady relied on the clairvoyant musings of such a person, referred to as "Joan in San Francisco," dumbfounded the presidential assistant. But Deaver reassured him that this astrologer, as opposed to the many he had had to deal with over the years, was at least sensible.

"Look, you should've had to deal with some of the others, especially Jeane Dixon," he told Henkel. "Then you'd know that at least this one is not totally out of her mind."

Henkel had questioned Deaver's sanity in the past for the strange last-minute changes he had made in the President's schedule, the odd hesitations and unusual delays, the peculiar times for arrivals and departures, the conflicting instructions he'd issue one day and countermand the next. "Now I finally understood the reason for all that craziness," Henkel said. "We had a good laugh about it, but then I realized that I would have to come up with the same asinine excuses that Mike had used, and develop the same creative cover stories for what the First Lady wanted done without telling anyone why she wanted it done."

The Reagans' reliance on Joan Quigley's computerized stargazing was a tightly kept secret within the White House. During the first term, it was known only to Deaver and Baker in the West Wing and Elaine Crispen in the East Wing. With the changing of the guard in 1985, more people had to be entrusted, including the new chief of staff, who was incredulous at first. "Stunned is more like it," said Don Regan many years later.

Fearful of anyone else finding out about her dependence on astrology, the First Lady did not even trust the White House switchboard. Afraid that operators might eavesdrop, she had the telephone company install a private line that bypassed the switchboards in the White House and at Camp David, where she carried on most of her conversations with the astrologer.

"If Nancy had to talk to the astrologer during the week, she had to pay extra," said Henkel. "I know because I caused a scheduling screw-up once, and she had to call during the week. She was so mad she wanted to charge me. She kept saying, 'This is costing me extra money because of you. This is costing me extra.'"

Every weekend, Henkel was paged on his beeper, a sign that the First Lady was trying to reach him and was ready to do business. Sitting in her cabin at Camp David with a phone in each hand—Joan Quigley on one, Henkel on the other—Mrs. Reagan began charting the President's schedule. Nancy proceeded on a day-by-day, hour-by-hour basis, sometimes fine-tuning arrivals and departures to the minute. She'd get the coming activities from Henkel and relay them to Quigley, who would check each date on her zodiac chart to see whether the stars predicted a good day or a bad day for the President. On the "bad" days, he was not to leave the White House because, according to the seer, he would be harmed; Henkel would have to propose alternate dates. The three of them would go back and forth for hours, with Henkel keeping scrupulous notes of each session so he could avoid "the threat days where you had to be careful," and capitalize on "the good days—the okay-to-travel days." Once the President's schedule was worked out in these three-way telephone sessions, Henkel would give the schedule to the Secret Service, the White House chief of staff, and the President's secretary so they all could mark their calendars accordingly. The procedure so confused Don Regan that he kept a color-coded calendar on his desk with green designating "good days," red for "bad days," and yellow for "iffy days." The President's schedule was then made up and resubmitted to Mrs. Reagan for final review. That way she knew what he was doing at all times.

Occasionally, the President upset things by spontaneously announcing that he wanted to go somewhere not sanctioned by the stars, like the opening game of the baseball season in Baltimore.

"That happened to be on one of the astrologer's 'bad days' when he [Reagan] was confined to quarters," said Henkel, "but I'll be damned if I'm going to tell the President of the United States that he can't go to a baseball game when he wants to. Don Regan came in after the staff meeting to tell me that the President wanted to roll in an hour, so I contacted the Secret Service and off we went to handle security arrangements at the stadium. En route, my buzzer started beeping and the commands came crackling over the radio that I was to call the switchboard immediately. I knew that it was the First Lady, so I radioed back on the Secret Service channel that I would call when I got to my destination. I didn't even say where that was, but by the time we got to the stadium, the President's secretary, Kathy Osborne, had told her what was happening.

"God, was she apoplectic when I called her back. She was just beside herself. 'Oh, Bill, how could you do this? You know better than to ever do something like this. How could you? You know that this is a black day.'

"I tried to explain that it was an unplanned, last-minute decision on the President's part, something that he had insisted on doing, and there wasn't much I could do to stop him. But she said, 'I don't care. You should've stopped him. You know better. You can't possibly secure the whole stadium. You should never have let him leave the White House.' Then she made the statement that really made my blood run cold. 'If anything happens to my husband today, I'll hold you responsible for the rest of my life. Do you hear me? I'll hold you responsible.'

"You don't know what pressure is until the First Lady tells you that the President's life is in your hands, that if anything happens to him, and he dies, *you* are his murderer. God, I was a walking zombie for the next two hours until we got him back to the White House safe and sound. Then I tried to stay out of her hair for the next few days."

Like dogs scampering under the bed during a thunderstorm, presidential aides scrambled for cover at the first sign of a Nancy storm.

"Deaver warned me about being too quick to answer any of her questions," said Henkel. "She's like a prosecutor with those questions of hers, and he said that a quick answer would snakebite you later, so the best thing to say was, 'I'll check it out and get back to you.'"

The Nancy storm grew into a howling gale when the news was released that her husband planned to visit the little cemetery in Bitburg, West Germany, in May of 1985 as part of the fortieth anniversary of the Allied victory in Europe. This visit was scheduled during the Economic Summit in Bonn.

The President had rejected making a ceremonial trip to a German concentration camp because his wife vetoed the trip as "too negative and depressing." So he promised instead to visit a cemetery that had been checked out by Henkel and Deaver. What they—and he—didn't know was that the cemetery held the graves of forty-nine Nazi storm troopers. Even after he was told, Reagan insisted on honoring the site. He was widely condemned for his insensitivity to the Holocaust, and Jewish groups in the United States, Europe, and the Soviet Union demonstrated against him. Many World War II veterans returned their medals, and a French newspaper gave him an "F in history."

Reagan responded by compounding his mistake. "We have to put the past behind us," he said. "The soldiers [buried in Bitburg] were victims, just as surely as the victims in the concentration camps."

Hearing the President of the United States equate the villains with the victims suggested to some Jews that he saw no difference between war and genocide. This provoked further bursts of outrage, including two resolutions introduced in the House of Representatives asking him not to visit the cemetery, coupled with a similar resolution signed by fifty-three senators.

The President's men tried to offer as rationale that Bitburg had been suggested by West German chancellor Helmut Kohl, who needed the visit as a U.S. gesture of reconciliation in order to win reelection. Without Kohl's Christian Democrats in power, they maintained, the United States would not be allowed to place missiles in Germany, and that would strategically cripple the President, who felt he could not negotiate with the Russians except from a position of strength.

Despite the political explanation, most people remained aghast that the President of the United States could be so obtuse about lending the prestige of his office to such a cemetery. Reagan, who fancied himself a hero to the Jewish people, could not understand the outrage.

In 1983, he had told Israel's prime minister, Yitzhak Shamir, that he had been an army photographer assigned to film the horror of the Nazi death camps. Two months later, he had spun the same fantasy for Simon Wiesenthal, the Nazi hunter for whom the Center for Holocaust Studies in Los Angeles is named. In 1985, six days before he went to Bitburg, he assured a group of foreign journalists that he was quite familiar with the Nazi SS because he had served in World War II. "Yes, I know all the bad things that happened in that war," the President said. "I was in uniform four years myself."

Historian Arthur M. Schlesinger, Jr., suggested Reagan had merely been in costume. "Mr. Reagan in fact is the only American president who was of military age during the Second World War and saw no service overseas," he wrote in the *Wall Street Journal.* "He fought the war on the film lots of Hollywood, slept in his own bed every night, and apparently got many of his ideas of what happened from subsequent study of the *Reader's Digest.*"

Elie Wiesel, who grew up in the death camps and lost his parents in Auschwitz, accepted the Congressional Gold Medal of Achievement from Reagan in April and then pleaded with him on national television not to lend his presence to a German military cemetery.

"May I, Mr. President, if it is possible at all, implore you to do something else, to find a way, another way, another site. That place, Mr. President, is not your place. Your place is with the victims of the SS."

Nancy feared the strong response to this eloquent man (who was to win the Nobel Prize in 1986 for his work in behalf of Holocaust victims) and was furious at him for shaming her husband.

"It's that man [Wiesel]," she told her astrologer. "He acts like he's crazy. It's his fault. He's a fanatic."

Yet she, too, pleaded with her husband to cancel the trip to the cemetery because the polls showed that a majority of Americans disapproved of the President's decision to lay a wreath at Bitburg. The issue crippled the White House in the spring of 1985, becoming the first great crisis in the Reagan presidency.

The First Lady begged her husband to change his mind, but he refused; he said he would look as weak and indecisive as Jimmy Carter if he vacillated. Former President Nixon and former Secretary of State Kissinger backed him up in his resolve, as did Patrick Buchanan, the new conservative communications director of the White House, who earned the First Lady's enduring enmity thereby.

The editorial opposition to Bitburg was overwhelming. The *Des Moines Register* said, "President Reagan has trifled with tragedy." The *Los Angeles Times* agreed: "Those who protest the Bitburg trip do not seek to give offense. Their wish is only that the President of the U.S. do nothing that could be interpreted as memorializing or dignifying the agents of Nazi criminality."

Watching her husband's approval rating plummet in the polls—one of the barometers by which she navigated—maddened the First Lady, who now blamed Mike Deaver. "You've got to tell him he can't go," she instructed him. "It will ruin his presidency. He will never recover." She became even angrier when she read newspaper reports that while Deaver was in Germany advancing the Bitburg trip, he had purchased a BMW automobile at a special discount.

The President remained adamant about visiting Bitburg, so Deaver scurried around trying to soften the damage by adding events to the itinerary that would placate the critics. But the First Lady was not pacified. In an uproar over what she saw as the ruination of her husband's presidency, she stormed into Deaver's office and again demanded that he cancel the trip. Deaver, who had admitted his mistake countless times to the President and apologized profusely for it, now became embroiled in the first ugly confrontation he had ever had with Nancy Reagan. He later admitted it was "very painful" and "emotional" for both of them.

"How could you do this to Ronnie," she screamed at him. "This will haunt him forever."

"Nancy, it's done," he said. "If going into a panic would help, I'd panic. But I'm trying to do my damnedest to make the best of a very difficult situation. Let me get on with it, please."

The First Lady nodded her head and, without another word, walked out while he went to work trying to salvage something out of the mess. But Nancy never forgave Mike Deaver. When he left the White House three months later, he wanted to have his big farewell party in the presidential residence rather than the Roosevelt Room, which is used for such affairs. His request was referred to the First Lady. She refused to honor him in the President's private quarters. "The Roosevelt Room will be sufficient," she said.

To repair the damage of Bitburg, Deaver shortened the wreath-laying ceremony to eight minutes and inserted a side trip to the concentration camp at Bergen-Belsen, where Anne Frank had died. He also canceled the Reagans' hour-long picnic with the villagers of Bitburg and arranged instead for the First Lady to lay flowers on the grave of West Germany's revered first chancellor, Konrad Adenauer.

As another diversion, he scheduled a visit to a drug rehabilitation center in Bonn, where Mrs. Reagan would present a check for $5,000 to the West German counterpart of the National Federation of Parents for Drug Free Youth of Silver Spring, Maryland.

Deaver also figured that the First Lady's refurbished image would lighten the damage of Bitburg. A recent *Time* cover story had applauded her as a political asset to her husband, and an equally favorable NBC-TV documentary had praised her to the skies. So he arranged for her to discuss her drug-abuse campaign with Pope John Paul II in Rome. The next day, Deaver arranged for her to attend a flamenco dance performance in Madrid, where she gamely tried to learn a few steps with castanets. Both events provided photo opportunities meant to soften the coverage of Bitburg. The last stop on the itinerary was Strasbourg, France, where Nancy would be photographed visiting the Château Rohan Museum.

The First Lady had insisted that the timing of their visits to the concentration camp and the cemetery be synchronized with the stars, so Deaver submitted his revised schedule to Joan Quigley. She insisted that the trip to Bergen-Belsen be made at 11:45 A.M. on May 5, 1985, because of "the positive position of the planets." She said she picked 2:45 P.M. for the eight-minute ceremony at Bitburg because her charts of the zodiac indicated that "the moon and Saturn in the third house" were propitious while "Neptune on the angle of the chart veiled the occasion and dimmed it."

The newsweeklies featured cover photographs of the President laying a wreath at Bergen-Belsen, not at Bitburg. That reinforced the First Lady's faith in her astrologer, who had claimed that she would "fix up the Bitburg thing."

"My biggest problem on that trip was coping with Nancy's damn hairdresser," said White House photographer Terry Arthur. "We had one photographer flying with the President on Air Force One to Bitburg, and I was to follow on the press helicopter, but at the last minute I was bumped because Julius wanted to go and take pictures for himself. I said, 'Don't you think it's kind of crazy to deny access to the White House photographer whose job it is to record history just so the First Lady's hairdresser can get a look-see with his little Brownie?" I finally ended up shoving my way onto the helicopter and sharing a seat with Julius. That's when I learned that he was the most important person on any presidential trip, next to the First Lady's personal maid, Anita Costello.

"During a rest stop in Venice, the White House wanted to release a picture of the President working on his briefing papers, so I was sent up to the huge baronial estate where the Reagans were staying. I walked into that cavernous building filled with hundreds of rooms and could hear a blaring television coming from a hallway off the entrance. I peeked in and saw Julius and Anita sitting there watching Italian cartoons at full volume. It was so strange. I felt like I was prowling around one of those spooky places in *Last Year at Marienbad*.

"Finally, I saw Jim Kuhn, the President's personal assistant, who said the Reagans were upstairs, so I headed for this enormous room with high ceilings, ornate columns, and intricate tapestries on the walls. The President and First Lady are sitting there in the dark watching a videotape of an old cowboy movie on a huge television set. She's in her bathrobe and he's dressed informally.

"Jim says, 'Mr. President, Terry is here to take the picture of you working on your papers.'

"'Oh, well, I better get some papers then,' said the President, continuing to watch the movie.

"Jim handed him his briefing folder and led him to a table where we spread out the papers. He buttoned up his shirt and asked where he should sit. I pointed to a table in front of one of the elaborate tapestries and he sat down. He obviously didn't know what the hell the papers were all about, but he looked at them while I took the picture. He put the papers back in the folder, handed the folder to Jim, and returned to the couch with Nancy to watch the cowboy movie. I went back to move the picture on the wire showing the President of the United States hard at work preparing for the upcoming summit."

The official White House staff photographers shot 8,000 to 10,000 pictures of the President every month—300 or so a day, whether he was at home or away. Before they could be released to the press, the First Lady scrutinized them and marked those that she approved "O.K. per N.R." She forbade the release of all candids and any pictures that made the President look sleepy, old, or less than robust. But she never vetoed photos of him on a horse, despite his disjointed attire. Reagan favored riding on a western saddle wearing master-of-the-hunt boots, a cowboy shirt, and English jodhpurs.

"We submitted contact sheets to her of all his pictures, but on hers, we had to have eight-by-tens blown up of every shot," said Arthur. "She'd go through them all and tear the corners of those that were not flattering enough to release. So she, in effect, controlled the entire photographic history of the Reagan years."

The First Lady spent hours poring over White House photographs. "She had to okay any picture with her in it," said another staff photographer. "Each box of 250 photos, all eight-by-tens, at $20 to $25 a print, costs about $6,000 a box, and we would send over boxes and boxes to Mrs. Reagan every few days. Half of them would be returned with the corners chewed. She would not take the time to look at contact sheets. Everything with her in it had to be blown up. What a waste of taxpayer money that was!"

When Ronald Reagan underwent surgery on July 13, 1985, the First Lady refused to let any of the White House photographers near him for twenty-four hours. "I don't care about a historical record," she said. "I don't want his picture taken." Mrs. Reagan had instructed White House press secretary Larry Speakes that he was simply to announce that the President would undergo surgery for the removal of a polyp. He was not allowed to use the word *massive.*

"At Mrs. Reagan's behest," Speakes said, "there was no mention of the words *cancer* or *malignant.*"

The President signed over the powers of his office to George Bush before he was anesthetized for removal of the cancerous polyp. The First Lady saw to it that no picture was taken showing the tubes carrying antibiotics running into his veins, the intravenous feeding tubes in both arms, and the nasal tubes removing gas and liquid from his stomach.

"He can't be seen this way," she told the White House photographers. "We don't want people to know it's this bad."

Two days later, though, she agreed to let the White House release a photograph of the President that she had artfully staged. All the tubes were temporarily removed, with the exception of the nasogastric tube, which was held in place by transparent tape. The picture showed her leaning over to kiss him, her face cleverly concealing the nose tube.

The surgeons had removed one polyp of five centimeters, two smaller polyps, and two feet of the President's large intestine. Over the next three years, they would remove twelve more polyps from his large intestine and three skin cancers from his face. Dr. Steven Rosenberg, chief surgeon at the National Cancer Institute, participated in the surgery, and announced the results of the biopsy on national television.

"The President has cancer," he said bluntly. When the Reagans heard that news broadcast and saw the detailed diagrams of the presidential intestines, plus videotapes of a proctoscopic instrument probing the inside of a colon, they were upset. Reacting viscerally to the word *cancer,* both rushed to deny it, she to herself and he to the world.

"I didn't have cancer," the President told reporters. "I had something inside of me that had cancer in it, and it was removed."

"That surgery was a result of the President's not listening to his doctors," said one of his physicians at Bethesda Naval Hospital. "He came in here in August of 1984, right before the reelection campaign, to have his prostate checked. We gave him a barium enema and that's when we discovered the first polyp. We advised him to have another enema because we needed to see more. Usually where there's one polyp, there are more, but he refused. He told me, 'I'm not having that damned procedure again.'

"He hadn't had a physical for two and one-half years, but when he did come, he came on a Friday so they could go to Camp David and not be hounded by the press. Made it look more casual just to stop en route. That way no one would get too suspicious.

"He came out right before the reelection campaign because he wanted a physical to show the world that he was healthy. He wanted the report issued certifying his good health. He promised us that he would be back after the election, but he didn't come back for eleven months. That's when we found the fungating thing in his cecum, which was cancer. He knew if we issued anything on the eve of the election hinting of cancer, he might not be reelected, so he wasn't going to give us a chance to find anything."

Two weeks after his colon surgery the President developed a sore on the right side of his nose, and the White House physician wanted it biopsied. Mrs. Reagan told Dr. Burton Smith that if the scab proved malignant, he was not to announce the fact. He was simply to say that the sore was an irritation caused by the President's nasal tube after his colon surgery.

She denied to reporters that a biopsy was being performed and told the hospital to send the tissue sample to the laboratory under a false name.

The biopsy showed the President had a small skin cancer. It was unrelated to the malignancy in his colon, but the First Lady felt the public would assume that he was cancer-prone. She was convinced that the uncertainty over the health of the oldest man ever to occupy the Oval Office would cause a crisis that could cripple his presidency. So she forbade Dr. Smith to say there had even been a biopsy. She fully intended to keep the information from everyone, including the White House press secretary, but his assistant, Mark Weinberg, cornered the President's doctor. Within minutes he had pried loose information that the First Lady did not want released. He called Larry Speakes.

"Don't dare breathe a word, but there is a problem," Weinberg said. "This thing on the nose, they've taken a biopsy from it."

He laid out the First Lady's deception and said she had dictated a statement declaring the President to be in excellent health without mentioning skin cancer. Speakes called Don Regan.

Unaccustomed to taking orders from a woman, the blunt White House chief of staff had had a bellyful of Nancy Reagan. She had strenuously objected to his using a helicopter to shuttle from the White House to the hospital for his daily visits with the President. "After all, *I'm* not traveling by helicopter," she said pointedly. He countered that it was necessary for him to save time, estimating the round-trip by car to Bethesda Naval Hospital would consume ten hours a week from his schedule. She was unsympathetic. Somehow, the next day's newspapers carried stories saying the self-important chief of staff was operating like a "prime minister." He didn't have to dip the stories in lemon juice to get the message. He canceled the helicopter.

"That was the beginning of the end for Don, but he didn't know it then," said one of Regan's top aides, "because he hadn't figured out how the First Lady operated. That 'prime minister' quote, which he could never overcome, came directly from her via her chief of staff to the reporter. Mrs. Reagan was much too smart ever to be quoted directly herself, but she got the point across anonymously and never left her fingerprints at the scene of the crime."

Shortly after the President's colon surgery, Regan had spoken to the First Lady about the need to make a frank disclosure of the facts should the tissue prove malignant. But she had disagreed. "All that," she told him, "has to be downplayed."

Now he had to tangle with her again over another dreaded biopsy. When she called him to say that a patch of skin on the President's nose was being tested for infection, he waited for her to finish her statement. "Nancy, have you told me everything?" he asked.

"What do you mean?"

"Is there any other problem with the nose? Are you sure that it isn't cancer?"

The rest of that day was spent on a relay of phone calls between the First Lady and the chief of staff, who was trying to persuade her to be candid about the President's skin cancer. She balked. He persisted.

"I won't be a part of this deception," said Don Regan.

"Oh, yes, you will."

Finally, the President entered the deliberations. "Yes, let's do it her way," he said. "Look, Don. Nancy is right."

At that point, the chief of staff became discouraged. He gave up and turned the problem back to the White House press secretary, who tried negotiating with Mrs. Reagan. She remained unmovable.

"Damnit, Larry," she said, "the President does not have cancer!"

"Just tell me what you want me to say," he replied. "Let me advise you that if you mislead the public, you'll make more problems for yourself than is necessary."

The next day, reporters noticed the Band-Aid on the President's nose. The White House physician, following instructions from the First Lady, said no biopsy had been performed on "the little pimple type of thing." Mrs. Reagan also denied a biopsy had been performed. Reporters kept asking questions. So Speakes drafted a statement, but the First Lady rejected it as "too medical and serious and right now could make people jump to conclusions we don't need." She held her ground about lying; she sent the statement back to Speakes, writing at the bottom:

Why can't we just say—You asked about the Band-Aid on the Pres. nose. He had had a pimple on his nose which he picked at and irritated it. After surgery adhesive tape was used to secure the tube that went down his nose. This further irritated the area so when the tape was removed the doctors, to avoid infection, treated it. Routine examination was done and nothing further is necessary. It was exactly what they thought—an irritation of the skin.

The next day the White House press office issued a misleading statement that omitted the words *cancer, malignant,* and *biopsy.* Unwilling to stake his credibility on Mrs. Reagan's deceitful language, yet not bold enough to defy her, Speakes did not put his name on the official release.

A few days later, the President admitted at a news conference that he had had a "basal cell carcinoma" removed from his nose, which made his press secretary look like a liar. Skeptical reporters passed along a new slogan: "Larry Speakes No Truth."

The truth was scarce around the Reagan White House, where the First Lady seemed to prefer falsehoods. She lied even when the truth would have served her better. "She would lie about anything," said one of her former press secretaries. "She lied whenever she saw the image going out of control or being sullied, like with the cancer business. . . . If I came to her with press questions about the kids, she would say, 'We're not going to talk about that. I don't think it's any of their business so I'll just tell them such and such.' And then she would make up a lie."

After the President's operation for colon cancer, the First Lady left it to the staff to call the Reagan children to tell them about their father's condition. She said that under no circumstances were they to come to Washington to visit him because it would be "too alarming" and "make the public think that the matter was serious." Her personal staff knew that she wanted the spotlight to herself. "She liked the fact that every day when she went out to the hospital, all the attention was on her as the worried wife," said one of her speech writers. After three weeks, reporters noticed that Ronald Reagan had had no contact with any of his four children. They reported that he had not seen or heard from them since his operation. Mrs. Reagan called Don Regan to get that impression corrected.

"How *could* he [Ronnie] talk to them?" she asked the chief of staff. "There was a tube in his nose, in his mouth, in his arm. There was no way he could have talked to them." She said that all her husband could do was nod and mumble, and only *she* could understand what he was saying.

The White House chief of staff would never admit it, nor would the men around him, but the First Lady controlled the presidency. It was Nancy Reagan, not Don Regan, who ran things in Ronald Reagan's White House. It was she who dictated the President's schedule, supervised his speeches, counseled his advisers, decided which interviews he should give, regulated his work load, decided his free time, directed his energies, and controlled access to the Oval Office.

While the men around the President readily acknowledged her influence, they publicly dismissed it as nothing more than wifely concern about his health and welfare. They stoutly maintained that she never entered the omnipotent male preserve of policy.

"She just gets involved in personnel and people things," said Mike Deaver.

"Mrs. Reagan, who leaves the issues to others, becomes deeply involved only when she perceives her husband's welfare is at stake," said former White House chief of staff James Baker.

Publicly, the men surrounding the Oval Office could not say anything more. They certainly could not acknowledge to the world the First Lady's hammerlock on the presidency, or admit that privately they referred to her as "Mrs. President." Instead, they kept silent to protect Ronald Reagan from being depicted as henpecked. For their own well-being they needed to have him appear stronger and more capable than he really was. He was the flag they were marching behind in the Reagan Revolution, and they could not afford to follow a weak standard-bearer carrying a flag that had faded. To do so would lessen their self-esteem and diminish their importance.

"It was disheartening for those of us committed to Ronald Reagan to have to admit how the First Lady dominated his presidency," said a top White House aide. "We believed in his ideals, and that finally was the way we justified our service to him. But it was heartbreaking to realize that he was so flawed in that he allowed his wife to do everything she did without objection.

"Bill Clark, who had been with Reagan since Sacramento, explained it by saying that the President wanted marital peace at any price. He had blamed himself for the failure of his first marriage to Jane Wyman and was traumatized by their divorce. So he allowed Nancy to run things in this marriage. To challenge her would only result in conflicts that would lead to marital discord, which, inevitably, could lead to a divorce, something he could never face again."

Much was written about the Reagans' ideal marriage, their unfolding love for each other. Each year on Nancy's birthday, he sent flowers to her mother in appreciation for her giving birth to such a special daughter. Nancy, in turn, gazed on him rapturously every time he delivered a speech, and she told the world: "My life began when I met Ronnie." They hugged openly, kissed frequently, and held hands publicly.

Despite their genuine affection for each other, they occasionally skirmished, especially when the long-suffering husband got fed up with his wife's incessant nagging. While the President ordinarily ignored his wife's importunings, White House aides heard him tell her to "stop pushing me," and to "get off my goddamned back." If others were present, he'd continue telling stories and ignore her. Only if she continued pushing on a subject he considered closed would he respond harshly.

"I was the pool reporter covering the July 4, 1986, celebration at the

Statue of Liberty," said Johanna Neuman of *USA Today.* "And I was with
the Reagans in the harbor where it was cold and windy. Nancy wanted to
leave and kept tugging at the President's sleeve, saying, 'I'm cold. Let's
get out of here.' He got so fed up with her that he told her to shut up."

"During the reelection campaign, Nancy was frantic because the President kept harping on abortion and prayer in the schools," recalled a
friend of the Reagans. "She wanted him to modify his stand, but she
couldn't get him to do it. So she tried her next ploy, which was to invite
three couples to the White House for dinner, briefing them beforehand:
'You tell him, because he won't listen to me. But he'll listen to you.'

"The couples arrived and midway through dinner Nancy nodded her
head at the first couple and said, 'Ronnie, they have something they want
to tell you.' The husband said his piece and Reagan nodded, but changed
the subject and started telling jokes. Minutes later, Nancy nodded to the
second couple, who screwed up their courage and broached the subject
of abortion.

"The President said, 'That reminds me,' and launched into one of his
Hollywood stories. Toward the end of dinner, Nancy signaled the third
couple and they managed to say their rehearsed piece. This time, the
President listened and said, 'I resent this. I'm angry and I know Nancy
has been telling you to do this because I won't listen to her, and I won't.'
That was that. He wouldn't change his hard-line position on abortion, no
matter what Nancy told him to do."

Usually, the President was unaware of his wife's stratagems, so she
continued to employ them on matters as minor as getting him to stop
wetting his hair and applying heavy hair lotion. At a White House dinner, she used sign language to signal a friend to compliment him on his
"more youthful-looking" hairstyle. The flattery worked, but it took a
while. "It was not until 1983 that Nancy and I finally got him off the wet
look, the Brylcreem and water program," said Mike Deaver.

Occasionally, the First Lady dismissed the President with a flip of the
wrist. "Run along, dear," she would say, shaking her hands as if she were
shooing away her little spaniel. "I remember I was up in the family
quarters meeting with her when the President came in early and obviously wanted to talk," recalled a member of Mrs. Reagan's senior staff.
" 'Honey, I've brought you some cookies,' he said, ready to sit down for
a good chat. She sent him scurrying with a quick 'Run along, dear, I'm
busy right now.' He backed off like a good doggie. I was stunned, but
after I saw her do that more than once, I realized she'd been shuffling
him off for years."

Others recall the First Lady's treating the President like a little boy,
urging him to change his clothes, take his nap, and not eat so much

dessert. After his cancer surgery, doctors had recommended a midday bath, and whether he was conferring with aides or chatting with friends, Nancy would interrupt him to say, "Honey, stop talking, go take your bath."

Ordinarily, the President did not mind his wife's nursemaiding, nor her policy-making. In fact, he gratefully acknowledged both in his weekly radio address to the country in July 1985, shortly before he checked out of the Bethesda Naval Hospital and returned to the White House.

"I'd like to indulge myself for a moment here," he said. "There's something I wanted to say and I wanted to say it with Nancy at my side, as she is right now, as she always has been. First Ladies aren't elected, and they don't receive a salary. They've mostly been private persons, forced to live public lives. And in my book, they've all been heroes. Abigail Adams helped invent America. Dolley Madison helped protect it. Eleanor Roosevelt was FDR's eyes and ears. And Nancy Reagan is my everything.

"When I look back on these days, Nancy, I'll remember your radiance and your strength, your support and for taking part in the business of this nation. I say for myself, but also on behalf of the nation, thank you, partner, thanks for everything. By the way, are you doing anything this evening?"

Ronald Reagan's devotion to his domineering wife did not surprise those who knew him well. "The man is inexorably drawn to tough, fierce women," said a friend of many years' standing. "Don't forget, he had a strong, domineering mother who influenced him greatly. His first wife was a heavy-duty number, and Nancy, too, wears emotional hobnail boots. Helene von Damm, who was his secretary for years, was another little toughie, and he was crazy about her. He's also nuts for Margaret Thatcher and Jeane Kirkpatrick, and they don't come much tougher than those two. He just likes ball-breaking women."

The First Lady tried not to be obvious. At White House state dinners, she allotted her husband a certain amount of time to talk to the reporters hovering on the sidelines. Then, with a prearranged flick of her eyes, she would signal one of the social aides, who would glide to the President's side and escort him back to the dinner. At events outside the White House, she clutched his hand. When he stopped to talk to reporters, she would give him a sharp tug to get him moving. That prompted the President to shrug, smile, and move on obediently.

• • •

While normally pleasant and passive, Ronald Reagan could be roused to anger, and his flashes of temper frequently accompanied flying objects. "When he gets mad, he throws things," said a presidential assistant. "He throws his glasses, his keys, his pencils. He flares quickly, but then it's over. Not so with Mrs. Reagan. She stews and simmers and never gets over it."

One day he lost his temper with his wife at the ranch, and some of the Secret Service agents who accompanied the easygoing President cheered. "The President and First Lady followed a routine when they went riding in the morning and afternoon," explained one agent. "He would clean and tack and saddle up the horses and when they were ready for riding, he'd ring the bell and Nancy would come out. She'd step up on the presidential riser—the white wooden three-step riser with the presidential seal in the middle that had been made just for the Reagans to mount their horses—and off they'd go.

"One day, though, he rang the bell and she didn't appear. He waited a few minutes and rang it again. No Mrs. Reagan. He waited a while longer and then rang it a third time. She still didn't appear. He started throwing stones down the hill [at the house]. He hit the red adobe tiles on the roof of the house, which the Reagans had replaced with plastic ones so they wouldn't crack. When she still didn't come out, he stormed down the hill and kicked open the side door of the house where he saw her on the phone. He grabbed the receiver out of her hand and ripped the cord out of the wall. He stormed back out and threw the white telephone in the pond, cursing loudly."

The First Lady admitted to "a few minor irritations now and then" with her husband, but asserted there was never any friction in more than thirty years of marriage. "We disagree. We don't fight," she said. For his part, the President spoke eloquently of his marriage: "There is no greater happiness for a man than approaching a door at the end of the day knowing someone on the other side of the door is waiting for the sound of his footsteps."

Mrs. Reagan was clever enough to know that she had to hide behind the sweet helpmate's façade in order to direct her husband's affairs through his top aides. So she was always careful to disavow publicly any interest in wielding power for herself, saying her only interest was in "what was good for Ronnie."

"I read that I make decisions and I'm the power behind the throne and that I get people fired. I don't understand where that comes from," she told U.S. News & World Report somewhat disingenuously. "I'm a people person. In other words, if people use my husband for their own agenda, I can see it from a distance . . . and I try to protect him."

Her daughter, Patti, pooh-poohed this protective pose, saying that her mother's commitment to her father was not simply for his benefit, but for what she got out of it as well.

"Patti was probably the first one to see how nakedly ambitious her mother really was," said a family friend, "and what angers her is Nancy's hypocrisy in saying that she's just acting in her husband's behalf. Patti maintains that her mother is acting just as much in her own interest as in her husband's. Nancy realized long ago that she could never have the life she wanted through her own talents, and that the only way she'd ever get it was through her husband's special gifts. What enrages the feminist in Patti is that her mother won't own up to her own ambitions."

"I submit that Nancy Reagan had her own political agenda," said former U.S. ambassador to Switzerland Faith Whittlesey, who worked in the Reagan White House for two years. "And that agenda was one which conformed to the world view of the *Washington Post* editorial page in that arms control is the most important goal of American foreign policy, whether or not that position enhances our national interest. The President supported arms to the Contras—Nancy was opposed. He supported SDI [Strategic Defense Initiative], school prayer, tuition tax credits, and the antiabortion movement. She was opposed, and she achieved her agenda by taking control of the White House personnel system and making sure that conservatives who supported the President on those issues never got jobs. The rest she accomplished through Deaver and Baker, working them like a puppet master."

By her husband's second term, the First Lady could no longer hide behind her wifely pose. Her political agility had become increasingly obvious, as her good friend George F. Will noticed during her husband's hospitalization.

"Fortunately for the president, and for a nation fixated by the presidency," Will wrote, "the first lady is a doctor's daughter who, if the 25th Amendment provided for transferring power to First Ladies, could have proven, in just eight hours, how formidable a person in a size four dress can be. In George Bush's eight hours as acting president, the deficit increased $200 million. Nancy never would have allowed that."

The writer Madeline L'Engle saw her former Smith classmate as the supreme dominatrix. "I remember in Leningrad seeing a throne with a hole behind it. The young czar sat on the throne while his sister stood behind him in the hole, telling him what to say. I see Nancy Reagan standing in the hole behind the President."

The comedian Robin Williams joshed, "I'm convinced that she dubs him. Ever notice when Nancy drinks water, Ronnie can't talk?"

The powerful First Lady was frequently compared with Mrs. Woodrow

Wilson. From 1919 to 1921, while President Wilson lay in bed incapacitated by a stroke, Mrs. Wilson more or less ran the White House. Wilson was never hospitalized, and his condition was hidden from the public. His wife guarded the door to his bedroom and admitted only the people needed most. In concert with the President's top aide and the President's physician, the President's wife presided.

In her autobiography, *My Memoir,* Mrs. Wilson, the former Edith Bolling Galt, wrote: "I studied every paper sent from the different Secretaries or Senators, and tried to digest and present in tabloid from the things that, despite my vigilance, had to go to the President. I, myself, never made a single decision regarding the disposition of public affairs. The only decision that was mine was what was important and what was not, and the very important decision of when to present matters to my husband."

By 1985, Nancy Reagan had far surpassed Edith Wilson. While President Reagan was not physically incapacitated, except when recuperating from the assassination attempt and from his colon operation, he was mentally disengaged from the daily routine of the presidency, especially during his second term. By then, most of his top aides admit, his faculties were failing and he was "operating on automatic." The President's mind was closed for repairs.

His failings became excruciatingly obvious during the first summit in Geneva in November of 1985. The First Lady had spent months persuading her husband to abandon his hard-line attitude toward the Soviet Union and to meet with its new leader to discuss arms reduction.

"I sat at the table with Ronald Reagan and the Swiss president during one of the Geneva meetings," said a State Department official, "and the National Security Council man and I both took notes, only his were doctored later for history to make the President look good. President Reagan kept saying, 'Our problems are suspicion and distrust.' He repeated it four times like a robot. The president of Switzerland looked at him and made a very eloquent speech about human rights coming from God, which distinguishes us from the Eastern bloc countries because they believe human rights are a gift of the state. Reagan didn't even react. He had memorized his line. 'Our problems are suspicion and distrust,' he said over and over like a broken record. I was quite alarmed. I thought he was absolutely gaga."

The White House press secretary also noticed that the President seemed "very tentative and stilted," especially compared with Gorbachev, who made several statements about the Soviet desire for peace. So Speakes fabricated some words for the President: "There is much that divides us, but I believe the world breathes easier because we are talking here together." The President had said so little on the subject that Speakes gave the phony quotation to reporters and attributed it to Reagan.

The First Lady had cooperated fully with Secretary of State George Shultz and national security adviser Robert McFarlane in preparing her husband for the Geneva summit, even suggesting that they make ten-minute video clips "because he loves to watch television." She had invited Suzanne Massie, the author of *Land of the Firebird: The Beauty of Old Russia,* to the White House to brief them on several occasions. Nancy Reagan had also contacted James Billington, the librarian of Congress, who recommended several books and films on Russia. And she had tried to keep the President away from hard-liners like Secretary of Defense Caspar Weinberger and CIA director William Casey, who believed only in continuing the military buildup.

While conservatives railed against the First Lady's "petticoat government," as Henry Cabot Lodge once called a wife-ridden presidency, liberals began to see her as the voice of reason and sanity within Ronald Reagan's White House. To them she was the wisest counselor in the President's administration, pushing him on nuclear disarmament treaties with the Soviet Union, an enforced cease-fire in the Middle East, and a peace drive to end the civil war in Nicaragua. To some Democrats, she looked like mankind's best hope for world peace.

The former Democratic speaker of the House of Representatives Jim Wright of Texas, who allied himself with the President in an overture of peace toward Central America, said, "He is almost in awe of the situation. He says openly, 'Nancy is determined I will go down in history as the President of Peace.' He thinks that she might even get what she wants because she usually does."

Whether she was motivated by a need to impress her friends on the editorial page of the *Washington Post* or to secure her husband's place in history as a peacemaker, she was the strongest person around the President, counseling him against indulging in his "evil empire" rhetoric.

"It was Nancy who pushed everybody on the Geneva summit," recalled Mike Deaver. "She felt strongly that it was not only in the interest of world peace but the correct move politically."

"She even had her astrologer do Gorbachev's chart," said Bill Henkel.

The First Lady's personal diary shows that she was meeting with White House officials during her husband's recuperation from cancer surgery in 1985 to discuss his first summit meeting with Mikhail Gorbachev.

July 30: Busy day. Meeting with Bob Tuttle [White House Personnel], then a meeting with Don Regan and Bill Henkel about the Geneva summit in November. Talked about where we'd be staying, what the plan was for the meetings with Ronnie and Gorbachev, and what I was supposed to be doing.

When the President was back in the Oval Office, his aides presented him with a detailed agenda for his first meeting with Gorbachev. Without even looking at it, the President said, "Have you shown this to Nancy?" "No, sir," they replied. "Well, get back to me after she's passed on it."

The State Department was unable to give the First Lady much pertinent information on her Soviet counterpart, so Nancy was not prepared for the highly educated, doctrinaire wife of the general secretary. At fifty-two, Raisa Gorbachev was twelve years younger than Nancy Reagan but not the least in awe of meeting her. This lack of deference irritated the American First Lady, who was accustomed to the gingerly respect reserved for a lioness.

A former professor of Marxist-Leninist theory at Moscow University, Mrs. Gorbachev was well grounded in the philosophical basis of Soviet policy and not at all hesitant about sharing her views. At the first dinner the Gorbachevs had with the Reagans, she expressed her opinions to the President, which annoyed the First Lady. As soon as the Gorbachevs left, Nancy Reagan said, "Who does that dame think she is."

Nancy's most lasting impression of the evening, besides Raisa's "damned monologue," was that Mikhail Gorbachev had never tasted a soufflé, which, to Nancy's way of thinking, marked him as less than sophisticated. She later confided how unimpressed she had been by Mrs. Gorbachev's appearance, which she described as "a little déclassé." Nancy mentioned Raisa's spike heels and the black velvet skirt she had worn to an afternoon luncheon, attire considered highly inappropriate by the First Lady's standards of fashion.

"She was shorter than I expected and her hair was more reddish than it appeared on television," Nancy said. "It became less red over the years. . . . She learned. It was fascinating."

A few weeks before going to Geneva, Nancy Reagan had indicated a certain amount of apprehension about meeting Mrs. Gorbachev. "I remember we were standing in the living room of Laurel Lodge at Camp David shortly before the President's Saturday morning radio address," recalled Terry Arthur. "Nancy came in and said she'd had a dream the night before. During her audience with the Pope, the Pope's ring had fallen on the floor. Nancy said she picked it up but couldn't find the Pope. She went back to where the purses were, and there was the Pope. But the Pope was a woman with red hair.

"I wrote that down at the time because I thought it was an interesting historical detail that the First Lady would talk about her dreams. Only after the Geneva summit did I realize that the red-haired lady she was dreaming about was probably Raisa."

In her memoirs, Mrs. Reagan admitted that she was nervous about that first meeting. "I didn't know what I would talk about with her," she wrote, "but I soon discovered that I needn't have worried. From the moment we met, she talked and talked and *talked*—so much that I could barely get a word in edgewise or otherwise. Perhaps it was insecurity on her part, but during about a dozen encounters in three different countries, my fundamental impression of Raisa Gorbachev was that she never stopped talking.

"Or lecturing, to be more accurate. Sometimes the subject was the Soviet Union and the glories of the Communist system. Sometimes it was Soviet art. More often than not, it was Marxism and Leninism. Once or twice, she even lectured me on the failings of the American political system. I wasn't prepared for this, and I didn't like it."

Raisa Gorbachev became a major irritant to the First Lady, but she had to put up with her for the President's sake. Concerned about his place in history, she now pushed Reagan to sign an arms control agreement with the Russians. She wanted him remembered as a man of peace, not a man of missiles. To that end, she had insisted that he avoid all appearances at military bases and ship dedications; she did not want him portrayed as a saber-rattling militarist. She also urged him to moderate his anti-Soviet rhetoric. "I would say, you know, 'This is unfair. It's not right. You are not trigger-happy,' " she said.

Two months before the November 1984 election, when the polls had shown Reagan's only vulnerability to be his bottomless hostility toward Russia, she had persuaded him to meet with the Soviet foreign minister, Andrei Gromyko. The seventy-five-year-old Russian, who had known every U.S. President since Roosevelt, had come to the White House for lunch, where he wisely engaged the First Lady in conversation.

"He turned to me and said, 'Is your husband for peace or war?' And I said, 'Peace,' " she recalled. "He was a little bit surprised . . . and he said, 'You sure?' And I said, 'Yes.'

"He said, 'Then why doesn't he accept our proposals?' And I said, 'Which proposals?' and with that people came up and we were interrupted. He turned to me and he said, 'You whisper peace into his ear

65.

66.

Adolfo, Nancy Reagan's favorite designer, who gave her everything she wanted from his collections free during her eight years in the White House.

Julius Bengtsson, Nancy Reagan's California hairdresser, who also provided his services for free throughout her years in the White house.

67.

Nancy Reagan being fitted for one of her free outfits from Gucci in Beverly Hills shortly after Ronald Reagan was elected President in 1980.

Carlo Celoni presenting Mrs. Reagan with one of Gucci's free handbags in 1980.

68.

*Nancy Reagan dancing
with Prince Charles.*

*Queen Elizabeth II and
Nancy Reagan.*

*The Reagans greet Prince Charles and Princess Diana at the
White House in 1985.*

The First Lady and the President welcome Margaret Thatcher to the Reagans' first state dinner at the White House in February 1981.

58.

59.

60.

61.

Imelda Marcos, first lady of the Philippines, with her good friend Nancy Reagan.

Nancy Reagan with one of her most generous benefactors, King Fahd of Saudi Arabia.

Nancy Reagan motions to Jehan Sadat, wife of Egyptian President Anwar Sadat.

55.

The former MGM starlet in her guest appearance on NBC's comedy show "Diff'rent Strokes."

Nancy Reagan with Gary Coleman on the set of "Diff'rent Strokes."

56.

First Lady Nancy Reagan is surprised on July 6, 1983, with a birthday cake from her staff at the White House.

57.

22

THE FIRST LADY WINCED when she read the corrosive portrait of herself in her daughter's novel. "It's hostile," she said. The President, who seemed to own more horses than books, dismissed *Home Front* as pulp fiction, saying, "I just hope she makes a lot of money."

"I tried to talk Patti out of writing that book, but she just wouldn't listen to me," said Dolores Robinson, Patti Davis's former personal manager. "We had a meeting at literary agent Irving 'Swifty' Lazar's house, and he tried, too. 'Do it after your parents are out of office,' he said. Swifty and I knew how close that book was going to be to Patti's real life and how embarrassing it would be for her parents, but she insisted. Her hatred for her mother was that strong."

The acting career that Patti Davis had dreamed of for herself had never developed. Expecting great opportunities after her father was elected President, she had hired Jay Bernstein, who had managed Farrah Fawcett and Suzanne Sommers. "I'm a star maker," he told reporters, "and I think Patti Davis will be a superstar within the year." He later admitted he represented her as a favor to a friend of her parents.

Bernstein arranged for Patti to sign an exclusive contract with NBC-TV Entertainment in 1981 for $100,000. She appeared in one episode of "Nero Wolfe," hosted a broadcast of a variety show, "The Midnight Special," and starred in a made-for-television movie about a male stripper. Her contract was not renewed.

"By then Patti had fired me and hired a very nice black lady manager every night.' And I said, 'Oh, I will. And I'll also whisper 'peace' in your ear.''

For the next four years, the First Lady whispered her messages in the President's ear, and, for the most part, he responded accordingly. He met four times with Mikhail Gorbachev, and on December 8, 1987, they signed the Intermediate-Range Nuclear Forces Treaty in the White House. The President even talked about eliminating all nuclear weapons. At that point, Mrs. Reagan began fantasizing about the Nobel Peace Prize as the capstone to his presidency, but on the eve of the third Soviet-American summit, that dream evaporated.

Without her permission, the President gave a long interview to Arnaud de Borchgrave, editor in chief of the conservative *Washington Times,* the Washington, D.C., newspaper financed by the Reverend Sun Myung Moon. In response to a question about pro-Soviet agents of influence in the U.S. Congress, the President complained that a Soviet "disinformation campaign" had made anticommunism in the United States "unfashionable." He spoke nostalgically of the good old days when Senator Joseph McCarthy, the Red-baiting Republican from Wisconsin, and the House Un-American Activities Committee would investigate suspected subversives.

"They've done away with those committees," Reagan said sadly. "That shows the success of what the Soviets were able to do in this country with making it unfashionable to be anti-Communist. . . . There is a disinformation campaign, we know, worldwide, and that disinformation campaign is very sophisticated and is very successful, including with a great many in the media and the press in America . . . and on Capitol Hill."

Apparently, the President still missed his Communist-bashing days as head of the Screen Actors Guild when he operated as a secret FBI source with a code designation all his own: Confidential Informant T-10. Despite the First Lady's best efforts, she had a long way to go before softening the rock-hard philosophy of her husband.

*Nancy Reagan presents
Brooke Astor with a
fashion award from the
Council of Fashion
Designers of America in
1987. Oscar de la Renta
stands at far left.*

*Raisa Gorbachev resists
the overture of First
Lady Nancy Reagan
during the Gorbachevs'
1987 trip to
Washington.*

70.

The First Lady rehearses the President on a speech delivered on September 14, 1986.

Secretary of State Alexander Haig and Secretary of the Treasury Donald Regan, two cabinet members who fell under the hammer of the First Lady and lost their positions.

73.

The image-conscious former First Lady tries to shield her husband's shorn head as he leaves the Mayo Clinic following brain surgery in 1989.

74.

One of the few existing photos of Nancy Reagan in a bathing suit. She is with her husband in Honolulu in April 1984.

Nancy Reagan and her husband strolling through Camp David.

named Dolores Robinson, who represents social activists like LeVar Burton, Margot Kidder, and Emilio Estevez," said Bernstein.

Under Robinson, Patti found work playing one of the rape victims in the CBS-TV movie *Night Partners* and a minor role in the feature film *Curse of the Pink Panther*. She got the latter role after meeting the producer at a memorial service for her godfather, William Holden. She tried unsuccessfully to interest Frank Sinatra in singing some of the songs she composed, then decided to sing them herself. She recorded a rock album in London, but it was never released. She returned to the United States to make her stage debut in a production of *Vanities* at the Cherry Hill Playhouse in Traverse City, Michigan. She starred in a production of the musical *The Pajama Game* in Birmingham, Alabama, and appeared as a pimp's assistant on the television show "Vega$." She also played television bits on "Fantasy Island," "The Love Boat," and "Here's Boomer," but she never established herself as an actress. Instead, she became famous as a caricature: the left-wing, vegetarian, I-love-Jane-Fonda daughter of the right-wing, carnivorous, I-can't-stand-Jane-Fonda President. Patti acknowledged that her career had been undistinguished, but she blamed the press.

"I wasn't given a chance to just do my work as an actor," she said. "A lot of it was the media's fault. . . . I assumed people would be interested in me at first because I'm Ronald Reagan's daughter, and then the interest would die out and they'd give me a chance. It was very stupid of me to think that. I was *always* just Ronald Reagan's daughter."

By 1986, she finally had figured out how to cash in on that relationship. After firing Dolores Robinson for trying to dissuade her, she accepted a $100,000 advance to collaborate on a novel about the daughter of a television star who becomes governor of California and then President of the United States. In the process, he sacrifices his children to his political ambitions. His clotheshorse of a wife is so obsessed with him that she has no interest in her children, except to preach chastity to them at every turn. The plot centers on the rebellious teenage daughter, who expresses her growing independence by opposing everything that her parents hold dear.

Advertised as an "autobiographical novel," the literary striptease unveiled most of Patti's life: her private school in Arizona, her poetry writing, her live-in lover, her illegal abortion, her relationship with her parents. "Almost everything in *Home Front* is based on the kernel of some real incident, but I'm not going to tell," she said. "I hope readers feel like they're looking through a keyhole into the life of somebody with a very unusual conflict."

Reviewers saw the book as a lethal weapon in the hands of a reckless child. "I don't know why Patti is so angry at her mother, but she is," said Dolores Robinson. "I wouldn't say Nancy Reagan was a great mother, but I wasn't there when Patti was growing up. I only met her as an adult, but I actually liked her mother. She's strong. A real woman-warrior type. I like those kinds of tough old girls who are inner-directed, know what they want, and go for it. Nancy Reagan created a life for herself and I admire that. She made her husband President of the United States, and then she ran the show for him. She took over. She controlled Ronald Reagan so much that she became President of the United States. No question.

"I used to get the biggest kick out of being in my office and having my secretary say, 'The White House is calling. They've got the First Lady on the line for you.' I'd pick up and Nancy would just be calling to see how things were going with Patti. 'Is she getting any work? Do you think there is something else she could be doing? Do you think she should continue to do what she's doing? Is it going to go anywhere for her?' She was very concerned about her daughter and her career. Both she and the President wanted Patti to be successful. This was before they had their last falling-out.

"I remember when I called the ranch for Patti once. She'd already left, but Nancy got on the phone. She had done the Michael Jackson radio show in Los Angeles a few days before and he had given her a rough time. She knew that Patti was scheduled to do the show the next day and she asked me if I had any control. Then she said, 'Oh, Dolores, my husband would like to speak to you,' and she put the President on the line. He said, 'I'm really concerned about Jackson pulling the same thing on Patti that he did on my wife. Can you make sure it won't happen?' I said I'd try. He said, 'Atta girl, Dolores.' My politics were totally opposed to the Reagans and they always knew that, but it didn't seem to make any difference in the way they treated me. One year, Patti took me to Nancy's big birthday party at the ranch, and I had a great time with all those rich folks. You can see me in the White House photograph; I'm the only little black face peering out of that all-white crowd.

"I really tried to be a friend to Patti and tell her that she had to stop blaming her parents and get on with her life. I said that once you turn eighteen, you have to stop pointing fingers and find a way to forgive your parents or to understand why they did what they did, and then get on with things. Patti would listen and then go on about her business. . . . I tried because I was amazed at the depth of her hatred. I shouldn't have been, though, considering how we met."

During the 1980 presidential campaign, Robinson and several friends were sharing a limousine with Patti Davis, but the entertainment representative had no idea that the long-haired brunette in the backseat was the Republican candidate's daughter. "I remember I started carrying on about Ronald Reagan, saying, 'If that son of a bitch wins, I'm leaving the country. I'm out of here. I'm packing up my kid and just clearing out.' There was an uncomfortable silence before someone pointed to Patti and said, 'Hey, Dolores, meet the son of a bitch's daughter.' Oh, God, I was so embarrassed, but Patti was great. She said, 'Don't worry. I feel the same way.' "

Patti never hid her revulsion toward her father's politics. Sometimes she would say, "I'm not against my father, but I am against his beliefs." She was much more vocal about her mother, telling friends that she couldn't abide her mother's manipulative ways.

"She told me that when she was growing up," said one friend, "she walked into a room and saw her mother putting words into Ronald Reagan's ear, giving him directions just like a puppet. 'And then you'll tell Patti why you're displeased about this, and then you'll say that you're upset about that and then . . .' They didn't know that Patti had walked in and caught them."

Watching her mother control her father disillusioned Patti, for she once had idolized Ronald Reagan. As she grew older, she realized that he was far too passive ever to stand up to his wife, so Patti appreciated the times he had sneaked off to meet her at airports to say hello even though her mother had forbidden any communication because Patti was "living in sin" with a bearded rock guitarist. Since then, though, the relationship between father and daughter had disintegrated over their sharp political disagreements, hence the portrayal of the President in her novel as a simpleminded dolt whose interest in politics precluded his spending time with his children.

It was a judgment that seemed particularly harsh to many, but not to Ronald Reagan.

"I didn't recognize anyone in the book," he said, "and certainly the happenings never happened."

Nothing condemned Nancy Reagan in the eyes of the public more than her daughter's attitude toward having children. One Hollywood director was speechless when Patti confided that she had had a hysterectomy in her twenties "in order to kill the gene pool." Publicly, she was more circumspect, saying only that having children was not important to her. "Kids are not in my top five things to do."

Patti had refused to be interviewed for the laudatory NBC-TV documentary on her mother because she did not want to be portrayed as part of a warm, nurturing family when none existed. Patti's husband, Paul Grilley, also refused to contribute to fraudulent bonhomie, and would not attend his father-in-law's second inaugural. Patti, though, did show up for the event. "She wore blue jeans in the official family photograph, which is why Mrs. Reagan made her stand in the back," said a member of the First Lady's staff. "And then Patti wrote that terrible book. We all felt so sorry for Mrs. Reagan after that."

Public sympathy poured in for the Reagans, even from their political adversaries, after their daughter's thinly veiled autobiography. "I can't believe someone would do that to their parents," said Eleanor Mondale, the twenty-six-year-old daughter of Reagan's 1984 Democratic opponent. "I come from a close family. Even the thought of embarrassing them makes me cringe."

Patti's siblings, scrambling for their own parental approval, agreed.

"I think it's disgusting," said Maureen Reagan.

"I'm just waiting for Dad and Nancy to write 'Children Dearest' next," said Michael Reagan.

"I don't think it was the classiest thing to do," said Ron Reagan. "I think it was wrong and in bad taste. I think someday she'll regret it."

The novel became a best-seller with paperback rights selling for $400,000. Patti hoped to sell movie rights as well so that she could play the lead, but Hollywood was not interested. She sent the book to her parents and a few weeks later called her brother to ask why she hadn't heard from anyone.

"What did you expect?" said Ron. "You've trashed us all in a terrible book. You made Mom and Dad into cartoon characters! Did you expect them to call you and tell you it's great?" Patti hung up on him and the two have not spoken since.

Home Front destroyed the last tenuous strand of Patti's relationship with her family. Her parents went on national television to tell Barbara Walters of ABC News how the book had left them "deeply hurt."

"I thought I was a good father," said the President, adding that having been in show business gave him more time to spend with his children than if he had had a nine-to-five job. "And maybe there were times when I should have been sterner than I was."

"I tried to be a good mother," said the First Lady. "I don't think anybody's perfect, but then, you know, there's no perfect parent and there's no perfect child." Her response—and her discomfort—reminded some viewers of King Lear: "How sharper than a serpent's tooth it is to have a thankless child."

Striking back at the viper in the family's nest, the First Lady sabotaged her daughter's book promotion tour. "We had sent her a copy of the publicity schedule as a courtesy," said the book's publicist, Judy Hilsinger. "We thought that she and the President might want to watch their daughter on some of the shows Patti was booked on. I never dreamed that Mrs. Reagan would do what she did, but two hours before Patti was to tape 'The Tonight Show' with Joan Rivers, she was canceled. The excuse was that Joan had read the book and didn't feel that what Patti had done to her mother was right. The White House denied all involvement, but I later found out that Mrs. Reagan had called Joan Rivers to say she was offended that Joan would be interviewing Patti and that she wanted her off the show. Joan was in shock and said, 'Well, gee, we don't have to talk about the book. We could talk about something else,' but Nancy said no. She made it very clear that she expected Patti to be taken off the show. Joan is not stupid. She did not want to offend her good friend the First Lady, who had invited her to a White House state dinner and to perform at the Republican National Convention. So she agreed to cancel Patti. Merv Griffin did the same thing. Phil Donahue didn't cave in like that, but he told us backstage that he had received a lot of White House pressure to cancel Patti as well."

For the rest of the Reagans' White House years, Patti was the family pariah. She became a nonperson, the phantom always noted in the press as absent from gatherings at Christmas, Thanksgiving, or birthdays, though the President and First Lady usually spent those holidays with friends, not family.

Having been publicly humiliated by her daughter, Nancy Reagan once again stopped speaking to Patti, so Patti heard from her only through the media, the megaphone that was her mother's principal means of communication. Nancy never realized how hurtful it was for her daughter to read her comments in the press, a practice she had started in 1966 when she told *Women's Wear Daily:* "Patti's long-legged, will be able to wear clothes well. She's tall—what I always wanted to be. But right at the moment we're going through that mother-daughter thing. All it takes is for me to say I like something for her to dislike it."

For the next twenty years, Nancy discussed her daughter with reporters, registering disapproval of her with long sighs and raised eyebrows, and then wondered why Patti recoiled from her. In 1984, the First Lady told society columnist Betty Beale that she did not understand her daughter and could not explain her feelings. "Patti is a grown woman, married and has her own life, and I can't worry about her anymore," she said. "I wrote an article for Mother's Day for my mother *[Family Weekly]*. I hope for Patti's sake—as I said in the article, the saddest thing is to be an 'if only' child. When it's too late to say, 'If only I had done this. If only I had done that.' I hope for her sake she will not be. But there's nothing I can do. That's a problem Patti's going to have to face and Patti's going to have to solve."

"Doesn't she realize what she's missing?" asked the columnist.

"No, she doesn't. I have a wonderful son. I really do. . . . Ron is a darling boy who more than makes up for everything. And Maureen, who now calls me 'Mother.' "

In 1987, Mrs. Reagan criticized Patti for not attending her grandmother's funeral, and told the Associated Press that she did not know how to reconcile with her daughter. "Not coming to Mother's services was really hard to take," she said. "Mother was very nice to Patti. I think I was more disappointed for Mother than for anything else." Nancy told the *Washington Post* that her daughter was "selfish and self-centered" for not attending her grandmother's funeral.

Patti chose not to publicly defend her actions. The grandmother she had known and loved had faded into senility long before she died. Afflicted with Alzheimer's in later life, she had often rebuked Patti for her political differences with her father. "She was very insulting to me at times, like 'You're criticizing your father publicly. You ought to shut up,' " said Patti, who never visited her grandmother after her grandfather died in 1982. She preferred to remember Edith Davis as the earthy surrogate mother she had been when Patti was going to school in Arizona. She also knew that despite the staged photographs released by the White House of the loving daughter with her pathetically senescent mother, Nancy and Edith had never been close. Patti did not want to contribute to further hypocrisy by attending the funeral, which was covered by the White House press corps as a media tribute to her mother rather than a celebration of her grandmother's life. Yet without a public explanation, it was Patti who looked cold and uncaring, not her mother. "Another crack in an already broken heart" is how the First Lady's press secretary described Patti's failure to join her family for the funeral.

The relationship between Nancy and her mother had always been distant and strained, despite Mrs. Reagan's statements to the contrary. The closest she ever came to admitting the emotional gulf that existed between them was to tell Donnie Radcliffe of the *Washington Post:* "I adored her, of course, but I was always sorry that I was so far away from her and I couldn't be with her more."

But a longtime friend of Mrs. Reagan said, "It was Loyal Davis that she really loved, and she still hasn't gotten over his death."

"Until Reagan became President, Nancy never called her parents," said one of the Davises' physicians. "A year would go by without Edith hearing from her. . . . I know because I was there."

"Nancy and her mother fought like cats and dogs, according to Marjorie, their housekeeper," said Shirley Singer, who lived next door to Edith and Loyal Davis in Scottsdale.

"I used to accompany Mrs. Reagan to Scottsdale to visit her mother, who was in a wheelchair by then," said a member of the First Lady's staff. "It was so sad. When Nancy would start to go, her mother would say, 'I love you, I love you, I love you,' and Nancy would back out of the room, not exactly responding in kind."

Uncommitted to a core of political principles herself, Nancy Reagan could not understand why her daughter felt impelled to oppose her father on political issues such as nuclear power. "Obviously, we disagree with her," the First Lady told reporters, adding, as she always did: "She's just being used by people with their own political agenda." Despite the devastation of Chernobyl, the President said Patti's opposition was based on "fairy tales" about dangers that did not exist.

"I really searched my soul, and I wrote them a long letter," said Patti. "I think they still feel I'm being used, or misinformed, but I'm just going to keep trying." She soon realized there were no grounds for discussion.

Patti believed that the biggest threat facing the world was the destruction of the environment. She couldn't understand how her father could support offshore drilling, cutting down forests, and the dismantling of the Environmental Protection Agency.

She became active in promoting the Marine Mammal Protection Act, which would stop the killing of dolphins by tuna fishermen, but she didn't talk to her father about it. "I didn't want to get my heart broken again," she said. "I couldn't have stood having him give me some *Reader's Digest* rationalization on why it had to go on."

Her second novel, *Deadfall,* castigated the Reagan administration for the war in Nicaragua, but by then her father had left office and few people cared about his daughter. The book sold so poorly that she was unable to get a contract with a reputable publisher for her third book. She filed for divorce and once on her own was barely able to pay her mortgage. She was living in a modest house in Santa Monica, only five miles from the Bel Air estate where her parents lived. They were worth more than $10 million, but she couldn't turn to them for help; they had disinherited her.

Determined to be a writer and finish her next book, she decided to sell an old four-page handwritten letter from her father warning against "compromising with the truth no matter how trivial." The letter had long been precious to her because those became the words by which she had chosen to live her life. The letter, estimated to be worth between $40,000 and $45,000, brought only $8,000.

Michael Reagan also approached the literary marketplace with family intimacies. In January 1987, he announced that he had sold the rights to his autobiography, *On the Outside Looking In,* and would be disclosing one "quite shocking thing" about his life that his father, mother, and stepmother would learn for the first time.

"Michael has not discussed this with the Reagans, or with his mother, Jane Wyman, because he feels they would disapprove," said his literary agent, Scott Meredith. "It's going to be a very frank book . . . a balanced account of his relationship with his father—more on the unfavorable than on the favorable side, but essentially balanced."

Hearing this news, the First Lady called her stepson.

"I've been asked to do a book about Dad for lots of money," he said.

"Of course," she said. "I could get lots of money for walking naked up and down Pennsylvania Avenue. It's a question of taste."

Nancy Reagan had good reason to be frightened by Michael's autobiography, for she had treated him like a communicable disease for most of his life. Having only recently reconciled her differences with him after a public feud and a few years of not speaking, she was only civil. But she never embraced him, or his wife and two children, as part of the family.

"I remember in one of our rare staff meetings, someone brought up the subject of grandchildren and asked Mrs. Reagan about hers," recalled an assistant to the First Lady. "She said, 'I don't have any grandchildren.' Period. End of subject."

Yet now, in an effort to soften her image, her staff issued statements about how much she loved being a grandmother. "It's that wonderful time in your life when you are able to enjoy the exchange of love between grandparent and grandchild without the daily responsibility that comes with being the parent," the First Lady told *McCall's* magazine. "We and our grandchildren, Cameron and Ashley Marie, all enjoy getting together for holidays and special celebrations. Since our coast-to-coast living arrangement doesn't allow those gatherings to happen very often, they are all the sweeter and more cherished and something we all look forward to."

"I think Michael's emotional neediness repelled her," said another member of the First Lady's staff. "He was so open and honest in wanting the Reagans' approval. Whenever he called, he knew that he would never get through to the President or First Lady. He accepted that he would have to talk to one of us, but he was always so cheerful and pleasant. You knew he didn't want to get off the phone. We were his lifeline to his parents."

During the months that Michael was working on his book, the First Lady tried to ingratiate herself with him to cushion what she thought would be a vengeful manuscript. She invited him and his family to the ranch for Thanksgiving, and she invited them to the White House. She made sure photographers took pictures of them celebrating Ashley's fourth birthday with her and the President, and the pictures were released to the press.

Shortly before his book was published, Michael visited the Reagans at the ranch to tell them his terrible secret. He said that at the age of eight he had been sexually molested by a camp counselor who had taken nude pictures of him. All his life, he said, he had lived with the fear of those pictures being published. He said he had recently started seeing a therapist and had decided against writing a negative book about the Reagans. Instead, he wanted to write one that would help victims of sexual abuse.

"Ronnie and I had absolutely no idea that anything like this had ever happened," said Nancy. "I don't know if we would have picked it up if Michael had been living with us—I'd like to think so—but I can't be sure. I knew Michael had problems, but *this?* I never dreamed of it."

After discussing the matter with her husband, the First Lady directed the White House press secretary to issue a public statement expressing the Reagans' full support for Michael and approval of his book. She could rise above the snide comments about her because they paled in comparison with the revolting picture he had drawn of Jane Wyman. He depicted her as a cruel and bloodless mother who neglected her children to pursue her career, her marriages, and her poodles.

Such a portrait of a woman Nancy despised suddenly endeared Michael to his stepmother. He had been telling television interviewers that he had always dreamed of being invited to a White House state dinner and flying on Air Force One while his father was President. So while Nancy was in California, she invited Michael to spend the night at the White House with his father and fly with him the next day on Air Force One to the ranch. Michael was thrilled.

"I've never been on Air Force One before," he told reporters. "I've never even spent so much time with Dad alone. Being next to him on a whole flight means I'll have spent more time with him in the air than I ever have on the ground."

The Reagan children seemed to court controversy as a way of getting their parents' attention, and none more blatantly than the favorite child, Ron, who freely admitted to cashing in on his father's presidency. "I'd be a fool not to," he said. "If people insist it's an unfair advantage, at some point you have to say, 'Who cares?' "

Before the first inaugural, he and his wife posed for a photographer from the Joffrey Ballet, who peddled the pictures to *New York* magazine, trying to sell a story on them.

"You should have seen the pictures of those two attention-getting fools

draped around each other in leopardskin on a bedspread in the most
sexual, provocative poses," recalled Marie Brenner, then a writer for the
magazine. "The editor showed them to me and said that Ron and Doria
wanted us to publish them. I told him to refuse unless I got to interview
them. I never thought they'd agree, but one half hour later my phone
rang and it was Doria Reagan saying, 'We'd love it if you would come to
our apartment and interview us.' Can you believe it?"

Shamelessly self-promoting, Ron Reagan signed with the William Morris Agency in 1983 as soon as he gave up his $13,000-a-year job dancing
with the Joffrey. "Thank God, he won't be collecting unemployment
anymore," said the President, who had been humiliated when his son
filed for federal compensation benefits during the time he was not performing.

Ron then began a career as a freelance journalist, writing articles for
Playboy for $10,000 apiece, which also embarrassed his father. "I think
he could have picked a better place to put his stories," he said. "I don't
think he'll be indulging in pornographic material, but I wish he'd find
something more dignified to do." Ron also wrote for *Parade, Ladies'
Home Journal, Newsweek,* and the *Washington Post.* He pursued a career in
television as well, collecting $200,000 for an American Express commer-
cial showing him in a telephone booth calling the White House. He
signed a three-year contract with "Good Morning America" for
$250,000 to produce forty-five humorous features a year, with an unlim-
ited budget for travel and entertainment. He hosted "Saturday Night
Live" in his underpants, imitating Tom Cruise in the movie *Risky Business.*
That caused former television personality Henry Morgan to write the
president of NBC charging that the spectacle was "so unrelievedly shocking that it embarrassed me to think that it could be aired in my country."
The television evangelist Jimmy Swaggart declared the performance "an
abomination," but the Reagans applauded Ron's performance. "Like father, like son," said the President after someone explained the spoof to
him.

Ron next signed to make his movie debut in *Soul Man.* He starred in a
pay cable "Cinemax Comedy Experiment" and hosted a satirical revue
featuring puppets of his parents. He also posed for *Vanity Fair,* stripping
to his skivvies for photographer Annie Leibovitz.

"Cashing in?" he asked. "You betcha. And why not? It's exciting to be
the President's son. You get to meet a lot of people you would otherwise
never meet. You have access to top-secret information. It is intoxicating
to be so near the center."

"Mrs. Reagan liked all of Ron's publicity," said Shirley Watkins, "except for the AIDS thing he did. That really upset her."

· · ·

Angry at his parents for ignoring the AIDS epidemic, the First Family's son agreed in 1986 to introduce a documentary promoting safe sex. Appearing before television cameras holding a prophylactic in one hand and spermicide in the other, he announced: "This is a condom, and this is spermicide. Get them and learn how to use them." He donated his $400 film fee to AIDS research, saying off camera that he and his wife had lost twelve friends to the disease. He criticized his father and his administration for irresponsible leadership: "The U.S. government is not moving fast enough to stop the spread of AIDS. We need more money for research to find a cure. We need more explicit education about how to be safe. Let someone you know in Washington know that you don't think enough is being done. Write your congressman, or write someone higher up."

Ron also criticized Secretary of Education William Bennett for curtailing information about AIDS in schools. "Our Secretary of Education issues a pamphlet supposedly dealing with the problem, but he's not doing any good. He never really mentions drug use, homosexuality, or preventive measures like condoms. From the start, there has been a singular lack of attention paid to this in Washington," he said. "Come on, goddamn it, how many people have to die before you get out and say something?"

The President called Secretary Bennett that evening to apologize for his son's remarks. Despite 21,000 deaths from AIDS, Ronald Reagan refused to discuss the disease or even to say the word aloud in public. He had turned down the suggestion of the surgeon general, C. Everett Koop, to educate the country by combining warnings about AIDS with his antinarcotics campaign. In fact, Reagan never discussed the disease with his surgeon general and never, according to a White House official, bothered to read Koop's report predicting 180,000 deaths from AIDS by 1991.

The President and First Lady did not focus on the seriousness of the AIDS epidemic until July 1985, when they heard that their friend Rock Hudson, who had recently attended a state dinner, was seeking treatment for AIDS in Paris. The President, then recuperating from his cancer surgery, asked his physician about the disease. That was more than five years after AIDS had been identified and had infected thousands of Americans.

"He accepted it like it was measles and it would go away," recalled Brigidier General John Hutton, who was Reagan's personal physician.

"He would say words to the effect: 'Is there a message in this?' Like, perhaps, people are supposed to modify their behaviors."

Reagan, who enjoyed mimicking homosexuals, now added AIDS jokes to his repertoire. "He loved to tell the one about the two doctors at the medical convention talking about treating AIDS patients," recalled an assistant. "One doctor said to the other: 'I've got the solution. I serve them a special dinner of crepes and filet of sole.'

" 'What does that do? It's not a cure.'

" 'No, it's not,' said the doctor, 'but the advantage is that I can just slide it under the door and I don't have to touch them.'

"Reagan always threw back his head and roared with laughter whenever he told that joke."

The President livened up one cabinet meeting by asking, "Why not invite Qaddafi to San Francisco, he likes to dress up so much?"

Quipped Secretary of State Shultz, "Why don't we give him AIDS?" Once again the President threw back his head and laughed uproariously.

Moderates on the White House staff who regarded AIDS as a medical disease worried that Ronald Reagan was spending too much time with his friend William F. Buckley, who advocated tattooing the upper forearm and buttocks of those who tested HIV-positive. "If somebody's got a sickness they could hurt somebody else with," said the President, "we should do something about it." Conservatives, who viewed AIDS as a moral issue, agreed. The White House drug adviser, Carlton E. Turner, said he believed that pot smoking led to homosexuality, and at the very least, homosexuals who used marijuana risked damage to their immune system and vulnerability to AIDS. He offered no scientific data for his claim, but said it was an observation from his visits to drug-treatment centers. White House infighting on the subject of AIDS rose to such a pitch that Reagan finally announced at a cabinet meeting, "I don't want to hear anything more about AIDS!"

The First Lady privately sided with homosexual leaders in opposing the mandatory testing that her husband supported, but she could not bring herself to go public on the issue. Until 1987, she refused to have her name associated in any way with AIDS.

She sent a message of support in 1985 to Elizabeth Taylor, who wanted her endorsement for a new national research foundation dedicated to searching for an AIDS cure, but Nancy would not attend the foundation's fund-raiser. The next year, she was honored with a humanitarian award for her efforts against drug abuse by AIDS fund-raisers in Arizona, who also hoped she would attend. Again, she declined, but sent a friend to accept her award. Months later, social arbiter Earl Blackwell, who publishes the *Celebrity Register,* issued invitations for a charity ball to raise money for AIDS. Emblazoned with a silver seal and red, white, and blue streamers, his $1,000-a-person invitation announced that the fundraiser would occur "Under the Distinguished Patronage of Mrs. Ronald Reagan." Although she had agreed to help him, the First Lady quickly dissociated herself from the event.

"She has nothing to do with AIDS and certainly is not a patron," said her press secretary.

The homosexual community, aware of Mrs. Reagan's coterie, could not understand her opposition to supporting research for a disease that threatened to infect hundreds of thousands of homosexuals by the end of the decade. Their attitude toward the First Lady surfaced in a play entitled *Unfinished Business: The New AIDS Show*, first performed in San Francisco in 1984.

The series of campy, humorous sketches, showing how people confronted and dealt with AIDS, included one in which an actor, talking about the day when he couldn't bear to watch his friend suffer anymore, looked up to the skies to plead, "Don't take him! Take me instead."

His dying friend said, "You know you don't mean that."

"You're right," said the actor, again directing his pleading eyes to the heavens. "Take Nancy Reagan instead!"

"I remember when Liz Taylor sent another letter asking the First Lady to attend a fund-raising dinner for AIDS research in 1987," said Shirley Watkins. "There was a tremendous amount of discussion about it because Mrs. Reagan felt it would be politically embarrassing for her to attend. She said that AIDS was not something she should be identified with, but because of her friendship with Liz Taylor she had to be careful. A letter was drafted and sent declining the invitation and wishing her well."

Ignoring the First Lady's rebuff, Elizabeth Taylor, chairing the event for the nonprofit American Foundation for AIDS Research, called the White House to speak to Nancy personally.

"You and the President have got to take this AIDS thing seriously," she said. "I want you to be there for that fund-raising dinner. It's in Washington on a Sunday evening, and you'll be back from Camp David in time to attend. You'll hurt yourselves if you aren't there."

Nancy reluctantly agreed and called her favorite speech writer, Landon Parvin, to prepare remarks for the President, who would be speaking publicly about AIDS after six years of silence. She decided that Ronald Reagan could not recommend mandatory testing because it would touch off a bitter demonstration, but she allowed him to call for routine testing of federal prisoners, immigrants, and marriage license applicants. This still caused an uncomfortable amount of booing and hissing from homosexual activists that evening, prompting the Reagans to leave early.

A reporter asked the departing President if "Just Say No" to sexual intercourse was the best policy he could recommend to teenagers for avoiding AIDS.

"That's a pretty good answer," the President said. "Yes."

Having now publicly acknowledged the disease, Reagan agreed to appoint a presidential commission to make recommendations on the medical, legal, ethical, social, and economic effects of the disease. To satisfy vociferous homosexual leaders, Nancy insisted that he name a homosexual to the thirteen-member board. "You'll look bad if you don't," she told him. Despite the counsel of his conservative advisers, he followed her advice. By doing so, he spared himself a massive protest from the homosexual community.

As soon as she saw that it was politically correct and even fashionable to support AIDS events, the First Lady allowed her name to be used as honorary chairman of a benefit in New York City organized by her high-society friends Ann Bass and Nan Kempner. But Nancy would not attend.

"She wanted to confine herself to drug abuse," said Shirley Watkins, "because she could get more public mileage out of 'Just Say No' than she ever could out of AIDS."

The First Lady had profited handsomely from embracing the social concern of drug abuse. Since the start of her campaign in 1982, the Gallup poll had chosen her every year as one of the "Ten Most Admired Women" in the world. She addressed the United Nations and was publicly honored for shining a national spotlight on the problem. She also received an honorary doctorate from Georgetown University. Money poured in from individuals, corporations, and foreign countries eager to contribute to *her* cause. In fact, so much money came into the White House that the First Lady's chief of staff at the time, James Rosebush, suggested in 1985 setting up the Nancy Reagan Drug Abuse Fund, a permanent endowment to be administered by the Community Foundation of Greater Washington, Inc.

"Mrs. Reagan wanted to set up a private foundation in her name, but the law prohibited that while she was in the White House, so they came to us," said a foundation official. "We did not want this fund controlled by Mrs. Reagan, so we suggested that she name an advisory committee to record the contributions and make recommendations on the disbursements."

The First Lady chose for her advisory committee: Joseph L. Albritton, chairman and chief executive officer of the Riggs National Bank of Washington, D.C.; John Kester, an attorney with Williams & Connolly; Nancy Reynolds, her former aide from Sacramento; the columnist George F. Will; and Richard Helms, the former director of the Central Intelligence Agency. Helms, a former U.S. ambassador to Iran, wore his perjury conviction for his testimony before the Senate Foreign Relations Committee on CIA operations in Chile as a badge of honor. And he relished his reputation as "The Man Who Kept the Secrets." All of this impressed Nancy Reagan, who made him chairman of her committee.

From the time Nancy had moved into the White House, she had curried favor with Arab oil potentates. Now it was their turn. With Mideast countries pressing her husband to extract concessions from Israel for a peace treaty, she was in a position to extract barrels of money from them. In February 1985, while the Reagan administration was considering a request from Saudi Arabia to buy sophisticated AWACS surveillance planes, King Fahd gave her $1 million for her drug fund. Twenty months later, an Egyptian businessman with ties to Saudi Arabia gave her $100,000, and the next month a Saudi tycoon delivered another check from King Fahd for $1 million. These petrodollars, combined with money the First Lady raised from her celebrity tennis tournaments at the White House every year, swelled the assets of the fund to $3.8 million.

Even the Sultan of Brunei, said to be the wealthiest man in the world, contributed to the Nancy Reagan Drug Abuse Fund—$500,000. (A year later, the Sultan gave to another Reagan pet cause—Lieutenant Colonel Oliver North's Iran-Contra fund: $10 million.)

The First Lady's drug-abuse campaign drew her to visit Phoenix Academy in Westchester County, New York, just north of Manhattan, in the fall of 1986. The director, Dr. Mitchell Rosenthal, escorted her through the sprawling complex of red-brick buildings that served as home and school for 250 young recovering drug addicts. Mrs. Reagan was interested in Phoenix House because of its stature as the nation's largest nonprofit drug-rehabilitation program. Dr. Rosenthal, a psychiatrist and the driving force behind Phoenix House, suggested to her that they join forces and establish a facility in Los Angeles that would bear her name.

"Let me think about it," she told him. A few weeks later, she sent Richard Helms, Jack Courtemanche, her new chief of staff, and George Scharffenberger, CEO of *Home Life,* who managed the Reagans' blind trust, to look at the site and make recommendations. She very much wanted to have an important facility bearing her name, and her advisers wanted to make it possible for her.

Letters and proposals discussing the Nancy Reagan Drug Center flew back and forth between Helms and Rosenthal. They agreed that it would provide extensive space for children, set aside an office for the First Lady

when she left the White House, and be convenient to Bel Air, which is
where she wanted to live. Dr. Rosenthal spent two years looking for the
ideal site, and he found it when the Lake View Medical Center in the San
Fernando Valley went bankrupt. The estimated site acquisition plus re-
modeling the existing center would cost about $10 million. Helms flew
to Los Angeles to negotiate the details and arranged for Phoenix House
to buy the center intact for $7.7 million. He authorized a $200,000
down payment from the Nancy Reagan Drug Abuse Fund, and the bankruptcy judge gave Phoenix House six and a half months to raise the rest
of the money.

"With the $3.8 million in the Nancy Reagan Drug Abuse Fund which
she had pledged to us, we felt we were on our way," said Jo Ann Burton,
former director of development for Phoenix House in Los Angeles.
"While Mitch had no qualms about aligning himself and his organization
with the First Lady, others were a little dubious about her commitment to
the program. She said that federal law prohibited her from raising money
while in the White House, and she forbade us to go to her personal
friends for funds because she wanted all of them to give to the Ronald
Reagan presidential library. The library took preference over everything."

Even so, Mrs. Reagan convinced the Phoenix House board of her
sincerity when she said she was in the drug-abuse fight for life. She
reassured them of her commitment to fund-raising for the center by making Merv Griffin head of the capitalization drive. One board member
said, "She chose Merv because he's rich and they both share the same
astrologer."

Griffin, who says he's worth "over $1 billion on paper" and probably
"$200 million in cash," agreed to hold a fund-raising breakfast in the
tennis pavilion of his four-acre Beverly Hills estate. The First Lady said
she would attend the breakfast, make a brief speech, and then, to skirt the
law prohibiting her from fund-raising, leave while Griffin made the sales
pitch.

"Merv had recommended Suzanne Marx, a doctor's wife from Los
Angeles, to do volunteer fund-raising," a Phoenix House executive said.
"She was superb because of her indefatigable energy and her awe of Mrs.
Reagan, which meant that she would gladly endure the First Lady's lofty
attitude. At their first meeting to discuss the project, Suzanne arrived
with all the statistics on the Betty Ford Clinic—a $9.6 million facility that
was funded entirely by private benefactors and continues private fund-
raising to finance special programs and projects. Mrs. Reagan got very
arch when Betty Ford's name was mentioned. 'I don't want to know
anything about Mrs. Ford's little project,' she said. Later, Mitch [Rosen-

thal] told us that Betty Ford is a name you don't *ever* mention around Nancy Reagan.

"We submitted an impressive list of two hundred powerful people from which to fund-raise. We thought the list should be bipartisan since drug abuse affects everyone, but obviously Mrs. Reagan thought otherwise because she axed the names of Michael Eisner, head of Disney Studios, and producer Norman Lear, both of whom are liberal Democrats. She wanted to cross off Marvin Davis, too, because she said he was too loud and vulgar, but we prevailed on that one. She added Frank Sinatra's name, but he refused to attend, and then sent a letter saying he was financially overcommitted for the next three years. He never gave a penny to the project."

The Griffin breakfast guests were multimillionaires all, including Michael King, president of King World; the billionaire developer David Murdock; the racetrack owner Marje Everett; the hotelier Barron Hilton; Unocal chairman Fred Hartley; Thrifty Drug chairman Leonard Straus; David Carpenter of TransAmerica; producers Grant Tinker and Jerry Weintraub; Fred Hayman of Giorgio's; architect Charles Luckman; Korn/Ferry International president Richard Ferry; "Dear Abby" columnist Abigail Van Buren; and attorney John Anderson, who had recently given $15 million to the UCLA Graduate School.

After the breakfast, the First Lady spoke to the guests. "I just want to put to rest the whole idea that my antidrug campaign was a p.r. thing created for me," she said. She cited a Sacramento interview when her husband was governor in which she talked about the need to combat drug abuse. She said that it had taken her the last five years to persuade the entertainment industry to stop making movies that glamorized drugs. "But there is still a tremendous need for education and for facilities to help youthful drug abusers," she said. "The final answer lies in taking the customers away from the product. . . . We've got to do it, and I need your help."

She then excused herself and left. Merv Griffin took over, telling the group that the First Lady planned to take an active role in the Nancy Reagan Drug Center. He quoted her as saying: " 'I cannot come back to the community and pour tea every day. I would go out of my mind.' "

He asked everyone for a generous contribution to put the First Lady's name in lights for Phoenix House, and Suzanne Marx followed up later by contacting all the potential givers in the group. John Anderson floored her when he said that he wouldn't give a dime to Mrs. Reagan's building because every time she met him she looked right through him as if he didn't exist.

"That man [Anderson]," said a Phoenix House executive, "had the capability of making the same $15 million donation to Phoenix House that he did to UCLA, but we lost any hope of ever involving him or his influential friends in our cause because of the First Lady's rudeness. That should've been a signal to us of what Nancy Reagan was really like, but, unfortunately, we were so focused on making the drug center happen that we closed our eyes to the danger signs along the way. None of us envisioned the disaster that was to occur; as negative as some of us might have been toward Nancy Reagan in the beginning, we never thought she would do what she finally did to us."

The Merv Griffin breakfast was expected to raise $5 million of the $10 million needed. Griffin pledged $500,000, but though the guests were among the wealthiest people in southern California, no one pledged a cent.

"That breakfast was a disaster because Nancy sat there playing the queen," recalled the Phoenix House executive. "She did not move. She did not make the rounds as she should have, greeting people personally and thanking them for coming. She sat there throughout as if they should come to her. That is not how you raise money."

In April of 1988, the First Lady committed herself to being the honorary chairman of a large dinner to introduce Phoenix House to the corporate community of Los Angeles. The board of directors voted to bestow their first public service award on Robert Erburu, chief executive officer of the Times Mirror Company, which owns the *Los Angeles Times*. Told that the First Lady would be presenting the award, Erburu accepted, and Phoenix House began selling tables to corporations that wanted to be represented.

"We reserved the Century Plaza for the evening and hired a professional organization to plan the party," said a board member. "We spent thousands of dollars on the event, ordering the invitations and the programs, because we wanted everything to be perfect. This was our chance to send a message to the community that we were legitimate. We were having some zoning problems on the proposed facility and getting opposition from the Lake View Terrace neighborhood, so this was more than just a dinner to us. It was our way of saying to the community that we are a substantial organization doing serious and creditable work in the field of drug abuse. Having the imprimatur of the most important, influential, and powerful newspaper in the area is no small thing for an organization such as ours, because the leading newspaper frequently determines how work is viewed in the community. Mrs. Reagan was aware of how crucial this evening was to us and to her drug center, but she felt abused by the *Los Angeles Times* and, of course, as we found out later, there was the small matter of Brooke Astor's dinner party."

Six weeks before the Phoenix House dinner, the First Lady's chief of staff called Dr. Rosenthal to say she would not be attending. "There's been a change in the schedule of such magnitude that my hands are tied," said Jack Courtemanche. Dr. Rosenthal called the White House to plead with Nancy, but she remained unmovable, falling back on her standard excuse. "I'm sorry, Mitch, but it's scheduling, and there's nothing I can do about it."

Hearing that the First Lady would no longer grace the gathering, the guest of honor quickly disengaged himself from the event, and those who had bought tables in his honor also began calling in their regrets. In the end, Phoenix House was forced to cancel the dinner at substantial expense. "Suddenly we looked like a flaky organization in the one city where we needed to establish our credentials," said a board member. "It was quite damaging to us. And all because Mrs. Reagan could not say no to a small dinner party invitation from Brooke Astor. We should've known then that we were traveling with a troublesome partner, but we still didn't foresee the catastrophe to come."

The impending calamity drew closer when the First Lady's advisers called Dr. Rosenthal to inquire about the size of the staff and the amount of office space Phoenix House was prepared to allocate for her. Dr. Rosenthal expected to provide an office for her in the Nancy Reagan Drug Abuse Center, but it turned out that Helms and Courtemanche had more in mind than just simple office space. They visualized a luxurious suite in Century City next door to the President's penthouse offices in Fox Plaza. They explained that, as First Lady, Mrs. Reagan had become accustomed to a White House staff costing more than $2 million a year. Upon retirement, she would be returning to California without so much as a secretary. Because she had no intention of paying for her own staff, and the federal government did not provide funds for former First Ladies, she expected Phoenix House to carry the load. She estimated the cost would be at least $300,000 a year.

Dr. Rosenthal listened to the proposal and then dutifully consulted with some of his board members, who expressed indignation. Mrs. Paul (Mickey) Ziffren threatened to resign if the nonprofit organization voted to underwrite such an expenditure. "It would be absolutely improper," she said. Phoenix House's charter requires it to devote its resources to caring for drug abusers, not for caring for the overprivileged.

As a result of the negative reaction by members, the board turned down Mrs. Reagan's request, and she took it as a personal insult. She felt that the *least* Phoenix House could do was to lay out $300,000 a year for her. After all, she had attracted a lot of rich people to Phoenix House, including Barron Hilton, who, in just one transaction, underwrote a fund-raising dinner guaranteeing the drug-rehabilitation program $1 million.

Hearing about her demands in Los Angeles made officials of the Community Foundation of Greater Washington uneasy, as they were administering the Nancy Reagan Drug Abuse Fund of almost $4 million. The board of directors suggested that the president, Lawrence Stinchcomb, try to get a better understanding of what Mrs. Reagan intended to do with that money when she left Washington. Stinchcomb called Helms and asked whether he would arrange a luncheon to discuss the matter.

"The advisory board was rounded up, but Larry was never able to penetrate the Nancy Reagan façade," said a foundation executive.

"We all showed up at Helms's house, and during the luncheon Larry started right in by asking Mrs. Reagan what she intended to do with the money we were managing. She smiled and turned to Helms, or Mr. Ambassador, as he preferred to be called.

" 'What do you think should happen to it, Dick?' she asked.

" 'I think the proposed Nancy Reagan Drug Abuse Center in California presents a wonderful opportunity to continue the marvelous work you've started here in Washington. We have such a splendid opportunity with that, and it's so close to the ranch.'

"Nancy Reynolds agreed, and Nancy Reagan smiled again. 'I really need to give this some thought. I'd like your ideas, Joe,' she said.

" 'I think a hospital should be built,' said Albritton, 'so that we can study why people get hooked on drugs.'

"Nancy Reynolds agreed with that, too, and then Nancy Reagan turned to George Will, who was always the dominant influence on her in these matters. He was her intellectual superior—aloof, articulate, and formidable. 'I'm sure you'll want to put the money into medical research, Nancy, because, after all, your father was a doctor who made such great contributions to medical science,' he said.

"Nancy Reynolds, who agreed with every suggestion made, clapped her hands and so did Nancy Reagan. 'Oh, yes, George, that is a wonderful idea,' she said.

"Nothing conclusive was decided at that luncheon," said the foundation executive, "but afterward Mrs. Reagan turned to Stinchcomb, and said, 'Gee, Larry, I've certainly got a lot to think about, don't I?' With that she put on her little red Adolfo coat and off she went. The next thing we knew, she'd set up her own private foundation in California and expected us to release all the money we were managing in the Nancy Reagan Drug Abuse Fund. That fund had been established as a permanent endowment and legally we could have kept it, but we did not want to risk unfavorable publicity that might have influenced future donors.

The day after the Reagans left office, Helms contacted us for the funds and we wired them to Mrs. Reagan's personal foundation. God only knows what she'll do with all that money now. I shudder to think."

Nancy's establishing her own nonprofit foundation troubled Dr. Mitchell Rosenthal, who could not understand why the First Lady would need such an endowment. After all, she was still committed to the Nancy Reagan Drug Abuse Center. She had pledged $5 million to Phoenix House for its new center, and on the basis of that pledge Phoenix House had already spent $600,000 and hired lawyers to deal with the zoning problems and permits. They hoped to open the facility by late 1989. For Dr. Rosenthal, who had dedicated his life to drug rehabilitation, the Los Angeles center was the capstone of his twenty-seven-year career. Now he was understandably nervous about his most important benefactor, and he sought reassurance from Helms, who dismissed the creation of the Nancy Reagan Foundation as nothing more than a way to finance a personal staff.

"Mr. Ambassador" did not realize how determined the First Lady was to maintain her White House standard of living. She knew that with her own foundation she could pay herself a munificent salary, hire a staff, and furnish high-priced offices filled with her favorite flowers. As long as her expenses pertained to foundation business, the foundation would also pay for her first-class travel, hotel suites, and entertainment plus a clipping service, magazine and newspaper subscriptions, postage, telephone, and stationery. For the previous eight years, all those expenses had been paid by taxpayers.

With her own foundation, she could make public service announcements on television and conduct a publicity campaign geared to reaping favorable press coverage and keeping her name in the public eye. She could operate like Brooke Astor, a genuine philanthropist, and make grants of any size to any antidrug program she approved without confining herself exclusively to Phoenix House. She could maintain her public posture of commitment to drug rehabilitation; she could also continue socializing with movie stars by sponsoring the celebrity tennis tournaments that would bring in at least $450,000 a year. She would not be required to give away much money—"only what is considered reasonable" is the way the California law is interpreted by the attorney general's office in Sacramento.* Best of all, she would be in absolute control of the money she raised and distributed, and not have to answer to anyone. Nor would she have to contend with an uproar like the one Phoenix House had touched off among the residents of Lake View Terrace, who

---

* By December of 1989, the Nancy Reagan Foundation had accumulated assets of $4,868,221 and distributed approximately 10 percent.

vociferously resented having a drug-abuse center in their neighborhood and threatened to picket the Reagans' home in Bel Air.

She seized on that threat as her best excuse and broke her longstanding commitment to Phoenix House. She said she no longer wanted the drug-abuse center in her name because she could not put up with protesters in her elegant new neighborhood. "I didn't go into private life to be picketed," she told Mickey Ziffren. "I just can't cope with picketing." She neglected to call Dr. Rosenthal, who learned of her decision in the newspapers.

In that instant, his dream dissolved, for he did not have the financial backing to proceed with the project without Mrs. Reagan. "It's such a waste," he said, surveying the deserted site that would have rehabilitated hundreds of drug-addicted young people. "Such a waste."

As much as Phoenix House lost by Mrs. Reagan's withdrawal from the project, she probably suffered more: A community that had once praised her now damned her. Suddenly, her "lifetime commitment" to fighting drug abuse looked fraudulent, and people who had believed in her felt betrayed. Yet she seemed not to understand why she was so heatedly denounced. "I don't think I deserve to be in the spot the Phoenix House supporters and the press have put me for having decided I was doing too much and for removing my name from the building of the L.A. treatment center," she complained. "I don't believe I deserve all this negative publicity when I have worked so hard."

The hard work definitely paid off—for Nancy Reagan. The Nancy Reagan Drug Abuse Fund worth $3.8 million was transferred from Washington, D.C., to the Nancy Reagan Foundation in Los Angeles. The foundation is situated in Nancy Reagan's suite of offices in Century City. The foundation is administered by Nancy Reagan, overseen by Nancy Reagan, and operated for the benefit of Nancy Reagan.

23

THE FIRST LADY BURST INTO TEARS. The waterworks started in November of 1987 when she heard someone on a television talk show speculate about impeaching the President over Iran-Contra. "I'll never forget the horror I felt," she said months later.

"She was so worried about impeachment," said a family friend, "she would have done anything to buy Congress off."

Her husband had fought with Congress over aid to the Contras, the U.S.-backed rebels in Nicaragua, whom he referred to as "the moral equal of our Founding Fathers." Congress had denied his plea for the aid and so, to circumvent Congress, Lieutenant Colonel Oliver North of the National Security Council had devised a complex scheme: Washington would sell arms to Iran in hopes of freeing American hostages, and revenues from those secret arms sales would pay for Reagan's covert war in Nicaragua. Eventually, the proceeds from the sales—$30 million—were funneled through Swiss bank accounts to the Contras.

On November 24, 1986, Attorney General Ed Meese discovered North's memo outlining the diversion. He advised the President the next day that he had to disclose the scheme immediately so he would not be accused of a cover-up and face possible impeachment. He also said Reagan had to fire North. The President called North on the telephone and said, "This is going to make a great movie one day," then he fired him. Afterward, the President commended the marine colonel publicly as a hero, and allowed the National Security Council director, Admiral John Poindexter, to resign gracefully.

The President's disclosure that the United States had been secretly selling weapons to the Ayatollah Khomeini, whose Iranian fanatics had taken Americans hostage and sponsored terrorists, dumbfounded people. Both Republicans and Democrats assailed the President, and former Presidents Gerald Ford and Jimmy Carter were stupefied.

"We've paid ransom, in effect, to the kidnappers of our hostages," said Carter. "The fact is that every terrorist in the world who reads a newspaper or listens to the radio knows that they've taken American hostages and we've paid them to get the hostages back. This is a very serious mistake in how to handle a kidnapping or hostage-taking."

"Whoever initiated this covert operation," said Ford, "and carried it out deserves some condemnation by certain people in the Congress, by people on the outside."

Once revered as the great communicator, President Reagan stammered when he went on television, stumbling into one falsehood after the other as he asserted that he didn't know anything about the secret arms sales to Iran or the diversion of funds to the Contras. "I was not fully informed," he said. Not even his own brother believed him. The next day, the President suffered the sharpest one-month drop in popularity ever recorded by public opinion polls measuring presidential job performance. For the first time in his presidency, Ronald Reagan's lack of credibility was certified.

The First Lady was livid. She blamed White House chief of staff Donald Regan for what she said was the worst crisis of her husband's presidency. She thought that Regan, who had described himself as "the de facto President" and "the second most important man in Washington," should shoulder the blame for the Iran-Contra mess. "After all, it happened on his watch," she said.

Regan rushed to dissociate himself from the crisis by telling the *New York Times:* "Some of us are like a shovel brigade that follow a parade down Main Street cleaning up after the elephant." That comment sent the First Lady into a sputtering rage. "I can't deal with that man anymore," she told her husband. She urged him to fire Regan, but the President balked.

Like a butcher going for the meat cleaver, she grabbed the telephone and called her hatchet men: Paul Laxalt, Stuart Spencer, and Michael Deaver, the latter currently under indictment on five counts of perjury for lying to a congressional subcommittee and a grand jury. As a result, he was being investigated by a special prosecutor, who was also accusing him of influence peddling. None of this stopped Deaver from joining forces with Laxalt and Spencer to do the First Lady's bidding. Her three myrmidons phoned reporters, who produced news stories quoting "family friends" and "White House insiders" as saying that Mrs. Reagan was hurt, stunned, and distressed by the crisis overwhelming her husband, and they said she wanted to get rid of Don Regan, CIA director Casey, and Secretary of State Shultz, who had opposed the Iran-Contra deal to no avail and then withdrawn from it.

Suspicion and accusation ricocheted around Washington, swamping talk shows and newspapers with rumors that Mrs. Reagan was consulting a group of longtime California supporters to persuade the President to fire his top aides. She denied the rumors. "I'm just talking to friends," she said.

A few days later, one of those friends, George Will, wrote: "The aides in close contact with President Reagan today are the least distinguished such group to serve any president in the postwar period."

By Thanksgiving, Donald Regan saw himself on the platter. "Sounds to me like I'm the turkey," he said.

"Don got his nuts cut off," said Dennis Thomas, one of Regan's top aides. "He didn't have a chance after Nancy decided he should go."

The First Lady told friends that the President's circuits were overloaded, and she began executing the duties of chief executive. Dismayed by his poor performance on television, she forbade press conferences and prohibited reporters' questions during photo opportunities. She instructed the White House press office that the President was to be totally isolated from the press.

Forlorn, Reagan acquiesced. He had not been so depressed and withdrawn since his first term as governor when it was disclosed that his administration was harboring a homosexual ring. Now, Iran-Contra had turned the country against him. "How can they really think I'm a liar?" he asked repeatedly. He was so crestfallen by his plunge in the polls that when he greeted the New York Giants after the Super Bowl and mentioned "our fans," he quickly amended himself. "Your fans, I should say. I don't have many fans anymore."

Her husband's vanishing popularity panicked Mrs. Reagan. "This was extremely disturbing to her—extremely," recalled Don Regan. "Because she knew that if that continued, the lame-duck image would really be pasted on this man, and he still had a lot of other things she hoped he could do."

Quickly assuming presidential prerogatives, the First Lady began dictating orders to the White House chief of staff. "She did it all with the telephone," said Regan's aide. "She would call Don at home every night and tell him to fire Secretary of Health and Human Services Margaret

Heckler. 'She's hurting Ronnie,' she'd say. Heckler was in the hospital at the time, so Don would say, 'Later. We'll do it later.'

"Nancy would call him the next day. 'Don, what have you done about Peggy Heckler? I want her fired.'

" 'But she's recuperating from a hysterectomy,' said Don.

" 'I don't care. Fire her.'

" 'I can't do it while she's in the hospital.'

" 'Get rid of the goddamned woman.'

"An hour later, Kathy Osborne, the President's secretary, would call Don. 'What about Peggy Heckler?' she'd ask. Two hours later, Stu Spencer would call and say, 'What about the Heckler dame?' Nancy had everyone running interference for her, but she was always the vague, shadowy presence in the background. That's the way she operated. She'd hit you first and then send in her reserves to wear you down. Once you were on the ropes, she'd come back and finish you off.

"Don waited too long on the Heckler matter and paid a price with the First Lady," said another Regan aide. "When Heckler was out of the hospital, he called to meet with her, but Peggy wouldn't do it. He finally had to ask Stu Spencer to meet with her at a hotel to work out terms. She'd resign, if she got appointed ambassador to Ireland. Regan got killed in the press for that one and branded inept, while it was actually the First Lady's doing.

"She did the same thing with Bill Casey. When he was in the hospital dying of a brain tumor around Christmas of 1987, she was calling Don six and eight times a day, demanding that he fire Casey because of his involvement in Iran-Contra.

" 'How's that going to look?' Don would say.

" 'He's hurting Ronnie.'

" 'The man is dying.'

" 'You're more interested in protecting Bill Casey than in protecting Ronnie. He's dragging Ronnie down. Fire him.' "

Believing that Regan was trying to protect the man who had brought *him* into the Reagan administration, the First Lady asked her stepbrother, Dr. Richard Davis, to call Casey's doctor about his prognosis. When she found out that the CIA director was indeed terminal, she was even more determined that he should walk the plank. After calling Casey's wife, Sophia, to wish her a Merry Christmas, Nancy called Don Regan and told him to fire Casey the next day.

"I told her that the President was probably going to send him a gentle letter soon, asking him to step aside," recalled Regan.

"Send it to his lawyer," snapped the First Lady, "because Sophia won't let it be delivered to Casey. And do it tomorrow."

Regan decided to visit his dying friend in the hospital instead, and took the Attorney General with him to obtain Casey's resignation. Afterward, he called Mrs. Reagan to say the deed had been done. "Good," she replied, slamming down the receiver.

A few days later, Regan's aide Dennis Thomas received a call from Mike Deaver inviting him for a drink after work. "I'd like to share some thoughts about rehabilitating the presidency," Deaver told Thomas. "Don really isn't helping himself or the President by staying on." Thomas disagreed, saying the President should not consent to a lynching party for his chief of staff because that would weaken Reagan's strength.

The First Lady was frustrated by her husband's refusal to fire his chief of staff. She nagged the President incessantly: "I was right about Stockman. I was right about Bill Clark. Why won't you listen to me about Don Regan?" Getting no place by herself, she started calling various members of Congress and asking them to tell the President how crucial it was for him to get rid of Regan, who had no support on Capitol Hill. The congressmen complied, and the President listened, but he did nothing—one of the few times he defied his wife.

Immobilized by the scandal swirling around him, Reagan seemed more distracted than ever. He couldn't understand why the American people didn't trust him, especially after he had appointed the Tower Commission to investigate what had happened; he had also named David Abshire, a former ambassador to NATO, as a special counselor to provide information to the investigating committees so no one could accuse Reagan of a cover-up. He still avoided apologizing for the arms sales to Iran beyond the televised admission that "mistakes were made." By whom, he didn't say. Although he blamed North and Poindexter privately, Reagan would not say so publicly. He left that to his wife, who kept telling reporters that the President had been misled. "He did not know what was going on," she said, "and that's not right. . . . He was badly served by the people on his staff." At her urging, Reagan gave North and Poindexter limited immunity to testify before the intelligence committees of Congress.

"They are the only ones who know what happened," the First Lady told the press. "No one else knows. Ronnie certainly doesn't know. That's why we are looking forward to the testimony of North and Poindexter."

Pursuing her campaign against Regan, she pressed Mike Deaver, who suggested she contact former Secretary of State William Rogers and Robert Strauss, the former chairman of the Democratic National Committee, outsiders whom the President might consider more objective. Nancy invited the two men to the White House family quarters to talk, and both advised the President of his liabilities, with Strauss bluntly suggesting he fire Regan. Reagan rejected the advice, saying he refused to throw his friend to the wolves, but the First Lady was grateful for the candor. She later called Strauss to thank him, saying that she agreed with everything he said.

"She's a smarter and tougher woman than I ever thought she was," Strauss confided to a friend. "But she apparently does not control her husband to the degree some people think. I believe the country would be better off if she did."

The President was scheduled for prostate surgery in January 1987, but the First Lady would not let the physicians at Bethesda Naval Hospital perform the surgery. Still smarting from the publicity surrounding his earlier cancer surgery, she called upon her father's friends at the Mayo Clinic and flew in a team of seven doctors to perform the prostate operation. She told them not to talk to the press, and they complied.

When the President entered the hospital, he was already disheartened by the scandal, and the surgery, common for men his age (seventy-six) but uncomfortable, left him enervated. The doctors suggested six weeks' rest, which his wife mandated. Once again she decided which photograph to release to the public. When a White House photographer showed up, she covered her husband's bare knees and ordered the photographer not to shoot. She quickly placed papers on the President's lap to make it look as if he had been working.

Before Christmas, the First Lady had called Dennis Thomas. "There is an absolute need to get the President out in public and show him as a leader who is in charge of the country," she said. "I want you to give me a plan of speeches and trips which will accomplish that when we return after the holidays."

But while the First Lady directed the presidency, her astrologer directed her. By the time Thomas reported back with his ninety-day plan, her San Francisco soothsayer had convinced Mrs. Reagan that the President should not appear in public for 120 days.

"Nancy gave me my plan with eighty-five days blacked out," recalled Thomas. "She said there were too many moons converging at once and the President couldn't travel. It was debilitating sitting in the White House, watching the President sink lower in the polls and knowing his judgments were being made by Nancy and her astrologers. There was another astrologer, so we weren't just dealing with Joan Quigley, but Nancy never gave us either name."

Eager for a second opinion to revive her husband's popularity, the First Lady had turned to her former seer, Jeane Dixon, who prepared written zodiac counsel and had it delivered to the White House—all free.

"Mrs. Dixon would call, and I would be sent to the East Gate to pick up her envelope for the First Lady," recalled one of Mrs. Reagan's secretaries. "I thought it was a joke and not to be taken seriously, but Elaine [Crispen] always rushed those envelopes right up to the family quarters."

Joan Quigley's astrological explanation for confining the President to the White House for four months was "the malevolent movements of Uranus and Saturn," which she said had turned against him. "These two planets were in Sagittarius, the sign that has so much to do with foreigners and foreign affairs and legal and judicial matters. . . . There is danger of impeachment during this period, and the danger of assassination is very real."

Relying primarily on her $3,000-a-month astrologer, the First Lady insisted the President stay inside the White House. She relented, though, and let him out long enough on January 27, 1987, to go to Capitol Hill to deliver the State of the Union message, but she took control of the speech he was to deliver.

"That was not unusual," said Dennis Thomas. *"All* of the President's speeches and remarks were delivered to Nancy Reagan before they were ever shown to the President. She edited them, made her suggestions, and they were all incorporated. Then he was given the speech."

The First Lady was determined to get rid of all right-wing rhetoric. "Don't you let Pat Buchanan have a single thing to do with writing Ronnie's State of the Union speech," she had told Don Regan. "His ideas aren't Ronald Reagan's ideas."

A few days before the speech, three drafts were submitted for the Reagans' consideration. The First Lady read each one, then called Regan to say that she was bringing in Ken Khachigian from California to rework the final draft.

"The parts about abortion have got to come out," she said. "I don't give a damn about the right-to-lifers. I'm cutting back on the Iran stuff, too. It's too long and it's not appropriate. Ronald Reagan's got to be shown to be in charge."

"She wanted the whole speech to be patriotic," Regan said later. "She wanted it all red, white, and blue."

With 62 percent of the country now convinced that he was lying about the scandal, the President delivered a State of the Union address that was his most confrontational. Once again, he declined to apologize for selling arms to Iran. His blustering manner set off partisan rounds of applause by the Republicans, who gave him standing ovations, while the Democrats, emboldened by his plummeting polls, sat on their hands.

The First Lady now dropped all public pretense about her feelings toward Don Regan and put on the boxing gloves. Calling him with daily orders, she enjoyed the obvious discomfort she inflicted each time he picked up the phone. "Oh, are you still here, Don?" she would ask with mock surprise.

By February, the chief of staff was determined to ignore her objections and schedule a press conference for the President, who held only forty-seven press conferences in his eight years in office—fewer than any President of the twentieth century.

"It simply has to be done," Regan said. "Otherwise, he looks like he's hiding."

"Absolutely not," said Mrs. Reagan.

The First Lady scrapped with the tough ex-marine until she was exhausted.

"I was furious," she said later. "When it was clear that I wasn't going to change his mind, I said, 'Okay, have your damn press conference.' "

"You bet I will," said Regan, slamming down the phone.

Days later, George Will wrote about the White House chief of staff in his syndicated column: "Nothing in his deplorable conduct of his office has been as contemptible as his clinging to it."

Regan was determined to hang on to his job until the Tower Commission report was published. He told the President he planned to resign after its publication and asked that his secretaries be kept on at the White House. The President agreed, but Mrs. Reagan had other plans. Minutes after the Tower report was issued, condemning Regan for "the chaos that descended upon the White House" and criticizing the President's sloth and ignorance by faulting his "personal management style," Nancy Reagan moved.

Having nudged her husband, a few days before, into secretly offering the chief of staff job to Howard Baker, the former Republican senator from Tennessee, she now had that news leaked to Cable News Network. When they called her for a comment, she told her press secretary to say that she wished Don Regan good luck and welcomed the arrival of Howard Baker. The First Lady's public statement caught both the President and the chief of staff by surprise, and denied Regan the dignified departure he had been promised. He stormed out of the White House that day, leaving a curt letter of resignation.

Four days later, a gleeful Nancy Reagan stood at the lectern of the American Camping Association to deliver a speech. "I don't think most people associate me with leeches or how to get them off," she said coyly. "But I know how to get them off. I'm an expert at it."

Publicly humiliated by the President's wife, Don Regan sought revenge. He joined the long list of former Reagan aides rushing to write memoirs. He was given an advance to $1 million for his. "I'll give some of the money to charity," he said. "Why do I need it when I'm worth thirty to forty million?"

Ronald Reagan's administration had spawned more critical, uninhibited, score-settling memoirs than had any other presidency. The first was former Secretary of State Alexander Haig's memoir, *Caveat,* followed by former Secretary of Education Terrel Bell's *The Thirteenth Man,* former Secretary of Interior James Watt's *The Courage of a Conservative,* former economic policy adviser Martin Anderson's *Revolution,* former director of the Office of Management and Budget David Stockman's *The Triumph of Politics,* former administrator of the Environmental Protection Agency Anne Gorsuch's *Are You Tough Enough?,* former deputy White House press secretary Larry Speakes's *Speaking Out,* former deputy chief of staff Michael Deaver's *Behind the Scenes,* former ambassador Helene von Damm's *At Reagan's Side,* former chief of staff to the First Lady James Rosebush's *First Lady, Public Wife,* former Secretary of Defense Caspar Weinberger's *Fighting for Peace,* former White House speech writer Peggy Noonan's *What I Saw at the Revolution,* and former chief of protocol Selwa "Lucky" Roosevelt's *Keeper of the Gate.*

All the books portrayed the President as an amiable, toothless grandfather figure, telling jokes and spinning tales about Hollywood's heyday. The First Lady was depicted as a cold, scheming virago. "Why do they always pick on Nancy so much?" asked the President, perplexed. Almost all the books appeared while Reagan was still in office, making the backstairs revelations even more embarrassing, especially for the First Lady, who resented the cascade of memoirs dumping on her husband's White House.

"I was furious when David Stockman revealed in a magazine interview that he didn't really believe in the economic plan he was supposed to be implementing," she said. "Had it been up to me, Stockman would have been out on the street that afternoon. . . . There's an implied trust when you're working for the president, *any* president, and David Stockman clearly violated it. . . . If Ronnie had thrown Stockman out when that story appeared, he would have made an example of him. It would have been a signal to everybody else who worked for Ronnie that he expected their loyalty. And who knows? Maybe we wouldn't have had so many kiss-and-tell books about the Reagan years."

Incensed by the disloyal chamberlains rushing into print, Nancy was particularly pained by Michael Deaver, a friend of twenty years. After his book came out in 1987, she stopped speaking to him. His book identified her as the closet liberal who softened U.S. policy toward the Soviet Union and cut the defense budget. After Deaver was convicted of perjury in 1987, he and his family were no longer invited to the Reagans'

Christmas dinner at the White House, and he was forced to resign as a trustee of the presidential library. He was replaced in that role by billionaire publisher Walter Annenberg, who admitted contacting the London advertising and public relations firm of Saatchi & Saatchi to advise them not to merge with Deaver's firm. Negotiations for the $18 million transaction—the price Saatchi & Saatchi was going to pay Deaver—were instantly dropped, leaving Deaver to wonder whether Nancy Reagan had instigated his financial ruin.

By the time the Speakes book was published, the former White House press secretary had accepted a $300,000 position with Merrill Lynch as vice president for corporate affairs. Mrs. Reagan called former White House aide Bill Henkel, also with Merrill Lynch. "I want you to go to the president of the company and tell him how displeased Ronnie and I are about Larry Speakes and his book," she told Henkel. Shortly after that, Speakes lost his job.

The most humiliating memoir by far for the Reagans was Don Regan's *For the Record,* published on Mother's Day 1988. The book disclosed that the First Lady, like the Emperor Augustus, Mary Todd Lincoln, and Adolf Hitler, relied on astrology. It was a proud, tough, bitter, angry memoir by the man who had described himself as the sweeper of elephant dung. "The metaphor holds," editorialized the *Washington Post.* "The only difference now is that Mr. Regan is no longer part of the solution, but part of the problem."

While no one questioned the information in the book, which became a number-one best-seller, the author was denounced by critics as petty, spiteful, and vindictive for betraying the confidences gained through presidential friendship—and for going after the President's wife.

"I would have preferred it if he decided to attack me," said President Reagan. "From what I hear, he's chosen to attack my wife, and I don't look kindly on that at all."

"I'm saying that those are the pimps and whores," said Frank Sinatra. "They're the ones who write the books about people with whom they had a kind of privy association and suddenly they're out making a buck because they got a pigeon."

"The book is destructive of the very process of government," said Brent Scowcroft, national security adviser to President Ford and a member of the Tower Commission that had criticized Regan and called Ronald Reagan lax. "This is very, very bad, particularly when the President is still sitting."

"Everyone wants to see Reagan go out with all his flags flying," said Robert Strauss. "But it's coming unglued right now. His people are just not loyal to him."

"The only time I ever knew the President to go into outer space for advice," said former Reagan aide Joe Canzeri, "was when he chose Don Regan to be his chief of staff."

In a swipe at the President's use of astrology, Speaker of the House Jim Wright said, "I'm glad the President was consulting somebody. I was getting worried there for a while."

Regan's book hurt the President and First Lady by exposing them to public ridicule. Comedians poked fun at them, working wisecracks about astrologers into their monologues. Johnny Carson suggested that overnight the White House had gone from playing "Hail to the Chief" to "That Old Black Magic." Mark Russell said that a reporter, knowing of Mrs. Reagan's interest in the occult, had asked her whether she had ever communed with disembodied spirits. "Why, yes," she replied. "I spoke to the President just this morning."

The japes were dispiriting to the Reagans. Aside from a few trusted aides, no one, not even their children, had ever known how much they relied on astrology. "I thought it was a media joke for a long time," said Ron Reagan. "Then I remember seeing Sam Donaldson on the Brinkley show treating it very seriously, so I finally called up and found out it was real, which was just as big a surprise to me as anyone else."

"I think there is probably a certain validity that people born under a sign have certain characteristics," said Patti Davis. "I can agree with it to that point, but I would *never* let someone tell me what to do with my life or when to leave the house or something. If someone said to me, 'Don't leave the house today because the stars are in a bad place,' I would make a point of leaving the house. . . . I'd be on a plane to South Africa!"

Nancy believed firmly that destiny had united her with Ronald Reagan. Extremely superstitious, she would not put a hat on her bed, walk under a ladder, or put shoes on a shelf higher than her head. She slept with her head and feet facing north and frequently knocked on wood. Ronald Reagan was equally influenced by superstition and the supernatural. He named his dog Lucky, carried good-luck coins in his pocket every day, and threw salt over his shoulder at meals. He believed in the magical charm of number 33, the existence of UFOs, and of Abraham Lincoln's ghost, which he swore inhabited the White House. He predicted the world would come to an Armageddon-like end "in our lifetime," and he subscribed to the destiny of dreams, citing one that he had regularly before he entered government.

"It was always the same thing, maybe a different locale or something," he said, "but I evidently had a yen for big rooms. And I would dream that I was in a big mansion, and I could buy it for a song. A man was showing it to me, and I would go from room to room, and maybe go into the living room, which was two stories high, and there was a balcony. And always, it was within my means to buy it. And I had this dream all the time. After we moved into the White House, I was *in* the big room. And I never had the dream since."

The President had proclaimed his belief in astrology to the newly elected president of Brazil, Tancredo Neves, when the two men met at the White House in 1985. Reagan marched up to Neves, Brazil's first civilian president after twenty-one years of military rule, extended his hand, and said, "Well, you know I've gotten word from someone I take very seriously and like very much, Danny Thomas, that your zodiac sign and mine are compatible and therefore we can't have anything but the best of relations between our two countries." The Brazilian president was left speechless.

While denying now that he had ever allowed stargazers to determine policy for him as President, Reagan would not disavow astrology. "I've not guided my life by it, but I won't answer the question the other way because I don't know enough about it to say there is something to it or not."

Trying to make her obsession appear innocent, the First Lady said she would continue consulting her "friend" in San Francisco. Regan had been unable to identify the First Lady's astrologer because he did not know her name. But when the press discovered her identity, Nancy called Joan Quigley to say her name had been leaked to the media, but that she must not speak to reporters.

"This must never come out! Never. . . . You must say nothing. Ever!"

"I will in no way injure you," said the astrologer. "But I will not refuse to be interviewed. . . . What will I do if someone asks about sensitive matters?"

"Lie if you have to," said Nancy, according to her astrologer.

Disregarding the First Lady's instructions, the astrologer accepted all media inquiries, posed for photographs, appeared on television, and spoke freely about her close association with the Reagans. Months later, she wrote a book entitled *What Does Joan Say? My Seven Years as White House Astrologer to Nancy and Ronald Reagan.* The First Lady never spoke to her again.

Despite Joan Quigley's inability to predict Iran-Contra or Don Regan's crushing memoir or the rupture of her own relationship with Mrs. Reagan, the astrologer claims she did foresee something "troubling" in the First Lady's chart in the fall of 1987 before their friendship foundered:

"Nancy's horoscope had indicated to me months in advance that she would develop breast cancer. I didn't want to alarm her by coming right out and telling her. I knew all too well what a worrier she was. So I did what I always do in such cases. I advised her to have monthly check-ups and frequent mammograms, certain the doctors would discover it the minute it developed."

The First Lady had had mammograms every December, but in the fall of 1987 she surprised her doctors at Bethesda Naval by scheduling an appointment in October. "Getting her out here for her annual check-up was usually hell," said one of her physicians. "We had to coerce her and start calling weeks in advance, but during the height of the Iran-Contra mess when her husband was having all his trouble, she actually called us and came out two months early for her mammogram.

"We found a microcalcification, and I didn't know what to attribute it to. I examined all her previous mammograms, and there had been nothing. She claimed on her medical records that there was no breast cancer in her family. Maybe her astrologer told her she should have her breasts checked. I don't know, but she came out here and that's what we found. She went against all medical advice in deciding to have her entire left breast removed and the underarm lymph nodes. I told her that the radical mastectomy was not called for. It was like taking a shotgun to kill a fly. Such a drastic procedure was totally unnecessary. She should've had a lumpectomy and then undergone radiation two times a week for six weeks. That would've meant a trip to Bethesda Naval Hospital two times a week for a half hour each time. There would have been no side effects —no nausea, no loss of hair, no mutilation. Only a minor sunburn in the breast area. There were other doctors who tried to tell her the same thing, including the Mayo Clinic doctors she had do the surgery, but she would not listen. She was determined to have that mastectomy.

"She did a grave injustice to American women by not saying publicly that the procedure she selected was against all medical advice she received, except for her antediluvian stepbrother, who is of the old school and believes that no matter what is found, the entire breast should be removed. She is so vain that I was flabbergasted when she decided to go ahead with it. I still don't understand why. I hope she didn't undergo that drastic operation simply to get her man off the pan."

Since Nancy had long ago stopped communicating with her natural father, Kenneth Robbins, and his relatives, she had no way of knowing that breast cancer ran in her family. Several of her paternal relatives had developed the disease, and it had caused the death of at least one great-aunt. One of her cousins was diagnosed with breast cancer around the same time, but the cousin chose to have a lumpectomy instead of having the entire breast removed.

"I just can't believe that Nancy would opt for the more extreme measure simply because she didn't want to disturb her White House routine," said her cousin. "That's deranged!"

Doctors around the country criticized Mrs. Reagan for her decision, and the executive director of the Breast Cancer Advisory Center said that she "set us back ten years." The First Lady strenuously disagreed. She appeared on a Barbara Walters television special and defended her decision, saying no one, especially doctors not knowledgeable about the case, had a right to criticize her.

"I couldn't possibly lead the kind of life I lead and keep the schedule that I do having radiation or chemotherapy," she said. "There'd be no way. Maybe if I'd been twenty years old, hadn't been married, hadn't had children, I would feel completely differently. But for me it was right."

What Nancy did not acknowledge was her deathly fear of radiation. She would not even consider the less radical procedure of a lumpectomy because it would require radiation treatments. "She's got a hang-up about it," said one of the Reagans' physicians. "She's terrified of radiation. So is the President. Nancy has got him convinced that radiation will turn them into crispy critters, I guess. I had to constantly tell her that the radiation from a mammography was one ten-thousandth of a rad, which was the minutest percentage of what the five hundred rads would be for breast cancer radiation. Once she understood that, she was better, but both of them are nuts on the subject.

"Going under the knife isn't as frightening to the Reagans as being X-rayed," said the physician. "Both of them have had numerous facelifts. From the scars behind his ears, I'd say the President has had two lifts, and she's probably had three or four. So they're not afraid of surgery, but they're spooked by radiation. It's incomprehensible to me."

The First Lady's schedule was inviolable to her. She felt she needed to be present during the U.S.-Soviet summit in Washington, which was scheduled to be held a few weeks after her surgery. She dared not be incapacitated because she had spent hours with her astrologer planning the exact time the Intermediate-Range Nuclear Forces Treaty should be signed, and Nancy wanted to make sure everything went according to the stargazer's plan. In retrospect, it might have been better had she been indisposed for this summit, because her negative feelings toward her Soviet counterpart became embarrassingly public during the Gorbachevs' visit.

Nancy was still fuming over Raisa Gorbachev's decision the year before to accompany her husband to the summit meeting at Reykjavik, Iceland, although wives had not been invited.

"That last-minute reversal struck me as a bit of one-upmanship," said Mrs. Reagan, who did not change her schedule to accompany the President. She became even more agitated as she sat in the White House watching Raisa on television in her silver fox fur and high-heeled suede boots, oozing *glasnost* glamour. "I was angry that Raisa had been there," she wrote in her memoir. "Her presence seemed frivolous."

The Iceland meeting had failed and ended in rancor. Gorbachev had insisted on a ten-year ban on the development and testing of strategic nuclear weapons. Reagan would not alter his commitment to the Strategic Defense Initiative (SDI). In the following months, both sides worked out a compromise resulting in the treaty that was to be signed at the December 1987 summit in Washington.

Jetloads of Soviets descended on the capital, where their armored black Zil limousines helped clog downtown traffic. Gorbachev, who understood the practice of public relations as well as Reagan, had dispatched 160 spokesmen to sing his praises. The hammer and sickle flew alongside the Stars and Stripes on the lampposts across the street from the White House as the excited city fell into the grip of "Gorby fever."

The First Lady did not join in the enthusiasm. She complained to the press that she had invited Mrs. Gorbachev for tea and a tour of the White House but had had to wait two weeks for a reply. Particularly vexing was Raisa's ready acceptance of a luncheon invitation from Pamela Harriman, the prominent Democratic fundraiser whose husband had been ambassador to Russia during World War II.

"I was offended," said Nancy Reagan. "In the circle we moved in, you don't ignore an invitation from the head of state or his wife."

She was so busy pointing out Mrs. Gorbachev's gaucheries that she committed her own. After all Nancy had done to bring about good relations between the United States and Russia, she was now sabotaging her efforts by not getting along with her Soviet counterpart.

"I missed you in Reykjavik," said Raisa upon her arrival.

"I was told women weren't invited," replied Nancy icily.

Haughty and disdainful in her free $2,100 dress by Oscar de la Renta, the First Lady promoted her fashion superiority by belittling her guest's attire.

"When she got off the plane in Washington," Nancy recalled in a television interview, "her skirt was down to her ankles, and then every day, the skirt would get shorter and shorter and shorter, and I had visions of all these little ladies over at the embassy sewing like crazy all night long to get that dress ready."

Taking the cue from her boss, the First Lady's press secretary looked askance when Mrs. Gorbachev arrived at the White House wearing a satin-collared black crepe dress with a rhinestone belt buckle, black stiletto heels, and sagging rhinestone-studded nylons. Elaine Crispen commented to reporters that such a "get-up seems a bit much for daytime . . . too cocktailish, don't you think?"

While their husbands departed for meetings, Mrs. Reagan served coffee in the Green Room to Mrs. Gorbachev and the wives of the Vice President, the Secretary of State, and the American ambassador to the Soviet Union. Nancy later complained that she had had to sit through another hour of Raisa's hectoring about the Marxist benefits of the USSR.

"She never once mentioned my recent breast cancer surgery, or asked me how I was feeling," Nancy said. "Nor did she offer condolences on the death of my mother."

Raisa returned to the White House the next day for tea and the tour of the mansion that she had requested. She irritated her hostess by gravitating toward the press, prompting a reporter to ask whether she would like to live in such a place.

"It's an official house," she said, surveying the opulence surrounding her. "I would say that humanly speaking a human being would like to live in a regular home. This is a museum."

Nancy gritted her teeth and pointed out the ethereal portrait of Pat Nixon. Raisa turned and headed toward the portrait of Lady Bird Johnson.

"This picture that we face, to what century does it belong? I would say it's a typical picture of the twentieth century."

She then peppered Nancy with questions: Was that a nineteenth-century chandelier? Did Jefferson live here? When was the White House built?

Unable to answer, Nancy turned to the White House guide for help. Clearly irritated now, the First Lady put her hand on Mrs. Gorbachev's arm to guide her away from the press, but Raisa jerked away, leaving Nancy struggling to control her temper.

"I'm not going to be able to show her the rest of the house," she told reporters, who seemed to be salivating for a fistfight. "Regrettably, we have to move on."

That evening, having read the reports of their feud, Raisa raised the subject with the First Lady.

"What is all this about our not getting along?"

"I have no idea," said Nancy. "It's all so silly."

Reporters later asked the First Lady about her forthcoming trip to Moscow for the final U.S.-Soviet summit of Reagan's presidency. "Are you looking forward to being a guest of Mrs. Gorbachev?" "I look forward to Russia," said Nancy dryly.

Six months later, in Moscow, she retaliated. Prepped by a crash course in Russian art and architecture, she met Mrs. Gorbachev for a tour of Assumption Cathedral to view the famous eight-hundred-year-old St. George and the Madonna and Child icons. In a rapid, tutorial tone, the Soviet First Lady began pointing out the historical significance of Russia's restored icons. Mrs. Reagan interrupted her.

"This cathedral now, is it mainly used as just a museum—wait," said Nancy, "I'm not finished yet—or also for religious activities?"

"Nyet," replied Mrs. Gorbachev, adding that such services stopped in 1917.

"Will there be a concert in the cathedral next month during the celebration of the millennium of Christianity?" Nancy asked pointedly.

"Nyet," said Raisa.

"Oh, yes," said Nancy. "The word *nyet*—that I understand."

She seemed quite pleased with herself for having jabbed at the sensitive issue of religious freedom. The women met again two days later at the Tretyakov Gallery, which contains the world's finest collection of Russian art. The gallery had been closed for repairs, but officials set up a special exhibit of icons for Mrs. Reagan. Mrs. Gorbachev arrived early and began talking to the assembled press.

"Did you have a look at the twelfth-century icon?" she asked reporters. "You are in luck to be able to see it. Maybe we'll have a conversation because you're on time and the guests are late."

She proceeded to describe the icons for reporters. "I would advise that you look at faces of the saints the way our icon painters painted them. They are quite open. They are friendly."

Minutes later, Mrs. Reagan rushed in; Mrs. Gorbachev greeted her with a handshake and presented her with a bouquet of roses and a book on the gallery.

"Mrs. Gorbachev has been talking with us," said Bill Greenwood of ABC News, "and we all think you should have equal time. She said there was no religious significance to the icons."

"I don't know how you can neglect the religious elements," Nancy said. "I mean, they're there for everyone to see them."

Mrs. Gorbachev tried to get the tour under way, but Mrs. Reagan stopped her.

"Now I want to say something," said Nancy, shaking her finger as the television cameras rolled. "I want to say something. Okay?"

"We have decided that there will be no interview in the Tretyakov. So please allow us to see the icons," said Mrs. Gorbachev, trying to get the First Lady away from the press.

"I want to talk," replied Mrs. Reagan with a hard edge, causing her hostess to retreat in silence. "I want to talk."

In reporting the final round of the powder-puff wars, the *New York Post* headlined its story: "Nancy: No Praisa for Raisa." All four U.S. networks ran the tape of the First Lady rudely interrupting and raising her eyes to heaven in disapproval of her hostess. That night at the Bolshoi Ballet, the USSR orchestra played the "Star-Spangled Banner," and Nancy stood listening to the national anthem with her right hand over her heart, the only American to salute correctly. The President, who didn't seem to know the words, looked as if he were singing "Old Mac-Donald Had a Farm."

The next day, the Reagans returned home. After viewing the television tapes of her contretemps with Raisa, the First Lady sent a White House courier to deliver a handwritten note to Bill Greenwood's home in Northwest Washington. It read: "Dear Bill: Thank you for giving me equal time! Nancy Reagan."

24

THE PRESIDENT WAS REQUIRED by the Office of Government Ethics
to make public in April every gift that he received, but that law was
ambiguous regarding the First Lady's gifts. So most of the expensive
presents Nancy received during her husband's eight years in office never
became public knowledge. Yet she had accumulated so many that it took
two months of packing and nine flights by Air Force transport planes to
move her gifts, her papers, and all her memorabilia out of the White
House.

Among her undisclosed treasures: a pair of large diamond earrings
from an Israeli diplomat's wife; an extraordinary necklace and earring set
from her friend Betty Wilson, a Pennzoil heiress; an emerald necklace
worth $60,000 from Imelda Marcos; an ornate sterling silver dresser set
monogrammed "N.R." from former White House aide Joe Canzeri; a tin
of caviar worth $1,500 from Kentucky horsebreeder Mary Lou Whitney;
a $1,500 watercolor by Chicago artist Victor Ing; a White House portrait
of Nancy worth $10,000 from the artist, Marian Pike.

But disclosed before she could leave the White House were the more
than $1 million worth of designer suits, dresses, and gowns that Nancy
had been accepting free since 1982, contrary to her promise not to do so.
Time magazine published the disclosure in the fall of 1988, saying Mrs.
Reagan had violated the Ethics in Government Act, that she had avoided
taxes on the clothes and might owe hundreds of thousands of dollars to
the IRS, and that the President, who had signed the income tax and

financial disclosure forms on which these alleged violations were concealed, technically had committed the same violations.

In the *Time* article, Chris Blazakis, a former executive with Galanos Originals, described the First Lady as greedy. He said that Galanos had asked her to select one of two fur jackets to go with the second inaugural gown he was designing for her. One was a $10,500 white mink, the other a $35,000 Russian sable. According to Blazakis, Nancy had wanted both, but Galanos convinced her that the American mink would be more appropriate and did not give her the sable.

At first, Nancy denied the *Time* account. She said she had paid for every item she had acquired in the last six years. Then Los Angeles designer David Hayes said she had borrowed sixty to eighty made-to-order outfits from him during the past eight years. He said she had returned more than half. Contradicted, the First Lady revised her story. She said she *had* borrowed some clothes, but claimed they had been returned. Other clothes, she said, had been received from "old friends" and did not have to be disclosed. She would decide about the rest when the President's term expired. The dresses she kept, she said, would be reported as gifts. Those she returned to designers would be considered loans and not listed.

Her press secretary tried to dismiss the flap. "She set her own little rule, and she broke her own little rule," said Elaine Crispen, sloughing off Mrs. Reagan's reneging on her six-year-old promise not to accept any more free clothes. "It's a woman's prerogative to change her mind."

The *Time* story stirred a torrent of publicity. The worst, from the First Lady's perspective, was William Safire's column in the *New York Times:* "For a public official's spouse to be 'on the take' is wrong, plain and simple. Nancy Reagan knew it, hid it for years, lied when caught, and now seeks to have a flock of taxpayer-paid press agents explain her ethical lapse away."

More than two hundred senior administration officials had been accused of illegal or unethical conduct in the seven years since Ronald Reagan took office. His administration had been the most corrupt in U.S. history. So many high-level Ronald Reagan appointees had been indicted or imprisoned that it seemed more than just a joke to say you couldn't walk twenty feet in Washington without leaving the scene of a crime. *American Politics* magazine ran a prayer in one issue: "Please, dear God, one week. Just five working days without some congressman or Cabinet member or low-level scum bucket being hauled through the headlines in another scandal." A cartoonist drew the front of the White House with the caption: "Will the last one indicted please turn out the lights?"

Now the First Lady became part of the sleaze. A year later, when the

Reagans left office, the Internal Revenue Service would begin an investigation into Mrs. Reagan's acceptance of clothes. Blazakis, who instigated the IRS probe, said that there was "a quid pro quo—direct compensation for services rendered" between Nancy Reagan and her designers when she was First Lady.

Garry Trudeau devoted a "Doonesbury" comic strip to the investigation, showing two IRS agents interviewing Mrs. Reagan:

"And do you know which designer lent you this beaded chiffon gown, Mrs. Reagan?" asked one.

"What possible *difference* could it make? I've already admitted I broke my own little rules!"

"Yes, ma'am, but at the IRS, we call them laws. You see, ma'am, the $1 million worth of gowns you 'borrowed' are worthless once you've worn them. You've enjoyed their full value. That's how haute couture works."

"Excuse me, but I don't need some tacky tax auditor to tell me about haute couture! I covered all this in my book! The only people who really care about my borrowing dresses are dumpy little size 10s who can't *stand* a woman who wears size 4!"

"Um. Well, actually, ma'am, we're both 42s," said one agent.

"I'm 42 long," said the other. "Can we get back to the beaded jobbie?"

Nancy Reagan never understood the ridicule. "In Europe, First Ladies borrow clothes all the time," she wrote in her memoir. "In France, for example, the wives of the presidents and prime ministers routinely wear dresses lent to them by such designers as Yves St. Laurent, Pierre Cardin and Christian Dior. The French government not only condones this practice but actually supports it as a way of helping one of the country's most important industries."

She didn't seem to grasp the distinction between borrowing and keeping—until faced with negative publicity. Only then did she start returning some of the "borrowed" designer clothes she had kept for six years.

Throughout her time in the White House, she had felt put upon by "all the silly little laws," as she called them, that she and the President had to abide by. She had chafed at having to pay for groceries. "We even had to pay for toilet paper!" she complained.

She had erupted in 1983 when the White House lawyer said that Queen Elizabeth and Prince Philip's anniversary present to the Reagans was not theirs to keep. The law states that any gift to the President from a

foreign official becomes government property if it's valued at more than
$180. "It was an engraved silver box and we had to *buy* it from the
United States government," she said. "Can you believe it? We had to *buy*
our own anniversary gift!"

The public disclosure of those gifts bothered her. "That's one thing I
won't miss about the White House," she said, "together with the fact
that our tax returns were published in the newspapers every April. I
hated that."

Each year, newspapers ran stories about the Reagans' taxes, noting
how their income had doubled since they had moved into the White
House. Yet their charitable contributions never exceeded 5 percent of
their income.

Year	Income	Gifts Received	Charitable Deductions
1980	$227,968	Not Available	$ 3,085
1981	$418,826	$31,534	$11,895
1982	$741,253	$18,590	$15,563
1983	$422,834	$ 8,856	$15,307
1984	$440,657	$ 7,156	$20,616
1985	$394,492	$ 7,104	$23,298
1986	$336,640	$13,806	$30,487
1987	$345,359	$ 3,977	$25,407
1988	Not Available	$25,083	Not Available

For the Reagans to charge Maureen Reagan $426 in interest on a
personal loan had seemed petty when published, especially in light of
their net worth of $4.4 million. Questions about their finances exasper-
ated the Reagans. So the First Lady made sure that the $3 million ad-
vance she was to receive for writing her memoir and the $8 million the
President was to be paid for his two books were deferred until after they
left the White House. That way, the amounts would not be subject to
public disclosure.

"Nancy talked a lot about feeling poor," said a close personal friend,
"and about the financial sacrifices she and Ronnie had made to go into
public service. He never talked about money, but she did all the time.
She said how upset she was that they didn't have anything after all their
years in government. That's why her friends gave her jewelry. Because
she had none and they had so much. They felt it's the least they could do
for someone who has given so much to public service. Holmes Tuttle and
Earle Jorgensen and 'the group' always helped the Reagans out. That's
why they bought them the house in Bel Air."

Nancy wanted to keep the transactions on that house a secret. She said it was nobody's business. She didn't even want anyone in "the group" identified. The story eventually leaked that two and a half years before the President left office, eighteen self-described "independently wealthy" individuals formed a corporation (Wall Management Co.) and chipped in at least $156,000 each to buy a house for $2.5 million. It contained 7,192 square feet and stood on 1.25 acres of land down the block from Zsa Zsa Gabor and Elizabeth Taylor. The friends, who did not identify themselves in the papers of incorporation, agreed to lease the house with its heated swimming pool and three-car garage to the Reagans for three years for $1,250 a month. Comparable houses in Bel Air leased for $15,000 a month.

A year after they left the White House, the Reagans bought their home from their friends. "We sold it to them for $3 million," said Henry Salvatori. "We had bought it for $2.5 million, put $490,000 into refurbishments and a lot of lawyers' fees. So we got our money back, plus a few bucks."

When Nancy had first been shown the three-bedroom house at 666 St. Cloud Road, she was dismayed. "This will be quite a comedown after the White House," she said. Her friends had tried to reassure her that with a few renovations, plus Ted Graber's decorating touches, the little estate could be made quite livable. After looking at houses for over a year, she had finally decided on the house on St. Cloud Road. Her first instruction was to get the address changed. She said that in the New Testament's Book of Revelation, the number 666 is associated with Satan. So the address was changed to 668.

The First Lady now felt that the publicity about the Bel Air house coming on top of the free designer clothes made her look grasping. "It's so unfair," she said. She told friends she was "fed up with living in a fishbowl" and could hardly wait to return home. Mentally, the President already seemed to be back in California chopping wood at his ranch. Only one duty remained for him in the White House and that was to help get Vice President George Bush elected as his successor.

He had wanted to endorse the Vice President shortly after Bush announced his candidacy, but the First Lady had made the President wait. "This is still your presidency and your White House," she told him. She had been secretly supporting the presidential hopes of Paul Laxalt and encouraging her friends to contribute to his campaign. Even after Laxalt dropped out of the race, Nancy would not support Bush, and she did not want his campaign to dominate the final months of her husband's presidency.

The First Lady had never forgiven Bush for running against Reagan in 1980 and for refusing to speak up to the President about Don Regan in

1987. She had felt that the Vice President had made her carry the burden of getting Regan fired by herself. Bush had called upon her in the family quarters to say that the White House chief of staff should be fired. Nancy agreed, and told Bush to tell the President how he felt. "Oh, Nancy," she had later quoted the Vice President as saying, "that's not my role."

"That's *exactly* your role," she said she had told him, knowing that he would never broach the subject with the President.

But even before that, the First Lady, who had nicknamed Bush "Whiney," disparaged him behind his back as weak and spineless. It was a favorite topic when she lunched with her friend George Will. On January 27, 1986, the First Lady and Will had had lunch in Shepherdstown, West Virginia, about an hour and a half from Washington. Three days later, Will wrote a column maligning the Vice President as "rancid," intellectually "dishonest," and "meddlesome." He saved the most wounding insult for the end. "The unpleasant sound Bush is emitting as he traipses from one conservative gathering to another," wrote Will, "is a thin, tinny 'arf'—the sound of a lapdog."

To certain friends, Nancy had peddled the story of "George and his girlfriend" that had been told to her about the evening of March 18, 1981, when some of "the group" were having dinner at Lion d'Or in Washington, D.C.

"Suddenly, there was a great commotion," recalled one of the five dinner guests, "as the security men accompanying the Secretary of State [Alexander Haig] and the Attorney General [William French Smith] converged on our table. They started jabbering into their walkie-talkies, and then whispered to Haig and Smith, who both jumped up and left the restaurant. The two men returned about forty-five minutes later, laughing their heads off. They said they had had to bail out George Bush, who'd been in a traffic accident with his girlfriend. Bush had not wanted the incident to appear on the D.C. police blotter, so he had his security men contact Haig and Smith. They took care of things for him, and then came back to dinner."

By the spring of 1988, the President was being pressured to formally endorse Bush, but the First Lady was still dragging her feet. She had already forced a cancellation of the President's appearance at a Bush rally held within walking distance of the White House.

Reagan, who advocated repeal of the Twenty-second Amendment, which limits a President to two full terms in office, said that in campaigning for Bush, he would be campaigning for his own place in history. Eventually, the First Lady agreed, knowing that the campaign would energize him and give him a chance to get out of Washington and talk about his administration's accomplishments before wildly enthusiastic crowds. Still, she managed to delay the presidential endorsement until May 11, 1988, when Reagan was scheduled to address 3,000 people at the annual Republican congressional fund-raising dinner in Washington. Advising him not to go overboard, she recommended a brief statement at the end of his speech. The President discussed the statement beforehand with Bush and endorsed him that evening. Reagan's restraint was noted in the next day's newspapers. The *Washington Post* carried a front-page headline: "Reagan Gives Bush a Terse Endorsement." Underneath ran a subhead: "Brevity of Remarks at Fund-Raising Dinner Baffles Republican Activists."

Nancy was right. The President did thrive on campaigning for Bush. "It rejuvenated him," said White House press secretary Marlin Fitzwater. The President began making at least one trip a week in Bush's behalf. But the First Lady did not accompany him. And her absence was never more glaring than in August at the Reagan-Bush rally at the Century Plaza Hotel in Los Angeles. The President and his wife were staying there for a few days, but Nancy said she could not attend because of a long-standing appointment concerning renovations on the Bel Air house. In fact, during the hotel rally, she was in her hotel room, several floors above.

People in the Bush campaign were worried that the First Lady's influence over the President might dull his enthusiasm for the Vice President. So they asked Stuart Spencer to talk to her. Spencer told her the best way to preserve her husband's legacy was to get his Vice President elected. She said she would not interfere, but she refused to campaign for Bush. So did her son. "Bush wouldn't ask me," said Ron Reagan. "I wouldn't do it, either." By election night, Nancy had almost reconciled herself to seeing George Bush in her husband's office, but she would never address him as "Mr. President."

Leaving the White House was another problem.

"Mom's buying sandbags," joked Ron Reagan. "She's piling them outside the Truman Balcony. They're going to have to fight to get her out of there."

After weeks of farewell events, the Reagans thought they were emotionally prepared to leave the nation's capital. But the preinaugural week had been torture for them, especially for the First Lady, as they properly stood aside from all the festivities to allow Bush his rightful place at center stage. On inaugural eve, the nation's capital blazed with lights, flags, and bunting in preparation for the most expensive inauguration in U.S. history. As the city sparkled with parties to celebrate the new administration, the Reagans sat in the White House eating dinner off television trays—and realizing just how wrenching their final day would be.

Plagued always by insomnia, Nancy Reagan said she slept fitfully her last night as First Lady. Tossing and turning, she mentally replayed the television news coverage of Barbara Bush getting raves merely for mocking her own matronliness.

"I want you to watch me all week and remember," Mrs. Bush had joked to luncheon guests at the Kennedy Center. "You may never see it again. . . . Notice the hair, the makeup, the designer clothes." She flashed open her jacket like a runway model and the audience roared with delight, cheering her and her indirect insult to the lacquered image of Nancy Reagan.

And then there had been the open comments of others.

"At last we will have a real First Lady in the White House—someone you feel could wash the dishes," said Pamela Peabody, the Republican sister-in-law of the former Democratic governor of Massachusetts Endicott "Chubb" Peabody.

Former U.S. Attorney General Elliot Richardson, who had attended the luncheon, had described Mrs. Bush as "a great asset to the President-elect. Her mask isn't going to slip because there isn't any mask."

Mrs. Reagan picked up her bedroom telephone and called a friend to complain about the wife of the President-elect. "It's so uncalled for," said the First Lady. "If it hadn't been for us, *they* wouldn't even be here."

Nancy Reagan resented turning over the White House to the Bushes. She had never felt comfortable with these patricians whose Eastern roots were bound by traditions of old-family money and social standing. She envied their spontaneity and their surefootedness. She was intimidated by the easy way they moved within the elite stratum of society that she cared so much about. But what bothered her most right now was the invidious comparison being drawn between her and her successor, a jolly woman who made fun of herself as the answered prayer of "fat, white-haired, wrinkled ladies."

The First Lady was stung by *Newsweek*'s promise that Barbara Bush would be "refreshingly real after Nancy" and *Time*'s cover story saying Mrs. Bush would bring "a refreshing new style to the White House." Mrs. Reagan seethed every time she read about the closeness of the Bush family, their five loving children and ten little grandchildren, who scampered all over everything, enchanting photographers with their boisterousness. Each joyous photograph of the Bushes seemed like a personal affront to Nancy, further underscoring the wretched relations she had with her own children. Only Maureen Reagan, the daughter of her husband's first marriage, was in Washington to share the last goodbye.

Rising at 7:00 A.M. on January 20, 1989, Nancy, who would be First Lady for only five more hours, sipped black coffee and turned on the morning news shows. At the same time, she skimmed the style sections of five newspapers, a routine after eight years in the White House. Again, she was confronted with replays of Barbara Bush's performance the day before.

Tearfully, Nancy Reagan summoned her hairdresser and her secretary while her personal maid, Anita Costello, laid out her inaugural outfit—a red dress and a red coat, the color Mrs. Reagan had long ago made her own. She had made it clear then that no other official wife could wear red when sharing a platform with her.

Grudgingly, she made arrangements with the White House flower room to leave a small white orchid for Mrs. Bush. Only after the President said he was leaving a whimsical letter ("Don't let the turkeys get you down!") for Mr. Bush in his dressing room did she decide to slip a short note into an empty drawer in the bedroom welcoming the new First Lady to the White House.

The President left for the Oval Office to take one last sentimental look around. He wanted to touch the desk carved of timber from the H.M.S. *Resolute* and to gaze at the Rose Garden, where he had fed the squirrels that scurried across his windowsill each fall gathering their food for winter.

He received his last daily schedule from his personal secretary, Kathleen Osborne. He nodded solemnly when his national security adviser appeared to make his daily report. "The world is quiet today, Mr. President," said Lieutenant General Colin Powell.

An inveterate letter-writer, the President sat down to write one more missive to George Bush, telling him "to carry on and walk with God." Reagan's last official act as President was to sign a letter of appreciation to the British prime minister, Margaret Thatcher, his staunchest ally. He made his last telephone call as President to Susan Nofziger Piland, the daughter of his former press secretary Lyn Nofziger. She was hospitalized fighting the cancer that would kill her four months later.

Upstairs in the White House, the maids moved quietly in and out of the presidential bedroom as the First Lady started opening and closing drawers to make sure she'd packed everything. Finally, her press secretary told her to stop. "If you leave something behind," she said, "they'll send it to you. They have your address."

The maids who serve all first families knew how much Mrs. Reagan hated leaving her royal roost. Although she had been packing for months and saying she wanted to leave, she now seemed to be dragging things out as long as she could to stall her departure.

One White House maid said Mrs. Reagan "had gotten a little nicer in the last year," but most of the domestic staff would not miss the imperious First Lady. She had been aloof and distant from the beginning, treating all of them as a czarina treats her serfs. The Reagans had been an abrupt change from the embracing warmth of Jimmy and Rosalynn Carter and the easy informality of Jerry and Betty Ford. "This administration is not interested in us as people," said Matty Mayfield. "They just want the house cleaned."

The maids who remembered having to drop everything simply to iron a last-minute wrinkle out of Nancy Reagan's gown the night of a state dinner would not be sorry to say goodbye to the demanding perfectionist. She had made them remain available around the clock when her friend Gloria Vanderbilt had stayed in the White House, even though Miss Vanderbilt had brought her own maids. Nancy had installed buzzers in every upstairs room when she moved in so she could summon the maids instantly. "If it was slave times, she'd been a good massa," said one, who resented having to give up the laundry room television set, which was the maids' only diversion during drying cycles. "Nancy had it taken out because she didn't want us to watch the soap operas."

The Reagans did not leave little mementos for the White House domestic staff as the Carters and Johnsons had done; nor did they consider leaving something more valuable for the White House, like the impressionist painting of water lilies by Claude Monet that the Kennedy family had left in memory of the assassinated President. The Reagans were grateful for their eight years in the White House, the most rewarding of their lives, but they left no memento of their gratitude.

On their last morning, they walked through all the rooms of the family quarters together and then walked down the central hallway into the yellow oval room, and lingered on the Truman Balcony, overlooking the greenswards of the Ellipse and the Jefferson Memorial. They looked at each other with tears in their eyes as a White House photographer took their picture. Later, the President confided, "I looked out at old Tom, and old Tom was looking back."

By 10:30 A.M., the Reagans were composed and ready to meet the President-elect and his wife, the Vice President-elect and his wife, and the congressional delegation sent to escort them all to Capitol Hill. As her last social duty as First Lady, Mrs. Reagan served coffee and pastries in the Blue Room. No more than correctly cordial to George and Barbara Bush, she hugged the handsome House Majority Leader, Thomas S.

Foley, always one of her favorites, and warmly greeted Dan and Marilyn Quayle, taking them aside for a few private words.

"My heart went out to the two of you during this whole campaign," she said, referring to the negative press coverage of the former Indiana senator for his evasion of military service and his frequent malaprops. "What was done to you was wrong. I prayed for you. I screamed at the TV. . . . Now it's your opportunity to show what you can do for the country. And Ronnie and I have always supported you, and I know how much he thinks of Dan in particular."

Touched by the First Lady's words, the Vice President-elect and his wife beamed. "She was just really lovely," said Marilyn Quayle.

Someone on the other side of the room inquired about the white bandage and splint on the President's left hand. Reagan said he still had a little discomfort from the corrective surgery performed on his ring finger two weeks before. "But I don't think they'll have to shoot me," he joked.

A military aide informed the President that the limousines were ready for the last motorcade of the Reagan era. Once again, the White House photographers stepped in to record the scene as the seventy-seven-year-old President was helped into his black topcoat and billowing white silk scarf. Holding his wife's hand, he walked to the front of the White House, followed by the Bushes and Quayles and the congressmen for the mile-and-a-half ride up Pennsylvania Avenue.

"It was very poignant . . . talking about how sad it was for them," said Marilyn Quayle. "Everyone was weeping."

At 11:34 A.M., the tall, robust figure of the fortieth President of the United States, finally showing a little gray hair at his temples, his only concession to age besides the hearing aids he now wore in both ears, stood erect at the top of the west portico of the Capitol, a stirring sight in the cold sunshine. A hush fell over the crowd as the U.S. Marine Band struck up "Hail to the Chief" in final homage to their commander in chief. Ronald Reagan paused for a few moments, then, gripping his wife's hand, walked down the steps to his seat on the platform.

Television cameras followed the Reagans' every move, and showed the President as he went out of his way to be warm to the Bushes, seemingly proud to be the first man in sixty years to turn over the office to a successor of his own party. The First Lady held back, keeping herself distant. She smiled briefly to a few people but mostly looked straight ahead, never loosening her grip on her husband's hand.

At 12:03 P.M., the Chief Justice of the United States administered the thirty-five-word oath of office to George Herbert Walker Bush. He raised his right hand and rested his left on two Bibles held by his wife—one a family Bible, the other used by George Washington at the first inaugural in 1789.

Army cannons thundered a twenty-one-gun salute, signaling the orderly transfer of constitutional power that had just occurred.

The new President took the podium for his inaugural address. Turning to the man he had served so faithfully for eight years, Bush said, "There is a man here who earned a lasting place in our hearts and in our history. President Reagan, on behalf of our nation, I thank you for the wonderful things you have done for America." The crowds cheered the gracious tribute, and Ronald Reagan smiled in appreciation as Nancy choked back tears. When she heard Bush call for a "kinder and gentler nation," she flinched. Later, she said she felt that was a slap at her husband's presidency.

At 12:50 P.M., the new President and his wife escorted the Reagans to a waiting helicopter on the east front of the Capitol, where the two men exchanged salutes in a moving farewell. The Marine One helicopter was assigned to carry only the President of the United States. So after the oath-taking, it was renamed "Nighthawk" to carry the former President and his wife to Andrews Air Force Base for the final leg of their journey home. There, the Reagans would board the same plane they had been using, but the radio code of Air Force One had been changed to indicate that the President was no longer aboard.

The helicopter lifted off, swooped down the west front of the Capitol, and circled twice before flying over the White House and heading for Maryland. "There's our little cottage," said Reagan as they flew over 1600 Pennsylvania Avenue.

A waiting crowd of 2,000 people waved placards and cheered as the helicopter came into view at Andrews Air Force Base, where Reagan had insisted on reviewing the troops one last time. For years, Nancy had kept these military enthusiasms of his in check, refusing to let him be photographed with the B-1 bomber or to christen navy ships for fear that a warmongering image might stay fixed in people's minds and obliterate all she had done to mold his place in history. She had been unable to obtain for him the Nobel Peace Prize that she had coveted, but she did take pride in his leaving office as the most popular President of the postwar era and the first to complete his terms unburdened by defeat. Even *Pravda*, the official Soviet newspaper, was praising him as "a premier American."

The band played "Ruffles and Flourishes," after which Nancy left the helicopter and stood where her toe marks had been indicated with masking tape on the podium. From there she watched her husband walk up and down inspecting the honor guard, made up of a platoon from each of the five branches of military service. He received a twenty-one-gun salute as the television cameras lingered on a child's placard that said, "So long, Gipper."

Weighing barely 105 pounds, Nancy Reagan shivered in the cold wind as her husband finished his ceremonial duties. He then walked to the podium and took her arm, leading her to the waiting plane. Suddenly, she veered to the left and dashed over to embrace George Opfer, her favorite Secret Service man. He had broken the news of the attempted assassination of her husband in March 1981 and had been in her security detail ever since. "I'll miss you so much," she whispered to him before rejoining her husband. At the top of the steps to the plane, both Reagans turned to face the screaming crowd. They smiled gamely and waved goodbye before ducking into the cabin.

The plane lifted off at 1:10 P.M. as the public address system carried the country tenor of Lee Greenwood singing "God Bless the U.S.A.," the Reagan campaign anthem. On board were a few close friends—Stuart Spencer and Reagan's last chief of staff, Kenneth Duberstein, Elaine Crispen, and Julius, the hairdresser—who were making the journey to California with the Reagans to cushion the pain of reentry.

The Reagans walked past the vanity photographs of themselves with heads of state and went into their private cabin to change clothes. A few hours later, they reappeared, wearing sweatpants and navy blue air force windbreakers with the presidential seal. Both looked sad and worn as they walked to the aft cabin, where they surprised the pool of reporters by offering them cake and California champagne. The Reagans, who had always avoided the traveling press on their plane, now wanted to talk about their feelings about leaving Washington and the White House.

"It was hard to say goodbye," admitted the former President. "It's been a time of tears for a great many people and certainly for us. But returning to California means a return to a life we did love very much. California isn't a place in my mind; it's a way of life, so that's the sweet part of this bittersweet experience."

The man who had once looked so youthful suddenly seemed old. Pluckily, he said he refused to consider the word *retirement*. He vowed to remain active and speak out on the issues he believed in, but it was as if he were trying to convince himself of his continuing role on the political stage.

"And he never took a nap either," interjected Nancy, who even to the end was sensitive about news accounts—and jokes—about his napping. "In eight years, he never took a nap."

"She sometimes gets edgy because she thinks I should be able to take a nap," Reagan said apologetically.

The reporters asked whether he would consider resuming his acting career. "Well," he said, "there is a lingering feeling that that would look a little bit like trying to cash in on this job that I've had."

"No," said Nancy, interrupting again. "You don't go back."

The former First Lady remained misty-eyed for most of the flight, but by the time the plane was ready to land in Los Angeles, she had changed her clothes yet again and was trying to cheer up.

As the plane began its descent, the uniformed bands of the Salvation Army and the University of Southern California struck up "California, Here I Come," and the festive crowd assembled at the airport cheered and shouted. The door swung open into the sunshine and Ronald Reagan appeared at the top of the stairs, his lopsided grin making him look engaging and appreciative.

"We hadn't really expected this," he said.

"Four more years, four more years," screamed the assembled fans, swinging their "Welcome Home" placards as the band kept playing.

Nancy smiled brightly for the first time all day when she saw "the girls" in a little blond cluster waving and waiting to welcome her home. They stood in a special roped-off section near a sign that read: "The King and Queen Return."

The mayor of Los Angeles, Tom Bradley, presented the Reagans with a citation and comedian Rich Little gave them a set of personalized license plates: "The Prez," and "F L Nancy." The actor Robert Stack thanked Reagan for making "us all proud to be Americans again" and praised Nancy for "bringing marriage back . . . into the American language."

"I introduced him at the airport when he came home, which I wouldn't have been able to do if it hadn't passed Nancy's okay," said Stack later. "I was very honored."

The former President took the microphone. "There aren't enough words to say what's really in our hearts," he said. "When you have to stay eight years away from California, except for an occasional visit,* you live in a perpetual state of homesickness." He said he was grateful for having been given "temporary custody over the United States," and he acknowledged the potency of his presidency by turning to his wife. "She worked harder than I did," he said. Few would ever disagree.

Within minutes, the couple, escorted by a small retinue of Secret Service agents, were en route to their new home in a limousine with no presidential flags and a motorcade with no sirens. As private citizens, the

* Ronald Reagan spent more than 436 days of his presidency in California—over one year of his eight in office. This included 338 vacation days at Rancho del Cielo, his ranch above Santa Barbara.

Reagans no longer had to suffer the traveling press, so the reporters who had accompanied them to write about their last presidential flight returned to the plane. There, presidential stewards were stripping the bulkheads and cabins of all Reagan photographs, throwing them into trash bags with discarded magazines and newspapers, and replacing them with pictures of George and Barbara Bush.

At the Reagans' new home in Bel Air, in one of southern California's most exclusive enclaves, neighbors had tied red, white, and blue balloons to an oak tree. Even Bel Air's Democrats welcomed the Reagans. "We don't care what house they live in here," said Jerri and Walter Shenson, "as long as it's not the White House." But there were no bands or crowds or placards.

"Just packing boxes all over the place," said Nancy in one of her first phone calls to her friend Harriet Deutsch.

Also waiting for the Reagans were two visitors from New York. Literary agent Morton Janklow and Richard Snyder, chairman of the board of Simon & Schuster, had flown in to present the two-book publishing contract, much of which had been worked out while the Reagans were still in the White House. The contract, which called for one volume of the President's key speeches and one of his memoirs, would pay Ronald Reagan $8 million. It was more money than he had ever made in his life. Still, he was in no hurry to address himself to the business at hand.

"A book is the last thing I want to think about right now," he said.

"I don't care," said his wife. "We both have to do them." She handed him a pen. "You sign this." Reagan then asked everyone in the room whether this was the best deal he could get. He was assured that it was.

So, sighing with resignation, the former President of the United States took the pen from his wife, walked over to the table, and did as he was told.

EPILOGUE

THE POOR REVIEWS started as soon as the Reagans returned to California. Without their scriptwriters, press secretaries, and advance teams, they floundered. They no longer had three-by-five cards to prompt them or toe marks to guide them. Out of the spotlight of the White House, they lost their luster.

"They're not the center of attention anymore," said their thirty-year-old son, Ron Reagan. "They're performers. These are theater people, these are actors. That was like the greatest role they could ever have. The greatest audience. Playing to a packed house wherever they went. And now it's over."

In retirement, the Reagans took their biggest pratfall. Their act, which had drawn raves in Washington, D.C., was now bombarded with boos. The jeering started when they began hawking the prestige of the presidency and selling themselves to the highest bidder. Like the Duke and Duchess of Windsor, the Reagans acted as if they expected to be life's royal guests. Wherever they went, they arrived with both hands out.

They had walked into retirement with assets exceeding $4 million. Within a year their net worth would soar to more than $10 million. As a former U.S. President, Reagan was entitled to a pension of $99,500 a year, plus his governor's pension from California of $29,711. He would also receive $1.2 million in transition funds from the federal government to set up his retirement offices, and taxpayers also paid for the Reagans' Secret Service protection, which costs about $8 million a year.

Nancy Reagan had accepted a position on Revlon's board of directors for $100,000 a year. She agreed to pose for Blackgama's "What Becomes a Legend Most" series in exchange for a mink coat worth more than $15,000. During one week, she turned down an invitation to speak to California state officials at a drug-abuse conference for $500, but accepted a speaking engagement from Toyota for $30,000.

Ronald Reagan accepted a $20,000 purebred horse from the Canadian Mounted Police, plus a $600 pair of blue jeans and a $3,600 western jacket from composer Marvin Hamlisch. The former President, who now charged $50,000 a speech, collected over $750,000 in his first three weeks of retirement by making fifteen speeches—the same speech—in twenty-one days. Out of the White House, the Reagans had obviously hit pay dirt.

They had set the tone for the eighties—a decade of corporate greed that featured hostile takeovers and leveraged buyouts. The Reagans mortgaged the presidency in much the same way the corporate raiders leveraged productive assets to bleed them dry of cash and equity. Reagan policies of deregulation had established a lucrative environment for these banking buccaneers and junk-bond pirates. Laws were unenforced and regulations, if not abolished, were ignored. People like Ivan Boesky, Michael Milken, and Donald Trump became instantly recognizable as billionaires, illustrations of the term *Reaganomics*. The Reagan Revolution had launched the era of big bucks, and the Reagans themselves were now determined to cash in.

In their rush, they abandoned all pretense of good taste. No longer directed by public relations specialists, the former President and First Lady did not know how to comport themselves with dignity. They did not recognize the unwritten rules associated with their former high office. They obviously had never read Harry S Truman's book *Mr. Citizen,* in which he wrote that the most unbelievable aspect of leaving the White House was the number of job offers thrust at him. One proposal, requiring only an hour of his time, guaranteed him a half million dollars.

"I turned down all of those offers," Truman wrote. "I knew that they were not interested in hiring Harry Truman, the person, but what they wanted to hire was the former President of the United States. I could never lend myself to any transaction, however respectable, that would commercialize on the prestige and the dignity of the office of the Presidency."

By contrast, the Reagans seemed determined to offend public sensibilities. Their first social event was excessive even by Hollywood standards. They were the guests of honor at a "Welcome Home" party thrown by Sheik Mouffak al Midani, one of the munificent Saudi contributors to the

Nancy Reagan Foundation. The sheik's party, held in a $40 million mansion in Beverly Hills, featured albino peacocks in the front yard, swans in the reflecting pond, and belly dancers in the living room. Sixty male waiters in gold and purple lamé harem pants dashed about spooning caviar for 150 guests, all selected by Nancy Reagan. Half-naked men dressed as Nubian slaves glided around in turbans and skimpy trunks snapping Bic lighters. Their sole function was to light guests' cigarettes.

Those who had admired Reagan now squirmed with embarrassment as they watched the former President and First Lady lend their presence to such socializing. Some people felt he trivialized the presidency by attending such a party. Many blamed Nancy, saying *she* was the social climber, not him. A few shrugged uncomfortably watching them embrace the jet-set life: flying to New York for a dinner party with Brooke Astor, to the Bahamas to celebrate Reagan's seventy-ninth birthday, to Paris for a party with the Rothschilds, to London for lunch with the Queen at Buckingham Palace. "We went to England," said Nancy, "so Ronnie could accept an honorary knighthood."

The discomfiture of Reagan supporters increased in May 1989 when the Reagans made no effort to attend the funeral of Lyn Nofziger's daughter, Susan. There was no call, no note, no flowers—nothing to comfort Nofziger, the former press secretary who had devoted twenty-four years of his life to Ronald Reagan. The only consolation the Nofzigers received was the photograph of Reagan making his last call as President to their daughter, which was sent by Reagan's secretary. There was never a personal word from the Reagans themselves.

The reservoir of goodwill that had accompanied the former President and First Lady as they left the White House started running dry in retirement. With each new story detailing their latest commercial venture, their popularity slipped. As they huckstered themselves for profit, they sank lower in the public opinion polls. Six months into retirement, public opinion polls rated them as the most unpopular first couple in history. With their trip to Japan, the dam of disapproval burst.

In the fall of 1989, Ronald Reagan accepted a $2 million honorarium —"proudly and honorably," said his spokesman, Mark Weinberg—from Fujisankei Communications Group in Tokyo for a ten-day trip requiring two twenty-minute speeches and a few guest appearances. The Japanese honored the former President with the Grand Cordon of the Supreme Order of the Chrysanthemum, the highest decoration in Japan. A fitting tribute for the man whose administration preached free trade with Japan, causing the United States to suffer an annual $50 million deficit from which it has yet to recover. In addition to the $2 million fee paid to the Reagans, the Japanese government donated $2 million to the Reagan presidential library.

At a time of growing controversy over Japanese investment in the United States, Reagan traveled to Japan to defend Japanese purchases of American companies and specifically angered the Hollywood community by applauding Sony Corp.'s buyout of Columbia Pictures.

"I don't think there's anything wrong with that," he said. "Probably we might see some improvements . . . [because] I'm not too proud of Hollywood these days with the immorality that is shown in pictures and the vulgarity. I just have a feeling that maybe Hollywood needs some outsiders to bring back decency and good taste to some of the pictures that are being made."

So many irate letters to the editor appeared in the *Los Angeles Times* protesting his comments that when the former President returned home, he said he was "misinterpreted." A few days later, he apologized to the Hollywood Radio and Television Society, prompting someone to quip that the apology came only after the check had cleared.

"The thing with Japan—that really pushed it over the edge," said the Reagans' daughter, Patti Davis.

The *New York Times* editorial page concurred: "Former Presidents haven't always comported themselves with dignity after leaving the Oval Office. But none have plunged so blatantly into pure commercialism."

"It demeans us all to see him so available," wrote Larry Gelbart, the creator of "M*A*S*H," in a *Times* op-ed piece, "so eager to please for a price, to become 'Rent-a-Ron,' the performing presidential seal."

The most popular President since World War II now looked like a common hustler. Herblock drew a cartoon of him sitting in a chair next to a book of astrology charts and suitcases. He was holding up a piece of paper with a circle resembling Japan's Rising Sun surrounded by dollar signs. "Well, Nancy," he says, "the signs were certainly right for the Japanese trip."

Other cartoonists depicted Reagan putting a "For Rent" sign on the presidency. One showed him standing on the presidential seal with his mouth wide open being fed $100 bills with Japanese chopsticks. The former First Lady was shown wearing a button that said, "Just $ay Dough." Another drew her in a kimono stuffing money into her pockets. The caption said: "Don't $ay Noh!"

"Well, $2 million was the price that was offered," she told reporters with pique. "What were we supposed to do—say we'd do it for less? Besides, they got both of us for that price. It was a two for the price of one thing, you know. . . . A twofer."

"I just thought that in 16 years I hadn't made any kind of money," said the former President, defending himself. "But I was happy at the same time that I was able to carry on what I had been doing in office, which was to bring about the elimination of the last few restrictions on free trade between our two countries."

When Thomas Jefferson and John Adams left the presidency, they corresponded with each other about the direction of the country. John Quincy Adams became a U.S. congressman and one of slavery's most eloquent opponents. William Howard Taft became Chief Justice of the United States. Herbert Hoover chaired a commission that paved the way for reorganizing the federal government after World War II. Jimmy Carter pursued peace settlements in Ethiopia, Northern Ireland, and Central America, and his Carter Center in Atlanta dispensed $16 million a year to various causes ranging from agricultural programs in Ghana to seminars on resolving conflicts between nations. In their spare time, the Carters built houses for the homeless. Once Richard Nixon left the White House, he gave up his Secret Service contingent, declined honorariums and board memberships, and did not travel at government expense. As a former President, Ronald Reagan made his greatest contribution to himself: He became a multimillionaire.

The Reagans were hurt as they watched their popularity plummet, and in desperation they turned to the public relations firm of Burston-Marsteller. Weeks later, Ronald Reagan made a public service announcement for the Pediatric AIDS Foundation that constituted an apology for the indifference of his administration toward AIDS. "Maybe it's time we all learned something new," he said. "I'm not asking you to send money. I'm asking for something much more important—your understanding."

The former First Lady decided not to pose for the Blackgama "What Becomes a Legend Most" ad. She disbursed $50,000 worth of grants through the Nancy Reagan Foundation, and when reporters began investigating what had happened to the $3.8 million she had collected when she was in the White House, she hurriedly gave away some more. Within ten days she made twelve grants through her foundation, totaling $217,000.

Still criticized for abandoning Phoenix House, she struggled to regain her visibility as the nation's leading antidrug crusader. She discussed her problem with Los Angeles police chief Daryl F. Gates, who had testified before Congress that casual drug users should be shot. The police chief suggested she might want to accompany him on a drug raid in the inner city. Assured that the press would be alerted, Nancy accepted.

Like Calamity Jane and Wild Bill Hickok, the former First Lady and the police chief headed into the drug-infested wilds of south-central Los

Angeles on the evening of April 6, 1989. Mrs. Reagan dressed for the occasion by wearing blue jeans, pink Nike running shoes, and a navy nylon police department jacket made especially for her, with "Nancy" embroidered on the breast pocket. *People* magazine described the style as "Full Meddle Jacket."

Escorted by a contingent of Secret Service agents, plus a herd of reporters and photographers, Mrs. Reagan and Chief Gates waited in an air-conditioned motor home eating fruit salad while a SWAT team lobbed three rounds of tear gas into a small stucco house a few hundred feet away. The police confiscated a gram of rock cocaine and arrested fourteen men and women on drug charges. The suspects stumbled out with their hands over their heads. Once they were loaded into a police van, Chief Gates escorted Mrs. Reagan into the house, whose metal front door had been riddled with bullet holes from a previous raid.

As the former First Lady walked inside she was hailed by several residents who had gathered to watch. "Hey, Nancy Reagan. She's over here in the ghetto," shouted one. She emerged a few minutes later and ran back into the motor home to freshen her makeup before speaking to reporters.

"I found this experience very, very depressing," she told the press, fluffing her hair. "I saw people on the floor, rooms that were unfurnished . . . all very depressing. . . . These people have no lives left. They're beyond the point of teaching and rehabilitating. . . . It's very sad."

"I tried to keep her back," said Chief Gates, grinning widely for photographers. "She wouldn't stay back. She had to be right up front and she was right up front. We gave her the opportunity to see what the dope trade is all about. She's a very courageous woman."

"I was able to see them busting in," she said. "I always see the other end—kids who are in rehabilitation."

After meeting the press, she and the chief got into a Cadillac and drove away from the ghetto, leaving behind residents who told reporters they felt exploited.

The next day's *New York Post* featured a front-page photograph of the former First Lady with her lips pursed in disapproval. She was wearing her LAPD "Nancy" jacket and counting the bullet holes in the door of the crack house. The picture of Nancy Reagan as drug buster ran above the headline: "Who Ya Gonna Call?"

The former First Lady looked foolish. Her campaign against drug abuse was now comic fodder for late-night television. A few nights later, Johnny Carson mentioned the drug bust in his monologue. "Nancy's going on from there," said the comedian. "She was last seen on a motorcycle writing tickets to women who were caught buying dresses off-the-rack."

The final blow to the magic of Ronald Reagan's presidency came from the most astonishing source—the former First Lady herself. The woman who cared so much about her husband and his place in history unwittingly delivered a crippling blow to both when she wrote her memoirs. Entitled *My Turn* and written for her by William Novak, the book gave Mrs. Reagan's version of her eight years in the White House. "I tried," she said, "not to be *too* vindictive."

"Although there is a certain dignity in silence which I find appealing," she wrote, "I have decided that for me, for our children and for the historical record, I want to tell my side of the story."

No other book would ever be so damaging to the Reagans as this memoir. Unconsciously, Nancy Reagan seemed hell-bent on destroying herself, her children, and her husband. Unintentionally, she showed her husband and herself to be heartbreakingly callous in their disregard of others. Inadvertently, she revealed meanness and spite, especially toward her children. She disclosed that her daughter, Patti, was conceived out of wedlock, and then she filled nine pages with the most hurtful, painful, embarrassing details about this child who she said had caused her so much suffering. She lacerated Patti for crying as a baby. For refusing to swallow her beans when she was two years old. For trying to run off with a kitchen worker from her boarding school when she was fourteen. For living with a rock star when she was twenty-four.

But apparently the biggest sin Patti committed, as recounted in Nancy's book, was not attending her grandmother's funeral. "When my mother died, there was no visit, no call, no wire, no flowers, no letter—nothing," wrote Nancy. "My mother deserved a lot better than that, and so, for that matter, did Patti's mother."

But years before, Nancy had ignored the funeral of *her* own grandmother, Nanee Robbins. There had been no visit, no call, no wire, no flowers, no letter then either. And Nancy had refused to contribute to a headstone for her grandmother's grave. She also had been too busy to attend the funeral of her aunt, Virginia Galbraith, the woman who had taken care of her as a child when her own mother, Edith Davis, was on the road. Nancy had never felt any compunction about ignoring the death of her father, Kenneth Robbins, because she had long since cut him out of her life. She did not understand that she was now seeing her own history repeated in her daughter.

In re-creating herself so many years ago, Nancy had not reckoned with one of life's universal verities—that the past is prologue. As Robert Penn Warren wrote in *All the King's Men*, "If you could not accept the past and its burden, there was no future, for without one there cannot be the other. . . . If you could accept the past you might hope for the future, for only out of the past can you make the future." Nancy did not realize that it is humanly impossible to cut the continuum that runs through every life, connecting the past to the present. Now she was being haunted by her daughter, whom she disliked, disowned, and disinherited.

Yet she had acknowledged the natural arc of retribution. "I am a big believer that eventually everything comes back to you," she had said many times. "You get back what you give out."

In her memoirs, the former First Lady settled scores with all her enemies—from her errant daughter to the arrogant Don Regan. In between, she sliced up her husband's closest advisers, including George Bush, Edwin Meese III, James A. Baker, David Stockman, Alexander M. Haig, James Watt, William Clark, William Casey, and even her former best friend, Mike Deaver. She slammed former governors Edmund G. Brown, Sr., and Edmund G. Brown, Jr., Jane Wyman, Betty Ford, Rosalynn Carter, Geraldine Ferraro, Barry Goldwater, Katharine Hepburn, and Raisa Gorbachev. She unloaded grudges carried for years against writers who had written negatively about her—Joan Didion, Gloria Steinem, Sally Quinn, William Safire. Those she despised she refused to mention by name—Helene von Damm, her husband's former secretary and later U.S. ambassador to Austria; James Rosebush, her White House chief of staff who served her for four years; and Muffie Brandon, her first White House social secretary. She did not acknowledge Anne Wrobleski, her White House projects director who developed her drug-abuse campaign. Despite their immense generosity, Adolfo and Julius were ignored, and because of petty squabbles, she also deleted the names of Betty Wilson and Jerry Zipkin—two of her oldest friends. People who had contributed hundreds of thousands of dollars to her husband's campaigns were inexplicably omitted—the Deutsches, Annenbergs, Salvatoris, William French Smiths, and Norman Spragues. Yet her newest friend, Katharine Graham, the chairman of the board of the Washington Post Company, was mentioned on twelve pages, and Meg Greenfield, the editor of the *Post*'s editorial page, was mentioned on six pages.

In almost four hundred pages, Nancy expressed no gratitude to anyone. Nor did she thank anyone—not her staff, the kitchen cabinet, "the group," or "the girls"—for devotion through the years to the Reagan cause. But she mentioned being "angry," "furious," "outraged," "annoyed," and "irritated" 102 times in the book.

By far the most devastating portrait was the one she painted of her husband. "Ronnie" emerges as a dim-witted idiot with the emotional maturity of a child and the judgment of a cocker spaniel—loving and romantic though he might be on occasion. She makes him look like a passive fool who cannot make a decision, and does not have the strength of mind to fire an incompetent. He is depicted as an abysmal executive who slides through his days on dirty jokes. He is shown as a terrible judge of character who cannot recognize crimes being committed in front of him nor summon the courage to confront the culprits. He's an adolescent who needs to be propped up with happy stories and martial music. A little-boy man who had to be coddled by his tough wife whom he calls "Mommy."

Mommy and *Ronnie.* "Yeah, well, that's us," said Nancy Reagan after her memoirs were published. "That's the way it is. . . . A lot of men like to be mothered."

For one book reviewer, Mrs. Reagan's startling between-the-lines description of her husband brought to life the joke about the Reagans ordering dinner in a restaurant:

"I'll have the meat and potatoes," Nancy says.
"And for the vegetable?" asks the waiter.
"He'll have the meat and potatoes, too."

The former First Lady could not completely drop her lacquered façade to step out of her masquerade as the little helpmate to the Great Man. She peeked out of her pages long enough to take a bow for being the one ameliorating voice amid the right-wing lunatic chorus surrounding her husband in the White House. She knew that without her intervention, Ronald Reagan never would have met with Mikhail Gorbachev, and never would have melted the cold war. She wanted to be given the credit she deserved for contributing to world peace. She wanted to be recognized for saving the Reagan presidency from catastrophe.

Unwittingly, she revealed herself as the engine that ran the presidency, the petite shadow hovering over the Oval Office. She showed that for their eight years in the White House, she was what she always claimed she was not—the puppet master pulling Ronald Reagan's strings. She left little doubt that she had been America's most formidable petticoat President.

The book became a number-one best-seller, but only for a few weeks. The stingingly negative reviews—"whining," "self-pitying," "mean-spirited"—discouraged buyers and sales plummeted, depriving Nancy Reagan of the approval she craved most. She did not understand the criticism, and as usual, she blamed the press for "misinterpreting" her book.

She retreated to her cocoon of luxury in Bel Air, where she and her husband lived amid their acquired riches, surrounded by servants and maids and Secret Service agents, almost replicating their White House existence. Even without Air Force One, they never had to fly commercial, because private planes were always provided by those who wanted to court their favor, and the Reagans encouraged such courting. They were like the ancient Chinese emperors who spent their time on the throne accumulating treasures for their tombs. After eight years in the White House, the former President and First Lady had learned one lesson—and they had learned it well: You *can* take it with you.

The Films of Nancy Davis

The Doctor and the Girl (MGM 1949)
Producer: Pandro S. Berman. Director: Curtis Bernhardt. Screenplay: Theodore Reeves. Cast: Glenn Ford, Charles Coburn, Gloria DeHaven, Janet Leigh, Warner Anderson, Nancy Davis.

East Side, West Side (MGM 1949)
Producer: Voldemar Vetluguin. Director: Mervyn LeRoy. Screenplay: Isobel Lennart. Cast: Barbara Stanwyck, James Mason, Ava Gardner, Van Heflin, Cyd Charisse, Gale Sondergaard, William Frawley, Nancy Davis.

Shadow on the Wall (MGM 1950)
Producer: Robert Sisk. Director: Patrick Jackson. Screenplay: William Ludwig. Cast: Ann Sothern, Zachary Scott, Nancy Davis, Gigi Perreau, Barbara Billingsley, Kristine Miller.

The Next Voice You Hear (MGM 1950)
Producer: Dore Schary. Director: William A. Wellman. Written by: Charles Schnee. Cast: James Whitmore, Nancy Davis, Lillian Bronson, Jeff Corey.

It's a Big Country (MGM 1951)
Producer: Robert Sisk. Directors: Richard Thorpe, John Sturges, Don Hartman, Don Weis, William A. Wellman, Charles Vidor, Clarence

Brown. Story for picture by: Dore Schary. Cast: Ethel Barrymore, Keefe Brasselle, Gary Cooper, Nancy Davis, Gene Kelly, Keenan Wynn, Fredric March, Van Johnson, James Whitmore.

Night into Morning (MGM 1951)

Producer: Edwin H. Knopf. Director: Fletcher Markle. Written by: Karl Tunberg and Leonard Spiegelgass. Cast: Ray Milland, John Hodiak, Nancy Davis, Lewis Stone, Jean Hagen, Rosemary DeCamp.

Shadow in the Sky (MGM 1951)

Producer: William H. Wright. Director: Fred M. Wilcox. Screenplay: Ben Maddow. Cast: Ralph Meeker, Nancy Davis, James Whitmore, Jean Hagen, Gladys Hurlbut.

Talk About a Stranger (MGM 1952)

Producer: Richard Goldstone. Director: David Bradley. Screenplay: Margaret Fitts. Cast: George Murphy, Nancy Davis, Billy Gray, Kurt Kasznar, Lewis Stone.

Donovan's Brain (United Artists 1953)

Producer: Tom Gries. Director: Felix Feist. Screenplay: Felix Feist. Cast: Lew Ayres, Gene Evans, Nancy Davis, Steve Brodie.

Hellcats of the Navy (Columbia Pictures 1957)

Producer: Charles Schneer. Director: Nathan Juran. Screenplay: David Lang and Raymond Marcus. Cast: Ronald Reagan, Nancy Davis, Arthur Franz, Harry Lauter, Selmer Jackson.

Crash Landing (Columbia Pictures 1958)

Producer: Sam Katzman. Director: Fred F. Sears. Written by: Fred Freiberger. Cast: Gary Merrill, Nancy Davis, Irene Hervey, Roger Smith.

The Television Shows of Nancy Davis

Schlitz Playhouse of Stars, episode "22 Sycamore Road," June 5, 1953, CBS. Producer: Meridian Pictures. Director: Bill Karn. Teleplay: Gail Ingram. Cast: Nancy Davis, Willard Parker, Myra Marsh, Ruth Lee, ViVi Janis, Richard Travis, Russell Hamer, Rudy Lee, John Hubbard.

Ford Theatre, episode "First Born," September 10, 1953, NBC. Producer: Irving Starr. Director: James Neilson. Teleplay: Karen DeWolf. Cast: Ronald Reagan, Nancy Davis, Paula Lorday, Tommy Rettig, Kathryn Card.

Schlitz Playhouse of Stars, episode "The Pearl Street Incident," May 14, 1954, CBS. Filmed by: Meridian Pictures. Director: Roy Kellino. Teleplay: Josephine and John T. Kelley. Cast: Nancy Davis, Horace McMahon, Jacqueline de Wit, Ted de Corsia, Tommy Ivo, Maudie Prickett, Fred Sherman, William Kennedy.

Climax, episode "Bail Out at 43,000," December 29, 1955, CBS. Director: John Frankenheimer. Teleplay: Paul Monash. Cast: Charlton Heston, Lee Marvin, Richard Boone, Nancy Davis.

General Electric Theatre, episode "That's the Man," April 15, 1956, CBS. Filmed by: Marada Corporation. Director: Ray Milland. Teleplay: N. B. Stone, Jr., and Joan Bourland. Cast: Irene Dunne, Richard Denning, Jo Ann Lilliquist, David Kasday, Lucien Littlefield, Elizabeth Patterson, Gordon Howard.

General Electric Theatre, episode "Turkey for the President," November 23, 1958, CBS. Producer: William Frye. Director: James Neilson. Teleplay: Jameson Brewer. Cast: Ronald Reagan, Nancy Davis, Ward Bond, Tommy Nolan, Joanne Davis, Warren Wade, Charles Seel.

General Electric Theatre, episode "The Playoff," November 20, 1960, CBS.

General Electric Theatre, episode "The Other Wise Man," December 25, 1960, CBS. Hosts: Ronald Reagan and Nancy Davis with their children Patricia and Ronald.

Zane Grey Theatre, episode "The Long Shadow," January 19, 1961, CBS. Director: Budd Boetticher. Cast: Nancy Davis, Scott Marlowe.

Tall Man, episode "Shadow of the Past," October 7, 1961, NBC.

General Electric Theatre, episode "Money and the Minister," November 26, 1961, CBS. Cast: Ronald Reagan, Nancy Davis, Fay Wray, Gary Merrill, Jaye P. Morgan, Ellen Corby.

Dick Powell Theatre, episode "Obituary for Mr. X," January 23, 1962, NBC.

87th Precinct, episode "King's Ransom," February 19, 1962, NBC.

Wagon Train, episode "The Sam Darland Story," December 26, 1962, ABC.

Notes

These chapter notes lay out the author's sources in writing each chapter of this book. The notes identify the people interviewed and the documents and publications examined. The summary is by no means all-inclusive, but it offers the reader a general review of some of the research involved.

CHAPTERS 1 AND 2

The birth certificate for Anne Frances Robbins came from the New York City Department of Health, Bureau of Vital Records. Records on the background of Edith Luckett researched at Petersburg Public Library in Petersburg, Virginia, plus city directories, church and school records, and birth, marriage, and death certificates; Berkshire Athenaeum in Pittsfield, Massachusetts, and Commonwealth of Massachusetts, State Department of Public Health Registry of Vital Records and Statistics for marriage certificate of Edith Luckett and Kenneth Robbins, as well as U.S. Army discharge papers of Kenneth Robbins and articles from the *Berkshire Eagle* of November 5, 1962, September 23, 1983, and January 29, 1985. U.S. Census for 1850, 1880, 1900, and 1910 from the National Archives, Washington, D.C. Birth and death certificates from the Vital Records Division of the Department of Human Resources, District of Columbia. The *Daily Index* and *Daily Express* in Petersburg, Virginia, for the marriage announcement of Sarah Whitlock and Charles Luckett.

Court records in Petersburg, Virginia, for the marriage bonds of Edward H. Whitlock and Martha A. Wells.

City directories from 1872 to 1948 in the District of Columbia were checked as well as map plats in the Columbia Historical Society in Washington, D.C. Death records from Joseph Birch & Sons Funeral Home in Washington, D.C., and burial records from the Congressional Cemetery in Washington, D.C.

For details of the suicide of Raleigh Luckett: *Evening Star* and *Washington Post* from July 2 to 12, 1907.

Interviews with Les Weinrott: May 9 and 15, June 7, and July 19, 1989; Kathleen Young: June 10 and 16 and October 14 and 23, 1988; Marian Robinson: June 10, 1988.

CHAPTER 3

Records include the marriage license of Loyal Davis and Edith L. Robbins, plus church records of the Fourth Presbyterian Church in Chicago. Trow's General Directory of New York City, R. L. Polk & Co., Vols. 124–133; Manhattan telephone directories for 1928 and 1929. Recorder of Deeds for Montgomery County, Maryland, for information on the home of Audley Galbraith. The Chicago Historical Society for Social Registers, city directories, Who's Who, Casino Club membership lists. Adoption records of Anne Frances Robbins, April 19, 1938, Cook County Circuit Court, Chicago, Illinois.

Books include *The Robber Barons* by Matthew Josephson (San Marcos, Calif.: Harvest, 1934); *History of the American Fortunes* by Gustavus Myers (New York: Modern Library Giant, 1907); *The Inheritors* by John Tebbel (New York: G. P. Putnam's Sons, 1962); *The Big Spenders* by Lucius Beebe (New York: Doubleday, 1966); *Clout: Mayor Daley and His City* by Len O'Connor (Chicago: Henry Regnery Company, 1975); *Make-Believe: The Story of Nancy and Ronald Reagan* by Laurence Leamer (New York: Harper & Row, 1983); *A Surgeon's Odyssey* by Loyal Davis, M.D. (New York: Doubleday, 1973); *Go in Peace* by Loyal Davis (New York: Van Rees Press, 1954); *J. B. Murphy: Stormy Petrel of Surgery* by Loyal Davis, M.D. (New York: G. P. Putnam's Sons, 1938); *Nancy* by Nancy Reagan with Bill Libby (New York: William Morrow and Company, Inc., 1980); *Early Reagan* by Anne Edwards (New York: William Morrow and Company, Inc., 1987).

Articles consulted include "The Remaking of a First Lady" by Susan Crosland, *Sunday Times of London Magazine*, March 11, 1985; "My Father Had to Earn My Love" by Nancy Reagan, *McCall's*, June 1983; "A Find at a Flea Market Sheds Light on Nancy Reagan's Life with Her Real

Father" written by Michelle Green, reported by David Grogan, *People* magazine, July 18, 1983. *Women's Wear Daily*, December 2, 1980; *Chicago Sun Times*, November 5, 1950; *Chicago Daily News*, April 26, 1981; the obituary notice of Mrs. Laura H. Davis, *Chicago Daily News*, September 26, 1945.

Interviews with Kathleen Young: June 10 and 16 and October 14 and 23, 1988; Les Weinrott: May 9 and 15, June 7, and July 19, 1989; Patsy Bullitt Collins: June 20, 1989; Jody Jacobs: September 8, 1987; David Grogan: January 4, 1989; Garry Clifford: January 4 and 5, 1989; Dr. Ray Weston: October 12, 1989; Lilyan Neiman Ordower: July 13 and 18, 1989; Mary Newhauser Dove: April 10, 1989; Carolyn Huddle Wells: April 10, 1989; LeRoy O. King: April 10 and June 18, 1989; Joan Kay Dilbow: April 6, 1988; Ken Cummins: June 20, 1989; confidential interview with publicist: June 20, 1989; confidential interviews with a classmate of Nancy Davis from Girls Latin: April 10 and 19 and May 9, 1989; Enoch Nappen: October 25, November 23, and December 3, 1988; Barry Morrison of Chicago Anti-Defamation League: June 27, 1989; Robert McCloud: June 17 and 20, 1989; Charlotte Galbraith Ramage: April 6 and 21 and May 19, 1989; correspondence and interview with Eileen Bailey: March 12, May 30, and June 7 and 9, 1989; Dr. Gerry Becker: June 2 and 7, 1989; Elizabeth Gillespie Kramer: June 2, 1989; Jane Beckwith Crowe: June 16, 1989.

CHAPTER 4

Records from the Smith College archives included Smith *Alumnae Quarterly*, August 1943; college bulletins, 1939–43; Rally Day programs, 1942–43; school newspaper *(The Sophian)*, 1939–43; drama playbills; college yearbook of 1943; *Life* magazine of December 30, 1940; Smith College Club of Washington, D.C., 1987 Directory; Smith College Alumnae Register of 1987.

Articles from the *Chicago Sun*, May 19, 1940; *New York Times*, July 3, 1942; "A Private Talk with Nancy Reagan" by Charlotte Curtis, *Ladies' Home Journal*, June 1981; *Avenue M* (Chicago), January 1989; *Chicago Tribune*, December 21, 1939.

Interviews with Dick Pate: April 27, and July 6 and 12, 1989; Daniel Stuckey: June 28, 1989; Eleanor Lincoln Terry: June 28, 1989; Sally Gavin See: April 27 and June 28, 1989; Racine Tucker: July 6, 1989; Charles Williamson: April 3 and 15, 1990; confidential interview with one of Frank Birney's closest friends from Princeton: April 17, 1990; Mary Ann Guitar: April 25 and 26, 1989; Jean Upham Sauter: March 8, 1989; Harline Ward Hurst: March 27, 1989; Ann Teal Bradley: March

24, 1989; Barbara Balensweig Wilk: March 24, 1989; Juliette Harvey
Guthrie: March 24, 1989; Mary Heald Dickert: June 28, 1989; Madeline
L'Engle: April 18, 1989; Amy Ward Beir: April 5, 1989; Pat O'Brian
Hayes: March 14, 1989; Ruth Jeffers Wellington: April 6, 1989; Priscilla
Blackett Rogers: July 6, 10, and 11, 1989; I. Newton Perry: April 13,
1989; John Farrington, Jr.: July 13, 1989; Jim McCahey: May 8, 1989;
Geoffrey Montgomery Talbot Jones: April 28, 1989; Robert Marquardt:
January 10, 1990; Mrs. Nathan Hatch: January 9, 1990; Mrs. Albert
McIntyre: October 4, 1989; correspondence with Jean Struben Harris:
April 9 and 23, 1989; Ann Keyser Rawley: March 23, 1989.

CHAPTER 5

Records from FBI files on Mrs. Loyal (Edith) Davis and Mayor Ed Kelly
obtained under Freedom of Information Act. Author also obtained access
to the legal and production files of Nancy Davis at the MGM studios in
Culver City, California.

Books include *The Mayors: The Chicago Political Tradition*, edited by
Paul M. Green and Melvin G. Holli (Carbondale, Ill.: Southern Illinois
University Press, 1987); *Captive City* by Ovid Demaris (New York: Lyle
Stuart, Inc., 1969); *Kup's Chicago* by Irv Kupcinet (Cleveland and New
York: World Publishing Co., 1962); *Big Bill of Chicago* by Lloyd Wendt
and Herman Kogan (New York: Bobbs-Merrill Company, Inc., 1953);
Syndicate City: The Chicago Crime Cartel and What to Do About It by Alson J.
Smith (Chicago: Henry Regnery Company, 1954).

Articles include reviews of *Lute Song* in *Time*, February 18, 1946; *New
York Times*, February 7, 1946; *Life*, March 4, 1946; *New Yorker*, February
16, 1946. Regarding Edith Davis as an undercover policewoman: *Chicago
Daily Times, Chicago Sun, Chicago Tribune, Chicago Daily News*, June 4–12,
1943; "MGM: Mammoth of the Movies" by Ezra Goodman, *Coronet*,
May 1949.

Interviews with Les Weinrott: May 9 and 15, June 7, and July 19,
1989; Richard Goldstone: October 18 and 24, 1988; Norma Connolly:
November 8 and 9, 1988; Norman Panama: November 11, 1988; Dorothy Manners: October 14, 1988; Joe Naar: September 6, 1989; Kathryn
Grayson: August 17, 1989; confidential interviews regarding Nancy Reagan's dealing with Sidney Korshak: October 5 and 14 and November 1,
1988; confidential interview with Max Allentuck's secretary: August 14,
1989; Charles Williamson: April 1, 1990; James Karen: February 24,
1989, and correspondence of March 6, 1989; Dr. Gerry Becker: June 2,
1989; Ward Patton III: July 2, 1989; Dr. Morton Smith-Peterson: July
20, 1989; Harline Ward Hurst: March 27, 1989; Bill Whorf: July 20,

1989; Mary Ann Guitar: April 25 and 26, 1989; Anne Edwards: August 4, 1988; Gottfried Reinhardt: October 8, 1988; Lillian Burns Sidney: October 9, 1988; Lucille Ryman Carroll: October 20, 1988; Ann Sothern: October 13, 1988; Rupert Allen: October 13 and 28, 1988; Joseph J. Cohn: October 10, 1988; Jill Schary Robinson: August 22, 1989; Pandro Berman: October 10, 1988; Arlene Sellers: November 13, 1988.

As to Nancy Reagan's assertion that her name was on a mailing list to receive "Communist" propaganda:

Three women of approximately the same age in Hollywood were named Nancy Davis. One of them was Nancy Strauss Davis, a political liberal married to producer Jerome Davis. She and her husband signed an appeal to the U.S. Supreme Court in 1949 to reverse the conviction of John Howard Lawson and Dalton Trumbo, two of the Hollywood Ten. The list of the signers was printed in the *Hollywood Reporter* of October 28, 1949.

"My wife, who died a few years after we had divorced and remarried other people, was an aspiring actress and a member of the Screen Actors Guild," recalled Jerry Davis on October 21, 1988. "Nancy and I both signed the amicus brief to the Supreme Court in 1949, but we weren't Communists. We simply believed that Lawson and Trumbo should not be persecuted for their beliefs."

In 1953, after Nancy Davis Reagan was dropped by MGM, she tried to get movie work with Columbia Pictures. The studio automatically investigated her background, discovered that a Nancy Davis had signed the amicus brief, and wrote to her. Mrs. Reagan responded with a blistering letter to B. B. Kahane, vice president of Columbia Pictures. He wrote back to her on January 7, 1953, and said, in part:

As you are aware, we make a check on all actors, writers, directors, et al. being considered for employment. This is a regular routine. The investigation is made by a reputable organization in New York under retainer to our Company.

If the report we receive indicates that the subject of the inquiry was identified or connected in any way or to any extent with the Communist Party or organizations or activities which supported or "fronted" for the Party, we request an explanation from the subject. . . . Yours is one of such cases. We regret very much that it has upset you and we ask your indulgence.

I received a call from Jack Dales [secretary of the Screen Actors Guild] and he told me that there was another Nancy Davis and that the citation did not refer to you. I immediately and gladly accepted this and considered the matter disposed of. . . .

I question whether your criticism of the organization which checks for us is justified. I am sure that they would not deliberately misrepresent or attempt to harm any one. Their job is to bring to our attention any information they can gather from all sources touching upon the subject. If they find that a Nancy Davis signed the Amicus Curiae brief for the convicted Hollywood Ten they have to report that fact to us. . . .

Of course we could have taken it for granted that the wife of Ronald Reagan could not possibly be of questionable loyalty and could have disregarded that report. But as the citation was merely the signing of the Amicus Curiae brief and many persons signed this brief who we have been convinced are not now and never were Communists or sympathizers, we informed you of the citation, believing that a satisfactory explanation would be forthcoming. . . .

Nancy Davis Reagan's reference to the other Nancy Davis as a "Communist" angered the third Nancy Davis, a former ice skater, who felt her reputation was sullied by Mrs. Reagan's pronouncements.

"Nancy Reagan has been lying about me for years," said Nancy Davis Hunt on October 15, 1988. She added:

I never was a Communist. I told Reagan back in the fifties that if she didn't stop saying I was a Communist, I'd sue her. . . . He called me in 1953 and said I had to change my name. I told him I didn't want to. I'd worked at all the studios as Nancy Davis, but he was the boss [president of the Screen Actors Guild] and could've cost me my membership so I did as I was told. . . . I was hurt to have to change my name because it wasn't fair. I was there first. I felt Nancy Davis Reagan should change her name. . . . When she became First Lady and started saying I was a Communist, I thought it was very cruel of her, but there was nothing I could do. I work in a snack bar in Ventura, California. I'm a nobody and she's married to the President of the United States.

As to Nancy Davis's reputation in Hollywood:
In *Make Believe: The Story of Nancy and Ronald Reagan* (New York: Harper & Row, 1983), author Laurence Leamer told of an interview with Benny Thau's receptionist in which she stated that she "had orders that on Saturday morning Nancy was to be sent directly into Benny Thau's suite." Leamer later confided to this author and others that the

receptionist had told him that she found "condoms in Thau's wastebasket after every visit from Nancy." Leamer said he did not include the information because his book was published in 1983, when Nancy Davis Reagan was First Lady of the United States. "I did not want to offend her," he said.

A few years later, Anne Edwards, who wrote *Early Reagan* (New York: William Morrow & Co., 1987), said she had interviewed Benny Thau at the Motion Picture and Television Hospital before he died in 1983. Edwards quoted Thau as saying that Nancy Davis was renowned in Hollywood for performing oral sex. "He said . . . she not only slept around, she performed that act and she performed it not only in the evening but in offices. That was what he told me. . . . That was really one of the reasons that she got a contract, and that was one of the reasons that she was very popular on the [MGM] lot." Anne Edwards told the author on August 8, 1988, that she did not print what Thau said because it "was too scandalous, too tasteless . . . and, after all, my book was really about Ronald Reagan, not Nancy."

In 1988, Peter Lawford's widow wrote a biography of her husband with Ted Schwarz, *The Peter Lawford Story: Life with Monroe, the Kennedys and the Rat Pack* (New York: Carroll & Graf Publishers, Inc., 1988). In it, she quoted Lawford as saying that Nancy Davis's "goal was to be an actress; her avocation was to have a good time . . . When she was single, Nancy Davis was known for giving the best head in Hollywood. . . . Then Peter told of driving to the Phoenix area with Nancy and Bob Walker. Nancy would visit her parents, Dr. and Mrs. Loyal Davis, while Peter and Walker picked up girls at Arizona State University in Tempe, a Phoenix suburb. He claimed that she entertained them orally on those trips, apparently playing with whichever man was not driving at the moment."

In the February 1989 issue of *Spy* magazine, a multiple choice quiz on Nancy Reagan contained this question:

> According to Peter Lawford, as a young actress Nancy earned the admiration of many of her fellow actors. What was she known for?
>
> (a) Her anti-Communist zealotry
>
> (b) Her dedicated work for the USO
>
> (c) The good-natured way she laughed it off when people mistook her for Nanette Fabray
>
> (d) Her concern that rampant materialism was corrupting the American way of life
>
> (e) Giving the best head in Hollywood
>
> *Spy* said the correct answer was (e).

As to Ronald Reagan as an informant for the FBI:
The author obtained documents from the Justice Department under the Freedom of Information Act pertaining to FBI informants Ronald Reagan (T-10) and Jane Wyman (T-9):

> T-10 advised Special Agent [blacked out] that he has been made a member of a committee headed by L. B. Mayer, the purpose of which allegedly is to "purge" the motion picture industry of Communist Party members, which committee was an outgrowth of the Thomas Committee hearings in Washington and the subsequent meeting of motion picture producers in New York City. . . .
> T-10 stated it is his firm conviction that Congress should declare, first of all, by statute, that the Communist Party is not a legal Party, but is a foreign-inspired conspiracy. Secondly, Congress should define what organizations are Communist-controlled so that membership therein could be construed as an indication of disloyalty. He felt that lacking such a definitive stand on the part of the Government it would be very difficult for any committee of motion picture people to conduct any type of cleansing of their own household.

In an interview on November 2, 1988, Mark Locher, public relations director of the Screen Actors Guild, spoke of Ronald Reagan's actions during the 1950s. "It was a dark and terrible time for the Screen Actors Guild," said Locher. "When Gale Sondergaard came to the board and asked for protection against those who were calling actors Communists and subpoenaing them to testify, Ronald Reagan said, 'Too bad. It's your duty to testify.' Then he went back to Washington as an FBI informer and named names."

CHAPTER 6

Records include the February 29, 1952, marriage license application of Ronald Reagan and Nancy Davis; the MGM legal and production files on Nancy Davis; the Collections files at the Academy of Motion Picture Arts and Sciences; the legal files of the Screen Actors Guild; and the minutes of SAG meetings. Doris Lilly provided copies of all her letters from Ronald Reagan. Carol Perry Wilson of the office of external affairs of the National Spiritual Assembly of the Bahais of the United States provided background material on the Bahais, along with a copy of the statement made by President Ronald Reagan in behalf of the Bahais in Iran on May 17, 1983.

Books include *Early Reagan* by Anne Edwards (New York: William

Morrow and Company, Inc., 1987); *Make Believe* by Laurence Leamer (New York: Harper & Row, 1983); *Case History of a Movie* by Dore Schary as told to Charles Palmer (New York: Random House, 1950); *Confessions of a Hollywood Columnist* by Sheilah Graham (New York: William Morrow and Company, Inc., 1969); *On the Outside Looking In* by Michael Reagan with Joe Hyams (New York: Zebra Books, 1988); *First Father, First Daughter: A Memoir* by Maureen Reagan (Boston: Little, Brown, 1988); *Heyday* by Dore Schary (Boston: Little, Brown, 1979); *Reagan's America: Innocents at Home* by Garry Wills (New York: Doubleday, 1987); *Viveka . . . Viveca* by Viveca Lindfors (New York: Everest House, Publishers, 1981).

Articles include the *Los Angeles Herald-Examiner* series on Nancy Reagan by Wanda McDaniel: "When Ronnie Was Running as a Bachelor" by Rogers Worthington, *Chicago Tribune,* September 11, 1980; "Why Reagan Moved from Left to Right" by Jack Anderson and Les Whitten, *New York Daily News,* August 18, 1976; "Reagan: Long in Spotlight, Still Enigmatic" by Robert Scheer, *Los Angeles Times,* June 25, 1980; "Nancy Reagan: Where's the Rest of Her?" by Louise Farr, *Los Angeles Magazine,* September 1980.

Interviews include Jacqueline Park: April 14 and 17 and December 21, 1988, October 14, 1989; Charles Palmer: October 25, 1988; Selene Walters: April 19, 1989, and correspondence: April 17 and 26, June 12, and October 16, 1989, and September 20, 1990; Mary Sinclair: December 5, 1988; Gottfried Reinhardt: October 8, 1988; confidential interview with a former MGM assistant director: October 17, 1988; Paula Raymond: October 17 and November 1, 1988; Richard Brooks: October 18, 1988; Kathleen Young: October 23, 1988; Brian Daly of the Little Brown Church: September 13, 1989; Mrs. Ralph Greenson: February 19, 1990; James Whitmore: October 25, 1988; Rosemary DeCamp: December 9, 1988; Doris Lilly: February 19 and March 3, 1989, and correspondence: February 17 and 28 and March 6, 1989; Ann Doran: August 16, 1989; Jim Lewis: April 7, 8, 21, 1989; Betty Lasky: April 6, 1989; Richard Epstein: January 15, 22, and 29, March 5, 24, and 26, April 6, 7, 9, and 20, and July 6, 1989, and correspondence: April 12, July 3, October 20, and December 13 and 28, 1989, January 18, 1990; Rose Murchison: April 6 and 7, 1989; Donald Murchison: September 6, 1989; John Cook: March 26 and 27, 1989; O. Z. Whitehead: April 6 and 7, 1989; David Bradley: October 13, 1988; Senator George Murphy: September 18, 1988; Fletcher Markle: October 10, 1988.

As to the other women in Ronald Reagan's life:

Chicago Sun Times columnist Irv Kupcinet wrote in his autobiography,

Kup: A Man, an Era, a City with Paul Neimark (Chicago: Bonus Books, 1988):

One story about the president [Reagan] that never saw the light of print occurred when he was courting the beautiful red-haired Rhonda Fleming. Reagan, then a handsome bachelor, was mad about the girl.

Rhonda was fond of Ronnie, but not in love. And one night Reagan was so frustrated that he pulled out a gun and fired a shot at her. I'm sure he was wide of the mark purposely, but he did scare the romance out of their idyll. I often have wondered what the course of history might have been . . . !

Rhonda Fleming, who appeared in four films with Reagan, denied the story. "Oh, awful," she said in an interview on June 15, 1989. "That was crazy. As I told you, we weren't social on or off [the set], certainly didn't have a romance. [At that time], I think I was married to this doctor I was very much in love with for ten years. I can't imagine . . . how he [Kup] could come out with this absolute lie. It's a joke. There was a time I was going to write him [Kup] a scathing letter, but I decided it wasn't worth it. Paul Harvey called me and was going to use it on his radio show. Now, this is a gentleman. I told Paul that's a lie, that's trash. . . . And he didn't use it. . . . There was never any romance between Ronnie Reagan and me. . . . If he was fond of me or had a crush on me, I didn't know it." Kupcinet stands by the story as reported in his book.

As to Ronald Reagan's relationship with Christine Larson:
One of Miss Larson's closest friends, who was interviewed for this book, called former President Reagan in June of 1989 to tell him that the author knew of his intimate relationship with Miss Larson and was planning to write about it. Reagan returned the telephone call to say that he had "no recollection whatsoever" of Christine Larson and that the period between his marriages was passed with only casual dating, without a serious relationship. Even the close friend was surprised by Ronald Reagan's professed lapse of memory.

As to Ronald Reagan's first marriage:
Jane Wyman has never talked for publication about her relationship with Ronald Reagan. It is not out of loyalty that she keeps her counsel, but because she considers that marriage to be a mistake she'd rather forget. Further, she views herself as one of the premier actresses of her era and her career has always been her top priority. She married three

times after Reagan, twice to the same man, but all three marriages ended in divorce.

As to Ronald Reagan's love letters to Doris Lilly:
Lilly sold two of Reagan's letters at auction, and both were purchased for $4,400 by financier Malcolm Forbes. He gave them to Nancy Reagan, but, at her request, he waited until after Reagan left office so that she would not have to declare them as gifts.

"That bitch is so jealous of any other woman who knew Ronnie," said Doris Lilly, "that she'll probably destroy the letters so that future generations won't know there was anyone else but her in his life. It's a damn shame that Malcolm gave them to her, because those letters should be preserved as a part of history."

CHAPTER 7

Books include *The Glory and the Dream* by William Manchester (New York: Bantam Books, 1973); *The Ragman's Son* by Kirk Douglas (New York: Simon and Schuster, 1988); *The Girl Next Door . . . And How She Grew* by Jane Powell (New York: William Morrow and Company, Inc., 1988); *Ronald Reagan: His Life and Rise to the Presidency* by Bill Boyarsky (New York: Random House, 1981); *The Politics of Glamour: Ideology and Democracy in the Screen Actors Guild* by David F. Prindle (Madison, Wisc.: University of Wisconsin Press, 1988); *Where's the Rest of Me?* by Ronald Reagan (New York: Dell Publishing Co., Inc., 1965); *My Turn* by Nancy Reagan with William Novak (New York: Random House, 1989).

Articles include "Blacklist? Never Heard of It" by Larry Ceplair, *Nation,* January 31, 1981; "Reagan's Multiple Duties" by Richard Dyer MacCann, *Christian Science Monitor,* December 21, 1954; "There's No Show Business Like MCA's Business" by Edward T. Thompson, *Fortune,* July 1960; "That Reagan Boy" by J. Hoberman, *Village Voice,* September 10–16, 1980; "Nancy Reagan: Smiling but Reserved" by Nan Nichols, *Sacramento Bee,* November 2, 1977; "When Ronnie Played Vegas" by Terry Mulgannon, *Los Angeles Magazine,* April 1983; "New Info on Reagan, MCA Waiver Probe," *Variety,* April 18, 1984.

Interviews include Barbara Ling: February 8 and 9, 1989; Chet Migden: November 9, 1988; Blaine Waller: September 19, 1989; Ann Doran: August 16, 1989; Ursula Taylor Schacker: April 8 and 11, 1989; Irv Kupcinet: May 9, 1989; Frank Casey: April 5 and 6, 1989; Lew Ayres: November 2, 1988; Irene Hervey: October 27, 1988; confidential interview with close friend of Nancy Reagan: September 16, 1989; John Bradford: September 13, 1989; Buff Cobb Martin: September 20,

1989; Steve Halpern: October 26 and 28, 1988; Patti Davis: October 11 and 19, 1989; confidential interview with childhood friend of Patti Davis: November 27, 1990.

As to Patti's relationship with her mother:

In her autobiographical novel, *Home Front,* Patti had the main character's mother tell her that she had been stubborn from the time she was conceived, clinging to her mother's ribs and refusing to come out to be born.

"Actually, that story of birth was what was told to me," said Patti on October 19, 1989. "I really did take that from my life and I did come back with a biology book one time and say, 'This can't happen . . . You can't hold on to a woman's ribs in the womb,' [but] my mother insisted that it was true. . . . I don't know how anyone could come up with a story like that and say it with a straight face, but she did."

CHAPTER 8

Records include copies of correspondence and other documents from the presidential libraries of John F. Kennedy, Lyndon Baines Johnson, Richard M. Nixon, Gerald R. Ford, and Jimmy Carter. Obituary notice of Mrs. Charles A. Galbraith (Nancy's aunt): *Atlanta Journal,* August 10, 1966. Transcript of CBS Reports "What About Ronald Reagan?" December 12, 1967, reporters Harry Reasoner and Bill Stout, producer Gene DePoris, executive producer Sam Zelman.

Books include *Death of a President* by William Manchester (New York: Harper & Row, 1967), *Reagan* by Lou Cannon (New York: G. P. Putnam's Sons, 1982), *Nixon: The Education of a Politician 1913–1962* by Stephen E. Ambrose (New York: Simon and Schuster, 1987); *His Way: The Unauthorized Biography of Frank Sinatra* by Kitty Kelley (New York: Bantam Books, 1986).

Articles include "Red Threat Is Cited," *New York Times,* May 9, 1961; "The Best Years of Our Lives" by Gore Vidal, *New York Review of Books,* September 29, 1983; "When Reagan Was Reagan" by Nicholas Lemann, *New York Review of Books,* January 15, 1987; "Reagan Warns of Hollywood Red Invasion," *Hollywood Citizen-News,* March 6, 1961; "Reagan Assails JFK's Key Plans," *Los Angeles Mirror,* January 3, 1962; "Ronald Reagan Pits His Voice Against JFK's," *Los Angeles Mirror,* June 17, 1961; "Dutch Reagan, All-American" by Joel Kotkin and Paul Grabowicz, *Esquire,* August 1980.

Interviews include Charlotte Galbraith Ramage: April 6 and 21 and May 19, 1989; Kathleen Young: June 10 and 16 and October 14 and 23,

1988; Dr. Gerry Becker; June 2 and 7, 1989; Philip Dunne: October 25, 26, and 31 and November 8 and 9, 1988, and correspondence: November 20 and 30, 1988, and January 16 and March 9, 1990; Amanda Dunne: October 25, 26, 28, and 30 and November 8, 1988, and correspondence: February 27, 1989; Brad Dexter: June 2, 1987, December 26, 1988, and December 19, 1989; Gene Kelly: November 21, 1988; Janet Leigh: October 17, 1988; Gene Nelson: October 24 and 26, 1988; confidential interview with former executive of Four Star Productions: April 7, 1988; Jean Kinney: radio interview of October 27, 1964; Mrs. Kirk Douglas: September 11, 1989; Patty Sue Stanton: October 12, 1988; Bob and Sabrina Schiller: October 28, 1988; Patti Davis: October 11 and 19, 1989, and correspondence: November 13, 17, and 30 and December 6, 1988, and October 13, 1989; confidential interview with the mother of Ron Reagan's best friend: November 5, 1990.

As to the assassination of John F. Kennedy:
After the Warren Commission report was published in 1964, Dr. Loyal Davis, who edited the official journal of the American College of Surgeons, wrote to the three pathologists who performed the autopsy of the President at the U.S. Naval Medical Center in Bethesda, Maryland. Knowing that Kennedy had Addison's disease, Dr. Davis asked why information regarding Kennedy's adrenal glands was omitted from the Warren Commission report. Dr. Davis did not receive an answer from any of the pathologists, but he did receive a letter from Dr. George Barkley, the White House physician to President Kennedy. The letter read: "All the pertinent facts concerning the late President Kennedy were supplied to the Warren Commission for their information and evaluation. All other medical records have been placed in a permanent receptacle here that will remain for reference at some future date. These medical files are being held under the same conditions as the President's private papers."

CHAPTER 9

Records include transcripts of "The Real Life of Ronald Reagan" on "Frontline," January 19, 1989, narrated by Garry Wills; and "The Jennings–Koppel Report" on ABC News, April 23, 1987, anchored by Peter Jennings and Ted Koppel.

Articles include "At Home with the Reagans" by Judy Cool, *Los Angeles Herald Examiner,* October 30, 1966; "Nancy Reagan: A Woman of Many Faces" by Lynn Rosellini, *Washington Star,* April 14, 1980; "I Am Worried for Ronald" by Jimmy Breslin, *New York World Journal Tribune,*

November 6, 1966; "The Real Ronald Reagan Stands Up" by Richard Oulahan and William Lamb, *Life*, January 21, 1966. Stories about Reagan's swearing in as thirty-third governor of California are from *Sacramento Union* and *Sacramento Bee*.

Interviews include Patti Davis: October 11 and 19, 1989; Ron Reagan on "The Larry King Show," March 3, 1988; Charis Webb: October 10, 1988; Nancy Dutton: June 19, 1988; Irving Wallace: November 13, 1988; Bernice Brown: October 17 and 19, 1988; former governor Edmund "Jerry" Brown and Kathleen Brown: October 15, 1988; Marian Darmsted: February 28, 1989; Martin Smith: February 8, 1989; Jim Wrightson: March 3, 1989; Virginia Lehman: June 3, 1988; Jody Jacobs: October 28, 1989; Henry Salvatori: September 18 and October 30, 1990.

As to Nancy Reagan's plastic surgery:
"I was a college student at the time Mrs. Reagan came in for her surgery with Dr. Irvine, and I was supposed to take her patient history," recalled a former medical secretary on May 30, 1989. "She was very rude and quite miffed that I did not know who she was or what her husband did. The office manager, who overheard the conversation, had to take me aside and explain who the Reagans were. . . . I recognized celebrities like Lana Turner . . . but I didn't recognize Nancy Reagan. . . . I've never forgotten her, though, because of her rudeness."

As to Michael Reagan attending various schools:
1949: Kindergarten: Buckley School in North Hollywood, California
1950: Grades 1 and 2: Chadwick Boarding School, Palos Verdes, California
1953: Grade 3: Warner Avenue School, Westwood, California
1954: Grades 4 and 5: Good Shepherd School, Beverly Hills, California
1956: Grades 5 and 6: St. John's Military Academy, Los Angeles, California
1958: Grades 7 and 8: Horace Ensign School, Newport, California
1959: Grades 9 to 11: Loyola High School, Los Angeles, California
1962: Grades 11 (repeat) and 12: Judson High School, Scottsdale, Arizona
1964: Freshman for six months at Arizona State University, Tempe, Arizona
1965: Freshman: Valley State College, Los Angeles, California

As to Ronald Reagan's cabinet appointments as governor:
"The amazing thing," said Henry Salvatori (interviewed September 18 and October 30, 1990), "is that right after Ronnie won the election [in 1966], he asked us to choose his cabinet. He did not have one man or woman that he had met during the campaign that he said, 'Hey, I think you ought to come aboard.' So we [kitchen cabinet] had to make all his appointments for Sacramento. . . . We did the same thing when he became President, too."

CHAPTER 10

Records include a confidential memo dated August 23, 1967, from Vice President Hubert H. Humphrey to President Lyndon Johnson concerning Barry Goldwater's talk with Ronald Reagan, from the files of the Lyndon B. Johnson Presidential Library. Memo dated July 2, 1969, from Harry S. Dent to President Nixon, from the files of the Richard M. Nixon Presidential Library. Oral History of Verne Orr, director of Department of Motor Vehicles and director of Reagan's Department of Finance, Volume 400/420, University of California at Berkeley, interviewed by Gabrielle Morris in 1982 and 1983.

Books include *The White Album* by Joan Didion (New York: Simon and Schuster, 1979); *College: A Smith Mosaic* by Jacqueline Van Voris (West Springfield, Mass.: Smith College at the M. J. O'Malley Company, 1975); *The Right Places* by Stephen Birmingham (Boston: Little, Brown, 1967).

Articles include "Not Great, Not Brilliant, But a Good Show" by Julius Duscha, *New York Times Magazine,* December 10, 1967; "What About Ronald Reagan?" by Jack Star, *Look,* July 23, 1968; "A Private Talk with Nancy Reagan" by Charlotte Curtis, *Ladies' Home Journal,* June 1981; "The Reagan Question" by Robert Scheer, *Playboy,* August 1980; "Reagan Bitter; Regents OK One Lecture," *Los Angeles Herald-Examiner,* September 21, 1968; "Luncheon with Nancy Reagan" by Gwen Dobson, *Evening Star,* March 10, 1972; "Nancy Reagan—Does She Run the State or the House?" by Nancy Skelton, *Sacramento Bee,* July 10, 1968; "Where's the Rest of Ronald Reagan?" by Jules Witcover and Richard M. Cohen, *Esquire,* March 1976; "The Fallen Knight," editorial from *Washington Star,* November 7, 1967; "A Conversation with Mrs. Reagan" by Mary Lou Loper, *Los Angeles Times,* February 26, 1973; "Pretty Nancy" by Joan Didion, *Saturday Evening Post,* June 1, 1968; "Conversations with Nancy" by George Christy, *West Magazine,* June 27, 1971.

Interviews include Susan Granger: May 14 and December 18, 1987, and January 10, 15, 22, and 23 and September 15, 1989, and correspondence: October 20, 1988, January 3 and 28 and February 2 and 9, 1989; Warren Steibel: November 7, 13, and 17, 1989, and correspondence: November 8, 1989; Leonore Hershey: June 7, 1988; Jody Jacobs: January 11 and July 13, 1987, and October 28, 1989; Stanley Gordon: January 21, 1989; Lyn Nofziger: August 19, 1989; Anne Garbeff: March 29 and 30, 1989; Pat Franich: March 28, 1990; Matt Franich: August 17, 1989; Martin Smith: February 8, 1989, and correspondence: February 10, 1989; Judy Dallenmere: January 16, 1989; Kate Beardsley: January 25, 1989; Sheldon Davis: June 30, October 5 and 14, and November 1, 1988; John Monahan: October 24, 1988; Clarence Newton: February 1, 1989; Stanley Tretick: March 20, 1987; correspondence with Jack Star: May 5, 10, and 19, 1988; Gordon Davidson: October 25, 1988; Patricia Taylor: October 12 and 26, 1988, February 7 and 8, 1989, and January 3, 1990, and correspondence: February 14, 1989; Murray Deutchman, attorney for Patricia Taylor, January 3, 1990.

As to the Reagans' attendance at the 1968 GOP convention in Miami:
"I was there writing a column for the *New York Post,*" recalled Doris Lilly, one of Ronald Reagan's former lovers, in an interview on February 13, 1989. "I remember interviewing Betsy Bloomingdale and she told me that she and Nancy were ironing their dresses. All these two dames care about are dresses. I think that if their house was on fire and they had to choose between their clothes and their children, they'd grab their clothes. . . . When I saw Ronnie, who was now governor of California, I said, 'Oh, Governor,' and introduced myself. He said, 'Well, I know who *you* are,' and without thinking he put his arms around me. Nancy gave me a look to kill . . . and he pulled back like a shot because he realized what he had done. But he was so happy to see me. Boy, was he lucky. Nobody got a picture. I said hello to him and hello to Betsy Bloomingdale and Nancy Reagan wouldn't even look at me."

As to Governor and Mrs. Reagan experimenting with marijuana at a dinner party at Betsy and Alfred Bloomingdale's:
In an effort to verify Bloomingdale's story twenty years later, several calls were made to people who had been invited to the Bloomingdales' for dinner at various times to see if any of them recalled the evening that Alfred Bloomingdale passed around a joint of marijuana.

Janet DeCordova, wife of "Tonight Show" producer Fred DeCordova, said that the incident did not occur at any of the dinner parties she had attended at the Bloomingdales' home. "Big deal, if he [Alfred] did pass a joint," she said on March 29, 1989, "but he didn't. Big deal, if he did."

"I've never heard the story," said Gloria Stewart, wife of Jimmy Stewart, on August 8, 1989.

"I wasn't there, but I wouldn't put it past the man [Alfred Bloomingdale]," said Ursula Taylor Schacker on April 8 and 11, 1989.

As to the Sacramento house purchased for Governor and Mrs. Reagan in 1969:

The wealthy political backers of Reagan who paid $150,000 for the 92-year-old Victorian house were: Leland M. Kaiser, San Francisco insurance securities executive; Jaquelin H. Hume, San Francisco industrialist; Holmes Tuttle, Los Angeles automobile dealer; Henry Salvatori, Los Angeles industrialist; Fritz Burns, Los Angeles businessman; Charles and Howard Cook, Los Angeles financiers; Roy P. Crocker, Pasadena businessman; Justin Dart, Rexall Drug executive; J. R. and J. S. Fluor, Los Angeles executives of Fluor Corp.; Edward Gaver, Roos-Atkins chain executive; Wayne Griffin, Los Angeles businessman; Earle Jorgensen, Los Angeles industrialist.

CHAPTER 11

Records include Steve Allen's open letter to Frank Sinatra, September 7, 1970; menu from the private files of Mrs. William Goetz for the dinner in honor of the Reagans on December 18, 1971.

Books include *First Lady's Lady* by Sheila Rabb Weidenfeld (New York: G.P. Putnam's Sons, 1979); *Confessions of an Ex-Secret Service Agent* by George Rush (New York: Donald I. Fine Publishers Inc., 1988); *Home Front* by Patti Davis (New York: Crown Publishers Inc., 1986).

Articles include "Wife Nancy as the Little Woman" by Karl Fleming, *New York,* December 15, 1975; "The Governor's Extraordinary Gesture," *Newhall Signal,* February 3, 1969; "Nancy Reagan Opposes Drugs, Women's Lib, Unrestricted Abortions" by Edith M. Lederer, Associated Press, July 10, 1970; "Patti Davis" by Gloria Steinem, *Ms.,* January 1986; "The Mafia and Frank Sinatra" by Leonard Aronson, *Chicago Today,* September 11, 1970; "N.D.R. . . . The Girl Behind the Man" by Jody Jacobs, *Women's Wear Daily,* October 31, 1969; "Sinatra Explodes Political Bomb" by Joyce Haber, *Los Angeles Times,* July 14, 1970; "The Essential Ronald Reagan . . . Traumatic as Apple Pie" by Lewis Armstrong, *Cosmopolitan,* February 1967.

Interviews include Nancy Reynolds: August 13, 1982; Linda Douglas: October 17, 1988; Mary Bogdonovich Dexter: December 26, 1988; David Columbia: October 13, 1988; a former White House aide from the First Lady's staff: March 25, 1989; Patti Davis: October 19, 1989; Carlo Celoni: October 11, 1988; Ellen Pollon: October 11, 1988.

As to the published comments of Betty Ford regarding Nancy Reagan:
These comments drew several critical letters, prompting Mrs. Ford's staff to draft the following reply:

Dear ———,

Thank you for writing to convey your esteem and affection for Mrs. Nancy Reagan.

Mrs. Ford, too, was disturbed by media accounts of events at the Republican National Convention which implied a lack of graciousness on her part regarding Mrs. Reagan.

You will be interested to know these accounts, as well as certain remarks attributed to Mrs. Ford which appeared in *Time* magazine, were inaccurate. Because of the size of the Convention Hall, Mrs. Ford, who was at one end of the hall, was unable to see Mrs. Reagan at the other end and was unaware of the origin of the many spontaneous demonstrations during that highly emotional time.

Mrs. Ford has deep respect and admiration for Mrs. Reagan and regrets that a totally different impression resulted.

Mrs. Ford appreciates your sharing your thoughts and sends her good wishes.

Sincerely,

CHAPTER 12

Records include Nancy Davis Reagan's letter to her cousin Marian Robinson, which Professor Robinson provided on July 5, 1988. Book proposal of Michael Reagan with Joe Hyams for the Scott Meredith Literary Agency.

Books include *Exile: The Unquiet Oblivion of Richard M. Nixon* by Robert Sam Anson (New York: Simon and Schuster, 1984); *Witness to Power: The Nixon Years* by John Ehrlichman (New York: Simon and Schuster, 1982).

Articles include "Reagan Assailed on Tax Liability" by Wallace Turner, *New York Times,* May 9, 1971; "Nancy Reagan: Smiling . . . but Reserved" by Nan Nichols, *Sacramento Bee,* November 2, 1977; "First Son: Ron Reagan" by Natalie Gittelson, *McCall's,* July 1986; "Citizen Reagan," *Newsweek,* January 6, 1975; "Mrs. Reagan Hits Loose Morality," United Press International, May 15, 1972; " 'Delay Marriage' Says Mrs. Reagan," Associated Press, April 24, 1972.

Interviews include Sanford Hollander: May 12, 1989; Kathleen Young: October 23, 1988; Les Weinrott; May 15, 1989; Peter Hayes: December 11 and 12, 1989; John Ehrlichman: December 12, 1989; Mary Pettus: July 15, 1989; Gene Nelson: October 26, 1988; Alice Braemer: December 1, 1989; John West: January 24, 1990; Carroll Righter's personal secretary: October 14 and 15, 1988; confidential source from Governor Reagan's staff: January 12, 1990.

As to the death of Nancy's father, Kenneth Robbins:
Ken's will was signed and executed on December 10, 1969, when Robbins visited his attorney, Sanford Hollander.

"It was a simple will witnessed by myself and my former secretary," recalled the lawyer, "and it left everything to Kathleen Young, appointing her the executrix. Ken told me about his daughter, who was the wife of the governor of California at the time, and he confided certain things about her which I cannot repeat. Those confidences will go with me to the grave and be intact when Ken and I finally meet again."

CHAPTER 13

Records include videotape of "Coping," a television show moderated by Richard Carlson, former KABC-TV newscaster in Los Angeles and now director of Voice of America.

Books include *My Turn* by Nancy Reagan with William Novak (New York: Random House, 1990); *Revolution* by Martin Anderson (New York: Harcourt Brace Jovanovich, 1988); *Landslide: The Unmaking of the President, 1984–1988* by Jane Mayer and Doyle McManus (Boston: Houghton Mifflin, 1988).

Articles include "Ronald Reagan Up Close" by Peter Goldman, *Newsweek*, July 21, 1980; "Peach-Pit Conservative or Closet Moderate?" by Richard J. Whalen, *New York Times Magazine*, February 22, 1976; "Patti Davis, Fictionally Speaking" by Donnie Radcliffe, *Washington Post*, September 25, 1989; "Ron Reagan Talks About Being a Son and a Celebrity" by Peter Ross Range, *Us*, August 26, 1986; "A Gamble Gone Wrong," *Time*, August 9, 1976.

Interviews include David Keene: January 18, 1989; John West: January 24, 1990; John Sears: January 25, 1990; Vic Gold: January 6, 1989; Gene Nelson: October 26, 1988; confidential interview with former top aide to Reagan from 1966 to 1982: November 29, 1989, and January 12, 1990; confidential interview with former 1976 campaign aide: May 16, 1988, and January 12, 1990; confidential interview with close friend of Kris Harmon Nelson: January 2, 1990; confidential interview with

Secret Service agent: January 12, 1990; correspondence with Kris Harmon Nelson: January 2, 1989; confidential interview with former employee of Deaver & Hannaford: January 12, 1990, and correspondence: January 26, 1990; Peter Sorum: September 22, 1988; Henry Salvatori: September 18 and October 30, 1990; Robert Goldwater: March 7, 1989.

As to Reagan's 1976 presidential campaign:
"I told Ronnie he should never make that race," said Henry Salvatori. "I said he shouldn't run against an incumbent President because he could not win. I was supporting President Ford at the time and I told Ronnie to wait until next time [but] he was induced by a lot of other people who said, 'Run, run, run.' I thought it was ridiculous."

Nancy Reagan never forgave Salvatori for his defection in 1976, despite the millions of dollars Salvatori went on to raise for Reagan's 1980 and 1984 presidential campaigns.

As to Nancy Reagan at the 1976 GOP convention where her husband tried to get the Republican nomination for President:
"Nancy told me later," said Gene Nelson, "when Pennsylvania went for Ford that the chairman of the delegation had been threatened that his father would be ruined if he didn't throw all the votes to Ford."

The chairman of the Pennsylvania delegation was Drew Lewis, who denied Nancy Reagan's story to Gene Nelson. "I was for Ford from the beginning," said Lewis (interviewed February 20, 1989), "and I delivered the entire Pennsylvania delegation to him, minus ten votes. I never said I would be for Ronald Reagan. Never."

Lewis, who became Secretary of Transportation during Reagan's first White House term, characterized Mrs. Reagan as extremely difficult at times. "She could be a real pain in the ass," he said. "No mistake about it. She hated Linda Gosden Robinson [wife of James D. Robinson III, chairman and chief executive of American Express] and when I hired Linda, Nancy did not like it one bit. As I went through a White House receiving line, Nancy pulled me over and whispered in my ear, 'Don't hire Linda. She's terrible. She's nothing but trouble and she will turn on you.' I hired Linda anyway because I think she's terrific and there wasn't much Nancy could do about it."

CHAPTER 14

Books include *Behind the Scenes* by Michael Deaver (New York: William Morrow and Company, Inc., 1987).

Articles include "Around Town" by William F. Buckley, Jr., *New Yorker,* January 31, 1983; "At Home with Ron and Doria Reagan" by Marie Brenner, *New York,* December 22, 1980; "From Film Star to Candidate" by Howell Raines, *New York Times,* July 17, 1980; "Nancy Reagan: Reflections" by Jody Jacobs, *Women's Wear Daily,* December 10, 1976; "It's Not Like Taking Candy from a Baby" by Judy Bachrach, *Washington Star,* October 14, 1980.

Interviews include Martin Smith: February 8, 1989; Maureen Kindel: October 17, 1988; Charles Orme: December 12, 1989; Clarence Newton: February 1, 1989; Bill Roemer: January 31, 1989; John West: January 24, 1990; Julia Knickerbocker: February 12 and April 17, 1988; confidential interview with top presidential aide: February 20, 1990; Reverend John Doran: March 11, 1989; Gene Nelson: October 26, 1988; Nancy Collins: February 4, 1990; Laurence Barrett: February 5, 1990; correspondence with Judy Bachrach: June 13, 1989; Peter McCoy: July 12 and 13, 1989; Narda Zaccino: March 11, 1989; Robert Scheer: March 11, 1989; David Keene: January 18, 1989; Susan Stamberg: October 30, 1989.

As to gossip columnist Liz Smith's relationship with Nancy Reagan:
Smith wrote a column dealing with Nancy Reagan's defection from Phoenix House that was to appear in the *Los Angeles Times* on January 30, 1990. Smith called her editor at the *Times* after reading the column to Nancy Reagan and said that Mrs. Reagan had yelled at her for using the word *defection.*

"I didn't defect," Nancy Reagan told Liz Smith. So Smith told the editor to change the copy so that "Mrs. Reagan's defection from Phoenix House" would read "Mrs. Reagan's removal of her name from the Phoenix House drug program."

Mrs. Reagan also objected to another paragraph in Liz Smith's column, which read: "I have been told by close friends of Nancy Reagan that her impulsive decision to 'just say no' to the Phoenix House drug center in L.A. was a mistake she need not have and should not have made." At Mrs. Reagan's direction, Smith advised her editor to delete the word *impulsive.* The next day's column carried Nancy Reagan's rendition of what happened.

CHAPTER 15

Records include the telegram Jimmy Carter sent to Ronald Reagan, November 4, 1980, and transcript of Tom Brokaw's NBC-TV interview with the Reagans on October 7, 1980.

Books include *Looking Forward* by George Bush with Victor Gold (New York: Doubleday, 1987); *The Acting President* by Bob Schieffer and Gary Paul Gates (New York: E. P. Dutton, 1989); *Washington Rollercoaster* by Sondra Gotlieb (Toronto: Doubleday Canada Limited, 1990); *The Complete Book of U.S. Presidents* by William A. DeGregorio (New York: Dembner Books, 1984).

Articles include "The New Shape of American Politics" by William Schneider, *Atlantic Monthly,* January 1987; "Doubts About Bush 'Haunted' Reagan," Newhouse News Service, November 12, 1988; "Bush—His Secret Dream Came True" by Bill Peterson, *Washington Post,* July 18, 1980; "Mrs. Bush Happy to Settle for Second" by Bella Stumbo, *Los Angeles Times,* July 16, 1980; "Ronald Reagan's Total Woman" by Julie Baumgold, *New York,* July 28, 1980; "Star Reborn: Nancy Reagan," *Chicago Tribune,* October 30, 1980; "Busing Intensifies Problems: Nancy Reagan" by Janice Carter, *Cleveland Plain Dealer,* September 10, 1980; "Mrs. Reagan on Offensive" by Donnie Radcliffe, *Washington Post,* October 23, 1980.

Interviews include Bill Plante: January 13, 1990; Alan Hilton: January 3, 1990; Peter McCoy: July 13, 1989; George Romanos: July 7, 1989; Les Weinrott: May 9 and 15, June 7, and July 19, 1989; Michael Evans: September 26, 1988; Betsy Forsythe Hailey: February 23, 1989; confidential interview with one of Mrs. Reagan's White House secretaries: August 6, 1989; Dr. Daniel Ruge: February 26 and March 2, 1990; Patti Davis: October 11 and 19, 1989; Bill Henkel: March 22 and 28 and July 7, 1989; Joan Quigley: October 6, 1988, and July 6, 1990; confidential interview with a top Reagan presidential aide: February 20, 1990; Lou Cannon speech: January 10, 1989; Jody Powell: September 18, 1990.

As to Nancy Reagan's demands on her advance team:
The First Lady insisted that she receive a copy of *Women's Wear Daily* every day. "We had to cut a deal with the U.S. Postal Service in order to accommodate her," said an employee of Fairchild Publications. "*WWD* is printed in Vineland, New Jersey, and I guess it's mailed out from there, but it did not always arrive on time and Mrs. Reagan would get crazed if she didn't get her copy every day, so we had to make special arrangements for her to receive her daily copy at the White House."

CHAPTER 16

Books include *Power and Greed: Inside the Teamsters Empire of Corruption* by Allen Friedman and Ted Schwarz (New York: Watts, 1989).
Articles include "The Floating Party" by William Safire, *New York*

Times, January 8, 1981; "Star-Strangled Gala" by Mike Royko, *Chicago Sun-Times,* January 21, 1981; "Inaugural Spotlight Shifts to Sinatra and Show Biz" by Harold C. Schonberg, *New York Times,* January 20, 1981; "The Reagan-Teamster Link," *Newsweek,* December 29, 1980; "With a New First Lady, a New Style" by Leslie Bennetts, *New York Times,* January 21, 1981; "A Fabulous Birthday for Frank" by Wanda McDaniel, *Los Angeles Herald-Examiner,* December 15, 1980; "Reagan Asks for a First Waltz and Wins Hearts in the Capital" by Lynn Rosellini, *New York Times,* November 19, 1980; "At Home with Ron and Doria Reagan" by Marie Brenner, *New York* magazine, December 22, 1980.

Interviews include Jody Jacobs: January 11, 1987, and October 28, 1989; George Masters: December 4, 1989; Peter McCoy: July 13, 1989; Jewell Jackson McCabe: February 14, 1989; Joel Odum: January 5, 1989; Bill Fitzpatrick: April 8, 1989; Laura Young: February 26 and October 25, 1988, and correspondence: December 14, 1987, and February 6, 1988; Carlo Celoni: October 11, 1988; Joanne Carson: October 24, 26, and 27 and November 2, 1988; confidential interview with a member of Mrs. Reagan's senior White House staff: March 25, 1989; Ellen Pollon: October 9, 11, and 17 and November 10, 1988, and December 27, 1989; confidential interview with White House photographer: March 15 and April 8, 1989; Oscar de Lavin: January 2, March 15, and May 11, 1990; Mary Finch Hoyt: June 3, 1988; Robin Orr: October 17 and November 7, 1988; Peter Sorum: September 22, 1988; Michael Evans: September 26, 1988.

As to Frank Sinatra and the FBI:

"The FBI checks the names of anyone going into the White House," said FBI executive assistant director of investigations Buck Revell in an interview on October 16, 1989. "The White House counsel must send over all names. So in 1981, when Frank Sinatra's name [first] came up, the FBI prepared a 'letterhead memorandum' summarizing everything in its files. I didn't see it, but it was probably a ten- to fifty-page report, considering everything we have on Sinatra. The FBI does not characterize its information, except to indicate if it comes from wire taps, surveillance, or informants.

"Without characterizing Sinatra's ties to organized crime, that report told President Reagan that his friend could never be anything but a social friend. Considering the information in the government files on Sinatra, he could never be named ambassador or appointed to a federal commission. Nothing where he would have access to government information or have to be confirmed by Congress. We would never tell a President who his social friends can be, but that summary put the President on notice."

As to rumors of Ron Reagan's homosexuality:

"I have no doubt that Ron Jr. is gay," said homosexual playwright Larry Kramer (interviewed on June 30, 1989). "He is always with a gang of men . . . and besides, we know our own."

Kramer had stated his opinion on "The Larry King Show" in 1989 and received a letter from Ron Reagan that said, in part: "Ever since I became a ballet dancer (or, to be more precise, ever since my father decided to run for president while I was dancing), a certain element of the public and media has assumed I was homosexual. Similar elements, I suppose, believe black people feel an inordinate fondness for fried chicken and watermelon. I decided early not to dignify such insinuations by declaring my (exclusive) preference. In principle, I regard questions about a person's sexuality as invasive, anti-intellectual and irrevelant. Not that I take them to heart, mind you; such queries are a bit like the weather—only less interesting."

Ron Reagan said he felt Kramer's remarks were "wholly undeserved," an "unconscionable insult" and succeeded only in "smearing my wife by defaming our marriage." He asked for an apology but said his expectations in that regard were slight.

"It was an exceedingly well-written letter," said Kramer, "and I responded by saying, 'I am very well known in the gay world, and in New York. I cannot tell you how many men have told me of their knowledge of your gay life.' " Kramer says Reagan never answered his letter.

"I really feel that the Reagans sold their son down the river," said Kramer, who wrote *The Normal Heart.* "Why? Because he's gay and his friends are gay and her [Nancy Reagan's] friends are gay. . . . Roy Cohn was her big buddy . . . she made a call to Sloan-Kettering to get him on the experimental program for AZT when they weren't taking any more people. She was willing to do something like that, but to speak out publicly about AIDS, no. [She wouldn't even say] it was a public health emergency . . . and neither would the President. . . . They were so awful on the issue of AIDS. . . . I think the reason is in their sexual background."

As to Ron Reagan's comments regarding President Carter:

"After Ron told me that Jimmy Carter had the morals of a snake, which made the wires all around the world," said Marie Brenner in an interview on April 1, 1988, "his mother got on the phone to William Buckley, who wrote an entire column attacking the accuracy of my piece without ever once calling me, even though Ron Reagan had confirmed to the *Washington Post* the following week that he had told me."

The Buckley column, distributed by Universal Press Syndicate on January 15, 1981, said, in part:

Sensitive women—and men—are easily hurt by fabricated misrepresentations. *Time* magazine reports that Mrs. Reagan will not give press conferences. No wonder . . . Look what happened to her son. He was quoted, in an article in *New York* magazine, extensively reproduced, as saying unpleasant things about President Carter and disparaging things about the institution of marriage. Specifically he was quoted as saying that he would decline to shake the hand of the president of the United States at the inaugural ceremonies, in retaliation for the untruths spoken by the president about Ron's father. "First of all, I never said that I wouldn't shake hands with Mr. Carter," [Ron Reagan subsequently told Buckley]. "I said that I didn't know if I could, quickly adding that, given the inevitable circumstances of our meeting, I was sure I would. There followed a discussion of appropriate handshakes and salutations (dead fish, Sicilian kiss of death, etc.)—of course, that doesn't make such splashy copy."

Then young Reagan was quoted as saying that the institution of marriage was nothing more than a $20 license fee and clap test. That pronouncement, by the son of the first family, quite justifiably caused the eyebrows to rise, not because Ronald Reagan, fils, has any obligation to regurgitate only the views of Ronald Reagan, pere; but because to disparage the institution that binds in love and devotion tens of millions of people is a venture in tastelessness.

"As for the remark about marriage, 'What is marriage anyway?' should have read, 'Our marriage was . . .' This referred not to the institution itself, but rather the drab municipal bureaucracy we confronted. I also added that church weddings were another thing altogether—just fine for people of a particular religious persuasion."

Once again, a position rather considerably modified. But, once again, less splashy as copy.

As to Peter Sorum's inaugural evening advance assignment for the Reagans:
Getting the Reagans to the ten inaugural balls on time did not endear Sorum to the First Lady, who had never forgiven him for his service to Betty Ford during the 1976 campaign.

"True to her word, Nancy Reagan got her revenge against me," said Sorum, "and blocked my appointment to a government position in 1981 when I was selected to be vice president for public affairs for the Overseas Private Investment Corporation (OPIC). I went to Jim Baker, Reagan's chief of staff, and he said, 'I'm sorry I can't help you. You pissed off the one person I can't control—Nancy Reagan.' "

CHAPTER 17

Books include *Gambling with History: Reagan in the White House* by Laurence I. Barrett (New York: Penguin Books, 1984); *Thumbs Up: The Life and Courageous Comeback of White House Press Secretary Jim Brady* by Mollie Dickenson (New York: William Morrow and Company, Inc., 1987); *Lilly: Reminiscences of Lillian Hellman* by Peter Feibleman (New York: William Morrow and Company, Inc., 1988); *Keeper of the Gate* by Selwa "Lucky" Roosevelt (New York: Simon and Schuster, 1990).

Articles include "The Battle of the Bouillon Cups" by Marianne Means, Hearst newspaper syndicate, October 24, 1989; "Who's Who in the Administration" by Charles Peters, *Washington Monthly*, February 1984; "Life at Court" by Joan Didion, *New York Review of Books*, December 21, 1989; "Surprising Nancy Reagan with Sinatra and His Songs" by Jennifer Hirshberg, *Washington Star*, May 22, 1981; "White House Gets Reagan Imprint" by Susan Granger, Independent News Alliance, December 21, 1981; "Puttin' on the Ritz" by Emily Yoffe, *New Republic*, May 23, 1981; "Fighting Back" by Elizabeth Mehren and Betty Cuniberti, *Los Angeles Times Magazine*, March 22, 1987; "Nancy's Total Makeover" by Fred Barnes, *New Republic*, September 16, 1985; editorial by William Loeb, *Manchester Union-Leader*, March 20, 1981; "The Woman Who Would Be Queen" by Wanda McDaniel, *Los Angeles Herald-Examiner*, November 10, 1980; "The Saving of the President" by John Pekkanen, *Washingtonian Magazine*, August 1981; "Notebook: Styles of the President's Men" by Howell Raines, *New York Times*, September 2, 1981.

Interviews include Jody Jacobs: January 11, 1987; Dr. Daniel Ruge: March 2, 1990; Bill Henkel: March 28, 1989; Frances Borden: January 31, 1990; Dr. Gerry Becker: June 2, 1989; Elaine Crispen's response to a question-and-answer session, Public Relations Society of America, July 20, 1989; R. W. Apple: May 25, 1988; J. Roger Friedman: February 17, 1988; confidential interview with a senior member of Mrs. Reagan's White House staff: March 15 and 25, September 26, and October 25, 1989, February 11 and May 8, 1990; Shirley Watkins: July 8, 12, and 27, August 1, September 5 and 6, October 17 and 19, and December 7 and 8, 1988, January 11, March 12, April 3, and May 30, 1989, April 27, 1990; Karl Schoumacher: September 12, 1988; Peter McCoy: July 12 and 13, 1989; confidential interview with former Deaver aide: September 21, 1988, and March 15, 1989; Paul Weyrich: March 2, 1990; Kathleen Young: June 10 and 16 and October 14 and 23, 1988; correspondence with Milton A. ("Mickey") Rudin: April 7, 18, and 19, 1989; Sally Fleg: March 30 and April 6, 1989; John Pekkanen: May 1, 1990; Helen Boehm: April 17, 1990; Julia Malone: September 24 and 25, 1989; Bess Abel: October 31, 1989; Frank Sinatra on "The Larry King Show": May 13, 1988; Lee Cohen: April 5, 1989.

As to the outburst of Secretary of State Alexander Haig in the White House press room on March 30, 1981:

White House aides in the Office of Communications were so concerned about the overwrought behavior of the Secretary of State that Frank Ursomorso of the White House Office of Communications arranged a series of secret meetings with six specialists, including a psychologist, a lobbyist, and public relations specialists to discuss handling the problem.

"Haig had had a heart bypass operation . . . and he was becoming so emotional . . . that the White House staff was having difficulty with him," said Ursomorso (interviewed on May 1, 1990). "I didn't know how to deal with the problem so I called in a few experts. . . . We learned that people who have heart bypasses tend to feel subconsciously that maybe they are going to die and they overcompensate by going through a phase of urgency and push too hard."

The psychologist who participated in the secret sessions at the White House was asked to assess the President's public image after the assassination attempt. "They [White House aides] wanted to know at what point the President would lose the public's sympathy," said the psychologist in an interview on May 1, 1990. "I drew an analogy from the work I've done with widows, and told them that it takes about two years in terms of what people are feeling internally, but it's only about six weeks in terms of getting any attention. After six weeks' time, the public forgets and goes on with its life and leaves the bereft to deal privately with feelings of mourning and grief. That process takes about two years to deal with internally."

Ursomorso also admitted concern about the First Lady's negative public image. "Nancy Reagan was extremely interested in public exposure," he said. "She was a very strong person with all this energy . . . and if you really want to know the truth, I kind of avoided dealing with her. . . . But I had a rather vicious argument with Joe Canzeri [former White House aide] because he was doing things which I felt were making her look improper, like going to New York City all the time to social black-tie affairs. The Reagans should have been seen in Indianapolis in the heartland of the country instead of at all those glitzy New York parties."

As to the First Lady's private beauty salon in the White House family quarters:
One of Mrs. Reagan's senior staffers was scheduled to attend a reception at the National Gallery but worked so late getting the First Lady off to a party in New York that she had no time to get her own hair done. She turned to the First Lady's hairdresser for help.

"Oh, God, Julius," she said, "can you do anything for me? My hair's a fright."

"C'mon," said Julius. "Let's go upstairs to Madame's parlor."

The two went up to the private quarters and into the First Lady's beauty salon where Julius shampooed and set the woman's hair. As she was sitting under the dryer, the door opened and in walked President Reagan carrying a box of cookies.

"Sweetie, I've got some cookies for you," said the President, handing the box to the woman under the dryer.

"Oh, my God, Mr. President," gasped the staffer. "I think you've got the wrong sweetie."

"I guess so," he said and laughed.

"I was so terrified," said the staffer. "I knew I'd be fired if Mrs. Reagan ever found out what I had done. I never said a word to her; Julius never said a word, and God bless him, neither did the President."

A few weeks later, the staffer was photographed with the President and she sent the picture over to the Oval Office to be autographed. The picture was returned to her with the President's signature under which he wrote: "Your hair looks great!"

As to Nancy Reagan's relationship with British royalty:
The Prince and Princess of Wales visited the United States for three days in November 1985 and thereby threw the First Lady and her White House staff into a tailspin.

"We were instructed as a staff that we were not to be around when Princess Diana came to the White House," said Shirley Watkins, one of the First Lady's secretaries. "This was the only time such an order was ever given. We were told that if we were caught being anywhere near the Princess that it could result in termination of employment. Only those who were supposed to be there with Mrs. Reagan could be there—her press secretary, her personal secretary, and her chief of staff.

"Mrs. Reagan was more uptight about royalty than she was about anything else. She was always nervous . . . as though she wanted to outdo or be equal to royalty. She was constantly trying to be more like them. . . . All of us felt her nervousness. . . . I remember when Prince Charles came to the White House once, the social secretary, Muffie Brandon, was trying to get everything ready for his arrival. He showed up

early, and so Muffie jumped into the broom closet and hid because she
knew that it would not please Mrs. Reagan if Prince Charles saw her. So
Muffie stayed in the broom closet until the Prince left."

During the royal visit to Washington in 1985, the Reagans honored
the Prince and Princess with a private White House dinner. The First
Lady controlled the guest list of seventy-nine people, which included
Princess Diana's favorite entertainers: John Travolta, Tom Selleck, Neil
Diamond, Mikhail Baryshnikov, and Clint Eastwood. Mrs. Reagan also
invited Brooke Astor, Betsy Bloomingdale, Jerry Zipkin, and her decorator, Ted Graber, but did not include Barbara and George Bush. She
instructed Leontyne Price not to sing opera because President Reagan
did not like opera or heavy classical music. Instead, the First Lady asked
the opera star to sing a selection from *Porgy and Bess,* which she didn't
seem to know was an opera.

". . . Our foreign guests were often subjected to has-been popular
singers and other marginal performers who were not up to White House
standards," recalled former protocol chief Selwa "Lucky" Roosevelt,
who was embarrassed by the Reagans' lack of culture. "Even when they
had a great opera star such as Sherrill Milnes, they asked that he not sing
opera! I felt that the White House should showcase our finest musicians
and dancers, regardless of the personal tastes of the First Couple."

Mrs. Reagan had instructed the U.S. Marine Band to practice "Night
Fever," the theme song from John Travolta's hit movie, *Saturday Night
Fever.* After dinner, she approached Travolta and said the Princess was
hoping he would ask her to dance. He obliged and spun Diana gracefully
around the floor of the grand foyer. Neil Diamond sang "Sweet Caroline" and "You Don't Bring Me Flowers" to her, and then he, too, asked
the Princess to dance. She seemed thrilled with the movie star treatment
accorded her that evening.

"My impression was that she was very impressed with seeing people in
the flesh that she had seen on screen," said Peter Ustinov. "She seemed
euphoric."

And so was Nancy Reagan, who had spent weeks planning for the
three-day trip of the British royals. She was so excited to be in the public
presence of Diana that she breached royal etiquette by putting her arm
around the Princess's waist. This was not Nancy's only diplomatic gaffe.
She committed a similar faux pas in Japan and shocked Japanese television viewers when she crossed her legs and laughed in the presence of
the emperor of Japan.

As to Nancy Reagan's request for presents for the President:
Rex Allen, the movie actor who became famous as a singing cowboy,

once joked to Reagan about giving him a pair of cowboy boots if he ever became President. "I just said, 'Well, Ron, when you get to the White House, we'll make you up a pair with the presidential seal on them,' " said Allen, "and he laughed, and I laughed, and then a while back, Nancy called me at home one morning and she said, 'Ron never forgot about them boots. He wants them.' "

Allen quickly called Texas bootmaker Tony Lama and ordered four pairs of boots decorated with the presidential seal on which the American eagle was inlaid in brown frog skin. Allen delivered them to the President in his suite at the Century Plaza Hotel in Los Angeles on September 1, 1981.

"I said, 'I know you have a lot more important things to do than stand around and fool with us,' " said Allen. "He [the President] said, 'No, you know four pairs of boots in forty-five minutes—that's pretty good.'

"He acted like there was nothing else in the world he had to do," said Allen, "nothing else on his mind."

CHAPTER 18

Records include copies of Nancy Reagan's private calendars and internal White House memos, including one of James S. Rosebush to the First Lady's staff, December 12, 1985.

Books include *Nouveau Is Better Than No Riche at All* by Marilyn Bender with Monsieur Marc (New York: G.P. Putnam's Sons, 1983); *The Power Game: How Washington Really Works* by Hedrick Smith (New York: Random House, 1988); *What Does Joan Say?* by Joan Quigley (New York: Birch Lane Press, 1990).

Articles include "Splendor in the Grass" by Alexander Cockburn, *The Nation*, October 3, 1987; "The Social Climber's Guide to Washington," *National Review*, February 10, 1989; "Objets de Tacko" and "Tacko Update" by Charlotte Hays, *Washington Times*, November 29 and December 13, 1989; "The Second Toughest Job" by Margaret Truman, *Parade*, August 15, 1982; "Nancy Reagan: The First Two Years" by Elisabeth Bumiller and Donnie Radcliffe, *Washington Post*, January 22, 1983; "The Grooming of a First Lady" by Jane O'Hara, *Maclean's*, January 25, 1982; "Nancy's Total Makeover" by Fred Barnes, *New Republic*, September 16 and 23, 1985; "Christmas Memories" by Nancy Reagan, *Washington Post*, December 16, 1982; "IRS May Tax Nancy's Free Dresses, Wardrobe," Associated Press, January 28, 1982.

Interviews include Shirley Watkins: July 8 and 12 and August 6, 1988; Marianne Means's interview with Sheila Tate: June 12, 1981; Patricia Sagon: September 17, 1988; Yetta Galiber: December 26, 1988, and

May 1, 1990; confidential interview with White House secretary: March 25 and October 25, 1989; Oscar de Lavin: January 2, March 15, and May 11, 1990; Joanne Carson: October 26, 1988; Matt Caufield: September 5, 1988; confidential interview with top Reagan presidential aide: February 20, 1990; Elaine Crispen speech: July 20, 1989; Charles Wick: September 15, 1987; confidential interview with senior member of First Lady's staff: January 15, 1989; confidential interview with close friend of Patti Davis: March 6 and 9, 1989; Reverend Donn Moomaw: January 31, 1989; confidential interview with top presidential aide: February 20, 1990; confidential interview with one of Mrs. Reagan's White House secretaries: August 6 and 8, 1989; confidential interview with one of the people who accompanied the Reagans to the Wicks' Christmas party: February 14 and 20, 1990; confidential interview of state dinner guest who sat at Mrs. Reagan's table: May 11, 1990; Anne Keagy: May 11, 1990; Sheldon Cohen: May 31, 1990; confidential interview with one of the First Lady's speech writers: October 11 and 28 and November 2, 1990.

CHAPTER 19

Records include Justice Department files on Alfred S. Bloomingdale obtained through the Freedom of Information Act, his last will and testament, his letters to Vicki Morgan, and her deposition; lists of all Reagan contributors from the Federal Elections Commission.

Books include *On Bended Knee: The Press and the Reagan Presidency* by Mark Hertsgaard (New York: Farrar, Straus & Giroux, 1988); *Vicki* by Joyce Milton and Ann Louise Bardach (New York: St. Martin's Press, 1986); *Beautiful Bad Girl: The Vicki Morgan Story* by Gordon Basichis (Santa Barbara, Calif.: Santa Barbara Press, 1985).

Articles include an editorial in *Washington Post,* April 25, 1985; "The Need for Tolerance" by Nancy Reagan, *McCall's,* November 1986; "Final Toast for the Queen in California," London *Times,* March 5, 1983; "The Pleasure of Her Company" by Donnie Radcliffe, *Washington Post,* March 5, 1983; "The Social Event of the Year for Her Majesty" by Betty Goodwin, *Los Angeles Herald-Examiner,* February 28, 1983; "Casing the Windsor Joint," London *Sunday Times,* June 6, 1982.

Interviews include Les Weinrott: May 9 and 15, June 7, and July 19, 1989; Eileen Bailey: May 30, 1989; Dr. Gerry Becker: June 2, 1989; Debbie Chenoweth: October 18, 1988; Jackie Rush: April 30, 1988; Jody Jacobs: January 11 and September 8, 1987; Lee Lescaze: June 7, 1990; Tom Chauncey: March 7 and 8, 1989; Reverend John Doran: March 11, 1989; Monsignor Robert J. Donohoe, March 11, 1989; confidential interview with senior member of the First Lady's staff: March 7, May 18, and October 4, 1989; confidential interview with close friend of Nancy Reagan: January 14, 1988; confidential interview with secretary of First Lady: August 6 and 8, 1989; Frank Sinatra's "tea break" comments: October 14, 1982.

As to the FBI files of Alfred Bloomingdale:
When President Reagan named Alfred Bloomingdale to the Foreign Intelligence Advisory Board, the appointment required FBI clearance, but the FBI investigators concentrated solely on interviews with people whom Bloomingdale had recommended. So it's hardly surprising to read the following from Bloomingdale's FBI files:

Justin Dart: "Bloomingdale is a very happily married man whose wife is an intimate friend of Nancy Reagan."

Earle Jorgensen: "Bloomingdale is a person of extremely high character who associates with competent and extremely fine people."

Ray Stark: "Bloomingdale is an emotionally stable individual . . . socially adaptable at all levels . . . enjoys a stable marriage and family life."

As to Nancy Reagan's cozy relationship with the Washington Post:
Post writer Colman McCarthy reviewed *To Love a Child: The Foster Grandparents Program* by Nancy Reagan with Jane Wilkie (Indianapolis: Bobbs-Merrill, 1982) for the *Washington Post* (December 5, 1982) and pronounced the book about the First Lady's involvement with the Foster Grandparents program simply an excuse for a "White House book party extravaganza for Nancy Reagan and Frank Sinatra."

"The language is a double-depressant of numbing, cliché-ridden prose that ranges from Lady Bountiful pitter-patter to tea room philosophizing. . . . The Foster Grandparents program deserves better."

McCarthy's review criticized the First Lady for not bothering to get to know the poor people she was writing about. "[She] gives no indication in these pages that she is remotely familiar with poverty or its causes."

"There was a big flap over that review," said Ron Kessler, former reporter for the *Washington Post* (interviewed on February 10, 1987), "and Mrs. Graham [chairman of the board of the Washington Post Company] got very upset with Colman McCarthy. Calls back and forth. The usual pressure. It was very harrying."

Katharine Graham called Mrs. Reagan to apologize and then called the editor of the "Book World" section and questioned the editor's judgment about assigning the review to McCarthy, a liberal who did not share the Reagans' politics.

McCarthy, interviewed on December 14, 1988, dismissed Mrs. Reagan's book, even six years later, as "absolute garbage, low grade, ghostwritten." He said of Mrs. Graham's interference: "You don't blame the hog for grunting. You blame the farmer for saying it was a symphony."

As to activities staged by Mrs. Reagan's White House staff to improve her image:

"I remember the Just Say No to Drugs march for second-, third-, fourth-, and fifth-grade kids in Washington, D.C.," said Shirley Watkins, one of the First Lady's secretaries. "The kids were going to march from the Capitol to the White House, and Mrs. Reagan was going to come out and make an appearance. What a mess that was. Mrs. Reagan's staff refused to make arrangements for bathroom facilities and beverages for the children, who arrived dripping with perspiration, throats parched, and in desperate need of toilets. Some of the kids started getting sick, others wet their pants standing around waiting for Mrs. Reagan to appear. I couldn't believe it, but she kept those kids waiting for thirty-five minutes. I asked Gahl Hodges where she was, and Gahl said, 'She's talking to Betsy Bloomingdale.' "

CHAPTER 20

Books include *The World Almanac and Book of Facts 1987* (New York: Scripps Howard Co., 1987); *William F. Buckley, Jr.: Patron Saint of the Conservatives* by John Judis (New York: Simon and Schuster, 1988); *Missile Envy: The Arms Race and Nuclear War* by D. Helen Caldicott (New York: William Morrow and Company, Inc., 1984); *Speaking Out* by Larry Speakes with Robert Pack (New York: Charles Scribner's Sons, 1988); *To Err Is Reagan* by Mark Green (San Francisco: Foundation for National Progress, 1987); *Ferraro: My Story* by Geraldine Ferraro (New York: Bantam Books, 1986); *The Quest for the Presidency 1984* by Peter Goldman and Tony Fuller (New York: Bantam Books, 1985); *Wake Us When It's Over* by Jack W. Germond and Jules Witcover (New York: Macmillan Publishing Company, 1985); *Behind the Scenes* by Michael K. Deaver with Mickey Herskowitz (New York: William Morrow and Company, Inc., 1988).

Articles include "The Choice for President," editorial, *Washington Post,* October 29, 1984; "Tap Dancing on Ron" by Owen Ullmann, Knight-Ridder newspapers, September 18, 1988; " 'Ethics Gap' Haunts Reagan" by Jerome R. Watson, *Chicago Sun-Times,* May 17, 1987; "The Ferraros of Newburgh" by Guy Hawtin and Jeff Wells, *New York Post,* October 18, 1984; "Mrs. R's R & R" by James A. Miller, *Life,* October 1983;

"President Nancy" by Fred Barnes, *New Republic,* March 23, 1987; "Co-Starring at the White House" by Kurt Andersen, Laurence I. Barrett, and Melissa Ludtke, *Time,* January 14, 1985; "The Feature Film" by Thomas M. DeFrank and Gerald C. Lubenow, *Newsweek,* September 3, 1984; "White House Successfully Limits News" by Robert Scheer, *Los Angeles Times,* August 20, 1984; "Patti Does It Her Own Way—Almost" by Kitty Bean Yancey, *USA Today,* August 14, 1984; "You Can't Always Take the Easy Way" by Cleveland Amory, *Parade,* December 4, 1988.

Interviews include Marian Robinson: June 10, 1988; George Romanos: July 7, 1989; Bill Henkel: July 7, 1989; Mrs. William Shannon: June 20, 1989; Helen Rees: June 7, 1989; confidential interview with top presidential aide: February 20, 1990; confidential interview with senior member of First Lady's staff: March 15 and 25, 1989; Shirley Watkins: July 8 and 12, 1988; confidential interview with one of Mrs. Reagan's physicians: March 9, 1989; confidential interview with senior member of First Lady's staff: October 4, 1989; Patti Davis: October 13, 1989; John Roberts: June 18, 1990; confidential interview with close friend of Nancy Reagan: January 10, 1989; Paul Weyrich: March 2, 1990; confidential interview with Deaver White House aide: February 14 and 20, 1990; Faith Whittlesey: June 15, 1990; Dolores Robinson: March 22 and 28, 1989; confidential interview with a child of one of the Reagans' closest friends: January 10, 1989.

As to Nancy Reagan's selection of guests for White House state dinners:
"We would get calls from Mrs. Reagan's office at the White House asking for people's addresses so she could invite them to a dinner," recalled an employee of *Women's Wear Daily.* "She got *Women's Wear* every day and the people who would appear most regularly in the Eye [gossip column] were the people Nancy Reagan would want to invite to the White House. . . . I remember when she called for [New York socialite] Nina Griscom's address. We couldn't give it out, but I called Nina and told her to call the White House because Mrs. Reagan wanted to invite her to dinner."

CHAPTER 21

Records include transcript of Nancy Reagan on "Good Morning America," ABC-TV, October 26, 1989.

Books include *For the Record: From Wall Street to Washington* by Donald T. Regan (New York: Harcourt Brace Jovanovich, 1988); *My Memoir* by Edith Wilson (Indianapolis: Bobbs-Merrill Co., 1939).

Articles include "The Burden of Bitburg" by Robert McAfee Brown,

Christian Century, May 22, 1985; "Presidential Luck" by George F. Will, *Washington Post,* July 17, 1985; "The Washingtonization of Nancy Reagan" by Bernard Weintraub, *New York Times,* March 26, 1985; "First Lady Says He's the Boss" by Jessica Lee and Johanna Neuman, *USA Today,* March 3, 1987; "The Morality of Bitburg" by Meg Greenfield, *Newsweek,* May 6, 1985; "German Soldiers Called 'Victims' " by David Hoffman, *Washington Post,* April 17, 1985.

Interviews include Joan Quigley: July 6, 1990; Dennis Thomas: September 21, 1988; Bill Henkel: March 28 and 29, 1989; Terry Arthur: April 22, 1988, May 18 and July 7, 1989; Lou Cannon: January 10, 1989; Madeline L'Engle: April 18, 1989; Lesley Stahl: June 18, 1988; Bill Fitzpatrick: March 15 and April 8, 1989; confidential interview with one of Mrs. Reagan's former press secretaries: January 15, 1989; confidential interview with physician from Bethesda Naval Hospital: March 9, 1989; Johanna Neuman: January 25 and 27, 1989; Faith Whittlesey: June 15, 1990.

As to Nancy Reagan's appearance:
In a letter to the author, Jean Harris wrote from the Bedford Hills Correctional Facility where she is serving time for the murder of Dr. Herman Tarnower:

> I wish I could reciprocate with something new and interesting about Nancy Davis Reagan, but I didn't know her at Smith. . . . I was surprised when I heard that the First Lady had gone to Smith; she is so unlike my rather stereotypical picture of a Smith girl, very down-to-earth, warm, competent, take-me-as-you-find-me. Barbara Bush has many of the qualities I find in old Smith friends. I picture Nancy holding her own very well in one of the French courts. . . .
> There's great interest in Mrs. Reagan even in spite of all those borrowed clothes, and all those pictures where there wasn't a hair out of place, or the sign of a stomach that sticks out a little bit. I for one could forgive her all that, but the sight of her standing with her husband watching the great ships pass [during the Fourth of July 1986 celebration of the Statue of Liberty]without a child or a grandchild by her side took her permanently off my Smith girl list.

CHAPTER 22

Records include papers of incorporation for the Nancy Reagan Foundation and the Ronald Reagan Presidential Library from the Registry of

Charitable Trusts, a division of the California Department of Justice and Attorney General's Office, Sacramento, California.

Books include *The Clothes Have No Emperor: A Chronicle of the American 80's* by Paul Slansky (New York: Fireside, 1989); *And the Band Played On* by Randy Shilts (New York: St. Martin's Press, 1987); *Home Front* by Patti Davis (New York: Crown Publishers, Inc., 1986); *Deadfall* by Patti Davis (New York: Crown Publishers, Inc., 1989).

Articles include "Just Say Dough" by Howard L. Rosenberg and Ellen Ladowsky, *New Republic,* March 26, 1990; "It's Grand to Be a Grandparent" by Nancy Reagan, *McCall's,* November 1986; "Helms Fined $2,000: CIA Director's Sentence: Suspended Jail Term" by Timothy S. Robinson, *Washington Post,* November 5, 1977; "Mitch's Mission" by Leslie Bennetts, *Vanity Fair,* October 1989; "Nancy Reagan Just Says No to Drug Clinic" by Jennifer Spevacek, *Washington Times,* September 5, 1989; "Reagan's Political AIDS Test" by Rowland Evans and Robert Novak, *Washington Post,* May 20, 1987; "Now, Only a Chopper Cuts It" by William Norwich, *New York Daily News,* January 24, 1990; "Report on the Reagan Four" by Lloyd Shearer, *Parade,* September 21, 1986.

Interviews include Ira Silverman: December 12, 1989, and March 1 and 7, 1990; confidential interview with member of First Lady's staff who accompanied her on trips to visit her mother: May 18, 1989; confidential interview with executive of Phoenix House: March 15, 1990; confidential interview with executive of the Community Foundation of Greater Washington, Inc.: March 10, 1988, March 28 and September 5, 1989; Jo Ann Burton: November 5, 1988; Dolores Robinson: March 22, 1989; confidential interview with close friend of Patti Davis: March 6, 1989; Shirley Singer: July 6, 1989; Eileen Bailey: May 30, 1989; Dr. Gerry Becker: June 2, 1989; confidential interview with former secretary on First Lady's staff: August 8, 1989; Marie Brenner: April 1, 1988; Jay Bernstein: March 15, 1989; Judy Hilsinger: September 7, 1988.

CHAPTER 23

Articles include "When Five-Alarm News Breaks Out, the Networks Call the Firemen" by Judy Flander, *Washington Journalism Review,* April 1989; "Gloves Come Off" by Maureen Santini, *New York Daily News,* June 2, 1988; "In Moscow, the First Ladies' Tour de Frost" by Donnie Radcliffe, *Washington Post,* May 30, 1988; "The Nancy and Raisa Show" by Naomi Schalit and Suzanne Donovan, *Washington Journalism Review,* March 1988; "Nancy Reagan Defends Her Decision to Have Mastectomy" by Tamar Lewin, *New York Times,* March 5, 1988; "Public Enemy No. 200" by Lars-Erik Nelson, *New York Daily News,* May 20, 1988;

"The Regan Book," editorial, *Washington Post,* May 10, 1988; "Stargazing Wars" by William Safire, *New York Times,* May 9, 1988.

Interviews include Dennis Thomas: September 21, 1988, and March 15, 1989; confidential interview with one of Mrs. Reagan's physicians: March 9, 1989; Joan Quigley: October 6, 1988, and July 6, 1990; confidential interview with one of Mrs. Reagan's White House secretaries: August 6 and 8, 1989; Bill Henkel: March 22 and 28 and July 7, 1989; Patti Davis: October 11 and 19, 1989.

As to Nancy Reagan's plan to get rid of White House chief of staff Donald T. Regan:

"I give Nancy great credit for keeping Reagan on course," said former Secretary of Transportation Drew Lewis. "I think she did an admirable job and she should be saluted. She performed a real public service by getting rid of Don Regan and by getting Ronald Reagan to thaw toward Russia.

"I was all set to be the chief of staff in 1985 before Regan was announced," said Lewis. "I had agreed to it but then I read in the papers that Don Regan got the nod. That was one of their worst mistakes. Jim Baker was terrific in the position. Nancy fell in love with him. He's very smooth and she prizes that, you know. She's a little too Adolfo/Galanos for my taste, but so what?"

As to Nancy Reagan's feelings toward Oliver North:

"Ollie North told me a story," said Paul Weyrich, "in which [the Reagans] were sitting together up in the residence as he gave the President a briefing on certain options. She [Nancy Reagan] turned to Ollie and said, 'I always thought that I liked you until now.' Ollie said it just turned his blood to ice the way she said it."

At the end of Reagan's presidency, Weyrich asked former senator Paul Laxalt to approach the President for a pardon for North. "I said, 'Look, the election is over, Bush has won and so Reagan is vindicated,' " said Weyrich. " 'For heaven's sake, pardon Ollie North. What's it going to cost? It's Christmas time. Even the media says the guy is a fall guy . . . that he was not the one making the decisions.' "

Laxalt carried the message to the President and called Weyrich back the next day. "He said he ran it up the flagpole," recalled Weyrich, "but the man just wasn't receptive because Nancy is so adamant against a pardon for North. What the heck business does she have determining a presidential policy like that?"

As to President Reagan's reliance on astrology:
While the First Lady was consulting Joan Quigley, the President was supposedly soliciting his own astrological advice.

"He would call me once or twice a month from Camp David," said Ed Helin (interviewed on October 25 and 30 and November 6, 1990), an astrology instructor with the Carroll Righter Institute in Los Angeles. "I have been working with Reagan since we first met on a movie set in 1949 when I started doing his charts. I became more involved with him through Carroll Righter, and when Mr. Righter became so ill, I took over and did most of Reagan's readings.

"As President, he was primarily concerned with the timing of events and how his popularity would be affected by his actions. He called me to determine the best timing for invading Grenada, for bombing Libya, for launching the *Challenger*—things like that.

"I was paid in cash by a local representative of the Republican National Committee. . . . He would come to my house with an envelope of cash every month or so. . . . No, I can't give you the man's name because I'm still doing astrological work for the Republican National Committee."

CHAPTER 24

Records include copies of the Reagans' tax returns for the years 1980–88; transcript of the Phil Donahue show, November 7, 1989.

Articles include "Nancy's Flub-dubs" by William Safire, *New York Times,* October 20, 1988; "Corruption's Everywhere but Few Are Going to Jail" by Carl T. Rowan, *New York Post,* July 31, 1990; "From Posh Retreat Reagans Sally Forth the Belles of Bel Air" by Michael Kilian, *San Jose Mercury-News,* April 25, 1989; Liz Smith column, October 18, 1989; "Seems So Long Ago, Nancy" by Georgina Howell, *British Vogue,* November 1989; "Reagans Leaving Amid Tears and Smiles" by Jeremiah O'Leary, *Washington Times,* January 20, 1989.

Interviews include Chris Blazakis: March 1, 1990; Joe Canzeri: September 3, 1989; confidential interview with close friend of Nancy Reagan: January 10, 1989; Henry Salvatori: September 18, 1990; Joel Odum: February 4, 1989; Robert Stack: September 14, 1989; David Horowitz: May 1989; Jerri Shenson: April 3, 1989.

As to Ronald Reagan signing contract to write his memoirs:
Before he signed to write his memoirs for Simon & Schuster, Reagan gave Edmund Morris unrestricted access to him to write about his presidency. Morris, who received a Pulitzer Prize for his biography of Theo-

dore Roosevelt, received a $3 million advance from Random House to write about the Reagan White House years. He was given a White House office in order to observe Reagan on a daily basis. He socialized with the Reagans at Camp David and traveled with them on Air Force One. He attended all summits and debriefed the President after every important event. Reagan sent letters to individuals Morris wanted to interview and asked them to provide whatever the writer wanted. No President ever gave a writer the unlimited access that Ronald Reagan gave to Edmund Morris.

To commemorate the anniversary of the Reagans' first date, Morris and his wife, Sylvia, gave a dinner party for the President and First Lady on November 15, 1987, in their house in Washington, D.C. Only eight guests were invited—all writers: Gay Talese and his wife, Nan; Robert Massie; Phyllis Rose; Anthony Haden-Guest; Marian Rodgers (researcher to Edmund Morris); and Kenneth Lynn and his wife, Valerie. Morris extended his invitations by asking each writer to send him a treatment of the dinner party and their reactions to the Reagans. Robert Massie, who wrote *Nicholas and Alexandra,* was the only writer to comply with his host's request.

"What bothered me about Reagan was his lack of curiosity as to what we did and what we thought about the world," wrote Massie. "There was a kind of impenetrable curtain hanging between us and the President. The curtain consisted partly of the Presidency. No one was going to ask a hard question or push for an answer. All of us were eating out of his hand, but it wasn't Ronald Reagan's hand. It was the hand of the American President, for whom all of us have a respect (in my case, approaching awe). Here, history is concentrated in a very dense mass. Here is unique and terrible power, not only over our lives, but over that of our race, the whole human future. And here he sits, telling movie stories. The stories are the other part of the curtain. None of us are actors; most of us have never seen a Ronald Reagan movie. The stories, within this context, are quite interesting. We laughed, perhaps a little harder than we should have, but the evening was so pleasant and he told them so well and with such good humor, that it was easy."

"The President was very nice, very charming," said Nan Talese, "but Hollywood stories are not my idea of great entertainment."

Mrs. Reagan must have shared her thoughts, because during her husband's ruminations she talked to Gay Talese, who was distinctly uncomfortable trying to listen to the President and the First Lady at the same time.

"I leaned down to try to hear what she was asking me," said Talese, "but I did not want to encourage her . . . I couldn't hear what the

President was saying, or anyone else for that matter, because Nancy kept talking to me. First, she asked me about myself and then she asked me what I thought of California. . . . In a way it was flattering, but in another way it was rude. I kept thinking, 'Jesus, she shouldn't be talking to me. She should be paying attention to him.' "

Morris had told the First Lady that all the guests would be writers with the emphasis on biographers; this was intentional, as she was embarking on her memoirs and now considered herself a writer.

"I remember sitting on the sofa with Mrs. Reagan," said Phyllis Rose, "and she said, 'I feel strange when I hear all you writers saying that your books will take five or seven years to write. I have no intention of spending that amount of time on *my* book.' "

The only writer mentioned all evening was Louis L'Amour, Reagan's favorite author.

"If I were to invite selected writers to meet the President," said Anthony Haden-Guest, "I would have put together a rather more imposing list, but then, of course, we would still have had the conversation about Louis L'Amour. Edmund was quite right . . . If he had had E. L. Doctorow and Harold Brodkey and all that, the conversation would have been more stilted, and the President still would not have known who they were."

Edmund and Sylvia Morris live in a house overlooking the rear of the Capitol dome. They invited the President to look at the view from their top-floor sitting room. Reagan went upstairs and looked at the dome that divides both houses of Congress. "Oh, boy," he said, rubbing his hands with glee. "I could finish those guys off with a .22 from up here." Relishing the prospect, he stared out the big glass windows until the Secret Service agents moved him back.

EPILOGUE

Articles include "Regan Exchanges Hisses with Nancy via 'Today' Show" by David Braaten, *Washington Times,* October 24, 1989; "Nixon or Fiction" by Roger J. Stone, *Washington Post,* November 4, 1989; Liz Smith column, *New York Daily News,* January 30, 1990; "First Family Reunion" by Karen Friefeld, *Newsday,* March 13, 1989; "Former First Lady, Gates on Scene as SWAT Team Carries Out Drug Raid" by Louis Sahagun, *Los Angeles Times,* April 19, 1989; "The Teflon Is Gone" by Martin Kasindorf, *Newsday,* March 13, 1990.

Interviews include Lieutenant Fred Nixon of the LAPD: April 17 and May 3, 1989.

As to Nancy Reagan's greediness:
In retirement, the former First Lady developed a money-saving trick to handle gifts of flowers from friends and fans. She let it be known that her personal florist was David Jones of Beverly Hills. But she told him not to send any of the flowers to her. Instead, when someone called Jones with an order for her, he was to call her. She then writes a thank-you note to the person who ordered the flowers. When she needs flowers, she simply orders from Jones on the credit she's piled up from the gifts that he has logged in for her.

As to Ronald Reagan's late conversion to voicing support for the victims of AIDS:
Heeding the advice of public relations specialists, the former President wrote an op-ed piece on Ryan White, who was infected with AIDS during a blood transfusion and died at the age of eighteen. The Reagans visited him during his dying days in the hospital, and the former President's article, entitled "We Owe It to Ryan," was published on April 11, 1990, in the *Washington Post.*

"How Nancy and I wish there had been a magic wand we could have waved to make it all go away," wrote Reagan. "Sadly, Ryan's is not the only life to have been cut short by AIDS. In a most poignant way, he told us of a health crisis in our country that has claimed too many victims. There have been too many funerals like his. There are too many patches in the quilt. We owe it to Ryan to make sure that the fear and ignorance that chased him from his home and his school will be eliminated. . . . It's the disease that's frightening, not the people who have it."

The editorial response to Reagan's column was resoundingly negative. "Of course, Ronnie and Nancy—who had a photo op with Ryan two weeks before his death—had the magic wand of presidential power at their disposal for eight long and inattentive years," wrote Doug Ireland in the *Village Voice* on April 24, 1990, "during which Reagan never even made a major speech on AIDS as tens of thousands died, so it's no surprise that this ghost-written obscenity failed to mention the world apart. . . ."

"Why does Ronald Reagan now feel that 'We owe it to Ryan to make sure that the fear and ignorance that chased him from his home and school will be eliminated'?" asked a letter to the editor of *Newsweek,* May 14, 1990. "He [Reagan] certainly didn't feel this way when he was in office. When the former president had a chance to endorse legislation that would have stopped exactly the kind of discrimination that chased Ryan from his hometown and school, he refused. Climbing on the bandwagon and trying to curry public favor by exploiting Ryan's death is disgraceful."

A homosexual man who said he had been fighting AIDS for three years wrote a letter to the editor of the *Washington Post,* saying Reagan's tribute to Ryan White was "one of the most infuriating and embittering things I've read in a long time.

"Reagan could have improved the survival chances of Ryan White and other people with AIDS by speaking out often and forcefully on AIDS," he wrote. "Instead, it took him seven years to make a speech about AIDS. In that time, 50,000 Americans contracted the disease, and 30,000 died of it. He could have pushed Congress to spend enough money to fight the disease. Instead, he initially requested no money and then requested insultingly insufficient amounts. Each year Congress had to appropriate more than his administration asked for. . . .

"That he had the nerve to eulogize Ryan White without first having taken responsibility, and asked forgiveness, for his eight years of inaction is an insult to those who have died of AIDS. . . ."

As to Nancy Reagan's promotion of her memoirs:
Barbara Walters of ABC-TV held a luncheon in honor of the former First Lady in New York on November 16, 1989, to which she invited twelve female journalists: gossip columnist Liz Smith; Aileen Mehle, also known as "Suzy"; Diane Sawyer of ABC-TV; Grace Mirabella, editor of *Mirabella;* Anna Wintour, editor in chief of *Vogue;* Shirley Lord, beauty director of *Vogue;* Jane Lane of Fairchild Publications, which publishes *W* and *Women's Wear Daily;* Joan Lunden of "Good Morning America"; Kathleen Sullivan, former co-host of "CBS Morning News"; Myrna Blythe, editor of *Ladies' Home Journal;* Tina Brown, editor of *Vanity Fair;* and Helen Gurley Brown, editor of *Cosmopolitan.*

"It was supposed to be an off-the-record luncheon," said one of the guests interviewed on December 6, 1989. "Barbara said, 'I don't even want it mentioned that it's going to be in my apartment, because, you know, I'm not in the habit of giving ladies' lunches at home.' Ladies, hell . . . a bunch of ax murderers is more like it.

"But we were all on our best behavior. . . . It was like the mah-jongg group . . . or Bingo night . . . all girl talk. . . . We sat at a round table. . . . Barbara Walters on one side of Mrs. Reagan and Suzy on the other . . . and Barbara said, 'I'm sure you all have questions for Mrs. Reagan about her book. . . .' "

One woman asked Nancy Reagan how her children felt about her memoirs. She said that she had sent the book to them, and then added, "But . . . you know, their books have never done very well."

"She made a very pointed comment about how much better her book was doing than the books of her children," said the luncheon guest. "It was like how pitiable they [the children] were. . . . She also talked about how much she hated Raisa Gorbachev, which I thought was pretty lousy manners to be bad-mouthing the Russian premier's wife.

"Nancy said the only reason people write negative things about her is that they don't know any better . . . and her apologists at the table said the only reason her book had gotten panned was because it had been reviewed by the wrong people. She agreed and exhorted us all to read the book.

Meeting the former First Lady was not a positive experience for this luncheon guest. "It was such a disappointment to be confronted by this sort of petty old bag . . . who seemed to bring out the worst in all the people at the table . . . Some people [i.e., Nancy Reagan] are so high strung that they have a way of casting a mood of tension and that's what that luncheon was like. . . ."

"Liz Smith then told her that she belonged to history and she was very pleased with that."

Bibliography

Adler, Bill. *Ronnie and Nancy: A Very Special Love Story.* New York: Crown Publishers, Inc., 1985

Ambrose, Stephen E. *Nixon: The Education of a Politician 1913–1962.* New York: Simon and Schuster, 1987.

Anderson, Martin. *Revolution.* New York: Harcourt Brace Jovanovich, Publishers, 1988.

Anson, Robert Sam. *Exile: The Unquiet Oblivion of Richard M. Nixon.* New York: Simon and Schuster, 1984.

Barrett, Laurence I. *Gambling with History: Reagan in the White House.* New York: Penguin Books, 1983.

Basichis, Gordon. *Beautiful Bad Girl: The Vicki Morgan Story.* Santa Barbara, Calif.: Santa Barbara Press, 1985.

Beebe, Lucius. *The Big Spenders.* New York: Doubleday, 1966.

Bender, Marilyn, with Monsieur Marc. *Nouveau Is Better Than No Riche at All.* New York: G. P. Putnam's Sons, 1983.

Birmingham, Stephen. *The Right Places.* Boston: Little, Brown & Company, 1967.

Blumenthal, Sidney, and Thomas Byrne Edsall, editors. *The Reagan Legacy.* New York: Pantheon Books, 1988.

Boyarsky, Bill. *Ronald Reagan: His Life and Rise to the Presidency.* New York: Random House, 1981.

Brown, Edmund G. "Pat," and Bill Brown. *Reagan: The Political Chameleon.* New York: Praeger Publishers, 1976.

Bush, George, with Victor Gold. *Looking Forward.* New York: Doubleday and Company, Inc., 1987.

Caldicott, D. Helen. *Missile Envy: The Arms Race and Nuclear War.* New York: William Morrow & Company, Inc., 1984.

Cannon, Lou. *Reagan.* New York: G. P. Putnam's Sons, 1982.

———. *Ronnie and Jessie: A Political Odyssey.* New York: Doubleday and Company, Inc., 1969.

Cooney, John. *The Annenbergs.* New York: Simon and Schuster, 1982.

Davis, James Kotsilibas, and Myrna Loy. *Myrna Loy.* New York: Alfred A. Knopf, 1987.

Davis, Loyal, M.D. *A Surgeon's Odyssey.* New York: Doubleday and Company, Inc., 1973.

———. *Go in Peace.* New York: G. P. Putnam's Sons, 1954.

———. *J. B. Murphy: Stormy Petrel of Surgery.* New York: G. P. Putnam's Sons, 1938.

Davis, Patti. *Deadfall.* New York: Crown Publishers, Inc., 1989.

———. *Home Front.* New York: Crown Publishers, Inc., 1986.

Deaver, Michael K., with Mickey Herskowitz. *Behind the Scenes.* New York: William Morrow & Company, Inc., 1987.

DeGregorio, William A. *The Complete Book of U.S. Presidents.* New York: Dembner Books, 1984.

Demaris, Ovid. *Captive City.* New York: Lyle Stuart, Inc., 1969.

Dickenson, Mollie. *Thumbs Up: The Life and Courageous Comeback of White House Press Secretary Jim Brady.* New York: William Morrow & Company, Inc., 1987.

Didion, Joan. *The White Album.* New York: Simon and Schuster, 1979.

Donaldson, Sam. *Hold On, Mr. President!* New York: Random House, 1987.

Douglas, Kirk. *The Ragman's Son.* New York: Simon and Schuster, 1988.

Dugger, Ronnie. *On Reagan: The Man and His Presidency.* New York: McGraw-Hill Book Company, 1983.

Eames, John Douglas. *The MGM Story.* New York: Crown Publishers, Inc., 1975.

Edwards, Anne. *Early Reagan.* New York: William Morrow & Company, Inc., 1987.

Eells, George. *Hedda and Louella.* New York: G. P. Putnam's Sons, 1972.

Ehrlichman, John. *Witness to Power: The Nixon Years.* New York: Simon and Schuster, 1982.

Fairchild, John. *Chic Savages.* New York: Simon and Schuster, 1989.

Feibleman, Peter. *Lilly: Reminiscences of Lillian Hellman.* New York: William Morrow & Company, Inc., 1988.

Ferraro, Geraldine A., with Linda Bird Francke. *Ferraro: My Story.* New York: Bantam Books, 1986.

Friedman, Alan, and Ted Schwarz. *Power and Greed: Inside the Teamsters Empire of Corruption.* New York: Franklin Watts, 1989.

Germond, Jack W., and Jules Witcover. *Blue Smoke and Mirrors: How Reagan Won and Why Carter Lost the Election of 1980.* New York: The Viking Press, 1981.

————. *Wake Us When It's Over.* New York: Macmillan Publishing Company, 1985.

Goldman, Peter, and Tony Fuller. *The Quest for the Presidency 1984.* New York: Bantam Books, 1985.

Goldwater, Barry M., with Jack Casserly. *Goldwater.* New York: Doubleday and Company, Inc., 1988.

Gotlieb, Sondra. *Washington Rollercoaster.* Toronto: Doubleday Canada Limited, 1990.

Graham, Sheilah. *Confessions of a Hollywood Columnist.* New York: William Morrow & Company, Inc., 1969.

Green, Mark. *To Err Is Reagan.* San Francisco: Foundation for National Progress, 1987.

Green, Paul M., and Melvin G. Holli, editors. *The Mayors: The Chicago Political Tradition.* Carbondale, Ill.: Southern Illinois University Press, 1987.

Hackett, Pat, editor. *The Andy Warhol Diaries.* New York: Warner Books, Inc., 1989.

Hagstrom, Jerry. *Beyond Reagan: The New Landscape of American Politics.* New York: W. W. Norton & Company, 1988.

Hannaford, Peter. *The Reagans: A Political Portrait.* New York: Coward-McCann, Inc., 1983.

Hertsgaard, Mark. *On Bended Knee: The Press and the Reagan Presidency.* New York: Farrar, Straus & Giroux, 1988.

Higham, Charles. *The Duchess of Windsor: The Secret Life.* New York: McGraw-Hill Book Company, 1988.

Hirschhorn, Clive. *The Warner Brothers Story.* New York: Crown Publishers, Inc., 1979.

Hopper, Hedda, with James Brough. *The Whole Truth and Nothing But.* New York: Doubleday and Company, Inc., 1963.

Josephson, Matthew. *The Robber Barons.* New York: Harcourt Brace & Company, 1934.

Judis, John B. *William F. Buckley, Jr.: Patron Saint of the Conservatives.* New York: Simon and Schuster, 1988.

Kahn, Gordon. *Hollywood on Trial.* New York: Boni & Gaer, 1948.

Kelley, Kitty. *His Way: The Unauthorized Biography of Frank Sinatra.* New York: Bantam Books, 1986.

Kupcinet, Irv. *Kup's Chicago.* Cleveland and New York: World Publishing Co., 1962.

———, with Paul Neimark. *Kup: A Man, an Era, a City.* Chicago: Bonus Books, 1988.

Leamer, Laurence. *Make-Believe: The Story of Nancy and Ronald Reagan.* New York: Harper & Row Publishers, 1983.

Leighton, Frances Spatz. *The Search for the Real Nancy Reagan.* New York: Macmillan Publishing Company, 1987.

Lindfors, Viveca. *Viveka . . . Viveca.* New York: Everest House Publishers, 1981.

Malatesta, Peter. *Party Politics.* Englewood Cliffs, New Jersey: Prentice-Hall, Inc., 1982.

Manchester, William. *Death of a President.* New York: Harper & Row Publishers, 1967.

———. *The Glory and the Dream.* New York: Bantam Books, 1973.

Masters, George, and Norma Lee Browning. *The Masters Way to Beauty.* New York: E. P. Dutton, 1977.

Mayer, Jane, and Doyle McManus. *Landslide: The Unmaking of the President, 1984–1988.* Boston: Houghton Mifflin Company, 1988.

Milton, Joyce, and Ann Louise Bardach. *Vicki.* New York: St. Martin's Press, 1986.

Myers, Gustavus. *History of the Great American Fortunes.* New York: Modern Library Giant, 1907.

Neal, Patricia, with Richard DeNeut. *As I Am.* New York: Simon and Schuster, 1988.

Noonan, Peggy. *What I Saw at the Revolution.* New York: Random House, 1990.

O'Connor, Len. *Clout: Mayor Daley and His City.* Chicago: Henry Regnery Company, 1975.

Patterson, Bradley H., Jr. *The Ring of Power: The White House Staff and Its Expanding Role in Government.* New York: Basic Books, Inc., Publishers, 1988.

Powell, Jane. *The Girl Next Door and How She Grew.* New York: William Morrow and Company, Inc., 1988.

Powell, Jody. *The Other Side of the Story.* New York: William Morrow & Company, Inc., 1984.

Prindle, David F. *The Politics of Glamour: Ideology and Democracy in the Screen Actors Guild.* Madison, Wisconsin: University of Wisconsin Press, 1988.

Quigley, Joan. *"What Does Joan Say?"* New York: Birch Lane Press, 1990.

Radcliffe, Donnie. *Simply Barbara Bush.* New York: Warner Books, Inc., 1989.

Reagan, Maureen. *First Father, First Daughter: A Memoir.* Boston: Little, Brown and Company, 1989.

Reagan, Michael, with Joe Hyams. *On the Outside Looking In.* New York: Zebra Books, 1988.

Reagan, Nancy, with Bill Libby. *Nancy.* New York: William Morrow & Company, Inc., 1980.

———, with William Novak. *My Turn.* New York: Random House, 1989.

Reagan, Ronald. *Speaking My Mind.* New York: Simon and Schuster, 1989.

———, and Richard C. Hubler. *Where's the Rest of Me?* New York: Dell Publishing Company, Inc., 1965.

Regan, Donald T. *For the Record: From Wall Street to Washington.* New York: Harcourt Brace Jovanovich, Publishers, 1988.

Reinsch, J. Leonard. *Getting Elected: From Radio and Roosevelt to Television and Reagan.* New York: Hippocrene Books, 1988.

Roosevelt, Selwa "Lucky." *Keeper of the Gate.* New York: Simon and Schuster, 1990.

Rush, George. *Confessions of an Ex-Secret Service Agent.* New York: Donald I. Fine Publishers, Inc., 1988.

Schary, Dore. *Heyday.* Boston: Little, Brown and Company, 1979.

———, as told to Charles Palmer. *Case History of a Movie.* New York: Random House, 1950.

Schieffer, Bob, and Gary Paul Gates. *The Acting President.* New York: E. P. Dutton, 1989.

Seale, William. *The President's House: A History.* Washington, D.C.: White House Historical Association with the cooperation of the National Geographic Society, 1986.

Shilts, Randy. *And the Band Played On.* New York: St. Martin's Press, 1987.

Slansky, Paul. *The Clothes Have No Emperor: A Chronicle of the American 80s.* New York: Fireside, 1989.

Smith, Alson J. *Syndicate City: The Chicago Crime Cartel and What to Do About It.* Chicago: Henry Regnery Company, 1954.

Smith, Hedrick. *The Power Game: How Washington Really Works.* New York: Random House, 1988.

Speakes, Larry, with Robert Pack. *Speaking Out.* New York: Charles Scribner's Sons, 1988.

Spock, Benjamin. *Baby and Child Care.* New York: Pocket Books, Inc., 1946.

Strait, Raymond. *James Garner.* New York: St. Martin's Press, 1985.

Tebbel, John. *The Inheritors.* New York: G. P. Putnam's Sons, 1962.

Voris, Jacqueline Van. *College: A Smith Mosaic.* West Springfield, Massachusetts: O'Malley Company, 1975.

Wallace, Chris. *First Lady: A Portrait of Nancy Reagan.* New York: St. Martin's Press, 1986.

Weidenfeld, Sheila Rabb. *First Lady's Lady: With the Fords at the White House.* New York: G. P. Putnam's Sons, 1979.

Wendt, Lloyd, and Herman Kogan. *Big Bill of Chicago.* New York: Bobbs-Merrill Company, Inc., 1953.

White, Theodore H. *The Making of the President 1968.* New York: Atheneum Publishers, 1969.

Wills, Garry. *Reagan's America: Innocents at Home.* New York: Doubleday and Company, Inc., 1987.

Wilson, Edith. *My Memoir.* Indianapolis, Indiana: Bobbs-Merrill Company, 1939.

Winters, Shelley. *Shelley II.* New York: Simon and Schuster, 1989.

Index

KITTY KELLEY left her job on the editorial page of the *Washington Post* in 1971 to pursue free-lance writing. She has written for *The New York Times, Newsweek, Los Angeles Times,* and *Chicago Tribune,* as well as *Ladies' Home Journal, Good Housekeeping* and other women's magazines. Her previous books, *His Way: The Unauthorized Biography of Frank Sinatra, Jackie Oh!* and *Elizabeth Taylor: The Last Star,* were national best-sellers. She has received numerous awards, including the 1987 Outstanding Author Award from the American Society of Journalists and Authors "for her courageous writing on popular culture."